Practical Gardening Encyclopedia

Practical
Gardening
Encyclopedia

edited by Roy Hay
Consultant Editor George Elbert
Managing Editor Roger Davies

VNR VAN NOSTRAND REINHOLD COMPANY

NEW YORK CINCINNATI TORONTO LONDON MELBOURNE

Published in 1977 by Van Nostrand
Reinhold Company
A division of Litton Educational
Publishing, Inc.
450 West 33rd Street, New York,
NY 10001, U.S.A.

Published in Great Britain by Ward
Lock Ltd., London, a member of the
Pentos Group.

Contents

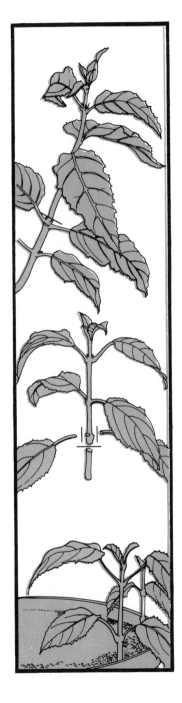

Acknowledgments

The publishers wish to thank the following for their contributions to this book and their assistance in its production.

A.C. Barber; Judith Beloff, Barrister; Michael Beloff, MA (Oxon) Barrister; Dr A.E. Beaumont; Dr Arthur Bing; R.J. Bisgrove, BSc, MLA; Alan Bloom; Ann Bonar, BSc (Hort); John Bond; Audrey V. Brooks, BSc, MIBiol; J.K. Burras, NDH; Mary Chaplin; Professor C.D.K. Cook; Michael J. Dawes, Dip Hort Kew; Dr A. Dick, BSc; Elly Beintema Photography & Picture Research; Alfred Evans; R.W. Gloyne, BSc, PhD; W. Godley, MIAgrE; Roger Grounds; A.J. Halstead, MSc; Geoff Hamilton; Harry Smith Horticultural Photographic Collection; Barry Hutton; Professor John Hyde; Clive F. Innes; Charles Jacquest; J.L.S. Keesing, BSc; J. Ross MacLennan; John D. Main, NDH, DHE; R.A. Martin, BSc; Brian Mathew, FLS; Merrist Wood Agricultural College; Paul Miles; Mrs Diana M. Miller; Barry Phillips, Dip Hort Kew; Publication Graphics, New Zealand; David Pycraft, Dip Hort; John Roberts; A. Russell-Smith; C.M. Simpson; Lionel P. Smith; Mavis Smith; Nils Solberg; Professor Edward Steppe; Professor Charles Straub; Professor Raymond Terry; Dr Peter Thompson; Neil G. Treseder, NDH; Arthur Turner; John Turpin, BSc (Hort); Brian Walkden; A.E.L. Walker, NDA, NDAgr; Ian G. Walls, NDH; Dr Max Walters; E.J. Winter, MC, MSc; J.R. Woodhams.

The photographs on pages 15, 18 and 19 are reproduced by permission of the Controller of Her Majesty's Stationery Office and are Crown Copyright. The pictures of tools on pages 102, 103 and 107 are reproduced courtesy of Stanley Tools Ltd. The picture of the geodetic greenhouse on page 119 is reproduced courtesy of Rosedale Engineers Ltd.

1. Introduction

How to Use This Book

This Encyclopedia is designed as a work of reference, but the arrangement of the information is thematic rather than alphabetical. This is to enable the reader who wants to pursue a subject in greater depth to read through a whole section or group of sections in logical order, while the index should be consulted by a reader with a specific problem or query. Each of the seventeen main sections is divided into a number of topics; for example, section 12, *Ornamental Plants*, covers *Annuals and Biennials*, *Herbaceous Perennials*, *Shrubs*, *Roses*, *Trees*, etc., and these again are often divided into self-contained sub-sections. So within *Ornamental Plants*: *Trees* there are sub-sections on 'Choosing a Tree', 'Planting Trees', 'After Care', 'Training' etc., followed by a list of recommended genera and species.

If you are planning a big new project in your garden, perhaps a new vegetable and fruit garden, then you should turn to section 13, *Edible Plants*, where you will find information about how much room fruit and vegetables need, how long you will have to wait for your crops, how much trouble they are and so on. The information should help you decide which fruit and vegetables you want to grow and this section will also give you most details of how to grow them.

If, however, you want to find out simply how to set about blanching leeks, look up 'Blanching' in the index. On page 153 you will find the topic explained within section 9, *Cultivation*. If you look up 'Leek', you will be referred to the same place, and you will also find that information about the soil pH leeks prefer is on page 17 (in the section on *Soil*), details about growing them under cloches are on page 130 (in the section on *Greenhouses*), there is information on planting (dibbling) on page 144 (again under *Cultivation*), and there are other references to the main *Edible Plants* section.

Using the Index

The entries in the index consist of plant names, of miscellaneous items such as pests and diseases or types of tool or equipment, and of references to the main topics and activities described in the Encyclopedia. You should use it either when you need information about a specific plant or topic or when you want to follow up a cross-reference from another part of the book. These appear in the text in *italic* type, with the title of the section followed by the topic (e.g. see *Design and Planning: Banks*). Look in the index for the topic; it is printed there in **bold** type to make it easier to find. If the cross-reference is to another topic within the section you are reading, the section title is omitted (e.g. within the section on soil, see *Improving Your Soil*); again this will be found by reference to the index. The section titles appear in the index as well, but you will find the page you are looking for more quickly by going straight to the topic. In the case of one or two shorter sections (e.g. *Climate* or *Pruning*) cross-references are made only to the section itself, but the required page will be quickly found.

Using the Plant Summaries

In the sections on *Design and Planning*, *Ornamental Plants* and *Gardens* you will find a number of plant summaries. These summaries are not meant to be absolutely comprehensive. They do not contain details of every genus, species and variety you might possibly come across, but they do contain details about most plants you are likely to find in nurserymen's catalogues and in garden centres. The details of size, form, colour and flowering season will help you to plan your garden more effectively, and the details of climate and soil preference should ensure you choose plants suitable for the particular situation of your garden.

The summaries are generally placed at

the end of each topic and are arranged in alphabetical order according to the plant genera. A typical entry is for astilbe, found on page 185 under *Ornamental Plants: Herbaceous Perennials:*

Astilbe 5 and 6, 20cm to 1·8m (8in to 6ft), *fls* feathery plumes of white, pink, red, June to August, *lvs* finely-divided, ferny, any soil, best near water. *A.* × *arendsii* 60 to 90cm (2 to 3ft) – vars include 'Bressingham Beauty', *fls* pink; 'Red Sentinel', *fls* brick-red; 'Gloria', *fls* white: *A.* × *crispa*, 20cm (8in), for rock gardens, *lvs* crinkled, *fls* white, pale pink or red.

The information following the genus name tells you the North American hardiness zone rating for the plant (see *Climate*), its height range, what the flowers look like, including colour, when the plant flowers, and whether the leaves have any distinctive features. It also tells you whether the plant prefers any particular type of soil or situation (including shade). This is general information about all the plants belonging to the genus. A number of recommended species may then follow – in this case *A.* × *arendsii* and *A.* × *crispa*. Recommended species are always divided by a colon. Within the recommended species we may also list a number of varieties – in the above case 'Bressingham Beauty', 'Red Sentinel' and 'Gloria'. Varieties are always divided by a semicolon. Where the species or variety has any feature which distinguishes it from the general description we give details. In the example above you can see that *A.* × *crispa* is one of the smallest astilbes, particularly suitable for rock gardens, and has crinkled leaves.

When the plant summaries refer to one species only the general information about the genus is omitted and specific information is given only about that species (and any varieties).

Naming Plants

Throughout the Encyclopedia we have used the botanical Latinized names for most plants as in the example just given. The reason for this immediately becomes clear when you realize that in English the foxglove has been known by at least 66 common or vernacular names, in French by 14, in German by 5, and so on. It is a very common plant found wild in most countries of Europe from the Azores to Norway and Hungary and is naturalized in North America. The total number of common names from all these countries is enormous. Further confusion arises when you consider that just one of its local names is lady's

fingers and this name has been applied to at least nine distinct British wild plants including the cowslip. However, the universal use by botanists of the Latinized names, *Digitalis purpurea* for the foxglove and *Primula veris* for the cowslip, overcomes all these regional and national barriers and anyone, whatever his native language, can understand at once exactly what plant is being referred to. Where a plant has one predominant common name we have often used this too.

Even more problems arise when the Latinized name of one plant is identical to the common name of a second. The most obvious example is the incorrect use of syringa as a common name for species of *Philadelphus*, also known as mock orange, whereas in fact *Syringa* is the generic name for lilac.

The full Latinized name of a plant consists of at least two parts and the main reason for this lies in the history of plant nomenclature. In the past, a relatively small range of plants was recognized for their food value and their herbal, medicinal or poisonous properties. Most people may have given them common names in the local dialects of their native tongue but the herbalists of the day gave them Latinized names because this was the universal language throughout the civilized world. Gradually, as communication between countries grew, more plants were discovered or raised in gardens and these were usually named by comparing the new plant with one already known. This led to plant names becoming very long and more or less incorporating a description of the plant as well as a comparison with a related species. For example, the native daffodil now known as *Narcissus pseudonarcissus* was called *Pseudonarcissus anglicus vulgaris*, the common English bastard daffodil. One garden form found by John Tradescant, a well known gardener of the early seventeenth century, had to be named *Pseudonarcissus aureus maximus anglicus flore pleno sive roseus Tradescanti* which translates to 'the greatest English yellow double bastard daffodil or John Tradescant's great rose daffodil'.

With about 250,000 species of flowering plants known today the problems would have been insurmountable had this system continued. In the mid-eighteenth century Carl Linnaeus, a Swedish botanist, developed a binomial system of nomenclature. Briefly, it involved the grouping together of plants which showed marked similarities, usually based on their reproductive mechanisms. The plant kingdom was divided into major divisions separating the algae, mosses, ferns, conifers and flowering plants. Each section was sub-divided to the level of families and families were separated into genera (singular genus). For example, within the flowering plants is the family *Primulaceae* containing 20 genera, one of which, *Primula*, includes the cowslip and the primrose. These two plants are quite distinct, although basically similar in their flower structures, and the genus *Primula* is therefore divided into species. A species is a unique unit which may show minor variations but in general breeds true from seed, and the cowslip and primrose are known as *Primula veris* and *Primula vulgaris* respectively. The first names refer to the genus, the second to the species and may be compared to the sur-names and forenames of people. In this way the name is reduced to two words, avoiding the unwieldy descriptions of the medieval botanists. The names of all the larger divi-sions are omitted as there should be no repetition of a generic name within the plant kingdom. Latin remains the universal language and by convention the name is always printed in italics (or underlined) with a capital initial letter for the generic name. As a form of shorthand, the generic name may be abbreviated to a single letter if it is repeated frequently in one context.

Although species are basically constant, variation may occur, as, for example, the occasional appearance of a double-flowered plant of *P. vulgaris*, and these plants may be selected by interested gardeners for dis-tribution. This plant is then a cultivar, a selected form which may only retain its characteristics by vegetative propagation such as division, cuttings or grafting. These man-made plants are given names in the language in which they were first coined and are written in Roman letters with capital initial letters and enclosed in single quota-tion marks. One very good double yellow primrose was named *P. vulgaris* 'Cloth of gold'. Small variations within a species which occur naturally and are maintained in the wild are known as varieties and are usu-ally written in italics with a lower case initial letter, for example *Calluna vulgaris alba* is a white form of the common heather. The distinction between cultivars and varieties is rarely useful to gardeners and throughout this book we have called them all varieties except where we use their Latin name.

A cross between two distinct species of a genus is know as a hybrid and there is a distinct method of representing this. For example the result of crossing the species *P. veris* and *P. vulgaris* is named *P.* × *var-iabilis*. A hybrid between two genera is typified by × *Cupressocyparis leylandii*, the well-known fast growing conifer used for hedging, which is a cross between *Cupressus macrocarpa* and *Chamaecyparis nootkaten-sis*. The rare cases of graft hybrids contain-ing tissues of two plants resulting from a graft instead of the more natural process of pollination may be written as in + *Labur-nocytisus adamii* which is a graft hybrid from *Laburnum anagyroides* and *Cytisus purpureus*.

Plant nomenclature seems confusing and complicated, but it is governed by a set of rules which need cause no major problems once they are understood. For wild species these rules are published in the Interna-tional Code of Botanical Nomenclature and for garden plants not derived directly from the wild in the International Code of Nomenclature of Cultivated Plants. The aim of these two publications is to bring stability and basically to ensure that one name is applied to one plant with no dupli-cation. Except in exceptional circum-stances, the name applied is the earliest recorded which is in accordance with the rules of the two codes. To ensure this, there must be an original Latin description of the plant when the name is first published and, in any serious botanical work, the abbrevia-tion of the name of the person, known as the authority, who first prepared this descrip-tion is given after the plant name. *Digitalis purpurea* L. indicates that this combination of generic and specific name was first applied by Linnaeus.

Unfortunately, despite the fact that the codes are attempts to simplify problems, it is not unusual for a plant to be known for many years under a name which further research proves not to be the first name. One of the best known recent examples is that of the well-known winter-flowering shrub, originally *Viburnum fragrans*. This had to be changed to *V. farreri* because it was found that *V. fragrans* was a name that had been given to a distinct species disco-vered several years earlier. For cultivated forms it is obvious that duplication of cul-tivar names would be disastrous and for many groups of plants there is an Interna-tional Registration Authority which may authorize or reject suggested names for newly developed forms.

So, although initially nomenclature may appear too difficult for the layman to under-stand, it is really a system designed to make the subject comprehensible to people of all nationalities.

2. Soil

Soil is the basic ingredient in which most garden plants grow, and a proper understanding of its nature, structure and properties is an essential prerequisite of successful cultivation. The soil in your garden limits the range of plants you can grow successfully but there is much you can do to change its character and increase its range.

Soil is an infinitely variable material: there is no chemical formula for it, and no two samples, even from the same garden, will be exactly similar. However, in most gardens two distinct layers of soil will be found. The first layer is the fertile top soil, which is usually dark in colour. Below this is the infertile subsoil which is usually lighter in colour. Gardeners are concerned with the top soil – this is where plants have their feeding roots. The anchoring roots of plants may penetrate the subsoil, but since it is generally infertile it should never be brought to the surface. In this book the word soil generally refers to top soil.

The Nature of Soil

Soil is composed of five main ingredients: 1) mineral particles, 2) humus, 3) micro flora and fauna, 4) air, and 5) water.

The mechanical characteristics of soil (its texture) are determined mainly by the size of the mineral particles.

The relative fertility is determined partly by the origin of the mineral particles and by the amount of humus present. The amount of humus also largely determines the relative populations of micro flora and fauna.

The amount of air in soil is determined by a combination of mineral particle size, humus and micro flora and fauna. Of these three factors, the mineral particle size is probably the most important.

The amount of water passing through soil is determined mainly by the mineral particle size. The amount of water retained by soil is determined mainly by the amount of humus (or organic matter) present.

None of these five factors is of undue importance on its own. What really matters is the relative proportions in which they are combined.

The Origins of Mineral Particles

The mineral particles in soil originate from the basic rocks of which the earth's crust is formed. The fertility of soil is directly related to the type of rock from which the mineral particles originally came. Over many years these rocks have been broken down into smaller and smaller fragments by extreme climatic conditions such as glaciation. The erosion of rocks is still going on under the action of wind, rain, sun, ice, and other agents such as lichen.

Basic Soil Types

There are three basic soil types, and each has its own particular characteristics. These are: 1) clay soils, 2) sandy soils, and 3) loam soils.

A clay soil is defined as one in which more than 30 per cent of the mineral particles measure 0·002mm or less in diameter. Such soils typically have an extremely sticky texture, and are considered hard to work. Their texture makes them very heavy and intractable. Clay soils tend to be very slow draining in winter, and to bake extremely hard in summer, but they are usually very rich in essential plant nutrients.

A sandy soil is defined as one in which 35 per cent of the mineral particles are between 0·10mm and 0·50mm in diameter. Such soils are typically fast draining, and low in essential plant nutrients, these having been largely leached away by very rapid drainage. Sandy soils are, however, very easy to work and often warm up early in the

Opposite: Make the most of what may seem to be unfortunate features of your soil. Here a wet shady area has been made into a very attractive marsh garden with plants that thrive in these conditions

spring making them very useful for growing early vegetables.

Loams are defined as soils in which one third of the mineral particles are clay, one third sand and one third silt. Loam soils are the ideal from a horticultural point of view, combining the best qualities of clay soils with the best qualities of sand soils, and ameliorating the deficiences of both. If you are fortunate enough to have a loam soil, try and preserve its condition.

A range of soils lie between the three basic soil types described above. In total, twelve categories are used to describe soil texture.

Extreme Soil Types

These soils generally occur under extreme climatic or geological conditions. They are not common but many gardeners do have to contend with them.

Stony soils are defined as soils which have over 35 per cent of their mineral particles at least 2mm in diameter. Often the particles are very much larger. Stony soils are almost totally unable to retain moisture and lack essential plant nutrients.

Peat soils have no mineral particles of a measurable size. They are composed entirely, or almost entirely of vegetation that has decayed under anaerobic (airless) conditions. Peat soils occur mainly in areas of extremely high rainfall, are usually extremely acid and contain very few essential plant nutrients.

Muck soils occur in dried up boglands which have not had enough time or enough plants for peat to form. They usually contain a very high proportion of silt particles but no humus and they are consequently virtually barren.

Gumbo or adobe soils are found in the west and far west regions of the USA in areas of very low rainfall. They are characterized by their extreme alkalinity. These soils are similar to clay in mineral particle size, and are usually extremely rich in essential plant nutrients. However, they generally contain insufficient moisture to make the nutrients readily available to the plants. The extreme alkalinity of these soils may also poison plants.

Determining Soil Type

When you take over a new garden it is wise to have an analysis of the soil done. You can have it done professionally, by a parks department in Britain, by the Department of Agriculture County Agent in the US, or by the Department of Agriculture, Ottawa, in Canada. You can do it much more cheaply yourself with one of the soil testing kits that are readily available in garden shops or garden centres. These kits will tell you how much your soil is deficient in nitrogen, phosphate, potash or lime, and how much of each of these essential plant foods should be applied to bring your soil into proper balance.

Another method: Put a little soil in the palm of your hand, moisten it gradually, rubbing it and moulding it with each addition of water until it reaches the point when you can mould it easily but it does not have any free water and will not stick to a polished surface. Press and mould the soil between your fingers and thumb several times and decide: how gritty or smooth it is, how sticky it is, whether it is plastic-like and how much 'polish' you can get on the surface. Grittiness is due to the presence of sand; smoothness is due to silt; stickiness, plasticity and cohesion are due to clay. Next roll the soil between the palms of your hands and try to form a ball. Note how easy this is. Then try to produce a sausage-like thread, and if this is possible, try to form the thread into a ring. By comparing your observations with the table opposite you can get some estimation of the soil texture.

The Function of Humus

Animal and vegetable remains are gradually broken down by the weather and by soil organisms. Humus is the substance which remains after the partial breakdown of this organic matter. It is a highly complex, microscopic, brown and black, colloidal (jellylike) material containing fats, carbohydrates and proteins.

Humus is important to the health of both soil and plants in four ways. 1) It acts as a store for plant foods which tend to adhere very tightly to the surface of humus particles, making them less likely to be lost from the soil through drainage. Humus is the only soil store for nitrogen. 2) It binds mineral particles together, preventing their erosion by wind and water and makes clay soils easier to work. 3) It is a reservoir for soil moisture but also helps improve drainage and passage of air through the soil. 4) It provides a source of food for soil flora and fauna which in itself is essential to healthy plant growth.

Many soils can be greatly improved by increasing the amount of humus present. See *Improving Your Soil*.

Micro-organisms

Soil contains a wide range of flora and fauna, varying from the smallest bacteria to the larger, visible organisms, such as earthworms and millipedes. All of these play a part in turning dead animal and vegetable matter into humus, in keeping the air and water channels in the soil open, and generally in maintaining the soil in good health.

GRITTINESS	SMOOTH-NESS	STICKINESS	BALL and THREAD FORMATION	TEXTURE
Extremely gritty	not smooth	not sticky	Balls collapse easily	SAND
Extremely gritty	not smooth	not sticky	Balls difficult to form	LOAMY SAND
Very gritty	not smooth	not sticky	Balls stick together, no threads	SANDY LOAM
Moderately gritty	slightly smooth	slightly sticky	Balls stick together, threads difficult to form	LOAM
Slightly gritty	slightly smooth	moderately sticky	Forms balls, threads and rings	CLAY LOAM
Very little grittiness	very smooth	slightly sticky	Balls stick together, threads difficult to form	SILT LOAM
Very little grittiness	extremely smooth	slightly sticky	Balls stick together, threads difficult to form. Slight polish	SILT
Very little grittiness	not smooth	extremely sticky	Balls, threads and rings easily formed. Plenty of polish	CLAY

A rich and varied soil micro-organism population is highly desirable. Micro-organisms thrive under exactly the same conditions as the roots of plants thrive; further, they compete for the same nutrients. In any soil which contains plenty of organic matter and has a rich micro-organism population, the micro-organisms continually compete with each other. This prevents any one specialized disease organism or fungus from gaining ascendancy. In the course of their activities, the soil organisms make many nutrients available to plants in a form in which the plants can readily use them.

Water

Water is important to plants in two ways. Firstly it is essential for photosynthesis: when there is a shortage or water available to a plant the rate of photosynthesis slows down and eventually stops. Secondly, since plants can only absorb nutrients in the form of weak solutions of mineral salts, water is essential to provide the medium in which the mineral salts are dissolved.

Water is held in the spaces between the soil particles. The size of these particles determines how much water is retained. The smaller the particles the more tightly the water is held; the larger the particles the more loosely it is held and the more rapidly it drains. The degree of tension with which the water is held between the soil particles affects the ability of the plant to use that water. In soils with extremely small particles, such as some clays, the water is held so tightly that plants can only draw on it with great difficulty.

Water can also move through the spaces between soil particles. The critical pore size for drainage is 0.05mm. If all the pores in a soil are smaller than this, there will be virtually no drainage. If they are all larger than this, there will be very little water retention. The ideal soil contains approximately equal quantities of pores above and below this critical size. The larger pores allow the free circulation of air, the smaller pores retain adequate water.

Air

The presence of air in the soil is essential for the healthy growth of plant roots and for the survival of vital micro-organisms.

The air in soil is contained in those pores which are larger than 0.05mm in diameter. During heavy rainfall these pores normally become filled with water, which moves rapidly through them flushing out toxic substances. The pores then quickly fill with air again. In soils with very small pores water may not be able to move rapidly enough through them to prevent its prolonged presence, causing permanent damage to the roots of the plants and to the micro-organism population. Water can force air out of soil pores, air cannot push water out of them.

The roots of plants and soil micro-organisms use soil air in the same way. They use the oxygen in the air in their metabolism and exhale carbon dioxide as a waste product. Large concentrations of carbon dioxide are poisonous to plants and to micro-organisms and when free movement of air through soil is interrupted a carbon dioxide build-up may occur. This build-up

Sandy soil

A ball made of sandy soil will fall apart if you try to make one

Clay soil

Clay soil can be formed into a ball

Forming the clay into a worm; clay moulds very easily

Forming clay soil into a ring

The clay ball and sandy soil ball compared; note the considerable difference in texture

can directly damage the roots of plants and upset the balance of the micro-organism population. Those micro-organisms which can survive best under conditions of high carbon dioxide concentrations are mainly unspecialized disease organisms. Under normal conditions there is healthy competition between these and the more beneficial micro-organisms – the disease organisms feed mainly off dead vegetable matter and the discarded cells from the growing tips of roots. But under high carbon dioxide concentrations, the disease organisms attack the roots themselves which further weakens plants already weakened by high concentrations of carbon dioxide.

To avoid problems of this type, it is essential that any soil should not only contain a high proportion of organic matter to ensure a balanced micro-organic population living in healthy competition within itself, but also adequate air movement. The optimum air content of a soil is about 10 per cent by volume. This is one reason why cultivation and planting should never be attempted on wet land, as the soil will compact and the roots be unable to develop properly.

Plant Foods and pH

Plants obtain the three most important nutrients – carbon, hydrogen and oxygen – from the air and water present in the soil. A good soil structure is absolutely necessary to ensure an adequate supply. Plants also absorb a number of other nutrients through their root hairs in the form of dilute solutions of mineral salts. The exact number of these nutrients which are necessary to plants is still unknown. At the last count 13 out of the dozens absorbed were thought to be essential. They are: nitrogen, phosphorus, potassium, calcium, magnesium, sulphur, iron, boron, manganese, molybdenum, zinc, copper and chlorine.

But even with these elements their exact role in plant nutrition is still only partly known. Nitrogen, phosphorus and sulphur are all constituents of the complex organic compounds from which plants are made. Potassium, iron, manganese and copper play an intermediate part in the building-up process without actually appearing in the plant tissues. Magnesium is found in chlorophyll and plays an essential role in photosynthesis. A number of these nutrients are needed by plants in relatively large amounts. These are known as the macro (or major) nutrients. The rest, though still essential, are needed in much smaller amounts and are known as the micro nutrients (or trace elements). It is rare to find a deficiency of micro nutrients in the soil.

Macro Nutrients

The major nutrients include nitrogen, phosphorus, potassium, calcium, magnesium and sulphur.

Nitrogen This nutrient is responsible for making plant leaves grow quickly. Plants which are not getting sufficient nitrogen grow slowly, tend to have small pale-green leaves (also a sign of shortages of magnesium or iron) and may not flower or fruit well. Poor flowering or fruiting may also be a sign of too much nitrogen. In this case it will also be accompanied by an excess of lush vegetative growth which is easily damaged by frost and susceptible to disease.

Most of the nitrogen in the soil is present as organic matter, but plants cannot use it until it has been broken down into simpler forms by micro-organisms. The first of these simpler forms which plants can use is ammonium ions. In a healthy soil the micro-organisms will then convert the ammonium ions into nitrates which can also be used by plants. Nitrates are only loosely held by the soil and are easily lost in rainwater draining away through the soil. Ammonium ions are much more firmly held by the soil.

Phosphorus This nutrient has a stimulating effect on root activity and helps plants grow to the right colour. Plants which are not getting enough phosphorus generally grow slowly and may have dull leaves which are tinged bronze or dull purple. Plants rarely suffer from too much phosphorus but it can make deficiences of other elements, such as zinc, much more serious. Most of the phosphorus in soil occurs as phosphate and is not readily available to plants. Some phosphate comes from soil organic matter but the vast majority of it is produced by the weathering of mineral matter. Plants need quite a lot of phosphate when they are young to help them build up a good root system. Established plants may need much less. Very little phosphate dissolves in the water found in soil and so is not washed out of the soil by rainwater.

Potassium This element helps plants to produce firm growth and, to some extent, can offset the lush vegetative growth produced by too much nitrogen. It also helps plants when they are forming their flowers and helps fruit trees to produce good quality fruit with a long storage life. Plants which are suffering from a lack of potassium produce a range of different symptoms. As with most other deficiences, plants do not grow as well as you would expect and the edges of their older leaves often go either greyish-brown or bronze. Some plants may be stunted. Too much potassium can lead to a deficiency in magnesium. Potassium is present in the soil as potassium ions and is

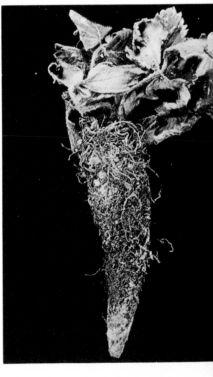

The result of planting a strawberry plant with a dibber (see *Tools and Equipment: Cultivating the Soil*): the roots are confined to the dibble hole

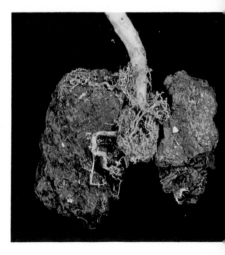

A brussels sprout plant with roots compacted through incorrect use of a dibber

15

formed through the weathering of mineral matter. (A little comes from the decomposition of organic matter.) Potassium is strongly held by the soil and only a little is lost in drainage water: Losses are heaviest on light, sandy soils.

Calcium This element is used by plants to build their cell walls. Soils with an excess of calcium are generally alkaline; those with a deficiency are acid. On acid soils plants may show symptoms of a deficiency of calcium or symptoms due to injury by an excess of other elements, such as manganese and aluminium, which dissolve more easily in soil water under acid conditions. Excess calcium may reduce the ability of plants to take up boron, iron and magnesium and so induce symptoms of deficiencies of these elements. See *Changing the Soil pH*.

Magnesium This element is used by plants to form chlorophyll. Plants suffering from a shortage of magnesium generally have pale leaves and much interveinal yellowing. The exact symptoms often vary from plant to plant. Magnesium can be found in various forms in the soil but is generally dissolved by soil water as either magnesium bicarbonate or magnesium sulphate. Plants take up a lot of magnesium when they are growing rapidly but almost stop as they approach maturity. This can make it quite difficult to treat magnesium deficiencies in mature plants.

Sulphur This element is continually being added to the soil through atmospheric pollution and is often one of the constituents of simple fertilizers. For these reasons sulphur deficiences are rare.

Micro Nutrients

These are needed by plants in tiny quantities and most are toxic to plants if too much is present. The margin between the right amount of micro nutrients and a toxic dose can be very small. Fortunately shortages of micro nutrients are rare and an adequate supply can generally be maintained by a regular programme of adding bulky organic materials to the soil. See *Improving Your Soil*. The wrong soil acidity or alkalinity can sometimes be responsible for micro nutrient deficiencies.

Acid or Alkaline?

The degree of acidity or alkalinity of a soil is measured on a scale called the pH (= potential Hydrogen) scale. A soil with a pH of 7 is neutral. One with a pH less than 7 is acid and one with a pH greater than 7 is alkaline. The pH scale is a logarithmic one so a soil with a pH of 4 is 10 times more acidic than one with a pH of 5 and 100 times more acidic than one with a pH of 6. Soils never reach the extremes of the scale. A very acid moorland or peat soil may have a pH of around 3·5; the most alkaline limey/calcareous soil may have a pH of between 8 and 9.

Plant Preferences

The table opposite outlines the pH ranges ideal for some plants. Plants may still grow, and sometimes flourish, outside these ranges but if you want to make sure of success it is best to stay within the figures given.

Shrubs and flowers vary a lot in their pH preferences. Rhododendrons, on one hand, like an acid soil but will not flourish at a pH much below 4·5. Lilacs, on the other hand, much prefer alkaline soils.

Vegetables generally grow best on a slightly acid to neutral soil. Potatoes grow well at a higher pH but to reduce the risk of potato scab *Streptomyces scabies* it is wise to keep the pH low – around 5·5. Most members of the brassica family will grow well at a fairly low pH but to reduce the risk of club root *Plasmodiophora brassicae* it is best to keep the pH around 6·5 to 7.

Coarse grasses grow well in slightly alkaline soil. Fine grasses grow well under acidic conditions. Keeping an ornamental lawn acid helps to make sure that only the right sort of grasses flourish.

Most fruits grow best on a slightly acid soil. Blueberries are the exception. They prefer a pH between 4 and 5.

Measuring pH

It is possible to get some idea of the pH of your soil by looking to see what plants grow well in your garden and in those of your neighbours. Weeds may also be good indicators of soil pH. Bracken, common sorrel, daisy, plantain, scentless mayweed, sheep's sorrel, sow thistle and spurrey can all indicate an acid soil. Bladder campion, campanula, salad burnet and scarlet pimpernel could mean an alkaline soil. At best, critical observations will give a rough estimate of soil pH. To get something better some sort of measurement is needed. You can do this yourself by using a pH testing kit or have it done professionally by a laboratory. Under *Determining Soil Type* we list those people who are likely to do textural analyses of soils. Most would measure soil pH too. Before sending samples, check whether they are able to do the measurement and how they want the sample to be taken. In most cases, samples will have to be taken from four or five different parts of the garden. Make sure that there is no confusion over the sort of measurement needed. A soil analysis is quite different from a soil pH measurement – see *Improving Your Soil*. Details for altering the pH of a soil are also given in this section.

pH Preferences of Plants

Vegetables	pH
Asparagus	6 to 7.5
Beetroot	6.5 to 7.5
Beans	6.5 to 7.5
Broccoli	6 to 7
Brussels Sprouts	6 to 7.5
Cabbages	6.5 to 7.5
Carrots	6 to 7.5
Cauliflowers	6.5 to 7.5
Celery	6.5 to 7.5
Cucumbers and Marrows	5.5 to 6.5
Leeks	6.5 to 7.5
Lettuces	6.5 to 7.5
Mushrooms	7 to 8
Onions	6.5 to 7.5
Parsley	5.5 to 6.5
Parsnips	6.5 to 7.5
Peas	6 to 7
Potatoes	5.5 to 6.5
Rhubarb	6.5 to 7.5
Spinach	6.5 to 7.5
Sweet Corn	6 to 7
Tomatoes	5.5 to 6.5
Turnips and Swedes	6 to 7

Flower and Shrubs	pH
Camellias	4.5 to 5.5
Carnations	6 to 7.5
Chrysanthemums	6 to 7
Delphiniums	6.5 to 7.5
Heathers	4.5 to 6
Hydrangeas (blue)	4.5 to 5
Hydrangeas (red)	7 to 7.5
Petunias	6 to 7
Rhododendrons and Azaleas	4.5 to 5.5
Roses	5.5 to 7
Zinnias	6 to 7.5

Fruits	pH
Apples	5.5 to 7
Blackberries	5.5 to 6.5
Black currants	6.5 to 7
Blueberries	4.5 to 5.5
Cherries	5.5 to 6.5
Grapes	5.5 to 6.5
Peaches	5.5 to 6.5
Pears	5.5 to 7
Plums	5.5 to 6.5
Raspberries	5 to 7
Red currants	5 to 6.5
Strawberries	5.5 to 7

Lawn grasses	pH
Browntop	4.5 to 6
Fescue – Chewings	5.5 to 6.5
Creeping Red	5.5 to 6.5
Sheep's	5 to 6
Ryegrass	6 to 7
Timothy	6 to 7

Improving Your Soil

Nearly all soils will benefit through some chemical or physical improvement. Clay soil can be made to drain faster and can be made easier to work. Sandy soils can be made to hold more water and plant nutrients. Acid soil can be made more alkaline and so on.

The first thing to do in any campaign of soil improvement is to make sure that the soil is well drained, particularly if it is clay, silt or fine sand. Then you can improve the top soil by adding bulky organic materials, changing the pH or by adding fertilizers.

Drainage

If soil becomes waterlogged and all the air is excluded from the pores then the roots of plants will start to die, disease organisms will step in and encourage further root damage, and plants may eventually die altogether. Unimpeded drainage through the soil is essential and is the prime consideration in soil improvement.

The Reasons for Poor Drainage

There are four main reasons for poor drainage.

On soils with a high proportion of clay, silt or fine sand, the pores between the mineral particles may be so small that water simply cannot pass through them easily.

The second and third reasons are similar – both are due to some sort of obstruction in the soil. If a soil is dug year after year to the same depth, then a hard impervious layer (a pan) can develop just below the level of cultivation. Even if the upper layers of soil drain freely then it is still possible to have poor drainage due to a layer of impervious material, such as compacted clay, in the subsoil. This impervious layer could be 1m (3ft) or more down.

The fourth reason is that the soil in your garden may be below the level of the water table in your area.

Establishing the Cause

The best way to find out whether drainage is poor is to dig a deep hole, to observe the colour of the soil as you go deeper and then to watch what happens to the water in the hole and in the surrounding soil. The hole needs to be about 1.2m (4ft) deep and about 1m (3ft) across. Do not dig it during a period of heavy rain.

Soil gets its colour from organic matter and soil minerals, from iron hydroxide in particular. The exact colour of these things depends upon how wet or acidic the soil has been in the past. A good, deep, well-drained soil will be a dark brown on the surface and will become lighter as the hole goes deeper. A mixture of browns and greys shows that the soil gets waterlogged from time to time – probably in very wet winters in the UK. A soil which is almost totally grey or bluish-grey is very poorly drained. Black layers of organic matter can also indicate very poor drainage.

Soils often change colour dramatically in going from the top soil to the subsoil. Do not confuse this sort of colour change with colour changes in the top soil. If the soil in your hole does not indicate poor drainage do not think that all is well – sometimes the signs of poor drainage are faint as the natural colour of the soil itself makes them difficult to detect.

If the hole starts filling with water while you are digging it or very soon afterwards even though no rain has fallen, look carefully to see from where the water is coming. If it is pouring into the hole from about the depth you normally dig to, then the probable cause of poor drainage is a hard pan. If the water then drains out of the hole after a few days, the answer to the drainage problem is simple – dig deeper and break up this hard pan. If it does not drain away, land drains may be necessary – see below.

If water gradually seeps into the bottom of the hole from all over the sides of the hole and does not drain away, then the water table in your area may be too high. Many plants will be happy growing in sandy loam with a water table 50 to 60cm (20 to 24in) below the surface of the soil, in a silty loam with a water table 75 to 90cm (30 to 36in) deep or in a clay loam with a water table $1 \cdot 0$ to $1 \cdot 1$m (40 to 44in) down. Soils with water tables at higher levels than these need land drains.

If the hole stays reasonably dry until it rains but takes more than four or five days to dry out again after rain, it is likely that there is some sort of obstruction below the level of the bottom of the hole which prevents water draining through. Again land drains will help.

Installing Drains

Land drains are porous clay pipes laid end to end with a steady fall from high to low ground. The drains are usually laid in a herringbone fashion, with branches coming out of a main drain, and should empty into a ditch, sewer or soakaway.

Surface capping, with a cracked cap on silt loam; note the beet seedling below the cap which has failed to emerge

Start by putting a stick into the ground where you want the pipes to terminate. Ideally this should be in the lowest part of the garden and it helps if it is as close to one corner as is possible. Next, using string and pegs, mark out a line diagonally across the garden for the main drain. Mark out the secondary drains at roughly 5m (16ft) intervals, staggering them so that they enter the main drain from each side alternately. If drainage is very poor the interval can be reduced to 3m (10ft). Secondary drains more than 6m (20ft) long should have a series of tertiary drains leading into them.

The tops of all drains should be at least 30cm (12in) below the top of the soil: 45cm (18in) is much better. The minimum workable drop for drains is $2 \cdot 5$cm in 2m (1in in 6ft) but if possible aim for $2 \cdot 5$cm in 1m (1in in 3ft). By combining the length of the drains with the drop and minimum depth, you can calculate the depth of the main drain entering the soakaway. If this is prohibitively deep then the drains are too long and a series of shorter drains terminating in a number of soakaways will be required.

Start the digging operations at the soakaway. The larger and deeper it goes the longer it will last. It should, at the very least, go below the level of any subsoil obstruction such as impermeable clay or rock. A soakaway 1m square (3½ft by 3½ft) by $1 \cdot 5$m (5ft) deep is an absolute minimum. Dig the sides of the soakaway vertically and line them with bricks. Do not put any mortar between those bricks which are below any impermeable subsoil layer. Use mortar on bricks above the impermeable layer and set the exit for the main drain into the brickwork. Fill the soakaway with broken bricks and rubble to about 30cm (1ft) from the top, cover the bricks with a layer of turf turned upside down and finish off by covering the whole thing with top soil. Dig the trenches for the drain checking the fall as you dig and again when you've finished. Drains should be laid on a layer of gravel so allow an extra 2 to 5cm (1 to 2in) in your calculations for depth. Remember to allow for the depth of the drain itself too. Lay the drains end to end on top of the gravel. The pipes should always be laid so that the clean-cut end is lower on the slope than the

Sub-surface compaction; the compacted zone is 8cm (3in) thick, 15cm (6in) below the surface

Laying drains

Construction of walls

Filling soakaway

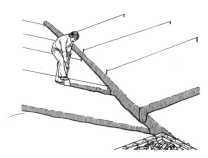

Excavation for drains

Covering the drain with gravel and
turned over turf

end with a shoulder (some land drains do not have shoulders). Cover the drain with more gravel, turned-over turf and finally with soil. Channels of rough rubble with turf and soil on top may be laid as an alternative to land drains.

If a high water table is the problem then a soakaway, no matter how deeply dug, will not solve the problem. The water will have to be collected and removed. Line the soakaway with heavy duty plastic sheeting to collect the water. The soakaway can now be turned into a garden pool. Water can be pumped from the pool into sewers or into a permanent ditch (check with the necessary authorities first). The level of water in the pool should always be kept below the bottom of the outlet from the main drain. If you are not allowed to pump water into sewers and there is not a handy permanent ditch, then you will have to use the pumping power of plants to disperse unwanted water. All plants lose water from their leaves by transpiration; with some the losses can be amazingly high. This water is taken from the soil through the plant's roots. If water from the lined soakaway is pumped on to a marginal area planted with a group of *Picea sitchensis* which are underplanted with hardy bamboos of the *Phyllostachys* group, then transpiration losses from these plants should keep the marginal area from flooding. Willows can also transpire vast amounts of water. In the subtropical zones of North America the choice of pumping plants is much larger.

Soil Organic Matter

Soil organic matter is the remains of plant and animal life. It exists in the soil in various stages of decomposition; the most decomposed part is known as humus.

Humus is a very complex material consisting of fats, carbohydrates and proteins and is constantly changing through the action of soil micro-organisms. Humus has two very important properties. It can hold many times its weight of water and can bind soil particles together. Both properties make it useful for improving the water-holding capacity of sandy soils and improving drainage through clay soils. Humus is also the only natural source of nitrogen for plants and plays a very important part in the natural cycling of nitrogen. When plants die they are dragged into the soil by organisms such as earthworms. Here, more organisms, including fungi and bacteria, convert the plants into humus which decays to release ammonium ions. The ammonium ions are converted into nitrate by more bacteria and new plants absorb this nitrate and use it to form plant tissues. The whole nitrogen cycle is much more complicated than this and

over a number of years the level of organic matter in soils which are highly cultivated gradually falls. Organic matter is burned up very quickly in sandy or alkaline soils.

Adding bulky organic manures can improve the water-holding or draining capacity and the fertility of most soils. Bulky organic matter can either be dug into the top 10cm (4in) of soil or spread over the land as a mulch about 7cm (3in) deep and just left. When digging in use about one barrow-load to each square metre.

Bulky Organic Manures

There are dozens of different organic materials which can be used to increase the level of organic matter in soils. Some of the more common ones are listed below.

Farm animal manure Animal manure is generally a mixture of straw and animal droppings. Manure which contains a lot of undecomposed straw is known as long manure. Well-rotted manure is called short manure. Horse manure is fibrous and rots down quickly giving off a lot of heat: it is known as hot manure. Manures from cows and pigs ferment slowly and remain quite cool: they are cold manures. Long horse manure is generally best for clay soils, silts and fine sands. Cold manure can be used on coarse and medium sandy soils.

Poultry manure Manure from battery hens is simply hen droppings. Fresh hen droppings are difficult to handle, smelly and can damage young plants. Add them to the compost heap. Poultry manure from broiler houses often has wood chippings mixed in with it and manure from deep-litter houses often contains straw. Both are dryish, easy to handle and are useful on most soils.

Spent mushroom compost This is basically highly decomposed strawy horse manure. Because it is so well rotted, it is not quite as useful as long horse manure for opening up heavy soils. Before repeatedly using heavy quantities of spent mushroom compost, ask the supplier how much lime the compost contains (this could seriously upset the soil pH) and what insecticides have been used – BHC which is widely used in some regions in mushroom growing could taint root vegetables and damage some flowers.

Sewage sludge Air-dried sewage sludge may be available from some water authorities. Two forms are usually available: raw and digested. Digested sludge is raw sludge which has been through various processes to make it less bulky and less smelly than raw sludge. Both forms of sludge may contain disease organisms such as *salmonella* so it is a wise precaution not to use sewage sludge near fruit or vegetables which are eaten raw, lettuces for example. Sewage sludge also contains variable quantities of metals, some of which may be harmful. Analyses of the metal content of sludges are sometimes available with the sludge. In general it is best to rely on the expertise of the water authority but make sure that they know what the sewage sludge is to be used for.

Peat In regions with a humid temperate climate, plants growing on land which is swampy may not decompose completely when they die. Instead they turn into a partially rotted organic material known as peat. Near the surface of the peat bog where the peat is freshest it will probably be brown, fibrous, light and porous. Deeper down where it has rotted further it will be black and more heavy. Most peat is one of two types (or a mixture of both). Sedge (or fen) peats are the remains of reeds and sedges and are dark coloured and well decayed. Sphagnum peats are mainly the remains of sphagnum and other mosses and are generally lighter coloured, less well decayed and able to hold much more water than sedge peats.

Peat is extremely good at holding water and is invaluable on coarse, light, sandy soil. It can also be used as a mulch, as a base material for potting and seed mixes – see *Seed and Potting Growing Mixes*, and for forming raised peat beds – see *Gardens: Peat Gardens*.

Compost In a carefully designed and well-constructed compost bin most garden and household waste can be converted into good compost.

Siting of the bin is important. It must be in full sun and open to the elements and it must be handy for both the vegetable garden and the kitchen. The shape of the bin is also important. Round ones are most efficient but difficult to make. An old oil drum which has had hundreds of large holes punched in it so that its external surface is about half and half holes to solid matter is ideal. Square or rectangular bins are simpler to make and use and are only slightly less efficient. The bin should be free standing with an adequate circulation of air around all sides. If you build your bin out of bricks, planks, chestnut palings or whatever, remember to leave about as much air space as solid matter on the outside. Lining the bin with wire netting will stop the refuse from falling out. A very simple bin can be constructed out of wire netting and four corner stakes.

Always build compost heaps on soil, never on concrete or other impervious material. Start the heap off by putting fibrous material such as broad bean haulms at the bottom. Build up the refuse in layers. Lay down about 15cm (6in) of garden waste and then a 5cm (2in) layer of soil. Repeat the sandwich until the bin is full. You can put almost any garden refuse into the bin; lawn clippings, weeds, leaves and so on and most kitchen vegetable waste, potato peelings and peapods, for example. Almost anything organic can go on to the heap except animal remains. These tend to attract scavengers. Do not add woody waste as it takes too long to rot down. Keep the heap damp but not too wet. Water it in dry weather and cover it with a tarpaulin in very wet weather. A sprinkling of a handful of Nitro-chalk on each layer or sulphate of ammonia and ground limestone on alternate layers will supply some of the nitrogen needed by the bacteria when they are decomposing the organic matter. Do not use Nitro-chalk or limestone if the compost is to be used around lime-hating plants. Use garden soil or manure instead. Two or three weeks after the bin is full turn the heap so that the inside becomes the outside and vice versa. The heap should be ready to use within two months in summer. In winter it will take much longer. Good compost has a light, crumbly texture and a rich, dark-brown colour. Do not worry if it is not quite like this, it will still be useful as a bulky organic manure. It takes practice to make good compost.

Other bulky organic manures Leaf-mould is an excellent source of humus but it can vary according to the degree of decomposition and the kind of leaves from which it is made. Oak and beech leaves are by tradition the best. Seaweed is rich in potassium, iron, manganese and zinc and can be a valuable source of humus. Do not stack seaweed in the open. Dig it into the soil a few months before you intend to start your plants. Sawdust is often widely available from sawmills. It should be well-rotted before it is used. Domestic soot contains up to 6 per cent nitrogen. It also contains tars which may be harmful to plants and should be stored under cover for three to six months before it is used. Shredded tree bark can be used as a peat substitute and in some areas local materials such as shoddy (in weaving areas) and spent hops (near breweries) provide useful, cheap sources of organic matter for the garden.

Changing the Soil pH

If your soil is very alkaline there is not a lot you can do to reduce the alkalinity. You will probably do best by concentrating on plants, like lilacs for instance, which grow well on alkaline soils. See *Gardening on a Limey/Chalky Soil*. If you desperately want to grow lime-hating plants such as *Ericas* then you will have to grow them in a peat bed – see *Gardens: Peat Gardens*. If you want to lower the pH a little you could use

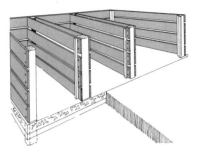

Timber compost bins

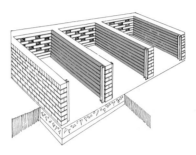

Three compost bins made from bricks. There are two timber battens to support a timber front. The floor is 15cm (6in) thick concrete on 10cm (4in) of hardcore

A detail of a timber slatted front to the compost bins above

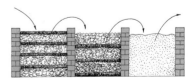

A three-bin cycle – on the left, the wide bands are organic matter, the narrow ones peat or soil plus activator. In the second year the compost is breaking down, and in the third it is ready for use.

Making a compost heap without a bin

Lay down and tread the bottom layer

Add a first layer of soil 5cm (2in) deep

Sprinkle some Nitro-chalk on the heap

Water the heap lightly

either flowers of sulphur at about 125g/m² (4oz/sq yd) or aluminium sulphate at much heavier doses. Aluminium sulphate can be used around hydrangeas to lower the pH and produce pink flowers. But aluminium is poisonous and aluminium sulphate should not be used near edible plants. Flowers of sulphur are much less obnoxious. Digging in and mulching with very acidic peats, and using acidic fertilizers like sulphate of ammonia will, over the years, marginally reduce the soil's pH.

Lime

If soil is very acid it can be left as it is – see *Gardening on an Acid Soil* – or it can be made less acid by using lime.

To a chemist lime is the popular name for calcium oxide. But to the gardener it is a name loosely used to cover chemical compounds containing calcium which can be used to reduce soil acidity. The most widely available form of lime is ground limestone or chalk: chemically calcium carbonate ($CaCO_3$). Hydrated or slaked lime is also easy to obtain. This is chemically calcium hydroxide ($Ca(OH)_2$). A third type of lime, quicklime, chemically calcium oxide (CaO), is much less widely available and should generally be avoided. Quicklime can cause skin burns if handled carelessly and is difficult to store safely.

Ground limestone or chalk often contains small amounts of magnesium. If lime contains a lot of magnesium it may be sold as magnesian limestone (at least 3 per cent actual magnesium) or burnt magnesian lime (at least 5½ per cent magnesium). In practice both magnesian limes contain about 10 per cent magnesium and are useful sources of this plant nutrient.

Neutralizing Value

The ability of a lime to reduce soil acidity is expressed in terms of a neutralizing value. The higher the neutralizing value the more effective the lime. Neutralizing values are expressed in terms of the chemical calcium oxide (CaO). One hundered kilos of a lime with a neutralizing value of 60 would have the same effect in reducing soil acidity as 60 kilos of calcium oxide. Ground limestone and chalk generally have a neutralizing value of around 55: hydrated lime around 70.

To compare the cost of using different limes you need to compare unit prices. In agriculture the unit price of lime is the cost per tonne/ton divided by its neutralizing value. You can use smaller quantities as long as all the limes being compared are in the same sized bags. The lower the unit price the cheaper the lime is to use.

Using Lime

Lime should generally be applied in the autumn after digging over the land in preparation for winter. It can either be spread on the surface of the soil or worked into the top 15cm (6in) but no deeper. Over-liming can do more damage than not liming at all so it is better to apply lime little and often rather than trying to make radical alterations to the soil pH over one season.

Nearly all proprietary brands of lime state clearly the suggested rates of application, and these should not be exceeded. If your soil test has shown only a small pH deficiency, then less than the amount stated can be used.

Different types of soil respond to liming in different ways. It takes much less lime to reduce the acidity of a sandy soil from pH5·5 to pH6·5 than it would to reduce the acidity of a clay soil by the same amount. The table below shows the amounts of lime needed to bring various types of soil to a pH of 6·5 – the pH at which most plants grow well. The table also shows the amount of lime needed to bring a peat soil to pH5·5. Plants grow just as well on a peat soil at this pH as they would on a mineral soil at 6·5 and any attempt to make peat soils any less acid could result in micro-element deficiencies. The numbers in the table refer to ground limestone or chalk. If hydrated lime is used the numbers should be reduced by 20 per cent.

Lime requirement for different soils using calcium carbonate with a neutralizing value of 50. Expressed in kg/m² (lbs/sq yd)

pH	loamy sands	sandy loams	loams	clay loams	clays	peat
6·0	0·1 (¼)	0·3 (½)	0·3 (½)	0·5 (1)	0·5 (1)	—
5·5	0·4 (¾)	0·5 (1)	0·7 (1¼)	1·1 (2)	1·2 (2¼)	0·8 (1½)
5·0	0·7 (1¼)	0·8 (1½)	1·1 (2)	1·5 (2¾)	1·8 (3¼)	1·8 (3¼)
4·5	1·0 (1¾)	1·1 (2)	1·6 (3)	2·0 (3½)	2·3 (4¼)	2·3 (4¼)
4·0	1·2 (2¼)	1·5 (2¾)	2·0 (3½)	2·6 (4¾)	3·0 (5½)	3·0 (5½)
3·5	1·5 (2¾)	2·0 (3½)	2·4 (4½)	3·0 (5½)	3·7 (6¾)	3·7 (6¾)

Supplying Plant Nutrients

If plants are to grow well they need an adequate supply of the basic plant nutrients. In established ornamental gardens regular mulching with bulky organic manures should provide enough nutrients to keep plants healthy. But in areas of the garden where plants are grown intensively and then removed – the vegetable garden, for example – extra nutrients may well have to be added. Extra nutrients are also essential when plants are establishing themselves soon after planting out. These extra nutrients are added as fertilizers.

The most important foods needed by plants are nitrogen, phosphorus, potassium and calcium. Most soils have adequate supplies of calcium so fertilizer treatments concentrate on supplying the extra amounts of nitrogen (N), phosphorus (P) and potassium (K).

Types of Fertilizer

Fertilizers are usually classified as either simple (sometimes called straight), compound or complete. Simple fertilizers supply one of the three basic nutrients, compound fertilizers supply two and complete fertilizers supply all three.

Fertilizers may also be called organic or inorganic. Organic fertilizers are generally those which are from animal or vegetable origin. Inorganic ones have been synthesized by man or dug out of the ground. In fact both organic and inorganic fertilizers are man-made and as far as the plant is concerned both supply nutrients equally well. If a sensible programme of adding bulky organic manures is adopted then claims that inorganic fertilizers destroy the soil structure and organic fertilizers help build it up can be safely ignored.

Manufacturers of fertilizers are required by law in the UK, the USA and in Canada to state on their packages the amounts of nitrogen, phosphorus and potassium in the fertilizer. Nitrogen is expressed in terms of the element nitrogen (N); phosphorus as phosphate (P_2O_5) and potassium as potash (K_2O). The amount of phosphate present may be further sub-divided into the phosphate which is readily soluble in water (and so quick-acting) and that which is insoluble. The table below shows some of the more widely available fertilizers and the amount of plant nutrient they contain.

Nitrogen fertilizers Nitrogen fertilizers are generally used in the spring when plants are growing well and can make use of the nitrogen to build up leaf tissues. The form of nitrogen in the fertilizer is important. Plants can use nitrate ions immediately but they are quickly washed out of the soil in drainage water. These fertilizers are best used as top dressings and applied when plants need a nitrogen boost – on spring cabbages in early spring perhaps. Fertilizers containing ammonium ions are slower acting. Plants can use some of the ammonium ions immediately but take up most of the nitrogen after the ammonium ions have been converted to nitrate ions by soil bacteria. Organic fertilizers such as dried blood and hoof-and-horn have most of their nitrogen bound up as complex organic molecules which have to be broken down before the

Fertilizers

	per cent nutrient	type of fertilizer	speed of action
Nitrogen fertilizers			
ammonium nitrate	34	inorganic	quick-acting
dried blood	12	organic	fairly quick-acting
hoof-and-horn	12	organic	quick-acting
nitrate of potash	13*	inorganic	quick-acting
nitrate of soda	16	inorganic	quick-acting
Nitro-chalk	25	inorganic	quick-acting
sulphate of ammonia	21	inorganic	fairly quick-acting
urea	46	inorganic	quick-acting
Phosphate fertilizers			
basic slag	14	inorganic	slow-acting
bone meal	24†	organic	slow-acting
superphosphate	19	inorganic	quick-acting
Potash fertilizers			
muriate of potash	60	inorganic	quick-acting
nitrate of potash	44	inorganic	quick-acting
sulphate of potash	50	inorganic	quick-acting

* also contains about 44 per cent potash
† contains variable amounts of nitrogen

plant can make use of them so these fertilizers are generally slower acting still. Because ammonium and organic fertilizers are slow acting they are useful for raking into seed beds before the seeds are sown.

Phosphate fertilizers Phosphate fertilizers divide roughly into two groups. Triple superphosphate, superphosphate and bone phosphate contain phosphate which dissolves in water and all three are quick acting. These are best for young plants which need a lot of phosphate fast – seedlings for example. Water-soluble phosphates are changed by the chemicals in the soil into forms which plants cannot use. Apply them near to seeds or young plants and keep the pH around the plants as near to neutral as possible. Bone meal and basic slag contain phosphate which will not immediately dissolve in water and both are slow acting. Slow-acting phosphate fertilizers are best for plants which have a long growing season or for digging into the soil when plants are being set out in their dormant season. Basic slag contains lime and its use should be avoided on alkaline soil.

Potash fertilizers All potash fertilizers supply potassium in the form of potassium ions which can be used by plants immediately. Potassium ions are not readily washed out of the soil in drainage water so potash fertilizers can be applied some time before the plant needs them. Some plants may be injured by the chloride ions in muriate of potash (potassium chloride), particularly fruit trees and bushes.

Common salt (sodium chloride) This may be beneficial or harmful to soil depending on the amount present. When agricultural salt is applied at 55 to 75g/m^2 (1½ to 2oz/sq yd) around root crops, celery and cabbage, the sodium replaces potassium and is said to improve the water and phosphate uptake.

If too much agricultural salt is used or where the soil is flooded by sea-water, then the structure of the soil is destroyed and it becomes impermeable to water. This effect is known as deflocculation and is due to the sodium displacing calcium and magnesium from clay particles. It is the reverse effect of calcium in lime binding clay particles together. Soil which has been flooded by sea-water can be reclaimed just before it is completely dried out by adding gypsum (calcium sulphate) at 300 to 1,500 g/m^2 (½ to 2½ lb/sq yd). The more clayey the soil, the more gypsum is needed.

Foliar feeds Plants originated in the sea and everything they needed for growth, including nutrients, was absorbed over the whole surface of the plant. Plants have now adapted to growing on land and taking up nutrients through their roots but they can still absorb small amounts of nutrients through their leaves. Applying nutrients to the leaves in the form of foliar feeds is a particularly useful technique for getting food into plants when their roots are not functioning properly. They promote root growth and therefore are valuable when applied to newly planted trees, shrubs, roses or indeed any plants.

Bulky organic manures As well as improving the structure of soils and supplying nutrient fuel for vital soil micro-organisms, bulky organic manures can themselves supply plant nutrients. Compared with fertilizers the amounts they supply are low and variable. The table shows the approximate NPK contents of bulky manures. It is not possible to give exact figures. The figure for horse manure, for example, depends upon

Bulky organic manures

	Approximate Percentage of Nutrients		
	nitrogen	phosphate	potash
horse manure	0·7	0·5	0·6
cow manure	0·6	0·3	0·7
sheep manure	0·6	0·3	0·7
pig manure	0·6	0·6	0·4
battery chicken manure	1·7	1·4	0·7
broiler chicken manure	2·4	2·2	1·4
deep-litter chicken manure	1·7	1·8	1·3
turkey manure	1·9	1·5	0·9
garden compost	1·5	2·0	0·7
mushroom compost	0·6	0·5	0·9
leaf-mould	0·4	0·2	0·3
peat	1·0	0	0
sawdust	0·2	0·1	0·1
seaweed	0·6	0·3	1·0
sewage sludge	1·0	0·6	0·2
soot	3·6	0·1	0·1
spent hops	1·1	0·3	0·1

what the horse has eaten, how much straw is mixed in the manure and how long and where the manure has been stored.

Improving Specific Soils

Improving the most common extremes of soil – sand, clay, acid and alkaline soils – is discussed separately on this and following pages. This section looks at how to improve some of the easiest and some of the most difficult, though less common, soils.

Loam soils These need little improvement and the aim should be to maintain them in good condition. In flower borders and areas where plants are not being continuously removed, regular mulches of bulky organic manures will keep the level of humus in the soil roughly right and will supply most of the basic nutrients needed by the plants. When setting out new plants dig in a phosphate fertilizer. On vegetable plots regular incorporation of bulky organic manures will help to replace the humus taken away from the soil when the crop is removed and will supply some nutrients. But fertilizers will be needed to supply the extra nutrients required by vegetables. Either follow the recomendations for individual vegetables given under *Edible Plants: Vegetables* or use a complete fertilizer. A 7:7:7 complete fertilizer (one with 7 per cent nitrogen, 7 per cent phosphate and 7 per cent potash) may be spread over the plot at about 70 to 140g/m² (2 to 4oz/sq yd) in spring.

Stony soils These are very rapid draining and hold very few plant nutrients. The more bulky organic manures you add the better. If you take out the stones you should replace each stone removed with a handful of coarse sand. The best way to garden on very stony soils is to garden above the soil rather than in it. Use a lot of bulky organic manure and simply spread it over the surface of the soil. Over the years these repeated dressings of manure will form a layer of fertile soil above the level of the original stony soil. Earthworms dragging the organic materials downwards will help improve the fertility of the original stony soil too. Compost is a particularly useful bulky manure for this technique.

Peat soils These have too much humus but lack nutrients and good drainage. Tackle drainage problems first then dig in bulky organic manures mixed with an equal proportion of very sharp sand. The particle size of the sand should be between 0·05mm and 2mm. Dig in this mixture a little deeper each year. The more sloppy bulky organic manures can be used on peat soils. These soils are very acid. You can reduce the acidity by adding lime or adjust your ideas to living with an acid soil – see *Gardening on an Acid Soil*.

Gumbo or Adobe soils These are rich in minerals but dry. Dig in as much bulky organic material as possible – the aim is to improve the water-holding capacity of the soil. These soils are very alkaline so you may need to adjust your gardening techniques to accommodate this – see *Gardening on a Limey/Chalky Soil*.

Muck soils These are dealt with in the same way as a peat soil but drainage is unlikely to be a problem.

Gardening on a Limey/Chalky Soil

Chalk is derived from the skeletons of sea creatures which were deposited on the sea floors many years ago. Subsequent changes in the surface of the earth have left these chalk beds as soft surface rocks often covered by no more than a thin layer of soil. Soils over limestone/chalk are usually strongly alkaline (pH 8 to 9) but in areas of heavy rainfall the thin layer of soil may have become acidic.

Some soils may be strongly alkaline because of repeated heavy liming. If no more lime is added to these soils, then they will slowly change to neutral or perhaps even acidic soils. But while these soils are strongly alkaline they have many of the disadvantages of a limestone/chalk soil and often lack their advantages.

Most limestone/chalk soils are very well drained and those with a deep layer of top soil are often quite fertile. Many limestone/chalk soils are, however, very shallow with the solid chalk no more than 75 to 100mm (3 to 4in) below the soil surface. Organic matter breaks down rapidly in limestone/chalk soils and, because of the alkalinity of these soils, some plant foods are less available to plants.

Improving the Soil

Soils over limestone/chalk may be light and sandy or heavy and clayey. In both cases it is likely that the soil will be low in humus and other organic matter and consequently limestone/chalk soils are often poor soils lacking in basic plant nutrients. Sandy soils over chalk are particularly poor. Annual applications of bulky organic materials like garden compost, leaf-mould, manure, peat and so on are essential to increase and maintain fertility. On shallow soils any well-rotted materials should be lightly forked or raked into the soil. Deep digging should be avoided as this will bring limestone/chalk particles to the surface and may increase the alkalinity of the soil.

Clayey limestone soils may be ridged in winter (see *Cultivation: Digging*); sandy soils do not need exposure to the winter

If you have an acid soil rhododendrons and azaleas will grow very successfully

weather and should be dug in mid or late winter (or in the early spring in parts of Northern America) while the soil is still moist and firm.

It is difficult to reduce permanently the alkalinity of a limestone/chalk soil. Using flowers of sulphur, aluminium sulphate, peat and acidic fertilizers may help in the short term.

Planting

Deciduous trees and shrubs can be planted immediately after the leaves have fallen off or at any other time during the winter, provided the soil is free from frost and snow. Plant evergreens and conifers in cool weather at the latter part of the year or in spring as they are beginning to make new growth. On heavy soils which are susceptible to water-logging in winter it is advisable to plant trees and shrubs in spring as soon as the soil is workable.

Planting trees and shrubs in deep limestone/chalky soil presents no special problems. When planting trees and shrubs in shallow soils, it will often be necessary to

excavate into the limestone/chalk itself to make a hole which is deep enough to hold all the roots. The first step is to remove the top soil carefully and pile it into a heap at the side of the hole. Then break up the limestone/chalk with a crowbar or something similar and remove it. Keep checking the size of the hole until it is deep enough to take the plant's roots easily with the tree or shrub set at its original depth and with its roots spread out well. Position any stakes as necessary. Before planting the tree in the hole, thrust the crowbar into the sides and bottom of the hole several times to splinter the solid limestone/chalk. This will improve drainage and make it easier for the roots of the tree or shrub to penetrate into the limestone/chalk. Line the hole with an acidic organic material such as peat. If such materials are unavailable, line the hole with other bulky organic manures which have been heavily dusted with flowers of sulphur. Both methods will help to counteract the strong alkalinity of the limestone/chalk in the early stages of the plant's establishment. Fill in the hole with good, fertile top soil. Do not put the lumps of broken-up limestone/chalk back into the hole. Water in well and mulch heavily, preferably with acidic materials.

Looking after Plants

On dry, poor, shallow soils, regular mulching is essential, particularly for young plants. Apply mulches in spring before the onset of drier weather. Renew mulches during the summer months if suitable material is available.

Unless the soil contains a high percentage of clay or has been well manured in previous seasons, plant nutrients added as fertilizers will be lost quickly, particularly in wet weather or when frequent watering is necessary. A generous application of fertilizers in the early spring at about 100 to 140g/m² (3 to 4oz/sq yd) will supply all the nutrients needed in the early part of the growing season. Later on further feeding will be necessary, particularly with nitrogen. Use sulphate of ammonia at about 10 to 20g/m² (¼ to ½oz/sq yd) at regular intervals whenever it looks necessary to stimulate leaf and shoot growth. Alterna-tively plants can be fed with light, but frequent, doses of soluble feed which will supply all three major plant nutrients. Do not use alkaline fertilizers such as bonemeal (for phosphate) and Nitro-chalk (for nitrogen).

Choosing Plants

Many plants will grow satisfactorily on slightly alkaline soils but few of these will tolerate the combination of alkalinity and shallowness of soil found on many limestone/chalk soils. Differences in tolerance occur even between plants in the same genus.

Most herbaceous plants grow on limestone/chalk soils including a number of lilies, *Lilium candidum* for example.

Many alpine or rock garden plants are also tolerant of limestone/chalk soils. A short list is given below.

Campanula	*Gentiana verna*
Dianthus	*Phlox*
Gentiana acaulis	*Saxifrage*

Trees and shrubs Rhododendrons, azaleas

Nearly all vegetables prefer a neutral or only slightly acid soil – this squash will grow best with a pH of around 6·5.

and camellias are unable to obtain or absorb sufficient amounts of iron, magnesium and other micro nutrients under alkaline conditions. To grow these plants successfully on limestone/chalk soils, it is necessary to isolate them from the natural soil environment. See *Gardens: Peat Gardens*. Roses grow best on heavy loam soils but they can be grown well if the ground is carefully prepared. Adding bulky organic manures, mulching and feeding with fertilizers are all essential. If conditions are very poor, choose the stronger-growing shrub roses or the floribunda varieties in preference to the weaker hybrid teas.

A list of trees and shrubs, which are among the most suitable for shallow limestone/chalk soils, is given below.

Trees

Acer negundo	*Crataegus*
Acer platanoides	*Malus*
Aesculus	*Prunus*
Cercis	*Sorbus*

Shrubs

Berberis	*Lonicera*
Buddleia davidii	*Olearia*
Ceanothus	*Paeonia*
Cistus	*Philadelphus*
Clematis	*Potentilla fruticosa*
Cotoneaster	*Senecio*
Deutzia	*Spartium junceum*
Forsythia	*Spiraea japonica*
Fuchsia	*Syringa*
Hebe	*Weigela*
Hypericum	

Conifers

Juniperus communis	*Thuja occidentalis*
Juniperus × media	*Thuja plicata*
Taxus baccata	

Fruits These do not grow well on limestone/chalk soils. Gooseberry is totally unsuitable; raspberry, plum and pear are not good; black currant and apple are variable, but usually not very good. If an attempt is to be made to grow fruit, it is essential to dig heavy dressings of organic matter into the soil before planting and apply more later as heavy annual mulches. Confining the choice of fertilizers to those which give an acidic reaction will help to keep the soil in the region of the roots more acid than elsewhere. For example, sulphate of ammonia applied at about 10g/m² (¼oz/sq yd) at two to three week intervals over the growing season will supply adequate nitrogen.

Vegetables These prefer a slightly acid soil but can be grown on limestone/chalky soils which have been heavily manured in previous years. Where little improvement is possible, asparagus (which grows naturally on limestone/chalk), onions, chicory and all the brassica family, including cabbage, cauliflower and turnips, will give the best results. Carrots, parsnips and parsley also usually grow well. When planting potatoes, line the trenches with peat or similar well-decomposed organic manures. Incorporate similar materials into the soil in quantity where lettuces, tomatoes, peas, celery and climbing beans are to be grown. Spinach and dwarf or bush beans may fail if the soil is strongly alkaline.

Lawns The grass on lawns over limestone/chalky soils often looks sparse and open and is highly susceptible to infestation by weeds and mosses. Regular feeding with fertilizers is essential to keep the grass growing well. In spring apply a complete fertilizer. A few weeks later, apply sulphate of ammonia at about 10 to 20g/m² (¼ to ½ oz/sq yd). Repeat this application every five to six weeks until grass growth slows down towards the end of spring. The fertilizer should be applied mixed with soil or sand to prevent scorching of the grass through uneven application and the lawn should be watered if the weather is dry. A top-dressing should be applied every year in late summer.

Gardening on an Acid Soil

Soils which do not contain natural deposits of limestone or chalk tend to become more and more acidic. Many factors contribute towards this increase in acidity including industrial pollution, soot, exhaust fumes from internal combustion engines, some fertilizers and the natural processes taking place in the soil, including ·absorption of calcium by plants. Acidity is not restricted to any particular type of soil; clay soils are just as likely to be acidic as sand.

Over the years some plants have adapted themselves to living on acid soils, others on alkaline soils. In general, those plants which grow well on alkaline soils will be successful on neutral or acid soils too but a few plants, such as azaleas, rhododendrons and heathers, will grow satisfactorily on acid soil only. Differences in tolerance occur not only between different genera but between different species of the same genus. Most ericas, for example, demand acid soil but *Erica carnea* will grow well on a neutral or slightly alkaline soil. Some magnolias will tolerate alkaline soils, others will not.

Improving the Soil

If soil is sandy or clayey it may need improvement because of its extreme texture. See *Gardening on a Sandy Soil* and *Gardening on a Clay Soil*. It is fairly easy to reduce the acidity of an acid soil by using lime or to increase it by incorporation of peat, for example.

Choosing the Plants

Soils which are moderately acid, with a pH between 5 and 5·5, provide the opportunity to grow quite a large number of plants which will not grow well on alkaline soils.

Herbaceous plants Many plants from alpine regions (see *Ornamental Plants: Alpines*) and from cool, acid soil areas such as the woodlands of Japan prefer an acid soil. The lily and primula families are good examples.

Trees and shrubs The genus *Rhododendron* is the most important group of acid-loving plants. They need a soil with a pH less than 5·5 but some will grow reasonably well up to about pH6. There are numerous gardens in North America and Europe where rhododendrons are grown almost exclusively. The genus *Rhododendron* contains many species and innumerable hybrids or varieties which vary from tiny dwarf alpines to tree-like plants which may grow 6 to 9m (20 to 30ft) high. In the UK alone there are over 500 species and 3,000 recorded hybrids. Most rhododendrons flower in spring but it is possible to plant a rhododendron garden which has blooms for up to eight months of the year in some areas. Azaleas are botanically rhododendrons and are invariably grown under the same conditions. Other acid-loving trees and shrubs include:

Calluna	*Eucryphia*
Camellia	*Hamamelis*
Cornus kousa	*Kalmia*
Embothrium	*Magnolia*
Enkianthus	*Pernettya*
Erica	*Pieris*

Fruits All fruit trees and bushes, except blueberry and bilberry, like a soil which is slightly acid. Blueberry and bilberry prefer considerable acidity in soils. For further details of preference of individual fruits see *pH Preferences of Plants*. Check the acidity of the soil before planting. If the pH is less than that required add lime to raise the pH to between 6·3 and 6·5.

Vegetables To grow vegetables successfully on acid soils, the pH should be raised and maintained at 6 to 7. This is usually done by adopting a three- or four-year cycle of crop rotation. Each year, in winter, lime is applied to the third or quarter of the vegetable garden which will be used to grow brassicas in the following season. For details see *Edible Plants: Vegetables*.

Gardening on a Clay Soil

Growing plants on clay soils is always a challenge. The list of problems is long. In wet weather they get very sticky and frequently become water-logged and if this lasts for long, perennial plants, shrubs and even trees may die. Clay soils are slow to dry out and warm up in spring and this may lead to delayed planting and subsequent low yields of vegetables. If vegetables are not harvested before winter sets in they may be lost through rotting. In dry weather, clay shrinks and forms rock-hard lumps and the soil may crack and tear tender plant roots. Young plants with undeveloped root systems may find it very difficult to establish themselves in clay soils, but clay soils are potentially rich in plant nutrients.

Improving the Soil

The first thing to look at is the drainage. See *Improving your Soil*. Organic manures and sharp sand will improve the texture of the soil. Add one part of very sharp sand (0·05mm to 2·0mm) to four parts of bulky organic manure every year. Do not bury the organic manure: keep it in the top 30cm (12in) of soil. The manure is best applied in the winter or late autumn followed by the sharp sand in the spring, just before planting. Sharp grit, broken bricks or weathered ashes (with the fine particles removed) can be used instead of sharp sand. Lime can make clay particles flocculate in small clusters and so improve workability and drainage. Add lime in winter or autumn but do not add it at the same time as bulky organic manures and do not use it on alkaline soils.

The weathering effects of wind, frost and rain can be utilized to open up clay soils. To get the best out of the weather, it is necessary to expose as large an area of soil as possible. This is done by a method called ridging. See *Cultivation: Digging*.

If your garden if far too large to do everything in one season, it is best to concentrate your efforts on a small area where plants will most appreciate the improvement.

Planting

Planting should be done when the soil is workable. Do not attempt it when conditions are wet and sticky underfoot. If the soil is waterlogged in winter, then it is advisable to delay planting until the soil dries out a little in the spring.

Deciduous plants should be planted before the leaf buds are far advanced. Evergreens can usually wait a further three or four weeks until their roots become active. If trees and shrubs arrive from the nursery in wet or frosty weather they should be heeled in until conditions improve. Heeling-in is a form of temporary planting. Make a shallow trench in a well-drained part of the garden. Place the roots of the trees and shrubs in the trench, close together, with stems angled at about 45 degrees. Heap the soil over the roots and

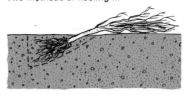

Two methods of heeling in

Lay the trees at an angle, and cover the roots with soil

lightly firm it. Alternatively, the plants can simply be laid on the surface of the soil and their roots covered deeply with leaf-mould or similar material.

Dig a hole which is deep and wide enough to take all the roots of the tree or shrub without overcrowding. Break up the soil at the bottom of the planting hole with a fork. Mix coarse sand or grit and leaf-mould or rough peat with the soil taken out of the hole. This will improve drainage around the plant and help the roots to establish quickly. Put this mixture around the plant roots and break down the sides of the planting hole as it is filled. A smooth-sided hole may act like a sump and collect and hold water around the roots of the plant. Do not use much peat in planting holes in heavy clay soils as this too may act as a sump.

Planting near Buildings
Do not plant vigorous-growing trees which need a lot of water close to houses or other buildings with relatively shallow foundations. In dry periods during the summer months, the roots of such trees could extract enough moisture from the clay to make it shrink and produce large deep cracks in the soil. These cracks can seriously damage the foundations of buildings. Many trees can cause damage but poplars and weeping willow seem to be the major offenders. Do not plant either in small gardens on clay soils. In larger gardens keep individual poplars and willows at least 20m (over 60ft) from buildings. If a row of poplars is grown as a windbreak keep at least 30m (100ft) between the trees and any building.

Looking after Plants
Clay soils are usually very fertile and regular application of bulky organic manures will satisfy most plants. If there is some doubt about fertility apply a general fertilizer a few days before sowing or planting. A 7 per cent nitrogen: 7 per cent phosphate: 7 per cent potash fertilizer could be applied at 100 to 140g/m² (3 to 4oz/sq yd).

Choosing Plants
On heavy clay soils it is best to choose plants which you know will survive. Look at neighbouring gardens to see what plants grow well for other people.

Herbaceous Plants Many herbaceous plants will grow well on clay soils. Some are listed below.

Achillea	Helianthus
Aster	Hemerocallis
Bergenia	Iris germanica
Campanula	Phlox
Geranium	Rudbeckia
Helenium	Solidago

Bulbs Most bulbous plants, including the popular tulips and daffodils, can be grown successfully on clay soils as long as provision is made to improve drainage. Good drainage is essential for plants grown from corms, such as crocuses and gladioli. On the lighter clay soils place a handful of coarse, sharp sand or grit underneath and around the bulb or corm. On wetter soils build a raised bed, at least 10cm (4in) high, to keep the bulb or corm above the natural soil level.

Trees and shrubs Ornamental trees and shrubs which will usually grow well on clay soils include:

Trees

Acer	Malus sp.
Betula sp.	Prunus sp.
Crataegus sp.	Salix sp.
Laburnum	Sorbus sp.

Shrubs

Aucuba	Ilex
Berberis	Juniperus sp.
Buddleia	Kerria
Chaenomeles	Mahonia
Colutea sp.	Philadelphus sp.
Corylus sp.	Potentilla
Cotoneaster	Pyracantha
Deutzia	Ribes sp.
Escallonia	Spiraea
Euonymus sp.	Symphoricarpos sp.
Forsythia	Syringa
Hedera	Viburnum

Fruits If the soil is well-drained, all hardy fruit crops can be attempted. Good drainage is particularly important for cherries, plums, strawberries and red currants. Use plenty of organic matter when preparing the ground for planting black currants and other bush fruit.

Vegetables Clay soils are slow to warm up in the spring and so cloches and cold frames are essential to produce early spring salads such as lettuces, radishes and onions. Early crops could also be grown on raised beds filled with lighter soil. The most suitable vegetables for clay soils are broad beans, red or salad beetroot, brassicas, onions, peas and seakale.

Lawns On clay soils, it pays to spend a lot of time preparing the site of a new lawn. Providing adequate drainage is essential. Seed sowing in autumn is possible but a spring-sown lawn is more likely to succeed. Dig the soil in early winter, allow it to over-winter and break it down in spring ready for sowing the seed in April (ten days after the average frost free date in North America). Soils which are impossible to rake finely enough for seed can be turfed in early winter. Before laying the turf place 25mm (1in) or so of sharp sand, grit or weathered ash over the soil to assist aeration and drainage.

Gardening on a Sandy Soil

The advantages of sandy soils are basically physical and mechanical. Because they are usually composed of relatively large, rough particles and have fairly large air spaces between the particles, they warm up quickly in spring and are easy to dig at almost any time of the year. But their disadvantages tend to outweigh their advantages. The large air spaces mean that sandy soils have low moisture retention and rapidly dry out after rain. They also contain very little humus and clay which means that their nutrient reserves are low. Extra nutrients added as fertilizers cannot be held long by sandy soils and are quickly washed out by natural rainfall or through the frequent watering which becomes necessary in dry weather.

Improving the Soil

The size of the mineral particles in sandy soils can vary from very coarse large particles which give good drainage to very fine sands which may be as poorly drained as heavy clays. If the particles are coarse, dig in as much bulky organic manure as possible. If the particles are very small then the best thing to do is to garden on top of the soil rather than in it. Organic matter breaks down quite quickly in sandy soils, particularly if they are strongly alkaline. To maintain a reasonable level of soil fertility it is essential to repeat the addition of organic matter every year.

Planting

This should only be done when the soil is moist. Dry seed beds should be watered thoroughly before seeds are sown and at frequent intervals afterwards until the seedlings are established.

Trees and shrubs should be planted as soon as cool moist conditions start to set in in the autumn. It is essential to have finished planting trees and shrubs well before drier conditions arrive with spring. Conifers and evergreens, in particular, will benefit from being planted in the garden in early autumn.

Add plenty of leaf-mould or peat to planting holes before setting out trees or shrubs. A double handful of bonemeal can be mixed in with each bucketful of organic matter. After planting, firm the soil well so that a slight depression is left around the plant. Soak the soil well, allow to drain, rake the surface slightly and then place a thick mulch around the plant.

Looking after Plants

Most of the attention given to plants on sandy soils should be aimed at overcoming the free draining properties of these soils.

Annual mulching is essential for fruit trees and will benefit ornamental trees, shrubs and herbaceous plants. Apply the mulch in the spring well before dry weather sets in. In hot weather sandy soils lose their water very rapidly and plants may die quite suddenly. All parts of the garden should be checked at regular intervals, daily if possible, and watered when necessary. Take care not to allow fine sands to dry out: they become very difficult to remoisten.

Plant nutrients are quickly washed out of sandy soils and all plants, including lawns, will benefit from light and frequent applications of fertilizers. These are always best applied in showery weather or scorching may occur.

Choosing Plants

Many annuals, bulbs and herbaceous plants will thrive in a dry sandy soil provided that the soil has been prepared well and a lot of attention is given to subsequent feeding and watering. When choosing trees and shrubs it is best to pick those which are tolerant of dry sandy conditions. Some are listed below. For further details of size, flowers and so on, see *Ornamental Plants*.

Trees

Crataegus	*Laburnum*

Shrubs

Berberis sp.	*Hypericum*
Calluna	*Lonicera*
Chaenomeles sp.	*Olearia*
Colutea arborescens	*Potentilla*
Cotoneaster	*Robinia*
Cytisus	*Salvia*
Elaeagnus	*Senecio*
Fuchsia	*Spartium junceum*
Genista	*Tamarix* sp.
Hebe	*Yucca*

Vegetables On very sandy, dry soils all vegetables are likely to grow poorly and give low yields but if the soil is improved by digging in bulky organic manures then most vegetables can be attempted and grown successfully. The most difficult vegetables to grow satisfactorily are broccoli, cauliflowers, lettuce and spinach; root vegetables such as carrots and parsnips are the most successful. Give potatoes a good start by planting them in furrows or trenches which have been well lined with a bulky organic manure. Plant tomatoes in shallow trenches on soil which has been previously well-manured. As the plants grow place 25 to 50mm (1 to 2in) of leaf-mould or similar organic material around the base of the plants and along the trench. Keep this material moist so that stem roots grow from the tomato plants into it.

Seed and Potting Growing Mixes

When plants are grown in pots, trays or tubs, you have much more control over the composition of the growing medium around their roots than when they are grown in the open garden. The growing medium can be formulated so that it has: a good physical structure with an adequate supply of air and the ability to hold enough, but not too much, water; total freedom from pests, diseases and weeds; and an adequate, balanced supply of plant nutrients.

The growing medium (or seed and potting growing mix) can be either soil-based or soilless. Soil-based growing mixes are mixtures of loamy soil, peat and coarse sand or grit with an additional supply of plant nutrients and lime to balance the acidity of the peat. Soilless growing mixes are mixtures of sand and peat with nutrients and lime. The basic ingredients of growing mixes should be chosen and used with care.

Loam This should be made from the top 10 to 12cm (4 to 5in) of grass land which has been stacked with the grass side down (add lime if necessary to bring the pH to 6·3) for at least six months until it is thoroughly rotted. If turfy loam is unobtainable use good loamy soil with thin layers of strawy horse manure added to the stack at roughly 15cm (6in) intervals. A few weeks before the loam is needed, cover the top of the stack to make sure that the loam is dry enough for steam sterilization. Cut the stack by slicing the heap from top to bottom and pass the loam through a 12·5mm (½in) sieve. Before the loam is mixed with the other ingredients, it must be sterilized to remove harmful organisms. This is done by driving steam through the dry soil to heat it thoroughly and quickly.

Peat This is used in many growing mixes as a soil conditioner. Many soilless growing mixes are merely peat with nutrients. It aerates the growing mix and regulates the water-holding capacity of it. Choose a fibrous, granulated peat which is relatively undecomposed and does not crumble to a dust when it is handled. It should have fairly even particles between 3mm and 8mm (⅛ to ⅜in). Avoid fine, highly-decomposed black peats and those which contain coarse fibres. Sphagnum peat is usually satisfactory.

Sand The best sort of sand for garden use is usually obtained from open excavations called sand pits. During extraction it is washed to remove fine silt or clay particles and screened to remove coarse gravel. Never use sea-shore sand. It usually contains salt and is very often alkaline. Builders' sand is also unsuitable: it is often too fine and is also

alkaline. Sand is used to increase the porosity of growing media. It will not hold water and has no nutritional value. The ideal sand for potting mixes has particles between 1·5 and 3mm (¹⁄₁₆ to ⅛in) but in practice most sands available are much finer than this. Keep the sand dry at all times.

Soil-based Growing Mixes

Until about 40 years ago, soil-based growing mixes were made up in a very haphazard way. The composition of the mix varied from plant to plant and from grower to grower. Considerable research has shown that it is not necessary to use different composts for different plants and that simplification and standardization of soil-based growing mixes is possible. There are three basic mixtures which are now used:

For cuttings Mix together two parts of sphagnum moss peat with one part of loam and one part of coarse sand (all by volume).

For seed sowing Mix together two parts of loam with one part of peat and one part of sharp sand. Add to this mix ground limestone or chalk at 0·6g/l (0·6oz/cu ft) and superphosphate at 1·2g/l (1·2oz/cu ft).

For potting Mix together seven parts of loam with three parts of peat and two parts of coarse sand. The amount of fertilizer and lime this mixture needs depends on the type of plant it is to be used for and how long the plant will have to stay in the mix without additional feeding. There are three different formulations:

No. 1 Add ground limestone or chalk at 0·6g/l (0·6oz/cu ft), hoof-and-horn* at 1·2g/l (1·2oz/cu ft), superphosphate at 1·2g/l (1·2oz/cu ft) and sulphate of potash at 0·6g/l (0·6oz/cu ft).

No. 2 Add ground limestone or chalk at 1·2g/l (1·2oz/cu ft), hoof-and-horn* at 2·4g/l (2·4oz/cu ft), superphosphate at 2·4g/l (2·4oz/cu ft) and sulphate of potash at 1·2g/l (1·2oz/cu ft).

No. 3 Add ground limestone or chalk at 1·8g/l (1·8oz/cu ft), hoof-and-horn* at 3·5g/l (3·5oz/cu ft), superphosphate at 3·5g/l (3·5oz/cu ft) and sulphate of potash at 1·8g/l (1·8oz/cu ft).

Soilless Growing Mixes

Suitable loams for soil-based growing mixes are difficult to obtain, particularly in North America, and, in 1957, this led to the publication of work done by the University of California on soilless mixes using peat and sand with suitable fertilizers. Nowadays Cornell mixes are more widely used. Soilless growing mixes have several advantages over soil-based ones. They are lighter in weight, give more consistent results because peat and sand are less variable than loam, and are easier to prepare (sterilization is not

---

*This should be ⅛in grist. Finer grades should not be used since severe ammonia release would follow.

normally required). But they do have some drawbacks. Watering is often more critical than with soil-based mixes and there is a much smaller margin for error with fertilizer levels. Branded soilless mixes are widely available but they can be mixed quite easily at home. There are no hard and fast rules about the ideal proportions of peat to sand. Mixtures which have been used vary from one part of peat with three of sand to three of peat with one of sand. A 50:50 mix or the 3:1 peat:sand mix seem to be the most popular. These mixtures are neither too free-draining nor apt to waterlog. Fertilizers and lime must be added, using either a proprietary fertilizer or one of the following formulations:

Chemicals	standard mix g/l(oz/cu ft)	longer lasting g/l(oz/cu ft)
ammonium nitrate	0.37	—
ureaformaldehyde	—	0·6 (winter) 1·2 (summer)
potassium nitrate	0·78	0·78
superphosphate	1·56	1·56
dolomite lime	2·37	2·37
chalk or ground limestone	2·37	2·37
fritted trace elements (235A)	0·37	0·37

The standard mix will store indefinitely before it is used. A few weeks after potting feed plants in the standard mix with a liquid fertilizer. Those in the longer lasting mix have adequate nutrients for several months. To make a seed-sowing mixture, use half the quantity of fertilizers added to the standard mix but the same amount of lime. For a cutting mix add seven parts of coarse grit to one or two parts of soilless growing mix. Pot on the cuttings as soon as they root.

Mixing Seed and Potting Mixes

Thorough mixing is important. Moisten the peat and spread the ingredients in layers on a clean sterilized floor. Mix part of the sand with the fertilizers before scattering them evenly over the heap. Turn the heap several times to ensure thorough mixing.

Special Mixtures

Alpines These need a well-drained mix. Add one sixth part of coarse sand to a No.1 soil-based potting mix or use the soil-based seed-sowing mix with the potting No.1 fertilizers and chalk added.

Cacti Mix two parts of coarse grit to five parts of soil-based No.1 potting mix or two parts of coarse grit with four parts of soilless growing mix.

Orchids The standard growing medium for orchids is three parts osmunda fibre (the chopped-up root of tropical relatives of the royal fern *Osmunda regalis*) and one part sphagnum moss (not peat). Orchids will also grow in a wide variety of other materials including pulverized or chopped bark, polystyrene, bracken fronds and sphagnum moss peat. Orchid-growing media should be just moist, neither too wet nor completely dry. It should be kept in the greenhouse before it is used to keep it warm. A cold mix may damage the roots.

Tropical plants Mix three parts of peat with two of vermiculite and one of perlite. Add fertilizers when watering.

Hydroponics

Hydroponics is the technique of growing plants without soil in inert aggregate or in a solution of plant nutrients and is of comparatively recent origin. It dates back to 1929 when Dr W. F. Gericke in California demonstrated its practical possibilities. At the time it caused great interest and numerous installations were developed both under glass and out of doors, especially in warm countries where good soil was in short supply. But research has been slow and hydroponics has never been fully developed or accepted in temperate zones.

There are basically four forms of hydroponics. The simplest is a static system and uses tanks 20/23cm (8/9in) deep filled with nutrient solution. Plants have their roots suspended in this solution by using wire netting to support the top. The nutrient solution needs to be changed at regular intervals and must also be aerated. This system has now fallen out of favour and research is being concentrated on the three dynamic systems.

Flooded aggregate Tanks or plastic troughs are filled with a chemically inert material like gravel, coarse sand, vermiculite, lignite, ash, and so on. The nutrient solution trickles through this aggregate, and is collected and recirculated. Aeration is achieved by the aggregate but the nutrient solution needs regular checking and replacement.

Sub irrigation or drainage tanks Aggregate such as lignite or vermiculite is spread to a depth of 13 to 15cm (5 to 6in) in a plastic-lined trench or container which has drainage holes around the side about 7cm (3in) above the base. Nutrient solution is fed from the top and the surplus is allowed to drain away. The nutrient solution collected by the tank below the drainage holes is sucked up by the aggregate and the plants. This method seems wasteful of nutrient solution but is remarkably efficient if complete spectrum nutrient solutions are used.

Re-circulating nutrient systems Several re-circulating systems are now being developed. These systems use shallow troughs and no aggregate.

Mulching, showing the area to be mulched, and the method of application

3. Climate

The relationship between the surrounding physical conditions (the climate) and the growth of plants, shrubs and trees is very complex and by no means fully understood. Nevertheless if you want to grow plants well it is important for you to appreciate the principles involved, but it is not necessary to learn all the precise and intricate details.

Climate can be defined as the summary of the weather conditions, like sun, rain, temperature and wind, likely to be experienced. It can be considered in three stages: 1) general climate of your area, 2) local climate, and 3) microclimate around growing plants.

General climate This is usually described in geographical or meteorological textbooks and precise details can be found in officially published statistics. This type of information can only provide you with a broad description of weather and you should not regard it as an accurate account of conditions in your garden. The character of the general climate in your area will be determined by latitude, distance from the sea and by height above sea level. If you live near the centre of a large land mass you will experience greater variations from winter cold to summer heat, or in periods of dry or rainy weather than if you live on or near coasts especially those open to the prevailing winds, where far more equable conditions can be found.

Local climate This is a modification of the general conditions in your area, brought about by such effects as the slope and aspect of your garden, its position relative to neighbouring hills and valleys, the nature of its soil, its exposure to wind, and its proximity to large areas of water. If you live on a large level plain you can expect to experience a degree of uniformity of climate but if you live in undulating or hilly country, then you should expect to experience appreci-

able changes in garden climate over quite small areas.

Microclimate This is the actual climate surrounding the growing plant and it is the final modification of the general and local climate, and over which you, as a gardener, have some degree of control. For example, you can provide shelter from the wind, can select shaded or sunny sites, improve soil conditions, provide some protection against frost, and most important of all, can water your plants in dry conditions. By the use of heated glass or plastic structures, you can attempt to provide a very special kind of climate, but even so your efforts may be limited by the local conditions of sunshine and wind.

The garden climate can change so significantly over relatively small distances that it is almost impossible to provide reliable information in the form of small-scale maps, and local experience or the advice of an expert nurseryman in your area can be far better guides. You have, in effect, two choices of action. You can restrict your activities to growing plants which are known to do well in your area, or you can accept a challenge and try to grow something more unusual, but only with the realization that you may meet with occasional lack of success if you attempt the wellnigh impossible.

The Important Weather Conditions
The most significant aspects of weather which affect the growth of plants are: 1) temperature 2) sunshine, and 3) soil moisture. Other factors are also important. Frost can occur generally over wide areas in winter, but will be very local in incidence and intensity during the most critical periods of late spring and early autumn. Strong winds can cause structural damage and will always

Opposite: The most equable temperatures occur near the sea

tend to restrict the growth of plants. Long periods of high humidity or wet leaf surfaces will encourage the onset of many plant diseases and warm dry periods can provide suitable conditions for garden pests. Plants also react to length of day or length of darkness, but, unless you are using modern artificial lighting or shading techniques in a greenhouse, you do not often have to worry about this aspect of the weather, as it is one of the few factors which behaves in a regular annual fashion.

Temperature

The temperatures surrounding a plant and its roots are very important in determining its development through the various stages of its biological life. Temperature alone is not a good guide to the amount of growth as this depends more on energy from the sun, availability of soil moisture and nutrients, and plant genetic factors, but temperature does control such things as seed germination, change from leaf to flower or fruit production, and the progress towards maturity. For example, grass begins to grow appreciably on a lawn when the temperature rises above about 6°C (43°F), and the length of time that the temperature remains above this level is often referred to as the length of the growing season. Even in small countries like the UK this can vary from nearly the whole year in the extreme south-west to less than half this value in the colder and higher areas in the north.

Nevertheless, it is not a constant feature, and the start of the growing season can, in any one year, vary by as much as three to four weeks either side of the average date in a maritime climate where the temperature depends so much on the direction of the wind rather than the strength of the sun in the spring period. In continental countries,

with a less variable type of climate, the uncertainties are less, but even so you should plan your work in accordance with the weather of each individual year and not place too much reliance on an average figure.

Average temperatures decrease with the height of the ground above sea level, with the result that the length of the growing season becomes shorter on hills than in valleys. In the UK, the rate of decrease is about two to three weeks per 1,000 metres inland,

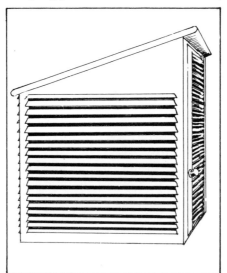

Right: Housing for a thermometer outside – the slatted sides allow free circulation of air while the box shades the thermometer from direct sun and shelters it from wind

Far right: Maximum and minimum thermometer

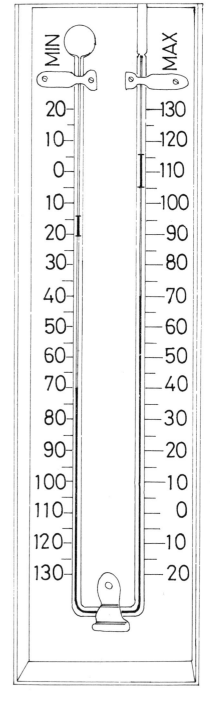

but it can be greater than this on the western coasts, where the relatively warm sea provides good growing conditions in the gardens near sea level. In the centre of large land masses, the rate of decrease can be less than that experienced elsewhere.

Very cold winter conditions provide the biggest threat to the survival of plants which are not completely hardy and, if an unseasonal mild spell encourages plants to start growing and is then followed by a return to wintry conditions, the growing plants can suffer extensive damage. Winters are generally most severe in inland areas, especially in large land masses such as Canada (and on eastern coasts), although a blanket of snow can help protect plants from damage from the cold air above. The least winter damage can be hoped for on western coasts and offshore islands, because the sea is always warmer than the land in winter and the prevailing westerly winds help to mitigate the cold. If the winds are blowing off the land towards the sea, this advantage disappears.

Summer temperatures will help to determine whether full maturity is reached in plants, especially in fruits such as apples, pears and peaches; a long growing season is not sufficient, it is the warmth that is needed.

Frost

This can damage plants in two ways:1) It can rupture the plant tissues, and 2) Freezing soil can interfere with the supply of water to plant roots. Frost is therefore one of the most worrying aspects of weather to the gardener, especially as the length of time between the last frost in spring and the first frost in autumn is invariably shorter than the length of the growing season determined by temperature.

In areas with a maritime climate the average date of last spring frost is an unreliable guide to the time of planting out of tender plants because there is such a large variation from year to year, sometimes up to a month either side of the average. Late frosts are also very local in incidence, being more frequent and more intense in valleys and sheltered places. The cold night air flows downhill until it meets an obstacle where it forms a 'frost pocket', or until it reaches a level 'frost plain'. The sites least liable to late frosts are those on hillsides with good air drainage to lower levels. Frosts are least likely close to coasts, and are most prevalent in inland areas. Air coming from a northerly direction, a clear sky at dusk, and a decreasing wind speed are all pointers towards a late spring frost. A strong wind and a cloudy sky will tend to prevent a late frost and if the air is moist, then frosts may be avoided even in clear still conditions by the formation of fog. Experience has also shown that late spring frosts are more likely to occur in a dry season, as dry soil cools more rapidly than one which is moist.

In continental climates such as the USA, the average date of the last spring frost is a much more reliable guide to planting time. Statistically it varies much less from year to year and is generally accurate to within 11 days (USA) of the average.

Frost hardiness, climatic zones and zone ratings In the UK plants have traditionally been divided into those which are hardy and those which are tender. A plant may be defined as hardy if it will tolerate an average winter in its own climate and in any other climate into which it is introduced. A plant may be regarded as tender if it is unable to survive an average winter, although all plants (with the exception of a few New Zealand ones) are hardy in their own habitat. The problem with the term tender is that it is so vague and tender plants can be found flourishing in areas where theoretically they should be unable to survive.

The gardener in North America is helped by the system of hardiness zones. The original hardiness maps were produced several decades ago and have been gradually updated as more and more reliable information has become available. The prime information represented on a zone map is the severity of winter, which is normally measured in day-degrees below zero (centigrade); however other factors such as soil have to be taken into account. For example clay soils take a long time to warm up in spring and are normally regarded as cold soils but sandy soils (which are normally regarded as warm) are so open in texture that frost can penetrate far deeper than it can in clay soils. It is factors like these which have led to the modification of the zone maps.

The whole of North America, including both the USA and Canada, is divided into ten hardiness zones numbered from 1 to 10. 1 is coldest, 10 is warmest. The system is quite simple to use. The first thing to do is to find out which zone you live in – see zone maps. When you read this book (or most plant catalogues) you will find a number after the plant, for example, *Liriope spicata* 5. This means if you live in zone 5 you can grow this plant in your zone. If the number were 6, that is one zone warmer than yours, you might just get away with a plant in a very sheltered position. You could also grow plants from zones 4, 3 and 2, and probably 1 as well.

The simplest way to help protect your plants against frost is to keep the soil moist, free from weeds and as compact as possible.

This enables heat to be conducted upwards during the night from the warmer soil beneath. Any form of cover over the plants will also help to prevent frost damage, although glass cover will not provide complete protection against a severe frost, and some forms of plastic cover may be even less effective.

The liability of a garden, or any particular part of a garden, to a damaging late frost can really only be decided by experience, but a site with least exposure to the open sky, and one at the highest level in the garden, stands the least chance of damage.

Sunshine

This provides both energy and light, either directly or in a diffuse manner through a cloud cover. Plants vary considerably in their requirements for light or shade, both in duration or amount. A sunny garden will be one in which there is a good extent of growth, provided that there is sufficient moisture in the soil within reach of the plant roots and a good standard of fertility in the soil. The ideal garden is one where there is a balance between warm sunshine and refreshing rain. Sunshine hours decrease with height above sea level.

In summer, the strength of the sunshine principally determines the amount of water used by transpiring plants, so that in fine weather much greater attention has to be paid to supplementary irrigation, especially

Above: Remember that local frost patterns may differ from those of your geographical region

Left above: Brush heavy snow off branches regularly or they will break

Left below: Bear in mind the time of day when various parts of your garden will be in sun or shade when planting

39

Rain Gauge

Funnel catches rain in a container inside a jam jar buried in the garden

Take out the inner container and measure the volume of rain caught. Relate this to the area of the top of the funnel

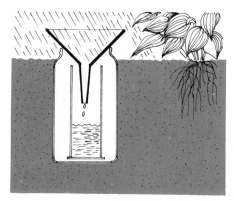

in the early part of a plant's life, when it may have a small root system. It is never wise to plant out young seedlings in a soil which has not been thoroughly watered, and the same rule applies when transplanting shrubs.

Rainfall

A country which has its rainfall distributed fairly uniformly throughout the year is always the best for a garden. The amount of rain that falls varies enormously from place to place, from season to season and from year to year. Any good atlas will show the long term averages for any land mass, and such maps are the best indicators of what plants can and cannot be expected to thrive in different areas. Such maps usually express rainfall in inches per annum but more detailed climatological atlases will also show the rainfall in inches or millimetres per month. Such maps are of necessity only generalizations and since significant differences can occur within quite small areas more detailed information can usually be obtained from nearby botanical gardens, horticultural experimental stations, schools or colleges. It is of course also possible to measure with a reasonable degree of accuracy the rainfall in your own garden (see opposite).

Soil moisture Plants need access to soil moisture to let them take in the necessary nutrients such as nitrogen, to maintain turgidity, and to enable them to transpire through their leaves. Soil moisture is gained by rainfall (or by watering), and is lost by direct evaporation from the soil surface or by extraction by the roots of the plants and trees. The maximum amount of water a soil will hold against the pull of gravity which would cause drainage is known as 'field capacity'. Soils vary in the amount of water which they can retain in this fashion. Very coarse sandy soil can only retain about 40mm of water for each 30cm depth (about 1½in per foot); the best soils with a good humus content can hold up to 65mm for each 30cm of depth (about 2½in per foot). The extent to which a plant can draw upon this reservoir of soil moisture will depend on its root system.

For successful growth, this reservoir of soil moisture available to plant roots must be maintained between fairly narrow limits. Too much rain or irrigation will cause waterlogging and leaching of nutrients; too little will cause wilting, and a severe shortage will bring about the loss of the plant.

At the end of winter, when the rainfall (or snow) has exceeded the very small losses from transpiration, the soil is usually at field capacity. Thereafter, as the strength of the sun increases, plants transpire more vigorously, and by the middle of the summer

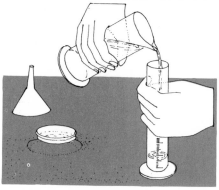

they can use as much as 25mm of water each week. In most gardens these losses are rarely replaced by the summer rainfall and what is known as a 'soil moisture deficit' builds up. Really successful gardeners make sure that this deficit rarely exceeds half the total amount of soil water available to the plant. At certain critical stages, such as when a strawberry is increasing in size, or when peas are filling the pods, it is wise to maintain even smaller deficits, and to keep the soil near capacity so that there is the least shortage of available water.

Most gardeners frequently water newly planted-out seedlings or transplanted shrubs to help them to become established, but new techniques have now become available to permit 'watering by calculation', so that the amount of water added can be found from the difference between the transpiration loss and the rainfall gain, thus providing a useful estimate of the soil moisture deficit. Specialist publications can explain how this can be done in a relatively simple way, but it is important that you take the trouble to measure the rainfall which actually falls on your own garden.

As a general rule, watering should be more frequent on light soils than on good loams, because the reservoir of water available to the plants is less, but the total amount of water added over a season need not be very different, as the water used is dependent on the weather. It is always wise to water before the plants show obvious signs of wilting, and any spell of dry days should prompt you to anticipate a soil moisture shortage, rather than wait until it occurs.

When water supplies are restricted, you must decide on your own selection of priorities. It is worth remembering that lawns will recover rapidly from a severe drought, even though they look brown and beyond recall. In the vegetable garden, it is probably the soft fruit and peas and beans that deserve the most attention.

In the autumn and winter months, rainfall generally exceeds the transpiration which is decreasing in amount in the weaker sunshine, so that the soil moisture deficit is made up and the soil returns to capacity. The excess rain then percolates through the soil and replenishes the streams, rivers, reservoirs and underground water supplies.

Wind

In addition to gales which can cause structural damage and breakage of plants, any form of moderate to strong wind can restrict growth in a garden. All gardens should therefore be designed to reduce the winds to a gentle level favourable for plants. This is best done by carefully designed hedges or (in bigger gardens) tree shelter-belts. These filter down the wind for a distance of seven to ten times their height, and should be sited to protect against the coldest winds and the prevailing winds, although much depends on the aspect of your garden. Walls and solid fences only provide effective shelter up to a distance of about five times their height; beyond this distance they can cause excessive turbulence and downdraughts which can bring about considerable damage. Badly designed shelter can take up too much land and possibly create small frost pockets, and there is always the problem of too much shading. Shelter is probably most needed near the coasts where the winds are always stronger than inland, and on hills rather than in valleys.

4. Design and Planning

A design for a garden must take into account the size and shape of the garden, whether it is level or sloping, how exposed it is, whether it faces north, south, east or west and what the soil is like. Most people have to build a garden by making the best of what they have got. But when a house move is planned, the garden of any prospective house should be examined carefully and its potential, or lack of it, should play a part in the decision of whether to purchase it.

Slope
A flat level garden is the easiest to deal with. It should be easy to apply the basic principles of design (see *Garden Design*) and will need the least work to turn these principles into reality. But, in practice, many gardens are far from level and can present quite a challenge to the garden designer. The end product can be quite fascinating but whether it is worth the effort depends on the slope of the garden itself, the keenness and ability of the designer, the amount of time at his disposal and the amount of money available. The sections on *Banks*, *Landscaping* and *Construction* should make the decision easier.

It will almost certainly be necessary to have assistance in work of this kind.

Exposure
A very exposed garden can present a lot of problems because plants will find it difficult to establish themselves if they are being blasted by strong winds. Fencing and screens will help by giving plants protection in the early part of their lives. See *Plant Screens*, *Hedges* and *Construction: Fencing*. But in very exposed areas fencing will have to be very rugged to withstand constant buffeting. Exposed gardens need patience – it will take some time before protection by trees and shrubs makes it possible to enjoy the pleasures of sitting out in the garden. Gardens by the sea suffer from exposure and also salt-laden winds.

Aspect
The direction a garden faces is known as its aspect. A south-facing garden will be warmer and sunnier than one facing north particularly if the north-facing one is close to a house. The situation is reversed in the southern hemisphere. Most vegetables and fruit trees and bushes prefer a sunny aspect but some ornamental plants will tolerate, and some even demand, shade. See *Gardens: Gardening in the Shade*.

Soil Conditions
Most plants prefer a medium soil with a good proportion of organic matter. This sort of soil is fairly easy to work too. Heavy, sticky clay soils are amongst the worst in a virgin garden: they are difficult to work and will need much improvement if plants are to grow well. For further details of soil types and how to improve them see *Soil*.

Garden Design
A well-designed garden brings together a harmonious collection of attractive plants in an aesthetically pleasing manner and fulfils and facilitates the functional demands put upon that garden. Three factors are important in any garden design: 1) the function of the garden, 2) its siting, and 3) the designer's knowledge of plants and how to combine them.`

A professional in garden design can plan a garden as he goes along. His experience will enable him to know, by instinct, what is right and what is wrong. A less experienced person should put all his ideas on a piece of paper and be fairly happy with the overall scheme before starting to work on it. Some

Opposite: This garden combines lawn, a border with shrubs, trees and spring bulbs, a rock garden and a greenhouse screened by trees

43

NEEDS LIST
Lawn
Sandpit
Swing ⎫
Climbing frame ⎬ Play area
Vegetable garden
Herb garden
Magnolia
Patio
Barbecue ⎫
Swimming pool ⎬ Fun area
Arbour
Bog garden

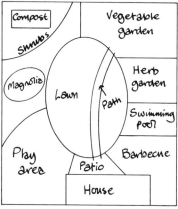

Conceptual plans A and B

final details can, and should, be left until work is well under way and a good idea of the final appearance can be visualized.

Function

The first step in designing a garden is to list all the important uses of the garden. This is your NEEDS list. An example of one is given to the left of this column. If you want to grow one or two plants in particular you can add them to your list. As a general rule, all gardens should provide a suitable setting for the house by emphasizing good architectural qualities and camouflaging the bad ones. A garden can also act as an extension to the home with sitting areas, and outdoor cooking facilities. It can provide somewhere to relax in private, unseen by neighbours; somewhere for children to play; somewhere to grow flowers for decorating the house or for growing fruit or vegetables.

The next step is to try and link the areas in your needs list in a logical manner. For the example given here you would start by drawing roughly on a piece of paper the shape of your garden and putting a circle in the middle of it labelled 'lawn'. Next draw another called 'play area', another called 'patio' and so on. Now organize it in terms of function. Does it make sense for the children to go across the vegetable garden to reach the swimming pool? Should their play area be near the house? Do you want a herb garden near the vegetable garden or near the kitchen door? This should lead to CONCEPTUAL PLAN A.

Now you have to start looking at the limitations imposed on your plan. Can you afford it? Do you have room for it? Does the space taken up by one of the areas justify the amount of use or pleasure you get from it? These questions effectively turn your needs list into a PRIORITIES list, the lowest priorities being the ones you drop first. Take another piece of paper with the shape of your garden drawn on it and re-arrange the circles in some sort of logical flow pattern in order of priority. For example you could think of a patio as a porchway into your garden turning left to the children's play area and right for the vegetable and herb garden. It may be that the play area while still existing need not have the three pieces of equipment. Alternatively, although it is nice to have herbs, you could restrict yourself in a small garden to a few in pots either indoors or out and gain a little more space that way. This should give CONCEPTUAL PLAN B.

Provisional Work

The next step is to combine your conceptual plan B with a study of your garden – its sunny and shaded corners, viewpoints,

changes in level, soil quality, prevailing winds.

Take time over this and think carefully about what you want. Before putting pencil to paper wander around the garden to get some idea of how big it is and where things will fit in. Think about how big the vegetable plot needs to be. Do you want to grow fruit? If there is not enough room for a separate fruit garden then some fruit trees could be accommodated in the ornamental part of the garden. But, be careful about what you plan to grow beneath fruit trees: some plants may be harmed by any spraying programme it is necessary to undertake. Think about whether those structures, such as a garden shed, which are normally considered as permanent features, can be moved. Think about where you want to put paths and whereabouts in the garden you want to put seats. Vegetables should usually be out of sight of the main windows but in full sun; seats should be sheltered from the wind, in a sunny corner with light shade in summer; cars and fuel stores require easy access to the road and children may need supervision from the house. A simple solution is not always possible but the end product should be a PROVISIONAL WORK PLAN.

Basic Principles of Design

The final step is to consider those factors which create a pleasing garden form. The most important ones are: 1) a definition of space, 2) a sense of proportion, 3) scale, 4) balance, 5) materials, and 6) good workmanship. The meaning of each of these is outlined below.

Space In buildings, a sense of space is clearly defined by floors, walls and ceilings. This sense of space is just as important in gardens but here it is more subtly formed by lawns or paving, by low plants and by a tree canopy.

In designing a garden there is a very strong tendency to concentrate on the real things which can be seen and touched – greenhouses, rockeries, sundials, flower beds, borders and so on – and to forget the vitally important space between them. A garden with too little space can feel cluttered and overbearing. But, equally well, one with too much space, even a garden overlooking beautiful countryside, can feel too flat, too bleak and uncomfortable no matter how interesting the plants are. Most gardens, even very small ones, benefit from an enclosure at least 1·8m (6ft) high. In large gardens the enclosure can be formed by trees and shrubs. In small gardens tall plants would probably take up too much lateral space and overfill the garden, so sheds, greenhouses and garages should be used to provide height where needed and should be supplemented with a combination of plants and light, open fencing. Plant-covered trellises are particularly suitable.

Proportion The relationship between the height, width and length of any garden feature is known as proportion. A well-proportioned garden will also take into account the interaction of the proportion of an individual feature with that of its surroundings. For example, a large lawn surrounded by a narrow flower border looks totally out of proportion. Reshaping and enlarging the planting areas or breaking-up the size of the lawn with a group of shrubs or trees will restore proportion.

One of the more important aspects of proportion is the relationship between the size of a space and the height of the enclosure surrounding it. As a rough guide, it is best to aim for an enclosure which has a height between one-half and one-fifth of the width of the space it surrounds. Taller enclosures feel overbearing, smaller ones feel bleak.

The relationship between the length and width of a space determines the direction of movement within the space. A space in which length and width are similar will give a calm restful appearance with no incentive to move from it; spaces with lengths 1½ to 2½ times their widths are calm with sufficient linearity to encourage observers to wander slowly along, but, if the length greatly exceeds three times the width, then the space takes on the appearance of a corridor with no incentive to stay within it. The same principles apply whether the garden is formal or informal but the principles become more difficult to apply directly in an irregular, flowing design. In very small gardens only a single space is possible. In larger gardens it is possible, and very desirable, to introduce a variety of spaces perhaps using pergolas, rows of cordon fruit or changes in level to divide them.

Harmonizing a garden like this does not mean that there cannot be contrast. A garden full of similar shapes and similar materials can become very dull. Bring two contrasting shapes together and one immediately starts to emphasize the basic qualities of the other. For example, a single-storey house surrounded by beds of low, scrambling shrubs can be enhanced by planting a strong vertical subject such as a cypress nearby.

Scale Scale is the direct relationship of any garden feature with the size of the human figure or a house. If the actual sizes of various parts of the garden are so small that free movement is constantly inhibited – stooping under arches, stepping around plants along a narrow path or teetering up and down

steep flights of steps, then the garden will appear cramped and confining. With slightly larger features and an occasional inhibition of free movement, the effect is intimate. Larger still and the effect becomes gracious, then grand and finally grandiose – too large for human comfort and a suitable setting only for large fêtes and pageants. While proportions of spaces should vary, it is desirable to keep the scale of a garden more or less constant and in keeping with the house. One should not, for example, plan a broad sweeping drive up to a little bungalow, or a little cottage garden that will huddle at the portico of a Palladian mansion.

Balance A garden which has many large trees on one side and few on the opposite side will feel as if it is toppling over – overbalanced in one direction. A well-balanced garden does not necessarily have to be a symmetrical one (the same on both sides) but it should have nearly equal 'weights' on both sides.

Materials Care should be taken with the choice of materials so that they are appropriate to each other, to the scale of the garden and blend well with the house. One common error is to think about each part of the garden separately with the result that too much emphasis is placed on making the various pieces interesting in themselves. Strongly textured or coloured paving, intricate fence or wall panels, ornate garden buildings and contorted plastic pools may be appealing as separate items in garden catalogues but are often too individualistic to be worked into a pleasant garden scene. As with interior design, so in gardens one needs to set the general scene with rather neutral materials like paving, grass, walls or background planting and only then to add accents of brighter note – a pot or statue or bright flowers.

The placing of statues, pots and so on should be done with care so that attention is focused on them. The most important question is where the viewer is standing. Should the focal point be in line with the kitchen window? Opposite the dining-room window? Or, perhaps, at the far end of the garden so that it can be seen by someone standing in the garden? Only the person who uses the garden can answer these questions.

Building materials themselves have characteristic qualities: stone varies from soft waterworn limestone to angular sandstone or polished marble; wood can be natural trunks or branches, rough-sawn planks or smoothly finished sections and both wood and stone can be used in a rough-hewn state or delicately carved. By choosing the materials carefully, gardens

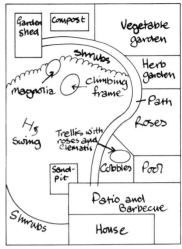

Provisional work plan

may vary from those which are very natural with paving of tree-trunk sections, steps of earth held up by logs and paths of gravel or sand to very sophisticated gardens with paving and steps of tiles, garden structures of polished steel and glass, and restrained planting of bold foliage plants. Over the years, most gardens gradually assume the character of their owner, more often than not without any conscious effort on his part. If possible, it is best to get most of this character stamped on the garden at the very beginning so that the garden does not become a scene of constant chopping and changing.

A town garden; paving will be more suitable than grass for nearly all such gardens; here the formal concrete path is softened by plants overflowing on to it

Good workmanship A well-designed garden can be ruined by lack of attention and poor workmanship. Joints in paving or the edges of lawns and flower or shrub beds should align with doors and windows on the house; on patios and paths any paving slabs or bricks should fit into the area to be paved without unnecessary cutting and all parts of the garden should be so shaped that they are pleasing in themselves and fit together with the other pieces like the parts of a jigsaw. The latter point applies particularly to any flat surface, such as a lawn, which can be seen in its entirety. If the garden looks as though pieces have been cut out for flower

Remember that a garden will need space for recreational facilities

A centre path can spoil the proportion of a small garden; here the constantly rising level makes it an attractive feature

beds, paths, sheds, and so on and what is left over is put down to grass then no amount of careful cultivation will provide a pleasing design. If on the other hand, the lawn is a carefully planned shape and fits with all the other carefully planned shapes, the design is immediately appealing. The need for good workmanship also continues into the construction and maintenance of the garden. You should .always trim hedges purposefully to a particular shape instead of merely cutting off the new growth at infrequent intervals; concrete should be even in texture and neatly laid; grass should be regularly mown and trimmed; if this is not possible it should be replaced by an area of rolled gravel or other inexpensive surfacing. With this sort of care the least inspiring garden can be given a new lease of life at little expense. It will at least look cared for. Even putting out the garbage can in the exact centre of a paving slab instead of dumping it just anywhere can make a difference.

From Paper to the Ground

Once the above points have been considered and a work plan reached, it is essential to transfer the curvature of lawns, flower beds and so on on to the ground so that some impression of the final appearance can be achieved.

Hose pipes, rope, string, pegs, garden canes (or poles), old sacks and a long tape measure all have a part to play in this. First, decide on a reference point on both plan and in the garden, a long fence or hedge is ideal. Next, lay out the hose and rope to mark the edges of all borders or lawns, use the string and pegs for more formal straight edged beds. Continue to lay and re-lay the shapes until a satisfactory outline is achieved. Use the canes with sacks draped over them to give some idea of what the trees and larger shrubs will eventually look like. Finally transfer the plan back on to paper – this time on to squared paper by measuring the distances between the outline of the shapes and the reference fence or hedge. When the shape is a formal one or has a gradual curve then measurements at roughly 3m (10ft) intervals will suffice. Sharp curves will need measurements at more frequent intervals.

The accurate plan will enable the shapes to be recreated later when much of the basic digging or movement of soil is finished.

Choosing the Plants

The choice of plants is often the most difficult part of garden making but it is made easier if one thinks of the form, shape and proportion of the garden first and then chooses plants to meet the basic requirements. In making the garden, enclosure can be achieved with walls, fences, shrubs or hedges; the floor can be paving, grass, ivy, heather or other low planting and focal points can be statues, fountains or eye-catching specimen plants. The decision to use plants or other materials depends on personal taste and finance. Plants take up more room than walls and are less amenable to walking on than paving, but they do have an appeal which man-made materials cannot reproduce.

Trees are of first importance in providing structure. The choice of species will depend on the soil and climate of the particular garden but attention should be given to selecting plants to provide a good background for the garden rather than a brilliant display of colour. Trees can be roughly divided into four groups according to their shape: rounded, vertical, horizontal and weeping. A fifth group can be formed by those which provide some special sort of decoration. Trees can be grouped closely provided they are all of the same kind. Mixed groups of trees tend to compete with each other and give the appearance of striving for existence. See *Ornamental Plants*: *Trees*.

Choosing shrubs and small trees comes next. Except in the case of a hedge, always avoid planning a solid, even wall of shrubs of similar height with the tallest at the back of the border, falling gradually to the smallest ones at the front. Make the rear of the border (or enclosure) undulating and bring forward, here and there, a taller shrub to stand out among a group of smaller plants. See *Ornamental Plants*: *Shrubs*.

Herbaceous perennials, biennials and annuals can be used as low planting to ease the contrast between the vertical background and the horizontality of the central space.

In both tall and low planting a good proportion of evergreens should be included, not usually the sombre laurels, aucubas and privets but viburnums, cotoneasters, berberis, mahonias, yuccas and *Iris foetidissima* with variety of foliage texture and colour and in many instances flowers and fruit as additional bonuses. The evergreens should be grouped so that the garden is well furnished even in winter. The bays between groups can then be filled with plants for colour such as hardy and half-hardy annuals or, for a more permanent planting, bulbs with herbaceous perennials, dahlias, grasses or low shrubs can be used.

Colour in the Garden

Once the basic design for a garden has been created, colour can be incorporated into the overall plan. Colour can be used to emphasize the basic forms and shapes in the initial design but it should not be regarded as an end in itself. A collection of plants with colours of many varying shades and tones carelessly arranged does not make a garden. The use of colour in a garden is a personal thing but there are some basic rules which can act as a starting point:

1) An abundance of green foliage, of any texture, shape or form will act as a foil to any other colour and will help to disguise incorrect tones and shades.

2) Primary colours – red, yellow and blue – must never be used in close juxtaposition. However primary and close secondary colours can be used together. Red with yellow, blue with yellow, and blue with red are too blatant for good taste, but red with orange, orange with yellow, blue with mauve, and purple with yellow, in the right shades, can be most effective.

3) White can be used with any other colour but it must not be over-used as it is very intense and can overpower other colours. White is most successfully used with itself, with grey and with green.

Most gardens have plenty of green foliage which gives a good, basic, green framework to start from. A few gardens have purple- or bronze-leaved trees or shrubs and these can be difficult to work with. If you have dark-leaved plants make a virtue out of them and use oranges and yellows to harmonize.

The Theory of Colours

The simplest way to think about garden colours is to imagine the three primary colours set out around a clock face with yellow at 12 o'clock, red at 4 o'clock and blue at 8 o'clock. Between these colours are yellow-orange (1), orange (2), red-orange (3), red-purple (5), purple (6), blue-purple (7), blue-green (9), green (10) and yellow-green (11). The numbers in brackets refer to their positions on the clock face. The colour at each of these clock points is a hue and it can be thinned with white to a tint. The clarity or purity of a hue is its tone.

Hues which are radially opposite each other give good contrasts but they might be difficult to use together if they are in their most brilliant form. Hues in the same quarter of the clock face should harmonize, particularly when they have been adulterated by the addition of greys.

The tone of the hues decreases as you go down the clock (both sides) from yellow to purple. When using contrasting colours it is best to use a light (white-added) higher-toned colour with a full-tone (deep) lower-toned colour than vice versa. In other words light yellow with deep purple is a better combination than deep yellow with mauve (light purple).

Warmer colours (reds and yellows) tend to be more noticeable than the colder blues and this can be used to create a feeling of length or depth even in a small garden. Plant the warmer colours in the foreground and the less noticeable colours towards the backs of the borders.

The Character of Colours

Borders or gardens of one colour alone can be most interesting to make – the acquisition of plants with the right colour of leaves, flowers or fruit is time consuming but enjoyable.

Colours have various moods and qualities that can be utilized.

Red is warm and lively, and a group of red plants should be placed in a spot that usually seems cold; red used in a hot part of the garden can be stifling.

Blue is mystic, and will give a feeling of depth even to a short border or a small garden. To do this use the paler shades towards the extremities, and reserve the brighter, purer colours for closer to the position the garden is normally viewed from. If you want a sort of inverse perspective you can put the taller plants near the viewing position and dwarfer plants at the far end of the garden.

White is ghostlike, and shows up well against dark backgrounds. It is a particularly good colour to use if the garden is to be used or seen at night.

Mauve and purple are rich, heavy colours and should be carefully balanced with grey and green, and perhaps some gold or paler yellow.

Never be afraid to use contrasting colours – a group of blue plants can be enhanced by a skilfully placed group of white or cream flowers. The blues will seem more blue for the contrast, and the white or cream cleaner.

When planning a colour scheme, pay particular attention to the architectural surrounds of the house and garden walls. If these are built of coloured brick, it would be foolish to ignore this. Red flowers and foliage should not be grown against red brick – pink is excellent, as are cream and white. Yellow should not be grown against yellow brick – purple and mulberry colours are richer.

Natural stone walls or pale-painted or white-washed walls are the most versatile backgrounds since any plant colour can be used against them.

Creating an entire garden with plants of one colour which will flower and be pleasing to look at over a long period can be very difficult as gaps will always occur in the flowering period. Instead it is more practical to have a series of distinct colour arrange-

Opposite: Trees and shrubs give form
and contrast to the plants around them

Make sure that garden doors open
easily, preferably on to a hard surface,
and that steps are a reasonable height
and not slippery

Neutral stone colours make a setting for
a wide range of attractive plants in this
small formal garden

ments for specific times of year so that once
the colour has faded in one spot it can be
allowed to go relatively dormant while
attention is focused on another part of the
garden which is just coming into dominance. For example a spring border of bulbs
could be mainly white and cream during
March and April, later these could be grown
over with ferns for the rest of the year. A
May and June bed could then assume dominance, planted with flag irises and lupins in
blue and purple, with perhaps a purple lilac
and a rich, dark paeony. In July perhaps

plants such as heleniums, achilleas and
orange lilies could assume the main role.

Grey plants like yuccas, *Cineraria
maritima, Stachys lanata* and santolinas are
always satisfying to come upon after the
luxuriance of rich orange, yellow and red
schemes, since they are such complemen-
tary colours.

Certain plants are indispensable because
they have the qualities to enhance any colour scheme. Ferns of all kinds are useful
especially to cover areas where bulbs are
grown. *Bergenia cordifolia* has pink flowers

that can be used in any pastel-coloured or red and blue border. It also has splendid green foliage that is an excellent foil. *Stachys lanata* is an excellent plant for edging, its flowers are white and grey and it associates well with any other colour. White lilies, especially *Lilium candidum* and *L. regale* are of such purity and have such classic simplicity of line that they suit almost any border or group of plants. Similarly tree lupins, *Lupinus arboreus*, especially the creamy-yellow forms, associate with all colours except pure bright red.

Landscaping (Shaping Earth)

Landscaping is the art of shaping pleasing contours where none existed before. It is not often used in gardens but it can be of great value in giving immediate height to a garden and in creating a far more effective barrier against unsightly views or unwanted sound than the densest collection of trees and shrubs. Even slight undulations in the ground can materially improve a small informal garden by smoothing out the transition from horizontal to vertical shapes. Earth mounding, however, requires considerable physical effort and, more than in any other aspect of garden design, a simple, broad, unified result is essential. Scattering two or three sudden bumps on an otherwise flat lawn creates a ridiculous appearance which has been aptly termed 'mouse under the carpet' landscaping.

Planning

In nature, rolling landscapes seldom have slopes exceeding 1 in 20. This means that a 10m (30ft) width of garden is needed to accommodate a rise and fall of 0·5m (1½ft) even without allowing any additional room for gently rounding off the base and top of the mound. So in all but the largest gardens, the heights of mounds in landscapes should be thought of in centimetres or inches rather than in metres or feet. This is particularly important if the mounds are to be covered with grass.

If there is not enough room for a gradual mound, a one-sided slope ending in a nearly vertical retaining wall or rock slope can be made. A rock slope is associated with mountainous scenery and can be very much steeper than a grass-covered, undulating one.

The first step in planning a landscape is to decide on the distribution of the hills and the gently curving lines of the valleys. Always aim to create a single sweeping shape rather than a series of isolated bumps. Undulations which all have to come back to the same base level – say the fences in small

gardens – look unattractive. Overcome this by building small retaining walls to allow undulation right to the boundary but, if these are not possible, conceal the extent of mounding by extensive planting.

To avoid moving vast amounts of soil, it is essential to reinforce the natural features of the garden rather than to work against them. Water provides a flat, horizontal, reflecting surface which makes even the slightest slope easily perceived so it is a useful feature in a small garden and soil from the excavations of an informal pool can provide additional material for mounding. Continuous or stepping stone paths should run along the winding centre of a valley in order to emphasize the shape of the land.

Planting is very important. Trees with clearly visible trunks tend to flatten slight hills if they are planted on top of them and they provide competing height if they are planted in a valley. Ideally trees should be planted on the steeper parts of slopes and perpendicular to the slope rather than truly vertical. A group of trees or, on a smaller scale, shrubs can provide reinforcement to the outline of the soil shape by being planted on the top of mounds with the taller ones on the highest point. The boundaries of groups of trees and shrubs should not follow the shape of the soil in a smooth line around the contours but should form spurs dipping down the hill to emphasize the steepness of slope. This effect is very difficult to plan on paper and is best resolved finally on the ground.

The Mechanics

For details of how to move and shape earth see *Construction*.

Landscaping a Small Garden

You can create changes in level in a small garden by using raised beds, sunken areas, rock gardens and pools rather than gentle slopes and valleys. For example, you could have a pool, a sunken garden, a scree, a bog garden and a rock garden. The materials excavated from the sunken garden and pool could be used for the rock garden (and possibly a raised garden for bulbs too). The rock garden could be linked to the bog garden by the scree and the bog could then merge into the pool.

Plant Screens

A plant screen is a row of fast-growing plants, usually trees or tall shrubs, which is used to hide an unsightly building or view, to prevent the garden or part of it from being overlooked, or to give some shelter to the garden either from wind or from noise.

Hiding unsightly building is easy – you simply have to make sure the plants chosen to do the job will eventually be big and wide enough to do it properly. Providing a windbreak is a little more difficult as wind can play unpredictable tricks. The first thing to find out is whether or not you really need shelter and then find out where the best place for it is. One way of doing this is to push very light battens about 90cm long by 5 to 8cm wide by 1 to 2cm thick (3ft by 2 to 3in by ½in) into the soil at intervals around the garden. They must be pushed to exactly the same depth and the soil must be well-cultivated. Those battens which blow down first will indicate the windiest part of the garden and, if you repeat the whole process a number of times, the direction they usually fall in will indicate the prevailing wind direction.

Hedges and screens provide much better shelter than solid objects such as close-boarded fences. Research has shown that a hedge, which is about 50 per cent permeable, cuts down the wind speed and avoids deflecting the wind, which creates problems of turbulence. Windbreaks moderate the wind on the leeward side for a distance on the ground equal to 20 times the height of the screen but really effective shelter is only provided over about one half of this distance. Maximum shelter is provided in the area between five and six times the barrier height. When planting for shelter do not forget to take into account problems of shade which windbreaks may cause.

In many areas *Populus nigra* 'Italica', Lombardy poplar, and other poplars are often used as screens on industrial estates and agricultural land. For this purpose poplars have many advantages: they are cheap to buy, easy and quick to grow and tolerate industrial pollution. They also have many disadvantages: they have an extensive surface rooting system that robs soil of food and water and makes it unwise to use them near buildings; they produce suckers; they are susceptible to bacterial canker which causes unsightly lesions; and they have soft, brittle wood which often results in a relatively short life compared to most trees. All in all, for garden use, the disadvantages outweigh the advantages except in very large gardens.

When choosing screens for gardens the factors to be considered are:

1) How big and how wide each plant will grow (these figures are usually obtainable from most plant lists).
2) Whether the plant will thrive in the soil in your garden – some plants will not tolerate acid soils, some will not tolerate alkaline soils. Most plants commonly used for screens like deep, moist, fertile soils. The suitability of soil is particularly important in North America where soil types can vary a great deal.
3) How easy the plant will be to look after. Will it need regular clipping or pruning to keep it in bounds?
4) Do you want maximum shelter or cover all the year round? Evergreens generally grow more slowly than deciduous plants but give year-round cover.
5) How hardy is the plant? Again this is much more important in North America than in the UK – see hardiness ratings and zone maps. In the deep south of the USA, cluster palms and some of the more tolerant bamboos are often used as screens.
6) Will it resist drought well? Important in countries with continental climates.
7) How firmly anchored in the ground is it? Deep-rooting plants are much better choices for the Great Plains and Prairies of North America than shallow-rooting ones. Lists at the end of the book give both. Any of those listed as suitable for the Great Plains could also be used elsewhere.

Screen plants should be planted in the same way as an ornamental specimen tree or hedge – see *Hedges* and *Ornamental Plants: Trees*. When planting like specimen trees reduce the normal planting distances by about 50 per cent.

Hedges

A hedge is basically a continuous line of evenly-spaced woody plants which have been allowed to grow together. They are generally used in gardens to provide barriers against people or animals, to provide shelter or privacy, to mark the boundary of property or as a division between one part of the garden and another. A hedge might, for example, be used to divide a vegetable garden from a flower garden. All these things can be done by a fence too – see *Construction: Fences*.

Many hedging plants such as *Ligustrum ovalifolium*, privet, or *Prunus laurocerasus*, laurel, are so widely used that many people now look on them unfavourably, especially when they have been badly maintained. But both hedging plants satisfy most of the criteria for a good hedge – it should be capable of growing well when closely planted, should not become sparse near the bottom even when growing to a considerable height and, in most cases, the growth should be dense.

Choosing the Plants

Hedges can be formal or informal and evergreen, deciduous or coniferous. For a formal hedge, choose plants which stand up to

Plants for Screens

Deciduous screens

Up to 18m (60ft)
  Aesculus indica 4
  Populus × *euramericana* and vars 3
  Populus nigra 'Italica' 4
  Quercus canariensis 7
  Tilia × *europaeus* 3

9 to 12m (30 to 40ft)
  Acer negundo 2
  Aesculus hippocastanum 3
  Carpinus betulus 5
  Prunus avium 3
  Salix alba 2

Up to 9m (30ft)
  Betula pendula 2
  Sorbus aria 5
  Sorbus aucuparia 2

Evergreens

Up to 18m (60ft)
  × *Cupressocyparis leylandii* 5
  Cupressus macrocarpa (seaside only) 7
  Eucalyptus gunnii 8
  Pinus nigra 4

9 to 12m (30 to 40ft)
  Picea sitchensis 6
  Quercus ilex 9

Up to 9m (30ft)
  Arbutus unedo 8
  Ligustrum lucidum 7

Shrubs
  Buddleja globosa 7
  Deutzia scabra 4
  Ligustrum chinense 7
  Syringa sweginzowii 5

Climbers (for covering trellis)
  Clematis montana and vars 6
  Clematis vitalba 4
  Polygonum baldschuanicum 4
  Wisteria sinensis 5

Opposite: Small plants should be raised above ground level for the best effect

regular trimming and pruning; for an informal hedge choose those which do best when they are allowed to assume their natural shape with the minimum of pruning.

Ideally you should also think about matching the choice of plants to the type of soil, whether the hedge is on a slope or not, how exposed it will be and what the climate in your area is like. Fortunately the majority of common hedge plants tolerate a wide range of conditions, although for best results a deep, moist, fertile loamy soil and some degree of shelter is needed. Many hedge plants dislike heavy clay soils. A look at hedges in nearby gardens will show you what will, and what will not, grow well in your area. Visits to famous gardens to see mature hedges of many types should give you some ideas about the use of hedges creatively. Whatever sort of hedge you choose remember that it must blend well with the rest of your garden. Plain hedges are good for showing off flowers, statues and water, while colourful hedges, either flower or foliage, brighten up plain parts of the garden where there is little competition – to enhance the lawn perhaps. The table overleaf lists some of the more frequently used hedge plants with details of their important features. In southern USA *Carissa grandiflora* could be added.

Preparation for Planting

Try to avoid planting a hedge near a fence as this will make it very difficult to trim once it is established. If possible run a path along the bottom of the hedge: this will reduce the competition with other garden plants and make trimming easier. In comparison with most garden plants, hedge plants take a lot of nutrients from the soil and this should be taken into account both before planting and throughout the life of the hedge.

The first step is to cultivate the ground well and deal with perennial weeds, especially *Convolvulus arvensis*, lesser bindweed, *Calystegia sepium*, greater bindweed, and *Agropyron repens*, couch or twitch, as once the hedge is planted these weeds will be very difficult to control. Do this by digging the soil and allowing it to lie fallow (unplanted) for one growing season. Apply a herbicide while the soil is fallow (see *Pests and Diseases: Herbicides* for which one to use), and remove any weeds which the herbicide fails to kill by hand. In the autumn of that year start improving soil fertility by digging in as much well-rotted garden compost or farmyard manure as possible. Work it into the soil as deeply as is practical – say 25cm (10in) below the surface. Leave the soil to settle and plant the hedge in the following spring, when soil conditions are suitable.

Planting

You should take just as much care planting a hedge as you would if you were planting specimen trees. Make sure that the soil is not frozen, sodden with rain, or too dry and do not plant if a drying wind is blowing. If conditions are suitable use a garden hoe to mark the run of the hedge and mark the position for each plant with a cane. The distance between each plant depends on the type of hedge being planted (see table overleaf). If the roots of the plants feel dry, soak them for about 12 hours in a bucket of water before planting. When planting one-year seedlings or rooted cuttings, dig a trench which is large enough to hold the roots comfortably. For older plants, dig individual holes large enough to take the plant roots without their being cut or bent.

Plants in pots can be spaced out in their approximate planting positions but bare-rooted plants must be kept together with their roots covered. Look for the nursery soil mark on the stem (the part of the stem which was below soil level in the nursery should be a little paler than the part which was above the soil) and aim to plant to this depth. The soil should be put back over the roots in shallow layers and worked between the roots well by gently moving the plants up and down as the hole is being filled in. Do not overdo this; a movement of 2 to 5cm (1 to 2in) should be sufficient. Finally tread the soil firmly with both feet until the plant is firmly held in place. Most hedges, particularly evergreen ones, should be given some protection against cold, drying winds to prevent desiccation of the foliage. Anti-desiccant sprays can be applied to the leaves and temporary windshields of wattle or hessian can be erected. If a screen is put up, it should allow about 50 per cent of the wind to get through it. It should not be necessary to stake individual hedge plants, but in windy, exposed areas a number of short posts along each side of the hedge with wires stretched between them will stop the plants whipping backwards and forwards too much. After planting, give the plants plenty of water and a 5cm (2in) deep mulch.

Pruning

Hedges can be neatly trimmed and formal in shape or sprawling informal shrubs. They can be small-leaved, like *Buxus sempervirens* box or large-leaved like *Euonymus japonicus*. Whatever sort of hedge you want, or have got, it will need pruning for shape in the early part of its life and regular pruning or clipping once it is established.

Hedges with small leaves can be cut with hedge trimmers or clippers/shears but those with large leaves like *Prunus laurocerasus*, *P. lusitanica*, *Laurus nobilis* and *Aucuba*

japonica, should always be cut with pruning shears/secateurs or loppers. Never cut through large leaves with clippers/shears as the leaves will discolour around the cut edges and the hedge will look unsightly.

All newly-planted hedges should be encouraged to branch freely from as low down as possible. Start pruning as soon as the hedge is established and is beginning to make growth. Reduce the length of new shoots by about one half three or four times a year until the base of the hedge is evenly dense. Once established, evergreen hedges should be clipped occasionally from May to September and any hard pruning necessary should be done in May. Deciduous hedges should be pruned in autumn or winter.

When trimming a hedge, aim to form a wedge shape with the hedge narrower at the top than at the bottom. This will ensure that light gets to all parts of the hedge; hedges with vertical sides may suffer from dieback

Hedging Plants

E Evergreen D Deciduous		approx. height m	(ft)	formal or informal	planting distance cm	(in)	pruning
Berberis × *stenophylla* 6	E	2	(6)	I	45	(18)	clip lightly, immediately after flowering
Carpinus betulus 5 hornbeam	D	to 5	(16)	F or I	45	(18)	trim in autumn
Cornus sanguinea 4 common dogwood	D	1·5 to 2	(4 to 6)	I	45	(18)	prune most shoots to ground in March
Crataegus monogyna 4 hawthorn	D	to 3	(10)	I	30	(12)	prune hard in August
× *Cupressocyparis leylandii* 5 Leyland cypress	E	to 25	(80)	F	75	(30)	leave central shoot uncut until required height is reached then clip in late summer
Deutzia scabra and vars 4 and 5	D	to 3	(10)	I	45	(18)	remove two or three of the oldest stems each year
Elaeagnus pungens 2	E	to 3	(10)	I	45	(18)	best left unpruned
Escallonia macrantha 8	E	to 4	(13)	F	60	(24)	clip regularly, lightly in spring and again after flowering
Euonymus japonicus 7	E	4·5	(15)	F	60	(24)	use shears/secateurs to prune lightly in spring
Fagus sylvatica 5 beech	D	to 5	(16)	F	60	(24)	trim at end of summer
Ilex aquifolium 7 holly	E	to 6	(20)	F	60	(24)	clip in August each year
Lavandula spica 5 lavender	E	1	(3)	F	25	(9)	clip hard when flowers fade
Ligustrum ovalifolium 5 and 6 privet	D	3	(10)	F	45	(18)	trim frequently when young, as required on older plants, cut back hard in April to rejuvenate
Lonicera nitida 8	E	1·2	(4)	F	30	(12)	trim frequently when young, as required on older plants
Philadelphus sp 3 to 5 mock orange	D	5	(16)	I	45	(18)	after flowering cut back shoots that have borne flowers
Prunus laurocerasus 5 to 7 laurel	E	5	(16)	F or I	60	(24)	use shears/secateurs to maintain shape in spring
Rosa sp and hybrids 2 to 5	D	variable		I	30	(12)	see *Ornamental plants: Roses*
Taxus baccata 6 yew	E	to 4·5	(15)	F	45	(18)	trim to maintain shape in late summer

at the bottom. Always hold the clippers/ shears flat against the hedge and, if you find it difficult to trim a flat top by eye, use a piece of heavy twine stretched tightly between two posts as a guide.

Rejuvenating Old Hedges

Most hedges get bigger over the years, even with regular, hard trimming, and often have to be rejuvenated. This should be done over a three-year period.

features

wide hedges, *lvs* slender, dark green, *fls* orange on arching stems, small thorns

easily grown, *lvs* rough, bright, usually retained in winter

lvs rough green, bark red or yellow

very thorny, *lvs* bright, glossy green, *fls* heavily scented

fast growing, easy to establish from pots, *lvs* mid-green but drab

loose, upright habit, *lvs* rough, pointed, grey-green, *fls* pink or white over a long period

lvs lustrous green: vars 'Maculata' and 'Variegata' both variegated

lvs small, dense, *fls* red, pink or white, summer salt-resistant so good near the sea

good for industrial areas, many variegated vars available

good on chalky soils, *lvs* pale green, usually retained as brown *lvs* in winter

lvs prickly, deep green, fruits red

ideal to edge a path or terrace, *lvs* grey, *fls* purple, good scent

cheap, fast growing but common and needs a lot of maintenance: var 'Aureum', golden privet, *lvs* rich, yellow-green

fast growing, best as a narrow hedge, *lvs* small, glossy

broad, *fls* white, sweetly scented

lvs large, oval, glossy green

species better than floribunda or hybrid tea, *fls* generally white, pink, red or cream

long lived, slow growing, *lvs* fine, dark green

In the first year reduce all the branches on one side to within 15 to 23cm (6 to 9in) of the main stems of the hedge, clean out all dead leaves and weeds from the hedge, lightly fork in a dressing of steamed bonemeal or hoof-and-horn and then mulch well. For deciduous hedges this should be done between late autumn and early winter, and for evergreens between late May and the end of June. Water the hedge well over the following summer, particularly in dry weather. Growths should develop from dormant buds on the main stems and, with the stimulus of light and air, these should soon hide the cut face with foliage. In the following year, treat the other side of the hedge in the same way, and lightly trim young growths from the first side to encourage branching. In the third season, the top of the hedge should be reduced to just below the required height. In subsequent years, trim the hedge hard, especially the top.

Bedding

Bedding is a method of displaying garden plants in which the entire bed is changed once or more each year to maintain a brilliant display of colour and sometimes texture. The usual bedding cycle is to plant bulbs, biennials and low spring-flowering perennials in October for spring display – this is known as spring bedding. These plants are then removed in late May to make way for a summer display of annual and tender perennial flowers – summer bedding. Three less commonly seen types of bedding are foliage or sub-tropical bedding, plunge bedding and winter bedding, all of which are described below.

Boldness and simplicity should be the keynote of bedding. Avoid using too many small beds or too many different types of plant. Choose an open and sunny, or at least uniformly shaded, area for the bed. A geometrical design can easily be ruined if some plants flower late or are small because of nearby trees or uneven shading.

Spring Bedding

The plants used for spring display are mainly bulbs, biennials and low, spring-flowering perennials. They may be used alone or in combination.

May-flowering tulips are the most widely used bulbs and they are available in an enormous range of colours. Narcissi are sometimes used but they flower before most carpeting plants and grow so well in permanent situations that their use in bedding is hardly justified. Hyacinths are very expensive. If you use tulips by themselves then mix together tall and short varieties which

Other Hedging Plants

Up to 1·2m (4ft)
Berberis wilsonae 4
Buxus microphyllum koreana 5 and 6
Buxus sempervirens 'Suffruticosa' 6
Chaenomeles japonica 4
Cotoneaster sp 4
Hebe 7 to 10
Kerria japonica 4
Taxus cuspidata 'Nana' 4
Metasequoia glyptostroboides 5
Pyracantha coccinea 6
Syringa 2 to 5
Taxus cuspidata 'Capitata' 4
Thuja plicata 5
Thuja occidentalis 2

1·2m to 3m (4 to 10ft)
Berberis darwinii 9
Berberis thunbergii 3
Buddleia davidii 5
Fuchsia magellanica 5 and 6
Hibiscus syriaca 5 and 6
Ilex crenata 'Convexa' 5 and 6
Ribes sanguineum 5
Stephanandra 5
Taxus media 'Hicksii' 4
Viburnum tinus 7 and 8

3m to 9m (10 to 30ft)
Carpinus betulus 5
Carpinus caroliniana 2
Chamaeecyparis lawsoniana pisifera 3
Corylus avellana 3
Crataegus 3 and 4
Euonymus alatus 4
Ilex crenata 5 and 6
Ilex opaca 5

Over 9m (30ft)
Fagus 4 and 5
Pinus strobus 3
Salix pentandra 4
Tilia cordata 3
Tsuga canadensis 3

Regular clipping will give a thick, healthy hedge

flower at the same time. If you use tulips with other plants, such as the taller wallflowers, then tall varieties are better. You can plant early- and late-flowering tulips as a mixed bed to lengthen the flowering season but set them close together to avoid diluting the overall effect. In doing this placing them 7 to 10cm (3 to 4in) apart would not be too close.

Of the carpeting plants, myosotis is a true biennial and must be grown from seed each year. Most others are perennials but they flower so much better in the first season that these too are best treated as biennials. The six most important are arabis, aubrieta, cheiranthus, myosotis, primulas and violas. Arabis, aubrieta and wallflowers are most suitable for well-drained alkaline soils in

sunny positions. Myosotis, primulas and violas are especially suitable for moist, partially-shaded situations and for soils rich in humus.

Arabis albida, low spreading, *lvs* grey-green, *fls* white. In poorer soils it makes a good perennial edging plant. Treat as for aubrieta.

Aubrieta, generally similar to arabis but more compact, *fls* range from pink to red to lavender to purple. Propagation: slow and uneven in growth so seed should be sown May-June. Colour strains will give a reasonable proportion of plants with red or purple *fls*, but, for more uniform habit and colour, vegetative propagation is preferable. Cut plants very hard after flowering to

Remember colour as well as height and thickness when choosing screening plants

59

2cm (1in) and divide or use new shoots as soft cuttings in sandy growing mix.

Cheiranthus cheiri and *C. allionii*, wallflower and Siberian wallflower, *fls* include cream, yellow, apricot, mauve, orange and red with Siberian wallflower a very clear orange. The range of height is sufficient to make wallflowers bedding plants in their own right saving the expense of bulbs. Most are heavily scented and taller strains make excellent cut flowers. Propagation: sow seed in June (more compact plants are grown by sowing in July), thin after emergence and pinch out tips to encourage branching.

Myosotis, forget-me-not, *fls* dark or pale blue, or pinkish. Low compact plant which falls apart easily when transplanted. Propagation: sow seed late (July) to keep plants small and manageable. After flowering, good plants can be thrown in a spare corner to produce seedlings for next year.

Primula polyanthus, this is a highly developed plant, which has a very wide colour range. First year's *fls* large on long stems, subsequent seasons produce more but smaller flowers on shorter stems, *fls* shredded by sparrows, so beds should have a thin network of black cotton stretched above them to deter birds. Good by themselves, although lacking variation in height. Propagation: seed of newer strains is expensive, erratic to germinate and best sown under glass in June to July or, for larger plants, a whole year before required for planting out. Plants are sufficiently satisfactory perennials to warrant lifting and dividing the best plants for future years.

Viola (including pansy), sprawling but very free-flowering plants in enormous colour range. Violas have narrow one-coloured *fls*, pansies have rounder, larger *fls* blotched, whiskered or edged with darker colour. The distinction between the two has disappeared with the production of intermediate types. Propagation: sow seed in July. Some strains can produce a good autumn display from earlier sowings and will flower sporadically throughout the winter before the main display in late spring. Cuttings from young growth can be rooted quite readily if it is desired to perpetuate particularly good plants.

For less conventional schemes, early flowering herbaceous plants may be used. Dwarf doronicums and *Euphorbia epithymoides* associate well with late daffodils. *Dicentra eximia*, *Polemonium caeruleum* (grown perhaps as a biennial) and the foliage of *Anthemis cupaniana* or *Achillea* 'Moonshine' make good foils for deeper-coloured tulips. Some hardy annuals (*Nigella damascena*, *Limnanthes douglasii* and *Malcolmia maritima*) can be sown in autumn directly over tulips to provide suitable foliage and some flower.

Summer Bedding

This offers a much wider range of suitable plants than spring bedding. Hardy annuals and hardy herbaceous perennials usually have too short a flowering season although some of the latter may be used as foliage plants. Half-hardy annuals and tender perennials, however, will flower for most of the summer if they are planted out when the danger of frost is over – usually in late May to early June.

Most summer bedding schemes use three different plants. The main plants, such as salvias, should give the bed its bold colour. Lower plants can be used to edge the bed and taller dot-plants should be spaced throughout to relieve the overall flatness. The three types of plant can contrast or harmonize with each other. In practice, it is not wise to use three contrasting colours as a harmonizing edge and dot-plants with contrasting main plants produce a much better effect.

In large beds, one type of plant such as antirrhinums, salvias or tagetes, can be used alone to give a massed effect of one colour.

Many different summer-flowering plants are available but foliage plants should not be overlooked. Grey-leaved plants like *Helichrysum microphyllum*, *H. petiolatum*, *Centaurea ragusina* and the taller *Eucalyptus globulus*, or bright foliaged plants alternanthera, coleus, iresine, or bold-textured plants such as *Ricinus communis* and *Canna indica* give an air of distinction to bedding schemes as well as being more reliably permanent than flowers.

Half-hardy annuals In areas with cool climates half-hardy annuals can be sown in boxes under glass from January (for such slow growers as antirrhinums and lobelias)

to April or May (for the quick-growing zinnias and Coltness dahlias). Prick off seedlings into other boxes or small pots before they become crowded and gradually harden them off for planting out in June. In areas with warm climates they can be started from seed sown out of doors.

Ageratum, originally a tall loose plant but now with many very compact and uniform F₁ hybrids, *fls* fluffy blue, dwarf forms suitable for edging.

Antirrhinum, varying from 15cm (6in) to 1m (3 to 4ft), *fls* a wide range of colours. Intermediate types are most useful for bedding and rust-resistant strains should be used. Very useful alone or with other plants.

Begonia semperflorens, 15cm (6in), *fls* red, pink or white borne prolifically above light green to deep purple-brown *lvs*. Can be grown in shade.

Calceolaria integrifolia, 50cm (18in), *fls* bright lemon-yellow. Better used harmoniously with ageratum or fine-textured foliage than as fierce contrast. Also grown from cuttings.

Dahlia 'Coltness Gem', compact 35 to 50cm (15 to 18in), single dwarf bedding type easily grown from seed, *fls* wide range of colour.

Heliotrope, 35 to 50cm (15 to 18in) but can be trained as standard, formerly grown from cuttings but now often grown from seeds, *fls* mauve to deep purple over dark *lvs*, strong perfume.

Lobelia, compact edging plant or trailer, 10 to 15cm (4 to 6in), *fls* light or dark blue, some purple, white and almost red strains available.

Nemesia strumosa, *Penstemon hybrida*, *Phlox drummondii* and *Salpiglossis sinuata*, all bright multi-coloured slender plants 20 to 35cm (9 to 15in).

Petunia, compact or trailing plant, 35cm (15in), *fls* funnel-like, white, red, purple or striped. Good in hot weather.

Salvia splendens, 35 to 50cm (15 to 18in) with some dwarf, *fls* usually brilliant scarlet but purple and pink strains available. Best alone or with grey foliage.

Tagetes, French and African marigolds, 15 to 60cm (6 to 24in), *fls* brilliant and long lasting, orange to yellow on rounded plants. Some people dislike smell. Very reliable.

Tender perennials These can be propagated from cuttings rooted in August or September and grown slowly over winter in a cool or warm greenhouse. In warmer climates they can be overwintered outside. Pinch out the tops in early spring to promote bushy growth unless the plants are being grown as standards.

Plants with swollen roots or tubers (begonias, canna and dahlias) should be dried off during the autumn, stored in a frost-free place and started into growth early in the new year. In areas with cool climates new growth should be started by plunging them in moist peat in a warm greenhouse. More plants can then be propagated from cuttings taken from the new growth.

Begonia, tuberous and intermediate, pendulous types useful for hanging baskets, need good soil and adequate water, *fls* tuberous types are large and intermediate types are small, both available in many bright colours, *lvs* fleshy and brittle.

Dahlia, very popular in borders but the dwarfer compact types make reliable and colourful bedding plants. 'Park Princess', *fls* pink; 'Border Princess', *fls* apricot-orange; and 'Downham's Yellow', *fls* bright yellow.

Fuchsia, less obviously colourful than most bedding plants but very graceful with pendant flowers best displayed on standard plants, *fls* white, pink, red, purple and

Making an island bed. From left:

Dig the bed well in autumn incorporating manure or compost. Leave the soil surface rough

In spring break down the soil surface with a fork, rake it level, firm by treading and rake again

Use sharp sand to mark the lines along which the plants will be positioned

Plant the bed starting from the middle and working outwards

orange-red. Best used alone or with delicate foliage to avoid overpowering the fuchsias.

Pelargonium, zonal, ivy-leaved and variegated geranium, one of the showiest, most reliable and popular bedding plants. Zonal pelargoniums *fls* white, pink, red, orange and purple, with single or double flowers in large hemispherical trusses: ivy-leaved pelargoniums fewer in number but excellent for hanging baskets, a few have decorative *lvs*. Variegated pelargoniums, *lvs* variously marked with white, yellow, red, dark brown-black. Dwarfer types make good edging plants. Scented-leaved species useful where they can be handled (especially in gardens for the blind).

Foliage or Subtropical Bedding

This type of bedding relies entirely on splendid foliage to create an effect of subtropical luxuriance. A sheltered location is required to prevent wind damage. In large gardens, yucca, palms, cordyline, banana, tree ferns and other large plants can be used. In areas with cool climates these should be grown in large containers under glass and plunged outside each summer. In warm areas, they can be left outside all year round. Canna, chlorophytum and echeverias can be lifted, divided and replanted each year whilst *Eucalyptus globulus*, *Ricinus communis*, *Grevillea robusta*, coleus, iresine and many others are sufficiently fast growing to be raised from seed or cuttings each year. In areas with cold climates, the amount of seasonal planting necessary can be reduced by using a framework of hardy foliage plants and filling the spaces between them with subtropical plants in rotation with spring bedding plants. Ornamental grasses and bamboos, hardy ferns and hostas are useful for this purpose.

Carpet bedding is a special form of foliage bedding using very low, coloured-leaved plants to create patterns, which are often insignias or commemorative plaques. It is exceedingly expensive and the plants must be nipped back removing new growth and flower buds at least once a week to preserve the sharp outlines of the pattern.

Opposite: The very tall trees at the back of this garden could be overpowering, but here the colours and sizes of the flowers and shrubs in the bedding scheme below have been carefully graduated to soften the background

If you are afraid your garden will look bare in the first years before shrubs and trees are full-grown, fill the gaps with spring bulbs

Plunge Bedding

This is another expensive system of bedding and is of limited use in gardens. In a normal rotation of bedding plants there is a gap between removing the bulbs used for spring bedding until normal summer bedding plants start to flower. This gap can be closed by growing plants in large containers and plunging them into the beds just before they flower and removing them almost at once after flowering. Azaleas, delphiniums, hydrangeas and lupins are favourite plants for plunge bedding.

Winter Bedding

This is a type of plunge bedding using evergreens with decorative foliage. These are usually grown in containers or in a nursery area for several years and then plunged into a bed each autumn and removed in the following year to make way for summer bedding plants. The presence of winter greens in a bed usually limits the scope for spring bedding plants. But low clipped heathers and trailing ivies allow crocuses, narcissi or tulips to grow through them. Small spaces can be left between winter bedding plants so that tulips can be grown.

Banks

In horticulture a bank is a slope which separates two levels of a garden. It is not the side of a hill. If you have a sloping garden which you want to arrange as a series of terraces (see *Construction*) then you can hold the soil in place at the boundaries between levels by using retaining walls or banks. In the past banks were an important feature of garden design but, because they are costly and difficult to maintain, retaining walls are nowadays much more popular.

You can erect a bank quickly, at the expense of top soil, by using a bulldozer or you can make one by heaping soil on to a pile of rubble though the latter is really a sloping dry wall and is structurally and aesthetically different from a true bank.

If you use a bank in place of a retaining wall you will need to protect it against erosion. This can be done by using extensive plant cover. Banks with a slope of one in three or less are fairly easy and economical to make and cover. Banks with slopes of one in two or greater present more of a problem. But even one in two slopes can be handled satisfactorily with certain types of plants and perhaps a little bit of construction.

Plants for Banks

These must be capable of holding soil together well and must also look neat and attractive. Plants which grow rapidly, possess tenacious roots or have either a mass of stolons or rhizomes, or layer easily, are very effective. They should not look weedy, straggly or stubby and they should tolerate pruning and dry soil conditions. Because bank plants are characteristically those which grow rapidly they need to be cut back every so often to keep them within bounds. Even the best designed banks tend to erode somewhat and this means that during dry periods plants will suffer the effects of drought sooner than similar plants growing on level land. A list of plants able to tolerate these conditions is given opposite.

Bank plants can be conveniently divided into those for banks in the shade and those for banks in the sun. Banks in the shade are less subject to erosion than those in the sun, as they are often protected by existent shrubbery or trees but the choice of plants for shade is smaller and the time required to establish them is longer.

Banks in the shade The search for better ground cover plants for shaded situations is still continuing. The present favourites, ajugas, pachysandras, the ivies and vincas are relatively unattractive for most of the year. *Ophiopogon japonicus*, grows 15cm (6in) high and can be planted 15cm (6in) apart and is hardy in the USA north to Philadelphia.

Many northern native plants will do well on an acid bank in the shade. *Cornus canadensis* forms flat rosettes and produces large white flowers in late spring. *Maianthemum canadensis* and *Mitchella repens*, with pretty berries, *Linnaea borealis* with pink twin flowers and spreading habit, and the yellow-flowered *Lysimachia nummularia*, are charmers. When well established they form solid mats of foliage during the summer months. Of the grasses, *Poa trivialis* will tolerate partial shade.

South of the frost line in the USA *Dichondra repens* (too tender for UK gardens) gives outstanding ground cover for shade or sun, forming very low, solid mats, which require less mowing than grass. It has become very popular in California and has a future in all southern countries. *Nertera depressa* is almost as low as a moss and is covered with orange berries in summer. *Helxine soleirolii* is another excellent southern ground cover for shade.

Banks in the sun On sunny banks the junipers have become increasingly popular as new varieties have been developed for almost every conceivable situation and because they are in themselves most ornamental. They are deep-rooted, totally ground covering and needing no attention except pruning for appearance sake, and this makes them nearly ideal. There are many varieties of the species *Juniperus chinensis*, *J. communis*, *J. horizontalis*, *J.*

procumbens, *J. sabina* and *J. squamata* with habits varying from creeping and mat-like plants to semi-upright ones.

Of the herbaceous plants *Lotus corniculatus* and *Coronilla varia* have skyrocketed into popularity as coverings for banks. *C. varia* grows as a prostrate vine forming thick, rather deep 40cm (15in) masses of stems and leaves. During summer it bears a profusion of pink and white flower clusters. Sow seed at about 50g/10 m² (1oz/7sq yd) or 25 rooted cuttings will cover just over 9m² (100sq ft). *Lotus corniculatus* at about 100g/10m² (2oz/7sq yd) forms less of a tangle and the bright yellow flowers, borne throughout summer, are very showy. Both can be mown and grow better on poor soil with occasional liming. Polygonums are generally killed down to the ground by frost but recover in the spring. *P. affine* and *P. cuspidatum compactum* are low growing with wiry and leafy stems. *Ceratostigma plumbaginoides* bears handsome blue flowers and is evergreen in southern parts of the USA and deciduous elsewhere.

Of the vines, *Parthenocissus quinquefolia* provides excellent ground cover and is often overlooked. Varieties show brilliant red tints. In frost-free areas *Trachelospermum jasminoides* forms deep roots and supplies pretty white pin-wheel flowers, but it does have relatively few leaves.

Arctostaphylos uva-ursi is a succulent shrub which forms solid mats on sandy soil. More tolerant of clay soils are *A. edmondsii* and *A. hookeri*. *Cotoneaster microphylla* and related species and varieties root and spread easily.

The numbers after the botanical names are the hardiness zone ratings – see *Climate*.

botanical name	common name	situation	height m	(ft)
Ajuga repens 2 to 3	bugle	sun/shade	to 0·15	($\frac{1}{2}$)
Akebia quinata 4	five leaf akebia	sun	vine 7·5	(25)
Arabis alpina 3	alpine rockcress	sun	to 0·2	($\frac{3}{4}$)
Arctostaphylos uva-ursi 2	bearberry	sun	to 0·3	(1)
Berberis thunbergi 4	Japanese barberry	sun/shade	2·1	(7)
Calluna vulgaris 4	heather	sun	to 0·45	(1$\frac{1}{2}$)
Celastrus sp 2 to 4	bittersweet	sun/shade	twining vine	
Cerastium tomentosum 2 to 3	snow in summer	sun/shade	0·15	($\frac{1}{2}$)
Clematis paniculata 5	sweet autumn	sun	vine	
Cornus sericea 2	red osier dogwood	sun/shade	2·1	(7)
Cotoneaster dammeri 5	bearberry cotoneaster	sun/shade	0·3	(1)
Cotoneaster horizontalis 4	rock spray	sun/shade	0·9	(3)
Euonymus fortunei 5		sun/shade	vine to subshrub	
Forsythia 'Arnold Dwarf' 5	Arnold's dwarf forsythia	sun	0·6	(2)
Forsythia suspensa 5		sun/shade	to 3·0	(10)
Forsythia suspensa 'Sieboldi'	Siebold weeping forsythia	sun/shade	to 2·7	(9)
Hedera helix 5	English ivy	sun/shade	clinging vine	
Indigofera kirilowi 4	kirilow indigo	sun	0·9	(3)
Jasminum nudiflorum 5	winter jasmine	sun	vine to subshrub	
Juniperus horizontalis vars 2	creeping juniper	sun	ground cover	
Juniperus sabina 4	Savin's juniper	sun	ground cover	
Leucothoe fontanesiana 4	drooping leucothoe	shade	1·8	(6)
Lonicera japonica 'Halliana' 4	Hall's honeysuckle	sun	vine	
Lycium chinense 4	Chinese wolfberry	sun/shade	0·3	(1)
Myrica pennsylvanica 2	bayberry	sun/shade	2·7	(9)
Pachysandra terminalis 5	pachysandra	shade	to 0·3	(1)
Parthenocissus sp 3 to 8	Virginia creeper	sun	vine	
Phalaris arundinacea 'Picta' 3	ribbon grass	sun	to 1·2	(4)
Phlox subulata 2 to 3	moss-pink	sun	to 0·15	($\frac{1}{2}$)
Polygonum reynoutria 4	fleeceflower	shade	to 0·15	($\frac{1}{2}$)
Rhus aromatica 5	fragrant sumac	sun/shade	0·9	(3)
Rosa multiflora 5	Japanese rose	sun	3·0	(10)
Rosa rugosa 2	beach rose	sun	1·8	(6)
Rosa wichuraiana 5	memorial rose	sun	0·15	($\frac{1}{2}$)
Salix tristis 2	dwarf grey willow	sun	0·45	(1$\frac{1}{2}$)
Sedum acre 3	goldmoss stone crop	sun	0·05	($\frac{1}{6}$)
Vinca minor 5	periwinkle	shade	0·15	($\frac{1}{2}$)
Vitis sp 2 to 6	grape	sun/shade	vine	
Xanthorhiza simplicissima 4	yellow-root	sun/shade	0·6	(2)

5.Construction

Clearing the Site
Clearing the ground is the first, and most important, step in any kind of garden construction work. It must be done thoroughly and properly.

Rubbish
In some parts of the world builders leave behind lots of rubble such as bricks, concrete and so on in the gardens of new houses. Collect it and keep it. This debris can be used for foundations of walls, paths and patios and can even be used to form the foundations of a rock garden.

Trees and Shrubs
Unwanted trees close to the house or the garden boundary are best left for a specialist to remove. Large trees can also be difficult and dangerous to remove and, if you have any doubt about your ability to cope with them, you should leave them to a skilled tree surgeon who is properly qualified and fully insured. But others, particularly small ones, can be dealt with quite easily. Remove them in stages. First cut off the smaller branches with loppers and larger branches with a saw. Use a pruning or lopping saw with large, well-spaced teeth; an ordinary, carpentry saw may stick if you try to cut green wood with it. Then chop the tree down – make a cut on the side of the tree which faces the direction you want the tree to fall, then make a cut on the opposite side just above this. Leave the trunk fairly long so that you can get plenty of leverage to help remove the stump. Dig all around the stump to reveal the roots which can be cut with a mattock or axe. Rock the stump to and fro as you go. Small stumps can be removed by hand, large stumps may need a hand-operated winch. If you cannot remove the tree stump by hand, cut it close to the ground and bore large holes in the top surface. Fill the holes with a mixture of paraffin and brushwood killer and plug them with plasticine. The stump will then rot.

Weeds and Brambles
The easiest way of getting rid of grass, weeds and brambles is to spray them with a weedkiller. Use brushwood killer on brambles, nettles, thistles and large, taprooted weeds such as docks. Use a total weedkiller on the other weeds. See *Pests and Diseases: Herbicides*.

The more laborious, but much less expensive way, of getting rid of weeds is to chop them down with a sickle, power-driven scythe or even a large rotary lawn mower and then to dig the ground by hand, removing the roots and weeds as you go. Top growth from weeds and grass can be added to the compost heap, roots are better burned.

Cultivating the Soil
Large, badly-neglected gardens may need to be ploughed, harrowed and then finally tilled with a rotary cultivator. On heavy soils ploughing is best done just before the winter frosts set in. Take this opportunity to improve drainage and the condition of the soil. See *Soil*.

Shaping Soil
If your garden is on a steep slope you may want to level it and turn it into a series of terraced gardens. On the other hand, if it is large and flat, you may want to create a series of mounds and hollows by landscaping it – see *Design and Planning* for the basic principles. You may also need to level parts of the garden for putting up structures like greenhouses. Whatever sort of soil shaping exercise is to be carried out try to avoid

Opposite: Surfaces for walking or sitting on should always be firm and level

Removing a tree

Cut off the branches

Chop the tree down leaving a long stump. Use a mattock to sever the roots and winch the stump out

Large stumps can be killed by filling holes with ammonium sulphamate or 2,4,5-T. The holes should be plugged with plasticine

mixing the top soil with the subsoil: never bury the top soil and never bring the subsoil to the surface.

Landscaping

This is simply the reverse of levelling – the deliberate creation of hills and valleys. Even the smallest earth-shaping operation can mean moving several tonnes of earth so you may want to plan your garden to minimize the effort.

The best way to landscape large gardens is to remove all the topsoil from the area, to reshape the underlying subsoil using mechanical earth-moving equipment, and then to replace the topsoil uniformly.

For smaller gardens, remove the topsoil from about a third to half of the area which is to be lowest in the final scheme. Use the rest of the topsoil from this area, and if necessary some subsoil too, to make the hills. Churn up the whole of this roughly shaped area with a rotary cultivator and rake it to the desired shape. Then cover the whole area with a thin layer of the initially stock-piled topsoil. This thin layer of topsoil should be sufficient for establishing grass, but beds of flowers or shrubs on hills or valleys need deeper topsoil. To get this deeper topsoil you can reshape an area by a method analogous to double digging. Divide the area into two strips and remove the topsoil from one strip, reshape the subsoil and cover the reshaped subsoil with topsoil from the next strip. Reshape the subsoil in this strip and continue to work systematically across the whole garden. In practice this method has one drawback: it can be difficult to visualize the exact shape of the garden as you are shaping the subsoil in each individual strip. This means that it is necessary to keep going over the garden time and time again until the desired effect is obtained.

Levelling

Gardens which slope will need some levelling if they are to have a terrace, patio, pool and so on. If your garden slopes gently, you could have one terrace or patio, say, and leave the rest of the garden alone. But if it slopes steeply you may want to turn it into a series of smaller, level gardens separated from each other by retaining walls and connected by ramps or steps.

If you want to construct a series of steps or terraces, start the earth-moving job in short sections from the bottom upwards. The procedure for each section is exactly the same as described below, but build a retaining wall at the lower end of each terrace to hold the soil back.

Approximately half-way up the slope to be levelled, drive a peg of wood about 5cm

(2in) square into the ground until the top of the peg just protrudes from the ground. This is the master peg and should be painted a bright colour so that it is always readily discernible.

Drive another peg into the slope below this master peg until the tops of both pegs are level. This is done by balancing one end of a straight-edged board on top of the master peg and knocking the second peg into the ground until a spirit level, on top of the board, indicates that both pegs are level. Continue this procedure down to the bottom of the slope. Pegs should be spaced about 2m (6½ft) apart and the straight-edged board should be inverted at each step to prevent errors accumulating as the work proceeds.

Next take off all the topsoil and place it to one side. Move some of the subsoil from above the first master peg down the slope. Hammer more pegs into the ground above the master peg using the plank and spirit-level. Continue to move the subsoil until all the pegs protrude by the same amount. Replace the topsoil and level it off to the top of the pegs.

The soil at the bottom half of the slope may settle and fall below the level at the top. If this happens, either rake the topsoil level again or bring in fresh topsoil from outside the garden.

Concrete in Gardens

Concrete is one of the most useful and versatile materials available for jobs in and around the garden. It can be used to make solid paths, garage drives, patios, steps and bases for sectional buildings and garden walls. It is also one of the cheapest materials available, long-lasting, needing little maintenance, and is one of the easiest materials to use.

Concrete is made up of stones and sand held together by cement which acts as a sort of mineral glue. When water is added to the mixture, a chemical reaction takes place and the mixture hardens to a stone-like material. Mortar is simply another form of concrete but it contains cement and sand only. The cement in the mix begins to harden as soon as the water is added, so it is essential to use the concrete as quickly as possible. The hardening process cannot be reversed and freshly-mixed concrete or mortar should be used within an hour, at most, two hours after mixing. Ordinary cement is grey but slightly more expensive coloured cements are also available.

Small quantities of concrete can be mixed by hand or with a small power mixer. Large quantities can be obtained in ready-mix form for immediate use. Mortar tends to be

Levelling

About half-way up the slope knock a 5 cm (2 in) square peg into the ground. This is the master peg

Move top soil from the ground above the slope to the area *below* the bottom peg. Move subsoil from above the slope between the lower pegs

Knock other pegs into the ground further down the slope with their tops level with the master peg

Knock more pegs into the ground above the master peg and keep removing subsoil until these pegs are level with the master peg

Knock pegs into the ground across the plot again with their tops level with the master peg

Rake the whole area smooth and replace the top soil

used slowly and so only small quantities are needed at a time. It is usually best to mix these by hand.

Mix-it-yourself Concrete

Most jobs around the garden are too small to justify buying ready mixed concrete. If the quantity needed is large enough, it is worth hiring a mixer. Use sharp sand for concreting and soft sand for mortar. The stones can be either gravel or crushed stone and should vary in size between 5mm ($\frac{3}{16}$in) and 19mm ($\frac{3}{4}$in). The stones used for concrete which is to be laid thinly should be less than 10mm ($\frac{3}{8}$in) in size.

Mixes

The amounts of each ingredient in concrete should be measured carefully and thoroughly mixed before and after the water is added. The exact proportions of cement, sand and stone vary depending on what the concrete is to be used for.

For thick sections such as garage floors, foundations and drives, use a mixture of one part cement, two and a half parts of damp sand (most sand is damp and remains damp) and four parts of larger stones.

For medium sections like paths, steps, edging and anywhere where the concrete is to be laid less than 75mm (3in) thick, a stronger mix is needed. Use one part cement, two parts of damp sand and three parts of stones.

For thin sections, say concrete under 50mm (2in) thick, use one part cement and three parts sand.

For bedding paving use a mortar mix of one part cement and five parts sand.

It is always preferable to buy the sand and stones separately and mix them in the correct proportions yourself. But, for smaller

Making a Concrete Slab

Make a frame from 50 by 25 mm (2 by 1 in) softwood. The joint at one corner should be easy to open and close

Place the frame on a plastic sheet and scatter a layer of clean sand over the bottom

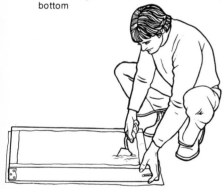

Fill the frame with a concrete mix making sure that there are no air bubbles in the corners

Level the surface with a long piece of wood

jobs, this is not always practical and combined aggregates or ballast which contain the sand and stones ready mixed, can be used. The amount of combined material needed is less than the sum of the separate materials because the sand in the combined material fills in the spaces between the stones. A mix of one part cement to five parts combined washed aggregate (ballast) is approximately the same as a 1:2½:4 mix. A mixture of one part of cement to three and three-quarters parts of washed ballast is approximately the same as the richer and stronger 1:2:3 mix. Never use straight-from-the-pit unwashed ballast, and always proportion the materials by volume, never by weight.

For small jobs it is best to get pre-packed, dry mixes which are available from builder's merchants, garden centres and many local hardware shops. These contain cement, sand and coarse aggregates already properly proportioned, and save a lot of trouble and mess.

Calculating the Quantities

Before buying the materials calculate carefully the amount of each material needed. To do this work out the area to be concreted in square metres (sq ft) and multiply this by the thickness of the concrete slab in mm (in). Divide the answer by 1,000 (12) and this gives the volume of the concrete needed in cubic metres (cu ft).

The volume of mixed concrete is less than the total volume of the components and this should be taken into account.

7½m³ (cu yd) of 1:2½:4 mix will yield about 5½m³ (cu yd) of concrete
6m³ (cu yd) of 1:2:3 mix will yield about 4⅓m³ (cu yd) of concrete
4m³ (cu yd) of 1:3 mix will yield about 3m³ (cu yd) of concrete

Sand, stones and combined aggregate are usually sold by volume. Cement is normally sold by the bag, which usually contains about 0·035m³ (1¼ cu ft) of cement. So the materials needed for a 2m³ (cu yd) slab of concrete with a 1:2½:4 mix would be

Opposite right: A concrete bowl makes an excellent plant container

Sequence showing how to set a post into the ground. *Top, left to right*: a hole borer, showing the soil carrying section; removing soil with a twisting action; testing the depth. *Bottom, left to right*: centring the post; replacing the soil

Cement $\dfrac{2}{5\frac{1}{2}} \times 1 = 0\cdot36\mathrm{m}^3$ (10 cu ft)

Sand $\dfrac{2}{5\frac{1}{2}} \times 2\frac{1}{2} = 0\cdot91\mathrm{m}^3$ (25 cu ft)

Stones $\dfrac{2}{5\frac{1}{2}} \times 4 = 1\cdot45\mathrm{m}^3$ (40 cu ft)

As a general rule, a one-bag mix (one bag of cement to the appropriate proportions of fine and coarse aggregate or combined ballast) will produce about $0\cdot17\mathrm{m}^3$ (6cu ft) of normal 1:2½:4 concrete or $0\cdot14\mathrm{m}^3$ (5cu ft) of the richer 1:2:3 mix.

Mixing

Mix the concrete on a clean, hard surface. Clean working conditions are necessary at all times but are essential when using coloured cement. Lay the stones down first in a roughly flat-topped, circular layer. Add the sand then mix. Then add the cement and mix again thoroughly. Form a crater in the middle and pour in water. Very roughly, six buckets of sand/cement/stones mixture will need one bucket of water: about half of this should be poured into the crater. Turn the mixture on the outside of the crater into the crater and continue turning, mixing and adding the rest of the water until it is even in colour and consistency. Take care not to use too much water. The ideal mix should be close-knit, and not wet and sloppy when it is tamped with the back of a shovel.

Ready-Mixed Concrete

Concrete can be bought ready mixed. It is usually delivered in trucks which hold from 3 to 6m³ (4 to 8cu yd). It is a very quick, and convenient, way of laying large quantities of concrete for jobs such as garage drives. It should be used as quickly as possible after delivery and this will mean a lot of work in a short time. Large quantities of ready mix are only really feasible if enough friends, relations and helpers can be pressed into service at the right time.

Before ordering ready mix, check the details of the best mixture for the job with the supplier and make sure that delivery vehicles have suitable access to the area to be concreted.

Laying Concrete

For details of how to use concrete see *Drives* and *Paths*. See *Paving* for details of making paving slabs.

Paving

Grass is the traditional material for covering large, flat areas in gardens. But it does not wear well and is slow to dry after rain. Paving is a more expensive alternative but in heavily used areas, its hard-wearing, low maintenance, quick-drying qualities increasingly justify the extra initial outlay. Most patios and paths are paved.

The Materials

Materials can be grouped into three categories: mass materials, small units and large units. In all cases, they should be laid on a compacted level base, preferably of rammed hardcore covered with rolled ballast. Good foundations are especially important for small blocks. Thought must be given to surface drainage.

Mass Materials

These are materials composed of a great many small pieces and include gravel, asphalt and concrete. They are the least expensive materials and the easiest to lay.

Gravel Gravel is a word used to cover a range of materials from crushed rocks to pebbles from beaches or river beds. Loose gravel is difficult to walk on, becomes rutted if driven over and is very difficult to keep free from leaves, litter and weeds. Gravel, rolled into a bituminous base, is easier to maintain. Loose gravel is sold by weight or by volume. Most producers specify the minimum quantity they are willing to sell – usually about 5 tonnes. The area covered by loose gravel depends on the size of the gravel particles: 1 tonne will cover about $9m^2$ (10 sq yd) to a depth of about 50mm (2in). Gravel paths need curbing to stop the gravel being tramped around the garden.

Asphalt This is a uniform matt black bituminous material. A salt-and-pepper finish can be given to larger areas by rolling in stone chips but this should not be overdone. It is flexible, can be used on irregular surfaces, but requires a firm edging to prevent it breaking away. Pre-cast white concrete edging is usually used but a less sharp contrast, which is perhaps more suitable for gardens, can be obtained by using brick or granite setts or other stone edgings. A chequer board of alternating brick squares and asphalt squares can be easily constructed using cold-rolled asphalt available in bags from larger garden centres. Because of its dark colour asphalt becomes very hot in sunshine and should not be used in small gardens unless adequately shaded. For further details see *Drives*.

Concrete Unlike gravel and asphalt, concrete is a rigid material and will crack if the ground settles unevenly beneath it. To avoid cracking, slabs should not be more than $2 \cdot 5m$ (8ft) square and never more than twice as long as they are wide. Small gaps – about 1 to 2cm (around ½in) – between slabs will allow for expansion and if these lines align with corners of the house, steps, pergola posts and other features the concrete area will fit satisfactorily into the garden.

Small Units

Bricks and other small blocks are more expensive than most other materials and are more difficult to lay but they can be used in small irregular areas and as patterns or edgings. Use high-quality exterior bricks and avoid those which are merely faced or of inferior quality. Treat them regularly with algicide to avoid dangerous slipperiness. Bricks and other small blocks can be used to create intricate patterns, sometimes using a combination of two colours for effect. Cobbles are much less expensive and very uncomfortable to walk on, but make excellent barriers at the edge of a path or terrace. Cobbles can be used as a decorative in-fill in other paving materials. Loose cobbles can also be used as a weed-suppressing mulch.

Large Units

These are basically large pieces of stone or concrete slabs laid together in a sort of jigsaw. See *Paths* for laying details.

Stone Large, flat pieces of natural stone can be used for paths, patios and terraces. Any sort of stone is satisfactory: sandstone is one of the most popular but it is very soft. Stones can generally be obtained in many different shades of yellow and orange. They need not fit together exactly as they are often bedded in concrete or cement. Stone is often sold, by weight, in random sizes. The area covered by each tonne depends on the average thickness and the density of the rock. If the stone is to be laid on concrete, it can be quite thin – no more than 25mm (1in), say. If it is to be laid on sand then 50mm (2in) will be more satisfactory. Ask the supplier what area each tonne will cover. Avoid obtaining slabs of different thicknesses as these can be very difficult to lay successfully.

Concrete slabs These are made by casting concrete in moulds. They are easy to handle and to lay and are available in many colours and in various shapes with different surface textures. They are generally made in sizes based on multiples of 225mm (9in) or

300mm (12in). Avoid using very big slabs in small paths and keep the small sizes away from path edges where they are liable to become displaced. Be careful with the arrangement of the joins. The pattern of joins can be used to emphasize or to play down the length, width or diagonal dimensions of the paved area.

Making concrete slabs Make a frame from 50mm by 25mm (2in by 1in) softwood to the desired size. Join three corners of the frame by tacking on strips of leather or tin. The joint at the fourth corner should be easy to open and close. Strong string wrapped around nails and kept under tension will make an adequate joint. Place the frame on a plastic sheet with a level hard surface below. Grease the insides of the frame to prevent the concrete sticking to it, scatter a 6mm (¼in) layer of clean sand over the inside of it and fill it with a concrete mix of one part cement to three of sharp sand. Coloured cement may be used. Push the mix into every corner to get rid of air bubbles by chopping it with a spade. Level the surface with a long piece of wood. The frame can be removed after a day or so but keep the slab covered by damp sacks or newspapers for at least four days. Store the slab, on end, for a further three weeks before use. Textured or completely smooth finishes can be given to the surface while the concrete is still damp.

Cutting

Stone and concrete slabs are cut in exactly the same way. Concrete slabs are more regular in thickness and texture and are generally the easier to cut. To cut straight lines, make the line and cut a shallow scratch all round the piece to be cut off using a cold chisel (or bolster) and hammer. Hit the slab face with the hammer along the line of the cut. When the ringing tone starts to deaden the slab is cracking apart. Trim off any remaining irregularities with a hammer and chisel.

To cut convex curved corners, mark the shape on one face of the slab and cut a scratch with a hammer and chisel. Place a piece of paper over the slab and trace the position and outline of the scratch. Cut the paper to the shape required and use this as a template to position the line for the scratch on the second face. Cut the scratch all round, as before, and tap along the scratch with a hammer until a portion cracks away. Trim off the excess.

To cut concave corners, cut a scratch along the curve as described above and cut an additional V-scratch into the concave corner. Cut out the V-shape very carefully and then chisel away at the curve with a small cold chisel.

To cut large holes, chip out a crater in the centre of the hole on each side of the slab until the chisel point breaks through. Carefully chip the hole to the required size.

To cut holes less than 10cm (4in) in diameter, drill a number of holes through the slab around the cirumference of the hole to be cut out. Position these small holes as close together as possible. Chisel out the waste carefully.

Choosing the Material

The cost of the different materials varies tremendously. Gravel, asphalt and concrete are the cheapest with paving stone the most expensive at around ten times as much. The cost of transportation is a large part of the price of any heavy material and savings can be made by using local materials which are also more in keeping than obviously foreign ones.

Paving small irregular areas or winding paths with large slabs involves a great deal of cutting and the final appearance may not be very satisfactory. Brightly coloured paving, especially mixtures of several bright colours look very gaudy and make it impossible to create a garden with a relaxed atmosphere.

Paths

The main purpose of a path is to give access to the various parts of the garden. It should provide a surface which is solid and dry and should, like all other garden features, make a contribution towards the appearance of the garden as a whole. It should also be non-slip and freely draining. The size and materials of a path will depend on its position in the garden and how much wear-and-tear it will be subjected to by garden users.

Paths in Vegetable Gardens

Paths in vegetable gardens should be functional rather than attractive. They should give convenient access with heavy loads to all parts of the vegetable plot, particularly in wet weather. In some vegetable gardens, it may be convenient to have a path, like paving slabs or duckboards, which is easily moved.

Sizes For walking behind a wheelbarrow, a path which is 35 to 40cm (15 to 18in) wide is usually sufficient but in larger gardens (or places where you are likely to use two- or four-wheeled barrows) it is more convenient to have a path which is 60 to 75cm (24 to 30in) wide so that the wheelbarrow can be stood on the firm, level path surface. If any motor-powered equipment is to be used in the vegetable garden then the path

Cutting a Concrete Slab

Make the shape on one face of the slab

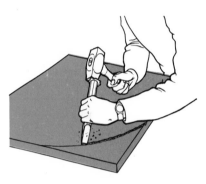

Cut a scratch with a hammer and chisel

Make a template of the scratch and trace it out on the opposite side. Cut another scratch

Tap along the scratch until the slab breaks

CONSTRUCTION

Top: A concrete paved area

Bottom: Brick paving is expensive but very attractive

Top: Brick paving complementing a brick wall

Bottom: A mixture of brick and concrete paving

Above: This woodland path is given an air of informality by the uneven edging

Left: A path should be wide enough to take a wheelbarrow

must be made sufficiently wide and strong enough to cope with it.

Materials On very light soils a path of trodden earth may be all that is needed. It can be kept free from weeds by annual applications of weedkillers such as simazine. Do not use any weedkiller which can seep sideways in the soil. This sort of path is very flexible. It can simply be dug up and another made somewhere else in the garden if the shape of the garden changes. On heavier soils, paths of trodden earth become muddy and sticky in wet weather but, if free-draining materials such as clinker or ashes are rolled into the surface, the drainage will be improved sufficiently to give a satisfactory path. Newly-made concrete slabs are relatively expensive and may crack unless they are laid on good foundations. A path made by pouring 75cm (3in) of strong mix concrete over a 25cm (1in) base of rolled coarse sand in short lengths will give a hard-wearing surface which could be removed at some later date. Grass paths are unsatisfactory in vegetable gardens. They develop ruts in their surface and their edges crumble as wheelbarrows bump on and off the path.

Soil brought onto the path by boots and tools can ruin mowers used to cut it.

Paths in the Ornamental Garden

In ornamental gardens a balance must be struck between function and appearance. Avoid running paths down the centre of the garden as these usually make it appear much narrower than it really is.

Sizes Be bold with paths in ornamental gardens. Aim for a minimum width of 1·5m (5ft) and, in very large gardens, increase this to 4 to 6m (15 to 20ft) to keep the path in scale with its surroundings. Any sort of hard surface presents a mowing problem if it is positioned next to a lawn. Avoid the troubles by leaving a 5cm (2in) gap between path and grass or by separating them with a border of flowers or herbs. In small narrow gardens, paths are best restricted to a narrow edging about 35cm (15in) or so wide between the border and the lawn. This gives enough room to get about the garden in wet weather and serves as a line to emphasize the shapes of the border and lawn. This sort of path allows plants to grow forward informally on to the path without having to resort to complicated mowing. Winding, uniformly wide paths look odd in perspective and need to be widened at each bend. Do this by marking the outline of the path directly on the ground rather than attempt to design it on paper.

Materials Various combinations of different types, textures and colours of materials can be used with considerable effect. See *Paving*. Edgings, insets of brick, mellow cut stone or impregnated wood planks can add character to gravel walks. Bricks or cobbles can be used between bays of concrete to create an interesting rhythm and a pleasing effect can be obtained by setting rectangular or large irregular slabs of stone or concrete into a path of loose gravel. Grass can make an attractive, wide path in many settings but it will not stand up to heavy wear and it should not be used in shaded situations. On heavy soils a grass path will need as much attention to foundations of hardcore, ballast and sand as any of the hard materials. For construction of grass surfaces, see *Lawns*.

Laying Paths

The basic principles involved in path laying are covered by the examples given below. Sensible application of these principles will enable you to adapt these instructions and to lay any kind of path successfully. For details of providing small cambers or falls see *Drives*.

Paving set in soil This is one of the easiest types of path to lay but it will need a lot of maintenance later to keep it weed-free and level. Sandstone or any other flat-surfaced rock can be used. Remove all weeds from the path area and apply a weedkiller. Rake the path area approximately level and set the stones on the soil. Brush loose soil into the joins. Planting is best done as the work progresses. A foundation of about 7·5cm (3in) of broken stones rammed into a 15cm (6in) deep trench and topped off with 2·5 to 5cm (1 to 2in) of soil will give a firmer foundation than soil alone.

Concrete slabs on sand Before ordering, make a sketch of the path on paper to determine the exact numbers, colours and sizes of slabs required. Remove all weeds and apply a weedkiller. Take out a trench and make foundations with about 7·5cm (3in) of rammed rubble. Top this off with 5cm (2in) of sharp sand or fine ash and rake level. Use a builder's spirit level on a 2m (6½ft) board to check the levelness of the sand before laying the paving. Paving near house walls should have a slight slope away from the house to let water drain away and should always be below the house damp-proof course. Narrow paths can be laid level. Lower the slabs gently on to the sand,

drive some sand under the edges and bed it in by tapping the slab all over with the handle of a large hammer. Lay more slabs edge to edge trimming and fitting as required and complete the job by brushing fine sand into all the joints. To make a more permanent bedding, a mixture of one part cement to six parts sand can be used in place of sand alone.

Stone set into concrete This gives one of the most durable attractive path surfaces it is possible to have. Natural stones or textured concrete slabs can be used. Prepare the path for concreting by erecting formwork. See *Drives*. Lay a 7·5cm (3in) deep layer of rammed, broken stones for a foundation. Make up the required concrete mix (see *Concrete*) and shovel it on to the rubble until the level of concrete is a little less than the thickness of the stone or paving below the formwork. Smooth the concrete surface by tamping with the edge of short board and check the level or slope with a spirit level. Scoop out a rough hollow in the wet concrete surface (do not remove the concrete), press the stone in place and bed it down with light blows from the hammer butt. Use battens laid across the formwork to check the height and level of the stones. Any concrete which squeezes up from around the stones should be trowelled back around them to bed them in firmly. Brush the surface when the concrete is partly dry to smooth the joints.

Remove the formwork after two to three days and smooth the rough path edges with fine cement.

Cemented, broken-slab paving Prepare the ground as for laying concrete slabs on sand. Sort out all the pieces and make up the path on the sand in jigsaw fashion. Put the larger pieces at the edges, for strength, and fill-in towards the middle with the smaller pieces. Work along the path, lifting each piece in turn and placing a generous quantity of mortar along the edges of each piece. Tap the piece down on the bed, fill in the joints with more and check all levels.

Bricks With this sort of paving the bricks are laid on edge and the depth of brick will, in many cases, provide sufficient foundations. Place the bricks on a 5cm (2in) layer of sharp sand or dry-mix concrete leaving gaps of about 10mm (⅜in) between them. Bed them in firmly using a hammer handle. Brush more sand or dry-mix concrete into the joints.

Concrete Concrete may be ordered ready mixed or as the separate ingredients. Details of the different mixes and how to calculate the amount needed are dealt with on p.69–71. Allow about 10 per cent extra for waste. Do not lay concrete when frost is expected.

Drives

Basically a drive is a large path which is capable of withstanding the heavier loads of motor vehicles and the occasional commercial vehicle. Most of the materials used for (and discussed under) *paths,* including paving slabs and broken paving, can be used on drives, provided they are given an adequate increase in the depth of the foundations. A drive can simply be two parallel tracks for the wheels with loose pebbles or gravel between them. But, more usually, they are a solid mass of concrete, gravel or coated macadam.

Gravel gives an easily laid, cheap drive surface. But it is noisy, needs a lot of attention to keep it weed-free, often needs raking level and it can be tramped into the house.

Concrete is more difficult to lay but it gives a hard-wearing almost maintenance-free surface.

Coated macadam consists of small pieces of stone (aggregate) coated with a tar or bitumen binder. When the binder is road tar the coated macadam is known as tarmacadam or 'tarmac'. Most coated macadams have to be laid hot and this is often left to the professionals. But laying hot coated macadam is not beyond the capabilities of the average handyman and the materials can be bought in bulk from a coating plant. Coated macadam can also be bought cold in pre-packed bags and is available in black, red and green. It blends better with the garden but may not be quite as durable as concrete.

Planning

Before starting to plan the drive out on paper, have a good look at the proposed site. In particular, note the position of drains and other services and check the legal or planning requirements necessary either to build over them or to move them. Visualize the various slopes the drive will need to have to make sure that rainwater drains off it and does not drain towards the house or garage. Think about the size it needs to be. In the UK a normal single automobile garage width is about 2·5m (8ft), in the USA and Canada it is about 3·0m (10ft). Constructing a drive exactly the same width as the garage allows precious little driveway to step out of the automobile on to. Give the drive an extension of at least 0·5m (1½ft) on the house side.

Look at the soil. On normal sound subsoil 15cm (6in) deep foundations will be adequate. On soft clay or other poor subsoils it may be necessary to increase the depth to 20cm (8in). A 10cm (4in) depth of concrete is adequate for ordinary automobiles on sound subsoil but this should be increased to 13cm (5in) on poor subsoils and another 5cm (2in) should be added if the drive is to be used by commercial vehicles. Finally, make a simple sketch to scale.

Ordering Materials

Drives can be thought of as having three layers – foundations, base course and wearing course.

For concrete drives the base course and wearing course are one thickness of concrete.

For coated macadam drives the base course may be concrete or it may be a coated macadam with large pieces of aggregate. In either case the wearing course is, of course, coated macadam. The table lists a number of different specifications for base course and wearing course coated macadams and shows what area of drive one tonne of each material will surface.

Specification	compacted thickness mm	coverage m²/tonne	(sq yd/ton)
Base course			
20mm nominal size open textured coated macadam	40	11	(13)
40mm nominal size open textured coated macadam	60	8	(10)
40mm nominal size single course coated macadam	60	8	(10)
Wearing course			
6mm nominal size medium textured coated macadam	15	31	(37)
10mm nominal size open textured coated macadam	20	23	(27)
10mm nominal size dense coated macadam	20	23	(27)
fine cold asphalt or fine-textured tarmacadam	20	23	(27)

Above left: An attractive mellow brick path

Above right: Geometrically designed brick path

Right: Spaced slabs give interest to a dark narrow path

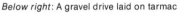
Left: A broken-slab path

Below left: A drive should complement the house it serves

Below right: A gravel drive laid on tarmac

Concrete may be ordered ready mixed or as the separate ingredients. Details of the different mixes and how to calculate the amount needed are dealt with under *Concrete in Gardens*.

Remember to allow about 10 per cent extra for waste.

Establish delivery times as closely as possible and make sure that delivery vehicles have adequate access to the area to be surfaced. If ready-mix concrete or hot coated macadam is to be laid, make sure that plenty of help is available – both set hard fairly quickly.

Laying the Drive

Clear away topsoil and plants, dig out roots and direct drains or re-lay them in a straight line across the drive. Treat the whole area with a weedkiller. Decide on a reference level – the damp-proof course of the house is useful: the top of the drive should be about 15cm (6in) below it.

Excavate the site for the foundations (arrangements will have to be made for removing this material – check to make sure that your use of a skip does not infringe laws or by-laws). Lay foundations of rubble and compact it well.

Set the level of the drive from the reference level using string, pegs and a builder's spirit level. Over large distances a hose pipe can be used by fixing one end of the hose to the reference level and fixing the other end loosely to a wooden stake. Fill the hose with water and raise or lower the hose at the staked end until the water comes to the top of the hosepipe at both ends. Mark the position of the hose on the stake: this is now level with the reference. Continue to set up pegs at regular intervals on the perimeter of the drive area. The drive must be sloped to one side to let rain water run off. Re-mark the pegs on one side to allow for a slope of about 1 in 60. If the drive slopes down towards the garage, take it to below the level of the garage floor making sure that there is an adequate slope for run off to one side.

Next make up a formwork of about 25mm (1in) thick wood which is at least as wide as the drive is to be thick. Set this on end and nail it to stout pegs which have been driven firmly into the ground. The tops of the pegs should be below the top of the wood used for the formwork. The top of the formwork should be set at the level of the final drive surface. The wood used for formwork can be bent into curves by cutting part way through the timber strip at roughly 25cm (10in) intervals. End to end joints between form strips should be backed up by additional pieces of timber and firmly pegged down.

For Concrete Drives

Set boards to act as expansion joints at right angles to the drive at 3m (10ft) intervals – these are necessary to prevent the concrete from cracking through alternating expansion and contraction in hot and cold weather. The boards should be moved slightly while the concrete is setting to make them easier to remove later. The joint should eventually be filled with mastic or bitumen. Place the concrete between the formwork evenly, working it into corners with a piece of wood. Spread the concrete evenly to about 12mm (½in) above the top of the formwork. Use a heavy tamping beam (a stout piece of wood at least the width of the drive and preferably with handles at both ends) to compact the concrete as soon as a length of about 50cm (1½ft) has been laid. Use a chopping motion to firm the concrete, keeping a steady rhythm and working from one end of the freshly laid concrete to the other. When the concrete is thoroughly compacted use the tamping board to remove any excess material by moving it backwards and forwards across the concrete with a sawing action. A rough finish (for grip on slopes) can be given to the

concrete surface by brushing it with a stiff broom.

Cover the concrete with plastic sheets, damp hessian or burlap to cure. Allow four days in warm weather and up to ten days in cold weather. Do not lay concrete when frost is expected. The drive can be used by light cars about seven days after concreting. In cold weather and with heavier vehicles it is wise to wait at least fourteen days.

For Coated Macadam Drives

These drives need a curb/kerb to prevent break-up of the macadam along its edge. Lay this first just inside the formwork on top of the drive foundations. For details see *Curbs/Kerbs*.

If hot-coated macadam is to be laid use hot tools, cover the heaps with tarpaulins to keep them warm and have plenty of help available. Rake the coated macadam level and to the desired thickness. If over-raking separates out some of the coarser aggregate add another shovelful of fresh coated macadam and re-rake. Compact the material as soon as possible. Use a vibrating roller in preference to a hand roller except where the coated macadam is to be laid over a concrete base. Keep the roller wet to prevent pick-up of the coated macadam.

Curbs/Kerbs

Curbs/kerbs are usually lines of bricks, concrete blocks or wood which are used to protect the edges of materials like asphalt and to keep materials like gravel enclosed in the path area. Curbs/kerbs are generally laid before a path or drive.

Concrete curbs/kerbs These are available in a range of sizes: 25cm by 7·5 to 10cm (12in by 3 to 4in) is quite popular. To lay them, spread a thick layer of concrete along the edges of the foundations and press each curb/kerb down into the concrete checking its height and levelness. A thin layer of concrete should be drawn up the inside face of the curbs/kerbs and any concrete which has oozed outside them should be rammed firm. The small gaps between the curbs/kerbs will allow water to drain away.

Brick curbs/kerbs These can be laid in exactly the same way as concrete curbs/kerbs or they can be set at an angle to give a dog's tooth effect. When laid at an angle they should be set on a wet concrete bed and a thin layer of concrete should be drawn up both sides.

Wood curbs/kerbs If wood is to be permanent it will need treating thoroughly with preservative. Ask the wood merchant about the possibility of obtaining pressure-treated wood. Supporting posts should be about 10cm by 2·5cm by 60cm long (4in by 1in by

Laying a Concrete Drive

Set the level for the drive using pegs and a builder's spirit level. Over large distances or around corners a hosepipe can be used

Tamp the concrete down

Attach the framework to the pegs and lay a layer of hardcore

Put in expansion joints at 3 m (10 ft) intervals

Give slopes a rough finish by sweeping the surface of the concrete with a stiff broom

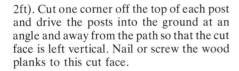

Work the concrete well into the corners

2ft). Cut one corner off the top of each post and drive the posts into the ground at an angle and away from the path so that the cut face is left vertical. Nail or screw the wood planks to this cut face.

Patios

Patios have developed from some of the earliest European gardens (the Moorish gardens in Spain) and from Persian gardens. Both were essentially a courtyard surrounded by the house on four sides. They were paved and plants in tubs were stood on the paving.

These gardens were usually found in deserts or desert areas and often had a water feature – usually called a canal. This feature was surrounded by bold foliage plants to create a cool, lush oasis feeling in contrast with the hot, dry landscape which was all around.

Nowadays the word patio is used more generally to describe a paved area in a garden but it should still be thought of as an area which contains more luxuriant vegetation than the surrounding garden. If you want the traditional water feature, see *Gardens: Water Gardens* for details of how to make and plant one.

Sites, Size and Shape

A patio can be almost any shape: it can be more or less square, circular, semi-circular or arc-shaped. It can be used as a suntrap, a place to grow plants that would not be hardy in the open garden, a place which can provide shelter from the sun (by building a pergola over it), somewhere in the garden which is out of view of the neighbours or as an outdoor extension to the house. The ideal position for a patio depends on which of these purposes are most important. For example, if a patio is to act as a suntrap, it might be impossible to position it next to the house. Instead it may have to be sited halfway down the garden.

If a patio is to be used as an extension to the house then it should generally have direct access through the main room. If the main room is at the side of the house which is in the shade for much of the day, then plant generously against the house and push out the paving to a more sunny spot. Allow ample room for garden furniture, plants, pools and other features and build the patio with a view to extending it in the future. There is much to be said for selecting garden furniture first and then designing the patio around it to make sure that there is adequate room.

Resist any attempt to create a patio by uniformly widening a concrete path. The result will be a wide path, not a patio. A much more successful approach is to reduce the apparent length of the path by blocking it from view and to widen the remainder

much more substantially. If the path runs along the full width of the house then the part of the width not occupied by paving can be filled with plants or the patio may be more definitely enclosed by a raised pool or by a permanent masonry seat. Seats built into the patio enclosure provide sitting space on a small patio with the minimum loss of room. A brick or concrete barbecue is also a useful divider.

The relationship of the patio to the rest of the garden is very important. A large patio leading on to a small lawn gives the garden an uncomfortable, unbalanced appearance. If there is not room for a patio which is large enough for your needs as well as a lawn, then one or the other should be sacrificed for the sake of the garden as a whole. The choice is between either extending the patio to provide a useful area of paving and surrounding this by lots of plants or reducing the patio to a large doorstep, just big enough to take a chair or two when the grass is wet, leaving adequate space for the lawn.

Opposite above: A macadam drive

Opposite below: A patio showing how levels can be broken up

Below: An impressive but restful patio design

Right: Patio 1
Small brick paved patio. The bricks
are laid flat and are continued into the
garden as boundaries for the lawn areas.
The bricks also border the tree and shrub
bed in the upper right-hand corners. Pots
can be placed on the patio for bulbs and
annuals

Far right: Patio 2
Patios made from brick circles surrounded
by contrasting white stone chips. This
patio is sited away from the house and the
example here is sheltered by trees and
shrubs

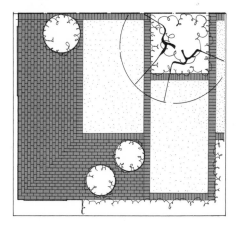

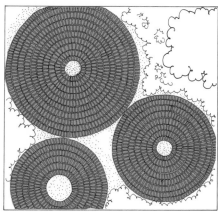

Right: Patio 3
York stone paving and bricks. The bricks
are laid flat. The edges to the patio are
softened with plants. This patio can be
built next to the house

Far right: Patio 4
Mixed patio with panels of bricks and
paving slabs between a concrete grid laid
in situ. The harsh lines to this sort of patio
need careful softening with trees and
plants

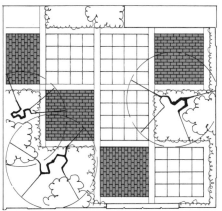

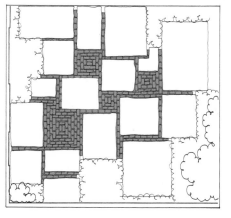

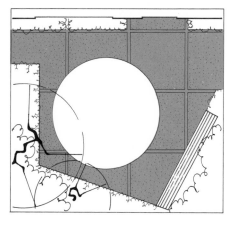

Left: Patio 5
A modern garden with concrete panels laid
in a wooden grid. The garden has a circular
lawn or gravelled area in the middle and is
screened by trees and shrubs on the
lefthand side. A bench seat completes the
garden

Designs

Patios look much better if they are enclosed
or partially enclosed (in small gardens any
form of enclosure may be impractical).
Screen-walls, trellises, arches, raised plant
containers and so on can be used to block
off unsightly views and to reveal carefully
framed vistas of the garden or more distant
landscape features.

A change of level also helps to emphasize
the identity of the patio and a sunken patio
can easily be made by raising the level of the
adjacent garden with soil excavated for the
patio. A sunken patio will need retaining
walls (see *Walls*) and great care must be
taken to make sure that it has adequate
drainage. It can also act as a frost pocket.

The positions of entrances to the patio
are important. If the main room of the
house gives access to the centre of the patio
and the exit to the rest of the garden is
positioned immediately opposite, then the
effect will be to minimize the apparent size
of the patio and to make it seem like a large
doorstep. If the access to the patio and the
exit to the garden are opposite each other

but offset towards one side of the patio, a secluded alcove is formed and a large area of useful space is created. Access and exit diagonally opposite each other will make the patio a more integral part of the house and garden but will cut it in two and make it less convenient to use.

Materials

Nearly all the materials listed under *Paving* can be used on patios. They should be laid by methods similar to those described for *Paths*. Make sure that the paving slopes slightly away from the house and meets it below the damp-proof course. Start at the house wall and work outwards away from it.

Select materials so that their texture and colour blend well with the house. Make sure that joins in paving align with doors, windows, steps, fence posts and other vertical lines around so that the patio is united with its surroundings.

Plants

The main purpose of a patio is for sitting outdoors and a careful selection of plants can add to this pleasure. Foliage plants give a more lasting attractive effect than do flowers and, because rainwater is often diverted from the paving to an adjacent border, there is ample scope for growing many bold waterside plants such as rodgersia, hosta, rheum and ligularia. Primulas and meconopsis provide attractive flowers in damp borders. On the drier, sunny side of a patio crocuses, tulips, agapanthus, nerines and the small kniphofias such as *K. macowanii,* provide a successful display of brilliant flowers among fatsia, acanthus, bocconia, artemisia and other bold or silver-leaved plants. For additional colour, azaleas, hydrangeas and other bright shrubs and bedding plants can be grown in tubs which should be moved to less conspicuous parts of the garden when they are not in flower. In winter tubs may need moving into the shelter of a greenhouse. Subtropical effects can be created by using plants such as yucca, opuntia, bergenia and palms. In the southern parts of North America tropical plants like palms, bananas, bromeliads and monsteras can be grown.

Terraces

A terrace is a large, level area built into, or on to, a sloping garden. The terrace may be covered by paving or by lawns and plants of various kinds.

Sloping gardens can often be planted informally but a level area around the house will provide a place for formal pools, flower gardens and outdoor furniture. In small gardens, one terrace may be all that is

Laying concrete slabs

Pressing down a gravel base

Spreading sand

Cementing the slabs

Checking the level

Top 3 on right: Checking the level above the patio

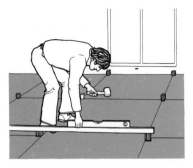

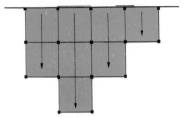

Sweeping off dried cement

Washing down

Above: A terrace and steps made of brick and broken slab paving

Colourful plantings soften the outlines
of these steps

necessary. In larger gardens, a series of terraces, with connecting steps, gives the garden a more elegant and more functional look. But the time, cost and effort involved in building terraces are considerable and even in large gardens it is normal to have only one or two terraces which merge into a less formal garden on the natural slope beyond. The top terrace might be a small, secluded paved area with a room for sitting outside the house. The bottom terrace might be a large area of lawn for children to play on.

Construction

The first step is to level the ground. Start with the bottom terrace and work upwards. See *Levelling*. The materials for laying on the ground are detailed under *Drives, Paths, Paving* and *Patios*. See *Walls* for building retaining walls.

Do not attempt to build retaining walls over 1·5m (5ft) high without the services of a building engineer. Walls below this height can be erected quite safely, with care. The retaining wall can be continued well above the terrace to emphasize the terrace from above. It will also make the terrace safer and will add height to the wall when it is seen from below. A wall 40 to 45cm (16 to 18in) higher than the terrace can be used for sitting on or a wall 1m or so (3 to 3½ft) higher than the terrace can be used for leaning on.

A dry stone wall is best for homes in the country while it is likely that a more finished brick or concrete block wall will be more suitable for town and suburban gardens.

A low terrace can be retained by a retaining wall or by a bank. Steep grassy banks are difficult to mow but they can be planted with ground-cover plants – see *Design and Planning: Banks*. Long, thin rock-gardens make very unsatisfactory terrace banks, especially when the uneven silhouette is seen from above.

Steps

In sloping gardens steps are essential for ease of movement but they add so much to the character of a garden that they are often introduced into flat gardens.

The most important requirement for any set of exterior steps is safety. Single steps are far too inconspicuous and may cause falls; small flights should be used instead. Make the treads out of durable, non-slip materials and slope them slightly sideways so that rainwater runs off them. Long flights of steps should be broken up into smaller flights with odd numbers of steps separated by level platforms of about 2m (7ft) square. The flights can change direction at each landing. The minimum tread – the flat part – should be 30cm (1ft) deep but 40cm (15in) is more desirable.

This wall supporting a slope with steps is filled with colourful trailing plants. It is a section of the wall shown on the facing page

Sizes

The main problem when designing steps is deciding how many to have and how high they should be. The ease of use and safety of a flight of steps depends mainly on the ratio of the depth of the tread to the height of the riser and how much each tread overhangs the riser. A good rule is to make the depth of the tread plus twice the height of the riser add up to 65cm (26in) for each step. The table below shows how the slope of the bank can modify this rule. The depth of tread can be varied by 2cm (¾in) and the height of the riser by 1cm (⅜in) to fit intermediate slopes.

Step sizes for various slopes

slope of bank	depth of tread cm (in)	height of riser cm (in)
1 in 2	33 (13)	16 (6½)
1 in 3	38 (15)	13 (5)
1 in 4·5	45 (18)	10 (4)
1 in 6	53 (21)	9 (3½)
1 in 8	60 (24)	7 (3)

Materials

Steps can be built from wood, stone, brick, concrete blocks or slabs, and concrete cast *in situ*. Bricks are often used for the risers and concrete or stone slabs for the treads. Wooden railway sleepers (railroad ties) can create an informal effect in rectangular gardens and are very easily made into steps and low walls.

Building Steps

Steps vary a lot in the amount of use they get. For steps used occasionally, bricks or stones bonded together with soil may be adequate but heavily trafficked steps are better bonded with cement. Cast concrete steps are very durable.

Cement or soil-bonded steps Smooth out the slope and mark out the position for the steps with pegs. Join all the pegs with string both across and up to the slope. Starting at the bottom of the slope, dig out the shape of the first step and make a hole at the very bottom of the slope for the bottom slab. Lay foundations. Cover them with about 25cm (1in) of sand raked level and lay the first slab. Make sure this first slab is dead level from front to back but slopes gently to one side. This can be done by adding or removing sand as necessary. Shape the soil for the second step. Tip soil (or cement) over the rear of this first slab, lay the risers on the soil (or cement) and bed them down firmly. When the risers reach the height of the first tread lay more sand (or cement) and lay the first tread. Repeat this process to the top of the slope.

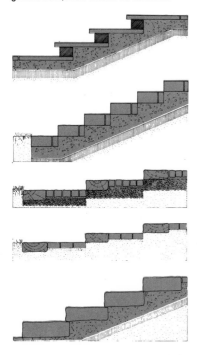

Different kinds of steps. *From top*: paving slabs; all-brick; railway sleepers (railroad ties); railway sleepers (railroad ties) with granite sets; rock treads on concrete

Cast concrete steps Smooth out the slope and erect deep formwork at each side (see *Drives*). Nail cross-boards which are the height of the risers to the formwork. The bottom cross-board should reach the ground, others up the slope should have a 5cm (2in) space below them. The upper edges of each cross-board should be level with the lower edge of the one above. Fill in each step with concrete and smooth flat with a short piece of wood. The formwork can be removed after four to five days.

Walls

The principle of laying bricks or stones on top of one another to form a wall is one of the most frequently used constructional techniques in the garden. Walls are used, for example, in the construction of raised flower beds and raised fish pools, for screening patios and terraces, for holding back steep banks and for defining the boundary of a property. The principles of bricklaying are used in building barbeques, constructing brick pergola supports and building stone garden seats.

Materials

Garden walls fall roughly into two types: 1) those built from man-made bricks and blocks which are usually held together by mortar, and 2) those made from irregularly-shaped natural stone and constructed without mortar.

Bricks and blocks Most manufactured wall materials are highly decorative. Solid bricks with textured faces giving a rough finish rather like a natural piece of weathered or worn stone are very popular; this sort of walling can be made to blend naturally with its immediate surroundings. Avoid using harsh, bright colours which can stand out like a sore thumb and be prepared for some colours to weather to a poor mottled shade. Brick and block colours widely available include natural (York stone), pink, light grey, dark grey, brown, sandstone, red, buff and green. The materials are generally available in a range of related sizes. Most are 50mm, 100mm or 150mm (2in, 4in or 6in) thick so, for example, two 50mm (2in) blocks could be used in a wall alongside one 100mm (4in) block. The depths and widths are also related in a similar fashion and half-blocks are available to produce the bonding effect.

Screen blocks Screen walling is highly decorative with an open pattern to each block. It is very useful where light is not to be excluded but, at the same time, some shelter and privacy is wanted – on patios, for example. Each block is a little less than 30cm square (12in by 12in) and about 9cm

(3½in) thick so that when it is all mortared together modules almost exactly 30cm (12in) square are produced. Screen walling often has interlocking pillars into which the blocks slide. This gives essential support and strength to large wall areas. The pillars are approximately 19cm (7½in) square. The finishing touches can be added by the use of capping and coping stone 1cm (⅜in) thick. A straight line can be maintained if a suitable length of cord is stretched from one corner brick to the other as the courses are built up. As the bricks are laid, the excess mortar should be carefully cut off. Never allow mortar to fall on to or remain on the face of the brickwork as it may stain. Wash off any surplus with a wet cloth. If a mortared wall is to be used to hold back a bank, weep holes should be left at intervals to allow water to escape from behind the wall. Double walls can be used as a form of plant container with drainage holes in the base of the walls and the cavity filled with good soil. These walls should always have ties to hold them together. Walls can generally be finished by constructing a pier.

Screen walls are erected in a similar manner, but the blocks are relatively fragile and must *not* be tapped too hard when they are laid. Very accurate level checks must be made all the time and the hollow pillars should be filled internally with mortar to reinforce them. For very high walls, the pillars can be reinforced by setting iron rods into the concrete foundations before they set and running these rods up the centre of the pillars. A screen effect can also be created by letting iron grills into an otherwise solid wall.

Natural stone This comes in various thicknesses and is rarely flat or regular in shape. Before the wall is built the pieces should be sorted out into groups of roughly equal thickness. Dressed stone, which has been cut to standard sizes, is also available but at a very high price.

Building Walls

Any wall needs good, well-prepared foundations. The depth and width of the foundations vary with the weight they will have to bear. A 90cm (3ft) high double wall, for example, needs foundations as deep as a single wall 1·8m (6ft) high. Always make the foundations at least 8cm (3in) wider on each side of the wall than the wall itself. For building walls more than 1·2m (4ft) high or retaining walls more than 90cm (3ft) high, its wise to seek professional advice as these walls will need buttresses or piers building-in at intervals. Walls about 1·8m (6ft) high should also be two courses thick and need frequent tie bricks. For most walls adequate foundations can be made by taking out a

Building a dry stone wall

Lay foundations of concrete on top of hardcore

Spread about 2·5cm (1in) of fine soil over the concrete, select the larger stones and press them into the soil

A free-standing wall should slope inwards towards the top (smallest stones at the top). Try to make each stone overlap the two below

A dry stone wall can be used to support a bank. Set each layer of stones further and further backwards. Soil can be inserted between the stones and plants planted as the wall is built

Above top: A wall made of broken slabs, with plants allowed to trail over the edge

Above centre: A screen block wall

Above: A low dry stone wall

Above right: Walls on three different levels

Right: Brick and concrete steps

A close-panelled fence brightened up with plants in pots

trench 23cm (9in) deep, filling the bottom 5cm (2in) or so with rubble and ramming it down well. Make up a concrete mix of one part of cement to four to five parts of mixed ballast and work it well into the trench to avoid air pockets. The surface of the concrete should finish just below soil level and should be trowelled quite smooth. If the concrete is laid level it will make subsequent building work much easier. Where a patio or other garden wall joins the house, it should be tied to the house wall and must have a damp-proof course at exactly the same level as the existing one on the house.

Dry stone wall Spread about a 2·5cm (1in) thickness of fine soil over the concrete, select the larger stones and press them down on to the soil and bed them in firmly. Firm more soil between each stone. If the wall is to support a raised bed or small bank, set each layer of stones progressively further and further backwards. Aim for an overall slope of 7·5 to 10cm (3 to 4in) for a 90cm (3ft) wall.

You can check this with a spirit level (with a vertical bubble) held against a piece of wood to show where vertical is. If the wall is self-supporting it should be wedge-shaped – narrower at the top than at the bottom. Try to make each stone overlap the joint between the two below and lean the faces of the stones backwards, rather than vertical, so that rainwater runs into the wall. Plant the faces as the wall is built.

Mortared wall Spread a layer of mortar (one part cement to six of sand – see *Concrete in Gardens*) down the centre of the concrete. Tap each brick or block into the mortar bed and check for vertical and horizontal levels with a spirit level. After the first brick or block is laid apply mortar to one end of all subsequent blocks. Try to keep the mortar between the bricks and blocks about 10mm (³⁄₈in) thick.

Fences

A fence can be used to: 1) increase the privacy of a garden, 2) mask some unsightly view, 3) support plants, 4) keep animals or children in or out of the garden, 5) mark out the boundary of the property, or 6) provide shelter from wind.

Types of Fence
There are literally dozens of different types of fencing, the most widely available are listed below.

Post and wire This is the simplest form of fencing available and is usually used only for marking out the boundaries of the garden. It will not deter children or animals and does not provide any privacy. If it is well built it can last for years. Concrete, wood or angled iron posts are used with two or three thick galvanized wires stretched between them. The posts should be set in concrete and the wires attached to the end posts and put under tension by using straining bolts. For longer wires, special strainers or tensioners can be used. Wood posts will need holes boring into them to take the straining bolts, concrete and angled iron posts usually have holes when bought. Attach the wires to the intermediate posts by using long steel staples (wood posts) or pieces of galvanized wire.

Wire netting This is available in a range of different gauges and mesh sizes. It will resist animals and children when new but does not last well. It can be attached to a post and wire fence by using twists of thin galvanized wire or simply stretched between posts.

Chainlink This looks rather like thick wire netting but it is constructed differently and is considerably stronger. It may be galvanized or plastic coated. A properly erected chain-fence can last for 20 years or

more. As with wire netting, it is available in a range of mesh and gauge sizes. Chainlink fences are erected on a post and wire fence. Unlike wire netting, this sort of fence should have every wire loop attached to the end posts. Failure to do this may result in the fence collapsing. With concrete posts, a thin, rigid metal strip should be passed through the end loops and this should be firmly attached to the end posts.

Ranch style This is the wooden equivalent of post and wire fencing. It will resist some larger animals but is easy for children to climb. It does not provide a great deal of privacy. Softwood fences will need repainting at regular intervals, hardwood fences may need varnishing or treating with preservative. Erection is simple but the rails should be screwed to the posts.

Paling This has short (generally 1m (3½ft) high) pieces of softwood attached vertically to two cross members. It provides more privacy than ranch style fencing but is not completely private because of the gaps between the vertical pieces and its lack of height. It will deter some small animals (not rabbits, mice and gophers) and is difficult for children to climb. Like ranch style fencing, it needs regular maintenance.

Wood trellis This can be obtained either as preformed panels which are simply nailed to supporting posts or as diamond-shaped expanding trellis which needs a support system built for it. To some extent it is child and animal proof but, because it is fragile, it is easily damaged by both. It has a very open appearance but privacy can be improved by using it as a support system for plants. Use blunt nails for attaching expanding trellis to its support system: sharp nails may split the thin trellis wood.

Vertical closeboard This consists of vertical wedge-shaped boards which are attached to two or three horizontal rails so that the boards overlap slightly. The vertical board should be covered with a capping to protect the end grain of the wood against the weather. It can be obtained as preformed panels or as individual pieces of wood. Panels are available up to 2m (6½ft) high. It is an extremely robust, animal and child-proof fence. And, provided the parts are erected well, it will last for many years. It offers almost complete privacy but looks overbearing in small gardens and is very expensive.

Woven panels These have strips of thin wood which are either interwoven or overlapped and the whole thing is mounted on a frame to give a panel. These panels are available in a range of heights up to 2m (6½ft) and are generally 2m (6½ft) long. Special, shorter panels can be obtained to fill in the end of a run of fencing. The panels

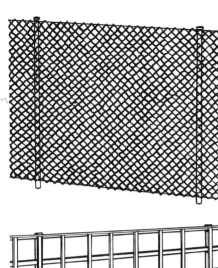

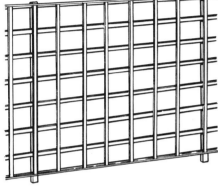

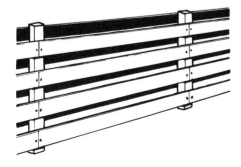

Different kinds of fence. *From top*: post and wire; open paling; woven panel; ranch style

will keep out animals, are not easily climbed and many are almost peep-proof. The panels are erected by nailing them to posts, which are erected one at a time as the work proceeds.

Posts

The ideal size for a post and the depth it should be buried in the ground depends upon the type of fence it will have to support. Open fences allow the wind to blow through them and will need less thick, less deeply buried posts than a closeboard fence. Small fences will need less support than tall fences. As a general guide, use posts which are 75mm square (3in by 3in) for all fences up to about 1·2m (4ft) high and for trellis and other open fences up to 2m (6½ft). For taller, closed fences use posts which are 100mm square (4in by 4in) or better still 100mm by 125mm (4in by 5in). Erect rectangular posts with the shortests dimension along the line of the fence. Fences up to 1·2m (4ft) should have posts set 3·8cm (18in) into the ground; 2m (6½ft) fences need posts which are buried 75cm to 90cm (2½ft to 3ft) deep.

Posts can be buried in the ground or set in concrete. The latter are sturdier but are much more difficult to replace. All wooden posts should be thoroughly treated with preservative. If possible, buy pressure-treated posts.

Pergolas

The word Pergola is Italian from the Latin *pergula* – a projecting roof. In garden terms it is a partly enclosed walk or an arbour, supporting climbing plants and providing protection from the direct heat of the sun. The classical pergola is a corridor of vertical columns supporting horizontal cross members, and links one building or garden feature with another. On the grand scale these can be seen in the grounds of country houses, perhaps with old brick columns supporting teak or oak cross members. They are often garlanded with venerable wisterias, roses and vines. A series of rustic arches forming an arbour may also be called a pergola, though such a structure dates from a later romantic age than the Roman original.

In smaller gardens a series of linked arches constructed from larch or pine poles will probably be more to scale than piers of brick or ornamental walling stone and supporting heavy timbers.

Building a Pergola

A pergola should not be too narrow: there should be room for two people to walk side by side without brushing against plants

Above: An open fence is attractive but does not give a lot of privacy

Right: Ranch-style fence

Centre: A combined wall-and-fence

Far right: Choose plants carefully to give your pergola maximum effect

Right: A diamond trellis fence

Centre: A pergola gives the opportunity to grow many climbing plants

Far right: A rustic pergola

94

Building a pergola with scaffolding poles

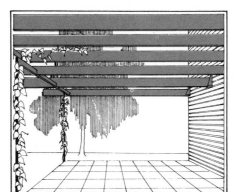

Modern pergola fixed to a house wall

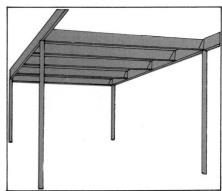

50cm (2in) scaffolding poles can be used as uprights

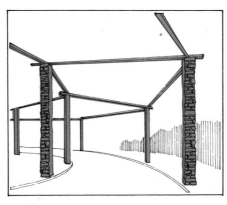

Traditional pergola with stone or brick piers

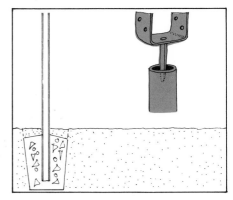

The base of each pole should be set in concrete and U-joints can be used to hold the long main beams

Rustic pergola

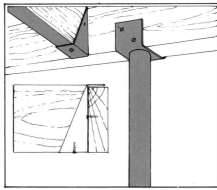

Use hangers to hold the cross beams. Hold the beams in place with screws

Building a rustic pergola

The uprights should be thicker than the cross members

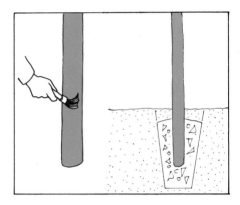

Coat the bottom of the uprights with preservative (a good soaking is better than brush treatment). Set the uprights in concrete

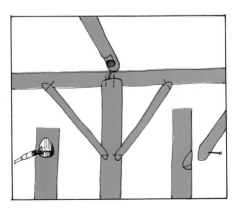

Shape the joints so that the poles fit into each other. Paint the cuts with preservative and hold the poles in place with nails or screws

trained onto the uprights. There should also be ample headroom. In theory the longitudinal distance between uprights should be greater than their height or their tranverse distance apart. But, in practice, it is best to fashion a pergola to your own taste. This applies when choosing the materials too. A more traditional pergola might be made as follows. Choose straight rustic poles about 75mm (3in) in diameter and about 2·7m (9ft) long for the uprights. Space these about 2·1 or 2·4m (7 or 8ft) apart down the length of the pergola, burying the bottom 60cm (2ft) in the ground. The bottom of the posts should be soaked well in preservative before they are erected. Secure the roof cross pieces to the uprights with nails or screws. If the rustic effect is to be emphasized, slimmer poles can be crisscrossed between the uprights. These will also add rigidity. Filling the sides of a pergola with trellis is another variation. Whatever sort of pergola is built care should be taken to make sure that the timbers used are stout enough to prevent sagging and to carry the considerable weight of mature climbers in full growth. For example, a modern pergola might be constructed of timber which has been cleanly trimmed and joined and either painted white or treated with a clear preservative.

Plants

Before planting enrich the ground thoroughly with well-rotted manure or some other bulky organic material. Make a planting mixture for covering the roots of shrubs by mixing a handful of bonemeal with the soil taken out of the hole at planting time. Actinidia, akebia, celastrus, clematis, hedera, jasminum, lonicera and passiflora can all be used with effect on pergolas. For further details see *Ornamental Plants.*

6. Tools and Equipment

Most garden tools fit into one of six categories: 1) tools for cultivating the soil, 2) tools for measuring and marking, 3) tools for carrying things, 4) tools for cutting, 5) tools for watering the garden, and 6) tools for looking after the lawn.

Cultivating the Soil

Some of the earliest drawings show gardeners working with tools which could be easily recognized today. Then, and now, the first requirement of the gardener was to dig or cultivate the soil.

Forks and Spades

The basic design of forks and spades is the same the whole world over but the way the design is executed varies from country to country. In the UK and North America both tools come in three basic sizes: digging, medium and border. Border tools are the smallest with heads measuring about 225mm by 140mm (9in × 5½in). Digging tools are the largest with heads measuring 315mm by 190mm (12½in × 7½in). All are fitted with T, D, or YD handle grips. In many European countries spades and forks have long shafts without grips.

Before buying a spade or fork there are a number of things to do. First, go through the motions of digging with the tool and get some idea whether it is too heavy or too light and whether the balance feels right. Look at the joint between the blade (or head) and the shaft. Solid socket tools are best, strapped tools only partly enclose the shaft and are often less robust. All joints must be smooth. Try the feel of the grip. D and YD grips suit most people better than the traditional T design but make sure that the hole in the grip is large enough for the hand to fit comfortably. Some tools are fitted with a tread – a strip of metal across the shoulder of the head. Treaded tools can be less wearing on footwear and may increase comfort. Stainless-steel tools are easier to dig with and easier to clean than ordinary steel tools but they are more expensive.

Hoes

There are two basic hoe designs: Dutch hoes with flat D-shaped blades and draw hoes with a swan neck. Dutch hoes are used for weeding, draw hoes can be used for weeding but are also used for earthing up and taking out drills when sowing seeds. A variation on the Dutch hoe design has wavy cutting edges on all sides which gives an increased cutting surface.

Rakes

The number of teeth in a rake can vary from 10 to 16; the more teeth a rake has the finer the soil surface can be raked. Heads with 10 to 12 teeth are most suitable for general seed bed preparation. Rakes with alloy handles are lighter than the ordinary ash handles and many people find them easier to use.

Trowels and Hand Forks

Most trowels are similar in design; look for one with a sturdy neck and with few indentations or channels which may prove difficult to clean.

Hand forks may have three or four flat tines or five twisted ones. Twisted tine forks are generally the more sturdy but weeds can slip between the tines. Flat-tined forks miss fewer weeds and are strong enough for use on light soil.

Mechanical Rototillers/ Cultivators

Nearly all mechanical rototillers/cultivators have a petrol/gasoline engine which drives a

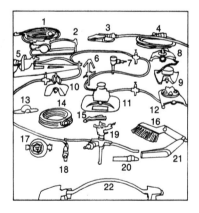

99

Dibbers, and how to use them. Many seedlings can be planted quickly using a dibber, but care must be exercised, particularly when the soil is wet, to avoid root compaction

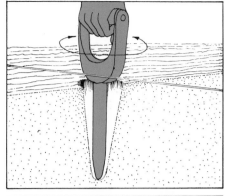

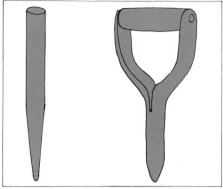

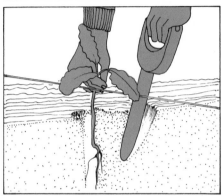

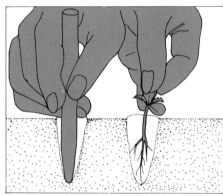

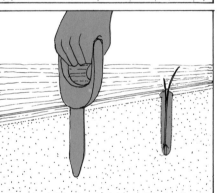

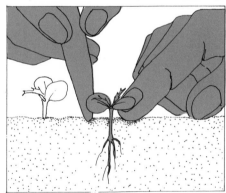

number of rotating cultivator blades. A few have diesel or paraffin engines. They can be divided into three groups: 1) Rototillers/cultivators with wheels and an arm which extends from the front of the machine. This arm has pairs of rotating blades set at the end. 2) Rototillers/cultivators with wheels and with blades behind the engine, and 3) Rototillers/cultivators without wheels and with blades set below the engine.

The basic job of a rototiller/cultivator is digging or turning over the soil: in the autumn to dig fairly coarsely and in the spring to produce a fine tilth. Most rototillers/cultivators can be adapted to hoeing or furrowing by attaching a frame (tool bar) with fixed blades. The engines on many rototillers/cultivators can be used to power many kinds of attachments – grass cutters or hedge trimmers for example.

Rototillers/cultivators in group 1) are generally light and manoeuvrable but are tiring to use on large areas of heavy soil. They are particularly suitable for small gardens with a variety of light jobs to do. Rototillers/cultivators in group 2) do not dig deeply but are very useful for maintaining large areas of garden already under cultivation – a professional market garden tool. Rototillers/cultivators in group 3) take a bit of getting used to, but once the knack of handling them has been acquired they are as easy to handle as those with wheels. These cultivators dig deeply and are suited to working under a variety of conditions. They can even be used when the soil is wet or when it is very dry.

100

Measuring and Marking

Measuring Rod

Many gardeners use their feet (or one of their feet) for measuring the distance between rows of plants but a 1·8m (6ft) rod with markings at 15cm (6in) intervals can make the job simpler and more accurate. Make one out of 25mm (1in) square softwood and paint each 15cm (6in) length alternately black and white.

Garden Line

A garden line for marking rows for seed drills can be made quite simply from thick garden twine and two small wood stakes. A more permanent tool is made from rotproof twine and metal stakes.

Labels

Labelling plants in the garden is largely a matter of personal choice. The two main purposes of labelling plants are: 1) to know where they are when they are dormant – particularly bulbs, and 2) to keep a trace of the names of new varieties to see which do well. The type of label is largely determined by the purpose you want it for. The most temporary, and cheapest, label is made from paper or soft card and simply ties on to the plant: one season is the most to expect from this sort. For vegetable gardens a large whitewashed wooden tally is ideal. The tally can be whitewashed and reused each year with the name of the vegetable painted on it in black. This sort of label would clearly look out of place in the ornamental garden and here plastic labels with names inscribed in Indian ink or anodized zinc labels with names either pencilled on or imprinted on to them last well. Probably the longest-lasting labels are made from laminated plastic with the name engraved in the surface. For propagating plants (seed trays), plastic labels are ideal since they can easily be sterilized. Write on them with a soft pencil.

Carrying

Wheelbarrows and Carts

In the UK most garden wheelbarrows have one wheel and a carrying capacity between 50 and 100 litres (about 2 to 4cu ft). Garden carts or trucks have two wheels mounted directly below the bin and capacities generally in excess of 80 litres (3cu ft). Wheelbarrows are the easier to use on rough, bumpy ground, when space is restricted and for getting up and down steps. Garden carts take unevenly distributed loads more efficiently. When buying either a wheelbarrow or cart, make sure that the handles are at a comfortable distance apart, that the bin is far enough forward to be out of the way of your legs and that it is big enough for the jobs you have in mind. Some wheelbarrows take extensions which can almost double their capacity. Wheelbarrows usually have galvanized steel bins; a few have plastic ones. Plastic bins will not corrode and are waterproof, but may be damaged by dropping heavy objects in them. Galvanized bins generally become chipped with use and eventually rust. Garden carts may have metal, wood or glass fibre bins. Some bins are detachable and the remaining cart frame can be used for carrying dustbins/garbage cans and so on.

Fertilizer and Seed Spreaders

There are four basic types of spreader. The simplest is a plastic bucket with a hole in the bottom partially covered by a scatter plate. The bucket is twisted by hand from side to side to spread the fertilizer. Most fertilizer spreaders have a hopper mounted on two wheels. Some simply have holes in the bottom of the hopper and an agitator (or paddle) to keep the fertilizer running freely inside it: others have a conveyor belt at the bottom of the hopper and distribute the fertilizer from the front of the spreader. The fourth type of spreader has a hopper and a spinning rotor. Some spreaders are adjustable for application rate. The conveyor belt type spreaders distribute fertilizers and seed most evenly and most accurately; the spinning rotor type is useful for large areas.

Pruning

Pruning Shears/Secateurs

These vary in size from small, lightweight flower gatherers to large, heavy pruning shears/secateurs best suited for pruning lots of shrubs and trees. A general-purpose tool about 20cm (8in) long is all most people need. For pruning branches over 20mm (¾in) across, heavy pruning shears/secateurs with extended handles are needed. These are often called lopping shears, long-handled pruners, shrub pruners, bush pruners and so on.

Pruning shears/secateurs have three types of blade arrangement: anvil, curved and parrot-beak. Anvil pruning shears/secateurs have a flat, soft platform (usually metal but sometimes plastic) and a sharpened steel top blade. The sharpened blade cuts through the wood on to the platform below. Curved-blade and parrot-beak tools both act like scissors: with curved-blade tools, only the top blade is sharpened; with parrot-beak tools both blades usually are. Most pruning shears/secateurs have a single-lever cutting action; a few have a

An assortment of hoes, rakes, trowels and handforks

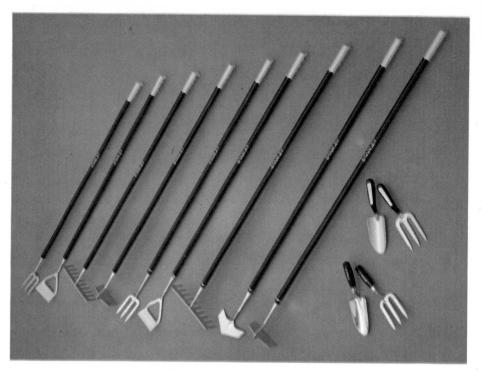

double-lever action, which should need less effort, and one has both double-lever and ratchet action. Some tools have replaceable blades, and some manufacturers offer a blade sharpening service. Anvil pruning shears/secateurs generally need less effort to cut with than curved-blade or parrot-beak models but may not cut the wood quite as cleanly.

Saws
Some pruning saws look rather like woodworking panel saws but have two cutting edges – a coarse one for basic work and a fine one for fine work. They also have different teeth: a normal woodworking saw would jam if you tried to cut through green wood. The coarse edges usually cut on both push and pull; fine edges cut on pull only. Grecian saws have curved blades and cut on the pull only. Some have tubular steel handles which will take a broom handle, others have extension poles. Bow saws are used mainly for cutting logs but can be used for pruning too.

Tree Pruners
Tree pruners have handles 2·4, 3·0, 3·6 and 4·2m (8, 10, 12 and 14ft) long and can be used for pruning trees without using a ladder. Most have a hooked cutting head and a blade operated by a cable or rod attached to a lever at the bottom of the handle. They take some getting used to and branches 20mm (¾in) thick are the maximum most people can manage.

Knives
Pruning knives have a curved blade which cuts into the wood as the blade is drawn rapidly across it. The wood should be held firmly against the blade by the thumb positioned just sufficiently above the blade to avoid being cut by it. They are not as easy to use as secateurs. Budding knives usually have straight blades and a tapered handle. The end of the handle is inserted into the cut to open up the bark to take the bud. See *Propagation: Budding*.

Shears
Hand shears come in a range of different sizes and weights. For hedge cutting, choose the lightest which will cope with the task. Some shears have a pruning notch at the bottom of the blade to cut thicker branches. For cutting lawn edges, make sure that the blades and handles are at a sufficient angle to keep your hands well clear of the ground. For both jobs, check that the handles are a comfortable diameter and that the blades are neither too loose nor too tight. Most people prefer smooth handles to those with fingergrips.

Power trimmers are generally electrically operated – either from the mains or a battery. Many are integral tools, some are attachments to electric drills. Choose a light trimmer and make sure that the balance feels right. Heavy duty trimmers will cut branches up to 20mm (¾in) in diameter, lighter models are useful for 10mm (⅜in) branches. Mains electric trimmers have

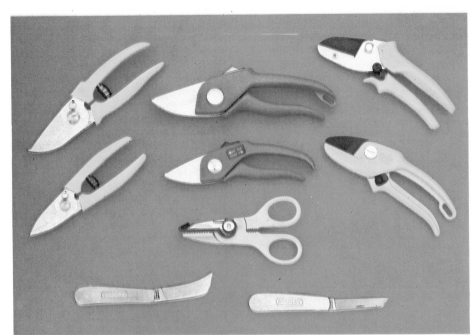

Above: Pruning shears/secateurs. Long-handled ones are also available

Below: An electric hedge clipper and an assortment of hand shears

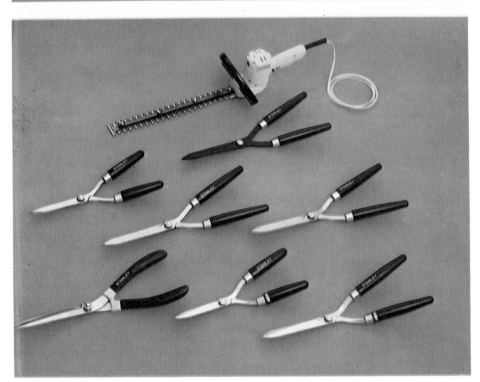

cables which can get in the way and may even be dangerous if the trimmer is being used while standing on a step ladder. Battery operated trimmers usually run for about one hour on a full charge. Electric hedge trimmers should always be used with care, they can impart severe injuries if used carelessly. Be especially careful with the cable, and take care also if there are young children around the garden.

Watering Equipment

Hose/Hosepipes

A good hosepipe is the basis of any satisfactory watering system. Most garden hoses are made of plastic. Some have walls which are one continuous layer of plastic, some have a soft inner layer of plastic surrounded by a harder outer layer, and others have three-layer walls. Some hoses have a nylon or rayon reinforcing braid between the layers. Ribbed hoses are generally less easy to clean than smooth-walled hoses but they are easier to grip. Many one-layer hoses do not resist water pressures well and should be used in low water pressure areas only.

Two-layer hoses generally stand up to water pressure better but are rather inflexible and difficult to use. Three-layer and two-layer reinforced hoses have excellent bursting strengths and are flexible at both high and low temperatures. Never leave hoses lying in the sun with the water turned off at the spray end of the hose but not at the tap end – it could damage the hose and contaminate the mains water supply. And do not leave it outside in the depths of winter (make sure it is empty before winter arrives).

Hose Fittings

To change one standard hose fitting for another, the whole fitting has to be detached from the hose. With interchangeable fittings, one part can be left attached to the hose and the other part plugs into it. Most interchangeable fittings have a snap-in/snap-out connection.

Hose Reels

Hosepipes are easily damaged by hanging them over a nail or leaving them kinked up on the ground. A hose reel is a good way of keeping a hose tidy. Simple reels are just a metal or plastic reel on a stand – there is not much difference between them so the best policy is to choose the size needed. Through-feed reels are more complicated. With these, water runs from the tap, through the axis of the reel and into the hose itself. The reel can be mounted on a wall or on a trolley and it is only necessary to unwind as much hose as is needed.

Garden Sprinklers

Sprinklers can be divided into six different types: static, rotating, oscillating, travelling, sprinkler hoses and permanent sprinkler systems.

Static sprinklers generally have no moving parts: they work by forcing water up through a vertical tube. Most have a small spike which can be stuck into the ground, a few have their spray head at the top of a 90cm (3ft) pole. Static sprinklers generally produce a circular spray pattern and distribute the water quite evenly over the area being sprayed.

Rotating sprinklers have two or three arms which rotate about a central axis. Water comes up this axis along the arms and out of small holes. The jets of water from these small holes make the arms rotate. Many sprinklers have jets which can be adjusted for fineness of spray and for the area of ground covered by the spray. Pulse-jet sprinklers are rotating sprinklers with a large jet and a spring-loaded arm. The water throws the arm away from the jet assembly and the spring brings it back again to strike the jet assembly and make the

Labelling

T-shaped white plastic labels – use a special felt tipped pen or a wax pencil for writing on them

Moulded botanical label with the plant name embossed on it

Dymo tapes – these should be tied on to the plant

sprinkler rotate. Like static sprinklers, rotating sprinklers produce a circular spray pattern and spray evenly.

Oscillating sprinklers have a central spray bar with a number of holes in it. Water comes into this bar and makes it oscillate from side to side. The fineness of spray cannot be adjusted but the area covered by the spray can be altered by restricting the movement of the bar. The usual settings are full throw, left throw, right throw, half left throw and half right throw. Because the bar of an oscillating sprinkler spends most of its time at or near the ends of its travel, they deposit the water in two rectangles – one on either side of the sprinkler.

Travelling sprinklers are rotating sprinklers which move across the garden at the same time as spraying. They are actuated by the water pressure and some rewind the hose (and will follow the pattern defined by the hose) as they move.

Sprinkler hoses are basically hosepipes which have been flattened and have a row of holes along the top half. To avoid contaminating the mains water supply, it is advisable to keep sprinkler hoses at least 15cm (6in) clear of the soil – on a plank, for example.

Permanent sprinkler systems can be installed when a large area of garden needs regular watering – a large lawn, perhaps. These systems usually have a number of pop-up sprinkler heads connected to the mains by alkathene tube. The alkathene tube is buried deeper than fork penetration. The sprinkler heads in their off position are slightly below ground level so a lawn mower can run right over them. When the mains water is turned on, the sprinklers pop up and start spraying.

Watering cans These are available from around 500ml (1 pint) to about 15 litres; the smaller sizes are for indoor plants and greenhouses, the larger sizes for general garden use. Cans with long spouts are useful in the greenhouse and for using outside on deep borders.

Water-butts There are at least three good reasons for the gardener to store and use natural rainwater as much as possible. 1) Tap water may be treated chemically and in hardwater areas it may be too alkaline for acid-loving plants. 2) Collected rainwater is usually at a more suitable temperature for watering plants than water drawn directly from the cold tap. And last, but not least, 3) it is the responsibility of every gardener to use drinking water economically and to conserve supplies as much as possible.

Rainwater is usually collected from the roof guttering of a garage, home extension, greenhouse or any other outbuilding and fed through a shortened drainpipe into an

Wooden labels with one face painted white – a pencil can be used for writing on them

Plastic tag labels – use a pen and ink to write on them. They can be either tied to the plant or pushed into the growing mix in a pot

Plastic tag labels with a black face – scratch the name on them with a stylus

inconspicuously sited collection vessel, such as a water-butt. To take care of overflow, the butt should stand alongside a drain grid or have a piece of hosepipe inserted near the top of the butt and leading to a drain. You can also use a linked butt system where the

105

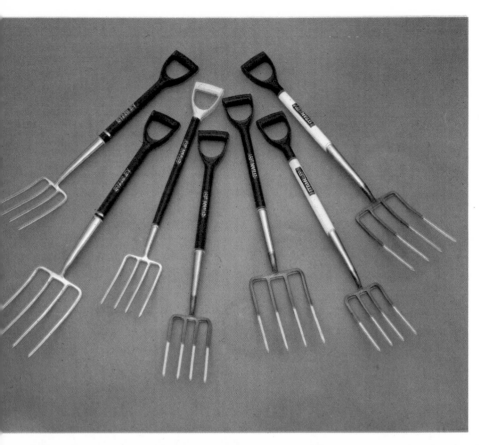

Opposite: A selection of lawn maintenance tools, including a mechanical sweeper, fertilizer spreader, half moon lawn edger, lawn aerator, lawn mower, electric grass trimmer, weeding tool, and a lawn sprinkler with hose and reel

Left: A selection of forks. Note the different types of shaft

Above: An electric rotary mower is light and easy to operate, but will not give the same finish as a heavier mower

Left: Spades come in many different sizes and weights – check that you can use it comfortably as well as its suitability for the work

Water-butts

Water-butt with lid and overflow pipe leading to rain-water drainage grate

Water-butt with overflow pipe leading to a soakaway filled with hardcore and topped with gravel

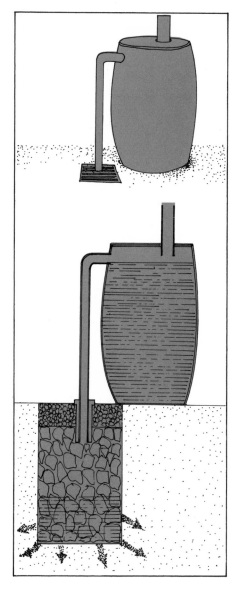

blades set in the shape of a cylinder. The spiral blades slice the grass against a fixed blade. Rotary lawnmowers generally have one flat blade which rotates rapidly and slashes through the grass. Cylinder mowers will give a close, neat cut but have difficulty cutting through grass over about 10cm (4in) high. Rotary lawnmowers will not give the same quality finish as cylinder mowers but are able to deal with longer grass: some will cut grass up to 45cm (18in) high. Lawn-mowers may be powered by hand, pet-rol/gasoline engine, mains electricity or by battery.

Hand lawnmowers are all cylinder mowers and generally have cutting widths from 25cm (10in) to 45cm (18in); 30cm (12in) is the most popular size. The finish given by a hand lawnmower mainly depends on the number of cuts a metre the mower makes, which in turn depends on the number of cutting blades the mower has on the spiral cylinder and on the gearing of the mower. Cylinder hand mowers can be further sub-divided into sidewheel mowers and roller mowers. Sidewheel mowers generally cut longer, thicker and tufted grass better than roller mowers but, unlike roller mowers, cannot be used over the edges of the lawn. Before buying a hand lawnmower, feel the weight of it, try the handles for comfort and look to see which way the grass clippings will be thrown – lawnmowers which throw clippings backwards are useful for getting right up to a wall or a flower border.

Petrol/gasoline mowers may be either cylin-der or rotary. Cylinder petrol/gasoline mowers are mostly roller mowers with cut-ting widths from 30cm (12in) to 50cm (20in). Rotary mowers generally have cut-ting widths from 30cm (12in) to 55cm (21in). Larger mowers often have ride-on facilities.

Cable/mains electric mowers may also be cylinder or rotary but many mains electric rotary lawnmowers do not have sufficient power to deal with really long or particu-larly tough grass. The main problem with all cable/mains electric mowers is the cable which becomes a nuisance when mowing round flower beds or obstacles. Never use them in damp conditions.

Battery mowers are generally cylinder mowers. They have two advantages over cable/mains electric mowers: they do not have the problem of the cable and they do not suffer from the inherent danger of run-ning off mains electricity. But they are heavier than cable/mains electric mowers and the battery limits the area of lawn which can be cut on one charge and it has to be topped up and periodically re-charged when the mower is not in use. As an approximate guide, a 30cm (12in) battery

overflow from one butt is used to fill the next. At one time, butts were wooden bar-rels which gave problems with leakage and cleaning. Plastic butts are now available which have the advantages of lightness, durability and hygiene. Much of the benefit of rainwater is lost once it is contaminated by micro-organisms or debris so a butt with a lid and thorough cleansing twice a year are both essential. Ideally, water to be used for plants should not have been standing in the butt for more than a week.

Looking after the Lawn

Lawnmowers
There are two distinctly different types of lawnmower: cylinder and rotary. Cylinder lawnmowers have a number of spiral cutting

mower will cut a 500m² (550sq yd) lawn with one charge of the battery and a 35cm (14in) mower with a heavy-duty battery may cut up to 1,800m² (2,000sq yd).

Adjusting a Lawnmower

The ideal height of cut for a lawn depends on the type of grass in the lawn – coarse grasses may be cut down to 25mm (1in), fine grasses are best cut shorter, 13mm (½in) say – and on the length of the grass to start with. In general most people do not alter the height of cut of their lawnmower frequently enough and this may be due to the difficulty in adjusting the height of some mowers. Choose one which is very easy to adjust. Cylinder mowers are generally adjusted by raising or lowering the rear roller. Some mowers have knurled knobs at each end of the cylinder which slide in a slot, others have nuts and bolts which need a spanner and others have levers and slots. Those with levers and slots are the easiest to adjust but the number of cutting heights is governed by the number of slots. Most rotary lawnmowers are adjusted by raising or lowering the body of the mower, a few are adjusted by raising or lowering the blade. Many rotary lawnmowers have independent height adjustments for each wheel, some have one lever which adjusts the height at all four wheels simultaneously.

Safety

Power-operated lawnmowers have blades which move at high speed and are potentially dangerous. Rotary mowers are regarded as being more hazardous than cylinder mowers. When using a rotary mower clear the lawn of sticks and stones before you start mowing, make sure that guards and grasscatchers are properly fitted, wear trousers and heavy shoes, keep your feet clear of the mower and be especially careful when starting, mow across slopes and not up and down them, never let anyone near the mower when it is running and never allow children to use it, never try to clear or pick up a blocked mower while it is still running and turn off and disconnect the mower from its power source (remove a spark plug or unplug the cable) before you leave it unattended.

Edging

Unsupported lawn edges are bound to crumble in places and will need reshaping from time to time. A half-moon lawn edger will cut a clean edge when it is pressed down against a taut line or plank. A spade is not designed for cutting lawn edges and should not be used for it. Aluminium or plastic strips inserted along the face of the lawn edge and tight up against the soil will support the edge of the lawn and reduce the need for trimming. Before inserting the strips the lawn edge should be cut cleanly and the strip should then be carefully tapped into place so that the bottom edge grips into the soil border and the top edge lies just below the level of the lawn.

Long-handled shears can be used for cutting the grass at lawn edges. For large lawns, more sophisticated tools are available which speed up the job considerably. Most of these work on the same principle: they have a roller or wheel which is pushed along the edge of the lawn and operates a special cutting wheel at the side of the tool.

Aeration

Lawns can build up a surface mat of dead, compressed vegetation which prevents water, air and nutrients from getting to the grass roots. They can also become compacted through using a roller or simply through hard wear. To chop up the surface mat the lawn will need scarifying. Many tools are available for this job: most have blades set around a cylinder – the blades slash into the lawn as the cylinder is pushed over it. Similar tools are available for spiking the lawn to ease compaction but the best tool for this job is a hollow-tine fork. These forks remove plugs of soil leaving holes which can be filled with sharp sand. For further details of lawn maintenance see *Lawns*.

Looking after Tools

The care of tools and equipment starts with good housing – keep your garden tools in a dry building with each tool placed or hung for easy visibility and access.

Digging and cutting tools will not perform effectively if the working edges are blunted with caked soil or rust. Clean all tools after use and wipe them over with an oily rag to deter rusting. Machines with moving parts – lawnmowers, for example – will need regular oiling and some mechanical and electrical tools must be given regular servicing.

7. How Plants Live

Plants are a complicated network of cells, each group having a different function. Plants grow by developing new cells and the rate of growth is controlled by a complicated control system. All growth requires a constant supply of energy and green plants, as distinct from animals, are capable of manufacturing their own food by the process of photosynthesis.

Germination

The starting point for most plant growth is a seed, which is a minute plant in an embryo state. Given suitable conditions, the young plant will emerge and grow into an adult plant. The initial awakening of the embryonic plant is called germination. To initiate growth the following conditions are necessary:

1) A supply of moisture to soften the protective seed coat and then to dissolve soluble chemicals (nutrients) for the plant to absorb through its roots.

2) Suitable air and soil (or growing medium) temperature. This temperature can vary from as low as 7°C (44°F) for cold region plants to as much as 27°C (80°F) for tropical plants. Most seeds have a period of dormancy in which they will not readily germinate and this period varies from plant to plant. This dormancy period can sometimes be broken by subjecting the seed to particularly low or high temperatures.

3) An adequate supply of air. This is necessary at germination – seeds sown too deeply often fail to grow through a lack of air – and later for the plant to grow through photosynthesis.

When all these factors combine, the tiny embryonic plant is stimulated and sets up a chain reaction by the release of plant auxins or chemical messengers. These messengers start and control cell development and the new plant emerges from the seed coat. In some cases the seed is left below the soil surface, in other cases the seed coat is taken above it.

The time taken for germination depends on the species and on the age of the seed. The ability of seed to germinate (its viability) also depends on its age. In general seeds with hard coats stay viable much longer than those with soft coats which readily absorb moisture.

Photosynthesis

The seed coat or cotyledon contains sufficient food reserves to sustain a young plant for a short period. Once the roots develop, they begin to draw on the moisture and dissolved chemical nutrients in the soil. Simultaneously the leaves start to manufacture carbohydrates by photosynthesis. During periods of light, air taken in through the pores in the leaves has the carbon dioxide part of it extracted and the oxygen and nitrogen part expelled. The carbon dioxide is converted into carbohydrates with the aid of chlorophyll, the green pigment, as a catalyst. Provided a plant has adequate supplies of nutrients, water and air, its rate of photosynthesis will depend on the level of light present. At high levels of light, plants will grow faster in an atmosphere which is enriched with carbon dioxide.

Respiration

Plants breathe continuously day and night by extracting the oxygen from air taken in through the pores in the leaves (and to a certain extent the stems and roots too). This oxygen is used to convert the carbohydrates, manufactured by photosynthesis, into sugars which the plant can either store or use as energy for cell division and, subsequently, growth. The rate of respiration depends on the air temperature and the rate of growth of the plant. Over a full day, photosynthesis and respiration should be roughly in balance in a healthy plant and the surplus of carbohydrates built up by the rate of photosynthesis exceeding the rate of respiration during the day should be used up by respiration at night when photosynthesis does not occur. If, however, a bright sunny day is followed by a cold clear night, a plant may develop an overall surplus and start to show signs of starch-filled leaves. On the other hand, if cloudy days are followed by warm nights – too much heat and too little light in a greenhouse, say – then the warm nights will use up the carbohydrates quickly and the plant will become drawn and spindly.

Transpiration

Plants keep cool by the process of transpiration which can be roughly thought of as the equivalent of perspiration in animals. Water absorbed by the plant roots passes up the xylem tissue in the stem to reach the leaves. In hot weather the leaf pores or stomata of a turgid plant open, water is lost through evaporation and this keeps the leaf surface cool. In cool weather or if the plant is flaccid, the stomata close. The rate of water loss is directly related to the temperature and amount of water vapour present in the air. But it also depends on an adequate flow from the roots to the leaves and this means that the roots and xylem should be healthy and there should be an adequate supply of water around the plant roots.

The flow of water within a plant acts as a transportation system for dissolved nutrients taken up from the soil.

Absorption of Water Through the Roots – Osmosis

A scientific definition of osmosis is that when a solution with a high concentration of dissolved salts is separated from one with a lower concentration of salts by a semi-permeable membrane, water will flow from the weaker to the stronger solution through the membrane in an attempt to equalize the concentrations. The driving force for this water flow is known as osmotic pressure. In plants the root hairs act as a semi-permeable membrane, the outer plant cells in them act as the concentrated solution and water in the soil acts as the weaker solution. So water flows from the soil into the outer cells in an attempt to equalize the concentrations. The next layer of cells in the plant now have a more concentrated solution of salts than the outer cells and so water flows from the outer cells into them and so on through the plant. This will continue to happen as long as the plant is able to extract water from the soil. There are two instances when it might not be able to do so.

1) If the amount of water in the soil is low, the surface tension of the water around the individual soil particles might be greater than the osmotic pressure and so water will stay in the soil.

2) If the concentration of salts in the soil is particularly high – this could happen in an over-fertilized pot plant – then water will tend to flow in the reverse direction, from the plant to the soil.

As well as taking up water from the soil, plant root hairs also take up soluble plant nutrients by the process of diffusion or absorption.

Translocation

Plants generally consist of roots, stems, leaves, flowers and perhaps fruits containing seeds. None of these parts exist in isolation and there is an ultimate co-relationship between each and every part in the different

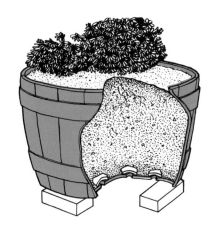

Many plants will live happily in containers with restricted root space

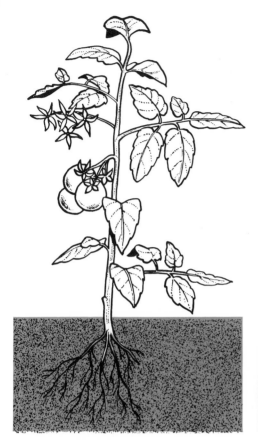

Far left: The growth of a tomato plant – fertilization occurs in the flowers, forming the fruit; photosynthesis, respiration, and transpiration take place in the leaves; the roots absorb water and soluble nutrients

Above: Hypogeal germination (bean)

Below: Epigeal germination (sycamore)

facets of growth. There is a tendency to think of applying fertilizers such as potash to encourage fruit formation and of nitrogen to encourage leaf growth. But the successful cultivation of any plant depends on a balanced diet suited to the needs of the particular plant being grown. The food synthesized in the leaves is also moved to the flowers or fruit as required by a process known as translocation. The main conducting tissue in this movement is the phloem. An upset in the plant's diet or cultivation conditions such as irregular watering or widely varying temperatures can disturb the normal movement of synthesized food and lead to physiological troubles – greenback and blossom end rot in tomatoes, for instance. See *Pests and Diseases: Plant Disorders*.

Pollination

Most flowering plants reproduce sexually by the interaction of male pollen with the female egg or ovary. This process relies on the male pollen grain reaching the ovary of the same or similar species, germinating and producing a pollen tube through which the male sperm can pass and fuse with the female egg. For further details see *Edible Plants: Fruit*.

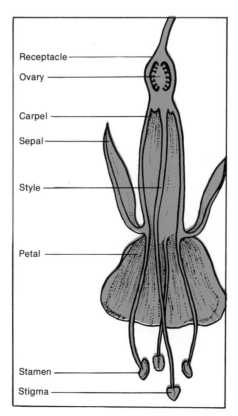

The reproductive organs of a typical flower (fuchsia)

Receptacle

Ovary

Carpel

Sepal

Style

Petal

Stamen

Stigma

113

8. Greenhouses

Greenhouses

A greenhouse is a light-admitting building or structure designed to trap heat from the sun and provide a more equable climate for plants which might not survive the rigours of the climate out of doors. Greenhouses can be artificially heated and used to produce crops out of their natural season.

From the definition above the greenhouse would seem to be almost entirely a temperate zone device, but it can also be used as a 'shade house' in warm climates to prevent damage by excessive sun and heavy tropical rain.

Shape

There are basically five different greenhouse shapes: span-roofed with a vertical wall, span-roofed with a sloping wall (including Dutch light types), lean-to, Mansard or curvilinear, and circular.

One of the most important aspects of the shape is the influence it has on the amount of light getting through the greenhouse. Light can be considered in two parts – direct rays from the sun and total illumination of the whole sky. Total illumination passes through the glass or plastic roof and walls of the greenhouse with almost equal efficiency. But the sun's rays can either be transmitted or reflected from the glass surface. The relationship between the amount transmitted and the amount reflected depends on the angle at which the sun's rays strike the glass surface. To get the maximum amount of light transmission (penetration) the sun's rays should strike the glass at right angles. If they strike it at 80° then about 80 per cent penetrates, at 70° about 70 per cent penetrates, at 60° about 60 per cent penetrates and so on.

The situation is complicated even more by the fact that the sun is never in any one position for long and is generally higher in the sky in summer than in winter. The difference between the angle at which the sun's rays strike the earth's surface in summer and in winter becomes greater the further you move away from the Equator. The table shows the relationship between latitude and the angle at which the sun's rays strike the earth's surface in summer and in winter. The ideal angle for the glass obviously has to be some sort of compromise and, as there is often much less light in winter than in summer, it is usual to concentrate on providing as much winter and early spring light as possible. The table shows the ideal glass angle for winter light: to get these figures you subtract the angle the sun's rays strike the ground from 90°.

Latitude	angle at summer solstice	angle at winter solstice	ideal glass angle for winter light
30	83½°	36½°	53½°
35	78½°	31½°	˙58½°
40	73½°	26½°	63½°
45	68½°	21½°	68½°
50	63½°	16½°	73½°
55	58½°	11½°	78½°
60	53½°	6½°	83½°

Cropping capacity

Round and curvilinear greenhouses let more light through than span-roofed greenhouses and in turn, span-roofed greenhouses with sloping walls transmit more light than those with vertical walls. Unfortunately the amount of area available for growing tall crops such as tomatoes and chrysanthemums is exactly the reverse of this order.

115

Size

There are three things to think about when deciding upon the size of a greenhouse. Firstly, will it fit where you want to put it? Secondly, is it big enough for your future needs? Most amateurs buy greenhouses which are too small for them: buy one size bigger than you think you will need. Finally, think about the sort of plants you intend to grow and how many, if any, paths you will need. If you have a path down the middle of a greenhouse which is 1·8m (6ft) wide by 2·4m (8ft) long and the path is about 60cm (2ft) wide then the available width of ground for growing plants is 1·2m (4ft). But if the greenhouse is 2·4m (8ft) wide then the available width increases to 1·8m (6ft) – a 50 per cent increase in growing area for a 33 per cent increase in overall width. But the wider house does not usually cost half as much again. Always compare the cost per square metre of growing area in different sized houses.

Materials

A greenhouse should be constructed so that glass or another transparent material is supported in a framework which offers maximum rigidity and strength, with minimum obstruction of the passage of solar heat and light. The relationship between the strength and size of members of the framework is given by the strength/bulk ratio: the higher the better.

Wood Hardwoods such as teak and oak were at one time popular. They are strong, which means that quite thin sections can be used to hold the glass, and they resist rotting well. But in recent years hardwoods have become very expensive and this has led to increased use of cheaper softwoods. Most softwoods have a good strength/bulk ratio but do not last well outside unless they are treated with preservative and preferably painted too. Western red cedar has been quite widely used in the past 20 years. It has an attractive appearance and is naturally resistant to decay, but it has a poor strength/bulk ratio. Wood readily lends itself to various systems of securing the glass. In the past decade, there has been a move away from the use of putty, which tends to harden and deteriorate, towards 'dry' glazing where glass is held in grooves.

Steel Steel has a very high strength/bulk ratio and produces very strong greenhouses. However, it has two major drawbacks. Firstly, it is prone to corrosion and must be galvanized or enamelled. But even if it is well treated, rust will, in time, break through and present difficult maintenance problems. Secondly, it is difficult to produce the shapes for 'dry' glazing systems and, in consequence, the glass is generally held in place by non-hardening, putty-like materials. Both problems can be overcome by using an internal framework of galvanized steel to give the greenhouse its basic strength and covering this on the outside with thin sections of wood which are used to hold the glass in place.

Aluminium alloys Aluminium alloys basically have a low strength/bulk ratio but they can be made remarkably strong through moulding or extrusion. Aluminium alloys are almost totally resistant to corrosion – they usually become pitted and covered by a whitish deposit in their early years but thereafter remain almost totally unaffected by the climate. The processes used to increase the basic strength of aluminium alloys can be utilized to produce simple 'dry' glazing systems. Some very sophisticated systems of retaining the glass have also been developed, including continuous bar-cap systems which give a complete seal against draughts and drips.

Reinforced concrete Reinforced concrete was for a time used in glasshouse construction, especially in cold climates, but has now largely been discarded because of its low strength/bulk ratio and light exclusion.

Glass or plastic? Since the 1960s rigid plastic, polythene and PVC have been increasingly used for greenhouse construction. Some of the latest non-glass greenhouses are extremely simple and cheap to erect and provide a high level of crop protection. Rigid plastic materials perform more or less the same function as glass. They are more efficient in some respects in transmitting light, and they can be readily shaped into curves but they are generally more expensive than glass. Plastic film materials such as polythene are much cheaper but break down through the action of ultra-violet sunlight and should be considered only as short-term materials needing regular replacement. In recent years the life of plastic has been considerably extended by the use of an ultra-violet inhibitor (UVI). Most plastics are unable, unlike glass, to trap reflected solar rays (see *Temperature Control*) and this results in rapid cooling when the sun goes down with much more condensation. However, this phenomenon does not affect the amount of artificial heat required to warm them above the outside temperature. The lack of air leaks from a plastic film greenhouse can, in many cases, make it much tighter and cheaper to heat than a greenhouse glazed conventionally with glass. It does however pose ventilation problems as a glazed house breathes – that is several changes of air an hour may be possible without opening or shutting ventilators. Make sure that plastic greenhouses are fitted with adequate ventilation.

Choosing a Site

A greenhouse must have good light and should be positioned so that it is sheltered from prevailing winds.

Light In summer, when the sun is high in the sky, most gardens have abundant light but in winter, when the sun is much lower, light is at a premium. For maximum winter light, site rectangular greenhouses east-west, but when a greenhouse is used mainly for summer crops, a north-south orientation will give a more even distribution of light.

Shelter A greenhouse on an exposed site can suffer physical damage to the structure and will also suffer from excessive heat loss. Wind can play strange tricks by bouncing off buildings and by creating areas of turbulence on the lee side of walls and fences. When providing shelter for a greenhouse, use a medium which will slow the speed of the wind and will not simply deflect it. A hedge as a screen is ideal. As a general guide, a screen will provide shelter for a distance equal to about 10 to 12 times the height of the screen itself. Maximum shelter is given in the region of five to six times the barrier height. For suitable plants for providing shelter see *Design and Planning: Hedges* and *Screens*. Make sure that a shelter hedge does not block out the light.

Other points Make sure that the greenhouse is not too far away from the house and that electricity and water are available if required. A hard path to the greenhouse will make access easier in wet weather. The path should be wide enough to stand a wheelbarrow on, should be even and well drained and made of non-slip materials. Try to choose a flat site as this will be a great deal easier to develop than a sloping one. For sloping sites see *Construction: Levelling*. Sloping sites may also have drainage problems. If the site is infested by difficult weeds such as couch grass start a weed-killing programme well before you start building the foundations – see *Pests and Diseases: Herbicides*.

Temperature Control

As well as providing light, the sun is also a source of heat. Greenhouses trap this heat by means of the so-called greenhouse principle. Short-wave radiation from the sun passes through the glass and is absorbed by things inside the greenhouse – benches, paths, plants and so on. In turn, things emit long-wave radiation but this cannot escape through the glass and is trapped and so heats the greenhouse. In summer the levels of solar energy are high and precautions may need to be taken to prevent over-heating – see *Ventilation* and *Shading*. In winter extra heat may be required. Green-

Light transmitted through greenhouses
(winter sun angle about 15°)

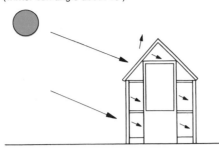

Vertical sides transmit more light than the roof (pitch 30°)

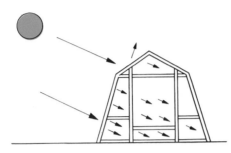

Angled side wall transmits even more light than a vertical wall

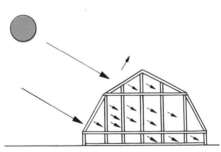

Curved greenhouse which nearly always offers part of the glass surface at more or less 90° to sun's rays

houses are usually divided into four categories according to their heating requirements.

Cold This sort of greenhouse is not artificially heated and has limited use. It can be used to grow either hardy plants such as peaches, nectarines, vines and alpines for the full year, or less hardy plants between spring and summer. How useful a completely cold greenhouse is depends greatly on the climate of the area. In very mild areas, where the incidence of frost is low, one can be used widely throughout the full year to forward the growth of many species of plants, particularly shrubby ones in pots, and protect them against wind and rain.

Cool This entails keeping the greenhouse environment completely free from frost and a minimum temperature of 5 to 7°C (40 to 45°F) is normal. A frost-protected greenhouse usually offers excellent scope for growing a wide range of plants at low cost. Frost protection can, however, mean a fairly expensive heating system in cold regions; in the temperate climate of the UK, for example, it is usual to think in terms of about 11°C (20°F) lift (see *Heating*

117

Above: A hanging basket adds greatly to the appearance of a greenhouse and releases growing space below

Right: Span-roofed aluminium greenhouse

Requirements) over outside temperatures, but it could mean a 30°C (50°F) lift in colder regions of the USA and Canada. Tender exotic plants cannot hope to survive in frost-protected greenhouses, except in the summer. Frost protection facilities, can, however, be turned to excellent advantage in the spring, when temperatures much greater than the minimum can usually be maintained. Propagating cases can be used with great effect in a frost-free greenhouse as they can ensure a high temperature level at low cost in a limited area within the greenhouse.

Intermediate An intermediate or warm greenhouse requires a minimum of 13°C (55°F) the full year round. This temperature will allow a very wide range of plants to be grown, including some exotic ones (especially house plants). Tender plants such as tomatoes or cucumbers can be planted very early but it should be noted that a lack of natural light cannot be made up by heat. Maintaining this temperature all year can be costly even in temperate regions such as the UK.

'Stove' or warm The name 'stove' is apt, as it involves a minimum of 18°C (65°F). Such a greenhouse allows unlimited scope for tender orchids and other plants requiring tropical conditions. 'Stove' temperatures

are common in botanic gardens or greenhouses of specialist plant collectors, but are uneconomic for amateur gardeners because of the high cost of maintaining the minimum temperature irrespective of weather conditions out of doors. A combined greenhouse/home heating system is the logical answer when stove conditions are desired.

Heating Requirements

If a greenhouse is warmer on the inside than on the outside then heat will flow from the warmer to the cooler area. The rate at which this heat flows depends on the insulating properties of the greenhouse materials and on the temperature difference between the inside and the outside. Any greenhouse heating system should be designed to cope with this loss of heat and should have a high enough output to provide enough heat in the coldest weather.

The difference between the temperature inside and outside is called the 'temperature lift'. In theory the temperature lift should be based on the lowest temperature which is likely to occur but, in practice, it is usually based on some arbitrary minimum temperature which is a little above the lowest temperature. For example, to provide an inside temperature of 13°C (55°F) when the temperature outside frequently falls to

−7°C (19°F), the heating system would have to be capable of providing a temperature lift of 20°C (36°F).

The insulating property of a greenhouse material is expressed in terms of its U value, which shows the power required to maintain a given temperature difference. The lower the U value the better the insulator. It is normally shown in watts (Btu per hour) per m² (sq ft) per deg C (deg F). The U values of different greenhouse materials are given below. These have been adjusted to take account of heat lost to the soil and through leaks and are a little higher than similar figures quoted elsewhere – in books concerned with central heating, for example.

Adjusted U values of greenhouse materials

	W/m² deg C	Btu/sq ft h deg F
Glass (including glazing bars)	8·0	1·4
12cm (4½in) Brickwork	3·6	0·63
25cm (9in) Brickwork	2·7	0·47
28cm (11in) Brickwork	1·7	0·30
10cm (4in) Concrete	4·2	0·75
15cm (6 in) Concrete	3·6	0·63
25mm (1in) Wood	2·8	0·5
Corrugated Asbestos Sheeting	8·0	1·4
Polythene Sheeting	8·0	1·4

The newest concept – a geodetic greenhouse (courtesy of Rosedale Engineers Ltd.)

To calculate the heat lost from the greenhouse, measure the external surface area of each material, multiply each by the appropriate U value given above and then multiply the total figure by the desired temperature lift. A very quick calculation can be obtained by multiplying the floor area in square metres (sq ft) of a very small greenhouse by 700 (125) for a 11°C (20°F) lift, 1,000 (190) for a 17°C (30°F) lift and by 1,400 (250) for a 22°C (40°F) lift. The total figure in watts (Btu) is the amount of heat which must be put into the greenhouse by any heating system. From the U values it is obvious that brick and wood are better insulators than glass and so greenhouses with brick or wood base walls are cheaper to heat than those with glass right down to the ground.

Double Glazing

It is an advantage in most cold areas to line a greenhouse with thin gauge clear plastic. In wooden-framed greenhouses, the plastic can be pinned on to the wood. In metal greenhouses, pieces of wood can be let into the grooves in the glazing bars and the plastic can be pinned to these. If all the greenhouse, apart from the vents, is covered then the heat loss will be reduced by about 25 per cent. In extremely cold areas, a double-glazed greenhouse could be considered but unless double glazing is carried out efficiently dirt and moisture can get trapped between the layers of glass.

Heating Equipment

Heat may be provided by 1) pipes filled with warm water, 2) electric convector or fan heaters, 3) oil or natural gas air heaters, and 4) electric tubular heaters or mineral insulated (MI) cables.

Water-filled pipe systems These work rather like house central heating. Water is heated in a boiler powered by electricity, gas, oil or solid fuel and is fed to pipes which act as radiators and heat the greenhouse. The pipes may be large-bore – about 10cm (4in) in diameter – or small-bore – usually 2·5 to 5cm (1 to 2in) across. Large-bore pipe systems usually work by gravity: small-bore pipe systems generally have an electrical pump. Both systems are expensive to operate and, because of the relatively large amounts of water being heated, it can be difficult to control the temperature of the greenhouse accurately. Small-bore systems are the easier to control. The pipes are generally set around three or four sides of the greenhouse and will heat it uniformly. When staging is used a 15cm (6in) gap should be left between the staging and the walls of the greenhouse to let the warm air rise. Boilers can be inside or outside the

greenhouse. Boilers sited inside are generally flued so that any products of the combustion, particularly sulphurous fumes from soild fuels, will not injure the plants.

Electric convector or fan heaters Both are excellent for providing heat for a greenhouse. They can be thermostatically controlled with a high degree of accuracy and they do not contaminate the air in any way. But the distribution of heat may not be quite as uniform as with water-filled pipes. Convector heaters rely on the natural convection currents within the greenhouse to distribute the heat and one centrally situated heater will provide very poor distribution. Fan heaters push the warm air around the greenhouse and care should be taken to avoid warm air blowing directly on to nearby plants.

Oil or natural gas air heaters Natural gas and paraffin are pure fuels and will, if burned correctly, produce only water vapour and carbon dioxide. This means that these fuels can be used to heat greenhouse air directly and do not need to be used in flued boilers. In winter, most plants prefer dry heat and the increase in humidity produced through using oil or natural gas air heaters can lead to trouble with winter fungoid diseases like grey mould, *Botrytis cinerea*. Water-producing fuels used in a plastic greenhouse (or one lined with polythene) are a particularly troublesome combination. Like convector heaters, there can be some difficulty in ensuring uniform distribution of heat.

Electric tubular heaters and mineral insulated cables Tubular heaters work directly from mains voltage electricity and should be set around the greenhouse perimeter about 15cm (6in) above the soil and in banks of one, two or three. Most have a loading of about 200 watts a metre length (60w/ft) – see *Heating Requirements* – and can be controlled by a thermostat. They give off quite a lot of radiant heat and can scorch nearby plants. Mineral insulated cables can be used when a relatively low heat output is required – see *Frames*. They are about as thick as a pencil and consist of a heating wire surrounded by an insulating material which is covered by a copper sheath.

Ventilation

Air in a greenhouse is heated by re-radiation of solar energy from solid objects and also, in some cases, by the input of artificial heat. Eventually there may come a time when the air becomes too warm for the plants' comfort, and when this happens the warm air in the greenhouse must be exchanged for cooler air from out of doors. As warm air rises, it is convenient to let it escape through exits at the highest point of the greenhouse. Cooler air usually gains entry through leaks where glass overlaps, for example, and through side vents set lower down the side of the greenhouse. Lean-to and circular greenhouses, in particular, should be provided with ample ventilation. Greenhouses used for alpine plants should also be well ventilated. In broad terms the area of the vents in a small greenhouse should be at least 25 to 30 per cent of the floor area. Vents are best operated automatically, either with electric motors operated by thermostats or, on a smaller scale, by expansion vent units. Ideally roof vents should be alternately positioned on both sides of the roof. Side vents should be set to match. If side vents are set at ground level, they should be covered by wire netting to prevent pests like mice and cats gaining entry.

Circulating fans are useful for mixing the air in a greenhouse and preventing cold or wet spots. Extractor fans pull air out of the greenhouse and there must obviously be provision to let fresh air in. Fans can also be used to pull air into a greenhouse but extractor fans are, in practice, the most reliable. In both cases the fans are controlled by an air thermostat and they must be large enough to be capable of moving sufficient quantities of air – consult fan suppliers for fuller details. Do not use domestic extractor fans – those designed for greenhouses have large blades which rotate slowly.

Absorbent pads or moisture jets can be used in conjunction with fans to wet the incoming air and raise the humidity of the greenhouse atmosphere.

Shading

In summer when solar radiation is high, a greenhouse may easily overheat and may need to be shaded. This can be achieved in four ways: 1) by applying green or white shading material to the outside or inside of the glass, 2) by using a roller or slatted blind inside or outside the greenhouse which can either be operated manually or by a thermostat or magic eye (photo electric cell), 3) by means of shading material applied to the outside of the greenhouse, or 4) by suspending green plastic or other material horizontally above the plants.

A further method is to run coloured water down the outside of the glass, but this system has its problems because the greenhouse must be completely drip proof.

Benching

Unless the greenhouse is used exclusively for growing ground crops, some kind of benching will be required. Most greenhouse benches are made of wooden slats about 10cm (4in) wide and about 19mm (¾in)

thick, set on bearers which are supported by legs about 75cm (30in) high. Angle iron and steel mesh benches are also available. Benches can either be of single row or tiered and should in all cases be strong enough to support considerable weight.

A completely solid bench with 75 to 100mm (3 to 4in) sides lined with polythene and containing 25mm (1in) of coarse gravel topped up with about 25mm (1in) of fine sand can be used as a capillary bench to water plants. The bench should be level and water can be supplied automatically from a header tank via a wick (usually fibre glass). The header tank can be filled by hand or from the mains water supply by means of a ball-cock valve system. Water can also be supplied to the bench from a dripping hose or by hand. Plants in pots spaced out on the capillary bed will obtain all their water by capillary pull. Plastic pots are better for this purpose than clay pots and the pots will need turning frequently to stop roots establishing in the sand. A 15cm (6in) gap should always be left between the bench and the outside of the glasshouse, especially where any form of artificial heat is being used.

Instead of heating the whole greenhouse to a high temperature, small areas can be warmed by using soil-warming cables. These can be used to heat a whole bench or part of it can be made into a propagating case. See *Propagation: Mist Propagation.*

A heated bench needs to be a trough about 15cm (6in) deep. Spread about 5cm (2in) of sand over the bottom of the bench and lay a soil-warming cable in loops along the bench leaving about 5 to 10cm (2 to 4in) between the loops. Cover the cables with another 5cm (2in) of sand. Boxes, pans or pots can be placed on this sand and the space between them should be filled with moist peat. The temperature of the bed can be controlled by a thermostat set across the run of the wires and just below the surface of the bed.

A propagating case can be made by covering part of the bench with glass or clear plastic sheeting supported on a wooden frame. Heating cables can also be attached to the sides of the wooden frame. By using the principles outlined above, a separate propagating case could be made quite simply. Small cases can be heated by an electric light bulb.

Lighting

There are two reasons why you may want to install artificial light in your greenhouse. You may simply want it so that you can see your way around your greenhouse in winter or at night. In this case a waterproof outdoor safety or burglar light properly installed should be sufficient. Check with the

Above: A polythene greenhouse

Right: Utilize all the space in a small greenhouse

appropriate wiring regulations or by-laws to make sure that your system is legal. You may also want to supplement natural daylight for your plants. Light affects plants in three ways: 1) the level of illumination affects the rate of growth, 2) the colour of the light affects the shape of the plant, and 3) the length of time a plant is illuminated may affect the initiation and development of flowers.

Tungsten filament lamps These are frequently used for home lighting and the light is produced by heating a filament to a high temperature. The light which comes out of these has a lot of long wavelength (red) radiation in it and tends to elongate plants. It is the cheapest type of supplementary lighting to install but, unless you have a particular job in mind – to control the flowering of chrysanthemums or simply to provide light so that you can continue to work after dark for example – then this would not be a worthwhile proposition. 100w lamps spaced 1·8m (6ft) apart along the length of the greenhouse should be adequate.

Discharge lamps These produce light by discharging electricity through a gas or vapour. The type of gas or vapour governs the colour of the light. Mercury vapour lamps can be used to supplement daylight, particularly during the winter months, and to increase the rate of photosynthesis. See *How Plants Live.* A 400w mercury vapour lamp is usually suspended about 90cm (3ft) above the plants being lit. If the inside of the lamp is coated with a fluorescent powder, some of the ultra-violet light given out by mercury vapour lamps can be converted into visible light.

Fluorescent tubular lamps These work like the mercury vapour lamps with fluorescent powder described above but contain a much lower pressure of mercury vapour. This means that much more of the ultra-violet light is converted into visible light and these lamps give off much less heat than mercury vapour lamps. The fluorescent powder used can be varied to give white, neutral or warm white light. Warm white is most suitable for horticultural purposes.

Frames

Frames are like miniature greenhouses; they admit light and trap heat from the sun and are used to forward, produce and propagate plants from seed or cuttings. They may be used both out of doors and inside a greenhouse. When used inside a greenhouse they form an area which can be kept readily and economically at higher temperatures than the surrounding greenhouse and are often used for propagation. The base of a frame is usually made of wood, brick or metal alloy and is taller at the back than at the front. This base supports a large, removable window which is often called a 'light'.

The type of frame used in the late 19th and the early part of the 20th century had a heavily constructed light with several sash bars and numerous panes of glass held in place by putty and nails. These lights measured about 180 by 120cm (6 by 4ft) and were supported on stout, brick-base walls. They were extremely heavy to handle and it often took two or more men to open the frame. This old-fashioned light frame has now been replaced by frames with Dutch lights which measure about 155 by 63cm (62 by 25in). Dutch lights have a single sheet of 24oz glass held in a wood frame. The wood can be either pressure-treated softwood or Western red cedar. The glass can be slid over the bottom rail and fits into grooves in the side rails and the top rail. It is held in position by a small spar secured by galvanized nails. Dutch lights are much lighter than the old-fashioned English lights and, because they do not have sash bars, they are also able to transmit much more light.

Several types of smaller patent cold frames more suitable for use in small gardens are available from manufacturers. These are often made of wood, galvanized steel or metal alloy and vary in size but are in the order of 150 by 80cm (5 by 2½ft). The light is often hinged to the rear of the base so that it can be opened but not removed.

Making a Frame

The easiest way to build a frame is to acquire an old glazed window – from a demolition site, say – and to build a base to fit. If this is not possible and you do not fancy building a light out of wood and glazing it then you can still make a light out of wood and plastic. But plastic-covered lights do not keep out frost as well as glass, mainly because plastics do not trap reflected heat from the sun. To make a plastic-covered light, make a framework out of wood measuring 6 to 8cm (2½ to 3½in) by 13 to 19mm (½ to ¾in). Lap the plastic around light spars of wood and then tack this on to the main framework. Alternatively you can make two frames out of 13mm (½in) wood and then trap the film plastic between them. There are no precise criteria for size of light, although 150 by 80cm (5 by 2½ft) is usual. Make the light in a warm atmosphere so that the plastic is fully stretched. If the plas-

A glass lean-to with a brick base

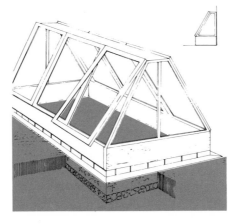

A modern frame with Dutch lights to catch the spring angle of the sun. The frame has a timber frame above a row of house bricks laid on a concrete strip over hardcore.

tic is put on to the framework on a cold day it will sag when the atmosphere is warmer. If you intend to glaze the light, design it around the standard-sized sheets of horticultural glass available at your glass merchant.

The base for frames can be made of brick, composition blocks, wood or asbestos. Brick and composition block walls provide better insulation than wood and should be used for frames which are to be heated for much of the year. A single course of bricks or blocks is usually adequate.

The ideal height for the base is largely dictated by the purpose for which the frame is to be used. For low-growing vegetables, such as lettuce, flower crops and bedding plants, a base which is 30cm (12in) high at the back and 23cm (9in) at the front is adequate. For taller-growing plants or alpines and plants in pots, increase the height at the back to 45cm (18in) and at the front to 38cm (15in). For low-growing plants, old wooden railroad ties/railway sleepers make an excellent strong and long lasting base. Secure the light to the base so that it will not be blown off by wind by either using hooks and eyes or by inserting nails in the frame of the light and base in a sort of zig-zag manner and then running a wire through them.

The traditional frame described above does not make full use of the available light and heat from the sun: in most areas the frame light will be set at the wrong angle for maximum penetration by the sun's rays. A more ideal frame can generally be made by setting the angle of the light much more vertically – see *Greenhouses* for the exact angles necessary. To do this you will need two lights: one set at the ideal angle to catch the sun's rays and the other set horizontally at the top of the frame to increase its overall depth. Frost will tend to settle on the horizontal light so, if possible, double-glaze it.

It is usual to have frames facing south (north in the southern hemisphere) for most activities. The exception is when the frame is to be used exclusively for shade-loving subjects such as ferns, or rhododendrons during propagation.

Heating Frames

The air and soil inside a frame can be heated at the same time by standing the frame on a hotbed. Or they can be heated separately by using soil- and air-warming equipment.

Hotbeds An old-fashioned but still very effective way of heating a frame is to stand it on a hotbed made from fresh horse manure mixed with an equal amount of leaves or old manure.

To make a hotbed mix fresh manure and leaves thoroughly and shape them into a conical heap. Water any dry parts as you build the heap. Within a few days the heap will become very hot and it should then be turned by putting the inside to the outside and vice-versa. After a few more days it should be hot enough to turn again. After the third turning level the heap out so that it is the same shape as the frame but about 30cm (1ft) larger all round. Tread the manure down firmly. The bed can be anything from 30 to 60cm (1 to 2ft) deep: the deeper the bed is, the warmer it will get and the longer it will retain its heat. Cover the bed with about 15cm (6in) of good topsoil, stand the frame on top of it and plunge a soil thermometer into the soil at the centre of the frame. After a few days the bed should get very hot. Do not sow any seeds or set out plants until the smell of ammonia has gone and the temperature recorded on the soil thermometer drops to about 24°C (75°F). A good hotbed will continue to heat a frame for about 10 weeks. The most useful time to make a hotbed is in the early spring so by the time it starts to cool in early summer the sun should be able to supply adequate heat for the plants.

Soil-warming equipment The soil can be readily warmed by using mains voltage soil-warming cables buried far enough below the soil surface to avoid being damaged by hand tools. A depth of 20 to 25cm (8 to 10in) is normal and the cables should be spaced to give a minimum loading of 81 watts/m² (7½ watts/sq ft). Before 1974 most soil-warming cables worked at a low voltage and were normally spaced about 15cm (6in) apart to give a loading of 70 watts/m² (6 watts/sq ft). But, because of the expense of transformers, low voltage wires have been superseded by mains voltage cables. Low voltage equipment may still be available in some countries.

Before buying a soil-warming set, measure the ground area and calculate the total loading by multiplying the area in m² (sq ft) occupied by the frame by the appropriate factor. A Dutch light covering about $2 \cdot 3m^2$ (25sq ft) will require a 187w loading and will use approximately one sixth of a unit of electricity an hour. A slightly lower or higher loading is of no consequence. To install the cables, excavate the soil completely to a depth of 20 to 25cm (8 to 10in) and space out the cables using hair pins or bits of wire to keep them in position. Avoid sharp bends. Replace the soil (or special growing mix) and make sure that the fittings for the supply of electricity are waterproof. The installation of mains voltage equipment must be carried out **in a competent manner**; if you do not feel capable of doing it, then seek professional help. **When cultivating the soil with any tools, shut off the electricity supply.**

The soil can also be warmed by circulating water through water-filled, plastic pipes buried about 20 to 25cm (8 to 10in) below the soil surface. It is not worth considering this type of system unless a pump-circulated hot-water system is used for greenhouse heating.

If the frame is to be used mainly for raising seedlings in boxes then the principles of bench warming (see *Benching*) apply. To make this sort of frame, lay the cables on 5cm (2in) of sand and cover them with a further 5cm (2in) layer. The cables should be spaced to give a loading of 86 to 130 w/m² (8 to 10w/sq ft).

Air-warming The first step is to calculate the heat load required. This can be done by calculating the surface area of each material the frame is composed of and multiplying each by its correct U-value. See *Heating Requirements*. But for all practical purposes, multiplying the ground area in m² by 86 will give a quick and accurate enough answer. The figure arrived at will be the number of watts for *each* degree Centigrade required above the outside temperature. (To get the equivalent figure in Btu lift deg F multiply the area in sq ft by $1 \cdot 4$.) This figure now needs converting into the amount of heat you need to put into the frame to keep it at the desired temperature. To do this multiply the figure by the temperature lift. The temperature lift is the difference between an average minimum winter temperature and the desired temperature inside the frame. For example, if complete frost protection is the aim, and if the average minimum outside temperature is $-7°C$ (20°F), a reasonable minimum temperature inside the frame might be 7°C (45°F) and to achieve this a 14°C (25°F) lift is required. The heat requirement can be supplied by mineral-insulated warming cables fitted on the side of the frame, or by tubular heaters. Tubular heaters normally have a loading of about 200w/m length (60w/ft). Mineral-insulated cables are normally bought as a set for a specific loading. Both mineral-insulated cables and tubular heaters are best controlled by an air thermostat (this thermostat should *not* be used to control the soil temperature as well).

If a frame is built against the base wall of a greenhouse it can be linked to the greenhouse heating system. If this is to be done, the frame should be on the south side of the greenhouse for maximum efficiency.

Watering
Plants in a frame can be watered by hand using a hose pipe or watering can. If the water pressure is sufficiently high (at least $2 \cdot 5$ bars/35psi) then a sprayline can be fitted. Lay-flat polythene can also be used for pot plants. A modern way of watering is to use the 'island bed' system. This is similar to a capillary bench and uses a capillary sand or fibre-glass bed with the flow of water controlled by a ball and cock device in a tank. This means that the tank must be connected to the domestic water supply. Trickle systems can be used for pot plants.

Ventilation
Frames usually need ventilating slightly in spring and autumn months. The amount of ventilation will need to be increased in early summer and by the middle of summer it may be necessary to remove the light completely.

Shading
During very hot weather, some plants will need shading and green plastic sheeting is a convenient material to use. Slats of wood screwed to a frame and oriented N/S with equal spaces of wood/no wood and various spray or paint-on materials can also be used.

Protection
In extremely cold weather, frames need extra protection from frost. This can be done in a variety of ways. Old sacks or straw can be used, as also can old carpets, but fibre-glass mats are more effective than either. Protection is really only necessary during extremely cold nights and should always be removed during the day to avoid plants becoming etiolated or drawn due to lack of light.

Using a Frame
Frames generally serve four purposes: to speed up the germination of seeds and the rooting of cuttings, to bring forward some crops, to protect plants like alpines from weather damage and to harden off plants raised in a greenhouse. See *Cloches* for forwarding crops.

A mini-climate can be created within the greenhouse by means of soil-warming cables in a growing box (courtesy of Humex)

Right: Double benching makes economical use of space

An aluminium and glass cold frame

Cloches

The basic objective of all cloches is to provide a congenial micro-climate which can be used to benefit plants at some stage of their life. Low-growing plants are often grown to maturity under cloches and tall-growing ones benefit during their early stages of growth. Plants grown under cloches will make an earlier start to life and grow more quickly, producing fruit, flowers and leaves sooner than they would if they had been grown completely unprotected out of doors. Cloches can also be used as transitional protection for plants from a greenhouse or frame.

Types of Cloches

There are several types of cloches and, whatever size or shape is used, they should always be anchored firmly to the ground.

Glass or plastic? Most cloches used to be made of glass but, because of the high risk of breakage, rigid, white translucent polypropylene sheeting is now often used instead. Thin plastic tubing or sheeting is also used. All plastic materials suffer to some extent through exposure to the ultra-violet content of natural light. The plastic will, in time, become cloudy and brittle. This factor must be weighed against the potential breakage factor of glass cloches when a decision is being made about which type to buy. Glass also traps reflected long waves from the sun, whereas plastic does not (see: *Greenhouses*), and this means that the climate

under glass cloches is warmer, on average, than under plastic ones.

Tent These have two sheets of 24oz glass measuring about 22 by 60cm (9 by 24in) clipped together by special galvanized wires. Such an arrangement only gives a 30 to 38cm (12 to 15in) width at the base and is very restrictive in cropping.

Barn These are shaped like a barn. Basically, two sheets of glass about 60 by 30cm (24 by 12in) form the roof, with two sheets 60 by 15cm (24 by 6in) forming the sides. Again wires are used to clip the glass together. This design gives cloches with a width of 60cm (24in) and a height in the centre of 23cm (9in). End sections are generally available and extra side pieces can be fitted to some barn cloches to raise the height to 36cm (14in).

Plastic tunnel These are made by stretching clear plastic sheeting over wire hoops. The hoops are made of heavy gauge fencing wire cut into lengths of 150cm (5ft). An 'eye' is made 15 to 20cm (6 to 8in) from each end and the hoop is bent into a semicircle. To make the cloche, space the hoops 60cm (2ft) apart in a straight line. At both ends of the row drive a 38 to 45cm (15 to 18in) long wooden stake into the ground at an oblique angle and about 40cm (2ft) from the end hoops. Tie one end of a 120cm (4ft) wide sheet of 38 micron transparent plastic to one stake, loosely stretch the plastic over the hoops and tie it to the second stake. Do this on a still, warm day: if it is done in cool

Cloches
The soil surface beneath a cloche may appear dry but water can flow to the roots of plants as shown

Far right: Rigid corrugated clear plastic sheets held in place by wire hoops

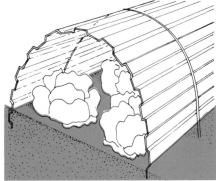

Rigid plastic cloche

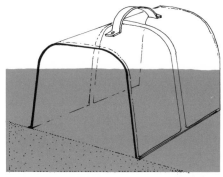

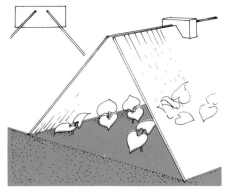

Plastic tunnel cloche. The plastic sheeting is draped over metal hoops and held in place by more hoops as shown. The plastic sheeting is drawn tight by tying it to a stake at each end of the cloche

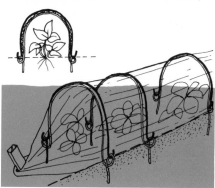

Above: Two panes of glass about 30 by 45cm (12 by 18in) forming a tent cloche. The panes can be held by inserting them in a block of wood as shown

weather the plastic will sag as the weather warms. Hold the plastic in position at each hoop by threading light wire through the eyes. In windy positions heap up the soil around the edge of the plastic sheeting, so that it is not easily disarranged. A wider cloche can be made by using slightly wider hoops and two widths of plastic held together by clothes pegs in the centre. This allows the tunnel to be opened up for planting, watering, picking and so on and the tunnel can also be opened on a wet day for a few hours to allow natural watering.

Cones These are used, mainly in North America, to give greater protection to individual plants.

Using Cloches
Choose a sunny, open site for positioning the cloches. Some shelter from strong winds is helpful but avoid, if possible, 'swirl' areas, caused by walls or solid buildings which deflect wind towards the ground at unusual angles. To let plants get the maximum benefit from the cover provided by cloches, the ground should be well drained and fertile. If the area has perennial weeds then it should not be used for cloche culture until the weeds have been eradicated. If a weed-killer is used then ample time should be allowed for the weedkilling chemicals to dissipate. To improve the soil condition at planting or sowing time, put cloches into position a week or so before they are required.

Plants under a narrow cloche may get enough water through the sideways seepage of natural rainfall and, in many instances, this can also be supplemented by opening up the cloches during periods of rain. But those under a wide cloche will probably need to be watered artificially. If there is a water supply point near the selected site, plants under the cloches can be watered by using lay-flat plastic or perforated hose running along the inside of the cloches.

Cloches are usually ventilated by lifting the roof glass or plastic. Cloches are seldom heated. The Belgians heat their cloches by warm-water-filled pipes in the soil below them. Soil warming cables could be used, but these are more effective in cold frames. (See *Frames*).

Planning Cloche Gardening

There are two approaches. You can use cloches merely to permit earlier sowing of a wide range of vegetables, flowers or bulbs. In this case place the cloches in position about three to four weeks before the normal sowing date, which can be advanced by two to three weeks. Or, you can adopt a more intensive approach and plan the ground in strips to allow the cloches to be used successionally. Once one sowing or one crop is finished the cloches are then moved on to another part of the ground.

Vegetable Growing Guide

This guide applies to growing vegetables under cloches or cones and in most cases it can be modified for growing vegetables in frames. For details of cultivation see *Edible Plants: Vegetables*). In the UK most vegetables can be sown under cloches about two to three weeks before the times given in the Vegetable Planning Chart (see *Edible Plants: Vegetables*). Dates for North America are given under the individual summaries below.

Bean, broad Use cloches or cones to cover an early crop sown six weeks before the average last frost date and to cover November-sown beans. Use varieties like 'Aquadulce' for autumn-sown beans or 'Early Longpod' for those sown in early spring. Remove cloches in April (or before) and use to cover lettuces or French beans.

Bean, French, kidney, snap or string Sow a single drill of seed at about the average date of the last frost or use cloches to cover seedlings planted out just after the last frost date. Remove cloches in May.

Bean, runner These are difficult to grow under cloches or frames because of their eventual height. Seed sown in pots can be started off under cloches or in frames at about the average date of the last frost (generally late April) for planting out in late May to early June. Seed can also be sown directly into the ground and the cloches removed when necessary.

Beetroot Sow early globe types about four weeks before the average date of the last

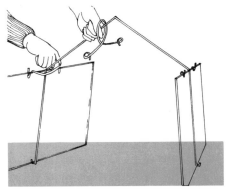

Putting up a glass barn cloche

Hold the main frame upright, put in the side glass panes first by clipping the spring over the edge of the glass

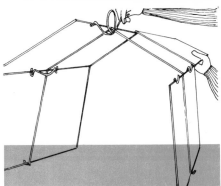

The springs which hold the side panes generally hold the bottom edges of the roof panes too. Clip the end of the handle loop over the first roof pane then slide in the other roof pane

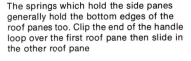

Clip the end of the handle loop over the outer side of the glass pane

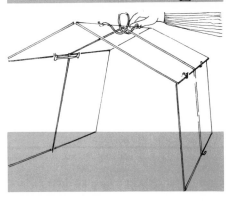

frost (generally early April). For the earliest crop keep the beetroot under the cloches until they are harvested. Alternatively the cloches can be removed in June.

Brassicas (broccoli, Brussels sprouts, cabbages and cauliflowers) Sow seed of all brassicas under cloches or in frames about four weeks before the average date of the last frost. Plant out in April or May.

Carrots Sow quick-maturing, forcing varieties about six weeks before the average date of the last frost. Carrots grow well on a hotbed beneath a frame – see *Frames*. Remove cloches in June.

Celery In areas with a long growing season, sow seed under cloches or in frames at about the average date of the last frost (generally April) for planting out of doors in May or June. Seedlings grown in a heated greenhouse or frame can be planted under

Cos lettuces growing under a cloche

Opposite: A conservatory should be a place to sit as well as to grow plants

cloches about three weeks after the average date of the last frost. Self-blanching varieties can be left to mature in frames or cloches.

Corn, sweet corn or maize In the UK, sow seed in small pots in a greenhouse in March or April or cold frames slightly later and plant out under cloches at the beginning of May. Remove the cloches in June. In Canada and the USA sow seed outside about one week after the last frost date.

Corn salad Sow seed up to ten weeks before the average date of the last frost.

Cucumbers An ideal crop for frames, but cloches can also be used. Seed is best sown in the greenhouse at about the average date of the last frost and planted out under cloches or in a frame four to six weeks later. Seed can also be sown directly under a cloche or in a frame about two to four weeks after the average date of the last frost.

Endive For timing see *Lettuce*. The most useful crop comes from seed sown in August in cold frames or under cloches.

Leeks In areas with mild winters seed can be sown in frames or under cloches about 10 to 12 weeks before the average date of the

last frost for raising plants to set out in May or June.

Lettuce In mild areas sow seed up to ten weeks before the average date of the last frost (generally early February) at two week intervals. Alternatively lettuces can be sown in January in a heated greenhouse and planted out in frames or under cloches in February or March. Remove the cloches in April so that they are then free for planting tomatoes or cucumbers which have been raised in a greenhouse.

Mint Cloches placed over established plants will allow the mint to be picked for most of the winter.

Mustard and Cress Broadcast the seed from four to eight weeks before the first autumn frost date (generally September to October) and repeat at intervals. The rate of growth will depend on the prevailing temperature.

Onions Sow seed under cloches or in frames about three to four weeks before the average date of the last frost (generally March) for planting out in April or May. Spring or salad onions can be left to mature under cloches or in frames. Cloches are use-

130

ful for raising onion sets; if seed is sown in May or June and the cloches left in position, the onion bulbs will ripen while they are very small.

Parsley Cloches are useful for covering established plants in autumn to allow parsley to be picked during the winter months. Plants can also be transferred to frames in September to October.

Peas Round-seeded peas can be sown two to three weeks earlier than the wrinkle-seeded varieties. Sow seed under cloches about eight weeks before the average date of the last frost (generally from early February to early March according to district). It is usual to sow one flat-bottomed drill under each cloche and remove the cloche by April or early May.

Radish Seeds of forcing radish can be sown broadcast about six to eight weeks before the average date of the last frost (generally from late February to mid March). For the earliest crops leave the cloches in place until the radishes are ready for picking.

Spinach An excellent crop for sowing under cloches. Sow summer spinach at two week intervals from eight weeks before the average date of the last frost (generally mid February to March). Sow winter spinach in September.

Tomatoes Only the largest types of cloches are suitable for growing tomatoes under. Set out greenhouse-raised plants about two to three weeks after the average date of the last frost (generally from late April to May). Select either dwarf varieties or those which can be trained along a wire about 30cm (12in) above ground level, or laid on a mulch of straw on the ground. Space the plants 90cm (3ft) apart.

Turnips Sow early turnips at intervals from two to three weeks before the average date of the last frost (generally in March and April). Remove the cloches in May or June.

Vegetable marrows In warm areas sow seed outdoors, under cloches, two to three weeks after the average date of the last frost. In other areas sow seed in a greenhouse about three to four weeks earlier. Plant out 60 to 90cm (2 to 3ft) apart in May. Restrict by training.

Fruit Growing Guide

For details of cultivation see *Edible Plants: Fruit*. Only two fruits are easily grown under cloches and in frames: these are strawberries and melons.

Strawberries Cover the plants in February or March and open the cloche or frame in good sunny weather during the day to allow pollination of the open flowers. It is usually necessary to water the plants to avoid small and deformed fruits. Strawberries under cloches or in frames usually produce fruit two to three weeks earlier than strawberries out of doors.

Melons For timing see *Vegetable Marrows*. Thin out the shoots and allow three to four melons to form. Pollination is required.

Flower Growing Guide

A tremendous range of flowers can be grown under cloches or in frames producing both earlier and larger-sized blooms. Of the many flowers under cloches the emphasis has been put on producing early flowers for cutting. Some of the more popular ones are listed below:

Bulbs Daffodils, snowdrops, most spring bulbs and gladioli, iris, anemones and ranunculus can be successfully grown under cloches and should flower about two to three weeks earlier than out of doors. In order to maximize space always plant the bulbs closer together than their normal outdoor planting distances. Daffodils and other narcissi can, for example, be planted 5 to 8cm (2 to 3in) apart.

Perennials Chrysanthemums, primulas, and pansies (including violas) are frequently grown under cloches.

Annuals Asters, calendulas, sweet peas, cornflowers, larkspur, annual mixed chrysanthemums, nigella and many rock plants, although hardy, can be protected against damp by cloches.

Conservatories

A conservatory is a place where a wide range of plants can be grown and kept in good condition without having to go outside to a greenhouse. Indeed the modern conservatory tends to be more of a sun lounge or an extension of the home, with plants simply as the main decor.

Early Conservatories

Victorian conservatories were usually extensive, ponderous structures linked on to the residence. They invariably had rounded roofs which gave them an aesthetic appeal and also trapped the maximum amount of solar heat by presenting a range of angles to the sun's rays. See *Greenhouses*. Very early conservatories often had a strong steel framework with glass held firmly in place with clips and putty. Hardwoods such as oak and teak were also extensively used.

Modern Conservatories

Early conservatories have little place in modern architecture. Nowadays modern conservatories tend to be either 'sun lounges' with solid roofs or a type of lean-to greenhouse which is often double-glazed, particularly in cold regions. Western red cedar, a soft but desirable wood of excellent appearance is often used in both types of conservatory. Metal alloy and enamelled steel can also be used, but wood tends to give a warmer atmosphere with less condensation, and this can be quite important, particularly in cold climates.

Using a Conservatory

Conservatories in the northern hemisphere are usually attached to the south- or west-facing walls of a house; west-facing ones are more pleasant in the evening. (The converse is true in the southern hemisphere.)

The main purpose of a conservatory should be to display pot plants or climbing shrubs to their best advantage and to maintain them in good condition. This means that heating and ventilation must be given careful consideration. Conservatories can often be heated by linking them to the existing house central heating system, but some provision will have to be made for heating the conservatory overnight when the domestic system is usually not in operation. In areas which have cool summers, house central-heating boilers which operate on natural gas or oil can be put in the conservatory, where the benefit of their constant warmth is considerable. In areas which have warm summers this sort of arrangement could create problems in warm weather when the boiler is in use for domestic warm water. There should be adequate provision for ventilation, either by vents or extraction fans. See *Ventilation*. Shading by blinds may be necessary in hot weather. Even in conservatories with solid roofs it may still be necessary to shade sunny windows.

Displays of plants in conservatories can be enhanced by modern materials such as gravel or sand trays, indoor window boxes, hanging baskets, wall brackets and other miscellaneous display materials. A wide range of contemporary furniture is now available for conservatories which is both decorative and comfortable.

Solariums

A solarium is a place which collects and makes the most of warmth from the sun and is often used for resting, recreation or therapeutic purposes. A solarium tends to be a place designed more for people and animals but the conditions inside it can be congenial for plants too.

An open-air solarium is a flat terrace or patio which is able to receive the maximum amount of sunshine and is generally protected from winds by either natural or artificial windbreaks. How well an open-air solarium works depends on the climate. In very warm countries, it may be desirable to provide some shade so that the sun can be avoided. Plants or plastic sheeting are generally used.

An indoor solarium is a totally enclosed building with a translucent roof and solid well-constructed side and end walls. The roof is suitably angled so that the maximum solar energy enters the building and raises the temperature appreciably. The walls are solid so that temperature remains high for as long as possible. Double-glazing also helps.

A solarium can be used as a source of solar heating for industrial and domestic buildings. In sophisticated solar heating systems, the sun's heat is used to warm large quantities of water. The heat from this water can be concentrated by a heat pump and used to provide domestic hot water and to heat buildings.

Obviously, the solarium creates an ideal climate for growing many species of plants. These, in turn, can help to provide an even more congenial restful aura for the solarium. Shrubs can be permanently planted in pockets of earth taken out of the paved floors or they can be planted in tubs. A wide range of pot plants and plants in decorative pools can be grown to perfection.

Growing Boxes

Growing boxes are small, mobile, artificially illuminated boxes in which plants are grown. They are not unlike terrariums (for details see *Specialist Gardens: Terrariums and Bottle Gardens*) but, whereas terrariums often have supplementary light, growing boxes admit no natural light at all; all the light is supplied artificially. Growing boxes are direct descendants of the growth cabinets used by research workers but they do not have the sophisticated equipment for cooling and heating of the latter.

Growing boxes can be put to a wide range of uses – for seed sowing, for rooting cuttings and for bringing on young plants quickly. They can be sited in a shed, garage or even in the house and may appeal, in particular, to gardeners who do not have greenhouses.

Making a Growing Box

The walls, top and bottom should be made of materials which have high thermal insulation such as compressed fibre glass sheeting. A reflective material, such as tin foil, should be used to line the inside of the top and banks of fluorescent tubes (preferably a mixture of warm white and daylight) should be attached to it by special waterproof clips. The lights should be spaced some 5 to 7·5cm (2 to 3in) apart. A typical growing box might be 150cm (5ft) long by 60cm

Even a small greenhouse can hold a wide range of different plants

Opposite: If you cannot have a conservatory, an elegant summerhouse could be an alternative

(2ft) wide by 60 to 90cm (2 to 3ft) high. Leave openings in the sheeting to allow adequate ventilation and make one side easily removable so that the plants can be watered and handled. Growing boxes can be equipped with a capillary watering system (see *Benching*) but precipitation of salts on the surface of the growing media through the high rate of evaporation caused by the heat from the lights can pose some problems.

Plants must be given a constant temperature environment which can be difficult to provide. During the 'light' periods the lamps may provide too much heat and during the periods of darkness, which some plants need, the temperature might drop too low. To overcome these problems sheets of plate glass can be installed below the lights to protect the plants from the excessive heat, and mineral-insulated cables, operated on an air thermostat, can be used in the dark periods.

Growing Rooms

A greenhouse is not the ideal place for raising young plants: it has low thermal insulation which means that it loses heat quickly and it is very difficult to avoid cold and hot pockets inside it. The main advantages of a greenhouse are shelter and a plentiful supply of natural light. But for years it has been known that many plants will grow successfully without any natural light at all provided that they are given sufficient artificial light. With this in mind it has been possible to construct buildings which have good thermal insulation and are free from draughts and hot or cold pockets. These buildings were mainly developed in the late 60s and early 70s and are known as growing rooms. The heat given off by artificial lights is often sufficient to provide most of the heat necessary, except during dark periods. Growing rooms must not be confused with the use of high-density lighting (see *Lighting*) to supplement natural daylight during periods when this is poor.

The early growing rooms or cabinets were developed by research workers to provide somewhere for them to carry out experiments on growing plants over twelve months of the year, irrespective of what the weather was like outside. See *Growing Boxes*. The growing boxes or cabinets they developed were highly sophisticated.

Commercial Growing Rooms

Most of the growing rooms now used by commercial growers are based on a highly insulated outer building with a smaller building made out of hardboard inside. The top and ends of this inner building are solid hardboard: the sides are pegboard. Plants (or seeds) are put on shelves inside this smaller building. About 30 to 45cm (12 to 18in) above each shelf is a battery of fluorescent tubes. The ideal number of tubes depends on the type of plants being raised but in general most growers choose between having an illumination level at the shelf of either 15,000 or 8,000 lux. A heater and a fan is sited on the top of the inner building so that warm or cold air can be circulated through the holes in the pegboard to keep the temperature inside constant. A thermostatically-operated vent is used to allow hot air to escape.

Growing Rooms for the Gardener

In order to reduce costs, many growers use much more rudimentary and practical growing rooms. A battery of fluorescent tubes is fitted to a reflector board suspended above the plants but the room itself is often a converted hut, glasshouse or even a plastic structure.

A growing room does not have to be a separate structure: it is possible to convert part of a garage or hut into one. The first thing to decide is how big it should be. Two benches 90cm (3ft) wide and $1 \cdot 5$m (5ft) long with 45 to 60cm (1½ to 2ft) between them will be adequate for most people. The benches can be made of any material which is strong enough to support the weight of the plants and soil. When a growing room is built inside another building, the outer shell can be made of polyurethane foam boarding with a PVC coating on the outside and a white, reflective coating on the inside. The inner shell should be made by nailing a hardboard top and ends on to a softwood frame. The sides should be pegboard. All the inside of the inner shell should be painted with a flat white paint and a gap of at least 23cm (9in) should be left between the inner and outer shells.

To get an illumination level of 15,000 lux, warm white fluorescent lights should be used at about 600 watts to the square metre (55w/sq ft) of bench. At this level a $1 \cdot 5$m by $0 \cdot 9$m (5ft by 3ft) bench would need eleven $1 \cdot 5$m (5ft) 80w fluorescent tubes. Similarly, an illumination level of 8,000 lux needs about 330w/m² (30w/sq ft) and a $1 \cdot 5$m by $0 \cdot 9$m (5ft by 3ft) bench would take six $1 \cdot 5$m (5ft) 80w tubes. Space the tubes so that they are closer at the edges of the bench than in the middle. A light meter can be used to check the evenness of illumination, but take care over the type used. A cosine-corrected meter should give the readings given above: a non-cosine-corrected meter will give lower readings – about three-quarters of those given.

A fan sited on top of the inner shell will be needed to ventilate the room. A two-bench room providing 15,000 lux needs a fan which is capable of moving about 28m³ of air a minute (1,000ft³/min). Larger or smaller rooms with higher or lower illumination need proportionately bigger or smaller fans. A vent (and cowl) will be needed on the side wall of the exterior shell and the fan should be built on to a sheet of hardboard dividing the space between the inner and outer shells to prevent the air being short-circuited.

A heater with about the same overall power as the fluorescent lights should be sited so that the fan blows air through it. The heater should be switched so that it cannot operate when the vent is open.

Intensity and Duration of Light

Apart from the intensity of light necessary for growing plants, the duration of light is also important. Many plants such as summer-flowering bedding plants benefit from being subjected for 24 hours a day to high light intensity, whereas other plants, such as chrysanthemums, are extremely sensitive to day length for their growth and bud development. Tomatoes must also have a dark period of at least 8 hours in every 24.

The table below gives some of the light and temperature information needed for a range of vegetables.

Plant	illumi-nation (lux)	hours of light a day	temperature light °C (°F)	dark °C (°F)	number of days in room
Aubergines	15,000	16	25 (78)	18 (65)	21
Cauliflowers	15,000	16	24 (75)	18 (65)	14 to 21
Celery	8,000	24	20 (68)	—	10
Lettuce	8,000	24	20 (68)	—	10
Mustard and Cress	8,000	24	21 (70)	—	3
Peppers	15,000	16	25 (78)	18 (65)	7 (after germination)
Tomatoes	15,000	16	23 (74)	19 (67)	21 (after germination)

It seems likely that with the economy of energy necessary today growing rooms or, more probably, growing boxes will become more and more used in both professional and amateur gardening circles. Much of the basic information such as exactly how much a plant will grow in a given period under the standard climate of the growing room has yet to be determined. When it is, the real value of the growing room may be realized. More precise information on the construction and use of growing rooms is available from electricity authorities, university research departments and advisory services in different countries.

Sheds

In earlier days, especially in the era when large garden staffs were employed on private estates or in private gardens, potting sheds were a very necessary part of gardening. They were used to give the gardeners shelter when they were mixing growing mixes, sowing seed or taking cuttings and potting plants. Now, with the advent of soilless mixes and the high cost of heating, most gardening activities are carried out in greenhouses or in sheds and garages whose prime purpose is not for gardening.

Modern sheds are used for many things. Their basic function is to store the equipment and accoutrements associated with outdoor activities including gardening and most will also be used to accommodate the overflow of household equipment. The secondary functions of the modern shed include: acting as a workshop, providing somewhere to store fruit and vegetables and providing space for some activities like propagating.

Choosing a Shed

When choosing a shed bear in mind the purpose for which you are going to use it. Most are free-standing buildings, but sheds attached to greenhouses and garages are also available.

Many people make a basic mistake by choosing a shed which is just big enough for their present needs without thinking about what they will need in the future. It is often the case that a $2 \cdot 1$ by $1 \cdot 5$m (7 by 5ft) shed which might be right now will be far too small in a couple of years time when a 3 by $2 \cdot 4$m (10 by 8ft) one might seem more suitable.

If a shed is to be used as a workshop or to provide extra space for propagation then it will need adequate natural light. If it is to be used mainly as a store, then the windows can be quite small and if it is to be sited well away from, and out of view of, the house then it may be wise to choose one which

does not have a window: this should help to deter vandals. Windows of sheds to be used as workshops should have some provision for opening them in the summer; for storage a permanently closed window is satisfactory.

When bulky items of equipment such as motorized lawn mowers and trolleys are to be stored, the doors must be wide enough to get the equipment in and out easily. Some sheds have double doors, others have sliding doors which may be useful if the shed is tucked away in some corner of the garden.

Sheds can be bought with or without a floor. Floors bought with sheds are usually floorboards nailed to lightweight timber joists. These make a shed feel warm and dry. But wooden floors tend to get damaged by heavy equipment and so some people prefer solid floors made of concrete or paving slabs.

Equipping a Shed

Guttering usually comes as an optional extra. Most people will find it worth having as it keeps the walls of the shed dry and the water can be collected and used for watering plants. Electricity for lighting and a power point for various items of equipment such as hedge cutters and power drills is essential if the shed is to be used as a workshop. It is useful to have a water supply near the shed for various activities such as watering plants, washing down equipment and flushing out sprayers.

A rack system along one of the walls is useful for storing hand tools. It will keep the tools off the floor and make them easy to find and ready when they are wanted. Shelves too should be fitted along at least one wall so that fertilizers can be stored off the ground and away from any dampness which could cause them to deteriorate. If insecticides, fungicides and weedkillers are to be stored, it is essential for the shed to have a cupboard which can be locked. As an extra safeguard, the cupboard should also be sited well out of reach of small children. Bins for soil, peat and other bulky materials are useful, if not imperative.

Maintenance

Brick-built and concrete sheds need very little maintenance. Wood sheds will require treating with preservative and some may need painting. Wood sheds often deteriorate around their bases and one of the main reasons for this is wet or damp foundations. Take extra care, when treating a shed with preservative, to make sure that the bottoms of the sides are well coated and never stand a shed directly on the soil.

9. Cultivation

Cultivating the Soil

Cultivating the soil is basically the process of moving soil particles with the intention of increasing aeration and improving drainage. This process will help create conditions under which plant roots thrive and useful soil bacteria become active and multiply. The bacteria will, in turn, break down the soil organic matter and liberate plant nutrients which can be taken up by plant roots. Cultivation is generally followed by an increase in soil fertility but, on regularly cultivated soils, the increased bacterial activity will lead to a drop in organic matter level. So it is essential to top up the organic matter in these soils by a programme of manuring. This is even more important on regularly cultivated soils where the naturally available organic matter is removed – taking vegetables from a vegetable plot, for example.

The main ways of cultivating the soil are digging, forking, raking and hoeing.

Digging

There are two main reasons for digging the soil: to destroy weeds and to break up the soil so that air and water can penetrate it more easily. An ample supply of air and good drainage are essential components of a fertile soil – see *Soil*. Most digging is done in the late autumn and early winter but do not attempt to dig heavy clay soils if they are very wet. The compaction caused by treading on the soil may do more harm than the digging will do good. Some people advocate no-digging techniques in which layers of organic matter are continuously added to the top of the soil and incorporated in it by earthworm activity. There is little doubt that on some soils these methods work well and on gravel soils it may be the best way of gardening but few people doubt that effective cultivation is well worthwhile and the

best method of ensuring a regular supply of good crops.

There are three principal systems of digging: plain digging where the soil is cultivated to one spade's depth, double digging (or bastard trenching) where it is cultivated to the depth of two spades and trenching where it is cultivated three spades deep. If soil is continuously dug to one spade's depth then a hard pan can build up just below this depth and hinder free drainage. Deeper digging can break up this hard pan.

In general when you are turning over an uncultivated part of the garden for the first time, it is wise to dig it at least to two spade's depth. If the soil is then used as a vegetable patch or a flower bed for bedding plants, it should be double dug approximately once every five years, being plain dug in the other four years. Double digging is laborious and it may help to divide the area of ground into five roughly equal portions and to double dig one fifth of the area each year, rotating it around the plot in subsequent years. If an area of garden is to be planted with perennial plants – herbaceous perennials, fruit trees, shrubs and so on – it should be double dug before these are put in.

With all three systems of digging it helps if you are methodical and neat: a garden line is essential to help you mark out the area to be dug. The first step in each system is to take out a trench of soil. If the area to be dug is fairly short, this soil should be transported to the far end of the plot but if it is fairly long then it helps to divide the plot lengthwise and to take out a trench which is only one half of the width of the plot and simply to move the soil across the lengthwise division. In the first case you will be working down the plot and filling in the last trench with the soil you took out of the first. In the second case you will be working down one side of the plot, turning around at

Opposite: Thorough cultivation of the ground in a new garden will pay dividends when your plants reach maturity

Plain (or single) Digging

Take out a trench about 25cm (10in) deep and about 25cm (10in) wide at one end of the plot. Transport the soil to the far end of the plot

Fill in the trench by taking out another trench alongside it

Always face the trench and turn the soil forward and over so that any weeds are buried at the bottom of the first trench

Repeat the process, filling in the final trench with the soil taken from the first one. Manure or compost can be placed at the bottom of each trench as you go

the end and working up the other side to where the soil for the last trench is waiting. The lengthwise division should be marked on the plot before you start by stretching the garden line down the middle and taking out a small notch or furrow in the soil with a spade.

When doing the actual digging there are two basic rules to follow. Always put the blade of the spade vertically into the soil: this means that the handle of the spade will be sloping slightly away from you and this, in turn, helps the process of levering the soil out. On some soils it may be advisable to drive the spade in at right angles to the trench before trying to lift the soil out. This helps get a clean cut and the maximum amount of soil on the spade. The second rule is that you should never mix top soil with subsoil. Some gardeners believe in some mixing of the two soils in an attempt to increase the overall depth of fertile soil, but it takes many years for subsoil to become fertile and, on the whole, it is best to reserve your efforts for increasing the fertility of the top soil.

Plain digging This can be done with a spade or, on heavier soils, with a fork. Dig a trench about 25 to 30cm (10 to 12in) wide and the depth of the spade or fork deep and move the soil. Then, facing the trench, dig a second trench and use the soil from this one to fill in the first trench. Twist the spade or fork a little when putting the soil into the first trench so that the upper layers of the soil and any weeds are put at the bottom of the first trench. Repeat the process down the plot filling in the final trench with the soil taken out of the first trench.

Double digging This is best done with a spade and a fork. Take out a trench about 60cm (2ft) wide and the depth of the spade deep and move the soil. Step into the bottom of this trench and use a fork to break up the soil at the bottom to the full depth of its tines. Take care to break up all the soil at the bottom of the trench, not just that in the middle. This means that the soil has now been cultivated to an overall depth of about 50cm (20in). Now use the garden line to mark another 60cm (2ft) trench alongside the first one. As this process will have to be repeated down the whole length of the plot, it helps if you have a 60cm (2ft) marker or mark the whole plot into 60cm (2ft) lengths before you start. Getting these measurements correct is absolutely essential if you are to move exactly the same amount of soil from trench to trench and to keep the plot level and avoid ending up with a series of ridges and valleys. Soil from the second trench should now be used to fill in the first one. To do this, turn so that you are digging across the trench and roughly divide the

Double Digging

Use a garden line to divide the plot lengthwise. Drive pegs in at 60cm (2ft) intervals. Take out a trench 60cm (2ft) wide and the depth of a spade deep. Move the soil as shown.

Fork over the bottom of the trench

Take out a second 60cm (2ft) trench and use the soil to fill in the first one. Note how the soil is dug and where each spadeful is placed

Manure can be spread over the bottom of the trench after forking or it can be spread over the surface to be dug

60cm (2ft) width of the trench into three widths of the spade. Use the spade to make a cut down the side of the garden line, make a parallel cut about a spade's width across the trench and remove a spadeful of soil from the ground nearest to the garden line. Put this soil in the equivalent place in the first trench so that it makes a good wall with the soil in the second trench which has yet to be removed. Take out the other two spadefuls to complete digging across the width of the trench and put these in the equivalent places in the first trench. Continue across the plot until the second trench is completely formed. Stand in the bottom of the second trench and throw all the crumbs up on to the soil on top of the first trench and break up the soil at the bottom of the second trench with fork. Move the garden line another 60cm (2ft) down the plot and continue.

When double digging a very grassy plot or lawn, move the turf from the first trench

along with the soil to the far end of the plot. Put the grass from the second trench face down at the bottom of the first trench after the soil at the bottom of the first trench has been forked over. Chop the grass with a spade and then continue as for normal double digging.

Trenching This method of cultivation involves digging the soil to a depth of about 75cm (30in). Take out a trench about 90cm (3ft) wide and move the soil as before. Now divide the soil at the bottom of the trench into two strips each 45cm (18in) wide. Remove the soil from the forward strip to a spade's depth and move this but keep it separate from the soil taken from the top of the trench. Fork over the soil at the bottom of this 50cm (20in) deep trench so that the overall depth of cultivation is 75cm (30in). Step on to the second 45cm (18in) wide strip and turn the soil on to the more forward 45cm (18in) wide strip as if you were double digging. Fork over the soil at the

Trenching

This method of digging cultivates the soil to a depth of about 75cm (30in). The shaded areas are those which are forked

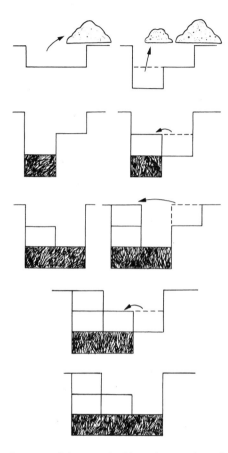

bottom of the trench this makes so that all the soil in the 90cm (3ft) wide trench has been dug to a depth of 75cm (30in). Mark out a 45cm (18in) wide trench alongside the first trench and turn the soil from the first spit of this trench on to the more forward 45cm (18in) strip of the first trench and turn the second spit of soil on to the 45cm (18in) wide strip of the first trench which has only been forked over. The new (second) trench will now be about 25cm (10in) deep and the bottom should be forked over. Mark out another 45cm (18in) wide trench and repeat as before.

Adding manure Digging is a good time to add manure or other bulky organic materials to the soil. Do not bury manures more than the depth of a spade deep: they should be used to increase the fertility of the top soil and are wasted lower down.

When single digging, spread the manure over the ground to be dug and scrape the manure on the ground for the next trench on to the sloping side of the previous trench. Use the soil from the ground you have just taken the manure from to fill in the trench

and cover the manure in it. After a bit of practice at digging, you will not need to scrape the manure into the trench but will be able to turn it in and bury it at the same time as you are digging out the next trench. You can use a similar system when double digging or trenching but remember in each case that the manure must not be buried deeper than the depth of a spade.

Ridging

This is a method of cultivating heavy, badly-drained soils so that the maximum soil area is exposed to the weathering action of winter frosts. Mark out the plot into an odd number of strips each about 75cm (30in) wide. Dig a small trench across one end of the first strip about 30cm (12in) wide, a spade's depth deep and the width of the first strip – 75cm (30in) – long. Put the soil from this trench in the corner of the plot diagonally opposite to it. Now dig across the first strip turning the soil forwards as you go. The soil from the centre of the strip should be turned straight forward and that from the right- and left-hand sides should be turned forwards and inwards to form a ridge. Turn round at the end of the first strip and work backwards along the second strip until the whole plot has been ridged. Ridging is best done in late autumn or early winter and the soil surface will need levelling in the following spring before sowing or planting. This can be done by forking.

Forking

Digging over the soil with a fork is a method of breaking up and levelling soil. Soil can be turned over and broken down by striking it with the back of the tines. A fork can be used when the soil in an established shrubbery or border needs aerating (but take care not to damage roots) or to prepare the ground before planting. On heavy soils a fork may be a better tool than a spade for digging.

Raking

The main object of raking is to produce a level, finely broken-down soil surface which is ready for sowing seeds into. A soil in this condition is said to have a good tilth. Raking alone will not produce a good tilth; it is merely one of the last stages in the process towards achieving it. A good tilth depends upon the overall condition of the soil and if it is difficult to achieve a crumbly seed bed in spring then steps should be taken towards improving the soil structure by adding bulky organic manures, sand or lime, or by winter digging – see *Soil*.

It takes some skill and judgment to achieve a satisfactory seed bed by raking. Do not attempt to rake if the soil surface is wet as the soil particles will tend to stick together and on heavy soils you may compact the upper layers of the top soil. Ideally raking should be done on a warm, dry day after the excess surface moisture has evaporated from the soil. It should not be done on a hot dry day as the soil surface might be too hard to break down well. The first step in preparing a seed bed is to hoe or lightly fork over the winter dug soil to a depth of about 8cm (3in) until the surface is well broken down and crumbly. Tread the bed to firm it. Then use the rake lightly with long sweeping strokes. The forward stroke should break down the soil particles, the backward stroke should collect stones and large, hard lumps of soil. Continue to rake the seed bed until it is absolutely level and fine. When broadcasting seeds, you can rake the bed in one direction only, leaving tiny furrows on the surface of the soil. Broadcast seed will fall into these furrows and raking the bed at right angles will then cover them.

Hoeing

The traditional way of keeping a garden free from weeds is to cultivate the top few centimetres of the soil surface and to chop weed seedlings down with a tool known as a hoe. As well as eliminating weeds, hoeing breaks up caked soil surfaces letting air and rainwater reach the roots of plants. The effect hoeing has on water already in the soil is open to dispute. Some people say that it reduces losses through evaporation by forming a mulch of loose soil on the surface. Others say that it increases water loss by exposing more soil surface to drying air.

To be really effective, hoeing should be started soon after seed sowing or planting while the soil is still quite friable and the weeds are small. Once the ground becomes hard and densely covered with weeds, hoeing will simply sever them at the soil surface leaving their crowns and roots behind to regenerate. At the same time the hoe will be difficult to control and could bounce off the hard ground causing damage to plants. Weed seedlings are best destroyed by cutting them off at the ground level and not by dragging them out of the soil, in which case they might easily take root again. To do this the hoe blade must be sharp.

There are two types of long-handled hoe and both are known by a variety of names.
Draw hoe This hoe generally has a half-moon blade attached at right angles to a swan-necked staff. The blade is usually turned slightly inwards. To hoe with this tool, you chop the soil by bringing the hoe blade down and towards you. Some people move slowly forwards while doing this, others move backwards. The soil rapidly brings the hoe blade to a halt once it hits it and so you have quite a lot of control over the tool.

A draw hoe is quite useful when working between irregularly spaced plants or on hard ground. An onion hoe is essentially a miniature draw hoe and can be used for accurate hoeing among delicate plants such as young onions.
Dutch hoe This tool is sometimes known as a push hoe. It has a rectangular blade set in more or less the same plane as the handle. To use it you push it shallowly into the soil in a series of short forward sweeps while walking slowly backwards. It is not as easy to use as the draw hoe.

Planting

One of the most critical stages in any plant's life is when it is being planted. There are a few basic rules: do not attempt to plant when the soil is too wet, too dry or too cold, make sure that you set the plants at the correct depth, and plant them firmly. See *Ornamental Plants* and *Gardens* for details of planting specific types of plant.
Soil conditions Ideally the soil should be wet enough to cling together when you squeeze it in your hand but fall apart again when you let it drop to the ground. Trees and shrubs are generally planted between the late autumn and early spring. In many areas, particularly in the UK, winters can be very wet and it is much better to plant in frosty conditions provided you can break down the soil. In many parts of North America the winter is too severe to allow winter planting and it all has to be done in the late autumn or early spring. If you can manage to break through the surface layer of frozen soil, you may find the soil beneath in an almost ideal state for planting.
Planting depth As a general rule, try to plant to the same depth as the plant was previously growing. For trees, shrubs and vines this usually means planting them to the soil mark on their stem. With herbaceous plants, it usually means planting them to the point at which the stem joins the roots, or a little lower.

A few plants like lupins and roses drive their roots deeply into the soil but most plants are much more shallow-rooting. When taking out planting holes, make the hole much wider than it is deep leaving plenty of room to spread the roots out without doubling them up at the ends.

Container-grown plants can be planted at any time as long as the soil conditions are suitable. Water them well before taking them out of their containers and take care not to disturb the rootball. In their normal planting season it may help if you tease out the roots a little before planting.

Protect evergreens by erecting a hessian screen on the windward side

Dibbling

A dibber is a simple pointed tool which can be used to make planting holes for seedlings and young plants. In the greenhouse it can be useful to have a range of home-made dibbers for the various stages of plant movement from seed tray to potting. A dibber for the open garden needs to be more robust and you can make one from the handle end of a broken spade or fork with about 23cm (9in) of the shaft attached. The shaft should be tapered to the end.

To use a dibber, make a hole by pushing the shaft into the soil and withdrawing it. Then, hold the young plant by a leaf and lower it into the hole to the correct depth. Push soil back into the hole by pushing the dibber into the soil at a shallow angle about 5cm (2in) from the stem of the plant. This action will firm the soil around the plant and, at the same time it will make a series of small hollows around it which will conduct water to the root area. Dibbling is an ideal method for planting vegetables from a seed bed, such as brassicas and leeks which quickly make new roots and grow away. Tiny seedlings can be pricked out with the aid of a small dibber. See diagram in *Tools and Equipment*. The main advantage of dibbling is that it is a quick and easy way of planting. But there are a number of drawbacks and these are:

1) Pushing the dibber into wet, heavy soil smears and compresses the walls of the hole making them difficult for the roots to penetrate. See illustrations in *Soil*.

2) The hole is often made deeper than the roots which means that they may be left suspended and in risk of drying out.

3) Roots must be forced into a narrow hole when their natural distribution may demand more space.

With the exception of tolerant vegetable plants, it is much safer to plant young plants with a trowel. Dibbers are often used when puddling.

Puddling

Setting out young plants in a planting hole filled with water is called puddling. It is not a procedure recommended for all kinds of plants on all types of soil but it can be used for young brassica plants and certain moisture-loving vegetables, such as celery and leeks.

In well-worked, light soil, the water poured into the planting hole may be enough to settle the roots firmly without further attention. On heavier soils, however, water is more likely to lodge in the planting hole and to seal it with a fine, sticky surface which is virtually impenetrable by fine roots instead of settling soil round the roots. On moist soils puddling should be avoided but where a bog, stream-side or pool margin garden is being made the ornamental plants, such as certain iris, gunnera, astilbes and some primulas, have well enough adapted to partially waterlogged soil conditions for puddling to be quite acceptable.

Staking and Supporting

There are many reasons why plants need support. Some, like peas and runner beans, are natural climbing plants and need support to keep their crops clear of the ground. Newly planted trees and shrubs, which have poorly established root systems and quite large tops, need support to prevent excess rocking and damage by wind. Flowers, like dahlias, which have large blooms also need support to prevent wind damage. Plants, like tomatoes, and fruit trees, like plums, may need support because the weight of the fruits can be too heavy for the plants to support by themselves.

Supports in the ornamental garden should be 1) sufficiently strong (this applies to other parts of the garden too), 2) situated so that they do not damage the plants they are supporting, and 3) inconspicuous.

Strength For supporting most annual bedding plants, a few small twigs should suffice. Most dahlias and other herbaceous plants can be supported by bamboo canes: these will be adequate for outdoor tomatoes too. For really heavy herbaceous plants it might be necessary to use $25 \times 25m$ (1in by 1in) softwood stakes and for supporting trees $50 \times 50m$ (2in by 2in) stakes are better. As a general guide, stakes for trees should be wider than the stem of the tree at planting time.

Positioning There are basically three methods of supporting trees. Vertical stakes should be driven into the soil on the windward side of the tree at planting time. Do this while the roots are visible so that none are damaged. The top of the stake should be positioned so that it is just below the lowest branch of the tree. If it is higher, some of the lower branches could be damaged by it as the tree rocks in windy weather. Ties are just as important as the stakes. If they are too tight they will either break or restrict the tree and interrupt the growth. If they are too loose, they will let the tree rock and the stake may chafe the trunk at the point of tying. Ties which can be adjusted as the stem or trunk grows are ideal but satisfactory home-made ties can be made from nylon stockings, heavy-duty polythene strips, bicycle inner tubes, rubber strips, sacking and, in fact, almost anything which is flexible, adjustable and durable. Use two ties to secure a tree. The first should be close to the crown of branches and the second lower down on the stem.

Trees which have branches heavily laden with fruit can be supported by a large stake driven in close to the trunk and protruding over the top of the branches. The branches can then be tied to the top of the stake to give a sort of maypole effect. Forked stakes can also be used to prop up individual branches and very weak branches can even be tied to two or three stronger ones with string or webbing.

Runner beans need substantial support because they present a large area to the wind. There are several widely used methods of support. The usual method involves a double row of stout bamboo poles or long hazel rods, about 2·1m (7ft) long, thrust in the ground so that each pair (one from each row) crosses at the top. Horizontal poles or rods should be laid in the V formed by the crossing poles and tied securely in place to form a rigid frame. A second method involves pushing the poles or rods in the ground vertically and securing them by stretching two or three rows of heavy twine between them and securing these to end poles which have additional supports – rather like tent guy lines. In a third method the poles or rods are pushed into the ground so that they all cross at the top rather like a wigwam. They should be firmly tied where they cross. A similar method involves using a central pole with wires tied to the top and anchored to the ground around the circumference of a circle about 75cm (30in) away from the pole. This method will take about 10 bean plants.

Peas can be supported by bushy twigs or by using nets stretched between vertical poles.

Mulching

A mulch is simply something which covers the surface of the soil around plants. It can be organic such as leaf-mould, peat, com-post, well-rotted animal manure, straw and so on. Or it can be man-made like black polythene or even tinfoil.

The reasons for mulching There are three reasons for mulching: 1) to prevent evap-oration of water from the soil surface through the action of sun or wind; 2) to keep weeds down and prevent some plants becoming mud-splashed in heavy rain; 3) to increase the organic content of the soil.

Using mulches Most mulches are applied in the spring just as new growth is about to begin. At this time weed seedlings will not be far advanced and can be effectively smothered and the soil will still be moist. Organic mulches should be spread at least 25 to 50mm (1 to 2in) deep, 75mm (3in) is better. Keep the mulching material away from the base of the plants being mulched. Acidic, organic mulches such as peat can be used to encourage better root development in naturally shallow-rooting shrubs like rhododendrons, azaleas and heathers and will help to keep the plant roots cool in the warmer summer months. Straw, peat and leaf-mould mulches have little food value and are best used between rows of herb-aceous plants. The more nutritious mulches like animal manure and good garden com-post are useful in the flower garden and on vegetable plots where their additional food supplies will be appreciated.

Sowing Seed Outside

Many flower seeds are sown broadcast by spreading them lightly and randomly over the area where they are to grow. Vegetable seeds, on the other hand, are generally sown in straight, narrow furrows or grooves made in a prepared seed bed. These grooves are known as drills and the process of taking them out and sowing seed therein is called drilling. Drills can be made in boxes of seed mix for sowing under glass but most are made in prepared seed beds out of doors. The thoroughness of the preparation of this bed will determine how easy it is to make a satisfactory drill.

A drill can vary in size from one with a flat bottom and up to 15cm (6in) wide for sow-ing peas and beans, to a shallow depression 12mm (½in) wide at the top and tapering to the base for sowing lettuce seeds. The depth of the drill depends on the size of the seed, the type of soil and the season. A rule of thumb is that the seed should be covered to twice its own diameter with soil. But if seed is sown early and there is a risk of frost damage at germination, drills should be made deeper. In sandy dry soils the drills should be deeper than in heavy wet soils to give more protection against loss through the seed drying out.

Planting a tree in the lawn. *From the top*: marking out a circle in the lawn; cutting out the turf; digging out the soil – keep subsoil and top soil separate; the grafting point; setting a stake in the hole before planting; tying the tree to the stake; securing the tree again after filling in the earth; the finished job

Drills are usually made with a draw hoe, but Dutch hoes, pointed sticks, garden rakes and spades can also be used. A garden line fixed at either end of the seed bed and secured tightly at soil level should be used to guide the tool so that a straight drill can be drawn. When using a draw hoe it should be held with one corner in the soil and with the bottom edge resting on a garden line. It should then be drawn along the line in a series of steady pulls making sure that the drill is the same depth throughout and not shallower at the ends than in the middle. A stick can be used in a similar way. To use a

Dutch hoe, hold it almost vertically with one corner in the soil and draw it sharply towards you. Rakes can be used by pressing the handle into the soil or by pulling a drill out using the end of the rake in the soil and the back of it resting on the garden line. A spade can be used to take out a wide, shallow trench for peas but on heavy soils it is better to use a draw hoe to avoid smearing the soil at the bottom of the drill.

Once the drill is made, the next step is to sow the seed. Always sow thinly – overcrowding usually weakens the seedlings and means more thinning out later. Larger seeds should be spaced out separately or sown in small pinches of three or four seeds every 5 to 10cm (2 to 4in) along the drill. Smaller seeds can be mixed with very fine sand to make thin, even sowing easier. When sowing seeds in double drills – for broad beans, for example – stagger the seeds along the drills.

Refill the drill by gently drawing the edges into the centre with a hoe, by scuffling with your feet so that the edges fall into the centre or by pulling the soil back into the drill with a rake. Finally, water the drill well and mark each end with a label, recording the particulars of the sowing on one of them. Some people prefer to water the drill before sowing the seed to avoid the risk of washing the seed deeper in the soil. In very sandy or very heavy soils, germinating seed can be given a better start by making the drill a little deeper than normal and lining it with moist peat.

Thinning
If plants are left crowded together they become spindly, weak and prone to disease. To give them a chance to reach healthy maturity they have to be thinned.

Thinning is very important for those plants which are sown where they are to mature – carrots, turnips, beetroot and other root vegetables and most hardy annuals, for example. Some plants may need thinning before they are eventually transplanted – like wallflowers and brassicas sown in a seed bed.

When thinning plants which are to be transplanted later, the operation can be done at one sweep. But thinning seedlings growing in their final quarters is best done in two operations. The first, when the seedlings are very small, should aim at reducing the number of plants in a row to about twice the eventual number, that is, the seedlings should be spaced at half their final distance apart. The second and final thinning operation can take place a few weeks later when the effects of the first have had time to show and any seedlings which have failed to grow can easily be seen. The first thinning should

be done very carefully, disturbing the seedlings left behind as little as possible. To do this, put one finger on the ground on either side of the seedling to be removed and draw the seedling out with the other hand. The final thinning can be done with a draw hoe and the thinnings either planted elsewhere or, in the case of vegetables, eaten. Never leave thinnings on the soil – they can encourage pests and diseases.

Thinning seedlings is most easily done when the soil is damp but not wet. After thinning make sure that the remaining seedlings are firmly planted and, in the case of carrots, that all gaps left behind where seedlings have been removed are filled in.

Hardening off
Plants growing in greenhouses, cold frames or in similar protected conditions have softer and more delicate tissue than plants accustomed to natural outdoor conditions. Placing plants grown indoors directly outside into a lower temperature and wind will lead to a check in growth, damage to tissues and wilting, because of rapid water loss from the leaves. This effect is most pronounced in spring when most transplanting is done. Later, in summer, when air and soil conditions are optimal for growth, plants experience much less change in their environment in going from a greenhouse or living room to the garden, and any check in growth will be minimal if the plants are kept well watered.

If the environment around plants is changed slowly, their cell tissue can adapt to the changes in temperature, sunlight and air movement by making thicker walls on the outer cells and by reducing pore apertures. Giving them time and slowly introducing plants to lower temperatures is known as hardening off. It is vital that plants are introduced to outdoor conditions in stages. In general plants raised under glass and artificially heated should first be allowed to become accustomed to a much lower temperature while they are still under glass. Ventilation should also be increased. Then they

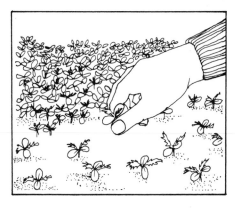

Thin the seedlings when they are large enough to handle easily. Take care not to disturb those which are to remain

should be transferred to an unheated (cold) frame with a sunny aspect. Keep the frame light closed at night and on cool days for the first week. Later, ventilation can be increased until the light can be removed altogether. Keep an eye on the plants. If they continue to grow while they are being hardened off, then all is well, but if they start to get brown streaks or blotches then slow down the acclimatization process, and close the light in the evening if the night is likely to be cold.

Sowing Seed Out of Doors – Broadcasting

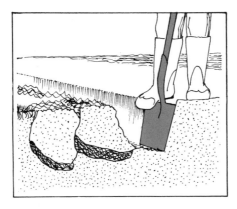

Dig the soil to at least one spade's depth in autumn, incorporating compost or manure. Leave the surface of the soil rough

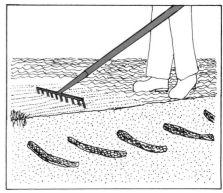

In spring rake the bed level

Firm by treading and rake again

Rake once more to produce a fine tilth

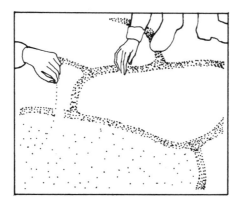

Mark out the areas to be sown with sharp sand and sow the seed thinly and evenly within its defined area

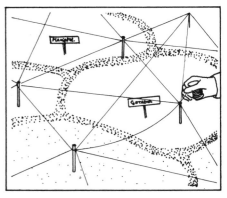

Label the areas and protect the young seed from birds by using black cotton stretched between short sticks

148

Potting

Potting is part of the programme of plant raising that begins with sowing the seed, continues with pricking out at a wider spacing in another container before the plant is given its first individual home in a small pot. This is the potting stage. As plants get older and bigger they need a richer food supply than a seed mix can provide and need moving into a potting mix. There are many proprietary soil-based and soilless mixes that are suitable for all stages of potting.

In the days when clay pots and soil-based mixes were used exclusively, it was the rule to improve drainage by placing pieces of broken earthenware pot, known as crocks, in the base of the clay pot over the drainage holes. But with the adoption of plastic pots and freely-draining potting mixes, this has been shown to be no longer essential.

The first priority in potting is to have clean pots, the second is to have a specially prepared, part-sterilized potting mix. The size of the pot is governed by the root area of the plant to be potted, and should permit room for new roots to extend before potting on to a larger pot becomes necessary.

For the first potting, fill a pot loosely to the rim with a potting mix which is just moist enough to cling together when squeezed in your hand but dry enough to fall apart if you drop it on to the potting bench. If it is soilless, it should be moister than this but not so wet as to drip water when you squeeze it tightly. Next make a depression to take the roots and gently lift the plant to be potted from its container first loosening the mix with a plant label or similar object and holding it by a leaf rather than by its stem. Some mix may have to be scooped from the pot to make a hole large enough to take the roots without doubling-up or spiralling them. When filled and settled, the plant should be buried to the same depth as before. The mix in the pot should then be gently pressed down with a finger of each hand and a little more potting mix added to bring the level to just below the rim. Finally the pot should be watered from a can with a fine rose and the plant stood in a slightly shaded position for a few days.

Once the plant fills the initial pot with roots, it is time for potting on to a larger size. This can only be judged accurately by examining the rootball. To do this, hold the base of the pot in one hand and put the fingers of your other on either side of the plant stem. Invert the pot and tap the rim against the edge of a bench or table. The whole rootball should fall out cleanly if the mix is well infiltrated by roots. If the roots run around the edge of the ball, it is time to make the transfer to a larger pot. Put a

Sowing Seed Out of Doors – Drilling

Dig the soil deeply in autumn. In spring break down the surface of the soil, firm by treading and rake to a fine tilth

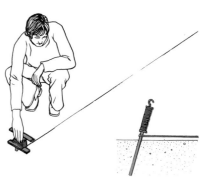

Stretch a line prior to taking out the drill. Push the stake at the end of the line into the soil at an angle so that as the stake is pushed down the line tightens

Take out a drill using a draw hoe with the blade resting on the line. Use your foot to prevent the line moving

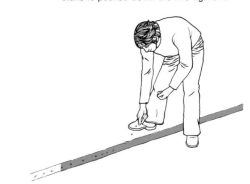

Sow seed thinly

Mark the end of the drill and cover the seeds by raking soil over them from both sides of the drill

crock for drainage in the base of the larger pot if a clay one is being used and cover it with a little potting mix.

Adjust the level of mix in the bottom so that the plant with its rootball intact will be just buried when the new pot is filled and settled. If the roots are matted and wound around the rootball, gently open up the base

Potting on. Removing the plant from its original pot; setting it in the centre of the new pot; firming the growing mix around the plant

of the ball to encourage the roots to explore the newly available space. With the ball centred in the new pot and held in place, trickle potting mix around the edges and firm it down with your fingers or with a dibber until the ball is just covered. The extent of firming varies from plant to plant. Older or more woody plants should be firmed more than younger or soft ones. For plants such as chrysanthemums which need heavy firming and large pots, it may be necessary to use a firming stick made out of a broom handle instead of your fingers. Finally, thoroughly water the plant. If young plants are grown in peat pots, the complete pot should be replanted but it is helpful to pull away the base first.

Forcing

Forcing induces plants to mature or bloom out of season. It might seem that the word forcing could be used to describe any form of protected cultivation but this is not necessarily the case. Greenhouses, for example. can be used to hasten the maturity of plants but they can also enable a plant from a warmer climate to adopt its natural growth programme in colder regions.

Evolution has ensured that plants mature, flower and make seed in the seasons most favourable to their survival. They have been programmed to experience seasonal changes in temperature and light, and only when the programme has been completed will they reach full maturity. This is why a plant will not necessarily flower earlier just because it is brought into the warmth of a greenhouse or room. The life cycle of plants is a very complex subject and is still not fully understood. But over the years experiment and experience have shown that many vegetables, bulbs, flowers and fruit can be successfully forced.

Forcing Vegetables

The purpose of forcing vegetables is to produce crops earlier than they would be ready if grown under normal conditions. Stools, crowns or roots of certain vegetables can be lifted and housed in an artificially heated forcing shed. This can be a garden shed, an area below a greenhouse bench a cellar or even a cupboard under the stairs or beneath the kitchen sink. Four important vegetables – rhubarb, seakale, Witloof chicory, and mint – are easily forced.

Rhubarb In the late autumn lift well-developed and ripened roots, which are at least two years old, and lay them outside on the soil surface to expose them to frost. From November (or just before the first heavy frosts) until February these roots should be kept in a forcing shed, placed close together with some well-rotted compost or finely-sifted soil around them and kept in darkness by blacking out the area around them with black plastic. Forcing starts at 7°C (44°F) and after ten days the temperature should be increased to 10°C (50°F) and then gradually to 15°C (60°F). Keep the roots moist but not saturated and the sticks should be ready to pull four to six weeks after forcing starts. Suitable varieties include 'Timperley Early', 'Prince Albert', 'Victoria' and 'The Sutton'.

Seakale Forced seakale provides an excellent vegetable crop in February and March. It can be forced *in situ* or under cover. Established plants are needed for both methods and those which have spent one year in a nursery bed and which were planted in April 50cm (20in) apart in both directions are most suitable. During the summer the bed will need weeding, at least three hoeings, and any flower heads should be removed as soon as they appear. Apply a mulch of organic matter in May to feed the plants and to conserve moisture. For outdoor forcing, cover the crowns in November with tall wooden boxes or old garbage cans/dustbins. These must be light tight, or the young growth will become bitter. Pull the shoots when they are about 15cm (6in) long. After cropping protect the crowns from frost. In the following summer feed the plants with plenty of organic matter. To force crowns indoors, lift them when they are well-ripened and their leaves have died down (usually in late November). Remove any straggling growth and bring the crowns indoors. Follow the general cultivation instructions given for rhubarb but start the temperature at 10°C (50°F) and increase it to 15°C (60°F).

Chicory and mint With chicory, follow a similar routine to seakale and rhubarb but keep the temperature around 10°C (50°F) as higher temperatures lead to less compact heads. See *Blanching*.

To produce out-of-season mint, plant matured roots in a well-manured bed in a light place in December and maintain a temperature of 18°C (65°F) and a humid atmosphere. Young shoots should be ready for cutting in about six weeks.

Forcing Bulbs

Most flowers which can be forced have flower embryos already formed within buds, scales or tunics ready for emergence when they receive the right amount of heat and moisture. If these flowering initials are not present then no amount of forcing will produce a flower.

Some plants have a relatively simple programme. Lily of the valley, for example, can be brought into flower at any time of the year as long as the rhizomes are chilled immediately before subjecting them to warmth. A number of spring-flowering bulbs will behave in the same way and can be brought into flower early by artificially simulating a season at the wrong time. Daffodil and tulip bulbs are subjected to cooling treatment, and hyacinths to heat treatment, which results in their flowering weeks before untreated bulbs.

Hyacinths, daffodils, crocuses and a number of tulips can be mildly forced by plunging them in a cool place after planting to let them develop an adequate root system before they are forced by heat. To do this plant the bulbs as soon as they are obtainable in pots or containers. Use ordinary potting mix if the pots have drainage holes; if not, use bulb fibre which contains charcoal. Plant the bulbs with their tips at the surface of the mix. Ideally, they should then be buried in the garden under 15cm (6in) of

Forcing rhubarb

151

Pricking Out

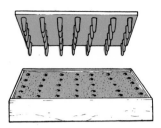

Fill a box with growing mix and firm. Holes can be made by using a small dibber but a multi-dibber makes the task easier

Always hold seedlings by their leaves. Lever them from the seed box by using a knife or plastic label

Never hold the stems

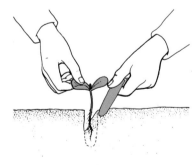

Use a small dibber to replace soil around the seedling when planting

soil or ashes with each pot wrapped in newspaper. If this is not possible they should be kept in an unheated cellar, cool cupboard, or cold frame, wrapped in newspaper to exclude light. If the containers were well wrapped and the mix well watered beforehand, the bulbs should not need any attention until about eight weeks later when they should be checked to see if they have pale shoots protruding about 2 to 5cm (1 to 2in) above the surface of the mix. The buds of tulips or hyacinths must be well clear of the neck of the bulb before they are brought into subdued light at a temperature around 10°C (50°F). Water as required to keep the mix moist. When the leaves are green and the flower bud can be seen swelling inside them, move the bulbs to a warmer room to hasten flowering. Once the bulbs have finished flowering, the flower heads (not the stalks) should be removed and the bulbs should be planted in the garden to recover. It may take a few years before they flower well again in the garden and they should be allowed at least three or four years to recover fully before forcing is attempted again.

Forcing Flowers and Fruit

A number of plants can be brought into a greenhouse to fruit or flower early and these include strawberries, fruit trees in tubs, a few herbaceous perennials such as astilbe, dicentra and helleborus and a number of flowering shrubs including azaleas, most flowering cherries, roses, forsythias, lilacs, philadelphus, spiraeas and viburnums. Use only strongly growing plants and grow them permanently in containers. Bury the containers to their rims in a bed of sand, ashes or soil during the summer while the plants are grown out of doors. In late autumn or early winter months bring the plants into a cool greenhouse or conservatory but do not give them a warm atmosphere until a few weeks before flowering. Spring-flowering shrubs for example should be brought into warmth in February and the temperature for the first two weeks should not exceed 10°C (50°F) with the lengthening days. Ventilate well. Forced plants will need careful treatment when they are returned to the open garden and should be well fed, watered and properly pruned. If this is done they can be mildly forced for a number of years.

A number of flowering pot plants purchased from florists are brought on out of their natural season. Shrubby azaleas can be set out in the garden after spring frosts and can be gently forced again in the following late autumn. The red-bracted poinsettias bought from florists are programmed by manipulation of day length and often

dwarfed chemically, so they will not perform in the same way again if they are kept in a greenhouse. Miniature pot chrysanthemums are treated similarly, but these can be planted in the open garden where they will grow into tall, unspectacular natural season chrysanthemums.

Blanching Celery – Trenching

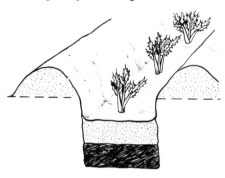

Take out a trench about 25cm (10in) across and the depth of a spade. Fork over the soil in the bottom of the trench and incorporate plenty of manure or compost. Return about 10cm (4in) of soil to the trench and plant the celery

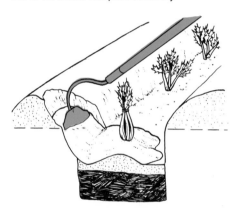

When the celery reaches about 30cm (12in) high, remove side shoots, tie the stalks just below the leaves and replace soil from either side of the trench

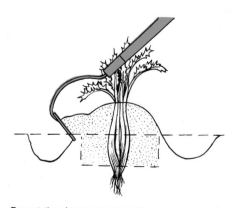

Repeat the above process at three-week intervals. In the final operation soil should be neatly mounded as shown

Blanching

Excluding or partially excluding light from stems or leaves of plants leads to growth with a reduced fibre content which is softer and more succulent than normal growth. This is known as blanching and blanched stems are longer and leaf blades smaller than those exposed to full light. Blanched parts are also pale in colour because the green colouring pigment, chlorophyll, cannot be produced in the absence of sunlight. This lack of colour can make some plants more attractive in appearance. Plants in darkness grow more quickly than those in light but their growth is weaker and as a rule they should not be blanched until they are well developed or until they are approaching maturity. Leeks are the exception: they should be blanched a little at a time from midsummer onwards.

Celery There are a number of ways of blanching celery. The simplest is by earthing up soil around the stalks. When the celery plant reaches about 30cm (1ft) high any small offsets around the base should be removed and soil from either side of the row should be drawn up to the base of the leaves. This should be repeated a second and a third time at about three week intervals. The soil is then sloped neatly on either side. Self-blanching varieties of celery are also available that produce pale leaf stalks without earthing-up. Take care to prevent soil working down into the heart of the plant. Some people tie paper collars around the stems before earthing them up but these may encourage slugs. Celery can also be blanched in clay drainpipes.

Chicory can be blanched under cover and because it is done indoors the plants are often said to have been forced, but this is strictly incorrect as no artificial heat is used. Chicory begins its life as an outdoor crop and forms a root which is not unlike a parsnip. The roots should be lifted in winter after being well-frosted and left exposed on the soil surface for a week or so. Then, with old leaves removed, they should be packed upright close together in boxes of moist soil with the crown of the root about 13cm (5in) below the soil surface and placed on the floor of a cool cellar or shed. Leaf buds should soon emerge from the crowns and a tightly furled head of leaves should grow to the surface. Once visible, the blanched chicory head should be severed at the root crown.

In a similar way, tasty tender leaves for salad can be produced from the dandelion root. Seakale and rhubarb can be blanched *in situ* by covering the plants with an inverted barrel. With rhubarb, a loose packing of straw generates a little heat and hastens elongation.

Mounding/Earthing up

There are several reasons why soil should be drawn up around the stems of some plants. It can promote new roots or shoots from the base of the stem – see *Propagation* – it can protect dormant crowns of herbaceous plants, such as *Lobelia cardinalis*, from winter cold and it can provide extra anchorage for plants.

Mounding/earthing up is almost always practised in the cultivation of potatoes. When a seed potato begins to grow it sends out underground stems, or stolons, from the eyes on the tuber. In well-worked soil, these stolons travel in all directions and new potatoes form on them. Some of the stolons come near the surface of the soil and new potatoes growing on these can protrude above ground. Once potatoes are exposed to light they rapidly turn green and are useless for eating. To ensure that all the new potatoes remain below ground and to encourage more extensive rooting and stolon activity, potatoes are usually mounded/earthed up by drawing up soil from between the rows and using it to make ridges along the plant rows. This can be done with a draw hoe. No harm is done if foliage is partly covered by soil, as it will soon extend above the ridge. The operation can be done in two stages and if the first stage is done just after the shoots start to appear, it will protect them against frost damage.

Mounding/Earthing up

Potatoes should be mounded/earthed up as soon as the tops appear above the soil. This will protect them against a late frost and will prevent the tubers from turning green through exposure to light

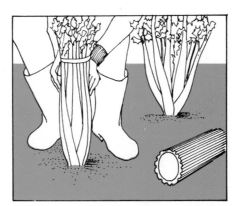

Blanching Celery – Clay Pipes

When the stalks reach about 30cm (12in) high, remove side shoots and tie the stalks together

Fit a clay pipe (or paper collar) around the stalks and gently mound the soil around the base of the clay pipe. Scatter slug pellets

10. Propagation

Propagation is the term used to denote the deliberate multiplication of plants. Its practice is one of the most creative and satisfying of all aspects of gardening. Plants can be propagated by sexual means (seed) or through vegetative propagation – division, layering, cuttings and grafting.

Sexual Propagation

This is confined only to seed, which is produced by fertilization of the ovary with male pollen. Its main advantage is that, since many plants produce enormous quantities of seed, it is possible to raise very large stocks of plants very quickly. Its second advantage is that by applying pollen from a selected male parent on to the stigma of a selected female plant a completely new or improved plant can often be produced. Its main disadvantage is that in many genera, eg *Pyracantha, Ilex, Rhododendron,* the species interbreed so freely that seedlings can differ greatly from the parent plant.

Vegetative Propagation

All other methods of propagating plants come into this category – division, layering, cuttings and grafting (q.v.). The advantage of vegetative propagation is that you can be sure that any plant you reproduce vegetatively will be genetically identical to the parent plant. This is particularly important in the propagation of specially fine forms of plants, or variegated plants.

Seed

A seed is a complete plant in embryo, but it is dormant. Before germination, it may need some preliminary treatment.

Preliminary Treatment

Seeds with very hard coats will take a very long time to germinate unless you carry out one of the three following pre-treatments: 1) soaking for 24 hours in water at blood temperature 38°C (98·4°F), 2) filing with a very fine file (such as a nail file) until the outer coating has been worn through, or 3) nicking – taking a small flake off the outer coat with the point of a sharp knife. With techniques 2) and 3) take care not to damage the soft matter inside the coat: that is the part of the seed that will germinate. If damaged at this stage it could rot before germinating. Berries (not *in sensu stricta* but as that term is normally used) should be stratified. To do this, crock a large clay pot, put in 50cm (2in) soil or seed mix, then a layer of seeds, then another 50cm (2in) of soil or seed mix, then a further layer of seeds and so on until the pot is almost full. Level off with soil or seed mix. Store under cold, moist conditions, and periodically turn the seeds in the mixture. The purpose of stratification is to allow the soft coating of the berries to rot without allowing the seeds to dry out. It usually takes one winter for the soft tissue to rot, but if you turn the mixture regularly, you will soon see when the seeds are clean. They can then be sown in the normal way.

Hardy Seeds

These are normally sown out of doors. Some seeds will only germinate after exposure to frost. If you live in an area where you do not get frost, you will have to sow these in pots and over-winter them in the freezer. The best time to sow hardy seeds is four weeks after the last killing frost in North America, March/April in the UK. The seed-bed should be prepared by digging it well in autumn and incorporating peat with the soil at one cubic metre of peat to every four square metres of soil (1cu yd/ 4sq yd). In spring the bed should be raked until it is level and has a fine tilth. If

Opposite: nearly all small trees and shrubs are propagated by grafting; most cannot be propagated by any other vegetative means

Sowing seed in pots

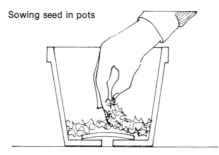

Place a crock over the drainage hole and cover with moss if a clay pot

Overfill the pot with a growing mix for seeds

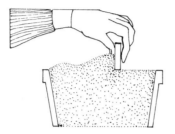

Remove the excess growing mix with a straight edge

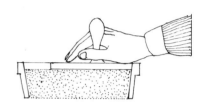

Compress the growing mix lightly using a flat circular piece of wood

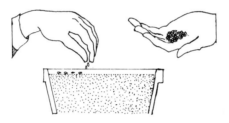

Sow the seed thinly

Sieve the mix over the seeds and cover the pot with a sheet of glass until the seeds germinate

the soil is heavy, sharp sand should also be added with the peat in the autumn at the rate of 1 cubic metre to 9m² (1cu yd/8sq yd). Sow the seed in drills. If the soil is dry, water the seed-bed the day before sowing. Make the drills by drawing the rake sideways along a line stretched across the seed-bed. Insert the seed and cover with soil using the rake. Do not water at this stage unless there is the possibility of the seed-bed drying out. Once the seeds have germinated keep them sufficiently well-watered to ensure steady, vigorous growth.

Tender Seeds
These seeds need artificial warmth to germinate. They will not germinate out of doors in areas where frost occurs. Most seeds in this group need only moderate temperatures, say 10°–21°C (50°–70°F), but some need very high temperatures. Sow the seeds in either pots or trays. Plastic containers are generally more satisfactory than wood or clay ones but will tend to break more easily.

Seed Mix
For slow-germinating seeds use a soil-based seed mix: for all other seeds use a soilless seed mix, and preferably one with a high proportion of sharp sand in it. For seeds of desert plants, add extra sand to ensure good drainage. For seeds of bog, peat or water plants use extra sphagnum peat to keep the mix wet. Use a lime-free mix for lime-hating plants (rhododendrons, camellias, ericas and others) – see *Soil*: *Gardening on an Acid Soil.*

156

Sowing seed in a box

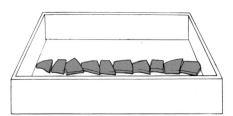

Put a line of crocks along the bottom of the box
(unless you are using a plastic box)

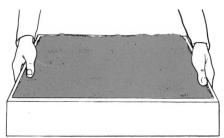

Slightly overfill the box with a seed growing mix
and then gently tap it to settle the mix

Remove excess mix with a straight edge

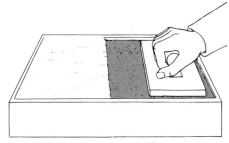

Firm gently with a rectangular template

Sow the seeds thinly. Large seeds can be sown
individually to prevent the necessity of pricking
them out later

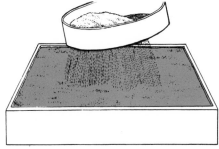

Cover the seed with sieved growing mix

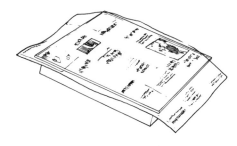

Place a newspaper and a sheet of glass over the
seedbox. Both should be removed as soon as the
seeds germinate

Planting Depth

Seeds should normally be covered by their
own thickness of seed mix. In the case of
very fine seed (callistemon and begonia),
sow on the surface and do not cover. Fine
seed germinates in 3–4 days or not at all.

Sowing the Seed

Sow the seed evenly and thinly. One way of
ensuring even distribution is to place the
seed in a teaspoon or on a folded sheet of
paper and then tap it gently while moving it
over the container.

Sowing seeds in Jiffy 7s. *Top left*: putting the pots in water to make them expand. *Top right*: preparing a planting hole. *Centre left*: putting the seed in. *Centre right*: leaving the pots to stand close together in a tray. *Bottom*: planting out the seedling, still in the Jiffy 7

Temperature Control

There are highly sophisticated propagating cases on the market which enable you to control exactly the temperature at which seeds germinate. If you do not have one you can still achieve high temperatures by placing the seed tray or pot, wrapped in plastic sheeting and sealed, on a radiator, boiler or in an airing cupboard. If seeds will only germinate in darkness (there are very few), cover the pot/tray with a cone/flat sheet of brown paper or tin-foil.

Watering

If seeds are in a propagating case or sealed in plastic sheeting they should not need watering until they have germinated. If sown in the open on a window-sill, water from below by lowering the pot or tray into water heated to room temperature. Do not allow the water to flood over the surface of the seed mix.

Treatment of Seedlings

Put these into individual pots or three to a pot as soon as their first pair of true leaves appears. The first leaves to appear will be the seed leaves (cotyledons): it is the second pair of leaves, which look like the leaves of the adult plant, that you need to watch for. In the case of monocotyledons (plants which produce only one seed-leaf – agaves and lilies) wait until the plants are large enough to handle.

Viability of Seeds

This can vary enormously. Parsnip is reliable for one season only. Most seeds will germinate up to a year after ripening, many for several years. Some seeds (paeonia and sorbus) may take up to three years to germinate. Check in a specialist work on propagation for germination time. Storage times for vegetable seeds are listed in the section on *Edible Plants*.

Remember that an opened packet of seeds cannot be expected to last as long as the time stated for a sealed one.

Division

This is the simplest method of increasing plants. It is used mainly for bulbs (in the loose sense) and herbaceous plants, but many shrubs can be increased by this method. Division basically involves separating large plants which have many growth buds into smaller plants each complete with its own growth bud and usually a root system too.

Simple Division

Lift the plant after it has finished flowering (as for primulas) or while it is dormant (most herbaceous perennials) and tease the roots apart with your fingers. A large clump can be divided into many pieces each about the size of a fist. With woody or tough-rooted plants use a sharp knife to cut the main roots, then tease them apart. With many tough herbaceous subjects the clump can simply be chopped into sections with a spade. With fibrous-rooted plants put two forks back to back in the centre of the clump, and divide the clump by easing the forks apart.

If the plant is divided soon after flowering, it pays to prepare the ground for planting before you lift and divide. Most plants will flag after division – do not worry, as long as they are well watered they will soon revive. With plants which have a large leaf system the divided roots may not be able to provide enough water for the leaves and it may be necessary to reduce the amount of foliage before replanting. Plants which spread usually have their most healthy and vigorous buds (which will provide the best flowers) towards the outside of the clump. Discard the old, woody centres after dividing the clump.

Plants with Woody Crowns

Division of plants like delphinium should be done in the spring. Lift the plants and wash the crowns to reveal the growth buds. Cut

Simple division

Tease the plants apart with your fingers

Plant only those plants with a good root system

Large plants can be chopped with a spade or by two forks inserted back to back if necessary

Plants with large leaf systems should have their foliage reduced before planting

159

Pot layering

Put growing mix in the outer (larger) pot until the rims are level. Thread the plant stem through and between the pots

Fill the space between the pots with growing mix

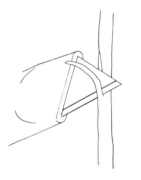

Woody stems may need to be split

through the crown with a sharp knife leaving at least one healthy bud and roots on each portion. Replant in well prepared soil or in boxes filled with potting mix until the new plant is established.

Tubers

Potatoes and Jerusalem artichokes can be propagated by simply cutting the tuber into pieces leaving each piece with at least one eye. Dahlias are rather different. The shoots do not arise from the tubers but from the crown – the base of the stem just above the point where the tubers are attached. Dahlias should be lifted in the autumn and the soil should be removed gently to reveal the small buds which will form the next season's growth. The tubers should be stored for the winter in boxes of dry sand or peat in a frost-free place. In spring, moisten the sand or peat so that the tubers begin to swell and then, a few days later, cut the stem vertically so that each portion has at least one strong growth bud, a portion of the stem and one or more tubers attached. Dahlias can also be propagated by means of cuttings.

Rhizomes

Dig up the plant after flowering and slice it into short sections about 5 to 8cm (2 to 3in) long, each with a strong new growth. Retain the youngest sections (those which grew in the previous year or in the current season) and throw away the older centres. The new portion needs only a few roots and one leaf or leaf bud. It should be planted horizontally with the rhizome half below the surface of the soil. When dividing irises by this method, the leaves should be shortened by half to reduce the loss of water.

Suckers

Many plants such as raspberries, lilacs and members of the berberis family throw up new stems from a creeping root: these are suckers. At the normal planting time (usually the dormant season) the suckers can be dug up, severed from their parent plant and replanted elsewhere. The sucker should have its own root system. Losses can be reduced by leaving the sucker in place and severing the root to the parent plant. When the sucker has recovered from the shock it can be dug up and replanted.

Layering

The technique of layering is used mainly for woody plants including climbers. The idea behind layering is to bring a growing branch which is partly severed or constricted into contact with the soil or a growing mix, and to allow it to root there. The great advan-

tage of layering is that the young plant is not severed from the parent plant until it has formed its own roots and is able to support itself. Three techniques are used: 1) layering, 2) pot-layering, 3) air-layering. Layering is best carried out in early spring before growth begins, or in early summer just as the new growth is ripening. Both layering and pot-layering can be done at any time of year, but rooting will only take place during the growing season.

Layering

Select a suitable branch or twig (one which can easily reach the soil) of the shrub or climber to be layered. At a point about 30cm (1ft) from the tip, make a slit on the underside of the branch using a sharp knife. The slit should be made from thicker wood towards the tip of the twig, should be at an angle of about 20° and should not penetrate more than one-third of the way through the twig. Open the slit by bending the end of the twig gently upwards. Make a hollow in the ground and put some sharp sand at the bottom. Work sharp sand into the slit and lower the layer into the hollow. Use a wooden or wire peg to hold the layer firmly in position. Insert a cane vertically against the layer and tie the tip to it with soft string. Replace soil and water well. Placing a stone over the layer helps retain moisture in the soil and so aids rooting. Label the layer with the date on which it was made and allow two growing seasons for rooting. Sever the new plant from the old with pruning shears/secateurs and let a further growing season pass before moving it.

Pot-layering

This technique is ideal for climbers which have very pliable stems or for plants which resent root disturbance, such as clematis. Take two flower-pots, a large one and a smaller one. There should be a difference of approximately 12mm (½in). Do not crock either pot. Place growing or seed mix, preferably soilless, in the bottom of the larger pot until there is enough to support the smaller pot so that its rim is level with the rim of the larger pot. Thread the stem to be layered through the drainage hole in the smaller pot. Place the smaller pot inside the larger pot, with the growing tip sticking out between the two rims. Fill the space between the two pots with growing mix. There is usually no need to slit the stem since the bend forced on it by having to go through the drainage hole and then grow upwards restricts sap-flow sufficiently to induce rooting. Only if the stem is thick and woody should it be slit as for normal layering. Allow two growing seasons before severing and planting.

Air-layering

This technique is used on plants where there is no branch or twig suitable for bending down to the soil, or where there is no soil to bend it down to, as, for example, in a greenhouse. Select a vigorous, upright shoot and make a slit as for normal layering, about 30cm (1ft) from the tip. Bend the shoot slightly so as to slightly open the slit and dust hormone rooting powder into it. Then push damp sphagnum moss into the slit, and close it. Wrap damp sphagnum moss tightly round the stem and wrap this in black or any other opaque plastic sheeting. Bind tightly with adhesive tape. Allow between six and nine months for rooting. Once severed, the young plant will need careful nursing in close conditions. The reason is that its roots will be water-roots (roots only capable of absorbing water). It will take time for them to develop into normal feeding roots.

Stooling

A stool is a mother plant which is cut back to encourage it to produce shoots which are then earthed up to induce them to root. The technique is very similar to layering, but is generally restricted to woody plants like ligustrum (privet), forsythia and cornus (dogwood). Most of the rootstocks on which popular varieties of apples and pears are budded or grafted are produced by stooling.

To produce rootstocks for fruit trees plant a young rootstock and cut it back to 45cm (18in) from the ground. In the following winter cut it back to about 3cm (1in) from the ground. In the spring anything from one to five shoots can be expected to grow and when most of these are 13cm (5in) high draw up well-cultivated soil to cover the shoots to about half their height. Earth up again when the shoots have grown a further 13cm (5in). Make a further, final earthing up (always with moist soil) in July or August, when the shoots are 45cm (18in) high.

In November or before hard frosts set in dig the soil away and cut the rooted stocks close to the stool with a sharp knife; they are now ready for planting out prior to budding. In the following spring more shoots will be produced and the earthing up can begin afresh. In the meantime, manure the soil. A well-managed stoolbed will produce rootstocks for at least 15 years.

Cuttings

Cuttings in general are not so easy to manage as layers since the young shoot which is to become the new plant is wholly severed from the parent plant. Lacking roots, it has no means of taking up plant foods or adequate moisture. The main problem with cuttings is that because of this they tend to wilt and dry out. Many techniques have been evolved to try to overcome this problem. In spite of its problems, cuttings are the main method used by nurserymen for increasing woody plants. You can get far more cuttings from a plant than you can layers. There are three parts of a plant from which cuttings can be taken – the stem, the leaf and the root. There are five types of stem cutting: 1) soft-wood or greenwood, 2) semi-hard, 3) hardwood, 4) nodal, and 5) internodal.

Soft-wood or Greenwood Cuttings

Soft-wood or greenwood cuttings are taken in late spring as soon as the base of the current season's growth begins to become firm. Select a vigorous growth between 10 and 15cm (4 and 6in) long and cut straight through it with a sharp knife. If the cutting is taken in the garden, drop it in a plastic bag and immediately seal the bag. When you are ready to plant the cutting, remove the lower leaves, dip the base in hormone rooting powder, tap the excess powder off the cut, and insert at least 5cm (2in) in a soilless potting mix. Water thoroughly, ideally with sterilized water, preferably containing a fungicide. The cuttings must then be kept close and given warmth from below. If you have a propagating case with soil-warming cables, use this. If it has mist propagation facilities, use these to keep the cuttings in good condition. If you do not have these facilities place a hoop of wire over the cuttings, making sure the bottom of the hoop touches the bottom of the pot. Place a plastic bag over this and seal it so that it is air-tight. Stand the cuttings on a source of heat such as a radiator or boiler to provide bottom heat. The cuttings will need full daylight, so if the heat-source is away from good light, supplement it by placing fluorescent tubes about 45cm (18in) above the cuttings. Allow about six to eight weeks for rooting.

Semi-hard Cuttings

These are taken from wood of the current season's growth as soon as the base of the growth has started to become woody. The cutting is taken with a heel. Take the cutting firmly between thumb and first finger (the thumb on the upper side of shoot) and give it a short, sharp tug downwards and outwards. Trim off the surplus bark and any bruised tissues with a sharp knife. Remove any soft, sappy growth at the growing tip of the cutting. Dip the rooting end of the cutting in hormone rooting powder and tap off

Taking a geranium cutting. Note where the cut is made and which buds and leaves are removed. Set the cuttings around the edge of a pot to root

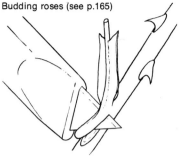

Budding roses (see p.165)

Take a well developed bud from halfway up a strong stem which has flowered

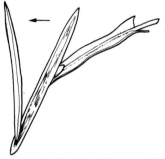

Remove the thin sliver of heartwood from the back of the bud

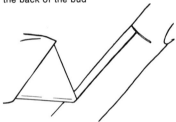

Make a T-shaped incision in the stock

Lift the corners of the bark and insert the bud

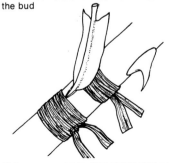

Cut away any protruding shield rind and bind

any surplus. Insert the cutting in a soilless potting mix and treat as for soft-wood or greenwood cuttings. Semi-hard cutttings will not wilt quite so quickly as soft-wood or greenwood cuttings.

Hardwood Cuttings

These are taken from deciduous shrubs, trees and climbers immediately after leaffall: with conifers and broadleaved evergreen trees they are taken as soon as the last leaves have fallen from neighbouring deciduous trees. The cuttings, which should be 40 to 60cm (16 to 24in) long, are taken in the same way as for semi-hard cuttings, with a heel. Prepare the heel in the same way as for the semi-hard cuttings. Open a V-shaped trench 25cm (10in) deep in a nursery bed, one side of which is vertical, the other sloping. Do this with a clean spade. Put a layer of sharp sand 25mm (1in) deep in the bottom of the trench. Insert the cuttings with the heel pressed into the sand. At least half the cutting should be in the soil. Replace the soil in the trench. Tread till firm. Water well. Retread after each frost: frost loosens the cuttings in the soil. Over winter the cuttings will callus. In spring they will start to root. Water regularly in spring since the cuttings will start to put on leaf growth before they have made roots. This is the moment when these cuttings are most at risk. Proprietary anti-transpirant sprays can be used to slow down transpiration and will reduce wilting while the cuttings are forming roots.

Nodal or Stem-section Cuttings

These may be taken from shrubs or climbers. Take the cutting when the plant is dormant. Select a vigorous shoot of the current season's growth, and sever as for a hardwood cutting. Make a cut straight through the wood a little above the heel. Make another cut immediately above the node. A node is a dormant growth bud. If there are two buds at the node rub one of them out with your thumb. Insert the section horizontally in the growing mix with the bud uppermost. Treat as for tender seeds.

Internodal Cuttings

These are used only for climbing plants with widely spaced nodes, especially grape vines. Select a vigorous stem of ripened wood in winter. Make a clean cut at equal distances above and below the node. About 5cm (2in) is ideal. Lay the cutting horizontally on the growing mix. Treat as for tender seeds.

Root Cuttings

Many plants with thick, fleshy roots can be increased by root sections. The Californian tree poppy *Romneya coulteri* is best increased this way. The whole plant is lifted and the required number of cuttings taken from the root, after which the parent plant is replanted. The cuttings should be about 2cm (¾in) thick at their thickest part, and about 10cm (4in) long. Make the cut nearest the parent plant with sharp pruning shears/secateurs and make it straight across the root. Make the cut nearest the root tip a sloping cut with a sharp knife. Always do this, then you will never make any mistake as to which way up to plant the cuttings. Plant these vertically, either in pots or seed-beds, the tops about 1·5cm (½in) below the surface. With plants that have eyes (growth buds) on the root cuttings (herbaceous paeonies, for example) plant the cuttings horizontally with the eye uppermost. With this group each cutting must have one eye, otherwise it will never grow. Both types of root cutting are best made in winter while the plant is dormant.

Cuttings from Leaves

There are two types of leaf cutting: 1) those in which the leaf itself will produce the new plant, 2) those in which the leaf stalk (petiole) will produce the new plant.

Leaf Cuttings

Take a leaf of the plant you want to propagate and lay it flat on a layer of fine sand 7mm (¼in) thick over the potting mix. Pin the leaf firmly in position – hairpins are ideal for this. Cut the mid-rib and main veins with the tip of a sharp pruning knife. Each cut should be no more than 7mm (¼in) long. Water well. Give plenty of light. Young plants will form on the side of the cut nearest the petiole. Forms of *Begonia rex* are normally increased by this method.

Leaf Petiole Cuttings

Take a leaf of the plant you want to increase and sever it from the parent plant with a sharp knife. Take care not to bruise the petiole in doing this. Make the cut cleanly. Insert the cuttings vertically into a soilless potting mix. Water well. Do not insert more than half the total length of the original petiole in the growing mix. *Saintpaulias* are usually increased in this way.

Mist propagation

If you place a soft-wood cutting on an open greenhouse bench or in an open frame, it will wilt through loss of water from the leaves by transpiration and may die. To reduce this loss of water, soft-wood cuttings are usually enclosed in a propagator or in a polythene bag – see *Cuttings*. But soft-wood cuttings can be rooted successfully in the open greenhouse or frame in full sunlight by

Taking a hydrangea cutting. *Top left*: A shoot of the correct length. *Top right*: strip the lower leaves off and cut across the shoot just below a leaf node. *Centre left*: dipping the cutting in rooting hormone. *Centre right*: setting the cutting in the centre of a pot and firming the potting mix. *Bottom*: the cutting covered with a polythene wrap to retain humidity and hasten rooting.

using mist propagation. The idea is to surround the cutting with a fine, mist-like spray of water which reduces transpiration from the leaves of the cutting and keeps the entire surface of the cutting cool and prevents wilting.

The basic equipment for mist propagation consists of a box about 15cm (6in) deep with a layer of 7mm (¼in) ballast at the bottom covered by an 8cm (3in) layer of 3mm (⅛in) grit or sharp sand which has soil warming cables buried in it. The box is topped up with a rooting medium for the cuttings. To prevent the rooting medium from becoming waterlogged, very porous ones are used – three parts of 3mm (⅛in) grit to one part of peat is fairly typical but vermiculite, perlite or pure sand could be used. The mist is provided by an artificial leaf (a sensing element) which is exposed to exactly the same conditions of light, humidity and temperature as the cuttings and turns a spray unit on or off when pre-set conditions are reached. Other, less sophisticated, devices are also available which simply turn the mist on and off at pre-set time intervals. With mist propagation cuttings can be rooted over a long season – from when the wood is very soft to later when the wood is half ripe. The root temperature for the cuttings should be maintained at about 24°C (75°F) and free circulation of air is essential.

163

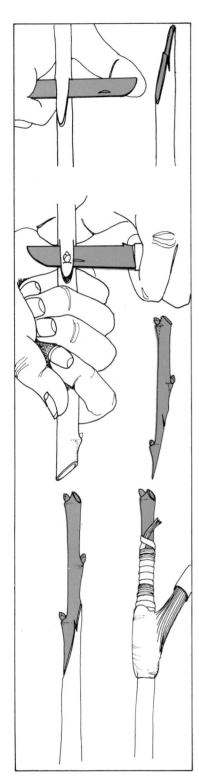

Whip and tongue grafting. *Top*: cutting the stock, and the prepared stock. *Centre*: cutting the scion – upwards, from just under a bud. *Bottom*: the two should fit neatly together, and should then be bound together with adhesive tape

When the cuttings have rooted they should be introduced to normal conditions in gradual steps. Some propagators have controls which allow the frequency of misting to be reduced. If this is not possible the cuttings should be covered by a wire frame with a sheet of polythene draped over it. The polythene should be removed in stages.

Hormones

Plant hormones are organic elements which are formed naturally in the tissues of plants and act as chemical messengers influencing the growth and development of the plant without necessarily taking part in it. They are not plant foods. Hormones have been extracted from plants or copied synthetically and can be used by the gardender to:
1) Aid root formation. Alpha-naphthalene-acetic acid, indolyl-butyric acid, beta-indolyl-acetic acid and naphthoxyacetic acid can be used to hasten the formation of roots by cuttings or layers. They are usually available as powders – the base of the cutting is dipped into the powder or the powder is sprinkled over the wounded part of a layer – and may be available in different strengths. The weakest strength is for softwood cuttings; the strongest for hardwood cuttings.
2) Aid pollination of fruit trees and to advance maturity and improve the colour of the fruits.
3) Reduce growth – growth retardants can be used to slow down the growth of lawns and hedges and to produce compact pots of chrysanthemums and poinsettias for the florist's shop. Methyl alpha-naphthalene acetate can be used to prevent premature sprouting of stored potatoes.
4) Kill weeds – see *Pests and Diseases: Herbicides*.

Grafting

Grafting is the name given to the operation of joining the rooting system and main stem of one plant (stock or rootstock) with a shoot of another plant (scion) so that they grow together and form one plant. Grafting may be used to propagate trees and shrubs because:
1) It provides a reliable method of propagation which can be used when other methods fail – for plants which do not root easily by layering or through cuttings and for plants which do not seed or those which produce seed which either is difficult to germinate or produces plants which are not true to type.
2) It can be used to produce artificial types of trees – shrubs can, for example, be made into trees.

3) By careful selection of the stock it is possible to influence the behaviour of the scion variety. For example, in the grafting of fruit trees the characteristics of the scion variety – taste of the fruit, season of maturity and keeping qualities – are retained but the overall size of the fruit tree and its rate of growth can be profoundly influenced by the rootstock.

Grafting can also be used to repair damage to the stems of young trees caused by rodents, disease or heavy frosts by providing a method of bridging gaps in the bark.

Two things are necessary to have a good chance of producing a successful graft. The stock and scion must be compatible – they should be varieties of the same species, species of the same genus or genera of the same family. There is no guarantee of successful grafting even when joining closely related varieties of the same species but, as a general rule, the closer the relationship between the scion and the stock the greater is the chance of success. Secondly, a good, firm contact between the cambium tissues of stock and scion is essential. Cambium tissue is found only in the roots and woody stems of dicotyledons and is a thin layer of green cells lying between the heartwood and the bark (or rind). This is why it is not possible to graft woody monocotyledons like palms. These cells are capable of producing callus growth which will knit together the stock and scion and protect the wounds. It is usually impossible to match the cambium layers of stock and scion at all points as the stems are seldom identical in diameter, so it is best to concentrate on obtaining a good match on one side only rather than a poor match on all sides.

The height of the graft union varies from plant to plant. Bush roses and most ornamental shrubs should be grafted as low as possible so that the union formed can be set just below ground level. Fruit trees are grafted at least 15cm (6in) above ground level to minimize the risk of roots being formed by the scion variety. Standard roses are generally budded about 1·5m (5ft) above ground level.

Tying and Sealing Materials

The simplest way of holding the stock and scion together while the graft is taking is to bind them with soft string or adhesive tape. Neither of these materials is flexible and they must be removed before they begin to constrict the plant. Rubber grafting strips are easy to handle, will stretch as the growth thickens and will eventually fall away when they are no longer needed. To limit the loss of moisture from cut surfaces, to prevent water seeping into the wounds and to keep disease organisms out, graft unions are usually sealed with a grafting wax or a bitumen emulsion.

Preparation of the Stocks and Scions

Grafting is usually carried out towards the end of the dormant season. Stocks should be young and free from disease. If the stocks have been grown in containers, they should be brought indoors into the warmth about seven to ten days before grafting to stir their roots into growth. Water stocks sparingly to prevent excessive bleeding when they are cut. Dormant scion wood should be taken from strong, one year old woody shoots in winter for grafting on to the stock in the following spring. To keep the shoots in good condition, they should be stored in cool, moist conditions. In the UK and less cold areas of Canada and the USA they can be bundled together and set vertically in sand or soil near to a north-facing wall. In extremely cold areas, they should be kept indoors in a cool place. Soft, or leafy, scion material must be kept in humid conditions and used as soon as possible.

Types of Graft

Over the years different types of graft have been developed for individual groups of plants and many books are full of complicated grafting operations. In fact, with a bit of care and reasonably good carpentry, it is possible to use just a few types of graft on a wide range of plants.

Whip and tongue This is the most frequently used graft for propagating fruit and ornamental trees. The stock and scion should both be about 13mm (½in) in diameter and the stock should be one to two years old. The scion should have four good buds and should be a piece from the middle of a one year old woody shoot stored over winter. The lowest bud should be about 19mm (¾in) above the base. Behead the stock about 15cm (6in) above ground level by making a sloping cut about 4cm (1½in) long. Make a matching cut across the base of the scion. A simple splice graft could now be made by binding the stock and scion together. Splice grafts are used to propagate brooms, clematis and roses. To get a better, more firm joint a downward cut should be made just below the apex of the stock to form an upward pointing tongue. A similar cut should be made in the stem so that the two tongues interlock and will hold the graft firmly together even before it is bound. Remove any growth which appears from the stock.

Saddle graft This method of grafting is suitable for all plants where the stock and scion are about equal in diameter but, in practice, is is mainly used to join a named rhododendron variety to the common rhododendron stock. A wedge-shaped piece of wood is cut from the stem to leave an inverted V and the stock is cut to fit. Saddle grafts do not need to be coated with grafting wax.

Approach graft This method of grafting permits the scion to retain its own rooting system until the union is complete and is sometimes used for propagating vines and nuts. The stock and scion are usually grown in separate pots placed side by side. A thin layer of wood is removed from each so that the two layers of cambium tissue are exposed. The wounded surfaces are then bound together and the union is covered with grafting wax. When the union is complete, the top growth of the stock is removed just above the union and the roots and stem of the scion are cut off just below the union.

Budding

Budding is a form of grafting which is mainly used to propagate roses but is becoming more and more widely used to propagate fruit trees too. The job is done between mid-June and the end of August. A well-developed leaf bud is slipped into a slit in the bark of the stock and bound in place until attachment is complete.

Shield budding This is mainly used for propagating roses. Buds are taken from about halfway up a strong stem which has flowered and are obtained by making a shallow upward cut from below the bud, going behind it and coming out well above it. A thin sliver of heartwood will be attached to the back of the bud and should be removed with care to avoid damaging the inner tissue of the bud. A T-shaped incision is made on the stock, the corners of the bark are lifted and the bud slipped into position. Any protruding shield rind is cut away at the top line of the T before tying.

Chip budding This is mainly used for propagating fruit trees. Buds are taken by making a cut starting above the bud and sloping down behind it. A second, downward sloping cut is then made below the bud so that it will cross the first cut and release the scion. A wedge-shaped piece is cut out of the stock to receive the bud.

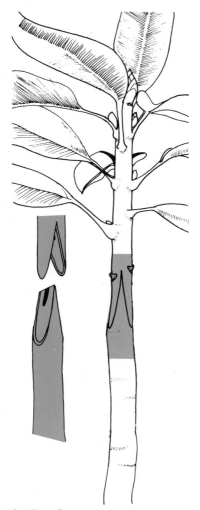

Saddle graft

11. Pruning

If trees and shrubs are left to grow naturally, many will eventually become a mass of tangled growth bearing small flowers and little fruit. By removing some of the growths the flowering, fruiting and health of such plants can be improved: the removal of these growths is known as pruning. There are four basic reasons for pruning:
1) to give the tree or shrubs a basic shape;
2) to improve the quality of flowers, fruit or leaves;
3) to regulate growth;
4) to remove damaged, diseased or dead wood and so maintain plant health; and
5) to maintain a balance between fruits or flowers and leaf or stem growth in a tree or shrub.

All pruning cuts should be made as cleanly as possible. Start the cut opposite a healthy bud and cut at an angle so that the cut finishes just above the bud. When training for shape make sure that the bud points in the required direction. The correct tools to be used for pruning are discussed under *Tools and Equipment*.

Training

The eventual framework of a tree or shrub can be formulated in its early years by careful pruning. Apple and pear trees can, for example, be trained as bushes, standards, half-standards, cordons, espaliers and pyramids – see *Edible Plants: Fruit* – and other trees can be pruned so that the lowest branch is high enough from the ground to allow you to walk beneath them in comfort. As a general rule the more artificial the shape, the more likely it is that pruning will be needed in later years to maintain the shape. Shaping trees and shrubs always means that they will start to flower and fruit later in life than they would have done if they had been allowed to grow naturally.

Deciduous Shrubs

After planting cut back the plant hard. This will encourage new shoots to develop near to ground level. Select three to five of the strongest shoots and reduce their length by about one half and cut back side shoots to two or three buds. In the following winter cut back the new shoots to about one half of their length and open up the centre of the bush by removing crossing branches.

Evergreen Shrubs

In late spring, after planting, remove the growing point of the three strongest growing shoots and thin out crowded branches.

Climbers

In late spring, after planting, cut back the stems to about one half or one third of their original length. This will encourage new growth from near ground level. Choose three to five strong shoots and train them along canes in the direction of their permanent support. At the end of the growing season reduce the length of the leaders by about one half and thin out crowded shoots. Repeat this process each year until the required framework has been built. Prune evergreen climbers less severely than deciduous ones – tip them.

Deciduous Trees

When young plants come from the nursery at the end of their first year's growth, they generally have a single straight stem and a few subsidiary shoots, known as feathers. In this form a tree is known as a whip. Remove all branches (feathers) on the lowest one third of the tree; reduce those on the middle third to two or three buds and leave those on the top third unpruned. Continue this process each year until the main stem has reached a height which is sufficient to allow branches to develop. Always remove any

Opposite: If you think you might like to try topiary, experiment with one plant first

167

branch which challenges the leader. Two methods of training are now possible.

Standards When the leader reaches about 2·2m (7½ft) remove the tip to encourage branching. This is best done during the autumn and this form of tree is particularly suitable for small trees such as mountain ash.

Central leader This is the shape for most large-growing trees. The central leader is allowed to grow on unchecked and branches growing 2·4m (8ft) or more from the ground are allowed to develop. Space the branches at intervals along and around the trunk to give the tree a good shape. Semi-pendulous trees may need a much longer clean trunk, perhaps as long as 4·5m (15ft). When pendulous trees are obtained from a nursery they are often allowed to droop on stems which are only about 2·1m (7ft) high. The height of the trunk can be increased by pruning back the leader to the point where it begins to bend over and reducing the length of the other branches. In the following autumn the strongest growing shoot should be selected and trained upwards to an eventual height of about 3·6m (12ft), removing the feathers by stages as described earlier. At this height the pendulous framework can be allowed to develop freely.

Evergreen Trees

These are normally sold by nurseries as a central leader with all branches retained. They can be trained in exactly the same way as deciduous central leaders but the side branches lower than 2·4m (8ft) are retained as long as possible.

Conifers

As with evergreens, conifers are sold as central leaders with all branches retained and they should be allowed to keep branches lower than 2·4m (8ft) as long as possible. Conifers like *Chamaecyparis* may develop several leaders which go unnoticed in their early years but later begin to fall outwards under the weight of their side branches. Dwarf growing conifers can be left to grow naturally even if they develop several central leaders.

For training fruit trees see *Edible plants: Fruit*. Wall shrubs can be trained horizontally as described for espalier fruit trees. For training roses see *Ornamental Plants: Roses*.

Topiary

Topiary is the art of training and clipping shrubs and trees into shapes like globes, pyramids and animal forms.

The best topiary is created from slow-growing evergreen trees which produce a dense cover of small leaves. *Buxus sempervirens*, box, and *Taxus baccata*, yew, are ideal. *Ilex aquifolium*, holly, can be shaped in detail but it has larger leaves and is overall less suitable. *Lonicera nitida* and species of *Ligustrum*, privet, have also been used. The statuesque nature of topiary does not harmonize well with small, informal gardens but this should not deter anyone with enough enthusiasm from having fun by shaping a single specimen. But be warned; it takes many years to create a well-formed cone or ball shape, and much longer to achieve, say, a peacock in all its glory.

It is best to choose a small, say 30 to 60cm (1 to 2ft), box or yew at the nursery which is well endowed with side shoots down to ground level. It should be planted in a well-prepared open site which is not exposed to cold winds or deeply shaded. A broad base needs to be established for any future shape to be built on: make this by restrained clipping in August or September. Always ensure that the tree has at least two central leaders. When the tree has reached the required size, bind these central leaders together at the top to make a framework which is subsequently filled in with side shoots and becomes a ball or cube shape. One or more of the central leaders can be allowed to grow on to form the neck or tail of a bird, say. If the tree is to have an unnatural shape, bend a stiff wire to the shape required, fix this to the base of the tree or to a stake or cane and tie nearby shoots of the tree to the wire. Eventually the tree will adopt this shape permanently and the supports can be removed.

Pruning Established Trees and Shrubs

Once a tree or shrub has become established the emphasis changes from pruning for shape to pruning to improve the quality of the flowers or fruit, to keep the amount of flowers or fruit in balance with the foliage and to keep the tree or shrub healthy.

Trees and shrubs vary in the amount of pruning they need. Some need little or no attention, others need drastic pruning every year. As a regular annual operation before any kind of pruning for flower, fruit or balance is done, all dead, damaged or diseased wood should be removed and crossing branches cut out. Thin weak shoots should either be removed completely or cut back hard. Shoots of variegated plants which are showing signs of reverting back to green should be traced to their point of origin and removed completely. All these tasks should be carried out in late spring when the damage caused by winter winds and frosts can be assessed.

Most established ornamental trees will need very little pruning other than described above. See *Edible Plants: Fruit* for pruning established fruit trees.

The best way of pruning established shrubs depends on when they flower and whether the flowers or foliage (or bark) are the most desired features. For pruning established roses see *Ornamental Plants: Roses*.

Summer to Early Autumn Flowering Shrubs

These bear flowers on shoots produced in the current year. If they are left unpruned, the shrubs will grow bigger but with less vigour and flowers and fruit will eventually be smaller and poorer. To give the flower-bearing shoots the longest time to grow, prune the shrub in early spring as soon as the buds start to swell. Cut last year's shoots back to one or two buds (or pairs of buds) from where they join the main stem (or ground level). Hard pruning, like this, will delay flowering. Another method of pruning can be used to extend the flowering period but still produce high quality flowers. This method involves cutting back one half of the shoots hard, as described above, and reducing the remainder to about one half or one third of their original length.

If fruits are not required, the shrubs should be dead-headed regularly by removing the flower head with, if possible, two or three buds on the flower stem. This will encourage further flowering.

Spring to Early Summer Flowering Shrubs

These generally bear flowers and fruit on shoots which grew in the previous year and are best pruned as soon as flowers begin to fade. Cut back all flowering wood to one or two buds (or pairs of buds) from where they join the older wood. If young growth is breaking cut back to where there is a strong shoot growing in the required direction. Thin out the remainder of the shoots and open up the centre of the bush. In wet seasons, when growth has been lush, thin the bushes further in later summer.

Shrubs Flowering on Spurs

Some shrubs produce their flowers on the same wood year after year. These shrubs grow strongly in their early years until flowering wood has been formed when growth slows. In the early years pruning should be restricted to the development of a framework and cutting back annual growth to about three or four buds. The main stems should be left unpruned. Later in life when the spurs have formed these should be cut back to between five and six leaves in the

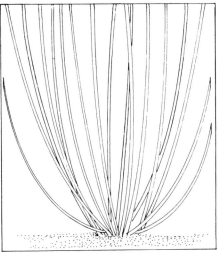

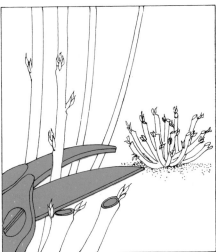

Cutting back growth in spring to one or two buds. Note the angle of the cuts

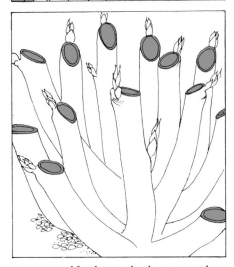

summer and further cut back to two or three buds in the autumn.

Foliage Shrubs

Some shrubs are not grown for their flowers or fruit but for their decorative foliage or

bark. Bark colouring is most intense on young shoots and these shrubs are pruned hard – almost to ground level – in the spring.

Evergreen Shrubs

Evergreens are pruned in spring just before growth begins. Damaged or diseased wood should be removed and the shrub thinned out and trimmed to shape.

Climbers

Follow the techniques outlined for deciduous and evergreen shrubs. Climbers on poles should always be pruned hard to make sure that the pole does not have to bear excessive weight. Climbers on trees need pruning only if the well-being of the tree is threatened.

Renovating Old Trees and Shrubs

Trees and shrubs which have been neglected and allowed to grow overcrowded can be renovated by cutting them hard back to the old framework or to ground level. The operation can be done in one season or over a period of two or three years. New growth should be encouraged by applying a general purpose fertilizer in the spring and new growths should be trained according to the type of tree or shrub.

Root Pruning

The vigour of a tree or shrub can be reduced by shortening or removing some of its roots and depriving it of some of its supply of soil nutrients.

Opposite: Topiary is not necessarily the preserve of very large formal gardens only

Well-pruned hedges and shrubs will greatly improve the appearance of a garden

Bark ringing – three methods

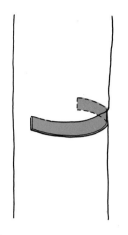

Take out a half ring of bark about 6 to 13mm (¼ to ½in) wide about 60cm (2ft) above the ground

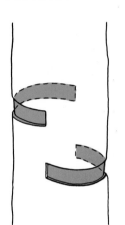

Take out two half rings with the second ring about 7 to 10cm (3 to 4in) above the first and on the opposite side of the tree

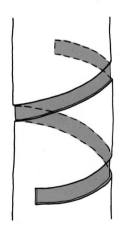

Take out a complete spiral with about 7 to 10cm (3 to 4in) between the ends of the spiral

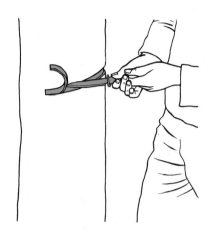

After making the cuts use the top of the knife to lever out the bark and the cambium layer below

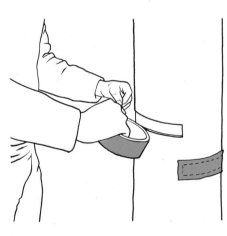

Cover the wound with adhesive tape

The best time to root prune trees is in the autumn. Take out a circular trench about 45cm (18in) deep at the same distance from the trunk as the outermost tips of the branches. Remove the soil with a fork and take care not to damage roots which are exposed. Cut through some of the thickest roots. The more roots you cut and the closer they are to the tree, the more severe the check will be. Re-lay the fibrous roots, cover them with soil and firm the soil in place. Root pruning has a similar result to *Bark Ringing*.

Bark Ringing

If a young tree is growing with too much vigour and is failing to make fruit buds, a ring of bark can be taken from the trunk to check the production of new wood. Bark ringing can be applied reasonably safely to apples and pears but should not be used on stone fruits (plums, peaches and cherries) which bleed or exude gum if they are cut in this way.

Bark ringing does have risks attached – removal of a complete ring of bark can lead to the death of a tree within a short time. For this reason many gardeners prefer to do it in stages, and to take out narrow rings of bark which the tree can heal by natural callusing. The ring of bark removed should be between 6 and 13mm (¼ to ½in) wide and should be taken out about 60cm (2ft) above the ground. Four alternatives are possible:
1) Take out a half ring of bark, then in the following year, take out another half ring 7 to 10cm (3 to 4in) above the first half ring and on the opposite side of the tree.
2) Take out both half rings, as described above, in the same year.
3) Take out a complete spiral with 7 to 10cm (3 to 4in) between the ends of the spiral.
4) Take out a complete ring.

Bark ringing should be done in May when a check will be given to the growth but the ring will have time to heal over during the summer. Use a sharp knife and cut right down to the heartwood. A piece of flexible metal or plastic can be used to make sure that the cut is level. Use the tip of the knife to lever out the bark and the cambium layer below. The wound can be bound with adhesive tape to prevent drying out. As a less effective, but safer, alternative to bark ringing the roots of a tree or shrub can be pruned – see *Root Pruning*.

Tree Surgery

Old trees often need some care and attention. Dead or diseased branches will need removing, holes in ancient trees will need filling and a main fork may need bracing to reduce the risk of splitting. All three jobs are well within the reach of the average gardener but if whole trees or large sections of trees are to be removed, it is worthwhile calling in a specialist tree surgeon who has the necessary skill, equipment and should be fully insured (it is worthwhile checking who pays in the event of any accident which may occur).

Removing Branches

Cut back dead or diseased branches to healthy tissue and always cut back lateral branches flush with the main branch. Try to make sure that all cut surfaces slope downwards so that rainwater runs off them. If several branches are to be removed, spread the job over several years to minimize the shock to the tree.

The dormant season is generally the safest time to remove branches but *Prunus* species should be tackled in May to reduce the risk of silver leaf infection and *Juglans* species (walnuts) should be pruned in leaf to reduce the risk of bleeding.

Branches should always be cut in such a way that the weight of the branch does not tear tissue from the trunk as it separates. If the branch is very heavy it should be removed in two sections. Cut the first section straight through at least 30cm (12in) from the final flush cut. Cut the second section by first making a cut on the underside of the branch extending about halfway through it and then making a second cut from above slightly further away from the main branch than the first cut. (This will also slant the cut surface downwards). Light branches can be removed in one by undercutting first. To reduce the risk of damage from falling branches, they should be supported by a rope slung over a higher (and larger) branch and held by a person below who is ready to lower the branch once the cut has been completed. Trim the cut surface with a sharp knife, paying particular attention to the edges and, when the wound is dry, apply a wound-sealing compound over the whole surface.

Filling Holes

Pare the edges of the hole with a sharp knife and cover the dried surface with a wound-sealing compound. Fill the hole with a stiff mortar mix: three parts of sand to one part cement. Alternatively a polystyrene filling sealed with bitumen can be used. Allow room for the tissue to grow and cover the opening of the hole.

Bracing

Drill through both limbs and pass a large bolt through a metal plate on the outer surface of each limb.

Removing a branch

Heavy branches should be removed in two parts. Make the first cut right through the branch at least 30cm (12in) from the final cut

Make a cut on the underside of the branch as close to the tree trunk as possible. Make a second cut from the top slightly further away from the tree trunk. The remaining stump should be cut as near flush with the tree trunk as possible.

Heavy branches need support. Use another (sturdy) branch

12. Ornamental Plants

Annuals and Biennials

Most of the flowers grown from seed for summer colour are either annuals or biennials.

Annuals are herbaceous plants which germinate, form a plant, flower, produce seed and die within one season. Their total life cycle need not necessarily take place within a calendar year; many annuals can be sown in the late autumn to stand the winter and to produce flowers in spring or early summer. Annuals can be divided into three groups according to their hardiness: hardy, half-hardy and tender.

Biennials grow roots and leaves in the year in which they are sown but do not flower until the second year. After flowering, they produce seed and die.

Many plants which are actually perennials produce their best show of flower in their first or second year and so are often treated as annuals or biennials in the garden. *Begonia semperflorens*, for example, is a perennial in its native country of Brazil but in cooler areas it will not overwinter and is treated as an annual. Wallflowers do not die after producing their first flowers but, because the plants become leggy, they are generally treated as biennials. Antirrhinums are also perennials but, because they too have a tendency to become leggy, they are often grown as annuals.

Soil Conditions

Most annuals and biennials will grow well in almost any garden soil but they do not like badly-drained, cold soils. In very rich soils annuals may produce too many leaves and very few flowers. *Salvia splendens, Lathyrus odoratus*, sweet pea, and *Helianthus annuus*, sunflower, are the most obvious exceptions to this rule. For most annuals, do not apply fertilizers to the soil before planting. On poor soils, a barrow-load of compost to every 10m² (12sq yd) should be dug in before planting and a general-purpose fertilizer (a 10:10:10 or 7:7:7 fertilizer) should be sprinkled around the plants at flowering time at about 70g/m² (2oz/sq yd).

Cultivation

Annuals and biennials are often grown as part of a formal bedding scheme (see *Design and Planning: Bedding*), for edging groups of plants (see *Edging Plants,* this section), as part of a herbaceous border or simply for cut flowers. If you want to grow annuals or biennials as part of a herbaceous border then plan the border on paper before you buy the seeds. In particular, select the size and colour of each group of plants with care. Try to avoid sharp contrasts – see *Design and Planning: Colour*.

Sowing seeds of annuals in their eventual flowering position is a very simple, and often highly successful, way of achieving a very colourful garden. Many annuals hate being moved and will do less well if they are started off under glass and transplanted. Those which should be sown *in situ* are indicated in the table overleaf. The main disadvantage is that in cooler areas half-hardy plants will have to be sown so late that their flowering period will be very short. Even hardy plants may flower very late.

Annual seeds vary tremendously in their size and shape and, as a general rule, smaller seeds will need the most care when sowing. Always sow seeds in a well-prepared seed bed. Dig the soil thoroughly, remove any weeds, allow the soil to settle for a week or two and then rake it to a very fine tilth. Mark out the areas for each type of flower with a sharp stick and then broadcast the seeds within these areas. Do not sow the seeds too thickly. Large seeds can be raked in or covered with a thin layer of soil; small seeds are best left uncovered but they

Annuals

	hardiness	situations	colours	number in a box 33 × 20cm (13 × 8in)	planting distance cm	(in)	uses	flowering time
Ageratum houstonianum	half-hardy	sun or shade	blue, white, pink	54	15 to 30	(6 to 12)	bedding, cut flowers, edging or pots	July to Oct
Alyssum maritimum	half-hardy to hardy	sun	white, pink, purple	54	15 to 30	(6 to 12)	edging	June to Sept
Antirrhinum majus, snapdragon	hardy to half-hardy	sun or semi-shade	various colours	54	23 to 45	(9 to 16)	bedding, border, cut flowers, edging or large pots	June to Aug
Begonia semperflorens	tender	sun or shade	pink, red, white mixed	40	10 to 15	(4 to 6)	edging, bedding or pot plants	June to Sept
Calendula officinalis	half-hardy to hardy	sun or semi-shade	orange, yellow, cream, mixed	54	30	(12)	bedding or cut flowers	May to Aug
Callistephus chinensis, Chinese aster	half-hardy	sun or semi-shade	mixed	54	30 to 45	(12 to 18)	bedding, edging or cut flowers	July to Sept
Centaurea cyanus, cornflower	hardy to half-hardy	sun or semi-shade	red, blue, pink, white, mixed	54	30 to 45	(12 to 18)	bedding, border or cut flowers	June to Sept
Chrysanthemum carinatum	half-hardy	sun	mixed	*in situ*	30 to 45	(12 to 18)	border or cut flowers	July to Sept
Chrysanthemum coronarium, summer chrysanthemum	hardy	sun or semi-shade	cream, yellow, white	*in situ*	30 to 45	(12 to 18)	cut flowers	July, Aug
Chrysanthemum paludesum	hardy	sun or semi-shade	white	*in situ*	15	(6)	bedding	July to Sept
Clarkia elegans	hardy	sun	red, pink, mixed	*in situ*	15	(6)	bedding or border	July, Aug
Cosmos bipinnatus	tender	sun or semi-shade	orange, pink, red, white, mixed	40	30 to 60	(12 to 24)	bedding, border or cut flowers	July to Sept
Dahlia (annual)	tender	sun or semi-shade	mixed	40	30 to 60	(12 to 24)	bedding, border or cut flowers	July to Oct
Delphinium consolida, larkspur	hardy to half-hardy	sun or semi-shade	blue, pink, red, white, mixed	54	30 to 45	(12 to 18)	bedding, border or cut flowers	June to Sept
Dimorphotheca sinuata, star of the Veldt	tender	sun	orange, white, mixed	54	30	(12)	bedding	July to Sept
Eschscholzia californica, Californian poppy	hardy	sun	mixed	*in situ*	23 to 30	(9 to 12)	cut flowers	June to Aug
Gaillardia pulchella, blanket flower	half-hardy	sun	mixed	40	30	(12)	bedding or cut flowers	July to Oct
Godetia, summer azalea	half-hardy	sun or semi-shade	mixed	*in situ*	30 to 45	(12 to 18)	bedding or cut flowers	June to Aug
Gypsophila elegans	hardy	sun	pink, red, white mixed	*in situ*	23 to 30	(9 to 12)	bedding or cut flowers	June to Sept
Helianthus annuus, sunflower	hardy	sun or semi-shade	mixed	*in situ*	60	(24)	bedding, border or cut flowers	July to Sept

should be gently pressed into the surface of the soil.

Half-hardy annuals are usually started off under glass. Sow the seeds in a seed mix in early spring at a temperature of about 16 to 21°C (60 to 70°F). When the seedlings are big enough to handle prick them off into a potting mix, spacing them between 3·5 and 4cm (1½ to 1¾in) apart.

Biennials are generally sown in rows out of doors in late summer and transplanted to a nursery bed at the beginning of the autumn. They are generally planted in their final flowering positions around the beginning of October and will flower the following spring or summer.

Both annuals and biennials are very easy to grow but they will handsomely reward a little care and attention. A number, such as antirrhinums, calendulas, nemesia, petunias and verbenas will produce a better display if you pinch out their tips while they are young to encourage them to form bushy plants. Most annuals and biennials start to die as soon as they have set seed particularly alyssum and nemesia. To keep them flowering over a longer period, the dead flower heads should be removed and with some, like lobelia, the whole plant can be trimmed back if it starts to get straggly. Several plants need support – twigs will do this admirably – and some like sunflowers will need staking.

	hardiness	situations	colours	number in a box 33 × 20cm (13 × 8in)	planting distance cm	(in)	uses	flowering time
Helichrysum bracteatum, strawflower	tender	sun	mixed	54	30	(12)	bedding, border or cut flowers	July to Sept
Iberis sempervirens, candytuft	hardy	sun	lilac, pink, red, white	54	15 to 23	(6 to 9)	bedding or cut flowers	May to Sept
Impatiens, busy lizzie	tender	sun	mixed	40	25	(10)	bedding, border or pots	July to Oct
Ipomoea purpurea, morning glory	hardy	sun	blue, pink, white, mixed	*in situ*	30	(12)	bedding	July to Oct
Lathyrus odoratus, sweet pea	hardy	sun	mixed	*in situ*	15 to 30	(6 to 12)	border or cut flowers	July to Oct
Lavatera trimestris, mallow	hardy	sun or semi-shade	pink, white	*in situ*	45 to 60	(18 to 24)	bedding	July to Sept
Linum grandiflorum, flax	hardy	sun or semi-shade	red, white	*in situ*	23	(9)	bedding	July, Aug
Lobelia erinus	half-hardy	sun or semi-shade	blue, white, carmine, mixed	54	15 to 23	(6 to 9)	bedding, edging or baskets	July to Oct
Matthiola incana, stock	half-hardy	sun	mixed	54	30	(12)	bedding or cut flowers	June to Sept
Mesembryanthemum criniflorum, Livingstone daisy	half-hardy	sun	mixed	54	30	(12)	bedding or edging	July to Oct
Mimulus, monkey flower	half-hardy	semi-shade or shade	red, mixed	40	30	(12)	bedding	July to Oct
Nemesia strumosa	half-hardy	sun or semi-shade	blue, orange, red, mixed	54	15 to 23	(6 to 9)	bedding	July to Sept
Nicotiana sanderae, tobacco plant	half-hardy	sun or semi-shade	green, red, white, mixed	40	45	(18)	bedding, border or cut flowers	July to Oct
Nigella damascena, love-in-a-mist	hardy	sun or semi-shade	blue, red, white, mixed	*in situ*	23	(9)	bedding or cut flowers	May to Aug
Petunia	half-hardy	sun	mixed	40	30	(12)	bedding	July to Oct

	hardiness	situations	colours	number in a box 33×20cm (13×8in)	planting distance cm	(in)	uses	flowering time
Phlox drummondii	half-hardy	sun or semi-shade	mixed	54	23	(9)	bedding	July to Oct
Portulaca grandiflora, sun plant	tender	sun or semi-shade	mixed	54	15 to 30	(6 to 12)	bedding or edging	July to Oct
Rudbeckia hirta, black-eyed Susan	hardy	sun	yellow, brown, mixed	40	30 to 45	(12 to 18)	bedding, border or cut flowers	Aug to Oct
Salvia splendens	tender	sun	pink, purple, red, white	40	30	(12)	bedding	July to Oct
Scabiosa atropurpurea, sweet scabious	hardy to half-hardy	sun or semi-shade	mixed	54	30	(12)	bedding, border or cut flowers	Aug to Oct
Tagetes erecta, African marigold	tender	sun	yellow, orange	54	23 to 30	(9 to 12)	bedding or edging	July to Oct'
Tagetes patula, French marigold	tender	sun	yellow, orange	54	23 to 30	(9 to 12)	bedding or edging	July to Oct
Tagetes tenuifolia, tagetes	tender	sun	yellow, orange	54	23 to 30	(9 to 12)	bedding or edging	July to Oct
Tropaeolum majus, nasturtium	hardy	sun or semi-shade	mixed	54	30	(12)	bedding	July to Sept
Verbena hortensis	tender	sun	mixed	54	30	(12)	bedding	July to Oct
Zinnia elegans	tender	sun	mixed	40	23 to 45	(9 to 18)	bedding, border, edging or cut flowers	July to Sept

French or African marigolds are popular annuals which grow well with most other garden plants. They are excellent both for bedding and for edging

178

Mix plantings in a herbaceous border so there is always something to catch the eye. Flowering plants in this border are set off by different varieties of hosta

Biennials

	hardiness (North America zone ratings)	situations	colours	number in a box 33 × 20cm (13 × 8in)	planting distance cm	(in)	uses	flowering time
Althaea rosea, hollyhock	hardy, 2 to 3	sun or semi-shade	pink, red, yellow, white	40	35	(14)	border	July to Aug
Bellis perennis, daisy	hardy, 3	sun or semi-shade	pink, red, white, mixed	40	15	(6)	bedding, border or cut flowers	May to July
Campanula media, Canterbury bell	hardy	sun or semi-shade	mixed	40	23 to 30	(9 to 12)	bedding or border	June to Aug
Cheiranthus × allionii, Siberian wallflower	hardy	sun or semi-shade	orange, yellow	54	23 to 30	(9 to 12)	bedding or large pots	April to July
Cheiranthus cheiri, wallflower	hardy	sun or semi-shade	mixed	40	23 to 30	(9 to 12)	bedding or border	April to May
Chrysanthemum leucanthemum, ox-eye daisy	hardy, 3	sun or semi-shade	white	54	30 to 45	(12 to 18)	border or cut flowers	May, June
Dianthus barbatus, sweet william	hardy	sun or semi-shade	mixed	54	23 to 30	(9 to 12)	bedding or cut flowers	June, July
Dianthus caryophyllus, carnation	hardy to half-hardy, 8	sun	red	54	23 to 30	(9 to 12)	bedding or cut flowers	June, July
Digitalis purpurea, foxglove	hardy, 4	sun or semi-shade	mixed	40	30 to 45	(12 to 18)	border	June, July
Lunaria annua, honesty	hardy	sun or shade	white, purple	54	30	(12)	border or cut flowers	May to July
Myosotis alpestris, forget-me-not	hardy	semi-shade	blue, pink, white	40	23	(9)	bedding or border	April, May
Papaver nudicaule, Iceland poppy	hardy	sun	mixed	*in situ*	30 to 45	(12 to 18)	bedding or border	June
Primula vulgaris, polyanthus	hardy, 5	sun or shade	mixed	40	15 to 23	(6 to 9)	bedding	April, May
Viola cornuta, viola	hardy, 6	sun or semi-shade	mixed	54	15	(6)	bedding	Mar to Aug
Viola tricolor	hardy, 4	sun or shade	mixed	54	15	(6)	bedding	Mar to Aug

Herbaceous Perennials

Perennials are plants which grow and continue to flower for many years. Herbaceous perennials are those which lack the permanent woody branch structure of shrubs and trees. Some, such as lupins, often die of old age after six or seven years, others, such as paeonies, can live for a long time. A few are evergreen but most of them die down to ground level in winter. Years ago most gardens had a border reserved solely for herbaceous perennials but this old concept has now lost favour mainly because of its drab appearance in winter and early spring. Today, the trend is towards mixed borders of shrubs, herbaceous perennials and other garden plants. The outstanding virtues of herbaceous perennials are the freshness of the new growth which comes from the soil each spring, the bright and conspicuous flowers which most species produce and the speed with which most plants grow to maturity. Many also have attractive leaves and the majority grow perfectly well on alkaline and heavy soils whereas most desirable shrubs and trees always seem to be those requiring light acid soil.

Using Herbaceous Perennials

A large number of plants of one individual herbaceous species may be planted in a large group to form a bed or used beneath shrubs as ground cover. But the more usual way to use herbaceous perennials is to prolong the season of interest by grouping together many different types so that some are nearly always in flower. In this sort of mixed planting, group together those herbaceous perennials which are in flower at the same time and set them against the neutral green background of plants not in flower. Most plants flower in June or between September and October. Plants which flower early in the year or in high summer are especially valuable. The many beautiful plants belonging to the genus *Helleborus* are winter-flowering herbaceous perennials and some of them are evergreen with good foliage as an additional asset. Because herbaceous perennials die down each year, bulbs can be planted between them to provide early spring flowers. When herbaceous perennials are used in conjunction with groups of shrubs, it is a good idea to choose shrubs which are most attractive in winter.

Planting and Propagation

Once herbaceous perennials have been planted they can often be left alone for many years. During this period perennial weeds, like couch grass and ground elder, which can grow around and among the perennials themselves can be very difficult to eradicate. So it is a good idea to prepare the ground thoroughly before planting, paying particular attention to any perennial weeds. The ground should be dug deeply and, if it is not in a really fertile condition, manure, compost or peat (see *Soil*) should be incorporated.

On light soils autumn planting is preferable for most species, but on heavy soils spring planting is more successful. A few plants, notably bearded iris and pyrethrum are best moved soon after flowering.

Most herbaceous plants are readily increased by dividing each plant into several smaller pieces but a few, especially lupins and delphiniums, are better propagated by cuttings prepared from young shoots. Plants can usually be grown cheaply and easily from seed but the end product will vary greatly in quality. A few important types are propagated by root cuttings – Japanese anemone, oriental poppy, *Anchusa italica* and phlox for example.

Maintenance

Routine maintenance of herbaceous perennials begins with the removal of weeds, general tidying and application of a general fertilizer in early spring. The shoots of over-crowded plants should be thinned out as they develop and weaker-growing plants should be staked before they start to collapse. To save work, plants which do not require staking or frequent division can be used – see opposite. The duration of flowering and the quality of the flowers can be improved by applying a mulch in the late spring when the soil has warmed up and by giving the plants copious quantities of water in dry periods. Removing dead flower heads also helps to prolong the flowering display.

To tidy up the border and to keep down pests and diseases herbaceous perennials are usually cut to the ground in the late autumn and the tops are then composted or burned.

Choosing the Plants

A selection of plants can be made for out of the ordinary purposes – in wet positions, beneath trees or in particularly exposed positions, for example. The soil conditions at planting time can be modified to some extent to accommodate most plants but it is nevertheless important to choose plants which grow satisfactorily in the soil and situation intended for them. With the wide range of choice this is not difficult.

To prolong the season of interest, especially in small gardens, choose plants which have good foliage. Some herbaceous perennials are evergreen or nearly so, and there are many sub-shrubby types (especially herbs) listed in most catalogues as herbaceous plants which will furnish the garden in winter. Some plants have particularly long flowering seasons but many of these do not have very conspicuous flowers. Short lists of plants for various purposes are given below. Use these lists to make your basic choices then turn to the individual plant summaries for more details. The numbers after the botanical names are the North America hardiness zone ratings – see *Climate*.

A Permanent Plants (not requiring frequent lifting, dividing and replanting)

Acanthus mollis 8, *fls* generally white or lilac, July to September

Alstroemeria aurantiaca 7, *fls* generally pink, yellow or orange, June to July

Anemone × hybrida (japonica) 5, wind flower, *fls* various colours, August to October

Aruncus sylvester 2 and 3, goat's beard, *fls* white, June

Astilbe 5 and 6, *fls* generally pink or red, June to August

Campanula lactiflora 5, bell flower, *fls* blue, June to August

Crambe cordifolia 6, seakale, *fls* white, summer

Dictamnus albus 2 and 3, burning bush, *fls* white, summer

Euphorbia 3 to 6, spurge, *fls* yellow or orange, April to August

Gypsophila paniculata 2 and 3, baby's breath, *fls* white, June to September

Hemerocallis 2 and 3, day lily, *fls* generally yellow, orange, pink or red, June to August

Kniphofia 6, red hot poker, torch lily, *fls* generally red or orange, June to October

Limonium latifolium 3, sea lavender, *fls* blue, July to September

Paeonia 3, paeony, *fls* white, pink or red, May to July

Papaver orientale 2 and 3, oriental poppy, *fls* red, white, orange, pink, May to June

Romneya 9, tree poppy, *fls* white, large, summer

B Tall plants (requiring no staking)

Aster novi-belgii 2 and 3, Michaelmas daisy, *fls* shades of red, pink, blue and purple

Campanula lactiflora 5, bell flower, *fls* blue, June to August

Cephalaria tatarica 2 and 3, giant scabious, *fls* yellow, summer

Echinops ritro 3, globe thistle, *fls* blue prickly thistle heads, June and July

Eupatorium purpureum 4, *fls* purple-rose, August to September

Hemerocallis 2 and 3, day lily, *fls* generally yellow, orange, pink or red, June to August

Kniphofia uvaria 6, red hot poker, *fls* coral-red becoming orange, summer

Onopordum arabicum 5, *fls* purple, thistle-like, July, *lvs* silver-grey

Perovskia atriplicifolia 2 and 3, Russian sage, *fls* lavender-blue, August to October

Verbascum olympicum 6, *fls* yellow, summer, early autumn, *lvs* grey, felted

C Plants for Dry, Alkaline Soils

Acanthus spinosus 8, bear's breeches, *fls* white, lilac lipped, July to September

Achillea filipendulina 2 and 3, yarrow, *fls* usually yellow, July to September

Agapanthus 'Headbourne Hybrids' 7, African lily, *fls* blue, July to September

Alstroemeria aurantiaca 7, *fls* pink, yellow, orange, June to July

Anemone × hybrida (japonica) 5, *fls* various colours, August to October

Anthemis tinctoria 3, *fls* shades of yellow, June to August

Centaurea montana 2 and 3, mountain knapweed, *fls* blue, white, pink, purple, cornflower-like, early summer

Crambe cordifolia 6, seakale, *fls* white, summer

Dictamnus albus 2 and 3, *fls* white, summer

Echinops ritro 3, globe thistle, *fls* blue, prickly thistle heads, June and July

Eremurus 3 to 6, foxtail lily, *fls* white, pink, amber, orange, yellow and copper, early summer

Gaillardia aristata 3, blanket flower, *fls* yellow and red, orange and red, browny-red, June to October

Gypsophila paniculata 2 and 3, baby's breath, *fls* white, June to September

Iris (bearded) 4 to 6, *fls* many shades, June to July

Limonium latifolium 3, sea lavender, *fls* blue, July to September

Macleaya cordata 3, *fls* ivory-white, June to August

Monarda didyma 4, bergamot, Oswego tea, *fls* scarlet, summer

Pulsatilla vulgaris 5, pasque flower, *fls* purple, pinks, reds, April to May

Romneya 9, tree poppy, *fls* white, large, summer

D Plants for Heavy and Wet Soils

Aruncus sylvester 2 and 3, goat's beard, *fls* white, June

Astilbe 5 and 6, *fls* generally pink or red, June to August

Caltha palustris 3, marsh marigold, *fls* golden yellow, spring

Euphorbia griffithii 5, *fls* orange, May and June

Gunnera manicata 7, prickly rhubarb, *lvs* 1·5 to 3m (5 to 10ft) diameter

Hemerocallis 2 and 3, day lily, *fls* generally yellow, orange, pink or red, June to August

Hosta 3 to 6, plantain lily, *fls* lilac, mauve, white, June to September

Iris ochroleuca 6, butterfly iris *fls* creamy white with yellow markings, June and July

Iris sibirica 3, *fls* blue, June

Ligularia clivorum 5, ragwort, *fls* yellow or orange, July to September

Lobelia fulgens 8, cardinal flower, *fls* brilliant scarlet, summer

Lysichitum 6, *fls* yellow or white, spring

Lysimachia punctata 6, yellow loosestrife, *fls* yellow, June to August

Mimulus 5, musk, *fls* yellow and red or brown, June to September

Peltiphyllum peltatum 5, umbrella plant, *fls* white or pale pink, mid-spring

Primula denticulata 4 and 5, *fls* shades of purple, rose, carmine or white with yellow eye, spring

Primula pulverulenta 5, *fls* claret-red with darker eye, summer

Rodgersia 5 and 6, *fls* white, pink, June and July

Trollius 2 to 4, globe flower, *fls* generally yellow, May and June

E Evergreen or Nearly Evergreen Plants (* means sub-shrubby or shrubby)

Alyssum saxatile 3, *fls* light yellow, spring

Anthemis cupaniana 3, *fls* white, June to August

Anthemis sancti-johannis 5, *fls* bright orange, June to August

Bergenia 2 and 3, bear's ears, *fls* pink, red, white, March to May

*Cheiranthus (annual in North America), wallflower, *fls* yellow, red, purple, mid-spring to early summer

Epimedium 3 to 5, *fls* red, pink, white, yellow, orange, April to June

Helleborus 3 to 6, *fls* greenish, white, purple, pink, January to April

Heuchera sanguinea 3, coral flower, *fls* deep or bright red, small bell-shaped, summer

*Iberis sempervirens 3, candytuft, *fls* white, early summer

Iris foetidissima 7, *fls* inconspicuous, orange berries in autumn

*Nepeta × faassenii 3, catmint, *fls* soft lavender, late spring to summer

*Ruta 'Jackman's Blue' 3, rue, *fls* yellow, June and July

*Salvia officinalis 3, common sage, *fls* purple or white, not very conspicuous, early summer

*Santolina 6 and 7, cotton lavender, *fls* yellow, mid-summer

F Plants with Good Foliage but not Evergreen

Acanthus spinosus 8, bear's breeches, *fls* white, lilac lipped, July to September

Alchemilla mollis 5, *fls* yellow, June to August

Anaphalis 3, *fls* white, July to September

Artemisia 3, wormwood, mainly grown for fern-like foliage

Aruncus sylvester 2 and 3, goat's beard, *fls* white, June

Brunnera macrophylla 3, *fls* blue, May and June

Coreopsis verticillata 6, *fls* golden, June to August

Dictamnus albus 2 and 3, burning bush, *fls* white, summer

Geranium 2 to 5, cranesbill, *fls* pink, blue, lilac, white, May to August

Gunnera manicata 7, prickly rhubarb, *lvs* 1·5 to 3m (5 to 10ft) diameter

Hemerocallis 2 and 3, day lily, *fls* generally yellow, orange, pink or red, June to August

Hosta 3 to 6, plantain lily, *fls* lilac, mauve, white, June to September

Macleaya cordata 3, *fls* ivory-white, June to August

Paeonia 3, paeony, *fls* white, pink or red, May to July

Rheum 3, ornamental rhubarb, *fls* creamy-yellow, red or white, summer

Rodgersia 5 and 6, *fls* white, pink, June and July

Stachys lanata 4, lamb's ears, donkey's ears, *fls* purple, July

G Plants Flowering for Two Months or More

Acanthus spinosus 8, bear's breeches, *fls* white, lilac lipped, July to September

Achillea 2 and 3, yarrow, *fls* usually yellow, May to September

Anemone × hybrida (japonica) 5, *fls* various colours, August to October

Brunnera macrophylla 3, *fls* blue, May and June

Buphthalmum salicifolium 3, ox-eye, *fls* yellow, summer

Catananche caerulea (annual in North America), cupid's dart, *fls* blue, June to August

Corydalis lutea 5, *fls* yellow, spring and summer

Dicentra eximia 2 and 3, fringed bleeding heart, *fls* rose-pink, late spring to summer

Euphorbia 3 to 6, spurge, *fls* yellow or orange, April to August

Helenium 3 to 5, sneezeweed, *fls* yellow, orange, red, August to September

Helleborus orientalis 6, Lenten rose, *fls* cream, pinkish purple, February and March

Hemerocallis 2 and 3, day lily, *fls* generally yellow, orange, pink or red, June to August

Kniphofia 'Maid of Orleans' 6, *fls* creamy-white, July to September

Kniphofia uvaria 6, red hot poker, *fls* coral red becoming orange, July to September

Papaver nudicaule 2, Iceland poppy, *fls* orange, salmon, yellow, white, summer

Polemonium caeruleum 2 and 3, Jacob's ladder, *fls* blue, late spring, early summer

Polygonum amplexicaule 6, knotweed, *fls* red, June to September

Potentilla 'Gibson's Scarlet' 2, *fls* red, June to September

Sanguisorba canadensis 3, burnet, *fls* whitish, summer

Tradescantia virginiana 4, *fls* blue, white, purple, June to early September

H Plants by Season of Flowering

Very early

Adonis vernalis 2 and 3, pheasant's eye, *fls* yellow

Bergenia 2 and 3, bear's ears, *fls* blue, pink, white

Cheiranthus (annual in North America), wallflower, *fls* yellow, red, purple

Doronicum 4, *fls* yellow

Euphorbia polychroma 4, *fls* bright yellow

Helleborus orientalis 6, Lenten rose, *fls* cream, pinkish purple

Pulsatilla vulgaris 5, pasque flower, *fls* purple, pinks, reds

May

Aquilegia 2 and 3, columbine, *fls* various colours

Brunnera macrophylla 3, *fls* blue

Centaurea montana 2 and 3, mountain knapweed, *fls* blue, white, pink, purple

Dicentra eximia 2 and 3, fringed bleeding heart, *fls* rose-pink

Geum 3 to 6, *fls* red, orange, yellow

Paeonia 3, *fls* white, pink, red

Papaver orientale 2 and 3, *fls* red, white, orange, pink

Polemonium caeruleum 2 and 3, Jacob's ladder, *fls* blue

Polygonum bistorta 3, *fls* pink, often again in autumn.

June

Achillea taygetea 'Moonshine' 2 and 3, *fls* lemon yellow

Anthemis cupaniana 3, *fls* white

Aruncus sylvester 2 and 3, goat's beard, *fls* white

It is not always necessary to put the largest plants at the back of the border; as long as nothing is hidden from sight, the variation in height can give a very pleasing effect

Centaurea dealbata 2 and 3, *fls* deep pink
Delphinium 2 and 3, *fls* blues, pink, white
Heuchera sanguinea 3, coral flower, *fls* deep or bright red
Iris 3 to 6, *fls* many shades
Kniphofia tubergenii 7, *fls* primrose-lemon
Lupinus 4, *fls* various colours
Pyrethrum 2 and 3, painted daisy, *fls* pink, red, white, again later if cut back after flowering
Tradescantia virginiana 4, *fls* blue, white, purple

July to August
Agapanthus 'Headbourne Hybrids' 7, African lily, *fls* blue
Chrysanthemum maximum 4, Shasta daisy, *fls* white
Coreopsis verticillata 6, *fls* golden
Erigeron speciosus, 2 and 3, *fls* pinks, blues, mauves
Helenium 3 to 5, sneezeweed, *fls* yellow, orange, red
Hemerocallis 2 and 3, day lily, *fls* generally yellow, orange, pink or red
Kniphofia 'Maid of Orleans' 6, *fls* creamy-white
Monarda didyma 4, bergamot, *fls* scarlet
Physostegia 'Summer Snow' 2 and 3, obedient plant, *fls* white
Potentilla, 'Gibson's Scarlet' 2, *fls* red
Sidalcea 8, *fls* mostly pink

September to October
Anaphalis nubigena 3, *fls* ivory-white
Aster novi-belgii 2 and 3, Michaelmas daisy, New York aster, *fls* shades of red, pink, blue and purple
Ceratostigma plumbaginoides 5 and 6, *fls* very bright blue
Chrysanthemum uliginosum 2 and 3, moon daisy, *fls* white
Eupatorium purpureum 4, *fls* purple-rose
Kniphofia galpinii 7, *fls* orange-yellow
Kniphofia nelsonii 7, *fls* orange-flame
Physostegia virginiana 'Vivid' 2 and 3, *fls* deep rose
Rudbeckia deamii 4, cone flower, *fls* yellow with black centre
Sedum spectabile 3, *fls* pink

Herbaceous Perennials
The numbers after the botanical names are the North America hardiness zone ratings – see *Climate*.

Acanthus, bear's breeches, *fls* white or lilac, in spikes, July to September, sun or light shade, ordinary soil. *A. mollis latifolius* 8, 1m (3ft): *A. spinosus* 8, 1·2m (4ft).

Achillea, yarrow, plate-like heads or airy sprays of *fls* on top of short and tall stems,

suitable for impressive clumps in large borders or for filling small pockets in rock gardens, *fls* May to September, any soil, sun or light shade. For borders *A. clypeolata* 3, 45cm (18in), *lvs* silvery, *fls* rich yellow heads, June to August: *A. filipendulina* 2 and 3, July to September, 'Coronation Gold', *fls* deep yellow; 'Gold Plate', similar but taller: *A. taygetea* 'Moonshine' 2–3, 45cm (18in), *lvs* silvery grey, *fls* lemon yellow, June to September: *A. tomentosa* 2–3, 15cm (6in), *lvs* grey green, ferny, *fls* yellow on short stems, July to September, superb plant for rock gardens.

Adonis vernalis 2 and 3, 20cm (8in), rock garden plant with *lvs* feathery green, short stems topped with flattish yellow daisy-like *fls*, March. Good rich soil, sun or light shade.

Agapanthus 7, African lily, 70cm (2½ft), the hardiest form is *Agapanthus* 'Headbourne Hybrids'. Fleshy stems terminate in spreading clusters of rich blue tube-shaped *fls*, July to September, *lvs* strap-shaped enclustering the flowering stems. Ideal for tubs on a sunny terrace or patio, or among border plants. Good rich soil in full sun, sheltered from cold winds.

Alchemilla, lady's mantle, foliage plant with rounded, finely-toothed *lvs* that have the ability to collect dew, *fls* yellow in airy sprays, June to August. *A. alpina* 3, 20cm (8in) ideal for rock gardens, *lvs* light green, *fls* yellow: *A. mollis* 5, to 45cm (18in), bigger sprays of tiny yellow *fls*, June to August. Any soil, sun or light shade.

Alstroemeria, Peruvian lily, *fls* a mixture of pink, yellow and orange, trumpet-shaped, June to July. Sheltered, sunny or lightly-shaded spot. *A. aurantiaca* 7, to 1m (3ft), 'Dover Orange', *fls* orange red; 'Lutea', *fls* yellow marked carmine red: *A. ligtu* 7, 60cm (2ft), *fls* shaded lilac, pink or purple.

Alyssum saxatile 3, 20cm (8in), creeping, cascading plant for rock gardens or walls in full sun, any well-drained soil, *fls* powder puff heads of bloom in various shades of yellow, April to June – vars lemon gold 'Citrinum', biscuit yellow 'Dudley Neville', double golden yellow 'Flore-pleno'.

Anaphalis, pearly everlasting, *lvs* silvery woolly, and flattish heads of white *fls*, August to September, sun or light shade, any soil, attractive carpeting plant for edge of border, good for flower arrangements in winter, as *fls* have a papery 'everlasting' texture. *A. nubigena* 3, 20cm (8in): *A. yedoensis* 3, taller, flowering from July.

Anemone × *hybrida (japonica)* 5, Japanese anemone, any soil, sun or light shade, 1·2m (4ft), *fls* saucer-shaped, August to October, named forms include semi-double pink 'Queen Charlotte', *fls* bright pink; 'September Charm', *fls* pure white; 'Louise Uhink': *A. vitifolia* 4, 60cm (2ft), *fls* white, copper coloured anthers.

Anthemis, *fls* daisy-like, plants with green or silvery grey ferny *lvs*, any soil, full sun or light shade. *A. cupaniana* 3, 30cm (1ft), *lvs* fine cut, *fls* small white, June to August: *A. nobilis* 'Treneague' 4, non-flowering chamomile, forms a bright green cushiony carpet or ornamental lawn: *A. sancti-johannis* 5, 45cm (18in), *fls* bright orange, June to August: *A. tinctoria* 3, 70cm (2½ft), *fls* yellow, June to August – vars 'E.C. Buxton' and 'Grallagh Gold'.

Aquilegia 2 and 3, columbine, *fls* distinctive, spurred, funnel-shaped borne on slender stems among maidenhair-like *lvs,* April to June, any well-drained soil, best in full sun, tall kinds make attractive border plants, small kinds are ideal for the rock garden. *A. flabellata*, 20cm (8in), *fls* white to violet-blue, May to July, rock garden plant: *A. longissima*, 70cm (2½ft), *fls* pale yellow, June to September: *A. vulgaris* hybrids, to 60cm (2ft), *fls* in shades of blue, red, pink and yellow, May to June.

Artemisia 3, silver-leaved foliage plant, excellent for brightening borders throughout the growing season, sun or light shade, any soil. *A. lactiflora* 3, white mugwort, 1·2m (4ft), *fls* tapering plumes of cream, August to September, needs a fairly moist soil in summer: *A. absinthium* 'Lambrook Silver' 2–3, wormwood, 60cm (2ft), *lvs* silvery white.

Aruncus sylvester 2 and 3, goat's beard, 1·8m (6ft), *fls* white plumes, June, *lvs* fern-like, any soil, sun or light shade, very adaptable.

Aster novi-belgii 2 and 3, Michaelmas daisy, New York aster, 70cm to 1·2m (2½ to 4ft), *fls* massed, daisy-like, many brilliant hues on top of sturdy stems, September to October, any well-drained soil, sun or light shade – vars include 'Ada Ballard', 1m (3ft), *fls* mauve; 'Chequers', 70cm (2½ft), *fls* purple-violet; 'Freda Ballard', 1m (3ft), *fls* semi-double, carmine; 'The Cardinal', 1·2m (4ft), *fls* rose-red.

Astilbe 5 and 6, 20cm to 1·8m (8in to 6ft), *fls* feathery plumes of white, pink, red, June to August, *lvs* finely-divided, ferny, any soil, best near water. *A.* × *arendsii* 60 to 90cm (2 to 3ft) – vars include 'Bressingham Beauty' *fls* pink; 'Red Sentinel', *fls* brick-red; 'Gloria', *fls* white: *A.* × *crispa*, 20cm (8in), for rock gardens, *lvs* crinkled, *fls* white, pale pink or red.

Bergenia 2 and 3, bear's ears, tough, leathery-leaved foliage plants for any aspect, *fls* spikes, bell-shaped, pink, red, white, March and April, *lvs* some kinds burnished coppery tints in cold weather in winter. *B. cordifolia purpurea*, *lvs* heart-shaped, *fls* lilac rose to purple: *B. crassifolia purpurea*, *fls* pink bell-shaped, January to April. 'Ballawley', a huge hybrid derived from crossing *B. beesiana* and *B. delavayi*, grows 60cm (2ft), *fls* fuchsia red, March to April. Hybrids of great merit include magenta-flowered 'Abendglut' (Evening Glow), March to April; and white- and pink-flowered 'Silberlicht' (Silver Light), April. Both of these hybrids are 70cm (2½ft). Any soil, sun or shade, ideal for ground cover under shrubs.

Brunnera macrophylla 3, 40cm (15in), effective shade-lover, *fls* intense blue forget-me-not-like in airy sprays, May and June, *lvs* large, matt green, heart-shaped, cover the ground. Any soil, provided it is fairly moist in summer, good in shade or full sun. *B. macrophylla* 'Variegata', *lvs* creamy-green variegated, *fls* blue.

Buphthalmum salicifolium 3, ox-eye, 70cm (2½ft), *fls* yellow, dark-centred, June and July. Ideal front-of-border plant. Related to helichrysum (everlasting flower). Any soil, sun or light shade.

Caltha palustris 3, marsh marigold, 25cm (10in), showy bog plant, attractive round the edge of a garden pool, any soil, sun or shade, *fls* kingcup-like, April and May, *lvs* rounded and shiny, *C.p.* 'Plena', *fls* double, golden; *C.p.* 'Alba', *fls* white, single, less vigorous.

Campanula lactiflora 5, bell flower, upright branching stems tipped with deep lavender blue or light lavender blue *fls*, June to August, any soil, specially good on chalk, shelter from cold winds. *C. lactiflora* 'Loddon Anna', 1·2m (4ft), *fls* greyish-pink; 'Pouffe', 20cm (8in), *fls* lavender; 'Prichard's Variety', 1m (3ft), *fls* lavender blue.

Catananche caerulea (annual in North America), cupid's dart, papery cornflower-like blooms are borne atop slender reed-like stems set with narrow greyish *lvs*, June to August. Ideal for winter flower arranging, as the *fls* are everlasting. Any soil, sun or light shade. Vars include 'Major', *fls* deep lavender-blue; 'Perry's White', *fls* white; 'Bicolor', *fls* blue and white.

Centaurea dealbata 2 and 3, 60cm (2ft), *fls* deep pink, thistle-like buds, June to September: *C. montana* 2 and 3, mountain knapweed, 45cm (18in), *fls* tufty heads, blue, white, pink or purple, May and June, *lvs* oblong, pointed, furnished with white hairs. Any soil, sun or very light shade.

Cephalaria tatarica 2 and 3, giant scabious, 1·5m (5ft), tall branching plant with shoots tipped with large yellow scabious *fls*, June and July. Ideal back of border plant for any soil in full sun, sheltered spot best to save winds blowing stems about.

Ceratostigma plumbaginoides 5 and 6, hardy plumbago, 30cm (1ft), *fls* small, sky-blue, July to November. Attractive ground-cover plants for sunny or lightly-shaded border.

Cheiranthus (annual in North America), wallflower, showy spring-flowering, short-lived perennials often grown as biennials, flamboyant heads of bloom in many brilliant colours, any soil, sun or shade. *C. × allionii*, Siberian wallflower, 40cm (15in) – vars 'Orange Queen', *fls* orange gold; 'Golden Bedder', *fls* orange, May to July: *C. cheiri*, 40cm (15in), many vars, *fls* range of colours, April to June; 'Blood Red'; 'Primrose Monarch'; 'Fire King'; 'Cloth of Gold'.

Chrysanthemum maximum 4, Shasta daisy, 70cm (2½ft), *fls* snow-white daisy-like with a pronounced golden eye of densely clustered stamens, June to August, any well-drained soil, full sun, excellent for cut flowers – vars 'Esther Read', *fls* white; 'H. Seibert', *fls* white with frilled petals; 'Wirral Supreme', *fls* double white, extra vigorous and tall: *C. uliginosum* 2–3, moon daisy, 1·8m (6ft), an imposing back-of-the-border plant, *fls* large, white single with green centres, October to November, *lvs* silvery grey-green, deeply cut, provide a pleasing foil.

Coreopsis verticillata 6, 45cm (18in), *fls* starry heads, golden-yellow top, ferny-leaved stems, June to August, any soil, sun or light shade. *C. grandiflora* 7–vars 'Baden-gold', 1m (3ft), *fls* golden yellow; 'Goldfinch', 20cm (8in), *fls* bright yellow; 'Sunburst', 70cm (2½ft), *fls* double rich yellow.

Corydalis lutea 5, 20cm (8in), *fls* spurred yellow in clusters on short stems among a cushion of ferny *lvs*, April to November. Ideal edge-of-border or rock plant for sun or shade, any well-drained soil.

Crambe cordifolia 6, ornamental seakale, 2·1m (7ft), tall branching stems misted with tiny white *fls*, July. Any soil, sun or light shade, best sheltered from strong winds, good for backing wide borders. Looks well against dark evergreen hedge.

Delphinium elatum 2 and 3, 1·2m (4ft), large group *fls*, majestic spikes, June to August. The more compact Belladonna varieties are ideal for smaller modern gardens and include 'Blue Bees', *fls* light blue; 'Peace', *fls* deep blue; 'Sensation', *fls* rose pink. Larger, to 1·8m (6ft), are the Pacific Hybrids, with immense *fls* clustered round imposing spikes. Among them are 'Astolat', *fls* pink; 'Black Knight', *fls* dark blue; 'Blue Jay', *fls* mid-blue, white-eyed; 'Galahad', *fls* pure white. Any deep, fertile, well-drained soil, full sun, sheltered from cold winds.

Dicentra eximia 2 and 3, fringed bleeding heart, 40cm (15in), *fls* sprays, rose-pink, locket or heart-shaped, May to September, *lvs* fern-like – var 'Alba', *fls* white. Ideal for deep shade or sun, any well-drained soil.

Dictamnus albus 2 and 3, burning bush, 60cm (2ft), *fls* spikes, spidery white or striped red, June and July, *fls* give off a volatile oil that can occasionally be ignited without endangering the plant. Any soil, sun or light shade, best in sheltered spot. 'Purpurea', *fls* pink with a red stripe, *lvs* shiny, finely saw edged.

Doronicum plantagineum 4, leopard's bane, 60cm (2ft), *fls* vivid buttercup-yellow daisy-like, April to June, *lvs* heart-shaped. Clump forming and ideal for sun or light shade, any well-drained soil. Good for edging borders. Vars include 'Harpur Crewe', *fls* 8cm (3in) across; 'Miss Mason', smaller.

Echinops ritro 3, globe thistle, 1·5m (5ft), imposing silver-grey foliage plant, stems topped with blue spheres of clustered blooms, June and July. Slightly prickly. Good for cutting for indoor decoration, any soil, best in full sun. Superb back of border plant, stake against gusty winds.

Epimedium 3 to 5, barrenwort, 15 to 30cm (6in to 1ft), attractive ground-cover plants valued for their exquisite miniature columbine-like *fls* in airy sprays, and mottled *lvs* which are often semi-evergreen. Any soil, sun, good for shade and keeping down weeds. *E. grandiflorum* 'Rose Queen', *fls* crimson carmine, June: *E. perralderianum*, *fls* yellow, June: *E. × rubrum*, *fls* crimson, May, *lvs* veined, reddish: *E. × youngianum* 'Niveum', *fls* white, April and May.

Eremurus 3 to 6, foxtail lily, ascending spikes of densely-packed starry *fls*, early summer. Ideal for a sheltered garden in full sun, deep rich soil. *E. olgae* 6, 1·5m (5ft), *fls* pink, June and July: *E.* 'Shelford Hybrids' 6, 2·1m (7ft), *fls* pink to glowing orange and copper, June and July: *E. stenophyllus bungei* 6, 1m (3ft), *fls* golden yellow with orange anthers, June.

Erigeron speciosus 2 and 3, fleabane, 45cm (18in), *fls* massed, daisy-like on leafy stems, June to August. Any well-drained soil, full sun. Good for rock gardens. Vars include 'Darkest of All', *fls* violet blue, single; 'Felicity', *fls* light pink, single; 'Gaiety', *fls* deep pink, semi-double; 'Prosperity', *fls* light violet, semi-double; 'Quakeress', *fls* lilac rose, semi-double.

Eupatorium purpureum 4, hemp agrimony, 1·8m (6ft), robust moisture-loving plant with stout stems enclasped by whorls of mid-green *lvs*, *fls* rose-red, August and September. Sun or light shade, but avoid dry spots.

Euphorbia, spurge, *fls* greeny yellow or orange red on sappy stems, April to August. For ground cover, rock gardens, swampy areas or woodland. *E. griffithii* 'Fireglow' 5, 60cm (2ft), *fls* rounded, flame-hued: *E. palustris* 3, 1m (3ft), *fls* sulphur yellow: *E. polychroma* 4, 45cm (18in), *fls* hummocks of bright sulphur yellow: *E. robbiae* 4, 40cm (16in), *fls* apple green, excellent for carpeting shaded areas: *E. sikkimensis* 6, 1·2m (4ft), *fls* chrome-yellow: *E. wulfenii* 6, 1·2m (4ft), *fls* bottle-brush heads of deep greenish-yellow on robust stems.

Gaillardia, blanket flower, 60cm (2ft) *fls* coppery red and yellow-zoned, daisy-like, June to October. Any soil, sun or light shade. Ideal front to middle of border plants. *G. aristata* 3–vars include 'Dazzler', *fls* orange-yellow, red-centred; 'Ipswich Beauty', *fls* orange, brownish-red; 'Wirral Flame', *fls* red with petals tipped gold.

Geranium, cranesbill, upright or spreading, *fls* saucer-shaped, *lvs* deeply cut. For borders, rock gardens and beneath shrubs, good for keeping down weeds.
For borders *G. grandiflorum* 2–3, 30cm (1ft), *fls* blue purple, June and July: *G. ibericum* 2–3, 45cm (18in), *fls* violet blue, July to August: *G. endressi* 'A. T. Johnson' 7, 30cm (1ft), *fls* silver pink, May to August: *G. psilostemon* 5, 70cm (2½ft), *fls* vivid magenta with a jet black eye, June to July.
For rock gardens *G.* × 'Ballerina' 3, 15cm (6in), *fls* pink, pencilled deep red: *G. dalmaticum* 2–3, 15cm (6in), *fls* light pink,

June to August, *lvs* glossy, rounded: *G. sanguineum* 3, bloody cranesbill, *fls* scarlet, June to September. Var 'Album', *fls* white.

Geum, avens, spreading *fls*, fiery colours, generally May to September. Any well-drained soil, sun or light shade. *G.* × *borisii* 3, edging plant, 30cm (12in), *fls* orange, scarlet: *G. chiloense* 6, 45cm (18in), 'Fire Opal', *fls* semi-double, scarlet; 'Lady Stratheden', *fls* double, yellow; 'Mrs Bradshaw', *fls* double, scarlet.

Gunnera manicata 7, giant ornamental rhubarb, 2·4m (8ft), for larger gardens in marshy soil, or on pond sides, *fls* large reddish brown cones, April and May, *lvs* to 3m (10ft), kidney-shaped, leaf stems thick, fleshy and prickly. Needs moisture in summer, any soil. Protect crowns by wrapping dying leaves over them in late autumn.

Gypsophila paniculata 2 and 3, baby's breath, *fls* clouds of white or pink on airy sprays, June to September. Any well-drained soil, full sun. Ideal for massing with foliage plants. Vars 'Bristol Fairy', 70cm (2½ft), *fls* double, white; 'Compacta Plena', 45cm (18in), *fls* double, white; 'Pink Star', *fls* double, pink.

Helenium autumnale 3, sneezeweed, midborder plant, *fls* disc-shaped with bobble centres on medium to tall stems, August to September. Any well-drained soil, full sun or light shade. Vars 'Bruno', 1m (3ft), *fls* mahogany; 'Butterpat', 1m (3ft), *fls* rich golden yellow; 'Pumilum Magnificum', 60cm (2ft), *fls* deep yellow.

Helleborus, *fls* cup-shaped, winter, *lvs* divided and often saw edged. Any soil, best in light shade. *H. argutifolius* 5, evergreen, 60cm (2ft), *fls* yellow green, March and April, *lvs* statuesque, three-lobed, spinyedged: *H. niger* 3, Christmas rose, 45cm (18in), *fls* white, January to March: *H. orientalis* 6, Lenten rose, 30cm (1ft), *fls* cream, pinkish purple, February and March.

Hemerocallis 2 and 3, day lily, 60cm to 1m (2 to 3ft), *fls* trumpet-shaped, yellow, orange, pinkish and coppery tinted, June to August. Best in deep loamy, moist soil that stays cool in dry summer months. Garden hybrids – 'Black Magic', *fls* yellowthroated, ruby purple; 'Hornby Castle', *fls* brick-red; 'Marion Vaughn', *fls* pale yellow; 'Pink Prelude'; 'Stafford', *fls* red.

Heuchera sanguinea 3, coral flower, 40cm (16in), *fls* deep or bright red, tiny, bellshaped, June to September, *lvs* heartshaped or rounded. Sun or light shade.

Hosta, plantain lily, grown for its long or broad or waved heart-shaped *lvs*, some variegated, *fls* white or pinkish lilac trumpets on spikes, summer. Any soil, ideally deep peaty loam, sun or shade. *H. albomarginata* 3, 45cm (18in), *lvs* white-edged, *fls* lilac, violet: *H. elata* 3, 1m (3ft), *lvs* wavy-edged, green, *fls* bluish violet, June and July: *H. fortunei* 'Aureomarginata' 3, 45cm (18in), *lvs* gold-edged green, *fls* lilac, July: *H. sieboldiana* 'Elegans' 3, 60cm (2ft), *lvs* crimped blue-green, rounded, *fls* pale lilac, July to August.

Iberis sempervirens 3, candytuft, 20cm (8in), rock plant for trailing over a dry stone wall or bank, *lvs* cushion of evergreen rosettes, *fls* white, May and June. Any soil, sun or very light shade.

Iris, fls many shades, June and July, *lvs* sword-shaped. The *fls* consist of six petals: three upright, known as the standards, and three drooping, called the falls. Bearded irises have tufts of silky hairs on the falls.
    Dwarf bearded – *I. pumila attica* 4, 15cm (6in), rock plants – vars 'Bee Wings', *fls* yellow with brown spotted falls; 'Orchid Flare', *fls* orchid pink.
    Intermediate and tall bearded – *I. germanica* 4, 70cm (2½ft); 'Chiltern Gold', *fls* yellow; 'Harbour Blue'; 'Langport Star', *fls* white; 'Techny Chimes', *fls* chrome yellow with orangy beard; 'Valimar', *fls* apricot.
    Beardless – *I. foetidissima* 7, stinking iris, gladdon, 45cm (18in), *fls* pale purple, June, scarlet seeds develop in autumn revealed through split seed pods: *I. ochroleuca* 6, butterfly iris, 1·2m (4ft), *fls* creamy white with yellow markings: *I. sibirica* 3, good on boggy soil, 70cm (2½ft), *fls* shades of blue – vars 'Violet Flare'; 'White Swirl': *I. spuria* 'Notha', 70cm (2½ft), *fls* rich purple.

Kniphofia 6–7, red hot poker, *fls* poker-like red, yellow, orange red, June to October, *lvs* slender, rush-like. For borders or rock gardens. June to July–'Bees' Sunset', 1m (3ft); *K. tubergenii*, 70cm (2½ft), lemon: July to September–'Bees' Lemon', 1·1m (3½ft); 'Maid of Orleans', 70cm (2½ft), creamy-white; *K. uvaria*, 1m (3ft), coral becoming orange-red: September to October–*K. galpinii*, 45cm (18in), orange-yellow; *K. nelsonii*, 70cm (2½ft), orange-flame; *K. rufa*, 60cm (2ft) yellow tipped with red.

Ligularia clivorum 5, ragwort, 1·2m (4ft), for waterside or moist garden, sun or light shade, keeps down weeds, *fls* orange or yellow, daisy-like, July to September – vars 'Desdemona', *fls* orange; 'Gregynog Gold', *fls* yellow, black anthers.

Limonium latifolium 3, sea lavender, 60cm (2ft), *fls* blue, July to September. Any soil, sun or light shade. For cutting for winter decoration – vars 'Blue Cloud', *fls* lavender blue; 'Violetta', *fls* violet blue.

Lobelia fulgens 8, cardinal flower, 70cm (2½ft), sun or light shade. In cold areas, lift plants in the autumn and over-winter in a cool greenhouse or frost-free frame, *fls* scarlet, *lvs* rosette, purple – vars 'Queen Victoria'; 'Bees' Flame'.

Lupinus polyphyllus 4, 1m (3ft), any soil, full sun, *fls* single and bicolour, May to July – vars 'Blue Jacket', *fls* blue and white; 'Blushing Bride', *fls* white; 'Cherry Pie', *fls* red; 'Elsie Waters', *fls* cream and pink; 'Serenade', *fls* red and crimson.

Lysichitum 6, American fake skunk cabbage (not to be confused with the skunk cabbage *Symplocarpus foetidus*), *fls* yellow or white, cowl-like, March to May, *lvs* broad, paddle-shaped, glossy, 60cm (2ft) long. Boggy soil, sun or light shade, sheltered from frost.

Lysimachia punctata 6, yellow loosestrife, 1m (3ft), vigorous spreading, *fls* bright yellow, cup-shaped, June to August. Any soil, sun or deep shade, excellent for keeping down weeds in wilder parts of the garden. *L. clethroides* 3, *fls* tapering cones, white, late summer.

Macleaya cordata 3, plume poppy, 1·8m (6ft), back of border plant, *fls* plumes, small, pearly-white, June to August, *lvs* deeply-lobed. Any soil, sun or light shade.

Mimulus 5, musk, 7 to 45cm (3 to 18in), spreading, for waterside or rock gardens, *fls* large, yellow and coppery red flushed or blotched. Sun or light shade, any moist soil. *M. × burnettii* 'A. T. Johnson', *fls* yellow spotted maroon, June to September: *M. cardinalis*, *fls* red, yellow throated, June to September: *M. luteus*, monkey musk, *fls* yellow, crimson or brown, May to August.

Monarda 4, bergamot, Oswego tea, *fls* rounded tassels top robust stems, June to September, *lvs* thick, hairy. Any soil, sun or light shade. *M. didyma* 70cm (2½ft), *fls* scarlet. Vars 'Croftway Pink'; 'Snow Maiden'; 'Blue Stocking'.

Nepeta × faassenii 3, catmint, 40cm (16in), edge-of-border plant, *lvs* silver-grey, aromatic, *fls* lilac lavender, May to September. Any soil, full sun – var 'Six Hills Giant'. Leave spent foliage uncut during winter.

Onopordum arabicum 5, Scots giant thistle, 2·4m (8ft), statuesque plant, *lvs* immense, prickly, silvered, *fls* purple thistle-like, July. Biennial, dying after flowering, self-sown seedlings appear in profusion the following year. Any soil, sun or very light shade.

Paeonia 3, paeony, fertile soil, sun or shade, *fls* globe or saucer-shaped single or double, late May to July, *lvs* bright reddish tints in autumn. *P. arietina*, 70cm (2½ft), *fls* single pink, May to June: *P. emodi*, 70cm (2½ft), *fls* single white, June to July: *P. lactiflora*, 1m (3ft), *fls* May to July – vars 'Albert Crousse', *fls* double carmine pink; 'Augustus John', *fls* single cherry rose; 'Bowl of Beauty', *fls* soft pink; 'Globe of Light', *fls* rose-pink: *P. mlokosewitschii*, 60cm (2ft), *fls* single yellow, April to May: *P. officinalis* 'Rubra-plena', 70cm (2½ft), *fls* double crimson-red.

Papaver nudicaule 2, Iceland poppy, 60cm (2ft), short-lived perennial usually grown as a biennial, *fls* cup-shaped, June to August, *lvs* deeply-lobed. Any well-drained soil, sun or light shade. Vars 'Kelmscott Strain', in shades of pink, orange, yellow, scarlet and white; 'Champagne Bubbles', in similar colours: *P. orientale* 2 and 3, oriental poppy, 70cm (2½ft), middle of border plants for any soil, in full sun, *fls* large, single or double chalice-like, many colours, May to June. Vars 'Enchantress'; 'King George'; 'Perry's White'; 'Salmon Glow'.

Peltiphyllum peltatum 5, umbrella plant, 70cm (2½ft), for watersides, *lvs* rounded, lobed, looking like umbrellas, on 60cm (2ft) stems, *fls* pink, bell-shaped, April.

Perovskia atriplicifolia 2 and 3, Russian sage, 1·2m (4ft), upright branched stems with small, lavender blue *fls*. Vars 'Blue Mist', *fls* light blue, July to September; 'Blue Spire', *fls* deep violet, August to October.

Phlox paniculata 4, 70cm (2½ft), *fls* tightly clustered, many shades, July to September. Any well-drained soil, full sun, sheltered from cold winds. Vars 'Graf Zeppelin', *fls* white, red-centred; 'Border Gem', *fls* violet blue; 'Dodo Hanbury Forbes', *fls* pink.

Physostegia virginiana 2 and 3, obedient plant. Vars 'Summer Snow', a pure white form, 1m (3ft), *fls* snapdragon-like, thickset heads about 15cm (6in) long, July to September; 'Vivid', 45cm (18in), *fls* deep rose, August to October.

Polemonium caeruleum 2 and 3, Jacob's ladder, 60cm (2ft), ground-covering, any soil, sun or light shade, *lvs* light green, *fls* sprays, blue or white, April to July.

Polygonum amplexicaule 6, knotweed, 1·2m (4ft), clump-forming, *lvs* large, heart-shaped, *fls* sprays, reddish, tiny, massed, June to September. Sun or light shade, any soil, specially useful for permanently moist places too wet to grow other herbaceous plants: *P. bistorta* 3, snakeweed, 1m (3ft), *fls* pink spikes, May and June, often again in autumn.

Potentilla atrosanguinea 2, spreading, *lvs* strawberry-like, *fls* cup-shaped or flattish, June to September. Any well-drained soil, full sun. 'Gibson's Scarlet', 30cm (1ft), *fls* red; 'William Rollison', 45cm (18in), *fls* semi-double, scarlet orange.

Primula denticulata 4 and 5, drumstick primrose, 30cm (1ft), *fls* purple, rose, carmine or white, March and April, *lvs* broad, crimped. For waterside planting or in moist, sheltered borders on deep rich soil, sun or light shade. Vars 'Alba', *fls* white; 'Ruby', *fls* rose purple: *P. bulleyana* 6, 70cm (2½ft), *fls* light orange, June to July: *P. pulverulenta* 5, 60cm (24in), *fls* red, pink or crimson, bell-shaped, June and July. Vars 'Bartley Strain', *fls* pink; 'Inverewe', *fls* orange scarlet; 'Red Hugh', *fls* brick red.

Pyrethrum 2 and 3, painted daisy, 70cm (2½ft), *fls* large, narrow-petalled, daisy-like, May to July, again later if cut back after flowering. Any soil, sun or shade. *P. roseum* – vars 'Avalanche', *fls* white; 'Brenda', *fls* pink; 'Evenglow', *fls* salmon; 'Kelway's Glorious', *fls* crimson; 'Carl Vogt', *fls* white, double; 'Prospero', *fls* pink, double; 'J. N. Twerdy', *fls* red, double.

Pulsatilla vulgaris 5, pasque flower, 30cm (1ft), *fls* purple, yellow-centred, cup-shaped, April to May, *lvs* ferny, very hairy. Good rock plant for sheltered garden. Vars 'Mrs Van der Elst', *fls* pale pink; 'Rubra', *fls* red; 'Budapest', *fls* reddish purple.

Rheum 3, ornamental rhubarb, grown for its handsome *lvs* and spikes of red or white *fls*, May and June. Moist soil, sun or light shade. *R. alexandrae*, 70cm (2½ft), *fls* creamy-yellow, May, *lvs* mid-green, oval: *R. palmatum*, sorrel rhubarb, 1·8m (5ft), *lvs* purple, deeply-cut, eventually fade to green, *fls* pinkish-red, bead-like, June and July.

Rodgersia 5 and 6, foliage plants for moist sheltered places, sun or light shade, any soil. *R. aesculifolia*, 1·5m (5ft), *lvs* huge, horse chestnut-like, *fls* plumes, white or pink, July:

189

R. tabularis, *lvs* green umbrellas 60cm (2ft) across, *fls* creamy-white, July to August.

Romneya 9, tree poppy, *fls* crumpled white, cup-shaped, June to September. Any well-drained soil in a sheltered part of the garden, in sun or light shade. Protect from frost by covering roots in autumn with plenty of straw or leaf-mould. *R. coulteri*, 2m (7ft), *lvs* deeply lobed, *fls* 10 to 12cm (4 to 5in) across: *R. trichocalyx*, similar, but smaller.

Rudbeckia deamii 4, cone flower, 1m (3ft), *fls* yellow, saucer-shaped, with blackish cone-like centres, July to September. Mid-to-back-of-border plant, any soil, sun or light shade.

Ruta, 'Jackman's Blue' 3, rue, 45cm (18in), best form of *Ruta graveolens*, *lvs* deep steel-blue, small, *fls* sulphur yellow, cupped, June and July. Edge-of-border plant, any soil, sun or shade, evergreen.

Salvia officinalis 3, common sage, 60cm (2ft), *lvs* furry, *fls* tubular violet-blue, June and July. Any soil, full sun.

Sanguisorba canadensis 3, burnet, clump-forming, *lvs* rosette, finely-divided, stems to 1·5m (5ft) high, *fls* white, bottle-brush-like, August to September. Sun or light shade, moist, rich soil, ideal for pond sides.

Santolina 6 and 7, cotton lavender, hummock-forming, *lvs* finely-divided, silvery, *fls* yellow, daisy-like, July. Any well-drained soil, full sun. *S. chamaecyparissus*, 45cm (18in), *lvs* silvery, woolly, *fls* yellow, July: *S. chamaecyparissus corsica*, dwarf species for rock garden, 30cm (1ft).

Sedum spectabile 3, ice plant, 40cm (15in), edging plant, *lvs* thick, round toothed, *fls* mushroom-like heads, tiny massed pinkish or reddish, August to October. Sun or light shade, any well-drained soil. Vars 'Brilliant', *fls* pink; 'September Ruby', *fls* pink; 'Iceberg', *fls* greenish white.

Sidalcea 8, mallow, 70cm (2½ft), *S. malvaeflora*, *fls* spikes, cup-shaped, June to August. Any well-drained soil, full sun. Shelter from strong winds. Vars 'Croftway Red', *fls* red; 'Loveliness', *fls* pink; 'Wm. Smith', *fls* pink.

Stachys lanata 4, lamb's ears, donkey's ears, 30cm (1ft), carpeting plant, *lvs* soft, furry, silvery-haired, *fls* short spikes, purple, July. For sunny borders, not suitable for shade or very wet soils. *S. macrantha*, betony, 60cm (2ft), *fls* purple, rose, violet, May to July, hairy green *lvs* form mat.

Tradescantia virginiana 4, trinity flower, spiderwort, border plant, *lvs* rush-like, pointed, *fls* on stems 60cm (2ft) high. June to September. Vars 'Caerulea Plena', *fls* blue; 'Isis', *fls* purple; 'J. C. Weguelin', *fls* violet blue; 'Osprey', *fls* white.

Trollius 2 to 4, globe flower, *fls* various shades of yellow and orange, globe-shaped, May to June, *lvs* deeply-cut and deep green. Best in rich deep soil, sun or shade. *T. × hybridus*, 70cm (2½ft). Vars 'Canary Bird', *fls* pale yellow; 'Golden Wonder', *fls* deep yellow; 'Orange Princess', *fls* orange yellow; 'Salamander', *fls* orange.

Verbascum olympicum 6, mullein, 2·4m (8ft), foliage plant. In its first year it develops a rosette of silver-felted hairy *lvs* the size of dinner plates; in its second year it sends up a slender spike topped with buttercup yellow *fls*. Any soil, full sun. Good for dry, stony gardens.

Viola 3, violet, carpeting plants, *lvs* dense, rounded, *fls* mauve, violet or white, most of the year. Any soil, specially lime/chalk, sun or light shade. *V. cornuta*, 20cm (8in), *fls* blue purple, or white, June to July: *V. labradorica*, prostrate weed suppressor, *lvs* purple, *fls* violet, April to May: *V. odorata*, sweet violet, *fls* shades of purple, violet, and white, February to April – vars 'Coeur d'Alsace', *fls* pink; 'Czar', *fls* violet; 'Marie Louise', *fls* mauve.

Shrubs

A shrub is a woody perennial – it develops one or several woody stems and does not die back to a bud at ground level after flowering, unless it is damaged by severe winter weather. Shrubs have many merits. They may bear an abundance of flowers, have decorative leaf form or colour, bear fruit or have colourful decorative bark.

When you choose a shrub, take into account three things: 1) your soil, 2) your local climate, and 3) where you intend to put it in your garden – against a wall, in shade or in full sun, for example. Some shrubs like azaleas, gaultherias and rhododendrons are lime haters and must generally be grown on acid soils that are rich in humus and very moist. If you garden on an alkaline soil, do not attempt to grow these but instead, make life much easier by choosing from those genera that enjoy alkaline conditions; *Berberis*, *Cistus*, *Cornus* and *Cytisus* are good examples. Some shrubs are very tender, others are very hardy. Your local climate will determine which of these you can grow well. In the shrub summaries we give North America hardiness zone ratings – see *Climate*. See *Gardens* for growing plants in shaded situations.

The next step is to look at labelled plants, either in botanic gardens, National Trust gardens or good public parks and see whether the plants you have chosen look as good in real life as they sound on paper. Revisit the plants at various times of the year so that you can evaluate their full beauty and usefulness.

Shrubs and trees form the permanent backbone and background of any garden. Shrubs can be used anywhere, either as specimen plants (magnolias and rhododendrons are often used in this way), or as part of a mixed border of herbaceous, climbing and wall plants, bulbs and ferns, or in a pure

Left: A well-planned herbaceous border. The plant in the foreground is *Centaurea montana* 'Rubra'

Below: In the larger garden leaf colour is as important as flower colour. This is especially true of a shrub border

shrub border. Many need little care and attention compared with most other garden plants and can act as useful habitats, and provide food, attracting birds and colourful insects.

Cultivation

Prepare the ground well by eradicating perennial weeds, deeply cultivating the whole area and enriching the soil with well-rotted compost or farmyard manure. If you garden on a dry, sandy soil dig in as much humus as possible to help to hold moisture. Dress heavy soils with sand and gravel to improve drainage. Apply one bucketful of each per square metre.

Planting

Shrubs with bare roots should be planted in the late autumn or spring. Evergreens are best planted in September or April and magnolias should be planted as the buds begin to burst. Plants purchased in containers can be planted at any time. Never plant bare-root shrubs when the soil is frozen or very wet. If it is, heel in the shrubs and wait for conditions to improve. When planting container-grown shrubs in the growing season, make sure that the soil is not too dry. If it is, the water in the rootball will move to dry soil at the sides of the planting hole.

Dig the hole for the shrub carefully making sure that it is deep enough and wide enough to hold the roots comfortably; do not bend the roots to get them into the hole. Snip off damaged roots with pruning shears/secateurs. Re-fill the hole a little at a time taking care to firm carefully each layer before proceeding on to the next. The final level of the soil should come up to the soil mark on the plant. Take care not to plant too deeply, particularly with shrubs which have been budded or grafted. If the soil is dry water the shrub and keep on watering in the first season if the dryness continues. Staking is not generally necessary but if a plant is loosened by wind then reduce its foliage lightly to prevent further rocking. Do not carry out this sort of pruning in the first year. Keep down weeds throughout the season to reduce competition and control pests and diseases as necessary.

When constructing a new shrub border you have three choices. You can plant it thickly to give a furnished effect and then remove some of them each year until a mature border is attained. In this sort of scheme it is often suggested that cheap shrubs should be used as fillers between choicer plants. But, unless a large proportion of the permanent shrubs require shelter in the early part of their life, this is a wasteful, expensive and time-consuming method of making a border. And you may find that you do not remove the coarser shrubs until they are spoiling the choicer ones and in some cases you may not remove them at all. Your second choice, which is much easier and less expensive, is to space the shrubs the correct distance apart and then carpet the whole area with ground-cover plants which can be removed. The final choice is to mulch the whole area with peat or leaf-mould, which will help to keep the soil moist and free from weeds and will later add to the humus in the soil.

Pruning

Most shrubs do not have to be pruned beyond the need to keep them healthy and uncongested. Most flower profusely if you leave them unpruned but they will benefit from judicious removal of old stems. You cannot keep a vigorous shrub in bounds by pruning it hard: in general the harder you prune it the more vigorous it will become. Some shrubs can, however, be restricted by pruning them in summer. If a shrub becomes weak or straggly, then it should be pruned and, as a safe rule, those that flower on old wood (generally in spring) should be pruned immediately the flowers have faded. Forsythia, kerria and lilac are typical of this group. Shrubs that flower on new wood (generally summer-flowering ones) should be pruned in the winter or spring before growth begins. Buddleias, *hydrangea paniculata* and indigoferas fall into this group. Shrubs like cornus, rubus and salix, which are grown for their brilliantly coloured bark, should be pruned very hard in early spring, although not all stems need to be removed. The faded trusses of shrubs such as magnolias, rhododendrons and syringas should be removed to prevent seed formation. For further details see *Pruning*.

Neglected Shrubs

If you take over a garden in which the shrubs have been neglected, it may well be worth trying to restore the best ones to health and vigour. The first thing to do is to identify the genera the shrubs belong to and then drastically prune them according to the rules outlined above.

Prune large evergreens very hard by cutting them back to the main framework in late June, when their growth is very vigorous. Severely prune deciduous plants after flowering, although you can remove dead, weak, or diseased wood at any time and allow young vigorous wood to take its place. Cover cuts more than 25mm (1 in) in diameter with a bituminous paint, to protect the wound from decay and insects.

Neglected, grafted plants, for example rhododendrons, will often be competing with shoots from the *Rh. ponticum* stock.

These are usually more vigorous and often produce pale-coloured flowers. Remove them at the base of the stem from which they arise.

After pruning, clear the surface of the border but do not dig it: if you do, roots of surface-rooting shrubs will be damaged. Apply a slow-acting fertilizer, such as sterilized bonemeal or hoof-and-horn, moisten the soil well and mulch the whole area with liberal amounts of compost.

Propagation
(see *Propagation* for further details)

Seed
Many shrubs are easily propagated by seed which, if fresh, will germinate freely. Sow seed to its own depth in pots of sterilized soil or growing mix and stand the pots in a cold frame without glass protection. Keep the soil or growing mix moist. Freezing will do no harm. Prick out the seedlings when they are large enough to handle.

Cuttings
Hardwood cuttings can be rooted in a sheltered border. In November cut strong growths of the current year's wood and trim it to lengths of about 20cm (8in) with buds at the top and bottom. Insert them to about two-thirds of their length in sandy, well-firmed soil. Keep the soil moist and weeded and leave the cuttings for about 16 months before moving. Berberis, buddleias, cornus cotoneasters, ribes, salix and weigelas can all be propagated in this way. Take softwood cuttings from late June until late August and root them under mist (see *Propagation*) or in a closed frame. When the plants have rooted, pot them on, overwinter them in a cold frame and plant them out in the following spring. Keep the cuttings on the dry side during winter when the plants are dormant. Most shrubs can be propagated in this way.

Layering
Most shrubs can be layered easily and this technique can be used to propagate shrubs which are not increased successfully by the above methods. See *Propagation* for details. Rooting may take up to three years and the roots tend to break off easily, so do not be in a hurry to move young plants.

Shrubs
More shrubs suitable for exposed positions can be found under *Gardens: Seaside Gardens*. See also *Climbing Plants* and *Wall Plants*. The numbers after the botanical names are the North America hardiness zone ratings – see *Climate*.

Abelia, grown mainly for its summer *fls*, likes full sun, lime-free soil. *A. chinensis* 5, to 1·5m (5ft), *fls* white, rose-tinted, freely produced, July, August: *A. × grandiflora* 5, to 3m (10ft), semi-evergreen, *fls* pink and white, July to September: *A. triflora* 7, over 3m (10ft), *fls* white or orange, May, June.

Abeliophyllum distichum 5, to 1m (3ft), well-drained soil, sunny position, *fls* fragrant, white, pink-tinged, February.

Amelanchier, snowy mespilus, grown mainly for its prolific white *fls*, spring, likes an open position, lime-free soil. *A. alnifolia* 4, to 3m (10ft), *fls* spring, fruits black: *A. canadensis* 4, to 3m (10ft): *A. stolonifera* 4, to 2·1m (7ft).

Arbutus, strawberry tree, evergreen, grown mainly for its creamy *fls* followed by scarlet fruits, generally 3 to 6m (10 to 20ft), dislikes wind. *A. andrachne* 8, likes lime-free soil, *fls* white, pitcher-shaped, spring: *A. menziesii* 7, to 18m (60ft), *fls* late spring, fruits orange-yellow: *A. unedo* 6, see *Gardens: Seaside Gardens*.

Berberis, barberries, huge group many of which are evergreen, *fls* vary from pale yellow to orange, spring, many species produce showy fruits or brilliant autumn colour, usually thorny. *B. aristata* 5, to 3m (10ft), *fls* yellow, berries red: *B. calliantha* 5, to 1·5m (5ft), *fls* crimson, fruits blue-black: *B. darwinii* 7, see *Gardens: Seaside Gardens*: *B. glaucocarpa* 8, over 3m (10ft), *fls* apricot-yellow: *B. × ottawensis* 5, see *Gardens: Seaside Gardens*. *B. sargentiana* 6, to 2m (6½ft), berries blue-black: *B. × stenophylla* 5, 3m (10ft), *fls* yellow, April: *B. taliensis* 5, to 1m (3ft), slow-growing, *fls* lemon yellow: *B. thunbergii* 4, see *Gardens: Seaside Gardens*: *B. vulgaris* 3, to 3m (10ft), berries red: *B. wilsoniae* 5, to 1·5m (5ft).

Buddleia, butterfly bush, grown mainly for its summer *fls*, thrives in almost any soil, full sun. *B. alternifolia* 5, to over 3m (10ft), *fls* lilac, June: *B. colvilei* 9, to over 3m (10ft), *fls* deep rose, June: *B. davidii* 5, and *B. globosa* 7, see *Gardens: Seaside Gardens*: *B. auriculata* 10, see *Wall Plants*: *B. × weyeriana* 5, *fls* orange-yellow, summer.

Callicarpa, neat shrub, grown mainly for the colour of its fruits in autumn, *fls* pink followed by purple fruits: *C. giraldiana* 5 and 6, to 3m (10ft), *lvs* purple in autumn, fruits deep lilac: *C. japonica* 5 and 6, to 1·5m (5ft), *fls* pink, fruits violet.

Calluna vulgaris 4, heather, many named forms, bright *fls* from July to November,

Shrub borders can provide colour and interest throughout the year. Shade need not be a problem; weigela and azaleas are growing well here under trees

colourful foliage. Plant in large patches of one type. Good for keeping weeds down. See *Gardens: Heather Gardens*.

Camellia, evergreen, grown mainly for its *fls*, likes an acid or peaty soil, can be grown in semi-shade or full sun. *C. japonica* 7, hundreds of varieties, *fls* white, pink or red, single or double, spring, good in north or east aspect: *C. saluenensis* 9, 3 to 4·5m (10 to 15ft), *fls* pink, spring: *C. sasanqua* 9, *fls* white, pink, crimson, single, semi-double, double, autumn and winter: *C. × williamsii* 7, 3m (10ft), *fls* white, pink to rose, single, semi-double, double, autumn to spring.

Caragana, thorny, shrubby, *fls* yellow, summer, *lvs* tiny, excellent on dry soils. *C. arborescens* 2, to 9m (30ft): *C. franchetiana* 6, to over 3m (10ft): *C. jubata* 3, to 1·5m (5ft), slow-growing, *fls* white, spring: *C. × sophorifolia* 2, over 3m (10ft).

Caryopteris, to 1·5m (5ft), *fls* late summer, *lvs* aromatic, likes a well-drained soil, warm, sunny position. *C. × clandonensis* 5, a few varieties, 60cm (2ft), *fls* blue.

Cassiope, dwarf plant, likes damp, acid soil, suitable for rock garden. *C. fastigiata* 2, to 30cm (1ft), *fls* white, April and May: *C. lycopodioides* 3, prostrate, *fls* white: *C. tetragona* 2, *fls* white, April and May.

Ceanothus, Californian lilacs, see also *Wall Plants*, variable habit, *fls* blue, rather short-lived, likes well-drained soil and wall protection. *C. cyaneus* 7, evergreen, *fls* early summer: *C. impressus* 9, evergreen, *fls* early spring: *C. rigidus* 8, evergreen, compact, *fls* spring.

Chaenomeles japonica 4, to 1·5m (5ft), *fls* orange, early spring, fruits large, yellow quinces, many varieties.

Cistus, sun rose, evergreen, usually to 1m (3ft), *fls* white, June and July, aromatic, likes very dry soil, shortlived. *C. × aguilari* 7, vigorous, *fls* very large: *C. albidus* 7, *fls* pale rose-lilac with yellow eye, *lvs* whitish-hoary: *C. crispus* 7, *C. × cyprius* 7, *C. ladaniferus* 7 and *C. laurifolius* 7, see *Gardens: Seaside Gardens*: *C. populifolius* 7, *fls* white, yellow basal stain: *C. salvifolius* 8, *fls* white, yellow basal stain.

Cornus, dogwood, large genus, to 3m (10ft), *fls* white, coloured bark. *C. alba* 2, *lvs* colour well in autumn, branches rich red in winter, fruits white or tinged blue: *C. florida* 4, *fls* May, rich foliage in the autumn: *C. kousa* 5, *lvs* rich bronze and crimson, strawberry-like fruits: *C. kousa chinensis* 5, slightly larger *fls*, *lvs* autumn tint: *C. mas* 4, cornelian cherry, *fls* small, yellow, February, *lvs* reddish-purple in the autumn, fruits bright red, cherry-like, edible: *C. nut-tallii* 7, *fls* white, sometimes flushed pink, May, *lvs* turn yellow, occasionally red in the autumn: *C. stolonifera* 2, dark red stems, fruits white – var 'Flaviramea' 2, noted for its rich shiny-yellow bark in winter. *C. alba* and *C. stolonifera* like boggy soil, others do well in sun or shade. See also *Gardens: Winter Gardens.*

Corylopsis, *fls* drooping yellow racemes, April, lime-free soil, sun or light shade,

A garden showing fresh spring colours. Take the heads off azaleas and rhododendrons after they have flowered to encourage the plants to put on new growth

shelter from cold winds. *C. pauciflora* 6, 1m (3ft), *fls* scented, fruits woody: *C. platypetala* 5, 3m (10ft), *fls* spring, fruits woody.

Corylus, hazel, over 3m (10ft), deciduous, slowly suckering shrub, mainly cultivated for edible nuts, thrives on heavy clay. *C. avellana* 3, *fls* yellow, lambs tails, February, *lvs* yellow in the autumn; vars 'Contorta' 3, has twisted spiralling stems; and 'Aurea' 3, has primrose yellow *lvs*: *C. cornuta* 4, beaked husk covers the nut.

Cotinus coggygria 5, smoke bush, to 4m (13ft), *fls* small, *lvs* rounded, good autumn tints; 'Royal Purple' 5, *lvs* rich purple; 'Atropurpureus' 5, *fls* pinkish.

Cotoneaster, huge genus of berrying shrubs, all sizes, mainly to 3m (10ft), *fls* white or pink-tinged, June, fruits usually red, sun or light shade, good for hedges or screens. *C. adpressus* 4, dwarf, widespreading shrub, good for rock gardens, *lvs* turn scarlet in the autumn, fruits bright red: *C.* × *aldenhamensis* 4, evergreen, to over 3m (10ft), widespreading habit: *C. congestus* 6, creeping evergreen, *lvs* small, bluish-green: *C. conspicuus* 5, evergreen: *C.* × 'Cornubia', semi-evergreen, grows over 6m (20ft): *C. dammeri* 5, evergreen, prostrate, ideal ground cover: *C. frigidus* 7, semi-evergreen, over 3m (10ft): *C. horizontalis* 4, see *Wall Plants*: *C. lacteus* 6, and *C. microphyllus* 5, see *Gardens: Seaside Gardens*: *C.* × *rothschildianus* 5, over 3m (10ft), distinctive, widespreading habit when young, fruits creamy yellow: *C. salicifolius* 6, 2·5m (8ft), evergreen: *C. simonsii* 5, semi-evergreen: *C.* × *watereri* 5, variable semi-evergreen hybrids, 9m (30ft).

Cytisus, brooms, vary from prostrate to 9m (30ft), *fls* mostly yellow, March to July, many hybrids, often brown-red and multi-coloured, enjoy dry, stony soils. *C. albus* 5, 1·8m (6ft), *fls* white: *C. battandieri* 7, 4·5m (15ft), deciduous, *fls* yellow, pineapple-scented, July: *C.* × *beanii* 5, dwarf shrub to 30cm (1ft), deciduous, *fls* May: *C.* × *kewensis* 6, semi-prostrate, deciduous, *fls* creamy yellow, May: *C. monspessulanus* 7, semi-evergreen, to 3m (10ft), *fls* April to June, subject to damage by severe frost: *C.* × *praecox* 5, to 1·5m (5ft), deciduous, *fls* creamy yellow, May: *C. scoparius* 5, common broom, deciduous, to 3m (10ft), *fls* May; vars with shades of crimson and yellow *fls* – 'Andreanus'; 'Dorothy Walpole'; 'Firefly'.

Daphne, some hummock-forming, others upright and well-branched, suitable for rock gardens, sweet-scented difficult shrubs, often very shortlived, *fls* from autumn to summer, any soil including lime/chalk, light shade or full sun, shelter from cold winds. *D. arbuscula* 4, evergreen, 15cm (6in), dwarf alpine shrublet, *fls* rose-pink, June, fruits brownish-yellow: *D.* × *burkwoodii* 5, semi-evergreen, to 1m (3ft), *fls* pale pink, May and June: *D. cneorum* 4, garland flower, 15cm (6in), *fls* rose-pink, April and May, fruits brownish-yellow: *D. mezereum* 4, deciduous, to 1·5m (5ft), *fls* purple-pink, February and March, fruits scarlet, poisonous: *D. odora* 7, evergreen, to 1·8m (6ft), *fls* winter and early spring.

Decaisnea fargesii 5, to 3m (10ft), deciduous, tender shrub for loamy, peaty soil, shelter from cold winds, *fls* yellow-green, early summer, fruits a long blue pod.

Deutzia, 1·8m (6ft), deciduous, hardy, any soil including lime/chalk, *fls* white or pink, bell-like, June, easy shrub but protect from icy winds in early spring. *D.* × *kalmiaeflora* 5, *fls* white, flushed carmine: *D.* × *rosea* 5, 1m (3ft), compact shrub, *fls* pink: *D. scabra* 4–5, to 3·6m (12ft), *fls* white, June and July; var 'Plena' 4–5, *fls* double, white flushed purple: *D. setchuenensis corymbifera* 4, *fls* white.

Elaeagnus, deciduous or evergreen, fast-growing, *fls* white, small, sweet-scented, generally October and November, excellent for seaside gardens. *E. glabra* 5, 3m (10ft), evergreen, *fls* autumn, fruits orange with silvery freckles: *E. pungens* and *E.* × *reflexa*, see *Gardens: Seaside Gardens*.

Erica, heath, evergreen, *fls* generally white and shades of pink, good for ground cover, possible to have ericas in flower most months of the year, prefer acid soils. See *Gardens: Heather Gardens* and *Seaside Gardens*.

Escallonia, evergreen, to 2·5m (8ft), *fls* pink, white, red, summer to early autumn, all soils including dry sand and lime/chalk, sun or light shade. *E. macrantha* 8, see *Gardens: Seaside Gardens*: *E.* × *iveyi* 8, *fls* white, July to August, protect from cold winds, best grown at the foot of a south-facing wall: *E. rubra* 8, to 3m (10ft), *fls* red, July, *lvs* aromatic when bruised.

Eucryphia, evergreen, cool, light-shaded woodland conditions on neutral or slightly acid soil, protect from cold winds and severe frosts, *fls* white, July to September. *E. glutinosa* 8, to 9m (30ft), *fls* July and August, *lvs* autumn colour: *E.* × *nymansensis* 8.

Euonymus, deciduous or evergreen, excellent on chalk, *fls* of little ornament, fruits pink, red, very attractive, sun or light shade. *E. alatus* 3, deciduous, to 1·8m (6ft), *lvs* fine autumn colour: *E. europaeus* 'Red Cascade' 3, spindle, deciduous, to 2·4m (8ft), fruits scarlet capsules, green stems: *E. fortunei* 5, evergreen, trailing or self-clinging climber, *fls* small, pale green, fruits pinkish capsules with orange seeds in the autumn: *E. japonicus*, see *Gardens: Seaside Gardens*.

Forsythia, *fls* yellow, spring, any soil including chalk, sun or light shade. *F. giraldiana* 4, over 3m (10ft), *fls* pale yellow, sometimes appear as early as late February: *F. × intermedia* 'Lynwood' 4, vigorous hybrid, up to 3m (10ft), *fls* late March and April: *F. suspensa* 5, rambling shrub up to 3m (10ft) higher against a wall, *fls* late March to April.

Fuchsia, tender flowering shrub, needs a warm sheltered sunny or lightly-shaded position. *F. gracilis* 5–6, slender habit, *fls* red and purple: *F. magellanica*, see *Gardens: Seaside Gardens*.

Gaultheria, evergreen, carpeting shrub, *fls* white, urn-shaped, late spring to early summer, followed by red or black berries, prefers acid soils and shade. *G. fragrantissima* 9, 1·2m (4ft), *fls* fragrant, fruits bright blue: *G. itoana* 8, 15cm (6in), creeping, fruits bright red: *G. procumbens* 3, 15cm (6in), partridge berry, creeping, fruits bright red: *G. shallon* 5, 1·8m (6ft), *fls* white, berries purple black.

Genista, broom, deciduous, upright or ground cover, best in light, poor soils, *fls* yellow, spring and summer, shortlived. *G. aetnensis* 6, Mount Etna broom, over 3m (10ft), *fls* July: *G. cinerea* 7, to 3·5m (11ft), *fls* June and July: *G. hispanica* 6, see *Gardens: Seaside Gardens*: *G. tinctoria* 2, Dyer's greenweed, to 60cm (2ft), *fls* June to September.

Hamamelis, witch hazel, deciduous, acid or neutral soil, shelter from cold winds, *fls* yellow, narrow petalled, late winter. *H. × intermedia* 5, over 3m (10ft), *fls* December to March: *H. japonica* 5, Japanese witch hazel, over 3m (10ft), *fls* December to March, *lvs* rich autumn colour: *H. mollis* 5, Chinese witch hazel, over 3m (10ft), *fls* fragrant, December to March, *lvs* autumn colour yellow; var 'Pallida' 5, *fls* sulphur yellow, *lvs* yellow in the autumn: *H. vernalis* 4, Ozark witch hazel, 1·2 to 1·8m (4 to 6ft), *fls* pale orange or copper, January and February, *lvs* in autumn usually butter yellow.

Hebe, evergreen, neat habit, *fls* usually white, good in maritime or industrial areas, can be damaged by frost, sun or light shade, carpeting forms make good ground cover plants. *H. albicans* 4, dwarf, dense, rounded: *H. brachysiphon* 5, to 1·5m (5ft) or more, *fls* June or July: *H. cupressoides* 9, up to 1·8m (6ft), *fls* small, pale blue, June and July: *H. hulkeana* 9, to 1·8m (6ft), *fls* blue, May and June: *H. pinguifolia* 6, dwarf to prostrate, 15cm (6in), suitable rock garden, *fls* July to August: *H. speciosa* 10, to 1·5m (5ft), *fls* dark, reddish-purple, *lvs* handsome, leathery. See also *Gardens: Seaside Gardens*.

Hibiscus, hardy forms mostly deciduous, in cold areas protect roots in winter, *fls* late summer to early autumn, full sun, shelter from frosty winds. *H. rosa-sinensis* 9, *fls* white, pink, red, yellow or multicoloured: *H. syriacus* 5, about 3m (10ft), *fls* shades purple or blue, open in succession between July and October; vars 'Ardens' 5, *fls* rose; 'Blue Bird' 5, *fls* mid-blue, red centred.

Hydrangea, deciduous and evergreen forms, *fls* summer and autumn, needs copious watering in summer, protect from frost in cold districts. *H. involucrata* 6 and 7, dwarf, Japanese species, *fls* blue or rosy-lilac surrounded by white: *H. macrophylla* 5 and 6, and vars to 3m (10ft), *fls* white, pink, red, blue or a combination of these – see *Gardens: Seaside Gardens*: *H. paniculata* 4, over 3m (10ft), *fls* creamy-white: *H. sargentiana* 7, to 3m (10ft), *fls* blue with white florets, July and August, shoots thickly covered with hairs and bristles.

Hypericum, St John's Wort, for well-drained soil, sun or light shade, generally to 1·5m (5ft), *fls* yellow, summer and autumn, red or black fruits in the autumn, for rock gardens, or carpeting under trees and borders. *H. calycinum* 6, rose of Sharon, evergreen, dwarf, to 60cm (2ft): *H. elatum* 5, *fls* pale yellow, fruits red; var 'Elstead' 5, brightly coloured fruits: *H. olympicum* 6, 30cm (1ft), rock gardens, *fls* yellow, July and August: *H. patulum* 'Hidcote' 5, 1·8m (6ft), *fls* yellow, saucer-shaped, July to September.

Kerria japonica 4, Jew's mallow, up to 1·8m (6ft), *fls* yellow, April and May, green stems effective in winter, sun or light shade, all soils; vars 'Pleniflora' 4, *fls* double, orange-yellow; 'Variegata' 4, *lvs* white edged.

Lavandula, lavender, evergreen, to 1·2m (4ft), *fls* blue, sometimes white, aromatic shrub, likes full sun, dry soil. *L. spica* 5; vars

'Hidcote' 5, 60cm (2ft), *fls* deep purple; 'Twickle Purple' 5, 1m (3ft), *fls* purple.

Ligustrum, privet, evergreen or semi-evergreen, *fls* white, heavily perfumed, summer and autumn, excellent in shade, fast growing. *L. delavayanum* 7, evergreen, to 3m (10ft), *fls* autumn, *lvs* large, glossy: *L. lucidum* 7, 3m (10ft), shelter from cold, frosty winds: *L. ovalifolium* 5, see *Gardens: Seaside Gardens*: *L. sinense* 7, deciduous, over 3m (10ft), *fls* July, fruits black-purple.

Magnolia, finest of all flowering shrubs, evergreen and deciduous, likes shelter from wind. *M. grandiflora* 7, to 15m (50ft), evergreen, *fls* creamy-white, July to September, fragrant: *M. liliflora* 6, 3m (10ft), *fls* purple flushed on outside, creamy-white within, late April to early June: *M. obovata* 5, 4·5m (15ft), *fls* creamy-white, June: *M. sinensis* 6, over 3m (10ft), *fls* white, June, lemon-scented: *M. × soulangeana* 5, over 3m (10ft), *fls* white with rose-purple basal stain, April to early May: *M. stellata* 5, to 3m (10ft), *fls* white, March and April, winter buds grey-hairy.

Mahonia, useful evergreen group for sun or shade, *fls* yellow, November to April, fruits purple, likes well-drained soil. *M. aquifolium* 5, and vars, Oregon grape, to 1·5m (5ft), *fls* early spring, followed by rich, black berries in summer, *lvs* sometimes turn red in winter: *M. × 'Charity'* 6, *fls* yellow, November to February: *M. japonica* 7, 2·4m (8ft), *fls* late autumn to early spring: *M. lomariifolia* 9, over 3m (10ft), *fls* winter: *M. nervosa* 5, dwarf species, *fls* May and June, *lvs* often red in winter.

Olearia, daisy bush, evergreen, to 2·4m (8ft), *fls* white or creamy-white, good on chalk soils, full sun. *O. haastii* 8, to 3m (10ft), *fls* July and August: *O. macrodonta* 8, New Zealand holly, to 3m (10ft), *fls* June, *lvs* holly-like, silvery-white beneath: *O. × scilloniensis* 9, 1·5m (5ft), *fls* May.

Pernettya mucronata 6 and 7, and vars, dense evergreen, useful for ground cover, to 1m (3ft), *fls* white, heath-like, May to June, fruits marble-like, ranging from white to purple, for acid soils and light shade; vars 'Alba' 7, white fruits; 'Bell's Seedling' 7, cherry red fruits.

Philadelphus, mock orange, to 2·4m (8ft), *fls* white, June and July, fragrant, deciduous, sun or light shade, well-drained soil. *P. coronarius* 4, to 3m (10ft); 'Aureus' 4, 2·1m (7ft), *fls* white, *lvs* yellow: *P. × splendens* 5, 3m (10ft), *fls* yellow anthers.

Potentilla fruticosa 2, and vars, to 1·5m (5ft), *fls* yellow, May to September, for full sun or light shade, good for hedging or carpeting the edges of a border.

Pyracantha, firethorn, evergreen, best in full sun, hardy, tolerates any soil including lime/chalk. *P. angustifolia* 7, yellow berries: *P. coccinea* 6, over 3m (10ft), *fls* white, June, fruit red, orange or yellow, often grown as a wall shrub, thorny: *P. × watereri* 5, orange-scarlet berries.

Rhododendron, huge genus of hardy, tender, evergreen and deciduous shrubs. Some make large towering bushes, others minute hummocks for the rock garden. Best in light shade, sheltered from cold frosty winds, on acid peaty soil that stays moist in summer. Woodland setting ideal for the larger species and hybrids. Grown mostly for their flamboyant *fls* early spring and summer; some also have magnificent foliage. Many hybrids and vars available; consult a specialist catalogue for choice. *Rh. arboreum* 7, 12m (40ft), tallest of the genus, *fls* ball headed clusters, blood-red, March and April: *Rh. augustinii* 6, 4·5m (15ft), *fls* funnel-shaped, blue to mauve, April and May: *Rh. falconeri* 8, 12m (40ft), *lvs* oblong, leathery, up to 30cm (1ft) long, *fls* rounded clusters, bell-shaped, creamy yellow, April, protect from cold winds: *Rh. fortunei* 6, 3m (10ft), *fls* clusters, funnel-shaped, pink, May, *lvs* oblong, blue-green beneath: *Rh. impeditum* 4, 30cm (1ft), *fls* mauve to purple blue, April and May: *Rh. lutescens* 7, 3m (10ft), *fls* funnel-shaped, yellow, January to April: *Rh. orbiculare* 6, 2·4m (8ft), *fls* pink, bell-shaped, April and May: *Rh. ponticum* 6, see *Gardens: Seaside Gardens*: *Rh. wardii* 7, 3m (10ft), *fls* primrose to canary yellow, saucer-shaped, May and June: *Rh. yakushimanum* 6, 1m (3ft), *fls* bell-shaped, pinkish white, May and June. Azaleas, *Rh. kiusianum* 6–7, main parent of the Kurume hybrids, evergreen, 1m (3ft), *fls* pink or purple, early May: *Rh. schlippenbachii* 4, 4·5m (15ft), *fls* white to pink speckled with scarlet.

Ribes, flowering currant, *fls* spring, easy shrubs, good in dryish soils, like sun, very hardy. *R. alpinum* 2, to 2m (6½ft), deciduous, *fls* greenish-yellow, fruits red: *R. americanum* 5, American black currant, to 1·8m (6ft), deciduous, *fls* yellowish, insipid, *lvs* crimson and yellow in the autumn: *R. sanguineum* 5, the popular flowering currant, to 3m (10ft), *fls* deep rose-pink, petals white, April, fruits black, bloomy: *R. speciosum* 4, semi-evergreen, to 3m (10ft), *fls* red, fuchsia-like, April and May, *lvs* shiny, fruits and stems reddish, bristly.

Left: Shrub borders featuring *Rhododendron discolor, Pinus sylvestris* and *Picea omorika*

Below; A colourful border of mixed azaleas with *Geranium macrorhizum*

Rosa, huge group of bush, climbing, deciduous and semi-evergreen shrubs, *fls* June and July, hips red in autumn, all soils except wet or acid ones. See *Roses*. *R. × alba* 4, rose of York, to 3m (10ft), *fls* white, richly scented: *R. centifolia* 5, cabbage rose, to 1·5m (5ft), *fls* pink, double: *R. helenae* 5, to over 6m (20ft), *fls* creamy-white, June: *R. hugonis* 5, to 2m (6½ft), *fls* yellow, single, *lvs* fern-like, bronze in autumn: *R. moyesii* 5, to over 3m (10ft), *fls* blood-crimson: *R. omeiensis* 6, Mount Omei rose, to 3m (10ft), *fls* white, May and early June, fruits crimson and yellow, edible, pear-shaped: *R. rubiginosa* 3, sweet briar, to 3m (10ft), *fls* pink, summer.

Rubus, brambles, scrambling, deciduous shrubs, sun or light shade. *R. biflorus* 4, to 3m (10ft), *fls* white, fruits yellow, edible, stems covered with white, waxy bloom: *R. deliciosus* 5, to 3m (10ft), *fls* white, like dog-roses, May and June, fruits purplish but seldom maturing, thornless: *R. phoenicolasius* 5, Japanese wineberry, 2·4m (8ft), stems have reddish hairs, fruits scarlet, edible, for arbour or trellis work: *R. spectabilis* 5, to 1·8m (6ft), *fls* magenta-rose, April, fragrant, fruits large, ovoid, orange-yellow, edible.

Skimmia, evergreen, dwarf, aromatic, fruits scarlet, plentiful, **any soil**, sun or light shade, protect **from cold winds**. *S. japonica* 7, to 1·5m (5ft), *fls* **white**, April and May: *S. laureola* 6, to 1·5m (5ft), *fls* greenish-yellow, spring, fragrant.

Spiraea, large genus, any well-drained soil, sun or light shade, excellent for hedges, *fls* white, summer. *S. × arguta* 4, bridal wreath, foam of May, to 1·8m (6ft), *fls* April and May: *S. × bumalda* 5, to 60cm (2ft), *fls* deep pink, *lvs* often variegated with pink and cream: *S. douglasii* 6, to 1·8m (6ft), *fls* purplish-rose, June and July: *S. japonica* 5, and vars, to 1·5m (5ft), *fls* pink, in large flattened heads, from midsummer onwards: *S. salicifolia* 6, bridewort, vigorous, *fls* pink, June and July.

Syringa, lilac, to 9m (30ft), *fls* May and June, any well-drained soil, sun or light shade. *S. × chinensis* 5, Rouen lilac, to 3m (10ft), *fls* lavender: *S. emodi* 5 and 6, Himalayan lilac, over 3m (10ft), *fls* pale lilac in bud, fading to white: *S. julianae* 5, to 2·4m (8ft), *fls* pale lilac: *S. × persica* 5, Persian lilac, to 2·4m (8ft), *fls* lilac: *S. vulgaris* 3, many vars including 'Blue Hyacinth'; 'Primrose'; 'Michel Buchner'.

Viburnum, deciduous and evergreen, *fls* all seasons according to types, some have rich red fruits, others superb in leaf, any soil, particularly lime/chalk, sun or light shade. *V. × bodnantense* 5, to over 3m (10ft), *fls* rose tinted, October onwards, scented: *V. buddleifolium* 6, nearly evergreen, to 3m (10ft), *fls* white, June, fruits red, finally black: *V. carlesii* 4, to 3m (10ft), *fls* white, June and July, fruits red: *V. davidii* 7, evergreen, to 1·5m (5ft), good for ground cover, *fls* white, June, fruits turquoise blue: *V. farreri* 6, over 3m (10ft), *fls* pink in bud, opening white, November onwards, fruits red: *V. henryi* 7, evergreen, to 3m (10ft), *fls* white, June, fruits red, then black: *V. lantana* 3, wayfaring tree, to over 3m (10ft), *fls* creamy-white, May and June, *lvs* sometimes dark crimson in the autumn, fruits red, turning to black: *V. macrocephalum* 6, see *Wall Plants*: *V. plicatum* 4, Japanese snowball, to 3m (10ft), *fls* white, May and early June: *V. rhytidophyllum* 5, evergreen, to over 3m (10ft), *fls* creamy-white, May, fruits red, finally black, plant two or more as single specimens, do not fruit freely: *V. tinus* 7 and 8, laurustinus, evergreen, to 3m (10ft), *fls* white, pink in bud, late autumn to early spring, fruits metallic blue, finally black.

Weigela, hardy, deciduous, *fls* foxglove-like, May and June, any well-drained soil, sun or light shade. *W. florida* 5, 1·8m (6ft), *fls* rose-pink, May and June: *W. florida* 'Folliis Purpureis' 6, *lvs* purple, *fls* pink; var 'Variegata' 5, *lvs* creamy-white margins: *W. middendorffiana* 4, 1·2m (4ft), *fls* sulphur-yellow, marked with orange on the lower lobes, April and May: *W. praecox* 5, to 3m (10ft), vigorous, *fls* rose-pink with yellow markings in the throat.

Roses

Wild roses are found mainly in temperate zones in the northern hemisphere although some occur on mountains further south. Many different bush and climbing species have evolved throughout the ages and today over 250 distinct species are recognized.

Classification of Roses

Roses are classified as belonging to three basic groups: species, old garden roses or modern garden roses. Each group is further sub-divided.

Species roses These include wild roses from various parts of the world along with natural or planned crosses. The majority of species roses are known by their botanical names and they are distinguished by their hardiness and resistance to pests and disease. Most species roses have single flowers with five petals and although they only bloom once a year many produce an outstandingly decorative crop of red hips during the autumn. Select species roses can be grown as shrubs in any garden where there is adequate space. Species such as *R. moyesii* 5, which grows to 2·4m (8ft) and has large, bottle-shaped hips in the autumn and *R. rubrifolia* 2, which grows 1·2 to 2·4m (4 to 8ft) high and is almost thornless, look good in any garden. *R. rugosa* 2, *R. willmottiae* 4 and *R. xanthina* 5 are also among the most beautiful. Where space is restricted then a short-growing variety such as *R. spinosissima* 4, the Scotch rose, is useful for low hedges.

Old garden roses These are hardy shrub roses which are hybrids or sports of species roses. A precise classification is difficult but alba, bourbon, boursalt, China, damask, gallica, hybrid musk, hybrid perpetual, moss, portland, provence, sweet briar and tea roses are usually included with non-climbing roses in this group. Noisettes and climbing tea are among the climbers. A few varieties from each of these groups are still available.

Modern garden roses These are now classified into non-climbing and climbing variants; the former include shrub, bush and miniature roses while the latter include ramblers, climbers and climbing miniatures.

Bush roses The repeat-flowering bush rose is by far the largest group and within it three types can be distinguished.

The hybrid tea rose is the most popular rose grown today. It is a descendant from the hybrid perpetual and produces large blooms often borne on a single stem.

Floribunda roses bear their flowers in clusters or large trusses and many open simultaneously. They produce a large splash of colour over a long season and are particularly useful for formal bedding. A few varieties in this group produce large blooms with many petals and such varieties are known as floribundas of the hybrid tea type.

Polyantha pompons are dwarf growing cluster roses with small flowers from which many of the modern floribundas were developed. They are rarely grown today.

Miniature roses These are dwarf, recurrent-flowering bushes usually 15cm (6in) to 30cm (12in) tall, with tiny well-formed flowers and small foliage. They are useful for edgings or in a rock garden.

Shrub roses Some of the modern shrub roses derived from species roses are vigorous, making large specimen bushes which flower only once a season. Others may have the characteristics of floribundas but are normally too tall for formal beds.

Ramblers These are climbing roses which usually flower only once a season and have vigorous, lax growth and small flowers.

Climbers These have stiffer stems than ramblers with moderate to vigorous growth and bear large flowers resembling hybrid teas. Several recent introductions are exceptionally free-flowering.

Planting

Most roses are sold with bare roots in temperate countries; they may be planted any time from late October until early April as long as the soil is neither too wet nor frozen. November is probably the best month to plant but in countries subject to severe winters, such as Canada and other northern parts of North America, roses are generally planted in the spring.

If roses arrive from the nursery during winter when soil conditions are unsuitable for planting then they should be heeled in at the foot of a hedge or in some other sheltered place. There they can be left for several months without any fear of harm provided that the roots are not over-crowded and that the roses are protected when it is frosty.

Once a rose is planted, it is not likely to be moved for many years, so like many other permanent members of the garden, time spent preparing the ground and in careful planting will reap rich dividends later. New beds should be dug well and have some organic material incorporated in the soil at least two months before the roses are to be planted. Roses should not be planted in any place which is surrounded by high hedges or trees, as it is absolutely essential to ensure that they have adequate circulation of air to reduce the likelihood of attack by fungal diseases. Drainage must be adequate.

When roses are planted in a bed, the smaller growing floribundas are usually spaced 45cm (18in) apart and the larger floribundas and hybrid teas are usually given 60cm (24in) between plants. A few vigorous growing varieties and some modern shrub roses need 90cm (36in) and tall-growing shrub roses and several species roses require about 180cm (72in).

Before planting mark the position of each rose with a cane, then dig a hole on the appropriate side of the cane about 30cm (12in) square and at least 15cm (6in) deep. Separate the roots and spread them out over a wide area inside the hole. Shorten any long tap roots to 25cm (10in) and cut back any damaged roots to healthy growth. On exposed sites, firm anchorage can be obtained by planting the roses with their roots pointing in the direction of the prevailing wind. Cover the roots with a spadeful of planting mixture made by mixing together equal parts of loam and peat and adding a handful of a slow-acting fertilizer such as coarse bonemeal. Firmly replace the top

Above: A rose garden at the height of its flowering season

Above right: Climbing rose 'Paul's Scarlet'

Right: A rose garden on the large scale

Opposite: A rose arch. Careful training is necessary in the early stages

soil so that the union of the rose with the rootstock is just below the surface of the soil. Make sure that the soil remains firm around newly planted bushes throughout their first winter. Newly planted standard roses must be firmly staked and climbers should be securely tied. See *Cultivation: Staking*. Established bushes can be moved and planted in an existing rose bed by a method similar to the one described above but in this case it is essential to use fresh soil in the bed. Roses may also be planted from containers. See *Cultivation: Planting*.

Pruning

Roses must be pruned to make sure that they produce the maximum number of quality blooms and to encourage growth from their base to form a well-balanced plant. Climatic conditions will influence the exact date of pruning but roses must be pruned while they are dormant before the sap starts to rise and growth becomes well established. In the northern areas of the UK this will generally be about mid-March while in the south the operation can usually be carried out a few weeks earlier. When pruning, the cut should be made about 6mm (¼in) above a bud or eye. The level of the cut is important; if it is too high, the snag left may decay and induce dieback, while if the cut is too low the bud may be damaged or the shoot coming from it may be insecure and liable to break off. If possible prune to an outward pointing bud so that an open and rounded plant is produced.

Newly-planted roses Bush roses should be pruned hard in their first year by shortening their growth to about 10 to 15cm (4 to 6in) above ground level, preferably to outward-pointing buds. Prune thin shoots more severely than thicker ones. Shrub and climbing roses (including ramblers) do best with the bare minimum of pruning the first year after planting. Tip their branches to the uppermost sound bud.

Established bush roses First cut out all dead wood and any late, soft growths, damaged shoots or weak growths. Prune the remaining sound wood to an outward pointing eye shortening the previous year's growth to about one-half in the case of floribundas and to about one-third in the case of hybrid teas. In general, vigorous-growing varieties with heavy wood do best with relatively light pruning, while less vigorous varieties with thin wood often benefit more by severe pruning to encourage new growth. Standard or tree roses require no special treatment and should be pruned in the same way as bushes.

Established shrub roses Shrubs, whether rose species or vigorous floribundas, should be pruned very lightly with their main branches being shortened to the first sound bud from their tip. Remove any weak or damaged shoots and keep the bush shapely.

Established climbers and ramblers Rambler roses with lax stems should be pruned late in September when flowering is completed. All the old wood, which has borne flowers, should be removed to the base and new wood should be supported by tying. Climbers, including sports of hybrid teas and floribundas with their more vigorous firm stems, should have the oldest wood removed and all the healthy, lateral growth should be shortened to three or four buds from the main stem. If in doubt prune climbers sparingly.

Summer pruning During the flowering season all spent flowers should be removed with a short portion of stem. In the case of floribundas, it may be necessary to delay this process until the last flowers are over. Long flowering stems should not be removed from newly planted roses as this will cause the plants to suffer through loss of foliage.

Cultivation

Roses thrive in soil which has an abundant supply of organic matter. The compost or manure dug into the bed when it was first made should last for a year or two but irrespective of the nature of the soil, more organic matter will have to be added if top-quality flowers are to be expected. Many types of organic material can be used. See *Soil*. Apply it in the spring, immediately after pruning, and lightly fork it under the surface of the soil without disturbing the roots of the bushes.

A well-balanced rose fertilizer, which includes trace elements, should be applied after the organic material at about 70 to 140g/m² (2 to 4oz/sq yd). A second flush of flowers and an August application of sulphate of potash at about 70g/m² (2oz/sq yd) will harden new growth and help it withstand the rigours of winter.

Foliar feeds are particularly useful on limey/chalky soils and for climbers grown against walls. They can usually be combined with a fungicide and applied at regular intervals as part of a preventive disease spraying programme. In warm countries, mulching with a layer of damp peat is an ideal means of retaining moisture. In really warm countries it might be necessary to irrigate the soil.

Roses can withstand reasonably low temperatures but in areas where frost is severe and prolonged they will not survive. In countries with cold winters, soil should be mounded around the base of the bush in late autumn. In countries with very cold winters, Canada for example, this may provide inadequate protection and the whole bush should be partially unearthed, bent over and completely buried in soil until the following spring. Cold, icy winds can be as devastating as frost and in exposed positions, roses benefit from having straw or heather tied around the head of the bush. All forms of protection should be removed when weather conditions improve.

Pests and Diseases

While roses are not trouble free, many recent introductions are much more vigorous and more resistant to diseases than many of their predecessors. Listed below are some of the more common pests and fungal infections likely to be encountered. Spraying against disease should be regarded as a preventive measure and it is wrong to wait until a disease is established before taking action. Spraying against pests can be undertaken when the pest or the symptoms of pest damage appear. See *Pests and Diseases* for descriptions of the symptoms and details of control.

Aphids or greenflies These usually appear in May or early June and affect young shoots and flowering buds. Aphids attack in all weathers but they are often at their worst in dry seasons.

Thrips or thunderflies These attack the outer petals of young flower buds just as they begin to show colour. If left untreated, the margins of the petals become discoloured and the blooms are greatly disfigured. Certain varieties are especially prone to infestation; roses grown under glass can also be affected.

Caterpillars There are several rose-infesting caterpillars. The common, green caterpillar which attacks in early May and eats the young leaves is best known. An equally troublesome pest is the 'rose maggot' or tortrix leaf-rolling caterpillar which produces a longitudinal downward curling of the leaves.

Leaf-rolling (rose) sawfly This pest is frequently seen in dry seasons from June onwards and also causes a downward rolling of the leaves. This upsets plant nutrition and eventually leads to a loss of vigour.

Chafers Several types of chafers can affect roses. In late June the adult beetles eat the flower buds and greatly disfigure the blooms.

Red spider mites In hot dry seasons, red spider mites infest roses grown out of doors but they are more frequently found on roses grown under glass. The small red mites live on the underside of the foliage and a severe attack can affect plant nutrition and can produce chlorosis and premature leaf fall.

Black spot This infection can be devastating and can lead to bushes being completely denuded of their foliage by early summer. As with mildew, certain varieties are highly susceptible to the disease. The first symptoms are round, raised, blackish spots which appear on the upper side of the leaves; eventually the whole leaf turns yellow and falls off.

Mildew Roses may be attacked by powdery or downy mildew. Powdery mildew is much more common. Some varieties are very susceptible to the disease.

Rust The problem of rust varies from country to country. In Scotland it is relatively rare, but in New Zealand, for example, rust is not uncommon. The disease affects susceptible varieties and appears in June as small reddish-yellow spots on the underside of the leaves. Later the leaves turn yellow and fall off so the health of the bush is seriously affected.

Rose suckers Suckers can grow from any rose which is not grown on its own roots. With certain understocks, for example *R. canina* 3, suckering is quite common while with others, such as *R. multiflora* 5, it can be quite rare. On standard roses suckers may arise from either the stem or the roots. See *Pests and Diseases*: *Plant Disorders*.

Varieties

A brief list of varieties which are readily available and which have performed satisfactorily in many countries is given below. The roses are listed alphabetically; details of colour and habit of growth will be found in most rose catalogues.

Hybrid Teas

'Alec's Red'	'Peer Gynt'
'Duke of Windsor'	'Piccadilly'
'Ernest H. Morse'	'Pink Favourite'
'Fragrant Cloud'	'Prima Ballerina'
'Grandpa Dickson'	'Rose Gaujard'
'King's Ransom'	'Royal Highness'
'Mischief'	'Stella'
'National Trust'	'Super Star'
'Pascali'	'Wendy Cussons'
'Peace'	'Whisky Mac'

Floribundas

'Allgold'	'Iceberg'
'Anna Wheatcroft'	'Jan Spek'
'Anne Cocker'	'Lilli Marlene'
'Apricot Nectar'	'Molly McGredy'
'City of Leeds'	'Orange Sensation'
'Dearest'	'Paddy McGredy'
'Elizabeth of Glamis'	'Picasso'
'Escapade'	'Pink Parfait'
'Evelyn Fison'	'Queen Elizabeth'
'Golden Slippers'	'Woburn Abbey'

Climbers

'Bantry Bay'	'Maigold'
'Casino'	'Mermaid'
'Danse du Feu'	'New Dawn'
'Golden Showers'	'Parkdirektor Riggers'
'Handel'	'Pink Perpétue'

Trees

A tree is normally defined as a woody perennial having a stem clear of branches to a height of 1·8 to 2·1m (6 to 7ft), although there are a few trees which generally form several branches near ground level.

Trees can be naturally separated into two groups – deciduous and evergreen. Deciduous trees lose their leaves each year, evergreens keep most of them. Evergreens can be further subdivided into those which bear flowers and those which bear cones. These differences are important because each group needs different cultural treatment. In general, deciduous trees have adapted, through evolution, to colder climates while broad-leaved evergreens are essentially tropical trees which have moved gradually into colder climates. Most deciduous trees are fully hardy while evergreens need shelter from winds and greater humidity.

Trees can be functional in the garden as well as decorative. They can be used to hide unsightly objects or views or they can be used to create two particular forms of micro-environment – dry soil and shade. A tree can pump enormous amounts of water from the soil and the sunny side of a deciduous tree provides almost ideal soil conditions for growing bulbs which like a dry soil in the summer and an adequate supply of moisture in the winter. The shaded side of a tree is useful for growing shade-loving plants.

Choosing a Tree

Trees can be decorative in 5 ways. They can 1) flower, 2) fruit, 3) have attractive leaf forms of spring or autumn colour, 4) have richly coloured twigs or bark, and 5) have a pleasing overall shape. The nearest thing to an ideal tree is one which provides

Standard rose 'Flor'

Above left: 'Masquerade'

Above right: The world famous rose 'Peace'

Left: Choose a tree carefully to set off your house and garden to their best advantage. This one is *Cedrus atlantica*

interest and beauty throughout the season and yet remains within the limits of a given area.

Obviously where space is restricted, the choice of species is also limited. *Juniperus scopulorum* 'Sky Rocket' 5 and the fastigiate cherry, *Prunus* 'Amanogawa' 5, will grow in very confined areas.

Trees can roughly be divided into four shapes: horizontal, rounded, vertical and weeping. The division is not an exact one; many trees fall into two or more of the groups. Horizontal trees are those with distinctly horizontal branches. Rounded trees are those with pear- or egg-shaped heads. Vertical trees are those which make a spire-shaped outline and weeping trees have either downward drooping branches or have branches which basically grow outwards or upwards with secondary branches which droop.

The summaries overleaf tell you about flowers, fruit, leaves and bark colour.

As well as depending on decorative factors, the selection of a tree also depends on local conditions such as the type of soil, whether there is any problem with pollution, and the climate, including rainfall, frost and temperature. The suitability of the soil is the first problem. Does the tree prefer an acid or alkaline soil? Climate is the second problem. Will the tree stand the winter? Look at the information given in the tree summaries and see also *Climate* and *Soil*.

It is totally unrealistic to expect an 'all-year-round' tree, but spring or summer flowers, followed by fruit, with perhaps a final splash of autumn colour linked with a diverse leaf form or unusual tree shape, provide much of interest.

Planting Trees

The main season for planting conventional bare-root trees is from October to March when most are dormant. Container-grown trees can be planted at almost any time of the year. The principles involved are basically the same for all types of trees. If the tree is delivered, check that it is in fact the species which was ordered. Then closely examine the roots and branches and remove any damaged parts. If the bark looks a little shrivelled, stand the roots in a bucket of water for two days. Next, select a sheltered position, dig a trench about 30cm (12in) deep and heel in the tree until planting. Trees treated in this way will stay in peak condition for two or three months until their eventual final position is ready for them. Do not plant in unfavourable weather conditions when soils are frozen or waterlogged.

How much care you take over planting may ultimately determine the success and establishment of the tree. Incorrect planting depth, inadequate holes, poor staking and lack of watering can result in the death of newly planted trees.

Choosing the site The siting of any tree requires imagination and forethought. Select a position where the tree will not only look attractive, but will blend in effectively with existing plants, without upsetting the balance or scale of the garden. Imaginative planting will utilize any special features possessed by the tree, to complement or highlight other noteworthy features in the garden.

Soil preparation Most garden soils, if they are not mistreated, are generally fairly free-draining: the obvious exception being where subsoils consist of heavy, wet clay. The lack of drainage is unlikely to be a problem unless pools of water remain on the soil after heavy rain. If drainage is a problem you can improve your soil condition by adding bulky organic manures (see *Soil*). Before applying any manure, remove all weeds, particularly perennial ones, to reduce possible competition with the young tree roots for nutrients.

Preparing the hole The size of hole is determined by the root spread of the tree. Spread the roots out and mark the shape of them on the ground. Allow an extra 25cm (10in) all round, for root development. When planting in a lawn remove and stack the turf. Dig a hole which is deep enough to plant the tree with the soil mark at ground level. The soil mark can easily be seen just above the top of the roots and indicates the depth that tree was originally planted in the nursery. Stack the top soil (usually a dark colour) and subsoil (lighter in colour) in two separate piles close to the hole. Fork over the base of the hole to a depth of 20cm (8in) to ensure good drainage and aeration. Add peat or leaf-mould to aid root establishment. Check to see if the sides of the hole have a glazed appearance. This effect is common on clay soils and will make the hole act like a sump. Remove it by lightly piercing the sides with a fork.

Staking Standards and large trees need support in the early part of their life: this is achieved by staking them. The size of the stake is determined by the length of the stem. After insertion, the stake should finish just under the lowest branch. Always insert stakes before planting and put them on the windward side of the tree. Driving in stakes after planting may damage the roots of the tree. When a tree is being planted near to the house, it is much more attractive to put the stake on the side of the tree which is away from the eye of the household. See *Cultivation: Staking and Supporting*.

Planting Lift the tree from the heeling-in area and carefully move it to its final planting position with its roots wrapped in hessian or plastic sheeting to stop them from drying out. Remove any broken or damaged parts of the roots with a knife or pruning shears/secateurs. Place the tree close to the stake but leave about a hand's width between them for stem development. If the tree has a crooked stem, place the bend away from the stake and pull it straight with tree ties after planting. Improve the top soil from the hole by mixing equal parts of peat or leaf-mould with it.

Planting a tree is a two-man operation: one man is needed to hold the tree while the second man replaces the soil in 20cm (8in) deep layers, firming each layer before going on to the next. Any air pockets should be filled by shaking the tree as the soil is put round the roots. Use your feet to firm the soil but take care to ensure that you apply an even pressure all round. Keep on checking the planting level as you put more soil back into the hole. This is very important as low planting induces basal stem rot and shallow planting allows the roots to dry out. Never allow the subsoil to come into direct contact with roots – return it to outer and upper portions of the hole. Finish planting by turning your spade upside down and use the handle to firm the soil between stake and the tree. Fork out any footmarks and apply a 5cm (2in) deep mulch around the base.

After Care

During the first growing season there are numerous important activities to attend to. Watering is the most important. Failure to provide an adequate supply of moisture to the roots may lead to the loss of the tree. Hot dry summers can aggravate this problem. Check the tree ties twice a year to make sure that they are not too tight. Constriction through over-tight tree ties can dramatically reduce growth. Keep the tree staked until its roots are sufficiently well developed and the tree is well enough anchored in the soil to stand on its own without support.

Control weeds either chemically or mechanically. You could try tying a circular plastic disc around the base of the tree. This is a new method and so far results look encouraging.

Training

Trees can be bought in various sizes ranging from one- or two-year-old forest transplants through to 20- to 25-year-old semi-mature trees.

If you choose a trained tree from a nursery, check it to make sure that any misshapen, badly angled, or diseased stems have been removed. Twin or double leading shoots, crossing or rubbing branches should also have been removed as they can threaten the safety of mature trees. A tree with a well-balanced system of branches exerts far less pressure on the roots than a lopsided crown and a well-trained tree is less likely to need tree surgery later during its life.

Training a one-year-old tree (maiden) is quite simple. Begin by tying it to a cane to ensure a straight stem or trunk. Then follow two rules: 1) keep a single leader, and 2) keep an open head by trimming out crossing branches. Over the first few years leave any side shoots which develop low down on the stem as they will assist stem thickening. If you want to grow a standard tree with a $1 \cdot 8$ to $2 \cdot 1$m (6 to 7ft) length of clear stem you should remove these after two years. If left longer the lower shoots will become branches. You can encourage strong fibrous roots to grow by cutting into the soil round the tree with a spade during its training period. This also discourages long single tap roots. Trees belonging to the genera *Betula*; *Populus* and *Salix* are amongst the quicker ones to train and take about three years. The majority of trees including those belonging to the genera *Aesculus*, *Malus*, *Prunus* and *Pyrus* take over four years, while *Castanea*, *Quercus* and *Ulmus* generally take five years.

Problems with Trees

The most frequent problem with trees is a direct result of underestimating the spread of the branches and roots with the result that foundations, gas mains, cables and street signs may be distorted or fractured through the pressure exerted by spreading roots and branches. To avoid these situations read and heed information regarding height and spread.

On heavy, clay soils, water taken up by tree roots may result in soil shrinkage and this might cause damage to the foundations of nearby buildings. Trees belonging to the genera *Populus*, *Quercus*, *Salix* and *Ulmus* are particularly troublesome. With the exception of *Quercus*, all four also provide another unwanted hazard: the unpredictable manner in which they shed their branches. None of these trees should be planted nearer to a building than their maximum branch spread, as root spread will be equal or even greater than this.

In autumn deciduous trees shed their leaves and these can block drains, and gutters, and in wet weather, can be very slippery to walk on. Some evergreens, notably the conifers, resent town and city pollution. Others such as the cedar, *Cedrus atlantica* 6 with its long horizontal limbs are prone to snow damage.

The seeds of some trees, for example the common yew, *Taxus baccata* 6, are poisonous, although the fleshy outer covering is edible. Equally dangerous are seeds of the laburnum, and consequently both trees must be used with care. The sap of the varnish tree, *Rhus verniciflua* 5, from the Himalayas, has been known to cause severe skin rash and irritation. And *R. toxicodendron* 5, poison ivy, a native of the USA is even more dangerous.

Looking after Trees

Once trees reach a certain age their ability to heal or mend after injury decreases and this leads to an increase in the amount of care and maintenance they need to remain healthy.

If a tree is so old and in such poor condition that it drops branches with little warning then have it inspected by a qualified tree surgeon to find out why the branch dropped and if the tree can be safely retained. Do not simply ignore it.

Tree maintenance generally means filling cavities in the branches or trunk, chopping off unwanted branches and bracing those which are unsteady which you do want to keep.

Cavities These occur through fungi, bacteria and other pathogens entering damaged branches or snags. Twin leaders or forked branches may trap leaves and water. The leaves may then rot and this may eventually lead to the formation of a cavity in the trunk. You can avoid this sort of problem by drilling holes and inserting drainage tubes. If you find a cavity, remove all the collected debris and cut back any rot to living tissue. Coat the cavity with a fungicidal sealant to prevent further infection, then either leave it open, but covered to prevent bird entry, or fill it with a special cavity filler foam or concrete – see *Pruning*.

Bracing Many mature trees have heavy, horizontal lateral branches, which move alarmingly in the wind. These can be removed – see *Pruning* – but when this might upset the balance of the tree or leave a conspicuous hole, the limb can be supported by using special galvanized multistrand cables with eye bolts or screw eyes until the need for support has passed.

Trees

The numbers after the botanical names are the North America hardiness zone ratings – see *Climate*.

Acacia, wattle, mainly evergreen trees suitable for milder areas and lime/chalk-free soil. *A. baileyana* 10, Cootamundra wattle, to 9m (30ft), *fls* yellow, late winter to early spring, *lvs* pendulous, divided into small leaflets: *A. dealbata* 9, silver wattle, to 18m (60ft), *fls* yellow, late winter to early spring, *lvs* fern-like, silvery green, not for exposed or frosty positions.

Acer, maple, mainly deciduous, very hardy, all soils including lime/chalk, *fls* on bare stems, March and April, good autumn leaf colours. *A. campestre* 4, field maple, 6m (20ft), *lvs* butter yellow in autumn: *A. capillipes* 5, 7m (25ft), *lvs* red in autumn, bark red-white striations: *A. griseum* 5, paperbark maple, 12m (40ft), *lvs* crimson in autumn, young stems red-cinnamon: *A. grosseri* 6, 6m (20ft), snake bark effect from green-white stems, *lvs* red, autumn: *A. japonicum* 'Aconitifolium' 5, Japanese maple, 12m (40ft), *fls* red, *lvs* crimson in October: *A. palmatum* 'Senkaki' 5, coral bark maple, to 3m (10ft), young branchlets coral red, *lvs* golden yellow in autumn: *A. platanoides* 'Crimson King' 3, large tree to above 15m (50ft), *lvs* crimson-red: *A. rubrum* 3, red or Canadian maple, 12m (40ft), *fls* red, *lvs* dark green, gold and scarlet in autumn.

Aesculus, horse chestnut, deciduous, *fls* large, summer, any soil. *A. × carnea* 3, pink horse chestnut, 21m (70ft), pyramidal when young, *fls* rose pink, May: *A. hippocastanum* 3, common horse chestnut, 27m (90ft), *fls* white, May, followed by conkers: *A. indica* 6, Indian horse chestnut, 30m (100ft), *fls* white, pink flushed, June, July: *A. pavia* 4, red buckeye, 6m (20ft), *fls* crimson red, June, fruits egg-shaped.

Ailanthus, tree of heaven, fast growing, tolerates atmospheric pollution, to 30m (100ft). *A. altissima* 4, *fls* greenish-yellow, fruits winged, red-brown on female trees, for sun or shade.

Alnus, alder, hardy, any soil apart from limey/chalky ones, wet or dry situations, *fls* before *lvs*, male catkins long, females short, woody cones. *A. cordata* 5, Italian alder, 16m (50ft): *A. glutinosa* 3, common alder, 25m (80ft), catkins yellow, March: *A. incana* 'Aurea' 2, small tree, orange branchlets, catkins yellow, *lvs* yellow-green: *A. rubra* 4, red alder, 16m (50ft).

Amelanchier, snowy mespilus, see *Shrubs*. *A. laevis* 4, 6m (20ft), *lvs* pink when young, spring, *fls* white, April: *A. lamarckii* 4, *fls* white, spring to early summer, *lvs* oval, copper-red, silky when young.

Arbutus, strawberry tree – see *Shrubs*.

Azara, small evergreen trees, best grown against a wall except in warmer climates. *A.*

dentata 8, 4·5m (15ft), *fls* yellow, June, *lvs* dark glossy green: *A. microphylla* 8, *fls* yellow, spring, very hardy: *A. serrata* 9, 5m (16ft), *fls* yellow, July, fruits white.

Betula, birch, deciduous, grown mainly for their attractive bark, most soils except shallow limey/chalky ones, generally short-lived. *B. ermani* 2, Russian rock birch, 12m (40ft), branches orange-brown, bark pinkish-white: *B. lenta* 3, cherry birch, 9m (30ft), *lvs* yellow in autumn: *B. pendula* 2, common silver birch, bark white with black horizontal markings – var 'Youngii' 2, Young's weeping birch, dome-shaped, pendulous: *B. utilis* 4, Himalayan birch, 20m (65ft), bark peeling dark coppery orange-brown.

Carpinus, hornbeam, deciduous, tolerates most soils including lime/chalk and heavy clay, used for hedging. *C. betulus* 5, common hornbeam, 21m (70ft), pyramidal, *lvs* yellow in autumn – vars 'Fastigiata' 5, 15m (50ft), pyramidal; 'Pendula' 5, small tree, branches pendulous.

Castanea, sweet chestnut, deciduous, spreading, 30m (100ft). *C. sativa* 5, likes a deep, loam soil, *fls* catkins, yellow-green, July, *lvs* hairy, nuts in a spiky case.

Catalpa, Indian bean tree, spreading, *fls* foxglove-like, late summer, well-drained soils, needs a sheltered position. *C. bignonioides* 4, 21m (70ft), *fls* white with yellow and purple markings, *lvs* heart-shaped – var 'Aurea', golden Indian bean, *lvs* large, yellow.

Cercidiphyllum, grown mainly for its autumn colour, any soil including lime/chalk. *C. japonicum* 4, Katsura tree, 15m (50ft), branches pendulous, deciduous, *lvs* yellow, red to pink in autumn, *fls* small, green sepals.

Cercis, deciduous, *lvs* heart-shaped. *C. siliquastrum* 6, Judas tree, 9m (30ft), rounded, spreading, *fls* dark pink, pea-like, May, seed pods brown, last through winter, any free-draining soil, needs full sun.

Cordyline, evergreen, slightly tender – see *Gardens: Seaside Gardens*.

Cornus – see *Shrubs*.

Crataegus, thorn, very hardy, tolerates dryness and excessive moisture, industrial pollution and exposed situations, widespreading with attractive autumn tints, *fls* generally white, May, June, fruits red. *C. crus-galli* 4, cockspur thorn, 9m (30ft): *C. ×*

lavallei 4, 9m (30ft), *lvs* red in autumn: *C. monogyna* 4, hawthorn, 9m (30ft), *fls* red, May: *C. oxyacantha* 'Paul's Scarlet' 4, 9m (30ft), *fls* double, scarlet: *C. prunifolia* 4, *lvs* red in autumn.

Davidia, hardy, deciduous, thrives on any soil, sun or shade. *D. involucrata* 6, pocket handkerchief tree, dove tree, ghost tree, 18m (60ft), white bracts, May, *lvs* green, fine hairs, fruit green, ovoid.

Embothrium, semi-evergreen tree, shade-loving, for sheltered position in a deep, moist, but well-drained soil, slightly tender. *E. coccineum* 8, Chilean firebush, 12m (40ft), *fls* orange-scarlet, June, *lvs* leathery.

Eucalyptus – see *Gardens: Seaside Gardens*. *E. niphophila* 2, snow gum, hardy, *lvs* long, leathery, bark green-grey in a patchwork pattern.

Eucryphia – see *Shrubs*.

Fagus, beech, hardy, deciduous, shallow-rooting, broad. *F. sylvatica* 4, common beech, tolerates limey/chalky soils, 35m (120ft), *lvs* red, bronze in autumn; 'Dawyck' 4, Dawyck beech, columnar, 15m (50ft); 'Pendula' 4, weeping beech, branches silvery, pendulous; 'Riversii' 4, purple beech, slow-growing, *lvs* dark purple.

Ficus carica 6, common fig, deciduous, 6m (20ft), *lvs* large, fruits pear-shaped, greenish-purple, edible.

Fraxinus, ash, hardy, fast-growing tree, thrives in almost any soil, tolerates wind-swept coastal and smoke-polluted areas. *F. excelsior* 3, common ash, deciduous, 30m (100ft), *fls* greenish-white; 'Jaspidea' 3, golden-yellow twigs, *lvs* clear yellow in autumn; 'Pendula' 3, weeping ash, fast-growing, branches hang stiffly: *F. ornus* 5, manna ash, black buds, *fls* white, May, fruit winged: *F. oxycarpa* 'Raywood' 4, *lvs* plum-purple in autumn.

Gleditschia, foliage tree with clustered thorns, all types of well-drained soils, tolerates atmospheric pollution. *G. triacanthos* 4, honey locust, 21m (70ft), quick growing, *fls* pea-like, green, pods shiny brown; 'Sunburst' 4, 12m (40ft), *lvs* bright yellow in summer.

Gymnocladus dioicus 4, Kentucky coffee tree, 27m (90ft), deciduous, tolerates hot, dry conditions, *lvs* pink tinged, yellow in autumn, *fls* small, greenish-white, June, pods oblong, tolerates either limey or chalky soils.

Hippophae – see *Gardens: Seaside Gardens*.

Ilex, holly, evergreen and deciduous trees. *I. aquifolium* 6, evergreen, 15m (50ft), *lvs* thick, dark green, leathery, *fls* small, white, berries red, tolerates atmospheric pollution; 'Argenteomarginata Pendula' 6, Perry's weeping silver holly, 9m (30ft), branches pendulous, *lvs* silver, berries; 'Bacciflava' 6, berries yellow; 'Ferox' 6, hedgehog holly, slow growing; 'Golden Queen' 6, young shoots green-reddish, *lvs* shiny, green-grey, broad yellow margin; 'Handsworth New Silver' 6, purple stemmed, *lvs* green with white border: *I. opaca* 5, American holly, evergreen, 15m (50ft), *lvs* green above yellow below, *fls* white, fruits small, red, dislikes limey/chalky soil.

Juglans, walnut, deciduous, fast growing, any soil, dislikes late frosts. *J. nigra* 4, black walnut, 45m (150ft), rounded crown, *fls* male catkins, fruit round: *J. regia* 5–6, common walnut, slow growing, 27m (90ft); 'Lacinita' 5–6, hanging branches, *lvs* deeply cut.

Koelreuteria, wide spreading, all soils, flowers best in hot dry summers, *fls* small, yellow, July and August. *K. paniculata* 5, golden rain tree, 11m (35ft).

Laburnum, deciduous, easily grown, all types of soil, *fls* yellow, pea-like, late spring and early summer, all parts of the plant are poisonous, particularly the seeds. *L. alpinum* 4, Scotch laburnum, 6m (20ft): *L. anagyroides* 5, common laburnum, 6m (20ft), upright, low branching: *L.* × *watereri* 4.

Laurus nobilis – see *Gardens: Seaside Gardens*.

Liquidambar, deciduous, most soils except shallow lime/chalk, young plants susceptible to frost, *lvs* maple-like, rich autumn tints. *L. formosana* 6, Chinese sweet gum, 35m (120ft): *L. styraciflua* 5, sweet gum, 45m (150ft), *lvs* crimson in autumn, *fls* yellow-green.

Liriodendron, tulip tree, fast growing, any fertile soil. *L. chinense* 6, Chinese tulip tree, deciduous, 15m (50ft), *fls* green outside, yellow inside, solitary, tulip-shaped, June, fruit October: *L. tulipifera* 4, 30m (100ft), *fls* greenish-yellow outside, orange inside, June, fruit October, *fls* on trees over 25 years only.

Magnolia – see *Shrubs*. *M. acuminata* 4, cucumber tree, deciduous, 30m (100ft), fast growing, pyramidal, *fls* small, yellowish, fruit like young cucumbers: *M. campbellii* 9, pink Himalayan tulip tree, 30m (100ft), *fls* pink, cup-shaped, March, likes lime-free soil, dislikes frost.

Malus, flowering crab, hardy, *fls* April and May, many have attractive fruits in autumn, easily grown. *M. baccata* 2, Siberian crab, 15m (50ft), upright, *fls* white, fragrant, fruit red-yellow: *M. floribunda* 4, 12m (40ft), deciduous, *fls* pink-red, fragrant; 'Golden Hornet' 4, 9m (30ft), initially upright, pendulous later, *fls* white, followed by bright yellow fruits: *M. hupehensis* 4, 9m (30ft), *lvs* greenish-purple, *fls* pink buds open white, fragrant, fruit green-yellow, small, autumn: *M.* × *lemoinei* 4, 7m (24ft), *lvs* bronze when young, red-purple to green later, *fls* deep purple-crimson, late summer: *M. prunifolia* 3, 6m (20ft), *fls* white, tinged pink, fruits red, conical: *M.* × *purpurea* 4, 7m (24ft), *lvs* dark green, shoots purplish, *fls* crimson, fruit crimson-purple in autumn: *M.* × *robusta* 3, 6m (20ft), *fls* white, pale pink, fruit large, scarlet, cherry-like: *M. sylvestris* 4, crab apple, 7m (24ft), *fls* white to pale pink, fruits green, red tinted: *M. toringoides* 5, cut leaf crab apple, 7m (24ft), *fls* creamy white, May, fruit yellow-red: *M. tschonoskii* 4, 12m (40ft), pyramidal, *lvs* colourful in autumn, *fls* white, tinged pink, fruit green-yellow.

Morus, mulberry, deciduous, most soils, particularly well-drained ones. *M. alba* 4, white mulberry, 13m (45ft), round, *lvs* heart-shaped, *fls* insignificant catkins, fruits edible, white to pink: *M. nigra* 6–7, black mulberry, 9m (30ft), edible fruit dark, black-red.

Nyssa, deciduous, noted for spectacular autumn foliage, for moist, lime-free soils. *N. sinensis* 7, *lvs* red, scarlet in the autumn: *N. sylvatica* 4, tupelo tree, deciduous, 18m (60ft), *lvs* yellow-scarlet in autumn, *fls* greenish, small, fruit egg-shaped, bluish-black.

Oxydendrum arboreum 5, sorrel tree, *fls* small, white, July, *lvs* brilliant scarlet in the autumn, not for dry or limey/chalky soils.

Parrotia persica 5, wide spreading, deciduous, lime tolerant, 12m (40ft), *fls* crimson, March, bark flaking, patchy, conspicuous, scarlet red to yellow autumn shades.

Paulownia, grown mainly for its magnificent summer *fls*, any deep, well-drained soil, full sun, sheltered from gales. *P. fargesii* 5, deciduous, 20m (65ft), *lvs* large, *fls* fragrant, dark purple, speckled throat: *P.*

tomentosa 5, empress tree, 15m (50ft), *fls* foxglove-like, pale lilac, mauve, May.

Phellodendron amurense 3, amur cork tree, deciduous, wide spreading, likes limey/chalky soils and full sun, 15m (50ft), *lvs* bright green, golden in autumn, *fls* small, white, bark deeply fissured.

Photinia serrulata 7, 12m (40ft), broad-headed, *lvs* copper red in spring, *fls* white, May, fruit small, red.

Platanus, plane, deciduous, wide spreading, most soils, dislikes shallow, limey/chalky ones, full sun. *P. hispanica* 5, London plane, 30m (100ft), *fls* small, bark white-grey patchwork, *lvs* maple-like.

Populus, poplar, hardy, fast growing, deciduous, unsuitable for confined areas – see *Design and Planning: Screens*. *P. alba* 3, white poplar, 30m (100ft), *lvs* initially white, *fls* catkins, tolerates limey/chalky, dry soils: *P. candicans* 'Aurora' 4, Ontario poplar, balm of Gilead, 30m (100ft), *lvs* variegated, creamy-white, pink tinted, green when old: *P. nigra* 'Italica' 2, Lombardy poplar, columnar, brittle branches. For Lombardy poplars used as a screen see *Design and Planning: Plant Screens*.

Prunus, a large genus of ornamental spring and summer flowering trees, grow well in any soil, need a sunny position. 'Accolade' 5, deciduous, 6m (20ft), *fls* purple in clusters, February: *P. avium* 3, gean, 12m (40ft), deciduous, *fls* small, white, fruit small, round; var 'Plena', *fls* semi-double, white: *P. cerasifera* 'Pissardii' 3, purple-leaved plum, 9m (30ft), *lvs* dark red in summer, purple in autumn, *fls* pink in bud opening white: *P.* × *hillieri* 'Spire' 4, 7m (24ft), pyramidal, *fls* soft pink, *lvs* turn rich red in autumn: *P. padus* 3, bird cherry, 15m (50ft), *fls* small, white, fragrant, May, fruit small, black, bitter taste: *P. persica* 5, peach, deciduous, 7m (24ft), *fls* pink, spring, fruit orange, round, furry: *P. sargentii* 4, Sargent's cherry, 12m (40ft), upright, *lvs* turn bronze red to yellow in autumn, *fls* deep pink, spring: *P.* × *schmittii* 3, quick-growing, conical, shiny, brown bark, *fls* pale pink, spring: *P. serrula* 5, red-brown bark, *fls* small white, fruit small, oval, red: *P. serrulata* 5–6, Japanese cherry, small, flat topped, deciduous, *fls* large, many vars; 'Amanogawa' 5, 9m (30ft), *lvs* greenish bronze, *fls* double pink, fragrant; 'Kanzan' 5, 10m (35ft), *fls* large, double, pink, *lvs* copper red at first, green later, grows well on limey/chalky soil; 'Shirofugen' 6, 9m (30ft), *lvs* copper coloured, *fls* double, purple in bud opening white, fading pink: *P.*

subhirtella 5, spring cherry, to 9m (30ft), *lvs* small, good autumn colours, *fls* pale pink, March ; 'Autumnalis' 5, autumn cherry, 7m (24ft), deciduous, *fls* tiny, double, white, late winter: *P.* × *yedoensis* 5, yashino cherry, 9m (30ft), flat topped, strong growing, arching branches, *fls* white, almond scented, March and April, fruits shiny black.

Pyrus, pear, deciduous, hardy, grows well on most soils, tolerates atmospheric pollution. *P. calleryana* 5, 12m (40ft), thorny branches, *fls* white, March, fruits small, brown; 'Bradford' 5, 13m (45ft), *lvs* good autumn colours, *fls* white, April: *P. communis* 4, common pear, 13m (45ft), *lvs* red tinted in autumn, *fls* white: *P. salicifolia* 'Pendula' 4, 6m (20ft), *lvs* silvery, willow-like, *fls* white, pendulous branches: *P. ussuriensis* 4, 13m (45ft), *lvs* bronze crimson in autumn, *fls* early, fruit yellow, hard.

Quercus, oak, large genus, evergreen and deciduous, *fls* as catkins, *lvs* some have good autumn colour, most like a deep, moist loam soil. *Q. cerris* 6, Turkey oak, rapid growing, 35m (120ft), good on lime/chalk soils, large acorns: *Q. coccinea* 4, scarlet oak, deciduous, 15m (50ft), *lvs* large, turning scarlet in the autumn, acorns, will not tolerate lime: *Q. ilex* 9, evergreen oak, broad, spreading, 25m (80ft), acorns in dry summers, tolerates shade and dry soils: *Q. robur* 5, common oak, deciduous, slow growing, long lived, 30m (100ft), acorns; 'Concordia' 5, golden oak, *lvs* golden yellow in spring and summer: *Q. rubra* 3, red oak, 25m (80ft), *lvs* red, scarlet in autumn.

Rhus, sumach, very hardy, deciduous. *R. typhina* 3, stag's horn sumach, wide headed, flat topped, *lvs* large, orange, purple red in autumn, fruits crimson, hairy; 'Laciniata' 3, *lvs* fern-like, suitable for dry, sandy soils.

Salix, willow, a large diverse genus most of which thrive on moist or dry soil, only a few are happy on lime/chalk. *S. alba* 2, white willow, deciduous, 25m (80ft), *lvs* furry, silver, *fls* catkins, spring, fast growing, branches brittle: *S. babylonica* 6, weeping willow, deciduous, pendulous branched, 18m (60ft), *lvs* long, slender, green above, blue-grey below, *fls* catkins, spring, not for confined areas: *S. matsudana* 4, Pekin willow, 15m (50ft), conical, *fls* catkins, spring; var 'Tortuosa', contorted willow, 12m (40ft), very striking, twisting, curling branches, *fls* spring.

Sophora, sun loving, deciduous and evergreen, well-drained soil. *S. japonica* 4,

213

pagoda tree, rounded, *fls* creamy-white, pea-like, late summer, pods crinkled, lobed; 'Pendula', weeping form: *S. microphylla* 8 and 9, see *Wall Plants*: *S. tetraptera* 9, kowhai, slightly tender, 4m (15ft), semi-deciduous, *fls* yellow, followed by pods.

Sorbus, large genus of mainly deciduous small, flowering, fruit and foliage trees, hardy, like well-drained soil. *S. aria* 5, whitebeam, deciduous, *lvs* upper surface white: *S. aucuparia* 2, mountain ash, rowan, 9m (30ft), *lvs* have good autumn colour, *fls* white; 'Beissneri' 2, 7m (24ft), upright, shoots orange red, *lvs* yellow green, fern-like; 'Xanthocarpa' 2, fruits amber yellow: *S. cashmiriana* 4, Kashmir mountain ash, 7m (24ft), *fls* pink, May, fruit large, white: *S. hupehensis* 3, Chinese mountain ash, 12m (40ft), upright, *lvs* blue green above, *fls* white, fruit white, pink; 'Joseph Rock' 4, 9m (30ft), *lvs* autumn colour, fruit yellow; 'Mitchellii' 3, deciduous, 15m (50ft), upright, *lvs* large, furry white below: *S. hybrida* 3, 6m (20ft) *lvs* ovate, oblong, mid-green leaflets, furry grey below, *fls* white, 10cm (4in) across, May, bright red fruits in late summer: *S. intermedia*, 5m (17ft), *lvs* toothed mid-green, hairy grey below, *fls* white, May: *S. terminalis* 4, *lvs* oval, yellow brown in autumn, *fls* white, fruit oval, brown: *S. vilmorinii* 5, 6m (20ft), spreading, *lvs* red, purple in autumn, *fls* small, white, fruit tiny, red, pink.

Stewartia, deciduous, thrives in semi-shade, moist, loamy soils. *S. koreana* 5, 15m (50ft), flaking bark, *lvs* orange red in autumn, *fls* large, creamy white: *S. pseudocamellia* 5, Japanese stewartia, 18m (60ft), peeling bark, *lvs* yellow-red in autumn, *fls* white, July, seeds winged.

Tilia, large genus, deciduous, fast growing. *T. cordata* 3, small leaved lime, *lvs* heart-shaped, reddish hair beneath, *fls* ivory, fragrant, July, followed by fruit: *T. × europaea* 3, common lime, 36m (120ft), vigorous, long lived: *T. petiolaris* 5, weeping silver lime, 24m (80ft), deciduous, weeping, *lvs* furry white below, *fls* fragrant.

Trachycarpus fortunei 8, Chusan palm, for mild areas, *lvs* palm-like, 1 to 1·5m (3 to 4½ft) across, *fls* yellow, fragrant, fruit blue-black.

Ulmus, elm, most soils, tolerates exposed positions. *U. glabra* 4, Wych or Scots elm, large dome-shaped, spreading pendulous branches: *U. × hollandica* 'Bea Schwarz' 4, 15m (50ft); 'Christine Buisman' 4: *U. vegeta* 5, 30m (100ft), ascending branches.

Conifers

Conifers are primitive, woody plants, mostly evergreen and, because of their beauty, form and colour, they are extensively grown in gardens. Once conifers formed a major part of the earth's vegetation cover but they are now reduced in types and distribution.

Conifers are characterized by an overall upright habit, generally with one trunk and radiating branches. The leaves are, in most cases, needle-like and rolled to prevent excess transpiration. The wood is soft, resinous, and is generally easily worked in carpentry. The male and female flowers are usually borne on the same tree with the male flowers often in bunches at the tips of the branches. Conifers are wind pollinated and the fertilized seed is borne naked on a woody structure, the cone, except in the genera *Ginkgo*, *Podocarpus*, *Cephalotaxus* and *Taxus* where it is enclosed by a fleshy covering.

Conifers can still be found in all climates and on all soil types. Most pines will grow on dry, sandy soil, and a large number are wind tolerant, although a more luxuriant tree will result from a moister situation. The spruces and firs must have adequate moisture, shelter and deep rich soils to be seen at their best. As a general guide, as long as the climatic conditions are suitable, it is possible to grow conifers in any soil type apart from shallow, limey/chalky soils, pure sand or peat or under waterlogged conditions. In gardens the most commonly grown genera are *Cedrus* and *Chamaecyparis* which can be obtained in many colour forms.

Conifers fall roughly into five groups according to their shape: conical, columnar, flat-topped domes, globular and prostrate or semi-prostrate. Conicals are cone-shaped, columnars are thinner and more upright, flat-topped domes are often hemispherical, globular are roughly round-shaped and prostrate or semi-prostrate are wide and often drooping.

Propagation

You can propagate all conifers most easily from seed; it should be fresh and sown as soon as it is available. Sow it either thinly in rows in a well-prepared bed, or, if there is little seed, in pots of a good, sterilized potting mix. Stand the pots in a cold frame and leave it open to the elements. Keep the mix moist and protect the seed from rodents until after germination in the following spring. Leave the seedlings in rows where they are for the first year, but keep potting on the seedlings in pots up to say a 13cm (5in) pot and grow them on in a cold frame or very cool greenhouse. At the end of the second year both the plants in pots and

A complete landscape can be created with conifers

Left: Conifers can make excellent windbreaks

Below: This small conifer makes an attractive edging to a drive

those in rows can either be planted out into their permanent quarters or grown on in a nursery bed.

Before planting out valuable conifers from pots, grow them for a while in wire baskets to minimize the total root disturbance. Baskets can easily be made from 2cm (¾in) galvanized wire netting and should be lined thinly with leaves, peat, moss or litter to prevent soil trickling through. Use the baskets like large pots.

Before moving conifers grown outside in rows to their permanent positions 'wrench' them regularly by putting a spade down one side of the plant about 12cm (6in) from the stem, and gently levering it. This action will cut about 25 per cent of the roots and strain others, and will help to form a compact root ball. The plants should be grown on until they are large enough for their permanent positions.

Conifers with needle-like leaves are difficult to propagate vegetatively (see *Propagation*). Some are grafted in specialist nurseries, particularly *Picea pungens* 'Koster' 2, *Pinus sylvestris* 'Aurea' and *Pinus sylvestris* 'Argentea' 2, but this operation is probably beyond the capabilities of most amateur gardeners because the problems caused by the resinous nature of conifers can only be overcome by an experienced propagator, knowing exactly when to select material for use.

However, those conifers with sprays of flattened foliage (the genera *Calocedrus*, *Chamaecyparis*, × *Cupressocyparis*, *Cupressus*, *Thuja*, *Thujopsis*) can be increased by cuttings. Time of selection is most important. The growths must be firm, and beginning to go woody at the base. Shoots 6 to 9cm (3 to 4in) long should be taken by gently tearing them back from the branch on which they are borne. Trim the 'heel' slightly and insert the cutting, after a dip in a proprietary rooting hormone preparation, into a close, shaded frame or under a mist propagation unit. Rooting is usually fairly slow. The rooted cuttings should be potted as soon as possible, and the procedure outlined for propagation from seed should then be followed. A simpler, but less reliable method is to take the cuttings in the autumn with the same type of material, insert them into a cold frame and leave them to root over the winter. The rooted cuttings should be left for a full season before transplanting them to a nursery bed or setting them out in their final position.

Planting in Permanent Positions
Conifers are large enough for their permanent positions when they are about 30 to 45cm (12 to 18in) high: this does not apply to dwarf conifers. If conifers are bought from a nursery or garden centre, make sure that a good, healthy plant is selected which is well furnished with foliage right down to the base of its stem. If it is not, it is unlikely to develop this foliage after planting. Plants bought should have their roots soaked in water overnight before planting. The basic principles for planting conifers are the same as for any other tree or shrub. Clear the land of perennial weeds, manure it well and cultivate it deeply. Make a hole which is large enough to hold the root ball comfortably. Lift the conifer carefully, with plenty of soil round the roots. If the roots are exposed and left to dry for any length of time it will mean a very severe setback, if not death to the conifer. Put the soil back into the hole carefully firming it as you go. The optimum planting time is mid to late September or mid to late April. Pines can be moved in midsummer (July to August) when the growth is firm. But this should only be done if the plants have been previously well watered, are carefully lifted and given some shade and shelter from wind while they are re-establishing themselves. Water well if the season is dry. An anti-desiccant can be used to cut down water loss through transpiration, and all conifers should be protected after planting with a light, wind-permeable screen.

There should be no need to stake conifers but weeds, pests and diseases must be controlled and the plants must be watered if the growing season is dry. A thick layer of peat around the base will help conifers to retain moisture.

Using Conifers
The colour of coniferous foliage can be 'heavy' in the garden, but careful selection will give the right atmosphere. A visit to national collections is useful for anyone contemplating planting conifers. Many have a distinctly upright habit, and can be used to give perpendicular lines to gardens, some form wide-based cones of foliage, and many pines are broad and round headed. Some make excellent hedge plants in the garden.

Some conifers need special soil, and climatic conditions and are not easy to grow.

Many conifers have produced small, dense growing variants (sports) and these types are commonly grown on rock gardens, although they can ultimately become too big and often overpower the alpine plants they are frequently put with.

Conifers
The numbers after the botanical names are the North America hardiness zone ratings – see *Climate*.

Abies, silver firs, large-growing, with short, broad needles, often white on the underside. Young cones usually brightly coloured. Prefer a deep soil and moist, sheltered site. Dislike industrial pollution and limey/chalky soils. *A. alba* 4, 45m (150ft), usually conical: *A. concolor* 4, Colorado fir, over 18m (60ft), *lvs* blue green, cones cylindrical, purple: *A. grandis* 6, grand fir, 45m (150ft), *lvs* fragrant when crushed, shade and lime tolerant: *A. spectabilis* 7, Himalayan silver fir, 21m (70ft), *lvs* dark green above, silver below, cones upright, purple, blue.

Araucaria araucana 7, monkey puzzle, evergreen, 30m (100ft), wide spreading, horizontal branches, up to 18m (60ft), *lvs* long, green, spirally arranged, cones large, prefers moist, mild climate.

Calocedrus decurrens 5, incense cedar, over 18m (60ft), columnar, erect branchlets of dark *lvs* in fan-like sprays.

Cedrus, cedar, usually large, horizontally-branched, conical tree, superb texture, most soils. *C. atlantica* 6, Atlas cedar, 30m (100ft), pyramidal when young; best in its blue-green form, *C. a. glauca* 7: *C. deodara* 7, evergreen, 45m (150ft), tips of branches drooping, lush, *lvs* mossy green, several vars including 'Aurea' with *lvs* golden-yellow, spring: *C. libani* 6, Lebanon cedar, over 18m (60ft), long-lived tree, conical when young but later branches generally assume a very horizontal line.

Cephalotaxus 5, over 3m (10ft), often prostrate, long, wide needles, fruits like small green plums. Likes limey/chalky soils and thrives in shade.

Chamaecyparis, large number of vars, both dwarf and large-growing and varying in form and colour. Prefers deep, moist soil. *C. lawsoniana* 5, Lawson cypress, over 18m (60ft), conical, *lvs* dark green, makes a good tall-growing screen quickly; 'Albospica', 9m (30ft), slow-growing, conical, *lvs* green splashed creamy white; 'Columnaris', to 15m (50ft), columnar, *lvs* grey-blue; 'Fletcheri', to 7m (24ft), columnar, dense, compact, slow-growing, *lvs* greenish-grey, often planted on rock gardens, but too large for this; 'Lanei', 9m (30ft), conical, *lvs* feathery butter-yellow sprays; 'Minima Aurea', to 1m (3ft), conical, *lvs* golden-yellow, excellent for rock gardens; 'Minima Glauca' 1m (3ft), compact, globular, *lvs* green-grey in vertical sprays; 'Stewartii', to 18m (60ft), conical, *lvs* green-gold: *C. nootkatensis* 4, over 18m (60ft), conical, but with very drooping habit, *lvs* pale green, pendulous, inner branches sparse: *C. obtusa* 3, generally over 18m (60ft), many vars; 'Nana', to 90cm (3ft), flat-topped dome, dwarf, densely packed, *lvs* very deep green in vertical sprays.

Cryptomeria japonica 5, Japanese cedar, over 18m (60ft), fast growing, columnar but broad, with spreading branches, *lvs* mid-green, warm red-brown bark; 'Elegans', to 4·5m (15ft), *lvs* green and bronze; 'Lobbii', about 18m (60ft), conical, *lvs* dense, dark green; 'Spiralis', to 1·5m (5ft), slow-growing, *lvs* bright green, twisted around stems.

× *Cupressocyparis leylandii* 5–6, Leyland cypress, over 18m (60ft), columnar, fast-growing hybrid, *lvs* drab green, tolerant of bad soil conditions, good for tall screens and seaside gardens, several colour selections; 'Castlewellan', golden Leyland, *lvs* bright yellow; 'Haggerston Grey', *lvs* grey-green, open habit; 'Naylor's Blue', *lvs* grey-green.

Cupressus, conical or columnar, does not transplant easily, will tolerate a wide range of soil conditions. *C. macrocarpa* 7, to 30m (100ft), fast-growing, *lvs* rich green, excellent on the coast; 'Donard Gold', *lvs* rich gold; 'Lutea', *lvs* greenish-gold: *C. sempervirens* 7, Italian cypress, to 18m (60ft), columnar, *lvs* dark green.

Fitzroya cupressoides 7, to 4·5m (15ft), cypress-like plant, *lvs* banded white, likes shelter from wind, needs moist conditions.

Ginkgo biloba 4, maidenhair tree, about 18m (60ft), deciduous, conical, *lvs* green, fan-shaped, which turn gold before falling, yellow small, plum-shaped fruits on female trees. Very hardy, tolerant of most soils, and industrial pollution.

Juniperus, juniper, large genus of varying sizes and habits. *J. chinensis* 4, Chinese juniper, to 18m (60ft), conical or columnar, *lvs* grey or grey-green; 'Aurea', slow-growing, *lvs* yellow, needs light shade; 'Pyramidalis', conical, slow-growing glaucous leaves: *J. communis* 2, variable usually about 3m (10ft); 'Compressa', to 60cm (2ft), columnar, slow-growing, *lvs* blue; 'Depressa', Canadian juniper, to 60cm (2ft), *lvs* yellowish or brown-green, silver backed; 'Hibernica', Irish juniper, compact, to 3m (10ft), upright, *lvs* silver-grey: *J. conferta* 5, shore juniper, prostrate, ground-cover plant with *lvs* a prickly apple-green carpet: *J. horizontalis* 2, creeping juniper, to 60cm (2ft), prostrate, *lvs* greyish, excellent ground cover; 'Bar Harbor', prostrate, grey foliage, spreading: *J.* × *media* 5, variable

217

hybrid; 'Pfitzeriana', to 1·5m (5ft), wide-spreading, drooping tips, *lvs* green; 'Pfitzeriana Aurea', *lvs* golden; 'Plumosa Aurea', branches tipped with gold: *J. sabina* 4, spreading habit, common, useful ground-cover plant; 'Hicksii', to 1·2m (4ft), spreading branches, *lvs* bluish; 'Tamariscifolia', to 60cm (2ft), *lvs* green, pungent: *J. squamata* 4, variable, tips of branches drooping; 'Meyeri', to 1·5m (5ft), semi-erect, bluish, *lvs* densely packed: *J. virginiana* 2, pencil cedar, to 18m (60ft), *lvs* deep green-blue; 'Skyrocket', *lvs* narrow, ascending, blue-grey.

Larix, larch, fast-growing, deciduous, *lvs* fresh green, needs good light. *L. decidua* 2, European larch, over 18m (60ft), *lvs* green: *L.* × *eurolepis* 4, Dunkeld larch, over 18m (60ft), very vigorous, an important forest tree: *L. kaempferi* 4, Japanese larch, over 18m (60ft), vigorous, *lvs* deeper green than *L. decidua*.

Metasequoia glyptostroboides 5, dawn redwood, to 30m (100ft), deciduous, brown bark, *lvs* pale green, pinkish-gold autumn colour. Easily grown and tolerant of most soils and pollution.

Picea, spruce, over 18m (60ft), conical. needs deep soil and adequate moisture, *lvs* most green, but some good blue forms. *P. abies* 2, Norway spruce, over 18m (60ft); 'Nidiformis', 60cm (2ft), dense, dwarf, flat-topped bush: *P. breweriana* 5, Brewer's weeping spruce, conical, weeping, slender hanging branches: *P. likiangensis* 6, to 18m (60ft), *lvs* blue-green, cones red-pink, purple, May: *P. omorika* 4, Serbian spruce, 18m (60ft), tall, slender, drooping shoots which turn upwards, *lvs* dark green: *P. pungens* 2, Colorado spruce, to 18m (60ft), conical, *lvs* green to green-grey; 'Glauca', 10m (35ft), slow-growing, stiff, blue-grey shoots: *P. smithiana* 6, over 18m (60ft), conical, hanging, upturned tips to shoots.

Pinus, pine, large genus of evergreen trees, conical when young, more bushy when older, excellent on sandy soils, cones often of great beauty, bark generally reddish, but sometimes grey, dislikes shade and industrial pollution. *P. armandii* 3, Armand's pine, to 18m (60ft): *P. bungeana* 4, lace-bark pine, about 10m (35ft), flaky bark often white: *P. jeffreyi* 5, over 18m (60ft), conical, *lvs* blue-green: *P. mugo* 2, mountain pine, over 3m (10ft), *lvs* blue-green, good ground cover, resists pollution: *P. nigra* 4, Austrian pine, over 18m (60ft), tolerates lime/chalk: *P. peuce* 4, Macedonian pine, to 18m (60ft), conical, *lvs* strap-like, pointed, blue-green: *P. pinea* 2, dwarf

Siberian pine, to 60cm (2ft), spreading, good ground cover: *P. sylvestris* 2, Scots pine, over 18m (60ft); 'Fastigiata', slender, low-growing, upright form: *P. wallichiana* 7, Bhutan pine, over 18m (60ft), *lvs* long, blue-green, slender brown cones.

Podocarpus, large genus of mostly hardy species, fruit fleshy, usually red, successful on most soil types. *P. alpinus* 9, to 60cm (2ft), spreading, *lvs* dark green: *P. andinus* 9, plum-fruited yew, about 10m (35ft), *lvs* green, fruits resemble damsons: *P. nivalis* 5, alpine totara, to 60cm (2ft), prostrate, *lvs* olive-green.

Pseudotsuga, variable size, conical, soft foliage, pendulous cones. *P. menziesii* 4 to 6, Oregon Douglas fir, over 18m (60ft), fast-growing, dislikes lime/chalk.

Sequoia sempervirens 7, Californian redwood, over 100m (350ft), thin red bark, branches pendulous, *lvs* dark green.

Sequoiadendron giganteum 6, big tree, to 80m (270ft), branches pendulous, *lvs* bluish, spongy, fissured, brown bark.

Taxodium distichum 4, swamp cypress, over 18m (60ft), deciduous, *lvs* soft green, excellent for damp or wet soils, deep brown autumn colour.

Taxus, yew, useful for hedging, very tolerant of shade and most soils including lime/chalk. *T. baccata* 6, English yew, about 4·5m (15ft), black-green leaves; 'Aurea', golden yew, 3m (10ft), compact, *lvs* golden yellow.

Thuja, arbor-vitae, small genus, most soils, conical, *lvs* flattened, aromatic. *T. koraiensis* 6, Korean arbor-vitae, variable size, *lvs* green, white below: *T. occidentalis* 2, American arbor-vitae, to 18m (60ft), columnar, likes limestone; 'Compacta', to 60cm (2ft), *lvs* flattened, green; 'Ericoides', to 1·5m (5ft), rounded; 'Rheingold', about 3m (10ft), conical, *lvs* gold: *T. orientalis* 6, Chinese arbor-vitae, variable size, roughly conical, upcurving branches; 'Aurea Nana', to 60cm (2ft), globular, *lvs* yellow-green 'Elegantissima', about 3m (10ft), columnar, *lvs* yellow-green: *T. plicata* 5, western red cedar, over 30m (100ft), fast-growing; 'Fastigiata', columnar, ascending branches; 'Zebrina', conical, *lvs* green, splashed yellow.

Torreya, variable size, evergreen, wide needles, fruits plum-like, tolerant of shade and limey/chalky soils. *T. californica* 7, Californian nutmeg, about 10m (35ft), conical, *lvs* green: *T. grandis* 8, about 3m (10ft), *lvs* yellow-green.

Tsuga, hemlock, fast-growing, evergreen tree, cone-like shape, tolerant to shade, prefers deep, moist, well-drained soils. *T. canadensis* 4, eastern hemlock, over 18m (60ft), good on lime soils: *T. diversifolia* 5, Northern Japanese hemlock, to 9m (30ft), horizontally branched, *lvs* deep green: *T. heterophylla* 6, western hemlock, over 18m (60ft), large, fast-growing, spreading branches, shade tolerant.

Bulbs, Corms and Tubers

Nearly all plants which have a swollen storage organ, enabling them to live through a period of dormancy, are commonly called bulbs. In fact, only a fraction of them are true bulbs, the rest are corms, tubers and rhizomes. All four types are generally found in most nurserymens' 'bulb' catalogues.

Bulbs

A true bulb has several fleshy scales (which are modified leaves) growing out of a solid piece of tissue known as the basal plate. The roots grow from this plate and usually die each year when the bulb goes into its resting state or dormancy. A few plants, such as some bulbous irises and some of the *Amaryllidaceae* family have perennial roots growing from the basal plate. It sometimes happens that within a genus some plants are true bulbs while others are not. *Iris* is a good example of this: *Iris reticulata* 5 is a true bulb, flag iris forms rhizomes while *I. unguicularis* 7 has fibrous roots and does not store large quantities of food.

The number of fleshy scales varies from just one in some fritillarias to many in lilies and daffodils, and the scales are covered with papery, usually brown, tunics as in tulips or uncovered like those of fritillarias.

During the so-called dormant period a bulb is, in fact, a hive of activity and internally the next season's plant is being built up using food stored within the scales. For example, in the centre of a flowering-size daffodil bulb in late summer is a complete tiny young plant with immature leaves, stem and flowers. In the late autumn, roots grow from the basal plate and in spring the tiny plant at the centre of the bulb expands and grows into the aerial portion of the plant. It is sometimes possible to alter this life cycle by speeding up some part of it. Some bulbs are specially 'prepared' for Christmas flowering, such as tulips, hyacinths and daffodils. These bulbs are usually planted in bowls for flowering indoors and it is essential to keep them very cool after planting to encourage the formation of roots.

Whether or not flowers will be formed in the coming season largely depends on the amount of food stored within the bulb and this, in turn, depends on how good the leaf growth was in the previous season. So it is very important to encourage the growth of healthy leaves and it is equally important to make sure that these leaves are left to complete their work and to die down naturally; do not cut them off prematurely. The flower stem of a bulb can also manufacture food so it is better after flowering to remove the dead flower head only and to leave the stem in place.

Propagation Most bulbs propagate themselves naturally but they do vary considerably in their method of reproduction. For example, the tulip bulb dies each year and is replaced by one or more new ones by its side, whereas a daffodil bulb is usually long-lived, and new bulbs form and live alongside the parent to form a clump. A few bulbs, such as *Cardiocrinum giganteum* 6, take many years to reach flowering size and then die after flowering. These 'monocarpic' types as they are called usually produce several small bulbs around the dying parent and these in turn grow on to flower and die. Other bulbs, some lilies for instance, have the ability to 'creep' sideways through the soil by producing stolons with a new bulb at the end. In this way the species propagates itself and has the advantage of moving into new soil instead of exhausting the nutrients in one place.

Most bulbs can be propagated by detaching these smaller bulbs (or offsets) and growing them in a suitable growing mix (if they are very small) or by planting them elsewhere in the garden. This is generally done after the leaves have died down. In a few instances new bulbs can be formed from individual bulb scales. The scales of fully-developed lilies can, for example, be detached by carefully lifting them away and snapping them off at their base. They can then be planted, pointing upwards and sticking up 1cm (½in) or so, in a very sandy growing mix and placed in a greenhouse or some other warm place. After a few months tiny bulb-shaped growths can be seen and these can be transplanted like normal offsets. Take care not to damage their fine, fragile roots. It may take three years to reach flowering stage.

Corms

These are swollen underground stems. Unlike bulbs, they are solid throughout and are not made up of separate layers or scales, but they do have a basal plate from which the roots grow. Corms are usually covered with a fibrous or papery tunic. If the tunic of a crocus or gladiolus is peeled off, a series of rings can be seen around the circumference. These correspond to the leaf scars on an ordinary aerial stem, and tiny axillary buds on these scars can often be seen. These axillary buds usually remain dormant but, if the main bud is damaged, they can come into growth.

Each year the corm shrivels away and is replaced by a new one; sometimes the new corm is formed on top of the old one (in crocus) or sometimes by its side (in colchicum). Corms do not form the basis of next season's leaves, stem and flowers internally during the dormant period. The body of the corm is solid storage material and next season's bud containing leaves and flowers is produced externally.

Tubers

These are thickened underground stems or roots which act as a store for plant foods. They differ from both bulbs and corms in three main ways: they are non-scaly, they do not have tunics and they do not possess a basal plate. Some tubers have buds (eyes) on their surface which are capable of producing stems and leaves. A typical example of this type is the potato and these are known as stem tubers. Others, like dahlias,

have no buds other than at the main growing point at the apex; these are root tubers.

Because tubers do not have a basal plate, they do not produce roots from a specific point and in cyclamen or *Anemone blanda* 6 roots grow from various parts of the tuber's surface.

Rhizomes

These are underground stems bearing leaf scars and axillary buds. They grow more or less horizontally and can be thought of as elongated tubers. Lily of the valley, bearded irises and *Anemone nemorosa* 4 are typical examples.

Growing Bulbs

In the rest of this section, the word 'bulb' has been used in its loose, nurseryman's catalogue sense to describe all underground, swollen storage organs.

Bulbs commonly found in the average garden may have originated in South America, South Africa, the Mediterranean region or even in the Middle East. Where a bulb from the southern hemisphere is brought to the northern hemisphere (and vice versa) there is obviously a problem of changing its growth pattern. So before

Bulb and corm depth planting chart for outside (bulbs shown with roots have roots when bought)

From left to right: tulip, scilla, hyacinth, crocus, narcissus and daffodil, snowdrop, crown imperial, fritillary, lily (candidum), most lilies, ranunculus

0cm (0in)
2·5cm (1in)
5cm (2in)
7·5cm (3in)
10cm (4in)
12·5cm (5in)
15cm (6in)
17·5cm (7in)
20cm (8in)
22·5cm (9in)

From left to right: stem rooting lilies (top dress as growth commences), nerines, crinum lily (mulch these two with straw or bracken for winter protection), winter aconite, gladiolus, anemone, acidanthera, montbretia, autumn crocus

0cm (0in)
2·5cm (1in)
5cm (2in)
7·5cm (3in)
10cm (4in)
12·5cm (5in)
15cm (6in)
17·5cm (7in)
20cm (8in)
22·5cm (9in)

deciding on which species of bulbs to buy and where to plant them, it is necessary to know where they originate from and to have some idea of the conditions under which they grow in nature.

Southern Hemisphere Bulbs

In the southern hemisphere, very few bulbs are found growing naturally outside South Africa and South America. When a bulb from one of these regions is brought to the northern hemisphere, there are two main problems to face: the different timing of the seasons and when the bulb generally receives most of the natural rainfall.

The different timing of the seasons is simple – a bulb from South Africa can, for example, simply alter its timing by about six months and flower in exactly the same season as before. So a summer-flowering bulb in South Africa becomes a summer-flowering one in the UK.

Most bulbs which come from the southern hemisphere make most of their growth during the rainy period. Some areas, for example the South West Cape area of South Africa and the area west of the Andes in South America, receive rainfall in the winter months and bulbs from these areas are winter-flowering. Other areas, the Eastern Cape and the area east of the Andes, for instance, receive summer rainfall and produce summer-flowering bulbs.

The summer-flowering plants create no problems in the northern hemisphere. They grow and flower during the best weather and then go dormant in the winter months. In cold areas, they should be lifted and stored in a frost-free place. The winter-flowering species are also quite satisfactory and present no great problem in the warmer parts of the northern hemisphere, such as south and west Britain and the Southern States of North America. But they are much more difficult in the colder areas since they try to grow through northern winters and are usually susceptible to frost. The gladiolus is a particularly good example of this problem since some species come from the South West Cape and others from the East Cape. Most summer gladiolus hybrids with large flowers have been raised from Eastern Cape (summer rainfall) species and are usually quite easy to grow in the northern hemisphere. The South West Cape species are, however, tricky because they usually grow from September until February and try to flower through the worst of a northern winter. In colder areas, these should be grown in a greenhouse for protection.

Northern Hemisphere Bulbs

The main areas for naturally-occurring

Naturalizing bulbs

Choose large bulbs for naturalizing. Do not use small ones – they will not compete well with existing plants or grass. Take a large handful of bulbs

Throw the bulbs into the air and leave them where they land

Plant the bulbs where they land. In lawns a bulb planter can be used – see page 224 – or the grass can be lifted, the bulb planted and the grass replaced

northern hemisphere bulbs are the Mediterranean region, the Middle East, and the Western States of North America. All of these areas have a fairly dry summer and this is the most important factor to bear in mind when cultivating species from these regions. Most of these bulbs have four definite stages in their growth pattern. The first is a period of dormancy during the dry summer weather, then in autumn, when cooler, damper conditions arrive, bulbs have a period of active root growth, and possibly grow some leaves as well. During the winter cold there is little activity, a sort of 'partial dormancy', but when spring and warmer weather arrives both roots and leaves grow rapidly and the plants flower and set seed before the hot, dry conditions of summer once again cause dormancy. A few species, for example some colchicums, produce leafless flowers in the autumn and then lie semi-dormant below ground until spring when leaves and seeds emerge.

The problem of growing bulbs from the northern hemisphere is generally not one of frost as most of the bulbs are quite hardy in the UK and North America. A few which occur naturally in the more southerly parts, for example North Africa and California, might be tender in very cold gardens. The real problem is supplying a warm, dry period in summer so that the bulbs can rest and form flower buds for the coming year. Some species will not form flower buds unless the bulbs are subjected to a period of relatively high temperatures and, in extreme cases, if the summer temperatures are too low, the plant will not start to grow at all during the following season, not even to produce leaves.

Raised beds In cool, wet areas, the garden will have to be modified to provide the essential summer warmth and dryness. There are various ways of achieving this.

The first and most simple way is to choose the best position in the garden and alter the soil. Soil near walls is usually drier than in the open garden and south-facing areas are warmer than north-facing ones (vice versa in the southern hemisphere). So, the soil just below a south-facing wall would be a good site. A light, well-drained soil is drier and warmer in summer than a heavy waterlogged one so the drainage of heavy soils must be improved either by digging in sharp sand and humus, or, in really wet places, by laying drains. See *Soil*. An even better way of providing the right conditions is to make a raised bed and fill it with a sharply-draining medium, the exact formula of which is not critical. The raised bed can be regular and made of bricks or concrete or, for a more attractive effect, natural walling stone can be used to make an irregularly shaped bed. This method has the advantage that rock plants can be grown in the walls making the whole bed a pleasant garden feature. See *Construction*: *Walls*. In areas which have especially wet summers, the bed can be covered with glass or plastic frame lights during the dormant season. Frame lights can also be used in cold districts to keep off the worst of the winter frosts.

Give the bulb bed a light, annual dressing of slow-acting fertilizer during late summer. This will then be washed down into the soil by the autumn rains. If the autumn season is especially dry, the bed should be watered artificially from September until the onset of winter: do not water the bed excessively during winter even if the soil is a little on the dryish side. In spring, when growth is at its most active, give the bed plenty of water until the foliage begins to turn yellow. Do not water the bed during the summer.

Rock gardens Basically rock gardens consist of raised pockets of soil which drain freely and so present ideal places for growing bulbs. There are quite a few species, for example *Crocus tomasinianus* 5, which will grow happily through ground cover of other plants but, on the whole, it is better to keep the two separate since ground-covering plants will stop the sun reaching the soil and raising the temperature.

Bulbs in the greenhouse Rare species and dwarf bulbs are best grown in pots in a cold or cool greenhouse. They should be grown in a well-drained growing mix and the pots should be left to dry off for the summer. The bulbs should normally be re-potted every year in late summer, but this can be done every other year if they are fed with a slow-acting fertilizer in alternate years. Plants such as the *Cyclamen* species make ideal pot plants for a show in the greenhouse from autumn to spring.

Bulbs from Mexico

The mountain regions of Mexico produce a considerable number of bulbs but not many of these are generally grown in gardens. They differ a lot from most northern hemisphere bulbs, and species such as *Tigridia pavonia* 6, the tiger flower, remain dormant in the winter and flower in mid to late summer. *Tigridia pavonia* is hardy in mild areas but, if the winters are cold enough to freeze the soil down to bulb level, it must be lifted and stored in a frost-free place and not planted again until the soil has warmed up in spring.

Other Mexican species in this category are *Polianthes* and some *Zephyranthes* and *Habranthus*.

Bulbs for Damp Soils

Although most bulbs grow naturally in areas where there is a dry period, and these must be treated in this way in gardens, there are bulbs which grow in damp meadows or in woodlands. Typical examples are snowdrops, *Leucojum aestivum* 4, *Erythronium* and many *Lilium* species. These plants can generally be grown easily in most soils which do not dry out excessively. In very dry areas, moisture might have to be supplied artificially. Snowdrops, for example, do not like dry sandy soils and must be given some shade, and extra humus must be added to the soil to retain moisture.

Bulbs in Grass

Bulbs are often particularly attractive when they are grown in grass. The secret of doing this well is to choose robust species which can compete successfully with the turf and also those which do not require a summer baking. Many bulbs sold for 'naturalizing' are small and will take many years to reach flowering size when they are in competition with the turf. Choose well-developed, flowering-size bulbs only.

An easy way to plant bulbs in grass is to strip off a layer of turf, place the bulbs in the exposed top soil and then roll the turf back in position. Species which are particularly effective in grass include the autumn-flowering *Crocus, C. speciosus* 5, *C. nudiflorus* 5 and *C. kotschyanus* 6, autumn *Colchicum* species, *Galanthus, Leucojum vernum* 4 and *L. aestivum* 4, *Ornithogalum umbellatum* 4 and *Fritillaria meleagris* 3, Autumn bulbs flower without leaves and look rather bare in the open border, so they are, perhaps, better grown in grass than anywhere else. The grass however should not be cut until the bulb foliage has yellowed and died and this will limit the choice of position to around fruit trees or ornamentals where grass can be left uncut. Do not plant them in a formal lawn which must be trimmed early in the season.

Wherever bulbs are planted, be it in raised beds, rock gardens, grass or mixed borders, they will benefit from an annual dressing of slow-acting fertilizer in the late summer.

Tropical Bulbs
Bulbs from tropical regions of the world, mostly tropical Africa and tropical South America, need minimum temperatures in the region of 15 to 21°C (60 to 70°F) and are usually treated as greenhouse or conservatory plants. They generally grow in the summer and should be kept dormant, warm and moderately dry in winter. Re-pot them every spring using a rich potting medium. Plants such as hymenocallis are very robust and need a lot of feeding to flower well. In warm areas, some tropical bulbs can be planted out in warm borders for the summer, or at least grown in large pots or tubs on a patio.

Species, like *Eucharis grandiflora* 9, which grow and flower in winter must be treated entirely as warm greenhouse plants.

Bulbs
The numbers after the botanical names are the North America hardiness zone ratings – see *Climate*.

Achimenes 10, to about 45cm (1½ft), *fls* generally blue, pink and red, normally midsummer, needs a temperature of at least 16 to 19°C (60 to 65°F).

Acidanthera murielae 9, to 90cm (3ft), *fls* white, strongly scented, August to October, likes well-drained soil. Lift before frosts.

Allium azureum (caeruleum) 2 and 3, to 60cm (2ft), *fls* deep sky-blue, summer: *A.*

beesianum, to 40cm (16in), *fls* bright blue: *A. christophii (albopilosum)* 4, to 38cm (15in): *A. karataviense* 5, to about 15cm (6in), *fls* rose pink, May: *A. moly* 2 and 3, to 30cm (12in), *fls* yellow, July.

Amaryllis belladonna 9, belladonna lily, to 60cm (2ft), *fls* white, pale pink to deep rose, August to October. Plant midsummer near a south-facing wall.

Anemone blanda 6, to 15cm (6in), *fls* blue, pink and white, winter and early spring, needs a well-drained soil, warmth and shelter: *A. fulgens* 5, *fls* vermilion or scarlet, May, needs moist but not wet soil. Also single 'de Caen' and double 'St Brigid'.

Begonia, tuberous, summer-flowering plant for bedding and pots. Double or single *fls* red, pink, salmon, yellow and white. *B. pendula* 10 used for hanging baskets: *B. multiflora* 10 vars useful for rock gardens. Must be lifted in winter.

Camassia esculenta 5, quamash, to 45cm (18in), *fls* light blue, needs a rich, moist soil.

Canna, a genus of about 50 species, to 3m (10ft), *fls* usually red or yellow, summer, needs a temperature of at least 16°C (60°F), generally grown in greenhouses.

Chionodoxa luciliae 4, to 15cm (6in), *fls* blue, pink or white, early spring. Plant in autumn.

Clivia miniata 10, evergreen, to 60cm (2ft), *fls* scarlet and yellow, spring and summer, usually grown in pots in a greenhouse.

Colchicum autumnale 4, to 8cm (3in), *fls* lilac, purple and white, autumn. Plant in midsummer: *C. speciosum* 4.

Corydalis solida 5, *fls* purple, late spring. Likes a moist, well-drained soil in semi-shade.

Crinum × powellii 7, to 90cm (3ft), *fls* red, autumn. Plant in a south-facing border and lift before frosts. Can be left in the ground in mild areas.

Crocosmia × crocosmiiflora 7, montbretia, to 90cm (3ft), *fls* orange to yellow, autumn. Plant in a south-facing border and lift before frosts.

Crocus, a genus of about 80 species, *fls* autumn or spring: *C. ancyrensis* 4, *fls* orange, winter: *C. aureus* 4, *fls* orange, spring: *C. biflorus* 5, *fls* white to lilac, spring: *C. chrysanthus* 4, *fls* orange, cream,

To use a bulb planter, push it into the ground with a twisting motion. Here it is being used in a lawn

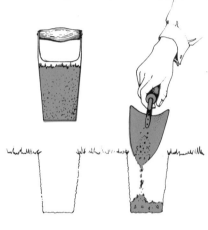

The tool will remove a plug of soil complete with turf (lefthand side). Put some sharp sand in the bottom of the hole

Plant the bulb and fill the hole by crumbling soil from the plug taken out by the bulb planter

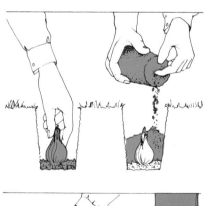

Replace the turf and firm it in place

gold, purple, blue and white, spring: *C. imperati* 7, *fls* purple, winter: *C. kotschyanus* 6, *fls* rosy lilac, autumn: *C. laevigatus fontenayi* 5, *fls* lilac, late autumn to winter: *C. speciosus* 5, *fls* lilac, autumn: *C. tomasinianus* 5, *fls* lavender, spring: *C. vernus* 4, *fls* white to purple, spring. See also *Gardens: Winter Gardens*.

Curtonus paniculatus 7, to 1·2m (4ft), *fls* orange-red, autumn.

Cyclamen, many species. Hardy species can be grown in open, suited to semi-shade. *C. coum* 6, *fls* carmine, winter: *C. linearifolium* 5, *fls* rose, autumn: *C. persicum* 9, *fls* white or rose, winter or spring, tender: *C. purpurascens* 5, *fls* carmine, autumn or spring: *C. vernale* 6, *fls* carmine, spring.

Dahlia 7, many vars classified by size and shape of *fls*. Two groups – Decorative and Cactus or semi-Cactus – divided into: Giant, *fls* over 25cm (10in), September to first hard frost; Large, *fls* 20 to 25cm (8 to 10in), August to first hard frost; Medium, *fls* 15 to 20cm (6 to 8in), mid-August to first hard frost; Small *fls* 10 to 15cm (4 to 6in), early August to first hard frost; Miniature, *fls* less than 10cm (4in), early August to first hard frost. Also Miniature Ball, Pompon and Dwarf Bedding.

Eranthis hyemalis 4, winter aconite, to 10cm (4in), *fls* yellow, spring. Best in rock gardens or in large drifts on lawns, does well in moist soil in partial shade.

Erythronium dens-canis 2 and 3, to 20cm (8in), *fls* violet, purple and white, late spring. Good for rock garden or front of flower border: *E. revolutum* 5, to 30cm (12in), *fls* cream: *E. tuolumnense* 5, to 30cm (12in), *fls* yellow, spring.

Eucharis grandiflora 9, to 25cm (10in), *fls* white. A stove plant needing a temperature of 18 to 21°C (65 to 70°F), rising to 27°C (80°F), in summer.

Eucomis bicolor 7, *fls* green, summer. Needs to be grown in a greenhouse in cold areas or in a sheltered spot in a warm garden in warmer climates.

Freesia 9, to about 45cm (18in), *fls* yellow, pink, lilac or white, spring. Usually grown in a greenhouse in cool climates.

Fritillaria imperialis 5, to 1·2m (4ft), *fls* bronze, yellow or red, spring. Needs very dry soil in summer and prefers acid-free conditions: *F. meleagris* 3, to 40cm (16in), *fls* purple, green and white, late spring.

Galanthus elwesii 4, to 25cm (10in), *fls* white, late winter, needs a warm, sunny position: *G. nivalis* 3, common snowdrop, to 20cm (8in), *fls* white, early spring. Best grown in a rock garden in a sheltered place or woodland.

Galtonia candicans 5, to 1·2m (4ft), *fls* white, midsummer, likes well-drained soil in a sunny position.

Gladiolus hybrids 9, a genus of over 150 species, many are worth cultivating in pots in cool greenhouses or in mixed flower borders: *G. byzantinus* 7, to 60cm (2ft), *fls* red, June. Many hybrids – Butterfly, 90cm (3ft), ruffled *fls*; 'Blue Goddess', *fls* blue; 'Green Woodpecker'; 'Pink Pearl': Nanus, 45cm (18in), *fls* pink or red. Large flowering vars also available.

Gloriosa superba 9, to 1·8m (6ft), *fls* orange and red, summer. Best in a greenhouse or conservatory in cool areas.

Gloxinia 10, true gloxinias are stove plants needing the same treatment as the florist's gloxinia which is *Sinningia speciosa* 10.

Habranthus robustus 10, *fls* rose, best grown in pots in a greenhouse.

Haemanthus coccineus 9, to 60cm (2ft), *fls* bright red, September, needs a warm position and better if grown in a greenhouse: *H. multiflorus* 10, to 90cm (3ft), *fls* red, April, more tender.

Hippeastrum 9, to 90cm (3ft), *fls* red or white or striped, February to May, needs a heated greenhouse, outstanding pot plant.

Hyacinthus orientalis 6, common hyacinth, to 30cm (12in), *fls* blue, purple, red, pink, white, cream or yellow. March to April; 'City of Haarlem', *fls* yellow; 'Delft Blue'; 'Jan Bos', *fls* red; 'Ostara', *fl* navy blue; 'Pink Pearl'.

Hymenocallis calathina 7, often known as *Ismene*, *fls* white, March and April, needs a greenhouse.

Iris, a genus of about 200 species. See introduction. *I. bucharica* 5, to 45cm (18in), *fls* yellow, April: *I. danfordiae* 5, *fls* yellow, January or February: *I. histrioides* 5, stem to 30cm (12in), *fls* blue-lilac, January: *I. reticulata* 5, *fls* violet-purple, February to March.

Ixia viridiflora 7, to 30cm (12in), *fls* green, May, June, best planted in a south-facing border or under a south wall.

Lachenalia pendula (*bulbifera*) 9, to 25cm (10in), *fls* deep purple, red and yellow, April, good for hanging baskets in a conservatory: *L. tricolor* (*aloides*) 9, to 30cm (12in), *fls* green, red and yellow, spring, grown as a pot plant.

Leucojum aestivum 4, summer snowflake, to 45cm (18in), *fls* white, spring, easily grown in ordinary soil: *L. autumnale* 5, *fls* white, autumn: *L. vernum* 4, spring snowflake, *fls* white, spring.

Lilium, lily, *fls* June to September, for border, woodland or large pots in a cool greenhouse. Many species – *L. auratum* 4, 1·8m (6ft), *fls* white with gold band through centre of petals, August: *L. candidum* 4, madonna lily, 1·2m (4ft), *fls* white, June, plant shallow. Trumpet vars, *fls* July and August; 'Golden Splendor', 1·5m (5ft), *fls* yellow; 'Green Dragon', 1·5m (5ft), *fls* white, flushed green; *L. longiflorum*, 1m (3½ft), *fls* white; 'Royale', 1·2m (4ft), *fls* white, streaked brown; 'Pink Pearl', *fls* pink; 'Royal Gold', 1·2m (4ft). *L. speciosum* vars, *fls* August and September; 'Album', 1·2m (4ft), *fls* white; 'Roseum', 1·2m (4ft), *fls* pink; 'Rubrum', 1·2m (4ft), *fls* red.

Montbretia – see *Crocosmia*.

Muscari armeniacum 4, grape hyacinth, to 30cm (12in), *fls* blue, May: *M. comosum* 4, to 30cm (12in), *fls* April.

Narcissus, a large genus consisting of many hundreds of named vars and species flowering from late winter until spring. Species include *N. bulbocodium* 6, hoop petticoat, *N. cyclamineus* 6, *N. minimus* 6 and *N. triandrus albus* 6, angel's tears. The genus is divided into various divisions of which the most important are the following:
Division 1 – commonly named 'daffodils'. These produce blooms with large cups in the shape of trumpets. Vars – 'Golden Harvest', *fls* golden-yellow; 'Trousseau', *fls* white perianth, rosy cream trumpet; 'Beersheba', *fls* white.
Division 2 – large cupped vars, usually the cups are rather flat. Vars – 'Carlton', *fls* yellow; 'Fortune', *fls* yellow with orange-red cup; 'Semper Avanti', *fls* white with orange cup.
Division 4 – double vars – 'Irene Copeland', *fls* creamy yellow; 'Texas', *fls* yellow and orange.
Division 8 – poetaz or bunch flowered. Var 'Geranium', *fls* 4 to 5 per stem, white with orange cups.
Division 9 – poeticus, old pheasant's eye – *fls* pure white, yellow and red eye.

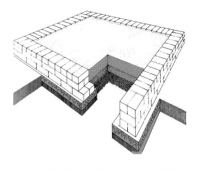

A raised bed for bulbs (see page 222)

Build the walls on a foundation of 10cm (4in) of hardcore topped by 15cm (6in) of concrete. The walls should be about 23cm (9in) thick (constructed as shown) with weep holes for drainage. Make the bed by first laying down 15cm (6in) of washed coarse pebbles, followed by 15cm (6in) of sandy loam and finally 8cm (3in) of sharp sand

Nerine bowdenii 9, to 45cm (18in), *fls* pale pink, September, needs a well-drained soil at the foot of a south-facing wall, protected from frost.

Ornithogalum thyrsoides 7, chincherinchee, to 45cm (18in), *fls* white or yellow, June, needs warmth and protection, lift in winter: *O. umbellatum* 4, star of Bethlehem, to 20cm (8in), *fls* white and green stripes, early summer.

Polianthes tuberosa 9, to 1·2m (4ft), *fls* white, any time, needs warmth and shelter.

Puschkinia libanotica (scilloides) 4, to 20cm (8in), *fls* blue or white.

Ranunculus asiaticus 8, garden ranunculus, to 38cm (15in), *fls* various colours, May, June, good for borders or rock gardens.

Richardia, see *Zantedeschia*.

Scilla campanulata (hispanica) 4, to 22cm (9in), *fls* blue, pink or white, May, needs dry, warm soil: *S. sibirica* 2 and 3, to 15cm (6in), *fls* blue, March: *S. tubergeniana* 3, to 15cm (6in), *fls* light blue, February and March.

Sparaxis tricolor 10, harlequin flower, to 60cm (2ft), *fls* orange and yellow, May, needs hot, dry conditions in summer, lift before frosts set in.

Lilium candidum, the Madonna lily

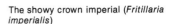
The showy crown imperial (*Fritillaria imperialis*)

Sternbergia lutea 7, to 20cm (8in), *fls* yellow, September, October, useful for planting in grass.

Tigridia pavonia 6, to 30cm (12in), *fls* yellow, white, red, last for 1 day, several in succession, lift in winter.

Tulipa 4, tulip, extensive genus divided into many different categories according to features like shape, time of flowering and colour.
Very early spring-flowering vars often called tulipa and are further divided:
T. dasystemon (*tarda*), small-flowering species, 8cm (3in), *fls* star-shaped, yellow and purple.
T. fosteriana 'Madame Lefeber', 38cm (15in), *fls* orange-scarlet. *T. greigii* 'Red Riding Hood', 38cm (15in), *fls* brilliant scarlet, *lvs* mottled.
T. kaufmanniana 'Heart's Delight', 22cm (9in), *fls* rose, white.
Large-flowered vars classified into:
Early single tulips, 'Keizerskroon', *fls* red and yellow; 'Prince of Austria', *fls* orange-red.
Darwin, *fls* large square heads on strong stems, 'Queen of Bartigons', *fls* salmon pink; 'Queen of the Night', *fls* maroon.
Lily-flowering tulips, *fls* waisted with pointed, reflexed petals.
Viridiflora – originate from species *T. viridiflora*, *fls* green on outside, 'Artist', *fls* rose, apricot and green; 'Greenland', *fls* pink and green.
Parrot, *fls* laciniated and crested petals, 'Blue Parrot', *fls* lavender-mauve; 'Fantasy', *fls* pink.

Vallota speciosa 10, to 45cm (18in), *fls* generally scarlet, July, August.

Zantedeschia aethiopica 10, arum lily, to 1·2m (4ft), *fls* yellow or red, spring, usually grown as a pot plant.

Zephyranthes candida 9, to 25cm (10in), *fls* September, October.

Aquatic Plants
Aquatic plants can roughly be defined as plants which live wholly or partly in water. They are attractive in their own right but can also perform important biological func-

tions in a fish pond. They can be divided into three kinds: oxygenating, floating and marginal. Oxygenating aquatic plants grow beneath the surface of water and help to remove carbon dioxide and generate oxygen. Both processes are very necessary to keep fish healthy and to keep water clear. Floating aquatic plants provide shade for fish and help to control the growth of algae. Water lilies, with their large leaves and attractive flowers, are probably the best-known plants in this group. Marginal plants are grown around the edges of a pool in varying depths of water.

Planting

In large pools plants can be grown directly in soil on the bottom of the pool or on ledges around the sides. In either case, the soil must be deep enough to hold the plants firmly, 10 to 13cm (4 to 5in) is a minimum. Particular care should be taken when planting water lilies. Plants bought from an aquatic centre may need some of their older leaves removed and some of their roots trimmed back. Spread out the roots before covering them with loam and leave part of the tuber slightly proud of the soil surface.

Some water lilies and many oxygenating plants grow vigorously and, in small pools, their growth should be controlled by planting them in containers. Open-weave plastic baskets are ideal but they should be lined with a material like turf placed upside down on the bottom and along the sides before filling them with good loamy soil. Before lowering baskets containing plants into the pool, spread a layer of pebbles or gravel over the soil surface to help prevent soil and plants from floating away. Some thin cord tied across the top of the basket will also help to keep the plants in place until they are established.

When stocking a pool for the first time it pays to put the containers in place two or three weeks before any fish go in. Fish can sometimes cause damage to young plants and this interval will help plants become established and grow well before it happens. For a new pool it is usually a good idea to purchase a balanced collection of plants suitable for the size of pool. Any special ones can be added at a later date when preferences are clearer.

Plants can be added to an old established pool at almost any time between April and the end of July when they are growing quickly. Again it pays to take precautions against fish damage by lowering the containers into the pool bit by bit so that by the time the plants are deep enough for the fish to disturb them their roots have got a firm hold on the growing mix which is in the container.

Oxygenators

A pool should have about five oxygenating plants to every square metre of pool surface (1 plant for every 2sq ft). So an average pool, about 2·2m by 1·2m (7ft by 4ft) needs about 14 oxygenating plants. It is a good idea to plant more at first and then reduce the number as they grow bigger.

Callitriche verna 6, a popular species of oxygenator, thread-like stems with small evergreen *lvs*.

Eleocharis acicularis 4, hair grass, *lvs* thread-like, pale to mid-green.

Elodea canadensis 4, strong growing and a particularly good oxygenator.

Hottonia palustris 5, water violet, to 30cm (12in), *lvs* fern-like, *fls* lavender, bloom above water, active October to May.

Myriophyllum spicatum 4, *lvs* green and bronze feather-like on long stems.

Ranunculus aquatilis 5, water crowfoot, *fls* white, standing slightly proud above the surface of the water, *lvs* three-lobed fern-like below water.

Floaters

Aponogeton distachyus 10, water hawthorn, *fls* white, sweet scented, April, *lvs* long, oval, glossy green, floating.

Hydrocharis morsus-ranae 5, frogbit, *fls* small, white in profusion, *lvs* dark green similar to a water lily.

Nymphaea 6 and 7, water lily, very wide range of species and varieties and only a few are mentioned here. Water depth varies according to variety but generally 30 to 60cm (1 to 2ft).
Pinks – 'Firecrest', 'Mrs Richmond', *N. odorata rosea*.
Reds – 'Charles de Meurville', 'Escarboucle', 'Rembrandt'.
Whites – 'Albatross', 'Candida', *N. odorata alba*.

Marginals

Marginals can be successfully planted in baskets or direct into soil on ledges around the sides of a pool. The water level should be just above the crown of the plant.

Acorus calamus 3, sweet flag, to 75cm (2½ft), grown for its erect strap-like sweet-scented foliage.

Alisma natans 5, water plantain, particularly suitable for small pools, water depth to

30cm (12in), *fls* small, white above the water surface.

Butomus umbellatus 5, to 90cm (3ft), *fls* rose pink in groups with the umbels up to 10cm (4in) deep, summer, *lvs* dark green, water depth 5 to 30cm (2 to 12in).

Calla palustris 2, bog arum, to 15cm (6in), *fls* white, spring, *lvs* glossy, heart-shaped. Water depth less than 10cm (4in) deep. Set in a small group along the pool margin it can be most attractive.

Iris laevigata 4, Japanese water iris, very adaptable, plants normally flower twice a year, *fls* various from white to ice-blue, May, June. Water depth 5cm (2in).

Mimulus luteus 7, to 30cm (1ft), *fls* deep yellow spotted with red, water depth to 8cm (3in).

Sagittaria japonica 5, Japanese arrowhead, to 60cm (2ft), *fls* white with a yellow centre, *lvs* pale green, narrow arrow shape.

Climbing Plants

Climbing plants are plants which have modified some part of themselves, generally their stems or leaves, to enable them to use other plants or objects for support. They do this to get their flowering parts off the ground and to reach the light. Because they use objects or plants for support, they have no need for a woody stem structure typical of shrubs and trees and so their stems are thin though very strong and flexible. The method used to get them to climb affects the way in which they should be used in the garden.

Types of Plants

There are basically four different types of climbing plants.

Twining stems These have thin young shoots which twist around a support plant or object. In most cases this support must be thin, about 2cm (1in) across, but a few plants such as convolvulus, wisteria and runner bean can climb supports more than 5cm (2in) across.

Tendrils A tendril is a modified leaf which will twist tightly around a thin support. Many vigorous plants use this method, particularly while they are young, for example mutisia, vitis and sweet peas.

Self-clinging sucker pads or **aerial roots** These can adhere to any rough, sound surface. When established and climbing, these plants need no extra support. Ivies use aerial roots and the Virginia creeper has sucker pads.

Scandent plants These are fast-growing plants which produce shoots that will grow through other woody plants and use them for support. These plants often have thorny shoots, for example, roses and rubus. Some, clematis for instance, use the petiole (stem) of their leaves to anchor their stems while scrambling over a support. *Solanum crispum* 8 is a typical scandent plant.

Supports

Most climbers are grown as wall plants, though many of them are not suited for such a position; other types of support are grossly under-used or totally neglected. Climbing plants are seen to their best advantage when they are allowed to grow naturally using other plants as support. For example, roses could be allowed to grow through a holly, or *Wisteria sinensis* through an old tree, where the hanging chains of the flowers could be appreciated fully. A recognition of climbing types, coupled with different support types can produce superb results.

Walls These should really only be used for plants which need the warmth and shelter a wall can provide (see *Wall Plants*), but climbers are usually grown against them. Do not use nails and string for tying plants to a wall. It is unsightly and may damage the wall. Provide wall support for climbers by putting up horizontal wires at about 30 to 45cm (12 to 18in) intervals and anchor these to the wall using metal wall strainers. The strainers should be sunk properly into the stone or brickwork, not the mortar. This method is unlikely to come loose at a later date. For narrow vertical panels, between windows, for example, sections of well-made trellis or lattice work are attractive, though not long lived. For further details see *Wall Plants*. They can be used to support plants like jasminum or lonicera which always look effective.

The ideal plants for walls are those which do not need regular pruning, those which form a woody framework, or those which can support themselves. Never try to grow large plants on small walls – they will quickly become too big and will need regular cutting to keep them in bounds. Instead try to keep the plant looking natural, and flowering or behaving as it would naturally. Vigorous, self-clinging climbers, such as ivies, can be allowed to climb up the walls of a house without much fear of damage to the wall. But, they should not be allowed to climb near drain-pipes, gutters, slates or tiles.

Pergolas These are wonderful supports for many plants but are often quite impractical in northern climates. Pergolas evolved in Italy, where cool, shaded walks are needed for relief from summer sun. All too often they become dark, dank tunnels through which the weaker, northern sun fails to filter. A pergola should be soundly constructed, preferably with brick or stone piers, and with a widely-spaced, beamed roof. Timber pergolas are not long-lived. Metal pergolas, though good, need regular maintenance. See *Construction: Pergolas*.

Pergola posts provide support for twining and scandent climbers but will not support tendril climbers unless some form of netting or trellis is stretched between them.

Pillars Many plants are best grown in borders on a pillar or stake. Leaving side branches on the stake will give the plant extra support. Tendril climbers are best grown in this way but scandent and twining climbers will grow up pillars or stakes too.

Tripods These can easily be made by wiring three sound stakes together. A wide-based plant will result.

Natural supports Almost any tree or shrub can be used as a support for climbers. Dead or dying plants that are difficult to remove, but are not harbouring pests or diseases, can be used as supports for vigorous climbers such as *Polygonum baldschuanicum* 4, the Russian vine. Living trees too, such as old fruit trees, make excellent supports. The tree chosen should not be one that is valuable in the garden for its own qualities. *Fagus sylvatica* 4 and most aesculus are poor climbing plant hosts.

Planting

Most climbers will grow in any ordinary garden soil but unless they are being grown as pillar plants in a border, it is likely that the soil in the site chosen will be rather impoverished. To encourage the climber to clothe its support quickly, the soil should be on the rich side and deeply and widely dug. See *Wall Plants* for preparing the soil near walls.

If the plant is to be grown through a tree or shrub, plant it well away from the main stem, so that the young climber is able to establish with the minimum competition from its host's roots. Take out a hole about 1m by 1m (3ft by 3ft) and 45cm (18in) deep about 1m (3ft) beyond the circle formed by the outer branches of the tree or shrub. Enrich the soil with manure or compost and line the hole with thin wood to prevent competition. Use nylon twine to get the climber into the tree or shrub and once it is established use rope or a chain to make the link. The rope or chain must be slack to stop the climber being pulled out of the ground in windy weather.

Planting should be done in the autumn or spring, when the soil is in good condition; not frozen, not too dry, nor wet with rain. Evergreen climbers should be planted in the spring. With container-grown plants, take care to ensure that the plant has been well watered before planting. Plants around pillars, pergolas or tripods should be planted at least 15cm (6in) away from their support. Young plants will need some form of temporary support until they can reach their permanent supports. Most climbers make little extension growth in their first season and should be loosely tied to bamboo canes to prevent damage. It should not be necessary to do any pruning in the first year but dead growths should be removed and weeds, pests and disease controlled.

Pruning

Pruning and training should begin the year after planting with the aim to encourage vigorous growths and to remove the weaker ones. For plants such as *Hydrangea petiolaris* 4, *Campsis radicans* 4 and *Clematis armandii* 7, make sure that a main framework is made as soon as possible. Climbers being grown over living trees should be encouraged to grow over the host in such a way that the climber gets as much light as possible.

When the main framework (if any) has been formed, the plant should be encouraged to fill its allotted space quickly and minimum pruning should be the aim. Prune according to flowering period. Plants which flower on one-year-old wood should be pruned immediately after flowering, *Jasminum nudiflorum* 5, for example. Plants that flower on older wood should not be pruned. Some species (some clematis) flower on new growth and can be cut back to a framework in spring as growth begins. Some, for example wisteria, need spurring to get flowering buds (cut back long growths to two to three buds). Only when a climber gets totally out of hand or is exceeding its allotted space should drastic pruning be given, and then the number of flowers may be very reduced for one season. For further details see *Pruning*.

Feeding

Climbing plants are greedy feeders and a top dressing of well-rotted compost is beneficial, especially after pruning. Plants can be mulched in the spring to help moisture retention, especially climbers near walls. This will eventually provide plant foods too. Do not give climbers too much fertilizer at once; small doses of fertilizer at regular intervals will keep them growing well. Spring and summer feeds of sulphate of ammonia, Nitrochalk or nitrate of soda at 35 to 70g/m^2 (1 to 2oz/sq yd) can be used as a stimulant. Do not use these feeds after August.

Pool with *Iris kaempferi*

Climbers

The numbers after the botanical names are the North America hardiness zone ratings – *see Climate*.

Hardy Climbers

Actinidia, climbing gooseberry, twining deciduous, *fls* generally white, *lvs* dark green, rounded, fruits many seeded, fleshy and elongated. Sun or semi-shade, vigorous, excellent for covering old walls or tall stumps. No pruning. Any soil, provided it is not limey/chalky, poor or badly drained. *A. arguta* 4, *fls* white, June, July, fruits greenish-yellow: *A. chinensis* 7, to 9m (30ft), *fls* creamy white, late summer, fruits green, turning brown: *A. kolomikta* 4, to 3m (10ft), *lvs* heart-shaped, green tipped with white or pink: *A. polygama* 4, to 6m (20ft), *fls* white, June, fruits yellow.

Akebia, twining, semi-evergreen, *fls* small, purple, fruits sausage-shaped, violet. Sun or shade, excellent for training over hedges, low trees, bushes or old stumps. Tender, plant in well-drained fertile soil where flowers escape spring frosts. *A. lobata* 7, (*trifoliata*), to 9m (30ft), *fls* dark purple, April: *A. quinata* 4, to 12m (40ft), *fls* red-purple, April.

Ampelopsis megalophylla 6, to 9m (30ft), strong but slow-growing, fruits top-shaped, purple at first, finally black.

Aristolochia durior (A. macrophylla) 4, Dutchman's pipe, deciduous, twining, to 9m (30ft), *fls* tubular, twisted, with expanded lobes, brown purple, June, *lvs* heart-shaped. Sun or shade, excellent for unsightly walls, fences, stumps, trees or on wooden supports such as pergolas. Foliage needs protection from icy winds or frosts in winter.

Campsis radicans 4, trumpet vine, to 6m (20ft) sparse aerial roots, deciduous, tall, strong-growing, *fls* tubular, clustered, orange-red, produced in great quantities in hot dry years, August, September, *lvs* toothed, bright green. Needs full sun, train over walls or roofs of out-houses or tree stumps. Prune hard to main framework in early spring.

Celastrus, twining and scandent, deciduous, very vigorous, *fls* insignificant, *lvs* oval, pale green seed coat, bright coloured, pea-size, yellow-orange, splitting to show scarlet seeds, male and female types must be planted, best grown on dead tree. Thrives

231

Left: Anti-clockwise twining stem –
convolvulus
Right: Clockwise twining stem –
honeysuckle

Left: Leaf tendrils – sweet pea

Right: Stem tendrils – grape vine

on all soils except dry and limey/chalky ones. Needs shelter from cold winds. *Celastrus scandens* 2, to 7m (23ft): *C. rugosus* 4, to 6m (20ft), *lvs* strongly toothed and wrinkled.

Clematis, tendrils, probably the most widely planted climber, can haul itself to the top of a small tree, then cascade flowering stems over it, enjoys soils with lime, and likes its roots shaded and heads in the sun. *C. armandii* 7, evergreen, to 6m (20ft), slightly tender, *fls* white or pink in clusters, no pruning. Subject to injury in severe winters, best planted on a warm, sunny wall: *C. × jackmanii* 5, vigorous plant to 3m (10ft), *fls* up to 15cm (6in) across, purple, July to October, prune to old wood when out of hand: *C. montana* 6, stems to 9m (30ft), *fls* white, May, very hardy: *C. tangutica* 5, weak climber to 4·5m (15ft), *fls* yellow, thick petals, August to September, followed by silky seed heads. Good for low walls, fences and trellises, large boulders and for garden banks.

Hedera, ivy, aerial roots, evergreen, high climbing, very hardy, *fls* insignificant, *lvs* lobed, sometimes variegated, berries black, will not damage a sound wall. Excellent habitat for small birds, clip annually in July. Good also for clothing bare ground beneath trees and banks. Grows well on any soil in sun or shade. *H. canariensis* 'Variegata' ('Gloire de Marengo') 7, to 6m (20ft), *lvs* deep green, silver margined, provide shelter from cold winds: *H. colchica dentata* 'Variegata' 5, similar to *H. canariensis* 'Variegata', but hardier, *lvs* green flushed with creamy yellow. Good for exposed gardens: *H. helix* 4, to 24m (80ft) – following vars grow to around 4·5m (15ft); 'Buttercup', soft yellow *lvs*; 'Goldheart', tapering *lvs* splashed with gold in the centre; 'Sagittaefolia', green, five-lobed, arrow-shaped *lvs*; 'Glacier' *lvs* silver variegated.

Hydrangea petiolaris 4, aerial roots, deciduous, to 18m (60ft), *fls* creamy white, May to June, borne on lateral shoots from climbing stems, *lvs* shiny, mid-green. For

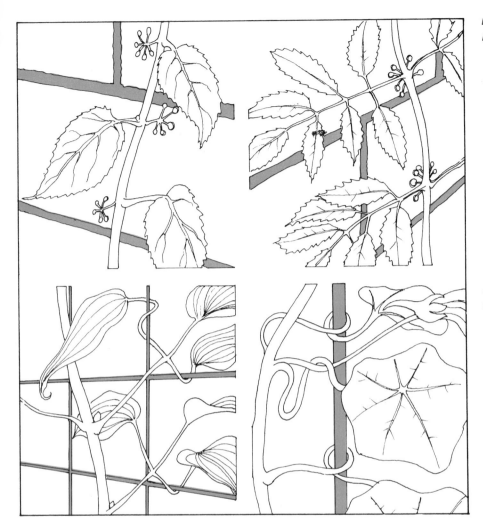

Left: Tendril sucker pads – ampelopsis
Right: Stem sucker pads – campsis vine

Left: Twining leaf-stalks – clematis
Right: Twining leaf stalks – nasturtium

sun or semi-shade, climbing trees or walls. Any well-drained site.

Jasminum, large genus, twining and scandent, deciduous or semi-evergreen, needs sun. Ordinary soil including lime/chalk. *J. nudiflorum* 5, winter jasmine, to 4·5m (15ft), *fls* yellow, November to February, cut off all flowering shoots in early spring, best grown on trellis and good for unsightly walls and banks: *J. officinale* 7, summer jasmine, to 9m (30ft), *fls* white, sweetly-scented, on vigorous twining stems, cut back hard when out of hand. Requires a sheltered corner if grown in cold northern districts.

Lathyrus, climbing pea, tendrils, to 1·8m (6ft) dies to ground in fall/autumn, *fls* lavender-violet or purple, pea-shaped, June to September, *lvs* grey-green, terminating in tendrils, stems square. Any well-drained soil, sun or light shade. *L. grandiflorus* 5: *L. latifolius* 3, everlasting pea, with white var 'White Pearl': *L. pubescens* 5.

Lonicera, honeysuckle, twining, vigorous, *fls* cream or red, sweetly scented. Subject to aphis attack, best in cool moist soil, no pruning. Best scrambling over other bushes or tree stumps, trellises or pergolas. *L. caprifolium* 5, to 6m (20ft), *fls* creamy-white, fragrant, June, July, berries orange-red: *L. etrusca* 7, deciduous or semi-evergreen, very vigorous, *fls* opening cream, deepening to yellow, June and July, *lvs* usually downy, at its best in sun: *L. japonica* 4, evergreen, to 9m (30ft), rampant, *fls* white, changing to yellow with age, continuously from June onwards. Excellent for covering and concealing unsightly objects: *L. periclymenum* 4, woodbine, vigorous, *fls* creamy-white within, darkening with age, purplish or yellowish outside, June to September, berries red – vars 'Belgica', *fls* purple-red, May and June; 'Serotina', *fls* red, purple and creamy white, July to October.

Mutisia, climbing gazania, tendrils, evergreen, *fls* large, gaudy 'daisy-like'. Needs shelter of wall, and light soil, no pruning. *M.*

233

clematis 10, *fls* red, summer and early autumn. For a conservatory: *M. ilicifolia* 10, to 3m (10ft), *fls* pale lilac or pink, summer.

Parthenocissus, sucker pads and tendrils, vigorous Asian climbers, 7 to 21m (24 to 70ft), *lvs* glossy, attractive at all times, no pruning. Good for clothing cold walls or fences. Any soil, sun or shade. *P. henryana* 8, *lvs* dark green or bronze with silvery-white veinal variegation, red in autumn, fruits dark blue: *P. quinquefolia* 3, Virginia creeper, *lvs* turn brilliant orange and scarlet in autumn, fruits blue-black.

Passiflora, passion flower, tendrils, 6 to 9m (20 to 30ft) generally grown in glasshouses, remove dead growth. Can be grown against south- or west-facing walls if sheltered from cold winds and frost. Any soil, full sun. *P. caerulea* 7 and 8, *fls* purplish, summer and autumn; 'Constance Elliott', white, can be grown on warm south wall.

Polygonum baldschuanicum 4, Russian vine, twining, fast-growing, deciduous, to 12m (40ft), very hardy, *fls* pink-white, June to July. Any well-drained soil, sun or deep shade. Ideal for training over an old tree, trellis or for camouflaging compost heaps. Cut back hard in early spring.

Rosa, hybrid climbing roses are probably the most common climbing, flowering plants, most are thorny, vigorous scramblers, *fls* pink, white, red, orange, yellow, many varieties are sweetly scented. Tolerant of most soils, but needing copious moisture. See *Roses* for varieties. Species mostly smaller flowered, but more freely flowering. *R. banksiae* 7, Banksian rose, to 7·5m (25ft), *fls* double, white, fragrant, May, June: *R. bracteata* 5, Macartney rose, evergreen, to 3m (10ft) *fls* white, lemon-scented, fruits orange-red: *R. filipes* 'Kiftsgate' 6, *fls* white, June, July, *lvs* light-green, copper tinted when young, fruits red: *R. setigera* 4, prairie rose, to 1·5m (5ft), *fls* rose-pink, July, August, fruits red.

Vitis, vines, large genus, tendrils, deciduous. Grown principally for colour of autumn foliage or for fruits. Remove some of the old shoots annually. *V. coignetiae* 5, to over 18m (60ft), strong-growing, *lvs* large, handsome, turn to crimson and scarlet in autumn, fruits black with purple bloom: *V. vinifera* 6 and vars, grape vine, have ornamental foliage as well as their edible fruits – vars 'Brandt' and 'Purpurea'.

Wisteria sinensis 5, Chinese wisteria, twining, vigorous, deciduous climber, needing support in early stages. Ideal for a south- or west-facing wall. Flower buds sensitive to frost. Arrange plants so that early morning sun does not fall on them. *Fls* long chains, mauve or white, May. Cut back young growths to two buds in autumn.

Tender Climbers

These can be grown outdoors in warm climates; elsewhere they need the protection of a cool greenhouse.

Bougainvillea glabra 10, a vigorous evergreen climber, to 6m (20ft), or in a pot to 1·8m (6ft), needs dry period to encourage *fls*, rose purple, orange or pink bracts. Prune out old growths when flowers fade.

Clerodendrum thomsonae 9, twining shrubby climber, 4·5m (15ft), *fls* creamy white with red centre, June to September, *lvs* dark green. Can be grown in large pot, thin shoots regularly.

Gloriosa simplex 10, slender stem arises annually from tuber, *fls* scarlet, yellow, reflexed. Needs rich, light moist soil.

Ipomoea, many sp and vars 7 to 10, to 2·4m (8ft), *fls* intense blue, lasting a few hours only, July to September. Cut back woody types hard in early spring. *I. tricolor* 'Flying Saucers', a perennial usually treated as an annual, is often grown outside.

Jasminum polyanthum 9, twining, evergreen, to 7·5m (25ft), *fls* white, very fragrant, May until late summer.

Passiflora edulis 10, tendrils, to 6m (20ft) *fls* sepals white, green without, corona with white filaments, banded with purple, June, fruits yellow or dull purple, pulp edible, August.

Petrea volubilis 10, twining, to 6m (20ft), *fls* purple, in hanging chains over a long period, mid-summer, *lvs* oval, leathery. Needs a large glasshouse to allow the trunk to develop, shorten growths by two-thirds annually.

Thunbergia mysorensis 10, twining climbers to 4·5m (15ft), *fls* hanging, red and dull yellow, *lvs* dark green, pointed. Remove thin shoots, cut back hard annually.

Wall Plants

There are three reasons why you might want to grow plants against a wall: 1) to make the wall look less bare, 2) to give shelter to plants which would be too tender to survive in the open garden, and 3) to help ripen the wood of plants which would not flower or fruit so effectively in the open garden. Most wall plants are shrubs and fruit trees and not true climbers.

In the northern hemisphere, when you want to grow plants which are much too tender to grow in the open garden, it is best to choose a wall which faces south or west. But if the plants are only slightly too tender then it is often better to choose one which faces north-west. The same plants grown against a south-facing wall may start to grow too early in spring and become victims of a late frost. Use the opposite compass points if you live in the southern hemisphere.

The aspect of a wall also governs the amount of shade plants get. In the northern hemisphere, plants grown against a north-facing wall will be in the shade for most of the day, against a south-facing wall they will have full sun for most of the day. East-facing walls get early morning sun but are shaded in the afternoon, whereas west-facing walls are shaded in the morning and sunny in the afternoon. Again you should use the opposite compass points in the southern hemisphere.

Any plant grown against a wall should be allowed to grow out from the wall producing an informal appearance and, as near as possible, assuming its own natural shape. Pruning should be restricted to improve health and to encourage flowering.

Preparing the Site

Soil against a wall is generally poor and should be improved before planting. Any rubble and house bricks should be removed and generous amount of organic matter dug in to aid water retention. Perennial weeds should also be eradicated. It is doubtful if any true wall plants are vigorous enough to damage foundations, but this possibility should be kept in mind. A deep trench against the wall, backed with a plastic sheet and refilled, will stop root invasion and safeguard foundations.

Planting

Dig a hole 1m (3ft) square and 60cm (2ft) deep, break up the base with a fork to give good drainage and refill the hole with a mixture of good garden soil, peat and sand. Firm and allow to settle.

Most young wall plants are bought with their roots in a pot and should be well watered before the pot is removed. If the roots are congested, tease them out gently and remove any crocks. Make a hole slightly bigger than the root ball of the plant and about 30 to 45cm (12 to 18in) away from the wall. Spread out the roots of the plant, put the soil back, firm it leaving a slight depression and water the plant in. If support is required in the first year, tie the plant loosely to a cane, not to its permanent support.

Supports for Wall Plants

Most wall plants will make a strong framework and need little support. For those needing some support, horizontal wires, fixed to strainers in the wall at 30 to 45cm (12 to 18in) intervals, are ideal. For further details see *Climbing Plants*. Trellises generally do not last very long. But they are pretty and if you decide to use one set it about 3cm (1in) clear of the wall by using wooden spacers or old cotton reels. If the wall behind the trellis needs regular attention, for painting for example, then arrange the trellis so that it can be taken down easily by attaching the top and bottom of it to wooden bars permanently fixed to the wall. The top attachment should be easily removable, by using hooks and eyes for example, and the bottom should be hinged so that the trellis (and plant) can be gently lowered away from the wall. Canes 2m (6ft) long arranged in a fan shape and attached to the wall also give firm support.

Wall Plants

The numbers after the botanical names are the North America hardiness zone ratings – see *Climate*.

Abutilon vitifolium 10, over 3m (10ft), needs a high wall, shortlived, *fls* pale-grey to violet, June to July, *lvs* grey-green, likes sun, propagate by cuttings. No pruning. *A. megapotamicum* 10 about 1·5m (5ft), *fls* red, a scandent climber.

Buddleia auriculata 10, rather tender, to 3m (10ft), *fls* small, sweetly-scented, buff-cream, late autumn, *lvs* small, dark green. No pruning.

Camellia japonica 7, (and its vars) excellent against a north wall, copious water is needed in dry periods even when the plant is established, otherwise newly formed buds may be shed. No pruning required. See also *Shrubs*.

Ceanothus, the best blue-flowering shrubs available, mostly evergreen and needing sun to ripen growths, *fls* borne in great profusion from April to autumn according to type, shortlived but fast-growing, remove dead shoots and longest new growths. *C. dentatus* 10, evergreen, *fls* bright blue, May: *C. impressus* 9 – see *Shrubs*: *C. × lobbianus* 10, evergreen, over 3m (10ft), *fls* bright blue, May: *C. × veitchianus* 10, evergreen, *fls* deep blue, May and June.

Left: Aerial roots – *Hedera helix*, ivy

Right: Aerial roots – *Monstera pertusa*, swiss cheese plant. See *Gardens: House Plants*

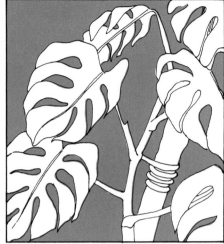

Chaenomeles (*Cydonia*) *speciosa* 4, to 3m (10ft), *fls* pink, red or white, in spring, thorny.

Chimonanthus praecox 7, winter sweet, up to 3m (10ft), very hardy but often grown near a door to take advantage of *fls* sweetly-scented, pale yellow, 'Luteus' best variety. No pruning.

Clianthus puniceus 9, lobster claw, scandent, semi-evergreen, very handsome, weak-stemmed plant, needing support, *fls* in large clusters, developing in autumn and opening the following spring, bright rose red, claw-like, *lvs* dark green. Will be killed in a hard winter, but easily propagated by short cuttings taken with a heel. Best on a west wall.

Cotoneaster horizontalis 4, common wall shrub, neat, *lvs* small. Better used in the open ground where it assumes a low habit of evenly spaced layers of growth.

Cytisus, broom, mostly hardy shrubs, *fls* cream, yellow or purple. *C. battandieri* 7, to 7m (23ft), *lvs* grey, hairy, needs a high warm wall.

Dendromecon rigidum 9, evergreen, over 3m (10ft), fast-growing. *Fls* bright yellow, poppy-like, *lvs* grey, pointed, very short-lived, but worth a warm corner.

Eriobotrya japonica 7, loquat, 8m (27ft), *fls* rarely produced, but white and fragrant, hawthorn-like, *lvs* bold, greyish, fruit extremely rare, pear-shaped, yellow.

Fremontodendron californicum 9, evergreen, 4m (13ft), shortlived but floriferous, *fls* bright yellow, five-petalled, *lvs* tough, three-lobed.

Garrya elliptica 8, very hardy, evergreen, 7m (23ft), *fls* male plant produces long tassels grey-green, March. Prefers north or east wall.

Magnolia grandiflora 7, superb architectural plant, 15m (50ft), *lvs* bold, lustrous. Takes some years to settle down before flowering. No pruning. Needs a large high wall.

Myrtus communis 8 and 9, common myrtle, evergreen, 1·5m (5ft), *fls* small creamy tassels, *lvs* small, branching shrub from base.

Olea europaea 9, olive, angular-shaped shrub, *fls* small, white, very rarely seen, *lvs* grey-green, fruit never in UK.

Punica granatum 7 and 8, pomegranate, deciduous, to 9m (30ft), makes a thin, twiggy shrub, *fls* borne in profusion, scarlet with fleshy petals and embryo fruit at base that generally fails to develop, but persists for some time, late summer, early in autumn, *lvs* narrow, glossy, yellow in autumn.

Pyracantha, firethorn, commonly used wall plant, generally clipped hard, better in the open, where its long arching branches have great elegance, very hardy – see *Shrubs*.

Sophora microphylla 8 and 9, kowhai, evergreen, 7m (23ft), *fls* bright yellow, April. No pruning.

Viburnum macrocephalum 6, snowball tree, semi-evergreen, 2m (6ft), *fls* large heads, white, sterile, summer, *lvs* neat, green. Rather tender. No pruning.

As well as woody plants, many herbaceous plants benefit from the shelter of walls.

Tripods

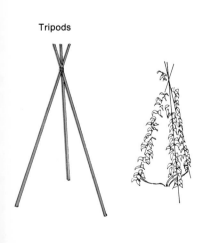

Such types as *Eryngium*, *Alstroemeria*, *Penstemon*, *Salvia* and *Sisyrinchium* and bulbs like *Amaryllis*, *Crinum*, *Habranthus*, *Vallota* and *Zantedeschia* will ripen properly and flower better with the protection of a wall.

Edging Plants

Edging plants are usually dwarf, spreading plants which are used to hide and break up the hard outline of the edges of flower beds or paths. They may be annuals, biennials, perennials, bulbous plants or even shrubs such as the dwarf evergreen box, *Buxus sempervirens* 'Suffruticosa'. Some carry large masses of flowers in season while others are important for the colour and nature of their foliage. Rock garden species, heathers and ground-cover plants can also be used for edging as long as they are compatible with other plants in the border and draw attention towards the border itself.

Alpine and Rock Garden Plants

Some alpine and rock garden plants are very attractive edging plants but, if they are used along the edges of herbaceous borders, suitable localized growing conditions may have to be provided. For instance, if lime-loving plants are used along the edges of paths then limestone chippings should be incorporated into the strip of soil which is being planted. For rock plants there should always be plenty of grit mixed with the soil.

Bulbs

Bulbs, particularly those which produce small or miniature flowers, can be planted along the edges of flower beds and usually look attractive in mixed borders too. Winter aconite, muscari, snowdrop, crocus and cyclamen provide interesting colour at otherwise drab times of the year and once flowering is over their foliage can be hidden by other edging plants starting to grow. Anemones have very pleasing foliage which adds to their value as edging plants.

Annuals

Hardy annuals can be sown outside where they are to flower, generally from March to June. But nearly all the best known dwarf annual edging plants are half-hardy types and need to be started under glass in most areas. They are planted once all threat of frost has gone – see *Annuals and Biennials* for details of situations, planting distances and flowering times.

Perennials

For details of planting, propagation and looking after perennials see *Herbaceous Perennials*.

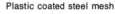
Supports for climbing plants

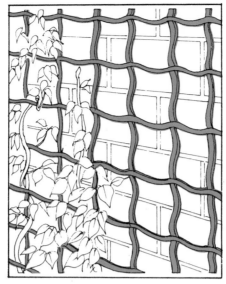

Plastic trellis fixed to a wall or fence
Wood diamond trellis

Plastic coated steel mesh

Chain link fencing

A well thought-out edging scheme – begonias behind corydalis

Heathers

Heathers are valuable for ground cover and are attractive as edging plants in mixed borders. In many cases the flowers of Erica and Calluna are not individually large but they are most effective *en masse*. Many heathers, particularly some of the newer varieties, have very colourful foliage which can make a great contribution to any garden in late winter and early spring. The range of colours is very wide and includes yellow, orange, red and green. Most species of Erica and Calluna need an acid soil but *Erica carnea* is very adaptable and is tolerant of a wide range of soils, including those which are alkaline. All heathers prefer a sandy soil and do least well on clay soils. Digging grit and peat in before planting will help to lighten the soil and provide conditions more suitable for heathers. Choose an open position where any sun can bring out the winter colour of the foliage. Many will, however, tolerate some shade.

Before planting apply an initial dressing of bonemeal at about 100g/m² (3oz/sq yd). Plant the young heathers deeply with their foliage touching the soil surface. They are best planted in groups along border edges – perhaps a dozen plants of one variety with 25 to 30cm (10 to 12in) between them. If they become crowded after a year or so they can easily be thinned out.

Varieties of *Calluna vulgaris* 4 will provide colour from June to December and then *Erica carnea* 5 and *Erica purpurascens* 7 will continue the sequence until May. See *Gardens: Heather Gardens*.

Foliage Plants

With a few exceptions, foliage is not as brightly coloured as the flowers of many border plants but the subtleties of colour, differences in texture and shape can be used to enrich any garden. Even with ordinary green foliage the colour of the leaf surface will vary – the undersurface is usually paler green, or a contrasting colour to the upper surface. And the colour of the leaves will vary with the season; spring foliage is fresher-looking than summer foliage and autumn foliage may be beautifully tinted with reds or golds.

The texture and shape of leaves can vary considerably. Some are woolly, sticky or crinkly, and others are waxy. Leaf shapes can be rounded, strap-shaped, spear-like or cut into fingers.

In most gardens, foliage plants are used as a foil for flowering plants with dull foliage, like aster, cotoneaster, philadelphus, phlox, solidago and syringa.

Foliage plants will set off the more brightly coloured flowers such as this red *Primula pulverulenta*

Lobelia and alyssum make an edging to this dahlia border

Left: An architectural plant is one with a distinct character

Below: Plants used architecturally break up the harsh concrete lines here

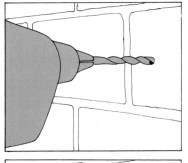

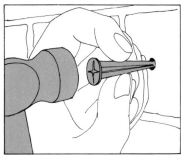

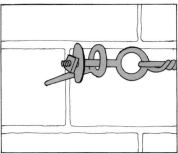

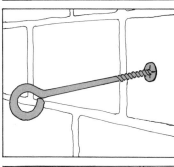

Supporting a wall plant by vine eyes and wires

Drill a hole into the wall and plug with a plastic wall plug. Screw a vine eye into the plug and fix wire to bolt eye. Use the nut to make the wire taught

Variegated Plants

Sometimes certain parts of leaves lack chlorophyll and these parts look white or yellow. This colour variegation may appear as irregular patches or blotches over the leaf surface, it may run along the leaf veins or it may be seen as regular bands or stripes. Variegation is often an inherited characteristic and may arise through a sport or mutation of a normally unvariegated plant. Many variegated plants are slower growing than their all-green counterparts because of their lack of chlorophyll and some tend to revert to their unvariegated form. If all-green leaves are seen on variegated plants, they should be removed as soon as possible. If they are left to grow they may, because of their greater vigour, crowd out the variegated leaves.

Some variegated plants can be propagated from seed but plants which are variegated because of mosaic virus disease or as a sport or mutation of a normally all-green plant should be propagated vegetatively.

Using Foliage Plants

There are two basic rules to follow when using plants with coloured foliage: never use a predominance of one colour and use plants with dark foliage sparingly. Bronze- and dark-leaved plants produce an overbearing effect. Blue and grey leaves are adaptations for hot, dry, sunny climates. These plants are less striking than purples and golds, and their colour cannot be seen to its best advantage unless they are in full light, with minimum shade but maximum shelter.

When choosing plants, make sure that the ones selected will actually grow and flourish in your garden. Most variegated plants like some shade to prevent damage by bright sunlight and all coloured-leaf plants are best grown in sheltered positions: many hate wind. Soil conditions must also be considered. Most plants will grow well in sandy, neutral soils, providing sufficient humus has been added to aid moisture retention, but many do not like heavy, clay soil. Make sure that plants preferring acid conditions are not being attempted where lime is found and vice versa. Many bold-foliaged plants come from woodland fringes, where there is light shade, ample humus and adequate moisture both in the soil and, more importantly, in the surrounding atmosphere. This is because the trees and shrubs in woodland areas give off water through transpiration and when they are packed closely together they prevent this water vapour from dispersing. Try to use bold-foliaged plants in similar situations in the garden.

To get the most out of foliage plants they should be planted where their form and colour can contrast with neighbours and where the colours they provide can extend the appeal of a garden long after the floral plants have faded. They can also be used to enliven an otherwise dull corner, either through colourful foliage or shape and texture.

Silver-leaved Plants

Most silver-leaved plants derive their distinctive coloration from a covering of hairs. These may be only on the leaves, but more often they occur on the stems as well. Some plants have a hairless, waxy surface giving them a blue-grey appearance. The whitest-looking plants have a thick covering of short hairs which are so close together that the leaves appear to be made from white felt, this effect is most pronounced on their upper surface. The most silvery-looking plants have long, fine hairs which reflect the light. Between these two extremes there is a wide range of intermediate plants which can be broadly described as silvery grey.

Silver-leaved plants should be used in association with green-leaved plants, in herbaceous or mixed borders, in rock gardens and in more formal arrangements. As well as being decorative in their own right, they provide a foil for more brightly coloured species growing amongst them. One of their great assets is their ability to provide interest for much of the year unlike the average garden plant which is showy only during the flowering season. In fact, many of the plants grown for their foliage have very insignificant flowers, and in these cases it is best if the flowers are cut off when they start to show. For the really ambitious gardener, an all white border can be very effective, or even a white garden. A dark hedge or screen of some form is necessary to show it up to best advantage.

Silver-foliaged plants are best propagated by cuttings or division as many do not set seed successfully and some are selected forms which will not come true from seed.

Silver-Leaved Plants

The numbers after the botanical names are the North America hardiness zone ratings – see *Climate*.

Anaphalis, see *Herbaceous Perennials*.

Artemisia a large genus of shrubs and herbaceous and rock plants, most are grey-leaved. *A. ludoviciana* 3, herbaceous, rather invasive, *lvs* white, woolly, *fls* wide spikes, silvery white, late summer: *A. absinthium* 'Lambrook Silver' 2–3, see *Herbaceous Perennials*.

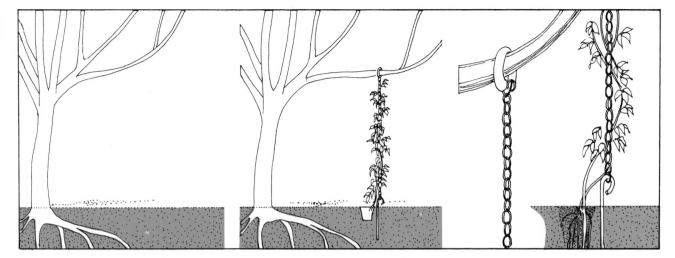

Convolvulus cneorum 9, perhaps the most beautiful of silver-leaved shrubs, 45 to 60cm (18 to 24in), *lvs* almost luminous when the sun catches the fine, silky hairs, *fls* pink-shaded, white, spring. It needs a dry, hot place, will not withstand cold winters.

Helichrysum angustifolium 6, shrub with a remarkable smell of curry, to 60cm (2ft), *lvs* silvery, needle-like, retained through the winter, *fls* small, yellow, should be cut off before they open. Hardy.

Senecio, related to the familiar garden weed groundsel, shrubby, very attractive plants, particularly forms of *S. maritima* 6 (often still called *S. cineraria*). Frequently grown as an annual for bedding displays. Hardy in all but the coldest of winters, *lvs* lobed, stems are covered with dense white hairs giving it a felted appearance, *fls* yellow, should be cut off; 'Silver Dust' is a particularly fine form with finely cut leaves.

Stachys lanata 4, popular cottage garden plant, *lvs* woolly which should be removed from the plant as they become old and be-draggled; 'Silver Carpet', non-flowering.

Tanacetum haradjanii 6, *lvs* silver-white, cut like fine filigree, held close to the ground to form a close mat, *fls* yellow, small, insignificant. One of the best of the small silver-foliage plants.

Architectural Plants

An architectural plant is one that has bold foliage and a distinct character. It can be used as a focal point in a garden, particularly in a small garden, rather like a sculpture. Many plants fall into this category including trees, shrubs, herbaceous plants, bulbs and annuals. Some are hardy, others are tender. Many of the tender ones can be

used as specimen plants in beds of summer flowers to draw the eye up and away from a mass of colour. *Canna indica* 10 and *Ricinus communis* 10 look particularly attractive when used like this. Architectural plants can also be used to give character to patios, to relieve the effect of the man-made materials, and with paving, walls and garden furniture. In these cases very bold plants are essential.

It is quite impossible to say categorically which plants go best in any particular situation but, generally, plants with clean lines to their form are best with constructed work, for example *Fatsia japonica* 7 and *Yucca gloriosa* 7 associate well with patios, while larger plants of statuesque proportions, like *Verbascum bombycinum* 6 and *Hosta sieboldiana* 3, are best in borders.

Because architectural plants embrace such a vast range of different types of plants, it is essential to have a clear knowledge of the species you are dealing with before trying to cultivate it. For example, *Verbascum bombycinum* 6 is a biennial and needs replanting annually. New seedlings should be raised and planted before the flowering plants are removed. This gives the new plants the long growing season they need. *Polygonum sacchalinense* 4 tends to be a wandering plant, and crops up where it is not required. Although it is generally not a nuisance, its stems must be stringently removed otherwise the form of the established clump will be dissipated.

It is very difficult to visualize where to place architectural plants in a new, unestablished garden. It is better to plan and plant the border and leave it to become established and then critically appraise various plant associations before attempting to plant architectural plants for effect. Do not be disappointed if you make several mistakes before finding the right position for the chosen plant.

Tree used as a support for a climber

Far left: Choose a suitable branch

Middle: Link the branch to the ground by a chain. Secure it to the ground with a sturdy hook. Plant the climber well away from the trunk of the tree

Right: Details of fixing the chain. On the left, protect the tree branch by sheathing the chain with a hosepipe

13. Edible Plants

Edible plants are those grown for their food value rather than for their visual appeal and are usually classified as either fruits or vegetables. The distinction between the two categories is not, however, clear-cut. The fruits of plants like cucumbers, marrows and tomatoes are generally treated as vegetables, while melons are thought of as fruits. Perhaps the best guide to which is which is to think of vegetables as plants eaten with the main course and fruits as those eaten as dessert. Herbs and mushrooms are usually classed as vegetables.

Fruit

Fruit growing is often divided into tree (or top) fruit and soft fruit. Top fruits include apples, pears, plums and cherries. The most important soft fruits are currants (black, red and white), gooseberries, raspberries and strawberries.

Top Fruits

Top fruits are generally composite plants consisting of a rootstock with a scion grafted or budded on to it. The scion variety determines the characteristics of the fruit itself and the rootstock influences the growth and cropping performance of the tree. The union between scion and rootstock should be at least 15cm (6in) above soil level – if it is lower than this there is a risk of the scion developing its own roots and influencing the overall behaviour of the tree. Trees on dwarfing rootstocks grow rapidly to their final size and usually start to bear fruit early in their life.

Shapes of Trees

Top fruits can be trained into a number of different shapes which vary in the amount of space they occupy and how quickly the tree starts to fruit.

Bushes Most fruit trees can be grown as bushes with closely spaced branches coming out of a main stem at a height of 60 to 90cm (2 to 3ft).

Standard and half-standards These are basically bushes with a main stem 1·2m (4ft) high for half-standards and 1·8m (6ft) for standards.

Cordons These have one, two or three straight stems with restricted side growths.

Pyramids These are shaped like a pyramid. The bottom branches generally start about 30cm (1ft) above the ground.

Espaliers These have pairs of branches growing from opposite sides of the main stem at roughly right angles to it.

Fans Fruits grown against a wall are often grown in the shape of a fan.

Soft Fruits

Soft fruits are grown on their own roots and start to crop much earlier than top fruits.

Planning the Fruit Garden

The first point to establish when planning a fruit garden is which fruits the climate will allow you to grow successfully. Late spring frosts are the biggest enemy of fruits. Top fruits are best grown towards the top of a sheltered slope. If other trees are used as windbreaks to provide the necessary shelter, make sure that these do not interrupt the flow of air down the slope and create frost pockets. Tender fruits can be grown as fans against south-facing walls.

Do not overcrowd a fruit garden. Choose the number of trees, variety and rootstock according to the space available. Cordons need least space; full standards need most. Planting distances are given in the individual fruit summaries.

Group together the same kinds of fruit to make routine feeding and spraying easier. This will also help pollination.

Opposite: raspberries are among the most delicious of summer fruits

243

Buying Fruit Trees and Bushes

Many countries run certification schemes covering the health of the more important fruit plants. These schemes may be statutory or voluntary. Most schemes are aimed at producing virus-free plants which are true to their name. Virus infections can greatly reduce the amount of fruit yielded by strawberries and raspberries, so for these two fruits in particular, it is essential to purchase virus-free stocks only.

When buying individual top fruits choose those with the largest tops. Make sure that the tops and roots do not show signs of shrivelling and that the union of scion with rootstock is well callused or healed.

Currants should have at least three or four sturdy growths. Raspberries should have clean canes with little sign of bark splitting or mottling and gooseberries should not be showing signs of dieback at the tips of their shoots.

Trees and bushes are sold at various stages in their development. Currant bushes, for example, can be bought as one-, two- or three-year-old bushes. As a general rule, the younger the plant the more likely it is to establish itself well, but some young plants do not qualify for certification and younger plants will take longer to reach their eventual size and to bear fruit.

Preparing the Ground

Soft fruits have a minimum useful life of five years; top fruits will go on being usefully productive for twenty years or indeed many more. Established fruits, particularly soft fruits, should be disturbed as little as possible. Make sure that the soil is well drained and improved as necessary (see *Soil*). Perennial weeds such as dandelion *Taraxacum officinale,* ground elder *Aegopodium podagraria* and couch grass *Agropyron repens* must be eradicated.

Planting

Most fruits are planted from the late autumn, through winter, to early spring. Strawberries are best planted in the late summer or the early autumn. If the soil is water-logged or frost-bound, delay planting until spring or until soil conditions improve. Heel in plants which arrive while the soil is unworkable. See *Soil: Gardening on a Clay Soil*. For details of planting and staking see *Ornamental Plants: Shrubs* and *Trees* and *Cultivation: Staking and Supporting.*

Propagation

Strawberries are propagated by rooting runners in the soil around the plants, or in nearby pots filled with growing mix. Raspberries sucker freely and new plants can easily be separated from the parent plant during the autumn. Both fruits are susceptible to severe virus infection and it is probably wiser to buy healthy new stocks rather than to propagate from old plants.

Currants and gooseberries are raised from hardwood cuttings. For black currants take cuttings about 20cm (8in) long in the autumn and insert about two-thirds of their length in the ground. Hardwood cuttings of gooseberries and red and white currants should be longer, about 30cm (12in), and should be inserted to half their length. Rub out the lower buds of gooseberries and red and white currants so that the bush is formed on a short stem.

Apples, pears, plums and cherries are all propagated by budding and grafting. See *Propagation.* Buy virus-free rootstocks from a specialist nurseryman.

Pollination

Pollination is the transfer of compatible pollen grains from a male donor flower to a female receptor flower. The pollen provides the male elements essential for the sequence of fertilization, formation of seeds, and development of fruit. Successful pollination depends on the kind of pollen which arrives on the styles, and whether it is able to germinate and grow down the styles to reach the ovules and fertilize them. If the pollen germinates but is unable to grow right down the styles, the pollen is incompatible. If it does not germinate, it is sterile. The number of chromosomes in fruit cells can vary from one variety to another. Diploids have 34 chromosomes and can divide nicely and regularly to produce pollen and ovules each with 17. Triploids have 51 chromosomes and divide irregularly and produce much sterile pollen. Many fruit trees are not self-fertile and will not set fruit with their own pollen. Consequently it is usually necessary to plant an additional pollinator variety which is compatible (see fruit summaries). Most soft fruits are self-fertile and additional varieties are not needed.

Pests and Diseases

Pests and diseases of deciduous fruit plants are often carried over from one season to the next and, if left untreated, can have serious consequences. Canker, for example, can kill established trees.

Fruit diseases are usually controlled by spraying with fungicide at regular intervals during the growing season. Pests are dealt with as and when they appear. Details of pests and their control are given in *Pests and Diseases.*

When spraying fruit plants try to get complete coverage of the plant, and take care to prevent sprays drifting on to nearby plants or fruit about to be harvested.

Apple

Malus pumila Cooking apples can be grown successfully on a wide range of different soils and will also tolerate some impedance in drainage. Dessert apples are much more sensitive to soil conditions but, nevertheless, will grow well on most soils provided the soil is at least 50cm (20in) deep. Most apples flower in April or May and may be damaged by late frosts. In general, susceptibility to frost damage increases as the development of the flower advances: a temperature which is harmless to a bud can severely damage a setting fruitlet. Avoid planting apples in exposed, windy places or in possible frost pockets – usually at the bottom of a slope.

Cultivation Planting distances depend upon the form of the tree, the rootstock, the scion material and on the nature of the soil. Rootstocks for apples can be roughly categorized as either dwarfing (M9), semi-dwarfing (M7, M26 and MM106), vigorous (M2 and M111) or very vigorous (MM104, M16 and M25). The scion material (variety) can also be grouped as shown on the right.

Combining the vigour of the scion material with the vigour of the rootstock gives the following approximate sizes for bush apple trees (measured across the head).

Rootstock	very vigorous scions	vigorous scions	weaker scions
	m (ft)	m (ft)	m (ft)
M9	5·2 (17)	3·7 (12)	3·0 (10)
M26	5·8 (19)	4·6 (15)	3·7 (12)
MM106, M7	6·4 (21)	5·2 (17)	4·0 (13)
M2, MM111	8·2 (27)	5·5 (18)	4·6 (15)
MM104	8·8 (29)	5·8 (19)	4·9 (16)
M25, M16	9·1 (30)	7·0 (23)	5·8 (19)

Cordon apples should be planted 75 to 90cm (2½ to 3ft) apart in rows which are 1·8m (6ft) apart. Espalier trees on dwarfing rootstocks can be planted as little as 3m (10ft) apart; on more vigorous rootstocks this distance should be increased to 4·5 to 5·5m (15 to 18ft). Dwarf pyramids can be planted 90cm (3ft) apart in rows which have 2m (6½ft) between them.

If the ground was well manured before planting then fertilizers will not be needed in the first year. In subsequent years apply sulphate of ammonia at 35g/m² (1oz/sq yd) and sulphate of potash at 25g/m² (¾oz/sq yd) every February or early spring. Add 70g/m² (2oz/sq yd) of superphosphate to the mixture every third year. Apply the fertilizers by hand around the root area.

Pollination Many apples will crop reasonably well without any obvious provision for cross pollination. But most will crop better and more consistently if a pollinator tree is provided. When triploids are grown two diploid pollinators should be planted to provide pollen for the triploid and for each other. Common triploids are 'Gravenstein', 'Ribston Pippin', 'Warner's King', 'Washington', 'Belle de Boskoop', 'Blenheim Orange', 'Bramley's Seedling', 'Crispin', 'Holstein', 'King of Tompkins County', 'Reinette du Canada', and 'Gascoyne's Scarlet'.

Pruning Apples may be pruned in the summer or in the dormant season. Pruning apples can be complicated but, at its simplest, can be confined to removing diseased or overcrowded branches, shortening growth where more vigour is needed and removing unwanted growths when training. It should be remembered that the less an apple tree is pruned the earlier in its life it will crop.

Bush Do not prune maiden trees in their first year. In the second winter select about four growths for branch leaders and cut these back by one-half to two-thirds, to an outward-pointing bud. In subsequent years the leading shoots should be shortened according to their vigour: remove one-third of vigorous growths, two-thirds of weak ones. Once the tree is established prune to maintain shape (outlined above) and to improve the quality of the fruit. With most apple varieties the laterals should be shortened during the dormant season to encourage the formation of fruiting buds and spurs close to the branch. Spur systems which become crowded should be thinned by removing some and cutting back others.

Half-standard and standard In the first year restrict pruning of maiden trees to pinching out vigorous laterals at about six leaves. At the two-year stage, cut the leader back to about 1·4m (4½ft) for half-standards, to 2m (6½ft) for standards, then prune in the same manner as for bush trees.

Cordon Do not prune in winter. Between the middle and end of July cut back all those shoots arising from the main stem which are 25cm (10in) or more long and have a woody base and dark leaves to three leaves past the basal cluster. Reduce existing side shoots or spurs to one leaf. In October prune any subsequent secondary growth to one bud.

Espalier In the first winter cut maiden trees back to a bud just above the first wire. Make sure that there are two good buds just below this one – growths from these two buds are trained horizontally to form the first tier. When growth starts rub out other buds and train the top bud vertically and the two lower buds at an angle of about 45°. At the

Apple scion material

very vigorous scions
'Laxton's Superb'
'Tydeman's Early'
'Ellison's Orange'
'Red Delicious'
'Crispin'
'Bramley's Seedling'
'Howgate Wonder'

vigorous scions
'Cox's Orange Pippin'
'Late Orange'
'Fortune'
'Worcester Pearmain'
'Ribston Pippin'
'Grenadier'
'Egremont Russet'

weaker scions
'Sunset'
'James Grieve'
'Lord Lambourne'
'Jonathan'
'Golden Delicious'

end of the season lower the shoots and tie them to the first wire. Repeat this process in the following winters until the top wire is reached when only two shoots which are to be trained along the wire should be allowed to grow. When the tiers reach the length required the leaders should be pruned back to 1cm (½in) each May. In July any current season's growth which comes directly from the tiers or previously pruned laterals is summer-pruned as for cordons.

Dwarf Pyramid In the first spring cut back maiden trees to about 50cm (20in) and shorten side shoots over 15cm (6in) long to five good buds. In the following winter or late autumn cut back the leader to leave about 25cm (10in) of new growth and cut back the laterals to about 20cm (8in) to a vertical pointing bud. In following years summer-prune in late July by cutting the mature branch leaders back to five or six leaves past the basal cluster. Laterals from the branches should be cut back to three leaves and growth from laterals and spurs should be cut back to one leaf past the basal cluster. Repeat the winter pruning until the bushes reach a height of about 2m (6½ft). At this stage restrict growth by cutting back the central leader in May.

Pests and diseases Apples may be infected by codling moth, apple sawfly, apple aphids, apple suckers, capsid bugs, winter moth and fruit tree red spider mites. Canker is the most serious disease of apples but scab, powdery mildew, brown rot, bitter pit, honey fungus and fire blight may all be troublesome.

Pear

In Europe the pear is derived from the species *Pyrus communis*. In North America pears are usually hybrids of the European pear and the Japanese Sand Pear, *P. serotina*. Pears can be grown successfully on a wide range of soil textures varying from sandy loam to clay loams but do not like very dry, light soils. Compared with apples they are much less tolerant of drought and much more tolerant of poor drainage. A soil depth of 45 to 53cm (18 to 21in) is generally needed to grow pears well. Pears flower before apples and are very sensitive to wind damage and so should be planted in sheltered parts of the garden. If a number of trees are to be planted they should be huddled together to give each other some degree of protection.

Cultivation Pears are almost exclusively grown on Malling Quince A rootstock which produces medium-sized trees. A few varieties such as 'Beurré Hardy', and 'Doyenné du Comice' can become too vigorous on this rootstock and may produce trees which are slow to start cropping.

These varieties should, where possible, be bought on Malling Quince C rootstock which is slightly less vigorous than Quince A. Some varieties make an unsatisfactory union when budded or grafted on to these rootstocks. These varieties are double worked – grafted on to an intermediate stock of a compatible pear such as 'Beurré Hardy' which itself is grafted on to the rootstock. 'Williams' Bon Chrétien' ('Bartlett' in the United States and Canada) is the most widely available double-worked pear.

Plant bush pears on Quince A rootstock about 3·5 to 4·5m (12 to 15ft) apart. Pears on Quince C can be planted closer together – about 3 to 4·3m (10 to 14ft) apart. Cordons can be planted 60 to 90cm (2 to 3ft) apart in the rows with about 1·8m (6ft) between rows. Dwarf pyramids can be planted 90cm (3ft) apart in the rows with 2m (6½ft) between the rows. Espaliers are generally set 4·5m (15ft) apart.

Pears need more nitrogen than apples. Each February apply a mixture of sulphate of ammonia at 45 to 70g/m² (1¼ to 2oz/sq yd) and sulphate of potash at 25 to 35g/m² (⅔ to 1oz/sq yd). Every third year add superphosphate at 70 to 90g/m² (2 to 2½oz/sq yd) to the mixture. Add more sulphate of ammonia to the mixture when the trees are grown in grass.

Pollination Very few fruits are produced from self-pollination. Most pear varieties are diploid, but a few are triploid and, as with apples, these should have two pollinators. Some varieties of pear are incompatible with other varieties even though they may flower at about the same time. In North America 'Anjou' and 'Bosc' are satisfactory pollinators for 'Bartlett' and 'Russet Bartlett'. The pears in the following two groups are self-incompatible and will not set fruit with the pollen of any other variety within the group.

Group 1 'Beurré d'Amanlis' and 'Conference'

Group 2 'Fondante d'Automne', 'Laxton's Progress', 'Laxton's Superb', 'Louise Bonne of Jersey', 'Précoce de Trevoux', 'Seckle' and 'Williams' Bon Chrétien'

Pruning The pruning techniques described under *Apples* can also be applied to pears. Pears mature a little earlier than apples and so most pruning can be done a week or two earlier. They can also be cut back harder than apples without much fear of producing over-vigorous growth.

Pests and diseases Birds and wasps are among the main pests but pears are also troubled by aphids, pear leaf blister mites and pear midge. Scab, fire blight, canker, brown rot and honey fungus are the main diseases.

Recommended varieties of Apple

UK (in order of flowering)
'Egremont Russet'
'Lord Lambourne'
'James Grieve'
'Sunset'
'Grenadier'
'Discovery'
'Malling Kent'
'Worcester Pearmain'
'Lane's Prince Albert'
'Red Charles Ross'

North America
'Puritan'
'Lodi'
'Caravel'
'Scotia'
'Golden Russet'
'Idared'
'McIntosh'
'Wealthy'
'Cortland'
'Empire'
'Delicious'
'Spartan'
'Golden Delicious'
'Northern Spy'

Recommended varieties of Pear

UK (in order of flowering)
'Packham's Triumph'
'Conference'
'Dr Jules Guyot'
'Williams' Bon Chrétien'
'Doyenné du Comice'
'Onward'

North America
'Anjou'
'Bartlett'
'Bosc'
'Clapp'
'Dawn'
'Dr Jules Guyot'
'Giffard'
'Kieffer'
'Magness'
'Russet Bartlett'

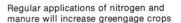
Regular applications of nitrogen and manure will increase greengage crops

Peaches and Nectarines

Prunus persica Peaches and nectarines are different in flavour but have a common origin. The main difference is in their skins: nectarines have a smooth skin, peaches have a furry one. Nectarines are a little less hardy than peaches and should always be grown in warm, sheltered places but both fruits need protection if they are to be grown successfully in cool climates. A soil with good drainage is essential for peaches and nectarines.

Cultivation Two rootstocks are commonly used: St Julien A (dwarfing) and Brompton (vigorous). In cool climates peaches and nectarines should be fan-trained against a south- or west- (in the northern hemisphere) facing wall. In warmer climates peaches may be grown as bushes. Fans should be spaced at 5·5 to 7·5m (18 to 24ft) intervals but, if space is restricted, both fruits will tolerate closer planting. Plant the trees 15 to 25cm (6 to 10in) away from the wall with the stem sloping slightly towards it. Use a system of wires to support the fan.

Care should be taken to avoid over feeding as this will induce the growth of foliage at the expense of fruit. A mulch of farmyard manure in May with a mixture of sulphate of ammonia at 20 to 25g/m² (½ to ¾oz/sq yd) and 20g/m² (½oz/sq yd) of sulphate of potash applied in April should be sufficient. Superphosphate at 50 to 70g/m² (1½ to 2oz/sq yd) can be added to the mixture every third year.

Pruning Two things should be remembered: 1) peaches fruit on the previous year's growth of wood and 2) fruit buds are plump and round and shoot buds are pointed.

For fan-trained trees cut maidens back to about 60cm (2ft) above the ground in the first spring after planting. Cut back to a good bud (or a lateral) and make sure that the tree has two other good buds below it. In

Recommended varieties of Peach

UK (in order of fruiting)
'Duke of York'
'Hale's Early'
'Peregrine'
'Rochester'
'Royal George'
'Noblesse'
'Bellegarde'
'Dymond'

North America
'Candor'
'Envoy'
'Garnet Beauty'
'Madison'
'Redcap'
'Veteran'

Recommended varieties of Nectarine

UK (in order of fruiting)
'Early Rivers'
'John Rivers'
'Lord Napier'
'Humboldt'
'Elruge'
'Pine Apple'

North America
'Nectared 4'
'Nectared 6'
'Pocahontas'
'Redgold'
'Sunglo'

Fruit tree forms

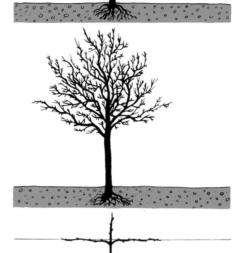

Fan – peaches, nectarines and plums are often grown like this

Half standard (or standard) – almost any kind of fruit tree can be grown in this way

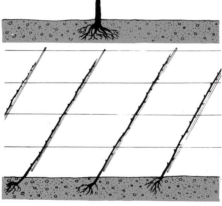

Espalier – usually apples and pears

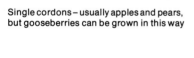

Single cordons – usually apples and pears, but gooseberries can be grown in this way

Bush on a leg

the following summer choose two good shoots on either side of the central shoot and about 25 to 30cm (10 to 12in) above the ground. Remove all other shoots. These shoots will form the first part of the framework of the fan. Cut out the main stem above these two shoots. Towards the end of the second winter cut back both side branches to a bud 30 to 45cm (12 to 18in) from the main stem. In the following summer allow the end shoot of each branch to grow along with three other shoots from each branch – preferably two on the upper side and one on the lower side. Rub out all other buds. At the end of the third winter cut back all the branches to a triple bud (two fruit buds and a wood bud) leaving about 60 to 75cm (24 to 30in) of ripened wood from the previous summer. Repeat this summer and winter treatment until the bush reaches the required size. In the next summer rub out all buds growing towards and away from the wall and thin buds growing upwards and downwards to about 10cm (4in) apart – these shoots will provide fruit in the following year. In the following spring again remove shoots growing towards and directly away from the wall. One or two shoots at the bottom of the previous year's growth should be allowed to grow on to provide the wood for the following year's fruit. Pinch out the terminal bud when it reaches about six leaves. Rub out side shoots which have fruit to about two leaves. Thin fruits to one peach to every 25cm (10in) of wood. This can usually be done in June and is necessary to ensure fruit of a good size.

Pests and diseases Aphids and glasshouse red spider mites are the main pests; peach leaf curl, canker, brown rot and honey fungus are the main diseases.

Plums (and Gages)

Prunus domestica Plums like heavy, deep – 50cm (20in) – soils with an adequate supply of moisture. They will tolerate poor drainage but not waterlogging. 'Early Rivers' tolerates poor drainage: 'Czar' and 'Monarch' are better on dry soils. Plums flower early in the year (April) and so need protection against spring frosts.

Cultivation Three rootstocks are commonly used: St Julien A, Brompton and Myrobalan B. St Julien A gives the smallest trees and Myrobalan B gives the largest. Plums are generally grown as half-standards or bushes planted about 3·5 to 4·5m (12 to 15ft) apart on St Julien A and 5·5 to 6m (18 to 20ft) on Myrobalan B.

Plums like liberal dressings of nitrogen and will benefit from annual mulches of farmyard manure supplemented by sulphate of ammonia at 20 to 25g/m² (½ to

¾oz/sq yd) mixed with sulphate of potash at 20g/m² (½oz/sq yd).

Pollination Many of the most widely available plums, such as 'Victoria' and 'Stanley', are self-compatible and will set fruit with their own pollen. Pollinators for partly or completely self-incompatible plums should be chosen according to their flowering time. However some varieties which flower at about the same time as each other will not set fruit with each other. Three groups of such varieties are known:

Group 1 'Jefferson', 'Coe's Golden Drop', 'Allgrove's Superb', 'Coe's Violet Gage' and 'Crimson Drop'

Group 2 'President', 'Late Orange', 'Old Greengage', 'Cambridge Gage'

Group 3 'Early Rivers' and 'Blue Rock'.

Avoid any varieties within these groups as pollinators for each other.

Pruning All pruning should be done in spring or summer to reduce the risk of silver leaf infection.

Cut back maiden trees in spring to about 1·3m (4½ft) for half-standards or 1m (3ft) for a bush. In the second year remove all the previous year's growth apart from three or four evenly spaced shoots. Cut these shoots back by about one-half in the spring. In future years prune the trees in spring and summer to maintain shape and health.

Plums can also be trained as a fan – see *Peaches* – but, unlike peaches, plums fruit on both old and new wood.

Pests and diseases Aphids and birds are the main pests. Silver leaf is the most serious disease. Cut out all branches with leaves which have a silvery discoloration.

Cherries

Prunus avium and *P. cerasus* A wide range of soil textures from sandy loams to clay loams will grow cherries but they do need a deep 90cm (3ft) soil which has an adequate supply of moisture in the summer. 'Early Rivers' will tolerate poor soil conditions better than most other varieties; 'Bigarreau Napoleon' does poorly on poorly drained soil. Cherries are very susceptible to attack by blossom wilt which is always most prevalent in moist conditions.

Cultivation Cherries are generally grown on Malling F 12/1 rootstock which is very vigorous and produces large trees. At least 5·5 to 7·5m (18 to 24ft) should be allowed between trees.

Mulch with well-rotted manure in the late spring and apply sulphate of potash at 20 to 25g/m² (½ to ¾oz/sq yd).

Pollination Most sweet cherries will not set fruits with their own pollen and at least two varieties should be planted to ensure a crop. Some compatible groups are listed on the right under *Recommended varieties*.

Pruning Cherries may be grown as a fan with the framework built up along the lines described under *Peaches*. Pruning should be carried out in summer to avoid infection by silver leaf.

Raspberry

Rubus idaeus A deep, well-drained soil with a minimum depth of 45cm (18in) is needed to grow raspberries successfully. 'Malling Promise' and 'Norfolk Giant' are very sensitive to poor drainage; 'Malling Jewel' is more tolerant. Raspberries flower in late May and early June and normally escape late spring frosts.

Cultivation Plant in rows with 60cm (2ft) between the plants and 1·8m (6ft) between the rows. If possible, run the rows north to south. Feed canes in March with sulphate of potash applied at 25g/m² (¾oz/sq yd).

Pruning After planting cut down the canes to three buds above the ground: do not allow canes to fruit in their first season. Secure subsequent new canes to horizontal support wires set 60cm (2ft), 1m (3ft) and 1·5m (5ft) above the ground. After fruiting cut off the old canes as close to the ground as possible. Select about eight new canes per plant and tie them securely to the support wires; cut out the remaining new canes. Towards the end of winter shorten the retained canes to 15cm (6in) above the top wire.

Pests and diseases Raspberry beetle and aphids are the main pests; spur blight, cane spot, honey fungus, grey mould and virus are the main diseases. Raspberries which have lost vigour, are cropping poorly and have blotched or yellow-mottled leaves may be virus infected and should be pulled up and burned.

Blackberry and Loganberry

Rubus sp. Almost any kind of soil can support blackberries and loganberries. Both flower after raspberries and are rarely troubled by frost.

Cultivation Both blackberries and loganberries need plenty of room and if space is limited one plant is a practical proposition. If more than one plant is required, they should be spaced 3m (10ft) apart. Apply a nitrogen fertilizer, such as sulphate of ammonia, in the spring at about 70g/m² (2oz/sq yd).

Pruning After planting cut down the young plant to 25cm (10in) above the ground. Tie in new growths to a system of strong support wires which has a top wire about 1·5m (5ft) above the ground. Cut out old canes immediately after fruiting.

Pests and diseases Raspberry beetle, cane spot, spur blight and virus diseases are the main problems.

Recommended varieties

Plums (and Gages)

UK (in order of flowering)
'Jefferson'
'Warwickshire Drooper'
'Victoria'
'Pershore Yellow Egg'
'Czar'

North America
'Bluefre'
'Bluebell'
'Damson'
'German Prune'
'Italian Prune' (Fellenberg)
'President'
'Queenston'
'Reine Claude'
'Stanley'
'Verity'

Sweet Cherries

UK
Group 1 'Noir de Guben'
     'Early Rivers'
     'Merton Glory'
Group 2 'Amber Heart'
     'Bigarreau Gaucher'
     'Bradbourne Black'
Group 3 'Frogmore Early'
     'Merton Glory'
     'Governor Wood'
Group 4 'Napoleon Bigarreau'
     'Bigarreau Gaucher'
     'Amber Heart'

North America
'Bing'
'Early Rivers'
'Napoleon'
'Stella' (self-fertile)
'Vogue'
'Windsor'

Acid Cherries (self-fertile)

UK
Morello cherry

North America
'Montmorency'
'Meteor'

Raspberries

UK (early to mid-season)
'Malling Promise' (not on clay soils)
'Malling Exploit'

UK (mid-season)
'Glen Clova'
'Malling Jewel'

North America (black varieties)
'Bristol'
'Dundee'

North America (red varieties)
'Bonanza'
'Madawaska'
'Newburgh'
'Sentinel'
'Thames'

Black Currant

Ribes nigrum Black currants require a moderately deep soil which can supply ample moisture throughout the growing season. They flower in April and May and are rarely affected by spring frosts.

Cultivation The bushes should be given plenty of room by setting them out 1m (3ft) apart with 2m (6½ft) between rows. Plant the bushes deeply. Black currants like heavy manuring and appreciate mulches of manure (which also helps conserve moisture) whenever it is available. Apply a nitrogen fertilizer – sulphate of ammonia on alkaline soils, Nitro chalk on others – in the spring at about 35g/m² (1oz/sq yd).

Pruning Cut the bush down to ground level immediately after planting. At the end of the first season one or two of the weaker canes should also be cut back to the ground to encourage further shoots in the following year. In future years cut out about a quarter to a third of the older wood after fruiting.

Pests and diseases The black currant gall mite is the most serious pest. It destroys buds and can transmit a virus disease commonly known as reversion. The mite causes abnormal enlargement of the buds. The effects are most apparent during the dormant season. Attacks of gall mite can be prevented by using lime sulphur washes in the early summer. Bushes suffering from reversion should be destroyed.

Red and White Currants

Ribes sativum Both currants like a moderately deep soil and will tolerate a fairly wide range of soil textures.

Cultivation Planting distances are similar to black currants. Red and white currants respond to liberal amounts of potash. Apply 25g/m² (¾oz/sq yd) in early spring.

Pruning The bushes are generally grown on a short leg which makes weed control much easier than with black currants and keeps the fruit high enough to avoid getting dirty in heavy rains. With newly planted bushes cut back each branch by about a half to an outside bud. In subsequent winters cut back the leading shoots by about one-half and shorten the laterals to within two buds of their base. Cut out old branches. At the end of June shorten the laterals to about five leaves; do not touch the leaders.

Pests and diseases Red currants are particularly prone to bird damage when ripening and bushes should be covered with netting.

Gooseberry

Ribes grossularia A good, well-drained loam soil which is at least 45cm (18in) deep is necessary for the successful cultivation of gooseberries. They will not tolerate impeded drainage.

Cultivation Space the bushes 1·4m (4½ft) apart with the same distance between rows. Plant firmly but not too deeply. Sulphate of potash at 25g/m² (¾oz/sq yd) can be applied in early spring.

Pruning Gooseberries are grown as bushes on short legs and any suckers which appear at ground level should be removed. In the early years, pruning should be directed towards the formation of a cup-shaped bush. To achieve this leading growths can be shortened to about half their length and laterals cut to about 8cm (3in). Once the bushes are established the older branches should be cut back even harder and some removed altogether. Cut out all crossing branches.

Pests and diseases Gooseberries are troubled by relatively few pests but are quite susceptible to mildew. American gooseberry mildew produces a white, powdery coating on leaves, shoots and fruits. Spray with 1½ per cent lime sulphur just before flowers open and repeat after the fruit has set. 'Careless', 'Early Sulphur', 'Leveller', 'Lord Derby', 'Roaring Lion' and 'Golden Drop' are sulphur-shy. For these varieties, other chemicals such as benomyl or dinocap can be used. Leaf spot, grey mould and honey fungus may also be troublesome.

Strawberry

Fragaria × ananassa Strawberries grow best on a well-drained soil which has a minimum depth of 40cm (15in). 'Cambridge Favourite' is tolerant to dryish conditions; 'Talisman' can cope with fairly poor drainage. Strawberries flower in April and early May and are easily damaged by spring frosts.

Cultivation Plant in rows with 30cm (1ft) between plants and 90cm (3ft) between rows. August is the best month for planting but it can be done successfully from July until the following April or May, provided soil and weather conditions are suitable. Make sure that the crown of the plant is set level with the soil, not buried, and that the roots are well covered. The plants will establish better if the blooms are cut off in the first season. Keep the fruit clean by covering the ground with straw, peat or black plastic sheeting just as the berries start to weigh down the trusses. Covering the ground any earlier will increase the risk of frost damage to the flowers and young fruit. Cut off all runners as they appear with a sharp hoe or knife: do not pull them off. After the fruit is picked, cut off the leaves about 10cm (4in) above the ground and remove them. Lightly fork in sulphate of potash at 20g/m² (½oz/sq yd). Do not use nitrogen fertilizers. After four years the bed will need replacing with fresh plants in a new part of the garden.

Pests and diseases Strawberries are troubled by a wide range of pests and diseases including aphids, slugs, red spider mites, eelworms, grey mould, strawberry mildew and various virus diseases. Plants with symptoms of virus diseases – leaves which are crinkled, have yellow edges, or with purplish or yellow blotching – should be dug up and burned.

Vegetable Growing

Vegetables need an open, sunny situation, a fertile friable soil and some shelter from strong winds. Good crops will not be produced if the vegetable plot is tucked away in some corner of the garden surrounded by mature trees or shrubs which deprive the soil of nutrients and moisture and shade the vegetables. If the garden is too small for a vegetable plot then some vegetables can still be grown among the flowers: the puckered leaves of savoy cabbages and the mauve leaves of beetroot can be quite effective in an ornamental garden.

Planning

The Vegetable Planning Chart gives much of the information needed to plan the vegetable garden and to buy the necessary seeds and fertilizers.

Soil Most vegetables prefer a rich, well-manured soil with a pH around 6 to 6·5. For growing vegetables on acid, alkaline, clay and sandy soils, see *Soil.*

To make the best use of the soil and to prevent the build-up of pests and diseases, the vegetables should be grouped together into similar types and the groups rotated around the vegetable garden each year.

The first group contains potatoes and other vegetables such as onions and tomatoes which like fresh manure and the most fertile ground. Apply liberal amounts of bulky organic manure to this area of the garden before the seeds are sown.

The second group (legumes) contains peas and beans. These vegetables can fix nitrogen from the atmosphere in the soil and make it available to any plants that follow them. They also appreciate the moisture-holding capacity of bulky organic manures.

The third group is the brassicas – Brussels sprouts, cabbages, cauliflowers and so on – and lettuces and other leaf vegetables. These are collectively known as greens and take large amounts of nitrogen from the soil. Brassicas are susceptible to club root disease and so most soils should be well limed before they are grown.

The fourth group is the root vegetables. These will generally tolerate some lime but dislike fresh manure.

To rotate the vegetables, divide the vegetable garden into four roughly equal areas and rotate as shown in the example below.

Vegetable Planning Chart

Hardiness The vegetables have been divided into three groups – hardy, half-hardy and tender – according to their frost hardiness. If you live in a cold area of the UK you should be able to sow hardy vegetables out of doors but you may have to start off some half-hardy vegetables under glass and some tender vegetables may not grow well out of doors at all. In warmer areas of the UK hardy and half-hardy vegetables can be sown out of doors but tender vegetables may have to be started off under glass. The Vegetable Planning Chart gives approximate planting and sowing dates for the UK. Planting and sowing dates for

First year
1st group   2nd group
4th group   3rd group

Second year
2nd group   3rd group
1st group   4th group

Third year
3rd group   4th group
2nd group   1st group

Fourth year
4th group   1st group
3rd group   2nd group

Dwarf runner beans. These are very convenient to grow for those who are unable to carry out the work involved for the tall varieties

North America are given in the individual vegetable summaries.

Weeks to harvest This is the time it takes from planting until the vegetable is ready to harvest. Knowing this time can be useful in two ways.

Firstly, it lets you know whether you can grow the vegetable out of doors in your area. If the interval between the first and last frosts in your area is less than the time it takes for the vegetable to grow, then you may not be able to grow the vegetable without starting it off under glass. Hardy seed can generally be sown out of doors in North America at about the time of the last frost; half-hardy seed about two weeks later and tender seed about four to six weeks after the last frost. In the UK where the first and last frosts are less severe, hardy seed can be sown outdoors in March or occasionally earlier, half-hardy from late April and tender from the beginning of June.

Secondly, by knowing how long a vegetable takes to reach maturity it is possible to squeeze in a quick maturing crop either before or after planting the main crop. This technique of slipping in crops before or after the main crop is generally known as catch cropping.

Planting distances The intervals between plants in a row and between rows are the minimum you should aim for. Use these distances when you are estimating the area to allow for each vegetable.

Fertilizers Each vegetable has its own particular nutritional requirements. The Chart

crop	UK sowing and harvesting dates			hardiness	weeks to harvest	days to germin-ation	seed needed for 10m (33ft) row	sowing depth mm (in)	space between plants cm (in)
	sow	plant	harvest						
Asparagus	April to May	April to May	April to July	hardy	150	7 to 21	random	38 (1½)	45 (18)
Aubergines	January under glass	June	July to October	tender	11 to 13	7 to 14	350 seeds	13 (½)	60 (24)
Bean, broad	October and March	March to April	May to June	hardy	12 to 14	7 to 14	275ml (½pt)	63 (2½)	15 (6)
Bean, butter or lima	May	May to June	September to October	tender	13 to 14	7 to 12	200 seeds	38 (1½)	15 (6)
Bean, French, kidney, snap or string	May	May to June	July to August	tender	12	6 to 14	150ml (¼pt)	38 (1½)	20 (8)
Beans, runner	May	May	August to October	half-hardy	12	6 to 14	275ml (½pt)	50 (2)	20 (8)
Beetroot	April to May	—	July to October	half-hardy	12	7 to 14	15g (½oz)	25 (1)	10 (4)
Broccoli	March	April to July	October to June	hardy	16 to 35	7 to 12	40–50 seeds	13 (½)	45 (18)
Brussels Sprout	March	April	August to March	hardy	16 to 30	7 to 12	40–50 seeds	38 (1½)	60 (24)
Cabbage, spring	July	September	April to June	hardy	34	7 to 12	40–50 seeds	13 (½)	45 (18)
Cabbage, summer, autumn	March to April	May to June	June to September	hardy	18 to 22	7 to 12	40–50 seeds	13 (½)	45 (18)
Cabbage, winter	April to May	June to July	October to March	hardy	26 to 30	7 to 12	40–50 seeds	13 (½)	45 (18)
Calabrese	April	May	July onwards	half-hardy	18 to 22	7 to 12	40–50 seeds	13 (½)	60 (24)
Carrot, early	February to March	—	May to June	hardy	12	10 to 21	7g (¼oz)	6 (¼)	5 (2)
Carrot, maincrop	April	—	September to March	hardy	20	10 to 21	7g (¼oz)	6 (¼)	10 (4)
Cauliflower, early	September under glass	late February	late May	hardy	32	7 to 12	40–50 seeds	13 (½)	50 (20)

lists the amounts of the three major nutrients, nitrogen (as sulphate of ammonia), phosphate (as superphosphate) and potash (as sulphate of potash), needed by each vegetable. So, for example, if you wanted to grow three 10m (33ft) rows of leeks at 30cm (1ft) apart, you would need to add fertilizers to a total area of 9m² (11sq yd). The mix for this area would be: 180g (5½oz) of sulphate of ammonia (9m² at 20g/m² = 180g), 225g (8¼oz) of superphosphate and 180g (5½oz) of sulphate of potash. The mix should be spread at 65g (20 + 25 + 20) to the square metre (1¾oz/sq yd).

If mixing individual fertilizers is too much bother, then a general fertilizer with twice as much nitrogen as phosphate or potash, (a 14·7·7 fertilizer, for example) could be used for most vegetables at 70 to 140g/m² (2 to 4oz/sq yd). For vegetables grown over winter use less nitrogen. For legumes use a fertilizer with more phosphate and no nitrogen.

Seed needed Many packets of vegetable seed contain more seeds than you are likely to need, particularly if the vegetable is started off under glass. The figures for the time seed keeps show how long seed can be stored in cool, dry conditions before it deteriorates seriously. A packet of brassica seed normally contains 7g (¼oz).

Days to germination This tells you how long you have to wait for seedlings to appear. The dates are very approximate. In cold weather some seeds may take much longer than stated.

space between rows cm (in)	fertilizer needed N	P	g/m² (oz/sq yd) K	years seed keeps	good yield for 10m (33ft) row as picked	soils	pests and diseases
90 (36)	50 (1½)	35 (1)	25 (¾)	1	15kg (33lb)	well-drained, humus-rich soil, pH 6·5	
120 (48)	25 (¾)	35 (1)	50 (1½)	5	50kg (110lb)	well-drained, humus-rich soil	bacterial wilts, fusarium
60 (24)	— —	35 (1)	25 (¾)	2	40kg (90lb)	well-drained soil, pH 7·0	aphis, chocolate spot, rust
75 (30)	— —	35 (1)	25 (¾)	3	15kg (33lb)	light, free-draining soil, ph 6·0	as beans, French
60 (24)	— —	35 (1)	25 (¾)	3	20kg (45lb)	well-drained, humus-rich soil, pH 7·0	anthracnose, black fly, halo blight, rust
120 (48)	— —	35 (1)	25 (¾)	2	40kg (90lb)	moisture-retentive, humus-rich soil, pH 6·5 to 7·0	as beans, French
30 (12)	35 (1)	35 (1)	35 (1)	1	20kg (45lb)	well-drained loam, pH 6·5	downy mildew, phoma
60 (24)	25 (¾)	35 (1)	35 (1)	3	20kg (45lb)	rich deeply-worked loam, pH 6·5, firm before planting	as cabbage, spring
60 (24)	45 (1¼)	45 (1¼)	50 (1½)	3	15kg (33lb)	rich deeply-worked loam, pH 6·5, firm before planting	as cabbage, spring
45 (18)	20 (½)	35 (1)	(1¼)	4	22 heads	as Brussels sprout	cabbage root fly, cabbage caterpillars, black rot, club root
45 (18)	50 (1½)	35 (1)	35 (1)	4	22 heads	as Brussels sprout	as cabbage, spring
45 (18)	50 (1½)	35 (1)	35 (1)	4	22 heads	as Brussels sprout	as cabbage, spring
60 (24)	25 (¾)	35 (1)	35 (1)	4	20kg (45lb)	as Brussels sprout	as cabbage, spring
30 (12)	no specialized requirements			3	15kg (33lb)	well-drained loam, free from fresh manure, pH 6·5	carrot fly, flea beetle
30 (12)	no specialized requirements			3	20kg (45lb)	as carrot, early	as carrot, early
50 (20)	25 (¾)	35 (1)	35 (1)	4	21 heads	rich, well-drained organic soil, pH 7·0, topdress in mid-April with general fertilizer	caterpillars, cabbage root fly, club root

crop	UK sowing and harvesting dates			hardiness	weeks to harvest	days to germin- ation	seed needed for 10m (33ft) row	sowing depth mm (in)	space between plants cm (in)
	sow	plant	harvest						
Cauliflower, summer	March to May	May to June	July to September	half-hardy	14 to 24	7 to 12	40–50 seeds	13 ($\frac{1}{2}$)	50 (20)
Cauliflower, winter	April to May	June to July	November to March	hardy	30 to 38	7 to 12	40–50 seeds	13 ($\frac{1}{2}$)	60 (24)
Celery, non-blanching	March	June	September	half-hardy	28 to 52	10 to 30	50 seeds	6 ($\frac{1}{4}$)	30 (12)
Celery, self-blanching	March	June	August	half-hardy	23	10 to 30	50 seeds	6 ($\frac{1}{4}$)	30 (12)
Corn	March	May	August	tender	14 to 16	6 to 12	14g ($\frac{1}{2}$oz)	38 (1$\frac{1}{2}$)	30 (12)
Cucumber, ridge	March under glass	June	August to October	tender	14	6 to 14	16 seeds	13 ($\frac{1}{2}$)	60 (24)
Kale	March to May	April to July	October to June	hardy	28	7 to 12	40–50 seeds	13 ($\frac{1}{2}$)	60 (24)
Leek	February	May to June	September	hardy	28	7 to 14	40–50 seeds	13 ($\frac{1}{2}$)	23 (9)
Lettuce	March to June	April to July	all year	half-hardy	7 to 14	4 to 12	4g ($\frac{1}{8}$oz)	13 ($\frac{1}{2}$)	23 (9)
Marrow and Pumpkins	March to April	June	August to October	half-hardy	8 to 14	5 to 14	16 seeds	19 ($\frac{3}{4}$)	60 (24)
Onion	September or February to April	April	September	hardy	24	7 to 14	4g ($\frac{1}{8}$oz)	13 ($\frac{1}{2}$)	15 (6)
Parsnip	March	—	November	hardy	36	20 to 60	7g ($\frac{1}{4}$oz)	13 ($\frac{1}{2}$)	15 (6)
Peas, early	November or February	February	May to June	hardy	14	6 to 15	275ml ($\frac{1}{2}$pt)	38 (1$\frac{1}{2}$)	8 (3)
Peas, 2nd early	March	March	June	hardy	14	6 to 15	275ml ($\frac{1}{2}$pt)	38 (1$\frac{1}{2}$)	8 (3)
Peas, maincrop	April to May	April to May	September	hardy	16	6 to 15	275ml ($\frac{1}{2}$pt)	38 (1$\frac{1}{2}$)	8 (3)
Pepper	March under glass	May to June	July to September	tender	16 to 24	10 to 25	30 seeds	6 ($\frac{1}{4}$)	45 (18)
Potato, early	—	April	June to July	half-hardy	16	7 to 21	1·6kg (3$\frac{1}{2}$lb)	100 (4)	38 (15)
Potato, maincrop	—	April	September	half-hardy	22	7 to 21	1·6kg (3$\frac{1}{2}$lb)	100 (4)	45 (18)
Radish	March to July	—	May to October	hardy	6	3 to 14	7g ($\frac{1}{4}$oz)	13 ($\frac{1}{2}$)	5 (2)
Shallot	January to March	—	July to August	hardy	26	7 to 14	1kg (2$\frac{1}{4}$lb)	25 (1)	15 (6)
Spinach, summer	February to May	—	May to September	hardy	12	6 to 14	14g ($\frac{1}{2}$oz)	13 ($\frac{1}{2}$)	23 (9)
Spinach, winter	August to April	—	November	hardy	14	6 to 14	14g ($\frac{1}{2}$oz)	13 ($\frac{1}{2}$)	23 (9)
Spinach, perpetual	April to July	—	July to March	hardy	14	7 to 14	14g ($\frac{1}{2}$oz)	13 ($\frac{1}{2}$)	30 (12)
Tomato, outdoor	February under glass	June	July onwards	tender	24	7 to 14	35 seeds	6 ($\frac{1}{4}$)	60 (24)
Turnip, early	March to June	—	June onwards	half-hardy	12	6 to 14	14g ($\frac{1}{2}$oz)	13 ($\frac{1}{2}$)	15 (6)

space between rows cm (in)	fertilizer needed N	P	g/m² (oz/sq yd) K	years seed keeps	good yield for 10m (33ft) row as picked	soils	pests and diseases
60 (24)	45 (1¼)	25 (¾)	20 (½)	4	21 heads	rich, well-drained organic soil, pH 7·0, topdress August onwards with general fertilizer	as cauliflower, early
60 (24)	25 (¾)	35 (1)	35 (1)	4	19 heads	rich, well-drained, frost free site, pH 7·0	as cauliflower, early
30 (12)	25 (¾)	20 (½)	20 (½)	5	40kg (90lb)	Deep, humus-rich, moist yet well-drained soil, pH 6·0 to 6·5, earth up stems from August	celery fly, heart rot, leaf spot
30 (12)	25 (¾)	20 (½)	20 (½)	5	40kg (90lb)	deep, humus-rich, moist yet well-drained soil, pH 6·0 to 6·5	as celery, non-blanching
30 (12)	50 (1½)	35 (1)	20 (½)	1	40 cobs	light, moisture-retentive, humus-rich soil, pH 6·5 to 7·0	damping off
90 (36)	50 (1½)	35 (1)	35 (1)	5	30	plant on mounds of rotted compost and soil, feed regularly	gummosis, leaf blotch
60 (24)	50 (1½)	35 (1)	35 (1)	4	15kg (33lb)	as cabbage, spring	as cabbage, spring
23 (9)	20 (½)	25 (¾)	20 (½)	3	15kg (33lb)	humus-rich soil, pH 6·0 to 6·5	eelworm, smut, white tip
23 (9)	50 (1½)	50 (1½)	35 (1)	1	44 heads	moisture-retentive, humus-rich soil, pH 6·5 to 7·0, rake in general fertilizer before sowing	botrytis, downy mildew, leaf aphis, mosaic, root aphis
90 (36)	35 (1)	35 (1)	35 (1)	4	10 to 20kg (22 to 44lb)	plant on mounds of rotted compost and soil, feed regularly	aphis, mildew
30 (12)	20 (½)	35 (1)	25 (¾)	4	15kg (33lb)	deeply-cultivated, well-drained, humus-rich soil, pH 6·0 to 6·5	downy mildew, onion fly, smut, white rot
45 (18)	no specialized requirements			1	15kg (33lb)	deep, porous soil, pH 6·5	canker, carrot fly
60 (24)	— —	35 (1)	35 (1)	2	25kg (55lb)	deep, humus-rich soil, pH 6·0 to 6·5, sheltered site	fusarium wilt, leaf spot, pea aphis, pea moth
75 (30)	— —	35 (1)	35 (1)	2	25kg (55lb)	deep, humus-rich soil, pH 6·0 to 6·5	as peas, early
120 (48)	— —	35 (1)	35 (1)	2	30kg (66lb)	as peas, second early	as peas, early
45 (18)	35 (1)	70 (2)	20 (½)	2	15kg (33lb)	deep, humus-rich, moist yet well-drained soil, pH 6·5	botrytis, fruit spot
60 (24)	80 (2¼)	60 (1¾)	35 (1)	—	20kg (45lb)	light, humus-rich soil, pH 5·5 to 6·5	blight, eelworm, scab, wart disease
75 (30)	80 (2¼)	60 (1¾)	35 (1)	—	25kg (55lb)	as potatoes, early	as potatoes, early
15 (6)	50 (1½)	25 (¾)	20 (½)	1	4kg (9lb)	humus-rich, porous soil worked to a tilth, pH 7·0	clubroot, radish fly, turnip fly
15 (6)	no specialized requirements			—	15kg (33lb)	light, sandy, free-draining soil, pH 6·0	onion fly
30 (12)	25 (¾)	25 (¾)	20 (½)	2	15kg (33lb)	rich, moist soil, pH 6·5, likes partial shade	downy mildew
30 (12)	— —	35 (1)	35 (1)	2	15kg (33lb)	rich, moist soil, pH 6·5, likes partial shade	as spinach, summer
38 (15)	25 (¾)	25 (¾)	20 (½)	2	15kg (33lb)	deep, rich soil which has been manured for a previous crop, pH 6·5	
90 (36)	25 (¾)	35 (1)	50 (1½)	3	25kg (55lb)	humus-rich, moisture-retentive soil, pH 6·0	botrytis, leaf mould, tomato mosaic virus
30 (12)	25 (¾)	35 (1)	20 (½)	2	15kg (33lb)	light, rich loam, pH 6·5 to 7·0	club root, mildew, turnip fly

Cultivation

Most vegetable seeds can be sown where they eventually produce the crop but with some it is easier, or sometimes essential, to sow the seed indoors in pots or trays or out of doors in a seed bed and later set them out as young plants.

Raising plants outside Choose a sunny position for the seed bed and dig it over very well in the autumn. In the spring, break down the rough clods by forking the soil lightly, apply either a general purpose fertilizer at about 70g/m² (2oz/sq yd) or the appropriate fertilizer mix given in the Vegetable Planning Chart and firm the soil to remove air pockets. Rake the bed level and remove stones and unbroken rough clods. Take out a seed drill with the corner of a rake or with a draw hoe and water the drill well. Sow the seed thinly along the drill, cover with loose soil and firm lightly with the back of the rake. Water the young plants before lifting them.

Raising plants under glass Carrots and other root crops cannot be transplanted, but most other vegetables can be successfully started off in pots on trays under glass. Sow the seed in shallow pans or seed boxes filled with soil-based or soilless growing mix: see *Soil*. Firm the growing medium gently before sowing, and make sure it is thoroughly damp. Sow thinly, to avoid damping off and cover the seeds with a little growing mix.

After sowing cover the containers with glass or place them in a germinating cabinet. The ideal temperature for germination varies considerably from vegetable to vegetable, but temperatures between 18 and 24°C (65 and 75°F) are usually adequate. When the seedlings are large enough to handle prick them off into boxes, pots, or into permanent beds. For further details see *Cultivation*.

Buying plants Look for fresh, green young plants. Avoid those which look too lush and green, those with poor root systems and those with yellowish leaves. Choose plants which have small fibrous roots which are preferably wrapped in moss or dampened newspaper.

Planting Dig over the ground well in advance of planting to give it time to settle. Add bulky manures or lime according to the rotation scheme. Make a hole which is large enough for the roots to spread naturally. Press the soil firmly around the plant's roots to make sure that they are not suspended in an air pocket. Test the firmness by pulling the young plant gently by a leaf. If the leaf starts to tear, the plant is firm enough; if the plant is pulled out, replant and firm. Water well after planting even if the soil seems moist.

Sowing seeds *in situ* Prepare the soil as outlined above and follow the seed bed preparation given under *Raising plants outside*. The fertilizers are shown in the Chart. Thin the seedlings by removing the weak ones first, leaving the strongest about 8cm (3in) apart. When the leaves start to touch, thin to the final spacing shown in the Chart. Some plants obtained from this second thinning can be eaten, particularly those like beetroot and lettuce. Remove thinnings to reduce the risk of pests and diseases.

Routine Maintenance

Weeds are a serious opposition to any vegetable. They can smother small seedlings and compete with established vegetables for available moisture and nutrients. Hoe the ground between plants regularly, chopping down the weed seedlings. When hoeing near vegetables, take care not to cut or break roots near the surface.

During the growing season vegetables will probably need watering. Decisions about when to water and how much to apply depend on the weather, the soil and the plants. See *Climate* for information on how weather and soil type affect the frequency of watering and see *Tools and Equipment* for details of watering equipment. Most vegetables will respond to adequate water supplies throughout their growing life but some need it at frequent intervals during a dry spell, while others benefit most if it is applied at a particular time, and others hardly benefit at all. In very dry spells, it may not be possible to water all vegetables, and so you will need to concentrate on giving water to those which will make most use of it – see below.

First priority
Beans, runner
 water before sowing and from the first signs of flowers until the end of summer
Cauliflowers, early summer
 water throughout life or 2 to 3 weeks before harvesting
Cauliflowers, summer and autumn
 water before sowing and throughout life or 2 to 3 weeks before harvesting
Celery, self-blanching
 water after planting and throughout life until the end of summer
Lettuces, summer
 water before sowing and throughout life until the end of summer
Potatoes, early
 water throughout life
Second priority
Beans, dwarf or French
 water before sowing and when flowering starts
Beetroot
 water before sowing and throughout life

Brussels sprouts
water-in young plants after transplanting

Cabbages, summer and autumn
water after sowing, and after transplanting and throughout life or 2 to 3 weeks before harvesting

Leeks
water after sowing, after transplanting and throughout life until the end of summer

Marrows
water after sowing, after transplanting and throughout life until the end of summer.

Third priority

Cabbages, spring
water after sowing and 2 to 3 weeks before harvesting

Cabbages, winter and Savoy
water before sowing and after transplanting

Cauliflower, winter
water before sowing and after transplanting

Lettuces, winter
water 2 to 3 weeks before cutting

Onions
water from late spring until the end of bulb swelling

Parsnips
water before sowing

Swedes
water before sowing.

Fourth priority (water in very dry spells only)

Beans, broad
water when flowering starts and when pods start to swell.

Carrots
water before sowing and throughout life. Do not water until plant reaches true four-leaf stage. Do not water at irregular intervals.

Asparagus
Unlikely to increase yields

Harvesting

Harvest vegetables when they are fresh and succulent: pick peas when the pods are green and just starting to swell, not when they are silvery. Cut cauliflowers when the internal leaves open away from the white curd. Pull roots when they are small and at their most succulent. Sow at regular intervals to get a succession of young vegetables. Choose early, second early, main crop, and late varieties to produce a continuity of supply.

The Vegetables

For UK planting and sowing times see Vegetable Planning Chart. Canadian and United States sowing and planting times are given below. The cultural details apply to all countries.

Asparagus *Asparagus officinalis* Sow seed outside about two weeks after the last frost. Leave for two years and discard any seedlings which produce berries (female plants). Plant two-year crowns in trenches 30 to 45cm (12 to 18in) wide and 25cm (10in) deep. Put 5cm (2in) of well-rotted manure or compost in the bottom of the trench. Topdress with bulky organic manure in late winter and apply fertilizers shown in the Planning Chart in early spring. Do not harvest until plants are three years old. Cut about 10cm (4in) below the soil level when the spears are about 7·5cm (3in) high. Continue to harvest until about eight weeks after the growth first begins in the spring.

Aubergine, eggplant *Solanum melongena* Sow seed indoors about seven weeks before last frost and transplant healthy plants to the garden after all danger of frost has gone. Do not hoe around plants: keep weeds down by mulching. Test for ripeness by pressing the side of the fruit gently: if the dent does not spring back, the fruit is ripe.

Bean, broad *Vicia faba* These are among the hardiest of the beans. For an early summer crop sow about eight weeks before the last frost. A March sowing will be ready in July. In Canada varieties such as 'Earliwax' and 'Early Puregold' are generally sown in May. In those areas which do not suffer severe winters (the UK for example) long pod varieties sown in November will produce crops in the following spring. Sow seed in double rows about 30cm (12in) apart. Stagger the seeds in each of the rows. Earth up soil around the stems of the plants to give a mound about 7·5cm (3in) high. Support the plants when they are 60cm (2ft) tall. Take out the tips when the first cluster of pods starts to swell to prevent blackfly attacks.

Bean, butter or lima *Phaseolus lunatus* This vegetable is not generally grown in the UK. Seed should not be sown until the soil warms to 16°C (60°F) which is usually two to three weeks after the average date of the last frost. Use cloches to protect young plants. Topdress with fertilizer shown in the Planning Chart about four weeks after planting. This plant grows best in warm weather but it will not set pods when the temperature exceeds 30°C (85°F). Both bush and pole varieties are available. Harvest when the seed has fully enlarged but before the pod starts to turn yellow.

Bean, French, kidney, snap or string *Phaseolus vulgaris* These beans will not tolerate frost and will only germinate when the soil temperature exceeds 10°C (50°F) and preferably 16°C (60°F). Like lima beans, most French beans will not set pods

Raking the soil to a fine tilth

Marking the row with a garden line

Taking out a drill with a hoe

Sowing the seeds

Using the back of the rake to cover the drill

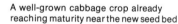

A well-grown cabbage crop already reaching maturity near the new seed bed

when the temperature exceeds 30°C (85°F). In Canada and the United States the time from sowing to harvesting is about 50 days and in most areas several spring crops and an autumn crop can be grown. The first sowing can be done safely about two weeks after the last frost but many gardeners try a sowing a few days before the average date of the last frost. Pick the pods before the beans in the pods begin to swell and continue to pick regularly to keep plants cropping. These beans have rather shallow root systems and weeds should be kept down by mulching rather than hoeing. Both bush and pole varieties are available.

Bean, runner *Phaseolus multiflorus* Sow seed outside about two weeks before the average date of the last frost. Prepare the soil by taking out a trench about 30cm (12in) wide and 25cm (10in) deep. Break up the soil at the bottom of the trench and line it with 10cm (4in) of well-rotted bulky organic manure. Return soil to the trench and firm. Leave for two weeks and insert poles or strings for beans to grow up. Poles should be at least 1·8m (6ft) high. The poles and strings can be arranged in straight lines or in the form of a wigwam with the poles lashed together at the top. Apply the fertilizers shown in the Planning Chart about 10cm (4in) from the plants. Mulch young plants. Pick the beans as soon as they reach a usable size and continue to pick regularly to keep plants cropping.

Beetroot *Beta vulgaris* Beet are fairly hardy and seed can be sown outside about six weeks before the average date of the last frost. Apply the fertilizer shown in the Planning Chart just before sowing. Take care to avoid damaging the roots when harvesting. Twist off the tops: do not cut the stems.

Broccoli, sprouting *Brassica oleracea italica* Sow in a seed bed at about the average date of the last frost. Lift the young plants and re-plant them about 2·5cm (1in) deeper about four weeks later. Cut the flower heads with as much stem as possible. Pick frequently to encourage cropping. Plants may need staking on exposed sites. Cultural requirements are basically the same as for cabbage and cauliflower.

Brussels sprout *Brassica oleracea gemmifera* Sow seed outside in seed beds at about the average date of the last frost. Transplant when plants are 10 to 15cm (4 to 6in) high. Plant firmly. Stake tall plants in the early autumn. Brussels sprouts are more difficult to grow than cabbage and are more sensitive to hot weather.

Cabbage, spring, summer, autumn and winter *Brassica oleracea capitata* Cabbages like a fairly cool, moist climate but can be grown successfully in the warmer areas by careful choice of varieties. Make the first sowing of summer cabbages in February and March in a cold frame and continue to sow at intervals until about four weeks after the average date of the last frost. Transplant after about four weeks when the cabbages are about 15cm (6in) high. Sow autumn and winter cabbages from August to September.

Calabrese *Brassica oleracea* See Broccoli, sprouting.

Carrot, early and maincrop *Daucus carota* Sow seed from eight weeks before the average date of the last frost until the middle of summer. Apply a general-purpose fertilizer to the seed bed before sowing. Sow seed thinly to avoid thinning. As the roots begin to swell pull soil into the rows to cover the crowns and to stop them turning green.

Cauliflower, early, summer and winter *Brassica oleracea botrytis cauliflora* Sow seed indoors up to four weeks before the average date of the last frost. Transplant cauliflowers from the last frost onwards. Bend the inner leaves over the curd to keep them white, and to protect winter and spring cauliflowers from frost. Use magnesian limestone instead of lime before planting.

Celery *Apium graveolens* Celery needs a growing season of 115 to 135 days and needs cool weather. It can be grown as a winter crop in areas with mild winters (southern USA and British Columbia), as a summer crop in areas with cool summers (UK) and as an autumn crop in areas which have a long growing period. It is generally not very successful in the middle states of the USA. Sow seed indoors about six weeks before the last frost, at a temperature around 18°C (65°F). Keep the seedlings at a temperature above 13°C (55°F) and plant them out about six to eight weeks after the average date of the last frost when they are 5 to 7·5cm (2 to 3in) tall. Self-blanching celery should be grown in blocks with the plants set 30cm (12in) apart each way. For non self-blanching celery, dig a trench 30cm (12in) wide by 45cm (18in) deep. Fork over the soil at the bottom of the trench and half re-fill the trench with soil enriched with a generous amount of well-rotted manure. Plant the seedlings down the centre of the trench. When the sticks are 30 to 35cm (12 to 14in) tall, start blanching by removing the shoots around the base of the plants, then gather the tops together and tie them with soft string. Fill in the trench and gather up soil around the leaves to form a ridge. Harvest about six weeks later.

Corn, sweet corn *Zea mays* Corn makes little growth below 10°C (50°F) and should not be planted out of doors until all danger of frost has passed. Successional sowings can be made at 10 day intervals until about 90 days before the average date of the first autumn frost. Sow seeds or plant seedlings in blocks to aid pollination. Apply the

Sowing runner beans in peat pots: sow one seed in each pot

Use a mini-dibber to plant seed at correct depth – 50mm (2in)

Keep the pots moist; the plants will be set out in them, and if the peat wall dries out, the roots will not be able to get through

nitrogen-rich fertilizer given in the Planning Chart at the time of sowing or planting and repeat the dose when the corn is 20 to 25cm (8 to 10in) high and again when it is 45cm (18in) high. Do not hoe the soil: keep weeds down by mulching with strawy manure or compost. Pick corn when the silks turn dark brown. Check the ripeness by puncturing a kernel with a thumb nail. If a milky liquid spurts out, the corn is ready for harvest; if the liquid is clear it is too early; if no milk spurts out the corn is over-ripe.

Cucumber *Cucumis sativus* This is a warm climate vegetable and should not be sown or planted out of doors until all danger of frost has passed. For early cucumbers seeds can be sown indoors and planted out some four to six weeks later. Some varieties need to be grown in a greenhouse or a cold frame. Prepare a 30cm (12in) deep bed of loam and well-rotted manure in approximately 50:50 proportions. Make mounds at roughly 60cm (2ft) intervals. When seedlings have two rough leaves, plant one seedling on each mound. In a greenhouse train the main stem upwards and along the roof. Spread the side shoots out horizontally. In a frame, plant the cucumber towards the centre and pinch out the tip of the plant when it is 15cm (6in) high. Train side shoots towards each corner of the frame. Remove male flowers. Water and spray plants often to keep the air humid. Keep the soil weed-free by applying a mulch.

Kale *Brassica oleracea acephala* This is a cool season vegetable and for an autumn crop seed should be sown outside about three to four months before the average date of the first frost in the autumn. For spring crops (UK and many seaboard areas of North America), sow seed in the autumn around the average time of the first frost.

Leek *Allium porrum* This vegetable requires a long growing season and seed may be sown indoors in February or outdoors in March. The young plants are planted out when they are 7·5cm (3in) tall. Dig a trench about 30cm (1ft) wide and 15cm (6in) deep. Enrich the bottom of the trench with well-rotted, bulky organic manure. Make holes in the bottom of the trench with a dibber. Drop a plant into each hole and fill the hole with water. Do not firm the plants in the holes. As the leeks grow, fill in the trench. Harvest as required.

Lettuce *Lactuca sativa* Four types of lettuce are grown – head, leaf, cos and asparagus. Head lettuce can be crisphead or butterhead. It is a cool season crop. Crisphead varieties will bolt if they are exposed to hot weather, butterhead lettuces are more tolerant of heat and leaf lettuces are tolerant enough to be grown throughout the summer in most parts of Canada and the USA. In areas with warm climates, lettuce should be grown as a spring and an autumn crop. Start sowing about four to six weeks before the average date of the last frost and make further sowings at about two week intervals. In areas with hot summers, do not sow head lettuce between mid April and mid July, and, in these areas, give leaf lettuce some shade at the height of summer to prevent excess bitterness in its leaves.

Marrow or squash *Cucurbita pepo* and **pumpkin** *Cucurbita maxima* Prepare soil as for cucumbers. Squashes and pumpkins are warm season vegetables and will not tolerate frost. Sow seed indoors three to four weeks before the average date of the last frost and set out the plants after all danger of frost has passed. To pollinate the female flowers (those with the embryo squash behind them) push the centre of the male flower into the centre of the female flower. Cut the summer squashes while they are small: cropping will be reduced if they are allowed to grow on. Winter squashes should remain on the plant until the rind is hard.

Onion *Allium cepa* Onions can be grown from seed or from sets. Bulbing is a function of day length and temperature so it is important to choose a variety which is known to grow well in your area. Plant sets in early spring or sow seed indoors in February for planting out about six weeks later. In areas with mild winters sow seed outside about six weeks before the average date of the first frost for a spring crop. When the tops of the onions start to turn yellow, bend the top growth over just above the bulb. Lift the bulbs when the tops have shrivelled, and dry them well before putting them into store.

Parsnip *Peucedanum sativum* This vegetable needs a long growing season (about 120 days in North America to over 200 in the UK) and should be sown so that it can be harvested after the roots have been exposed to frost. In early summer repeat the application of the fertilizer shown in the Planning Chart. Harvest the roots as required.

Pea *Pisum sativum* English peas are a cool climate crop. They germinate at soil temperatures above 4°C (39°F) and appear to grow most satisfactorily at temperatures between 10 and 16°C (50 and 60°F). They will tolerate temperatures in the low 20s (about 70°F) but in warmer areas they must be grown as a spring or an autumn crop. There are many different varieties. Dwarf peas reach a height of 30 to 45cm (12 to 18in) and need no support. Medium and tall varieties must be supported by netting or twiggy branches. Repeat seed sowings at two to three week intervals in double rows or in flat-bottomed drills scooped out with a spade. Peas are classified as early, second early or late or (North America) by the number of growing-degree-days (GDD) from sowing to harvest. A growing-degree-day is one degree (F) average temperature for one day above 40°F. So, for example, one day with an average temperature of 42°F would count as 2GDD but if the average temperature were 65°F it would count as 25GDD. Most varieties need between 1200 and 1700GDD and to get successional crops it is better to plant varieties with different GDD requirements rather than the same variety weekly or at two-weekly intervals.

Pepper *Capsicum annum* (sweet) *C. frutescens* (hot) These are hot climate plants and are only really successful in the UK if they are grown in a greenhouse or garden frame. In Canada and the United States they can be started indoors and planted out when all danger of frost has passed.

Potato *Solanum tuberosum* There are early, second early and main crop varieties. They differ in the time they take to reach maturity and their yield: early potatoes do not usually yield as heavily as main crop ones. Potatoes are grown from tubers. About ten to twelve weeks before the average date of the last frost stand the tubers on end in a box with the eyes uppermost. Place the box in a light, frost-proof place for the tubers to sprout. Potatoes can be planted in spring before all danger of frost has passed. Keep four to six good, well-sprouted eyes on each tuber and rub off all the others. Large tubers with many eyes can be cut in half, thirds or even quarters. Plant the tubers in V-shaped trenches with the sprouts upwards. As soon as the shoots appear above the ground, draw the soil from between the rows over them to form a ridge. This will protect the young shoots against late frosts and will prevent the tubers going green through exposure to light. Store harvested potatoes in the dark in a frost-free place.

Radish *Raphanus sativus* Sow seed in spring as soon as the ground can be worked. Repeat the sowing at two weekly intervals, until the middle of the summer. Radishes become strong-flavoured and woody during hot weather. In areas with hot summers they should be grown as a spring and an autumn crop making a final sowing about a month before the average date of the first autumn frost. Pull radishes while they are small.

Shallot *Allium cepa* These are grown from bulbs planted in spring as soon as the ground can be worked. They need a long growing season, a temperature above 21°C (70°F) in the summer, and a day length of at least 15 hours. When the new bulbs are well formed, draw soil away from them to aid ripening. Lift the bulbs when the tops turn yellow and leave them on a paved surface to dry out.

Spinach *Spinacia oleracea* This is a cool climate vegetable and can be grown as a spring or an autumn crop. New Zealand spinach is a warm-season plant and can be grown as a summer crop in areas where spinach will not thrive. Sow seed for summer spinach at roughly two weekly intervals from four weeks before the average date of the last frost until four weeks after it. In many areas with mild winters (UK and seaboard areas of North America) winter spinach can be sown at intervals between October and March for a spring crop. Take the centre out of each plant as soon as it reaches a usable size. This will encourage the buds below to grow. Pick the leaves regularly until the plants run to flower.

Sweet corn – see Corn.

Swiss chard, seakale beet, spinach beet or perpetual spinach *Beta circla* Sow seed where plants are to grow about two weeks after the average date of the last frost and repeat the sowing at two weekly intervals until late summer. Pick the outer leaves first.

Tomato *Lycopersicon esculentum* This is a warm season vegetable and will not tolerate frost. It can be grown as a bush or supported by stakes or a trellis. Sow seed indoors about ten weeks before the average date of the last frost for plants to be grown under glass and about four to six weeks later for plants to be grown outside. Plant outside seven to ten weeks after sowing. In very warm areas seed can be sown outside in early spring.

Under glass, plants can be grown in large pots, boxes of about 27l (1cu ft), beds of soil, bottomless rings on a bed of aggregate or in plastic bags filled with peat-based growing mix. Rub off side shoots as they appear and give the stem support. Water regularly and feed with liquid fertilizers as soon as the lowest flower truss shows signs of fruit. Ventilate freely and spray flowers with water to aid setting. Pinch out the top of the plant when it reaches the roof of the greenhouse. When plants are grown in rings, water should be given to the aggregate and fertilizer to the rings.

Turnip and swede *Brassica rapa* This vegetable can be grown as a spring and an autumn crop in the warmer areas of North America and as a summer crop in milder areas like the northern states and the UK. When grown as a summer crop seed is usually sown at intervals of three to four weeks from May onwards.

Herbs

Herbs are aromatic plants which are grown principally for seasoning foods. Some may also have medical and cosmetic uses.

The Herb Garden

Many herbs are attractive plants and merit a place in the ornamental garden for their looks alone.

Choose a place sheltered from the wind with sun for much of the day. Make sure that the herb garden is not sited in a frost pocket. Most herbs like a warm, light, well-drained soil. See *Soil* for improving heavy, wet soils.

Herb gardens are usually formal in design as this helps to define the individual herb beds and stops the collection becoming

Right: Capsicums. The red ones are green fruits which have been left on the plant

Below: Two different styles of herb garden; the one on this page a mass of colour and scent, on the facing page, one traditionally formal. In a small garden, a formal herb garden is probably the better idea

Above: Hoe between rows of vegetables to keep weeds down

A mushroom bed will generally crop over a three or four week period

rather rambling and unkempt. The most popular design is a symmetrical arrangement of small beds with paving or brick paths between them. The beds can be arranged, for example, in a chessboard pattern, or as a wheel with paving instead of spokes, or as a knot garden with beds outlined by shrubby or half-shrubby plants such as box, lavender, winter savory or hyssop. Plant the tall herbs at the centre or at the back of the bed; plant the dwarfs at the edges. Keep large-leaved plants away from those like thyme which have tiny leaves. Make sure that flower colours do not clash, and do not put the few shade-lovers in full sun.

The herb garden can be very practical and placed as near the kitchen door as possible. To achieve this, herbs can be mixed with the vegetables, or can become part of the herbaceous or mixed border. Some herbs such as chamomile, creeping thyme or pennyroyal can be used for paths or small lawns, and many others can be grown in a window box on the kitchen window-sill.

Looking after Herbs

Herbs are very easy plants to look after and demand relatively little attention. An established herb garden can last for years, so it is worthwhile making sure that the soil is light and well drained (see *Soil*) and that the site is free from perennial weeds, before the herbs are planted. In future years apply a sprinkling of a slow-acting general fertilizer every spring, and a little lime in winter. Remove weeds as soon as they are seen, and water the plants in prolonged dry periods. Give the plants a mulch of compost or leaf mould in spring. Some plants will need trimming after flowering, unless the seeds are needed. Tall plants should be supported. Pests and diseases are rare.

Harvesting and Storing

Harvesting herbs for drying and preserving should be done on a dry, warm, still day. Pick the leaves just before the plant flowers. Gather flowers just as they are fully open and collect seeds as they change colour and loosen in the seed case. Dry the plants in a dark, warm, airy place and store them in airtight containers.

The Herbs

Allium sativum, garlic, half-hardy bulbous plant, 30 to 60cm (1 to 2ft), pungent onion flavour and smell, grows world-wide, *lvs* grasslike, *fls* white, June. **Cultivation** plant segments of the bulb outdoors late February to early March, 15 to 23cm (6 to 9in) apart, just below soil surface; sun and good soil drainage are particularly important. Harvest in August.

Allium schoenoprasum, chives, hardy perennial dying down each autumn, 15 to 25cm (6 to 10in), mildly onion smelling, native of the northern hemisphere, *lvs* tubular, grass-like, *fls* lilac, June to July. **Cultivation** plant in fertile soil between September and April and divide every few years in autumn. **Propagation** division or seed sown outdoors in spring.

Artemisia dracunculus, French tarragon, perennial, evergreen in mild climates, 30 to 60cm (1 to 2ft), native of south Europe, *lvs* small, narrow, strongly aromatic, *fls* tiny, greyish. **Cultivation** plant in spring or September in a light, dryish soil with plenty of sun. Transplant after a few years to fresh soil to maintain flavour. Protect in severe weather. **Propagation** divide in spring.

Mentha, mint, hardy perennial, dying down in autumn, 30 to 60cm (1 to 2ft), native of north Europe, *lvs* rounded or narrow, pointed, *fls* white or purple, July to August. *M. citrata,* Eau de Cologne, rounded leaves; *M. piperita,* peppermint; *M. rotundifolia, lvs* smelling of apples – var *variegata,* green and cream-edged *lvs,* scented with pineapple; *M. spicata,* common mint. **Cultivation** plant between spring and autumn, in moist soil. **Propagation** divide in autumn or spring, or detach rooted stems. Pineapple mint less hardy, take cuttings and overwinter under glass.

Ocimum basilicum, basil, half-hardy annual from the tropics, 60 to 90cm (2 to 3 ft), *lvs* clove-scented, *fls* white, August. **Cultivation** sow seed under glass at 16°C (60°F) in March, prick out into boxes and plant out in late May.

Origanum majorana, marjoram, half-hardy annual, 20cm (8in) native of North Africa and Europe, *lvs* small, grey-green aromatic, *fls* white, summer. **Cultivation** sow seed outdoors in early May, and thin to 25cm (10in) apart. Keep well weeded. Trim back to 5cm (2in), lift in early fall/autumn and pot for winter use, keeping indoors.

Petroselinum crispum, parsley, biennial treated as annual, 15 to 30cm (6 to 12in), native of central and southern Europe, *lvs* much curled with strong-flavour. **Cultivation** sow outdoors March to May in heavy soil with some shade. Thin to 15cm (6in) and remove flowering stems. Sow in July for winter, protect from snow with cloches.

Rosmarinus officinalis, rosemary, evergreen shrub, killed by severe cold or wet soil, 1·5m (5ft), native of south Europe and Asia Minor, *lvs* narrow, small, pungently aromatic, *fls* tiny, blue-lilac, April to May. **Cultivation** plant in spring in well-drained soil in a sunny position. Pinch out tips in early years, to make more bushy. **Propagation** tip cuttings May to July in sandy growing mix under glass.

Runex scutatus, sorrel, perennial, native of Europe, *lvs* round, fleshy, *fls* insignificant, greenish, summer. **Cultivation** plant in spring on moist soil, remove flowering stems. **Propagation** by seed or division.

Salvia officinalis, sage, evergreen shrub, killed by severe cold or wet soil, native of Europe and the Mediterranean area, *lvs* grey-green, aromatic, *fls* purple or white, June. **Cultivation** plant in spring in sun and chalky soil, remove flowering stems. **Propagation** by seed sown in late April outdoors, or by layering in autumn.

Thymus vulgaris, thyme, evergreen shrublet, hardy except in severe weather, native of south Europe, *lvs* minute, strongly aromatic, *fls* purple, June to August. *T. citriodurus*, *lvs* lemon-scented. **Cultivation** plant in spring or by 5cm (2in) cuttings in early summer. Place cuttings in sandy potting mix, under glass; pot on when rooted and plant out in September. Lemon thyme needs winter protection.

Mushrooms

The most common natural species of edible fungi are *Psalliota campestris*, field mushroom and *P. arvensis*, horse mushroom. Neither of these species is cultivated: mushrooms grown commercially can be thought of as belonging to *P. hortensis* or *P. bispora*.

The life cycle of the mushroom has three stages: spores, spawn (or mycelium) and mushroom. Mushroom spores look like minute particles of brown powder. When the spores are placed on a suitable medium, well-rotted compost for example, they germinate and produce a mass of white fungus threads (mycelium). These threads permeate the compost and eventually throw up the mushrooms. Two things are essential for successful cultivation of mushrooms: the purchase of fresh, viable spawn and the preparation of good compost.

Preparing the Compost

Mushroom compost can be made from strawy horse manure or from straw alone. Making compost takes about five weeks and will need a lot of time and effort. Choose a composting site which is sheltered from the wind and preferably from rain too. A garage or car port with a concrete base and a nearby source of water is ideal. Only three tools are essential: a garden fork, a spade and a long, 45cm (18in) composting thermometer.

Horse manure About ½ tonne (10cwt) of strawy horse manure is needed to make a 9m² (30sq ft) mushroom bed. If the manure is very strawy, it will need a nitrogen booster adding. Poultry manure, pig manure, dried blood, urea, or sulphate of ammonia

can be used. Add poultry manure or pig manure at about 25kg to each half tonne of manure (½cwt/½ton) or use dried blood, urea or sulphate of ammonia at between 6 and 12kg/half tonne of manure (14 to 28lb/½ton). Make up a stack of manure about 1m (3½ft) by 1m (3½ft). Shake the manure out through a fork as the stack is being built, add the nitrogen booster evenly and add water if the manure looks dry. Put the composting thermometer in the top of the stack.

After five to seven days the temperature should have reached 60 to 70°C (140 to 160°F) and the stack will need turning. Take the stack apart and rebuild it systematically, turning the outside to the middle, the top to the bottom and so on. Add more water if the manure feels dry, and wet thoroughly any dry, white-grey patches. If the compost feels greasy, add gypsum (calcium sulphate) at about 6kg/½ tonne (14lb/½ton). Turn the compost at weekly intervals for about four to five weeks.

Good compost which is ready for use should be brown and should fall to pieces if it is rubbed between the fingers. If there is a smell of ammonia or if the compost is too dry, continue the composting process. **Straw** About 100kg (2cwt) of wheat or barley straw is needed to make a 9m² (30sq ft) mushroom bed. Chop the straw into 25cm (10in) lengths and wet thoroughly. Do this in stages adding more and more water daily for about a week. Make a stack adding a ready-prepared mushroom compost activator.

Boxing

Place the compost in boxes about 25cm (10in) deep and wait for it to cool down to about 25°C (77°F). At this temperature push pieces of spawn into the surface so that they are just covered and put the boxes in a dark, humid place.

In about six or seven days the mycelium threads should be visible spreading through the compost. Cover (case) the surface of the bed with a layer of sterilized loam and peat, or peat alone, about 4cm (1½in) deep. After eight to ten weeks the mushrooms should begin to appear and should be picked over regularly until the bed is exhausted. The mushrooms should appear in flushes at intervals of 12 to 14 days. When picking them, remove all the stalk from the bed as any left behind will rot and prevent the mycelium from spreading through the compost.

The bed usually lasts about three to four weeks after picking starts. When it is finished use the mushroom compost as a bulky organic manure around the garden and start again with fresh compost.

14. Lawns

A lawn is a basic feature of many gardens. It can be ornamental or can be a play area for children. The shape and size of a lawn is influenced by various factors but as far as is practical, the shape should be a simple one with a minimum of sharp angles to make mowing easier. Ideally a lawn should be positioned in full sun as grass in deep shade is difficult to maintain satisfactorily. In very shaded areas of the garden it is better to plant shade-tolerant shrubs and herbaceous plants rather than to struggle with grass, which is unlikely to grow successfully.

A New Lawn

A new lawn can be grown from seed or turf. The amount of preparation of the soil is roughly the same for both methods except that when laying turf the soil surface does not need to be raked quite as fine as for seed. The choice between the two is one of personal preference and the relative advantages and disadvantages listed below should be considered individually.

1) A lawn from seed will be considerably cheaper, perhaps three or four times cheaper, than one laid from turf.

2) After the ground has been prepared, sowing and raking in seed is much less work than laying turves.

3) Laying turves gives an almost instant lawn whereas it might be six to nine months before one grown from seed can be used by children.

4) There is a wide range of different grasses available when sowing seed and so the ideal mixture for a particular position or use can be selected. Turf may contain unwanted grasses and good turf can be difficult to obtain.

5) Turves deteriorate rapidly unless they are stored correctly but seed can be bought well in advance and does not deteriorate if the weather conditions are against preparing the lawn.

A third possibility is to make a lawn from plants of *Agrostis stolonifera*, creeping bent, but this grass is shallow rooting and can suffer severely in dry weather unless it is watered regularly.

Preparation

The first thing to consider is drainage. An otherwise good lawn can be ruined by being over-wet and unusable in winter – see *Soil*. A lawn with a slight slope, say 1 in 60, can be easy to maintain but if it is steeper than this, then you should consider levelling the area by a series of terraces. See *Cultivation: Levelling*. Soil texture should then be considered. If the ground has been heavily compacted by builders' lorries, double dig the soil. See *Cultivation: Digging*. If not, single digging is adequate. Improve light sandy soils, prone to drought, by digging in well-decayed organic material such as moist peat, garden compost or well-rotted manure at 4 to 6kg/m² (7 to 10lb/sq yd). The surface drainage of clay soils can be improved by working coarse, gritty sand at up to 8kg/m² (14 lb/sq yd) into the top 15cm (6in) of soil.

While doing these things remove the roots of any perennial weeds.

If the soil is very acid, a light dressing of lime can be applied after digging. The finer lawn grasses, however, prefer an acid soil and unless the soil is below pH 5, do not apply lime. Unnecessary liming can encourage coarser grasses, various weeds and earthworms. Casts from earthworms are unsightly, can make mowing difficult and if compressed, but not cleared, can quickly be colonized by moss or weeds.

Turf should be laid between October and February as the weather allows. Seed is best sown in April or September to October (see

Opposite: A well-kept lawn is of prime importance in the overall appearance of a garden

Sowing a lawn

Raking the surface

Marking out the area into small squares

Sowing the seed evenly; prepare the quantities for each small square in advance

below). Ideally the ground should be prepared a year before the lawn is made so that it can be left fallow and weeds which grow can be dealt with easily. If you do not want to do this, try to prepare the ground as far in advance as possible – in the autumn for a spring-sown lawn. Many annual weeds which germinate can then be cleared by hoeing or applying a contact weed killer based on paraquat.

One or two weeks before laying the lawn,

work a general fertilizer at 100 to 140g/m² (3 to 4oz/sq yd) into the top 15cm (6in) of soil.

The final stage of preparation is to make the ground level and firm. Hollows and humps are very difficult to correct when the grass is established. For small areas, the best method of firming is to carefully tread the entire area wearing boots or stout shoes and to apply constant even pressure by keeping your body weight on your heels. Then rake, correct the level by re-treading at right angles to the original treading and rake again until a fine level, stone-free surface is achieved. A roller can be used to consolidate large areas but firmness is usually less uniform. The ground is then ready to be sown or turfed.

Sowing Seed

The best time for sowing seed is when the soil is warm enough to ensure rapid germination and there is enough moisture available to help the seedlings to become rapidly established. In the UK the optimum time is generally in late April or May and again from mid-August to mid-September. In North America the autumn sowing should be a little later.

There are many different grass species but relatively few of them are suitable for lawns. Each species has its advantages and disadvantages and most lawn seed in the shops is a mixture – for example a drought-resistant species might be mixed with a less drought-resistant, but finer, species to give a lawn with a good appearance and some drought resistance. Do not choose a mixture with too many species as germination may be uneven and the finer constituents in the mixture are unlikely to make much contribution to the final lawn. For a hard-wearing lawn a suitable mixture might be 40 per cent Chewings fescue, 30 per cent perennial ryegrass and 30 per cent smooth-stalked meadowgrass/Kentucky bluegrass. Alternatively 20 per cent crested dog's tail could be substituted for 20 per cent of the smooth-stalked meadowgrass. An ornamental lawn subject to a reasonable amount of wear could be 80 per cent Chewings fescue and 20 per cent brown top bentgrass/colonial bentgrass. A mixture with roughly equal proportions of Chewings fescue, creeping red fescue and brown top bentgrass would be equally suitable. For shaded areas, you need a mixture with a higher proportion of rough-stalked meadowgrass/rough bluegrass and such a mixture could consist of 50 per cent rough-stalked meadowgrass/rough bluegrass, 30 per cent smooth-stalked meadowgrass/Kentucky bluegrass and 20 per cent creeping red fescue.

Turfing

Cut the turves to exactly the same size by laying them grass side downwards in a box and cutting the excess soil away with a sharp blade

Lay the turf going forward. Try to lay them so that the middle of each turf coincides with a joint between two turves in the previous row

Force sand or compost into the joints between the turves

The seed should be sown when the soil surface is dry but the soil below is still moist and when rain showers are expected. Divide the lawn area into squares one metre by one metre or strips one metre (1yd) wide using pegs and string. Divide the seed for the whole lawn in half – sow half in one direction and then sow the other half at right angles to it. Weigh out the seed according to the size of the squares or strips marked out. Ornamental mixtures can be sown at just over 35g/m² (1oz/sq yd) – 17g/m² in each of the two directions – harder-wearing mixtures should be sown at up to 50g/m² (1½oz/sq yd). Do not roll after sowing but rake the soil at right angles to the direction of the previous raking.

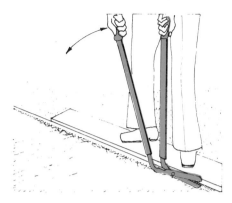

Cutting the edge of the lawn. Hold one handle steady and move the other up and down to cut. Cut against straight-edged board to get a good line

Laying Turf

Turfing is best carried out when grass is dormant or growing slowly. Where winters are mild, it can be done from October through to February. Where the winters are cold and long, it should be done as the colder weather approaches or as soon as conditions allow in early spring. Summer-laid turf needs very careful treatment to ensure satisfactory establishment.

Always try to have a look at the turf before buying it particularly if it is meadowland turf. Choose turf which is thick and healthy looking, has few weeds or coarse grasses, is cut flat along the bottom and is about 4cm (1½in) thick.

Before laying the turf make sure that each piece is of equal thickness. To do this, make a box the same size as the turves and about 4cm (1½in) thick. Trim the turves to fit the box. Lay them in it grass side down and trim off the excess soil by drawing a long knife across both edges of the box. Start turfing the lawn from one corner and work forwards laying the turves like housebricks. Leave a slight overlap all round the edge of the lawn and make sure that all turves are flat by adding or taking away soil as necessary. Once the turf is laid, fill in all the obvious joints with sandy soil and then top-dress the whole lawn with sandy soil worked in with the back of a rake.

An Established Lawn

Regular attention to mowing, raking, feeding, watering, aerating and weed control is necessary to maintain the appearance and health of an established lawn.

Mowing Under suitable conditions lawn grasses grow rapidly in late spring and usually need mowing twice a week. In summer and early spring once a week is usually sufficient. In mild winters mow occasionally, with the blades set high. Close mowing weakens the grass and encourages moss and weeds. Cut ornamental lawns from 15 to 20mm (½ to ¾in) and more hard-wearing

269

Above: Take care when planting a tree in a lawn – it can be difficult to maintain healthy grass around the base

Left: A lawn makes good contrast to a water feature

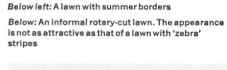

Below left: A lawn with summer borders

Below: An informal rotary-cut lawn. The appearance is not as attractive as that of a lawn with 'zebra' stripes

Left: An ornamental tree can look very effective in a lawn; give it its own small bed

Below: A quality lawn with herbaceous border

Edging

Use a garden line and a board to cut the lawn with a half-moon edging tool

Detail of the tool in use – the tool is inserted between the board and the garden line

Use a hosepipe to cut curved lawn edges. Put one foot on the hose to stop it moving

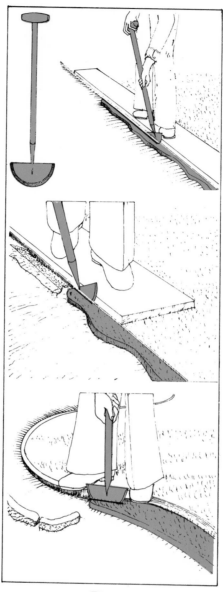

lawns from 20 to 25mm (¾ to 1in). Always collect the mowings. If they are left to decay on the lawn they can impede surface drainage and aeration and encourage worms.

Feeding Regular feeding is essential to maintain health, vigour and appearance. Grass grows vigorously for several months and takes considerable amounts of plant foods from the soil. Feed the lawn in early spring (March to April) as soon as the grass begins to grow freely. Use a general or proprietary lawn fertilizer. A lawn fertilizer for spring use can be made up as follows. For each square metre (sq yd) apply:
17g (½oz) sulphate of ammonia
50g (1½oz) superphosphate
8g (¼oz) sulphate of potash

Grass can be made greener and moss controlled by adding 8g (¼oz) of calcined sulphate of iron to the above mixture.

If there is a decline in vigour and loss of colour between spring and late summer, a nitrogenous fertilizer such as sulphate of ammonia can be applied at $17g/m^2$ (½oz/sq yd). This should be mixed with four times its weight of dry soil to ensure even distribution and to reduce the risk of any scorch damage to the grass from the concentrated fertilizer.

Feeding is not required in the colder months when there is little or no growth.

Apply all fertilizers when the soil is moist, preferably in showery weather, or water the grass well after application. If during the summer the turf has suffered from drought or compaction through heavy use, a high phosphate fertilizer can be applied in September after raking and spiking to relieve compaction. A mixture of 7 parts of bonemeal to 3 of sulphate of potash can be applied to $70g/m^2$ (2oz/sq yd).

Annual renovation In most areas September is a good month to renovate. Dead or matted turf, decaying mowings and

Right: Caring for the lawn. Top dress a lawn in autumn or early spring with a mixture of peat, sand and fertilizer.

272

Far left: Caring for the lawn mower. Keep it in top cutting condition by cleaning the blades thoroughly and oiling them every time you use the machine

Left: Choose a lawn food appropriate to the season. In spring a nitrogen based fertilizer will encourage healthy green growth, and in autumn a fertilizer with a high phosphate and potash content will aid healthy root development

debris should be removed by vigorous rakings. This will aerate the surface and let air, rainwater and any fertilizers applied get to the plant roots. Compaction can be relieved by spiking – this will improve air and moisture penetration to deeper roots and thus stimulate root development. Spiking tools range from a simple garden fork to large power-driven machines but all should give at least 8cm (3in) of penetration. On heavy, clay soils a hollow tine fork should be used. At each insertion this will remove cores or plugs of earth. These can be raked up and taken away, and a sand-based top-dressing can be spread over the lawn and worked into the holes. The top-dressing mixture can be prepared from sieved leaf mould or peat mixed with good quality loam soil or sand. The sand content can be increased on heavy soils, the organic content on light sandy soils. Top-dressings should be applied at the rate of 4 to 6kg/m² (7 to 10lb/sq yd) and should be worked well into the grass with the back of a rake or by similar means. Too heavy an application can kill finer grasses and allow weeds and moss to establish.

Bumps and hollows should be dealt with in early winter by peeling back the turf, then adding or removing earth before carefully replacing the turf. Edges can be maintained by using a half-moon-shaped lawn-edging tool against a plank to cut through the turf. After a while the lawn may become slightly smaller. This can be dealt with by cutting a strip of turf about 30cm (1ft) wide, moving it forward to form a new edge and re-seeding the soil left behind.

Weeds A number of different species of native plants can be found as troublesome weeds in lawns. These can be dug up individually or dealt with by applying a weed killer. See *Pests and Diseases*: *Herbicides*.

15. Pests and Diseases

Garden Insects and Other Pests

There are many hundreds of potentially damaging animals in a garden, but only those which cause visible damage or a reduction in yield from food plants can be called serious pests.

Sap-feeding Insects

Some examples of this type of insect pest are aphids, whitefly, scale insects and mealybug. Some of these insects excrete a substance known as honeydew which makes leaves sticky and encourages the growth of black sooty moulds. Honeydew is, in fact, the unused part of the sap which has passed through the insect's body. Some kinds of sap-feeding insect, like capsid bugs, leaf hoppers and thrips, do not produce honeydew.

Aphids (greenfly and blackfly) These insects can occur in vast numbers on the stems and foliage of many plants, including roses, fruit trees and broad beans. They may cause leaf curling, discoloration and stunted growth. Some aphids are capable of transmitting virus diseases from one plant to another.

Capsids These are medium-sized, fast-moving brown or green insects which feed on shoot tips and flower buds. They inject toxic chemicals as they feed which causes the death of tissues in the feeding area and this results in distorted flowers and tattered foliage. Fuchsias, hydrangeas, apples, chrysanthemums and dahlias are frequently attacked.

Leaf hoppers These small, yellow-coloured insects live and feed on the underside of the leaves and cause small white or yellow spots to appear on the upper leaf surface. As the common name suggests, this pest has a habit of jumping off the leaves when disturbed.

Many greenhouse plants, roses and rhododendrons are the main plants affected by this type of pest. The rhododendron leaf hopper helps to spread the disease known as bud blast which causes the flower buds to turn brown and die.

Mealybugs These are pinkish-grey insects which are often covered with a white, woolly material. They are related to scale insects and are common pests on cacti and succulents, and many plants under glass. They breed rapidly and must not be left untreated.

Scale insects These insects suck the sap of ornamental and fruit trees and herbaceous and greenhouse plants. They have flattened or rounded oval-shaped bodies and firmly attach themselves to stems and the underside of leaves. They vary in size: some are so small that they are almost invisible and look like small blisters. Some species are soft bodied, while others have a hard shell.

Thrips (thunder flies) These are tiny, thin yellow or black insects which are about 3mm (⅛in) long. Gladioli, peas, chrysanthemums and dahlias are some of the plants which may be damaged by thrips. Their feeding activities result in distorted flowers and pea pods with a silvery discoloration of the foliage and petals.

Whitefly These insects look like tiny white moths which drift off plants in clouds when they are disturbed. Both the adults and their scale-like larvae live and feed on the underside of leaves where eggs can also be found. Greenhouse plants and brassicas are particularly susceptible to this type of pest.

Flies

The roots of vegetables such as brassicas and onions are often eaten by the creamy white maggots of root flies. Heavy attacks result in stunted growth with discoloured foliage or the plants may wilt and die.

Opposite: Black spot on rose leaves

Carrot root fly The orange maggots of this fly burrow into the tap root of carrots causing reddening and wilting of the foliage. This allows the entry of fungi. Damaged carrots may not last in store during the winter.

Celery fly This lays its eggs on the foliage during summer, and the larvae attack the leaves causing them to blister and decay.

Onion fly The flies lay eggs in the soil in late spring, the maggots tunnel into the bulbs and make them useless.

Crane flies The grubs of crane flies are better known as leatherjackets. They are legless grey-coloured maggots which grow up to 3cm (1in) in length and are mainly a pest of lawns where they destroy the roots and cause dead patches.

Leaf miners These are the larvae of several insects which tunnel inside leaves, causing pale green or white discoloured areas. Chrysanthemums, holly, tomatoes and celery are frequently attacked. The adult flies appear from April onwards and lay eggs on the underside of leaf surfaces.

Sawflies Adult sawflies look rather like flying ants. The larvae cause damage to many fruit trees, roses and Solomon's seal. They often feed together in groups and they can often cause more damage than moth caterpillars.

Apple sawfly Adult sawflies lay their eggs on apple and plum blossom and the young grubs emerge and tunnel their way into the young fruitlets. The grub is white with ten pairs of legs and feeds in the apple flesh moving from one fruit to another and making a large sticky hole. Many fruits drop prematurely in June but those which reach maturity are deformed with ribbon-like scars on their surface.

Gooseberry sawfly The larvae of this insect are green and black speckled and feed on the foliage of gooseberry bushes causing so much damage that they may prevent the bush from fruiting.

Rose sawfly The black, shiny larvae feed on the leaf surfaces and make young leaves curl up tightly during the summer while the caterpillar feeds inside.

Rose slugworm This is the larva of several species of sawfly and looks like a green slimy slug with legs. It eats leaves of roses, peas and cherries and eventually strips them down to a skeleton.

Beetles

Chafer grubs and wireworms are beetle larvae and are found in greatest numbers in neglected or newly created gardens. The adult beetles select weedy areas and grassland for egg laying and when the land is cultivated, the pests concentrate their attentions on the cultivated plants. Seedlings, potato tubers and other root crops are mainly affected. Another group, weevils, are small, active beetles and both the larvae and the adults attack fruits and plants. Weevils are easily distinguished by their long snouts.

Cockchafers The adult beetles and the larvae can cause damage. The beetles attack the leaves of many trees and shrubs, while the fat, white larvae eat the roots of herbaceous plants, fruit and vegetables. The larvae have large bodies rather like a letter C and can live for three or four years in the soil before reaching maturity. Garden chafers have a similar diet to cockchafers but the larvae eat grass roots.

Flea beetles These small black and yellow beetles attack vegetables, mainly brassicas, and can riddle the leaf with holes or eat through young seedlings at ground level.

Raspberry beetle The adult beetle appears in May, eats the flowers of raspberries and related fruits and lays its eggs. The larvae eat their way into the young fruit.

Wireworms These orange-brown, thread-like tough grubs are the larvae of the click beetle. They grow up to 4cm (1½in) long and feed on the roots of plants. Symptoms of attack include yellowing and wilting of foliage.

Apple blossom weevil The adult weevils lay their eggs on the flowerbuds of apples, pears and quinces in March. The cream-coloured grubs which hatch eat the buds.

Pea and bean weevil The adult weevils chew at the edges of leaves and may also attack the growing shoots of young plants.

Vine weevil This is a legless grub and is mainly a greenhouse pest. The grubs, which have white bodies and brown heads, feed on cyclamen, begonias, fuchsias and primulas. The first sign of an infestation may be when a plant suddenly wilts and further investigation reveals that the root system has been eaten away.

Moths and Butterflies

Adult butterflies and moths feed only on nectar and are harmless. Their caterpillars, however, can eat large holes in the foliage and flowers of most plants. The only butterfly caterpillar pests feed on brassicas and are known as cabbage white butterflies. Some caterpillars attack fruit, such as the codling moth on apples, and others, such as the pea moth, attack seeds. Some caterpillars live in the soil and feed on the roots and stems of plants at soil level. These are called cutworms and are often overlooked because their dingy brown colour gives them good camouflage.

The life cycles of the various types are similar – they hatch out from eggs in the spring and begin to feed at once.

Buff-tip moth The fluffy, orange-striped caterpillars with black heads eat the foliage of fruit trees, particularly in midsummer.

Cabbage white butterfly The green and black and yellow caterpillars eat leaves and may completely strip a plant particularly brassicas. They also foul crops with their excrement.

Codling moth This is a pest of apples and pears. The moth lays eggs in leaves in June and July and the caterpillars tunnel into the fruit where they feed just under the skin before burrowing to the core. The caterpillars are small and pale pink and are the main cause of maggoty apples.

Cutworms These caterpillars live in the soil by day and come out at night to attack the roots, stems and leaves of many herbaceous plants and vegetables.

Pea moth These are pale yellowish green caterpillars which enter young pea pods and feed on the peas.

Tortrix moth There are many different species of tortrix caterpillar and they have different colours. All wriggle backwards when disturbed. They feed on the foliage of ornamental trees and shrubs (including roses).

Eelworms

With the exception of the cyst-forming types, eelworms are microscopic and identification has to be made on the symptoms they cause on plants. If possible, expert help should be sought to confirm the presence of eelworms when they are suspected. There is no chemical cure for this type of pest available to gardeners and affected plants should be destroyed and susceptible plants should not be grown in affected soil.

Leaf eelworms These live and feed inside the foliage of many plants, but they are most commonly found on chrysanthemums. Affected leaf areas turn brown and the infestation is often bounded in wedge-shaped areas by leaf veins.

Potato cyst eelworms This is the only cyst eelworm commonly occurring in gardens. It also attacks tomatoes. Affected potatoes produce tiny crops and the foliage turns yellow from the bottom of the stems upward, leaving a tuft of green leaves at the top. Careful examination of the roots will reveal spherical chestnut-brown cysts which are about the size of a pin head.

Stem and bulb eelworms These attack a wide range of plants, but they are mainly a problem on narcissi, onions and phlox. An infested narcissus produces distorted leaves and flowers and if the bulb is cut transversely, concentric rings of brown tissue can be seen where the eelworms have been feeding. The symptoms shown by young onions are sometimes known as 'bloat' describing the soft, swollen condition of the plants. Affected plants become very susceptible to diseases and often fail to complete their development. Infected phlox have short, thick shoots and distorted young leaves.

Mites

These are small, microscopic creatures related to the spider family. They reproduce rapidly in hot, dry summers and, unless they are controlled, they can lead to a reduction in crops. Many insecticides have little effect on mites.

Big bud mite These mites live inside currant leaf buds causing them to wither and fall off. With black currants the buds swell before they wither, with red and white currants they do not. See *Reversion*.

Bulb scale mite Bulbous plants with rust-coloured streaks on their foliage and flower stalks, poor blooms and weak growth may be suffering from this pest. It can be confirmed by the appearance of brown patches between the scales of the bulbs when they are lifted.

Fruit tree red spider mite These mites feed on the sap of trees such as apples and pears. They lay their red eggs on the bark and young shoots of trees. In a bad attack the leaves turn bronze and may drop prematurely. A few mites introduced into the garden on bought fruit trees may be killed off by insect predators already in the garden.

Greenhouse red spider mite These are a serious pest of many plants under glass. Carnations, chrysanthemums, melons, tomatoes, grapes and many pot plants can be affected. The mites suck sap and check growth of the plants.

Miscellaneous Soil Animals

This section includes millipedes, woodlice, ants and earwigs.

Ants These can be found in every garden, but they are usually only a serious nuisance in dry areas where their nest-building activities loosen the soil around plant roots and expose them to drought.

Earwigs With characteristic pincers at the tail end, these hardly need describing. They spend much of their time living in the soil, but climb up plants during the summer and they eat young leaves and flowers, particularly chrysanthemums and dahlias.

Slugs and snails These cause great damage in the garden by eating leaves, stems, flowers and roots of many garden plants. They are nocturnal animals hiding by day beneath stones or rubbish, particularly under hedges, and emerging at night to forage for food. There are many different types of slug varying in length from 2 to 15cm (½ to 6in). Among the most common are the grey field slug and the black garden slug.

277

Some slugs, known as keeled slugs, live underground most of the time and can drastically harm potatoes and other plants, particularly in wet seasons.

Woodlice and millipedes These are both common in soil which is rich in organic matter and they are mainly pests of young seedlings. Woodlice are slate grey in colour, about 1cm (½in) long, and they seek shelter when disturbed. Millipedes have long, thin, hard bodies with many legs and when disturbed they curl up like a watch spring. This distinguishes them from the similar, but beneficial, centipedes which run away when exposed.

Beneficial Animals
Not all insects and mites found on plants are harmful and some should be regarded as friends.

Towards the end of the summer, aphid colonies are often destroyed by predators and parasites. Ladybird beetles and their black larvae are well-known aphid predators, but equally important are the slug-like maggots of hoverflies which also devour aphids. Tiny parasitic wasps develop inside the bodies of aphids and the pest is killed when the full-grown wasp emerges. Caterpillars are also attacked in the same manner by parasitic wasps.

Aphis (blackfly) on an elder branch

278

Scale insects on a fern

For many years, biologists have tried to use predators and parasites to control pests. The most successful examples of biological control are with pests which have been accidentally introduced into a country where there were no natural checks to keep their numbers under control. The introduction of predators and parasites can sometimes restore the balance. There is little scope for this type of control in Britain or North America, where most garden pests are natives. Many greenhouse pests, however, have been introduced from warmer countries and the glasshouse red spider mite and the glasshouse whitefly can be controlled biologically. The former pest is controlled with a predatory mite, *Phytoseiulus persimilis* and the latter by a parasitic wasp, *Encarsia formosa*. These beneficial animals are reared in large numbers for commercial growers of crops such as cucumbers and tomatoes and some suppliers will also sell small quantities to amateur gardeners.

Garden Chemicals

Nowadays, we rely heavily on chemicals to keep our gardens looking nice. We use fertilizers to supply plant foods, herbicides to control weeds, insecticides to kill insects and fungicides to control fungal diseases. These last three are usually grouped together and called pesticides. This group also includes chemicals to kill slugs, snails and other garden pests.

Chemicals are usually classified as either organic or inorganic. But, in fact, the boundary between the two is rather artificial. Roughly, organic chemicals can be thought of as those containing carbon and generally of plant or animal origin. Inorganic chemicals do not contain carbon. They may occur naturally or they may be man-made.

Two distinct schools of thought exist with regard to inorganic and organic chemicals, especially concerning plant nutrition. Organic gardening enthusiasts insist that the use of inorganic chemicals for either plant nutrition or pest or disease control destroys the vital biological cycle of growth. They claim also that the vital balance of life in both plants and animals has been disturbed by the wholesale use of inorganic chemicals.

There can be no doubt that organically grown vegetables and fruit are of superb quality, but it is difficult to see how organic

279

husbandry could suddenly be interpolated in modern life on a world-wide scale as a complete substitute for inorganic chemicals. And it is difficult to see why it should be – many inorganic chemicals are just as 'natural' as organic ones. Whatever sort of chemical you use for plant nutrition, your aim should be the same – maintain the level of organic matter in the soil by adding plenty of bulky organic manures and keep the level of nutrients adequate by organic or inorganic fertilizers.

The large-scale use of some pesticides in the past has given cause for concern, and even in the garden any chemical is potentially dangerous if not used strictly in accordance with the manufacturer's directions. Regulations exist in different countries regarding the sale and distribution of certain chemicals and their approval or otherwise for agricultural and horticultural use. These regulations have been tightened up considerably in recent years mainly because of public pressure and damage to wild life.

Dusting

This is a method of applying a chemical in powder form to control a pest or disease. The active ingredient (insecticide or fungicide) is finely ground and mixed thoroughly with an inert carrier such as kaolin dust. The chemical must be evenly distributed throughout the dust, which should flow freely and should not cake. Some dusts can be applied by squeezing the puffer packs which they come in. Others need small hand bellows. Where there are only a few plants to treat a simple applicator can be made by putting the dust in a muslin bag and tying this to a stick. The bag can then be held over the plant and beaten with another stick. Dusting should always be done when the foliage is damp with dew or rain. For the control of diseases and pests which attack the top growth of plants, dusting is easier and cheaper than spraying, but it is not usually as effective and must be done much more frequently. Dusting, however, is often the best method for controlling soil-borne pests and diseases.

Relatively few fungicides or insecticides are applied to plant foliage as dusts – captan to control grey mould of chrysanthemum flowers and some foliage diseases, and dinocap to control powdery mildews are the exceptions. Most dusts are used for treating bulbs, corms and tubers and for application to the soil. Sulphur dust can be applied to the foliage to control powdery mildews and it can be used on dahlia tubers to prevent storage rot. Bordeaux powder (also known as copper lime dust) can be used to prevent storage rot of tubers and to protect collars

of plants such as polyanthus, cinerarias and iris against crown rots. It will also give some control of paeony wilt if it is applied in the same way. Quintozene can be used for dusting bulbs and corms to control storage diseases like gladiolus core rot. It can also be raked into the soil before planting bulbs to check some soil-borne diseases such as tulip fire and to give some control of the soil-borne fungus *Rhizoctonia solani*. Four per cent calomel dust can be raked into the soil to check club root and onion white rot. (It gives incidental suppression of cabbage root fly and onion fly as well.) Mercurized turf sand which often contains calomel, can be used to control some turf diseases and to eradicate moss. Thiram and captan can be used in dust form as seed dressings.

Very few insecticides are used as dusts. Derris dust will control caterpillars and sawflies. BHC dust can be used to control certain soil-borne pests such as weevils, wireworms and onion flies. Malathion can be used as a dust to control aphids, and pyrethrum to kill a wide range of pests.

Fumigation

This is a method of killing pests and fungal organisms by subjecting them to chemical fumes of sufficient concentration and toxicity to be lethal to them. Fumigation is most effective when it is carried out in confined spaces such as greenhouses, frames and solid buildings but outdoor plants can be treated by covering them with plastic sheeting or boxes to trap the fumes.

The first step in fumigating a greenhouse or shed is to calculate its cubic capacity by multiplying its length by breadth by average height. Chemicals for fumigation are usually obtained as smoke bombs, pellets or volcanoes. Each pellet or volcano will treat a certain volume of building. The volume may vary according to the pest or disease being controlled or the time of year the application is being made. Never exceed manufacturer's stated doses. For effective fumigation, it is important to reduce air leaks to a minimum to prevent fumes quickly escaping to the atmosphere and lowering their concentration inside the building. Leaky doors and ventilators should be temporarily sealed with wet newspapers or sacks. Fumigation is also more effective in still weather and when it is raining – rain helps to seal cracks.

Do not enter a greenhouse or shed until all the fumes have dissipated – many fumigating materials are harmful.

Insecticides

Insecticides are usually complex chemicals with special killing properties, acting against pests, particularly insects. Ideally they should not affect plants or man.

Formulations

Modern insecticides are generally so potent that the main problem in their use is how to apply very small quantities over relatively large areas. To this end, insecticides are sold in various easily diluted forms. The most widely available forms are aerosols, dusts and liquid concentrates. Aerosols and dusts are ready-to-use, liquid concentrates have to be mixed with water and are applied by sprayer but they generally work out much cheaper.

Liquid concentrates The commonest insecticide preparation is a liquid in which the chemical is dissolved in oil. Once diluted with water the oil breaks up into minute drops which disperse through the water. Each droplet contains a trace of insecticide and this is left on the plant surface after the water has evaporated from the diluted spray mixture. Diluted liquids can also be used as spot drenches to control root-feeding pests.

Aerosols Many insecticides are now available in aerosol cans. In these the chemical is mixed under pressure with an inert compound, known as the propellent. When the pressure is released by pressing the button a stream of liquid is forced out as fine drops. The propellent then rapidly evaporates to leave a string of insecticide particles.

Dusts In a dust the chemical is absorbed on to an inert clay. They can be sprinkled on to the soil to control soil pests which come to the surface to feed at night. They can also be worked into the soil to kill pests which feed only on plant roots. A useful modification is the puffer-pack containing pesticide mixed with fine talc dust which can be squirted around plant bases. Some dusts can be used to make up sprays. These 'wettable powders' must first be mixed with a very small quantity of water to form a cream before taking the mixture to its final dilution. See *Dusting*.

Granules Many soil-applied pesticides are broken down by soil-living bacteria and soon lose their potency. One way to overcome this lack of persistence is to mix the pesticide into a small ball or granule of inert material which releases the chemical over a longer period. These granules are usually sold in pepper-pot shakers. It is essential to get the granules at the right concentration around the plant. Do not spread pesticide granules like fertilizer.

Smokes Some pesticides are not easily destroyed by heat and these chemicals can be made into a sort of firework for fumigating greenhouses. The smoke from the firework settles as a very fine deposit of pesticide particles. See *Fumigation*.

Baits All the previous methods are aimed at killing any animal which feeds on treated plants. A bait which incorporates poison can offer a short cut in pest control, as the lure may be more attractive than the plant which is being protected. Baits are often used for rats, mice, slugs and snails. With slugs and snails the standard method of control is to use bran pellets dosed with a pesticide such as metaldehyde or methiocarb. When using baits, a knowledge of the animal's feeding behaviour is essential. Slugs and snails are most active on warm humid nights after rain, so there is little point in baiting during a drought. Both metaldehyde and methiocarb are stomach poisons so it is essential for the slugs and snails to eat the poisoned bait. Old, soggy pellets seem less attractive than fresh ones. There is now some evidence to show that slugs and snails are not actually attracted towards the bait but simply come across it in their normal wanderings. Many modern slug and snail killers come as small granules which must be spread over the soil surface. The old way of putting larger pellets under inverted flower pots (a must to keep birds away) still works.

Paints Some of the more volatile pesticides can be mixed into paints and resins so that the killing vapour is slowly released into the atmosphere.

How Insecticides Work

Most insecticides are contact poisons. They kill when the spray drop scores a direct hit on the insect or when the insect walks over a deposit of the chemical. Contact poisons may also be stomach poisons and are particularly effective against chewing insects such as caterpillars and beetles. To kill the pests effectively it is important to get the chemical into the right place – many insects, for example, spend most of their time on the undersides of leaves and with these there is little point in spraying the upper sides of leaf surfaces. These pesticides are usually non-selective and kill all insects including the beneficial ones.

Another group of insecticides contain systemic poisons which are absorbed by plant roots and leaves and are transported around the plant particularly into actively growing tissues. The only insects killed by systemic poisons are those which have mouthparts specially adapted to suck sap. Systemic insecticides kill aphids, scale insects, mealybugs, whitefly and red spider mites but do not affect caterpillars feeding piecemeal. Because the plant does most of the work in spreading the poison, concentrating it at points where it is most needed, systemic insecticides can be applied in smaller quantities and with much less need for

chemical	usual formulation	pests controlled	systemic?	interval days	do not use on
Carbamates					
Carbaryl	Dust and wettable powder	earthworms, caterpillars, capsids, earwigs and wasp nests	no	7	tender foliage and green-house plants
Pirimicarb	aerosol and liquid concentrate	aphids only	partially	14	cucumbers and soft fruit
Propoxur	wettable powder	aphids	no	7	clematis and fruit
Natural					
Bioresmethrin	aerosol	aphids, caterpillars, whitefly	no	—	some varieties of fuchsia and hydrangea
Derris	dust and liquid concentrate	aphids, caterpillars, beetles and red spider mite	no	1	—
Nicotine	liquid concentrate	aphids, thrips, leaf hoppers and leaf mites	no	2	—
Pyrethrum	aerosol, dust and liquid concentrate	aphids, whitefly and housefly	no	—	some varieties of fuchsia and hydrangea
Organochlorine					
BHC (lindane)	aerosol, dust, liquid concentrate and smoke cones	ants, aphids, caterpillars, earwigs, whitefly, wood-lice and soil pests like wireworms, leatherjackets and chafer grubs	no	14	beetroot, carrots, cucur-bits, potatoes, and soft fruit after flowering (all are tainted), hydrangeas and vines
Chlordane	liquid concentrate	earthworms	no	14	for use on turf only
Organophosphorus					
Bromophos	dust	cutworms, wireworms and root flies which affect carrots, onions and cabbages	no	—	—
Diazinon	aerosol and liquid concentrate	aphids, scale insects, mealybugs, caterpillars, red spider mites and whitefly	no	14	maidenhair fern, young tomatoes and cucumbers
Dichlorvos	impregnated plastic strips	whitefly and aphids (in a greenhouse)	no	1	cucumbers, roses and some chrysanthemums
Dimethoate	liquid concentrate	aphids, scale insects, mealybugs, capsids, white-fly and red spider mites	yes	7	asters, chrysanthemums, pileas, ornamental prunus, sage, salvia, rhus and ursinia
Fenitrothion	liquid concentrate	caterpillars, aphids, capsids and leaf hoppers	no	14	—
Formothion	liquid concentrate	aphids, scale insects, mealybugs, capsids, white-fly and red spider mites	yes	7	asters, begonias, chrysanthemums, Michael-mas daisies, nasturtiums, tagetes, zinnias and pot and greenhouse plants
Malathion	dust and liquid concentrate	aphids, whitefly, thrips, capsids, scale insects, mealybugs and red spider mites	no	4	antirrhinums, crassulas, ferns, gerberas, petunias, pileas, sweet peas, vines and zinnias
Menazon	liquid concentrate	aphids (including woolly aphids)	yes	14	—
Oxydemeton-methyl	aerosol	aphids and other sucking insects and mites	yes	21	greenhouse and pot plants
Pirimiphos-methyl	liquid concentrate	aphids, caterpillars, leaf miners, beetles and red spider mites	partially	7	celery, raspberries and strawberries after flowering

chemical	usual formulation	pests controlled	systemic?	interval days	do not use on
Trichlorphon	liquid concentrate	caterpillars, ants, earwigs, and root flies	no	2	cherries
Miscellaneous					
Lime sulphur	liquid concentrate	gall mites and big bud on black currants	no	applied in winter	do not use on sulphur-shy varieties
Tar oil winter washes (DNOC)	liquid concentrate	eggs of aphids, capsids, winter moth and fruit tree red spider mites	no	applied in winter (10)	plums on myrobalan stock or red currant 'Ruby Castle'
Slug and Snail Killers					
Metaldehyde	pellets and liquid concentrate	slugs and snails	no	7	—
Methiocarb	pellets	slugs and snails	no	7	—

accurate spray cover. They will also reach pests which are feeding in curled-up leaves and have the added advantage that the effect on beneficial insects which prey on the pests is reduced.

Most branded insecticides will contain several active ingredients. The 'cocktail' usually contains one systemic and one non-systemic poison to cope with sap-suckers and leaf-chewers simultaneously.

The Chemicals

Insecticides can be classified into four groups according to their chemical composition – natural insecticides, organochlorine compounds, organophosphorus compounds and carbamates. A fifth group contains those which do not fall satisfactorily into the above classifications.

The significance of these groups is connected with the problems of insecticide resistance which occurs when continual use of the same type of material kills off most of the susceptible individuals in an insect population and selects the more resistant ones. These resistant insects are immune to all the chemicals within a group and not just the one used. Ordinary garden spraying is unlikely to cause this, but it is possible to bring in resistant pests on plants which have come from a nursery where insecticides are used extensively. If resistance is suspected, the answer is to select a pesticide which belongs to a different group from that which is ineffective.

Natural insecticides At the turn of the century virtually the only reasonably safe insecticide available was nicotine extracted from tobacco plants. A little later, pyrethrum extracted from the flowers of a Persian chrysanthemum, and derris from the roots of South American plants, became available. All are non-selective, non-systemic insecticides. They have the advantages that they are generally safe to use (pure nicotine

is very poisonous) and, because they are derived from plants, they are unlikely to damage plants. Unfortunately, they are not very persistent and control insects for a short period only. To get good results they have to be sprayed directly on to the insects.

Organochlorine compounds The organochlorine compounds such as DDT and BHC (lindane) have special insecticidal powers and little or no directly damaging effects on plants or man. Most of these compounds are persistent and will kill insects even though only part of them (feet, perhaps) come into contact with the insecticide. Their persistence is one of the main reasons that they have largely gone out of favour in recent years. Most organochlorine chemicals present little hazard to the person who uses them but, because they break down so slowly, they tend to accumulate in the soil. More importantly, they become increasingly concentrated as they pass up a food chain – from plant to insect to small mammal to predatory bird and so on. Man accumulates excess organochlorine compounds in his fatty deposits. It has never been proved that the normal usage of chemicals like DDT has harmed man but the harmful effects on wild life are well known. Many such chemicals, DDT, aldrin and dieldrin, are no longer available in most countries for garden use and those which remain – BHC and chlordane – are likely to continue in short supply.

Organophosphorus compounds The organophosphorus compounds form the largest group of insecticides and have now largely replaced the organochlorines. They may be systemic, such as dimethoate, formothion, oxydemeton-methyl and menazon, or non-systemic, such as diazinon, dicotol fenitrothion, malathion and trichlorphon. They generally lack persistence and so present less of a hazard to wild life.

Unfortunately, the shorter life of these

283

chemicals means that plants are protected for shorter periods unless the chemicals are made up in forms which give slow release. Another snag of this group is that they act on the nervous systems of animals as well as insects and while some, for example malathion, are of very low toxicity to man, others, such as dimefox, can be extremely hazardous to use. Once the chemical has been diluted to working strength it is much safer, but the effects of an overdose may linger for up to six months weakening the operator's resistance to further exposure. Over and above the direct effects on the nervous system, some modern insecticides have been implicated as cancer agents. One can, however, overemphasize the danger. Provided common sense prevails and the simple rules outlined below are followed, there is little reason why anyone should not use an insecticide safely. These rules should be observed for all pesticides.

Avoid buying pesticides if no active ingredient is indicated on the label. In the UK use pesticides with the government approval mark. In North America consult Department of Agriculture bulletins or your county agricultural agent.

Follow the manufacturer's instructions

Keep to the recommended strength.

Store pesticides out of reach of children. Label the containers properly and NEVER STORE PESTICIDES IN DRINK BOTTLES.

Do not spray open flowers because pollinating insects such as bees may be killed.

Do not spray in windy weather. This is both dangerous and uneconomical because spray will drift into areas where it is not going to be required.

Wash out watering cans and sprayers after use.

Wash yourself after using pesticides.

Do not allow pesticides to get into watercourses and ponds. Most modern pesticides are efficient fish-killers.

Wash used containers and dispose of them safely.

If anyone feels ill after using pesticides and the symptoms do not quickly disappear, seek medical assistance. Have ready the name of the chemical used, how much has been used and how it got into the patient (by skin contact or by swallowing or by breathing).

Carbamate compounds Only three carbamate insecticides are widely available to gardeners – carbaryl, pirimicarb and propoxur. Of these, only pirimicarb has some systemic properties but even so it is mainly used as a contact insecticide. Carbaryl is effective against most chewing insects but pirimicarb is usually said to be specific to aphids.

Miscellaneous insecticides There is a miscellany of chemicals which are not insecticides but which have some pesticidal properties. A spray of soapy water is a well-known 'cure' for greenfly. Tar oils can be used to destroy the eggs of pests exposed on trees during the winter. A grade of petroleum oil (purified to eliminate chemicals which damage plants) is often sprayed on house plants to give them an extra shine. At the same time it smothers insect life. The mealybugs, which attack the roots of cacti, are easily controlled by mixing a mothball into the growing mix. Generally, however, it is better to rely on proprietary insecticides to gain effective and lasting control of a pest problem.

Suitability – for Plants

All insecticides have instructions for use written on them and these must be read and carefully followed. It is most important that the correct dilution is used. A stronger dose can be dangerous and may harm the plants. Some plants may be damaged by some insecticides, even when they are used at the correct strength. This is known as phytotoxicity and the manufacturer's instructions will list any of the more common plants which are liable to be damaged in this way. Many ornamental plants are readily damaged by insecticides. The usual symptoms are scorching on the margins or between the veins of the leaves. Growth may be checked and shoots may go blind. As a general rule, flowers and open buds should not be sprayed. Petals are easily scorched and some such as freesias lose their perfume. Ornamental plants vary considerably in their susceptibility to spray damage. Cacti are tolerant to most pesticides whereas other succulents can be killed. If you are going to treat a rare and precious house plant with an insecticide, do it cautiously until you are confident that the plant will come to no harm. If several plants are involved, treat one or two plants first and leave them for a week before going on to treat the rest.

Suitability – for Pests

A positive identification of the pest will make control more sure. When the pest is unknown, advice can usually be obtained from local or national gardening societies, or from books in the local library. A knowledge of the pest's biology and life cycle is often useful as this indicates the best time to take control measures. An example of this is the raspberry beetle which is at its most vulnerable when the adults are laying eggs. This stage occurs long before the damage to the fruit is noticed.

Insecticides vary in their ability to control

different stages in a pest's life-cycle. For example, a natural insecticide will kill adult greenhouse whitefly but it will not kill the whitefly's eggs or larvae. This particular pest's life-cycle is so short that all stages – eggs, larvae and fly – are present at the same time and this means that the pesticide will have to be re-applied to kill the adults from the original larvae or eggs before they in turn have a chance to lay eggs. On the other hand, greenfly, which also have a short life-cycle, do not usually have an egg stage and the immature stages are simply miniature versions of the adult. This means that all stages of the life-cycle can be controlled by one application of a pesticide.

Plant Diseases

Diseases of plants are caused by parasitic fungi, bacteria and viruses. Collectively these are known as plant pathogens and most are restricted to relatively few host plants which are often closely related botanically. The diseases can be classified according to the type of organism causing the trouble but, as this is often impossible to tell outside the laboratory, it makes more sense to classify them according to the symptoms they produce. Many, for example red core of strawberries, have common names which describe the symptoms.

Fungi Disease fungi are themselves plants but they do not have the green colouring (chlorophyll) or the vascular system of more advanced plants. Basically they consist of hyphae, or threads, which together make up the mycelium. Whether or not a fungus will thrive in a particular situation depends on the receptivity of the host plant to the fungus and suitable states of the soil, humidity and temperature. Fungi may live inside the host plant with only their fruiting bodies (which contain the spores necessary for reproduction) projecting through its surface. As fungi are so closely related to their hosts those actually living inside the host are very difficult to eradicate without harming the host itself. Other fungi, such as the powdery mildews, are more unusual – they grow superficially on leaf surfaces with only small anchors holding them in position. They are difficult, but possible, to eradicate. Prevention is much easier than cure.

Harmful fungi can be classified into two broad categories: 1) root-attacking fungi and 2) fungi attacking above ground portions of the plant. Root-attacking fungi generally live in the soil and enter plants through openings in their roots. The expression 'damping off' refers to seedlings which have been attacked by fungi entering through root ends broken during transplanting. Fungi which attack the above ground portions of plants are usually air-borne and generally enter plants through damaged surface tissue. Once fungi have entered, they reproduce rapidly and quickly become entrenched in the host plant. For example, on a cool, moist day a green healthy rose may become covered with a white mildew within eight hours.

Bacteria Most bacteria in the garden are harmless to plants and are essential for their well-being. They play an important role in the breakdown of humus in the soil and the maintenance of soil fertility – see *Soil*. Compared with fungi, relatively few bacteria cause plant diseases. Some of the more common diseases caused are: crown and leaf gall, bacterial canker of cherry and plum, fireblight and some soft rots.

Viruses Virus organisms are simpler than fungi or bacteria and can affect all types of plants. They may produce any or all the following symptoms: stunting, distortion, mottling of foliage and fruit, abnormal flowers and poor cropping. Marrows, sweet peas, lilies, strawberries and raspberries are very susceptible to infection. An unthrifty plant showing any of these symptoms should be destroyed, and in the case of soft fruit, only plants which are known to be free of viruses should be planted. Viruses are readily transmitted by vegetative propagation but unlike fungi and bacteria, they can only be spread from one plant to another by some external agency – insects, such as aphis, are often to blame.

Plant Diseases and their Control

Plant disease symptoms can be roughly divided into mildews, moulds, rots, cankers, distortions, leaf spots, rusts and root diseases. Each one is dealt with in turn below. A method of control is also suggested for each one; for further details of the chemicals involved see *Fungicides*.

Mildews

There are basically two mildews: downy and powdery.

Downy mildews Downy mildews invade plant cells and only the spore-bearing structures show on the leaf surface as a white or grey fuzz. Early stages of fungal attack can be seen as a yellowish blotching on the lower leaf surfaces of seedling brassicas, wallflowers and lettuces. These blotches are followed by a bloom of white or greyish-white spores and if left untreated the brassicas or wallflowers may be severely crippled and the lettuces may rot. Affected onion leaves wither and fall over.

Control Susceptible plants should be grown in well-drained soil on fresh ground each year and should never be allowed to become overcrowded. Zineb will control most downy mildews but dichlofluanid can be used on cauliflowers and thiram on lettuces. Diseased tissues should be burned.

American gooseberry mildew A white powdery fungal growth can be seen on young leaves, fruits and shrubs. In the late summer or early autumn the fungal growth becomes brown and felt-like and contains black spore cases. Severe dieback may result if gooseberries and other infected plants are left untreated.

Control Wash with lime sulphur, dinocap or quinomethionate just before the flowers grow, at fruit set and at fruit swelling. Benomyl can be applied to the open flowers and then twice more at two-week intervals. Do not use lime sulphur on sulphur-shy varieties – see *Edible plants*: *Fruit*.

Powdery mildews Plants suffering from these diseases are easily recognized as their leaves, stems, flowers or fruit may be covered with a white-grey powdery coating. The fungus causing the disease may be specific to the host plant – for example rose mildew will not affect any other type of plant – or it may have a wide host range attacking many types of herbaceous plants. The disease is superficial but if it is not combated it may result in a loss of leaves.

Control The fungi flourish in moist atmospheres, so avoid planting susceptible plants like roses in some part of the garden where the air circulation is known to be poor – a walled garden, for example. In greenhouses the disease can be checked by careful ventilation to reduce the humidity. Plants are more susceptible to infection when their roots are dry, so mulching and watering should help to prevent the disease. The fungicides benomyl, chloraniformethan, copper, dinocap, thiophanate-methyl and sulphur can be used on different types of plants.

Moulds

The commonest type of mould is *Botrytis cinerea*. It affects many plants and provides a great variety of symptoms which results in different names being given to the same disease. When it attacks lettuces and strawberries it produces a greyish mould which gives rise to its most common name of grey mould.

Grey mould This disease is most troublesome on strawberries, tomatoes, chrysanthemums and cyclamen but it also attacks cucumbers, melons, marrows, geraniums, roses, vines and many other plants. It may also be found on dying woody shoots where the fungus has entered through wounds caused by frost. Affected tissues die, become soft and may turn black. Later they become covered by a greyish-brown mould and rot quickly. The trouble may spread by

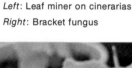
Left: Leaf miner on cinerarias
Right: Bracket fungus

contact between diseased and healthy parts of plants. The disease thrives in damp conditions and is often seen in autumn.

Control Dead and dying parts should be burnt, and greenhouses should be fumigated with tecnazene smokes and ventilated well to reduce the humidity. Benomyl, captan, dichlofluanid, thiophanate-methyl and thiram sprays can be used on various types of plants once the disease has appeared, but soft fruit should be sprayed as the first flowers open, repeating the application two or three more times at two-week intervals.

Lily disease This is caused by a species of botrytis and mainly attacks the Madonna lily *Lilium candidum*. It shows as brown blotches on the leaves and flowers, which wither from the bottom of the plant upwards and then rot. The disease is most severe in late spring and early summer.

Control This disease can usually be prevented by spraying with colloidal copper, Bordeaux mixture or benomyl as soon as the first leaves appear, repeating the application regularly until flowering. Badly affected parts of plants should be burned.

Paeony wilt This is due to another botrytis species which causes rotting at the base of paeony stems, which then collapse at ground level. The leaves and buds may also rot.

Control Affected shoots should be removed and the crowns dusted with dry Bordeaux powder. Herbaceous and tree paeonies should be sprayed regularly with captan, dichlofluanid or zineb commencing soon after they start to grow.

Tomato leaf mould This is a form of mildew and occurs on plants in cold, humid greenhouses. It can be first seen as pale yellow blotches on the upper surfaces of older leaves. The lower surfaces become covered with a greyish mould which changes colour to brownish violet.

Control Good ventilation and spraying with zineb may check the disease, but it is better to grow a variety resistant to the trouble.

Rots

Any disease which causes the disintegration and liquefaction of cells can be called a rot.

Brown rot Various fungi can cause rotting of top fruit, but brown rot is the most troublesome. It attacks apples, cherries, pears, plums and occasionally peaches and nectarines. The disease mainly infects the fruits which become covered with buff (light brown) coloured patches of fungus often arranged in concentric rings. Eventually the whole fruit rots, then withers and may hang on the tree in a mummified condition, for many months. Fruit spurs may also be attacked and killed.

Cucumber mosaic virus in courgette

Control Prompt removal of diseased fruits and dead shoots should control this disease. If not, spraying with tar oil wash in January and with captan at three-week intervals from late July to September will keep it down. During late summer sprays of thiophanate-methyl may check losses in store.

Soft rot This is characterized by a wet, evil-smelling yellowish rot which attacks the roots or stems of carrots, celery, cabbages, seakale, onions and a number of ornamental plants. It is caused by bacteria which enter through injured tissues and the disease may occur in the ground or in store. Blighted potatoes and bruised stored organs, including dahlia tubers, can be affected. Iris rhizomes and the crowns of pot plants during the growing season are also susceptible.

Control Diseased parts should be removed and burned and dry Bordeaux powder applied to cut surfaces. Drier conditions should be maintained.

Tomato and potato blight This is another rot. It causes black blotches on leaves which quickly spread so that the whole haulm withers. The disease may pass into the fruit and tubers, which rot rapidly.

Control Sprays of colloidal copper, Bordeaux mixture or maneb applied in July or August should check the disease, but in wet seasons efficient control may be impossible to achieve.

Cankers

This is a name given to a number of diseases which cause the skin of plants to split and decay. It is most frequently found on trees such as apples and cherries where the bark splits and the diseased area becomes covered by enlarged tissue growth. If it is allowed to go unchecked the growth may encircle a whole branch which may die. Cankers often enter plants through open wounds or through dead shoots resulting from bad pruning.

Fruit tree cankers Apple cankers are deep with the inner tissues exposed and occur on shoots and branches. They often result in dieback. Bacterial cankers of *Prunus* species, including plums and cherries, show as flattened elongated cankers exuding gum. Again dieback can occur.

Control Dying branches and diseased tissues should be cut out, taking the cut right back to healthy wood, and the wounds covered with a protective paint. Diseased apple trees should be sprayed with Bordeaux mixture just before leaf fall, at 50 per cent leaf fall, and at bud burst. For *Prunus* species, this fungicide should be applied in mid-August, mid-September and mid-October.

Fireblight This disease also causes cankers and progressive dieback. The flowers become blackened and shrivelled followed by the leaves becoming brown and withered and the shoots die back. Unlike canker, the leaves do not usually fall from affected branches of apples, pears and related ornamentals like sorbus and cotoneaster. In the UK if the disease is suspected, the Ministry of Agriculture must be notified and treatment will be recommended.

Silver leaf This disease mainly attacks plums but may also affect other fruit trees and Portuguese laurel. The fungus enters through a wound and causes dieback of shoots. It can kill branches or a whole tree if it is left untreated. A change in colour of the leaves from green to silvery green is an early symptom. Affected branches have a brown or purplish stain in the tissues and after the wood is dead the spore-bearing bodies appear on its surface as flattish, purplish-mauve growths. At this stage the disease can be passed on to other plants.

Control Affected branches should be cut out several centimetres behind where the stain ceases. Diseased trees may recover if well cared for.

Distortions

A distortion is some sort of unusual growth or swelling on the root, leaf or shoots of a plant.

Azalea gall This shows on the young, developing leaves or flower buds as swollen pinkish or greenish galls which later become covered with a white bloom of spores.

Control Galls should be removed and the shrubs sprayed with colloidal copper, Bordeaux mixture or zineb.

Club root This disease attacks cabbages and other brassicas including turnips and wallflowers. It is caused by a fungus which can lie dormant in the soil for many years. It is most troublesome on acid and wet soils and results in a swollen and distorted root system which eventually decays with an unpleasant odour. Affected plants usually wilt.

Control Liming and draining the soil will help plants and they can be coated with a paste made from calomel or have their planting holes dusted with four per cent calomel dust. The best treatment is to sterilize the soil with dazomet.

Peach leaf curl This is a disease of peaches and related trees caused by a fungus which attacks young leaves which turn pink, swell up and distort and then turn white and brown before falling prematurely.

Control Lime sulphur, colloidal copper or Bordeaux mixture applied twice in January or February and again at leaf fall will control it.

Leaf Spots

There are many leaf-spotting fungi, and most are specific to certain host plants. Rose black spot and apple and pear scab are the most common. Though the fungi causing these diseases are different, the cures are more or less the same.

Rose black spot This shows as round black blotches on yellowing leaves and will not affect any other type of plant. The spots increase in size until the leaf falls off. As with most diseases of this type, the fungus overwinters on fallen leaves, which should be raked up and burned.

Control Benomyl, captan, dichlofluanid, maneb or thiophanate-methyl applied initially as the leaves unfold and then regularly through the summer should check the disease. Removing the top few centimetres of soil from the rose bed in winter, burning it and replacing it with fresh soil in which roses have not been grown will help to get rid of over-wintering spores. The bed should be thickly mulched in spring as growth starts.

Apple and pear scab This shows as brown or blackish scabs on the fruit which often cracks. Olive-green spots appear on the leaves which may drop prematurely. Diseased shoots become blistered.

Control Remove any blistered shoots and spray with chemicals listed under rose black spot.

Rust

This is a name given to a range of fungal diseases. The one thing they have in common is that they all produce rusty coloured growths on the stems or leaves of affected plants. The rust spots are, in fact, brown, orange or yellow powdery masses of spores and the exact colour depends on the rust and the host. Rust affects antirrhinums, carnations, chrysanthemums, hollyhocks, mint, pelargoniums and roses. The size of the rust spots varies from small spots on antirrhinums, carnations and chrysanthemums to larger pustules on hollyhocks and mint.

Control Maneb may control some of these diseases though zineb is best on pelargoniums. Rust-resistant antirrhinums should be grown and new hollyhock plants raised every second year. All affected leaves or shoots should be removed and burned immediately. With mint, it is probably best to remove and burn the whole plant.

Root Diseases

Several fungi are soil-borne and attack susceptible plants such as petunias, China asters, pansies, polyanthus, sweet peas and beans causing them to wilt.

Black and violet root rots Both diseases cause affected roots to decay and turn either black or violet or purple. Black root rot affects peas, pansies and violets. Violet root rot is found mainly on vegetables such as carrots, beetroot and potatoes.

Control Rotation of vegetables and bedding plants should prevent these troubles but, once they have become established, soil sterilization with formalin or dazomet is the only cure.

Honey fungus This is the commonest root parasite and often causes the rapid death of woody plants. White fungal threads can be seen beneath the bark at ground level. The disease gets its name from honey-coloured, umbrella-shaped toadstools which appear on the soil surface near affected plants. Trees and shrubs are often mistakenly diagnosed to be suffering from drought as the above ground symptoms are similar to those caused by lack of water.

Control There is no totally effective cure but treatment of the soil with creosote sometimes works. Diseased bushes and trees should be removed and burned and specialist advice sought.

Bulb Diseases

These are often soil-borne. Tulip fire shows as a grey mould on rotting leaves, shoots and flowers. The fungus forms small black resting bodies on the bulb. Another fungus which causes grey bulb rot of tulips and hyacinths also forms black resting bodies on the bulbs, but in this case, the bulb rots in the ground so that no shoots emerge. Similar diseases occur on narcissus.

Control Unhealthy plants should be lifted and any bulbs showing rotting or bearing small black hard structures on or between their scales should be burned. The remainder should be dusted with quintozene which should also be raked into the soil on fresh ground before replanting. Gladioli are subject to numerous soil-borne diseases, most of which cause yellowing or even collapse of the foliage, sometimes accompanied by rotting of the corms. Control measures are as for tulip fire, but in addition the corms should be dipped in a solution of benomyl or captan before storing or planting.

Turf Diseases

There are five diseases which can cause browning or even death of turf.

Dollar spot Small patches about 5cm (2in) across appear on the surface of the lawn. These patches are brown at first but later become bleached.

Control Water the affected patches with calomel mixed with water and repeat at monthly intervals. Quintozene may also be used.

Fairy rings This disease produces a characteristic three-zoned ring on the lawn. The outer and inner zones are covered with green, vigorous grass while in the zone between them the grasses are brown and dying. The fruit bodies may appear in late summer towards the outer part of the ring.
Control Destroy the affected turf, spike the soil beneath and soak it with formalin.
Ophiobolus patch This disease produces depressed, circular straw or bronze coloured patches about 5cm (2in) across. Affected areas may increase in size and coalesce with others.
Control This disease is difficult to cure but it has been reported in North America that chlordane is effective.
Red thread This disease can be seen as pinkish patches from 8 to 15cm (3 to 6in) in diameter composed of dead grass with coral-red fungus growths.
Control Quintozene will give control of the disease.
Fusarium patch The symptoms are large brown patches covered with whitish fungus. Mycelium may be seen particularly after a snow fall which gives the disease its other common name of snow mould.
Control As for dollar spot.

Reversion

A lot of confusion surrounds this term as it is used to describe a number of different and quite separate occurrences.

The term may have originally been used to describe the dominance of an original parent species when varieties bred from it are allowed to cross pollinate and give rise to a new generation without selection. Under such circumstances there can be a high proportion of parent-type offspring and an almost total 'reversion' to the dominant type in the next generation.

The term is also commonly used to describe a vegetative (non-sexual) phenomenon. When a variety produces a flower of a different colour (chrysanthemums for example) or when a variegated shoot appears on an otherwise green shrub, it is known as producing a sport. Even apple trees have been known to sport fruit of a different colour on one branch. Such sports are often selected and increased vegetatively but, in turn, they are quite likely to bear flowers or shoots that 'sport back' to the original. They revert in fact. In most cases the sport can be preserved by the timely removal of reverted parts.

A further example of the use of the term reversion is to describe the change in character of a plant severely affected by a virus. Plant viruses can cause leaves to become uncharacteristic, even wild-looking. This can occur in tomatoes and strawberries and in black currant bushes.

Black currants suffer from a widespread virus that gives a nettle-head appearance to affected shoots and alters the vein pattern of leaves. This virus disease has unfortunately been called reversion, presumably because the leaves appear to have 'gone back' or reverted. In fact the virus is transmitted by a mite that lays its eggs in unfolding buds causing them to blow-out. For this reason the mite is known as big-bud mite. Affected black currant bushes produce more leaves than normal which are smaller, have fewer lobes and have fewer side veins branching from the main vein than in normal plants. The simplest way of telling whether a bush is infected is to count the number of veins on each side of the main vein. If fewer than five pairs are found in the height of summer and the leaves are crowded together at the ends of the branches looking like a nettle head, then it is likely the bush has the disease. There is no cure for the disease. Dig up infected bushes and burn them. To prevent the disease spreading, take steps to deal with the big-bud mite, aphis and other sucking insects which could transmit the disease.

Damping-off

This is a general name for a number of fungal diseases which attack the stems of young seedlings. These fungi thrive in damp, airless conditions, where weakly-growing plants are most at risk. Included in this group are *Pythium* species and *Phytophthora* rots, which attack seedlings close to soil level causing them to wilt and fall over in a short time. The bases of the seedling stems look dark and rotted. Damping-off diseases can also attack the stems of older plants, notably tomatoes. The disease is common under glass but rare in the open.

Although a number of fungi are responsible for damping off, it is not necessary for the gardener to recognize one from the other. Prevention and treatment is the same for all of them and is basically good hygiene and careful plant raising. The fungi are soil-borne so loam used for sowing mixes should be sterilized either by heat or with formalin, or soilless mixes should be used. Containers should always be perfectly clean or sterilized. Damping-off can be carried on seeds, so it is a wise precaution to treat them with a dressing containing captan or thiram before sowing. A dense mass of seedlings traps damp air and encourages damping-off, so sow them thinly and prick them out as soon as possible. The fungi may be carried in water and it is best to avoid using water which has been standing in the greenhouse or in a water butt for some time.

Give the seedlings as much ventilation as is safe and do not overwater them.

When damping-off does occur, an area of seedlings is usually affected. These should be carefully removed with the soil beneath them, and the remainder watered with Cheshunt compound, captan or thiram.

Fungicides

A true fungicide is a chemical which will kill a fungus without harming its plant host. In fact very few true fungicides are available to amateurs and the more generally accepted definition of a fungicide is any chemical which is effective in inhibiting, eradicating or preventing the fungal infection of plants.

Fungicides such as lime sulphur, which will kill powdery mildews, are said to have eradicant properties – they kill through contact with the fungus on the plant surface but do little harm to fungi growing inside plants. Formalin might be thought of as a soil-acting counterpart. Most garden fungicides merely inhibit fungal growth and act, therefore, as protectants and must be applied before infection occurs.

The first fungicides used were inorganic compounds and a few of this type are still available, but the majority now are organic compounds.

Inorganic Fungicides

These are mainly based on three chemicals: copper, sulphur or mercury.

Copper Fungicides

Copper salts are poisonous, but copper fungicides present few toxicity hazards to man if used properly. They must, however, be kept out of ponds and waterways as they can kill fish. Some copper fungicides are phytotoxic in that they can scorch the foliage of plants such as apples, pears and roses. They are, therefore, now used on a decreasing scale, but the following formulations are still available to amateurs.

Bordeaux mixture This is essentially a mixture of copper sulphate and lime. The small retail packs contain either the ingredients already mixed or in separate layers in the tin. The latter type of formulation is better as the chemicals are not actually mixed until the fungicide is to be used. The standard formula is 20g of copper sulphate and 20g of hydrated lime mixed in 2·5l of water (1¼oz of each chemical to 1gal of water). It should be used fresh as stored mixtures lose their adhesiveness. A reduction in the amount of lime will cause less spotting and burning of leaves. This fungicide controls a wide range of diseases including specific diseases such as azalea gall, clematis wilt and lily disease. It is also effective against leaf spots on many types of plants, bacterial canker and peach leaf curl on ornamental and fruiting *Prunus*, apple canker, raspberry diseases and potato and tomato blight. Avoid using Bordeaux mixture in wet, cool weather. Dry formulations of Bordeaux mixture can be used for dusting crowns of plants to prevent collar rot (caused by bacteria) or paeony wilt. Dahlia tubers can be dusted with it before storing them to prevent storage rots.

Cheshunt compound This fungicide is made up of two parts of copper sulphate to eleven parts of powdered ammonium carbonate. It can be used to control damping-off by applying it as a solution in water to soil before sowing or to seedlings after germination. It can also be used to give partial control of soil-borne diseases which affect bedding plants.

Other formulations of copper Powders which can be mixed with water (wettable powders) and liquid formulations of copper are also available and can be used as alternatives to Bordeaux mixture.

Sulphur Fungicides

These are relatively safe to humans and animals, but unfortunately can injure plants, particularly 'sulphur-shy' varieties of apples, pears, gooseberries and black currants. The following types are sold in small packs.

Sulphur sprays Wettable powder and liquid formulations can be used to control apple scab on certain varieties, but they are now usually used only to control powdery mildews on chrysanthemums and peaches.

Sulphur dusts Dusts of different fineness are sold as green and yellow sulphur and as flowers of sulphur. These can be used to control powdery mildew on strawberries and for the prevention of storage rots of dahlia tubers. They are sometimes vaporized and used in greenhouses to control grape mildew and powdery mildew in begonias. They can also be burned in empty greenhouses to fumigate them.

Lime sulphur This is very effective against peach leaf curl and can be used to control the same diseases as pure sulphur, but it is actually a solution of calcium polysulphides. It can also be used to destroy insects in their dormant stage. It stains buildings and should not be used when temperatures exceed 30°C (85°F).

Mercury Fungicides

These need careful handling as they are very poisonous, but some formulations are still very useful for the control of certain diseases.

Calomel (mercurous chloride) This is the most readily available fungicide which will give any control of club root disease of brassicas and onion white rot. It is usually sold as a four per cent dust and is used as a soil dressing.

Mercurial turf fungicides and turf sand These usually contain mercurous chloride as the active ingredient and can be applied as dusts to control such common turf diseases as red thread and snow mould (fusarium patch) and can also be applied to lichens.

Organic Fungicides

Most organic fungicides are highly complex substances. Some are closely related to each other and they can be classified into five groups.

Dithiocarbamates

Most dithiocarbamates can be irritating to the skin, eyes, nose and mouth. Although this is a large and probably the most important group of fungicides introduced in recent years, only those listed below can be used by gardeners.

Dazomet This fungicide is at present only available in large commercial packs. It is, however, such an effective and easily used soil sterilant that it is worthwhile buying it for use in gardens where club root and soil-borne disease of leguminous crops are troublesome. It is applied as granules which should be watered in and can be used both under glass and outside. It is best used between April and October, but can be applied later providing the treated area is kept covered with plastic sheeting for several months during the winter. Under glass, allow at least eight weeks before planting, outside less time is necessary. Dazomet also controls seedling weeds and couch.

Ferbam In North America this is one of the principal dithiocarbamate fungicides. It can be used to give general control of spot diseases including black spot on roses and will control rust on apples. It is available as a wettable powder and has virtually no toxicity to mammals.

Maneb This is a very efficient fungicide sold as a wettable powder for the control of several diseases including rust and black-spot on roses, tulip fire, leaf-spot diseases and tomato leaf mould. It is particularly valuable against blight on tomatoes and potatoes as it does not harden the foliage as do copper fungicides.

Thiram This fungicide can be used to control grey mould on ornamentals, lettuce and soft fruit, but, to avoid possible taint, it should not be applied to fruits to be processed. It will also control other diseases of ornamentals, fruit trees and bushes and lettuce downy mildew. Thiram alone is sold as a liquid, but it is also available in combination with insecticides and is a constituent of a hormone rooting powder.

Zineb This fungicide will control many diseases of ornamentals, vegetables and some fruit diseases including blight, brown root rot, botrytis, mildews, leaf spots and rusts. It is sold in small retail packs as a wettable powder.

Dinitro Fungicides

Although several dinitro fungicides are used in commercial horticulture only dinocap is available to amateurs. This fungicide was originally introduced as an acaricide (a chemical which kills mites) but is now more commonly used to control powdery mildews on ornamentals, fruit and vegetables. Wettable powder, liquid and smoke formulations are on the market. It can be irritating to skin, eyes and nose, is dangerous to fish and will damage some chrysanthemum varieties.

Chloronitrobenzenes

There are two of these useful fungicides available to amateurs.

Tecnazene This fungicide is very volatile and is, therefore, not very persistent in the open. It is used as a fumigant under glass for the control of grey mould on ornamentals and vegetables.

Quintozene (called PCNB in North America) This fungicide persists for a long time in the soil and is useful for the control of certain soil-borne fungi especially those affecting bulbs. It can also be used for dusting bulbs. Cucurbits may be damaged if planted in soil where quintozene has been previously worked in. It is also sold as a wettable powder for the control of turf diseases.

Systemic Fungicides

A true systemic fungicide is one which is absorbed and translocated by the plant (travels around inside the plant) which thereby becomes systemically toxic to the fungus. However, the fungicides sold to amateurs as systemics are only partially so. They are not translocated very far, particularly within woody plants, and have to be applied almost as frequently as other types. The following four 'systemics' are sold in small packs.

Benomyl This fungicide can be used as a spray, drench or dip to control a very wide range of diseases on ornamentals, fruit, vegetables and turf including apple and pear scab, leaf spots, powdery mildews and the grey mould fungus *Botrytis cinerea*. Unfortunately, strains of *Botrytis* and other fungi which are resistant to benomyl have developed in many localities so that it has lost its effectiveness for the control of these diseases. In some circumstances excessive use of benomyl, particularly on bulbous plants, has resulted in other fungi which are normally considered to be of no significance, causing more serious troubles.

Thiophanate-methyl This fungicide is very closely related to benomyl and therefore controls the same types of diseases. Strains of fungi resistant to one fungicide are also resistant to the other.

Triforine This is a comparatively new fungicide and is unrelated to the two former fungicides so that no strains of fungi resistant to it have yet developed. It also has slightly more systemic properties so is taken up better by woody plants and does not have to be applied so frequently. It is sold for the control of powdery mildew and black spot on roses, but can also be used against powdery mildews and certain other diseases of ornamentals and fruit.

Chloraniformethan Few formulations of this fungicide are available and it is generally sold to amateurs solely for the control of rose powdery mildew. It is unrelated to the previous fungicides.

Miscellaneous Fungicides

This group contains all those fungicides unrelated both to those in the groups above and also to each other.

Captan This fungicide can be used as a spray, dip, drench or seed dressing for the control of foliage and bulbous diseases and soil- and seed-borne fungi. It will not control powdery mildews so it is somewhat specific. It is of low toxicity to warm-blooded animals, but harmful to fish. It can produce a taint and should not be used on fruit for processing.

Dichlofluanid This fungicide is sold as a wettable powder against rose black spot, but controls a wide range of diseases on soft fruit including grey mould, although it must not be used on strawberries grown under glass or plastic sheets. It will also control certain other diseases of ornamentals and vegetables. Dichlofluanid is harmful to fish.

Dichloran This fungicide is available in the USA and effectively controls botrytis on lettuce and ornamental plants. It is usually applied as four per cent dust.

Forpet This fungicide is sold in the USA and is effective against mildews, black spot and many fungal diseases of fruit trees and bushes. It is sold as a wettable powder.

Formaldehyde Although this chemical is poisonous, irritating to skin, eyes, nose and mouth and must not be used near growing plants, it is a very useful substance for general disinfection of potting soils, glasshouse structures and implements and for the sterilization of soil under glass and outside. After treatment light soils must be left vacant for three weeks and heavy soils up to six weeks. When it is used as a soil drench 40 per cent commercial formaldehyde should be diluted with 50 parts of water and this used at the rate of $50 l/m^2$ (1 gal/sq ft). The soil should be covered for 24 hours and the area isolated.

Quinomethionate (USA) This fungicide can be used to control powdery mildews on roses, black currants, gooseberries and many pot plants under glass. It is sold as a wettable powder and is also effective as an acaricide for controlling red spider mites.

Choosing a Fungicide

Other chemicals can be used as fungicides, but since they are not sold specifically for this purpose they have not been included. Some diseases can be controlled by several different fungicides. It is not always possible to determine which will be the most useful for controlling a particular disease, as the effectiveness of some fungicides depends to a certain extent on the environmental conditions. It may, therefore, be necessary to experiment with different fungicides to find which gives the best control.

In the UK, whenever possible buy products which have been approved under the Agricultural Chemicals Approved Scheme run by the Ministry of Agriculture. These are identified by the approval mark consisting of a capital A surmounted by a crown, which guarantees that the products are safe when used according to the instructions and effective against the diseases listed on the label. However, some fungicides of very long standing, though safe and efficient, have never been submitted for approval and some of the newer fungicides have not been available long enough to collect the evidence necessary for approval. There is no reason why these safe and effective non-approved fungicides should not be used, and once a fungicide has been found to give good control of a disease and has not proved too expensive, there is no point in changing to one of a different type. In North America consult Department of Agriculture bulletins or your county agricultural agent.

To minimize any possible harmful effects arising from misuse of fungicides the following general rules should be observed.

Chemicals should be used only when really necessary.

A chemical which is recommended for the particular purpose in mind should be selected.

The instructions on the manufacturer's label must be followed implicitly.

Spraying and dusting should not be done in windy weather.

All equipment must be thoroughly cleaned after spraying.

Brown rot on apples and pears
Opposite: Rose mildew

Plant Disorders

Plant disorders are nearly always due to adverse cultural conditions and can arise as a result of incorrect planting or sowing, under or over watering, malnutrition, too dry or moist an atmosphere, too low or high a temperature and poor light. In general plants affected by one or more of these troubles show discoloration of foliage, lack of growth, poor cropping and even dieback. However, certain specific disorders are associated with definite unsuitable conditions as described below.

Irregular Watering

Tomatoes affected by irregular watering show a small circular brown spot at the base of the fruit – a condition known as blossom end rot. The spot usually increases in size fairly rapidly and becomes black. It is the result of a collapse of some fruit cells through lack of moisture. Appearance of this disorder indicates that two to three weeks earlier the soil was allowed to become too dry. Later fruits should develop normally, once a regular watering programme is maintained.

Vegetables and fruit often split when heavy rain follows a long period of drought. Carrots, in particular, split when they are watered artificially irregularly.

Dry Soil

Bud drop of camellias is usually due to drought at the time the flower buds were developing in early autumn. Mulching and watering should prevent this trouble from occurring.

Bulbous plants affected by drought at a critical stage of growth may suffer from blindness as the flower buds wither without opening. Drought can also lead to splitting of peach stones with subsequent rotting of the fruit.

Waterlogging

Affected plants die back as the roots are killed by lack of oxygen and show a bluish-black discoloration. In severe cases susceptible plants may be killed. Shoots of waterlogged plants often show peeling of the bark, which becomes papery. It is best to prevent such trouble by improving the texture of heavy soils and draining where possible.

Oedema is a trouble which can be due to waterlogging or too moist an atmosphere. It shows as small corky outgrowths on the lower leaf surfaces of ivy-leaved pelargoniums and camellias. The affected leaves should not be removed but drier conditions should be maintained.

Malnutrition

Most plants require feeding at some stage of growth but perennial plants, including trees and shrubs, should be fed at least once a year with a complete fertilizer. Neglected plants show discoloured foliage, premature leaf fall and dieback. It is often not possible to determine which food material is lacking, unless certain specific symptoms appear. Thus a deficiency of boron causes brown rings in swedes and turnips and browning and splitting of celery. A shortage of calcium within apple fruits results in bitter pit, which shows as small brown spots in the flesh. This trouble occurs on young trees on light hungry soils, particularly in a dry summer. It may be prevented by feeding, mulching and watering to keep growth even, accompanied by spraying with calcium nitrate in midsummer.

Greenback is a common disorder of tomatoes grown under glass. The fruits remain greenish around the stem and do not ripen evenly. It appears to be due to inadequate or unbalanced feeding and is most likely to occur in soils which lack potash and magnesium. Some varieties are highly susceptible while others are almost totally resistant.

Soil alkalinity can also lead to malnutrition as iron, manganese and magnesium are made unavailable to plants in soils having a high pH. Affected plants show yellowing between the veins and in severe cases the leaves may be almost white. Acid-loving shrubs such as rhododendrons and camellias are particularly susceptible to this trouble but all types can be affected where the pH is very high. It can be corrected by applying chelated compounds or fritted trace elements and by digging in acidic materials such as peat, crushed bracken or chemicals to reduce the alkalinity of the soil.

Chemical Damage

Careless use of chemicals may cause damage to plants. In particular, misuse of hormone weedkillers may cause severe distortion of foliage, but affected plants usually recover in due course.

There are numerous other disorders which can affect plants, and many diseases are worse on plants suffering from adverse cultural conditions. It is essential, therefore, to try to encourage healthy growth by good horticultural practices.

Suckers

These are growths arising from below ground, either from the lower sections of the main stem or stems, or from far-reaching roots. They are most frequently encountered in grafted plants and are generally regarded as undesirable.

The ability of roots to make suckers can be a considerable asset as it enables plants to be propagated vegetatively from their roots. Many herbaceous border plants can be increased this way, phlox, hollyhocks and gaillardias, for example. Raspberry canes often 'spawn' from their roots at some distance from the trained row. These suckers can be dug up and used to establish a fresh row of canes. In most cases, however, raspberries produce many more suckers than are needed and they have to be chop-ped off or dug out annually. Apart from the raspberry, few other woody garden plants throw useful suckers from their own roots. The elm tree and *Rhus typhina* are notable exceptions.

Suckers often grow from the roots of a stock plant on which the garden variety has been budded or grafted. These suckers will resemble the character of the rootstock and if they are left to grow they will eventually become a threat to the survival of the garden variety above. Roses which are budded on to 'wild' rose stock often produce suckers. These are usually quite easy to distinguish from the named variety as they nearly always have coarser, paler, smaller leaves and more small spines on their stems. These distinguishing features are helpful in deciding whether a basal growth is a sucker from below the union of stock and scion or a desirable new shoot of the actual variety coming from the scion at or just below soil level. Any shoot which appears to be a sucker should be traced back to its origin and torn off from the root with a sharp pull. Do not cut it off at soil level as a new growth bud (or buds) will develop to replace it and the trouble will be compounded. A flush of suckers may also arise at the base of grafted lilacs, magnolias and rhododendrons and should be treated similarly.

Bark Splitting

As a tree or shrub grows the outer bark layer is normally replaced so that it grows and expands with the tree. Under certain circumstances a tree's growth can slow down so much that the bark hardens and is unable to expand in the normal way and effectively begins to strangle the tree. This can happen when a tree goes through a period of impeded drainage causing damage to the roots or a lack of moisture or plant foods in the soil. Trees in this condition are said to be bark bound and the condition can be relieved by bark splitting. Sometimes a tree will relieve the tension itself by splitting naturally but if it does not the bark should be split longitudinally using a sharp knife. The split should be superficial penetrating through the bark to the cambium layer below. The best time to do this is in spring just as the tree starts to grow.

Weeds

In the broadest sense any plant which grows where it is not wanted can be called a weed. It is usual to look upon weeds as wild herbaceous plants but weeds can be woody, such as brambles, or even plants which were originally grown in gardens and have escaped from cultivation to become widely troublesome.

Like other garden plants, weeds can be divided into two groups – annuals and perennials.

Annual weeds complete their life cycle – germination of seed, growing, flowering, development of new seed and dying – within one growing season. Most annual weeds grow rapidly and seed freely. Some, such as groundsel, can produce three or four crops of weeds in the same season.

Perennial weeds continue their growth from one year to the next having an annual period of dormancy. The stems of herbaceous (non-woody) perennials die back to soil level at the end of their growing period but, by storing food in bulbs, tubers, fleshy rhizomes or roots, they can survive winter (or a period of drought) and resume growing when more favourable weather comes. Woody-stemmed perennial weeds, such as brambles and unwanted tree seedlings, do not rely on storing food in their roots but manage to overwinter on reserves of food stored in their branches. Perennials often multiply both by seed and vegetatively. Chickweed seeds, for example, will germinate at almost any time of the growing season and when its stems are cut each piece is capable of rooting and growing into an individual plant.

Annual weeds will generally be most troublesome in those parts of the garden that are heavily cropped and frequently replanted or sown such as vegetable plots and flower borders. In these parts of the garden the soil is too frequently cultivated to allow perennials to become established. In many cases, seeds lie dormant until conditions are just right for them to germinate and frequent cultivation can continually bring new seeds to the surface of the soil.

Perennial weeds will usually be most troublesome in areas where garden plants remain undisturbed for several years, for instance shrubberies, herbaceous borders, rock gardens and fruit gardens. In these areas, digging to remove deep-rooted perennial weeds might endanger the roots of the garden plants. Perennials with a low, spreading habit, such as plantain and daisy, can compete effectively with grass under closely mown conditions.

Controlling Weeds

There are many reasons for controlling weeds. Firstly, they are obviously unsightly in flower beds and borders, although many may be attractive when growing in fields or woods. Secondly, they strongly compete with cultivated plants for all the essentials of plant life: water, nutrients, light and space to develop. This means that plants, such as carrot and onion which germinate and grow slowly, can be quickly smothered by weed competition in the early stages of their life and this seriously affects both the quality and yield of the vegetables. Weeds left to grow unrestricted – in uncultivated parts of the garden, perhaps – can pose a risk to nearby garden or greenhouse plants by acting as hosts for disease, virus and pests, such as aphis, carrying over infestations from one year to the next.

Weeds can be removed, killed or prevented from growing by mechanical, cultural or chemical methods.

The simplest way of dealing with weeds is to remove them mechanically either by digging them up individually or by hoeing their tops off. Digging weeds up is an effective way of dealing with annuals and over a period of time it is effective against perennials too. But many perennials will regrow unless every bit of their root system is removed and this can be difficult to achieve. Hoeing is an efficient way of dealing with annuals but it must be done before the weeds set seed.

An abundance of one particular type of weed may mean something is wrong with the soil conditions. Horsetail could indicate that the soil is acidic, too heavy and badly needs its drainage improving. Docks and sorrel can also indicate a poorly drained, acid soil, Coltsfoot, dandelions and plantains thrive on heavy clay soils, sheep's sorrel and spurrey can indicate an acid soil or a light, sandy one and scarlet pimpernel and bladder campion could indicate alkalinity. Improving the soil conditions can effectively eradicate many of these weeds, but it may mean changing one weed problem into another, but different, one. For controlling weeds by chemical means see *Herbicides*.

Moss

There are many different genera and species of moss – in the UK alone around 600 are known. In some areas of the world they form the major vegetation of the land. Moss can grow where other plants find life impossible – in drains, gutters or on brickwork. But the gardener will probably find moss most troublesome when it grows on lawns. Invasion of a lawn by moss usually indicates that the soil is rather poor and wet with poor aeration. It may also be too acid or too alkaline. These are all conditions in which moss thrives but grasses find life difficult. Mosses need less light than grass so they usually inhabit the more shaded areas of a garden and it is not uncommon to see mosses spreading in the poor light conditions of late autumn.

Basically two types of moss are found on lawns. Mat-forming mosses can be found when the grass is kept cut very short and fern (or feather) mosses are usually found in longer grass. Mosses reproduce by spores which they produce twice a year – in spring and in autumn – just after their periods of active growth. The best way to eradicate moss on a lawn is to improve the soil conditions and encourage grass to grow again.

Poor drainage and poor aeration are the first things to tackle. If the lawn is laid over heavy soil in a natural hollow it may be impossible to improve drainage sufficiently, but most lawns will benefit from aeration of the top 5 to 10cm (2 to 4in) and removal of the dead surface 'mat'. Aeration is best achieved by removing plugs of soil and filling the holes left behind with a gritty compost (or a soil/sand/peat mixture). A hollow-tine fork is ideal for this. A certain degree of aeration can be achieved by using spiked rollers or by making holes with an ordinary garden fork. Again, gritty compost should be swept into the surface. To remove the mat, rake the lawn in spring and autumn with a wire lawn rake.

There is relatively little to be done about shade. Most grasses like full sun but *Poa trivialis* is more tolerant than most to shaded situations. Once drainage is improved, feed the lawn annually, and mow it lightly but often (though infrequently during dry spells). Avoid compaction through over-enthusiastic use of a heavy roller.

Moss can also be controlled by chemical means. Lawn sand is the standard treatment. This is a mixture of ammonium sulphate, ferrous sulphate and sand and it is usually applied at the rate of $140g/m^2$ (4oz/sq yd) in early spring when the grass is moist. If it does not rain within 48 hours of application, the lawn should be watered well. Lawn sand often scorches the grass and blackens the moss but the grass soon recovers. Dead moss should be raked away after a week or two. Mercurized lawn sand contains mercurous chloride as well as the other two chemicals. The mercury kills the moss spores and gives much longer lasting control than lawn sand alone.

Moss growing on garden soil can be dispersed by cultivation, on paths and hard surfaces it can be cleared by washing it down with caustic domestic chemicals. All these chemicals should be washed into drains and not on to the soil.

Herbicides

A chemical used to kill or control weeds is called a herbicide. You may want to use these in preference to cultural or mechanical control because they involve less effort and may be able to deal with problems which the other methods do not solve satisfactorily – weeds in paths or drives, for example.

How Herbicides Work

The chemicals used in herbicides fall broadly into three categories: contact, translocated and residual (or soil-acting). The branded products available in the shops may simply contain a single weedkilling chemical or may be mixtures of chemicals generally having different modes of action. Herbicides may also be selective or non-selective. Selective herbicides will kill some types of plant but not others. Non-selective (or total) herbicides kill all forms of plant life.

Contact These herbicides are applied to the foliage and destroy only those green parts of plants they come into direct contact with. They are most effective in killing annual weeds but, because they act by contact, complete coverage is essential. They will destroy the leaves and green stems of perennial weeds but have little or no effect on underground parts. They can be selective, such as ioxynil which can be used on newish lawns to control weeds without seriously harming the grass, or non-selective, such as paraquat and diquat mixtures which kill all green foliage with which they come into contact.

Contact herbicides usually have little or no residual effect in the soil.

Translocated These are usually absorbed into the weed through its leaves and stems and are able to move around inside the weed even into the roots of perennial weeds. Some translocated herbicides such as MCPA, 2,4-D, mecoprop, dicamba, dichlorprop and 2,4,5-T are selective. These are the so-called hormone herbicides and can be used on lawns to kill weeds but not the grass. They are most effective against broad-leaved weeds which have a large leaf area for chemical absorption; they tend to run off the narrow, erect grass leaves and little is absorbed. Grasses can, however, also be harmed by over-application. 2,4,5-T is often used to control woody-stemmed or shrubby weeds and docks and nettles. It is rarely used on lawns. These chemicals usually remain in the soil for two or three months, after which it is safe to plant. Dalapon is another weedkiller which is selective when it is applied at low concentrations. Like this it can be used among fruit trees and bushes to kill couch grass but it must be applied when the trees or bushes are dormant and least susceptible to harm. Other translocated herbicides such as aminotriazole (amitrole), ammonium sulphamate and sodium chlorate are non-selective and should not be used on, or near, ground where plants are growing. They are, however, very useful for keeping down difficult weeds in uncultivated areas. Land treated with ammonium sulphamate should not be planted for three months, with sodium chlorate for six months and with aminotriazole it is best to wait a year. Dalapon can also be used non-selectively at higher dose rates and ground treated with it should be left about two months before planting.

Residual These are taken up by plant roots and stay active in the soil for some time. They can roughly be divided into long-term and short-term herbicides.

Long-term residuals Some soil-acting herbicides, like atrazine and simazine, are relatively insoluble and remain in the top few centimetres of soil killing germinating weed seedlings over several months. They can be selective or non-selective depending on the concentration applied. When used selectively they must be applied at low concentrations and are generally applied to weed-free soil in the early spring: like this they have little effect on established weeds. At low concentrations they will be confined to the top of the soil and as the majority of tree and shrub roots penetrate well below this level, they can be used amongst many woody plants, including ornamental trees and shrubs, roses and fruit bushes. Some woody plants are particularly susceptible however and can be damaged even at very low dosage rates, flowering cherries, for example. Others, such as black currant, are shallow-rooting and do absorb some of the herbicide but with no apparent detrimental effect. Some herbaceous plants are tolerant of the long-term residuals but many kinds may be damaged. At higher doses long-term residuals can be used non-selectively, on paths and drives for example, to keep down all germinating annual and perennial weeds. At these high dose rates they will, in time, kill established weeds too.

Dichlobenil is also a long-term residual herbicide but, unlike many of the others, it will kill established weeds. It can be used at high doses as a non-selective herbicide or, at lower doses, as a selective herbicide for killing and keeping down weeds amongst woody plants.

Short-term residuals These are similar in action to long-term residuals and kill germinating weed-seedlings, but they remain effective only for about eight weeks. Chloroxuron and propachlor are examples. Propachlor can be applied at the time of sowing seed and used to control seedling weeds in the first few critical weeks amongst leeks, onions and members of the cabbage family. By the time the effects of the herbicide have worn off, the crop is sufficiently advanced to be little troubled by further weed development. It can also be used in flower beds, shrub beds and among other more established vegetables. Chloroxuron is similar but should be applied to vegetables after they have reached the five true leaf stage.

Pre-emergent or Post-emergent?

These words are sometimes used to describe herbicides. They can be confusing – some people use them to talk about herbicides which are applied before or after the crop, others use them to describe herbicides applied before or after the weeds have emerged. Here we have used them for the latter.

Chloroxuron is an example of a pre-emergent herbicide – one which is applied to the soil surface before the weeds have broken through. All pre-emergence chemicals are soil acting and they are most effective in a warm moist soil. Some of the chemical is in solution in the top layer of soil and prevents germination of the seed or kills the young root or shoot as it comes out of the seed coat. In a dry, loose soil weed seedlings may develop at a lower depth which does not contain enough herbicide and then grow through the inactive chemical in the dry upper layer. DCPA (Dacthal, not readily available in the UK) applied to a lawn in the spring before the soil warms sufficiently for crabgrass *Digitaria* species to germinate provides effective pre-emergence control of crabgrass.

A post-emergence treatment is applied to growing weeds. The chemicals may be of either the contact, systemic or residual (dichlobenil) type.

Using Herbicides

Weeds vary considerably in their reactions to herbicides. Some may be easily killed by a single treatment, others may need two or more repeat treatments, at intervals of several weeks, before being killed. A few may prove resistant to all attempts at chemical control.

Garden plants also vary considerably in their reaction to herbicides. There are many thousands of different plants in cultivation and within groups such as shrubs and herbaceous plants some genera may be killed or badly damaged by a single incautious application while others may remain unharmed. The time of year, weather conditions, soil type and rate applied can all affect degree of effectiveness and risk of damage to garden plants. Always follow the manufacturer's instructions.

Handling Most herbicides available are soluble powders or concentrated liquids which must be mixed with water. These can be applied by a low-pressure sprayer operating at around 2½ to 3½ bars (35 to 50psi) and fitted with a flat spray nozzle or through a watering can preferably fitted with a dribble bar. A few herbicides are granular – dichlobenil and simazine, for example. Some are combined with a fertilizer and are generally used on lawns.

For effective weed control the herbicide should be uniformly distributed over the foliage or the soil. For foliar spraying, the amount of active chemical *per unit volume* is most important. If you apply too concentrated a solution of the chemicals, it may kill the weeds less well not better. But for spraying existing weeds and for pre-emergence soil treatments the *amount of herbicide per unit area* is of prime importance. The volume of water used to dilute the herbicide is generally not critical and the herbicide should be mixed with the amount of water necessary to cover the desired area well. Granular herbicides are more convenient because they are ready to use and do not require dilution. They are also safer around growing plants because they fall off the foliage to the ground.

Safety What are some of the dangers of using herbicides? Potentially at risk are the people who put them on, animals – both pets and wild life – fish, people who eat produce from treated ground and plants.

Plants can be damaged by spraying the wrong plants or by using too high a concentration on susceptible plants. Avoid spraying herbicides with high-pressure sprayers with a small nozzle aperture on windy days as the chemical may drift to sensitive cultivated plants. If you have to spray near plants erect some sort of screen to make sure that the spray does not drift. This is particularly important when using lawn weedkillers near flower and shrub beds. In warm moist weather some forms of 2,4-D and, particularly 2,4,5-T, can produce fumes which are toxic to plants, so in this sort of weather, even if you take all the precautions to avoid spray drifts, some plants may be harmed through vapour drift. Never store these chemicals, or anything which has been used to apply them, near a greenhouse – some greenhouse plants, particularly tomatoes, are extremely sensitive to even the faintest trace. Persistence of a chemical in the soil gives a long-lasting effect but if the chemical is too persistent it may harm later crops. In order to control a wider range of weeds and reduce residues in the soil, combinations of herbicides at lower individual rates, such as simazine plus diphenamid, are used.

To reduce the risks to people and animals, it is important to exercise care in handling all herbicides, particularly concentrated liquids. Always read and follow manufacturer's instructions and wear rubber gloves when mixing and applying.

Always store herbicides in their original containers – never put them in soft drinks bottles. Keep them well away from children, preferably in a locked cupboard with other garden chemicals. Do not use herbicides near fish ponds or at flowering time on weeds visited by bees.

Lawns Selective herbicides of the 'hormone' group such as 2,4-D, dichlorprop and mecoprop, will control most lawn weeds without harming grasses. On established lawns, 2,4-D is effective against daisies and dandelions while MCPA is better against creeping buttercups. Clover and pearlwort are effectively controlled by dichlorprop and mecoprop. Most lawn weedkillers are mixtures of these chemicals. These chemicals are most effective when the weeds are growing well so an application of fertilizer two or three weeks before the herbicide is beneficial. It helps the grass to re-colonize the bare patches afterwards too. A weedkiller/fertilizer combined product is a simple way of doing this. Repeat treatment of most herbicides may be needed with resistant weed species.

Lawn sands, which are a mixture of ferrous sulphate and ammonium sulphate, have a contact weedkilling action on broad-leaved weeds. They may brown or blacken the grass too but this will eventually recover. Lawn sand must not be confused with mercurized lawn sand – see *Moss*.

Young grasses (under six months) can be damaged by selective herbicides but annual weeds can be controlled with special preparations based on ioxynil and morfamquat. These chemicals will also control speedwell in established lawns (speedwell is resistant to other selectives).

Annuals and biennials Contact herbicides, like paraquat and diquat, can be used after sowing and before seedlings emerge. They can also be used with care between established plants. Short-term residual herbicides like chloroxuron and propachlor can be used after planting out a number of biennial or tender perennial bedding plants like pansies, geraniums, fuchsias, antirrhinums and wallflowers.

Herbaceous perennials Do not use total or translocated herbicides on herbaceous perennials. Low doses of residual herbicides such as simazine can be used, but it is essential to clean the site thoroughly of all perennial weeds first. This is a very diverse group of plants, and whereas some are tolerant of the long- or short-term residuals, others can be severely damaged. Restrict their use to carefully selected groups, for example hemerocallis and nepeta or to block-plants of species such as paeonia and solidago. Apply the herbicides in early spring when beds are weed-free.

Bulbs Contact herbicides, like paraquat and diquat, can be used shortly before the bulb shoots show above the soil to kill any seedlings weeds present at that time. They can be used again after bulb foliage has died down, but it is essential to detach the foliage from the bulb and cultivate the bed first. Holes left after the removal of foliage can channel the herbicide down to the bulb if they are not earthed over. Research reports suggest that it may also be possible to use some of the short-term residual herbicides to control germinating weeds.

There is no safe chemical means of controlling perennial weeds in bulb beds.

Ornamental trees, shrubs and roses Total and translocated herbicides cannot be used safely amongst this group of plants. Contact herbicides can be used all year round but if they are applied in late winter to control weeds that grow during the winter and then followed with a low-dose application of a residual herbicide, such as simazine, weed seedlings will be controlled over several months. Dichlobenil can also be used and it can be applied to established weeds. Do not apply these herbicides to newly-planted or small ornamentals and do not use them on highly sandy soils.

Always check the range of products available to see if there are any which specifically mention their suitability for use amongst trees, shrubs or roses.

Tree and bush fruit Established annual weeds can be controlled by applying paraquat/diquat mixtures. Simazine can be used to control germinating weeds if low doses are applied in the spring. Dichlobenil can be used to control established weeds around trees and bushes which are more than two years old. It should be applied in late winter. Dalapon can be used to control couch grass: apply it in November. The tolerances and stages of development at which treatment can be safely made, vary from plant to plant, and it is essential to study manufacturers' recommendations carefully.

Vegetables Paraquat and diquat can be used immediately before sowing to kill weed seedlings that have sprouted in the interim between preparing the ground and sowing. They can also be used between rows of vegetables if they are applied carefully, using a dribble-bar. Propachlor can be used immediately after sowing seed of brassicas, onion, leeks and carrots and chloroxuron can be used once they have reached the five true leaf stage. Both of the latter keep ground weed-free for up to two months; they will do nothing about established weeds.

Paths and drives Path weedkillers usually combine a translocated herbicide such as MCPA with a residual herbicide such as simazine to give a quick and long-lasting kill. Aminotriazole may be added to control couch. Simazine and aminotriazole herbicides can be used on narrow paths as the herbicides do not creep sideways, but where tree or shrub roots pass under paths they may be harmful and it may be safer to use repeated doses of contact herbicides. Sodium chlorate should only be used on very infested paths. It moves around in the soil quickly – both downwards and sideways and should never be used near trees or shrubs you want to keep. Be particularly careful about using it on paths near trees: tree roots can spread for many metres.

New or neglected gardens The best herbicide for a new or neglected garden depends on the sort of weeds present. To clear the garden of most weeds use ammonium sulphamate or sodium chlorate. For grass weeds use dalapon. For broad-leaved weeds on lawns use a translocated weedkiller mixture. For difficult broad-leaves weeds such as docks and nettles or thistles use 2,4,5-T. For brambles and other shrubby weeds use 2,4,5-T.

16. Gardens

Rock Gardens

A rock garden is a composition of rocks and soil deliberately constructed to imitate a natural rock pavement or cliff and to provide a home for many small plants which naturally inhabit open, stony places.

Rocks have for many centuries played an important part in the gardens of China and Japan, with the rocks themselves of primary importance and usually having both symbolic significance and aesthetic appeal. It is more than likely that the oriental landscape gardens, particularly those of Japan, provided the seed of inspiration for western attempts to create special gardens designed particularly for the display of alpine and rock plants.

Raised and Sunken Gardens

Nowadays the emphasis is placed on the plants and on providing a suitable home for them but the rocks in the garden should not be without attraction. Natural rock should be used wherever possible and placed in such a way as to simulate natural rock outcrops. To achieve the imitation of a natural outcrop, you need sloping ground, either as a small artificial mound or a whole natural hillside. This requirement is the basis for the two main types of rock garden constructed today – raised and sunken. A raised rock garden is potentially the more natural and outcrops should be constructed on an area of naturally sloping land. On a normally flat site, height and contours can be produced by excavating soil and throwing it up into one, or a series of mounds with sunken paths. This is a sunken garden.

The soil removed when you are making a pond can form the beginning of a rock garden by turning it into an outcrop or series of outcrops mirrored in the water. If you intend to build a scree into the rock garden, then the soil removed when constructing this can be used too – see *Scree Gardens*. If you can obtain a load of top soil, perhaps from a building or road-making site, then a rock garden can be constructed in a flat garden without the toil of digging and earth moving.

Building a Rock Garden

Natural rock can be an expensive commodity and should be chosen with care. If possible, use the natural rock of the area where you live. It will generally be cheaper than rock from elsewhere and will fit into the landscape more convincingly. In very flat areas where clay is the only bedrock, use one of the sandstone or sandy limestone rocks with flat cleavage planes. Towering masses of water-worn limestone would look out of place.

Most rocks used for rock gardens are built up in layers or strata and split easily along the layer-lines. Before starting to build a rock garden, look at a quarry or cliff face to see these rocks in their natural state and lay them in a similar way with the layer-lines in the same plane.

The ideal position for a rock garden should be open to the sun and, if possible, sheltered from the cold and drying winds which can damage any plants which may have been stimulated into early growth through a mild, snowless winter. Do not build rock gardens near trees, especially if they are deciduous and shed large leaves in winter. Falling leaves can cover tiny plants with a soggy, killing layer.

Most plants from mountainous and other rocky areas need a well-drained soil to grow in. The natural rainfall in mountainous areas may be quite high but the nature of the soil makes sure that moisture does not stagnate around plant roots. Bear this in mind when constructing a rock garden on flat ground.

Opposite: Very few gardens have the benefit of a natural feature like this, but a wide variety of water gardens can be created on a smaller scale

Building a rock garden

Spread shingle over hardcore foundations for drainage

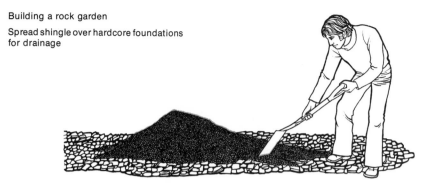

Select rocks carefully

Move large rocks into position with a sledge

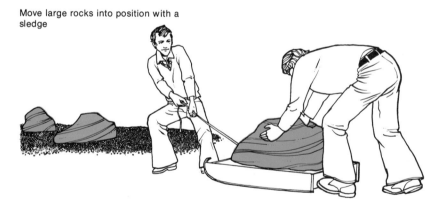

Firm the soil behind the rocks as they are positioned

If the part of the garden you choose is under turf, remove it and stack it nearby. Then dig out all the fertile top soil and keep it to use when the rocks are set in position. Mark out the areas where you want the mounds.

If the subsoil does not drain freely, put a 20cm (8in) deep layer of weathered clinker or rubble in the hole (you may have to remove more soil to do this). Cover the clinker or rubble with the turf turned upside down or with coarse gravel to prevent the soil from washing down and clogging the drainage. If the subsoil is sticky clay, it will probably be necessary to lay drains across the garden, leading them to a ditch, or to a pond or bog if this is to be a feature of the garden. Alternatively, you can dig a sump to take the drainage water. See *Soil*.

The next step is to put the rocks in position. Before starting to do this make a rough plan of where you want the outcrops to be and which rocks you want where. This usually has to be modified as you go along according to the type and size of rocks available but it should prevent your being left with all the wrong-sized rocks as you get towards the end.

Start with the larger rocks at the base, making sure that each one is firmly bedded and sloping down into the ground. The rocks should retain the soil, not vice versa. After these have been set and firmed in, add more soil and proceed with the next layer. Properly bedded-in rocks should be buried by about two-thirds of their bulk, only the most attractive face should be visible. In general the actual outcrops should not be too high, with plenty of ledges and pockets being left for the plants. Here and there, particularly if you are building a large rock garden, you can attempt to use more massive and vertical outcrops, but do this only if you can get really large rocks. If you build high vertical walls with small stones, the rock garden may collapse after prolonged rain or severe frost.

In general the top soil from the garden is good enough to construct a rock garden, but if it is a very heavy loam or a clay soil it is better to mix it with equal parts of sharp grit or even gravel with particles up to 13mm (½in) across. Whatever the soil, make a special growing mix to fill the pockets for the more choice plants. A mixture of four parts loamy soil, two parts moss peat, two parts coarse sand and two parts grit can be used. A fertilizer should be added to this mix. If good quality leaf-mould is available, it can be substituted for the peat or a 50/50 mix can be used.

For plants that need an acid rooting medium, use either lime-free loamy soil or substitute peat in its place.

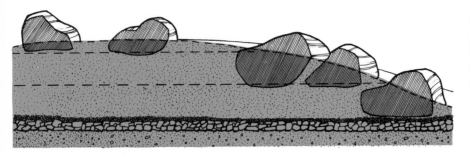

The rocks should be planted into a mound of soil (the soil is built up behind the rocks as work proceeds). When the first rock is placed, soil should be built up to the lower horizontal dotted line. When the second and third rocks are positioned it should be built up to the upper horizontal line. The curved dotted line is the soil mound line

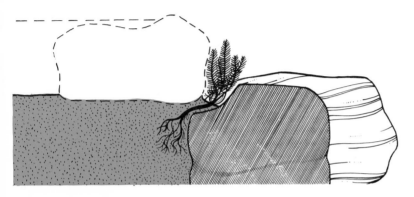

Planting should be carried out during construction. Spread the roots out well

Difficulties encountered if you try planting after construction.
Far left: no room for the plant
Near left: roots left dangling in an airpocket

Building a rock garden on a slope follows a similar pattern, though drainage preparations should not be needed. Strip off turf and top soil as before, then mark out the positions of the outcrops. Start at the lowest outcrop with the largest rocks and gradually work up the hillside, finishing with the smallest ones.

The narrower and more vertical ledges and outcrops should be planted as they are built – if you wait until the rock garden is finished, there might not be enough room to do the job properly. Planting the rest of the rock garden can take place when the whole outcrop or the whole rock garden is constructed. If you raise your own plants from seeds or cuttings, plant them out when they are small, straight from the seed pan or box. This is particularly important when they are to be grown in narrow crevices. Well-rooted, pot-grown plants are often difficult to plant in such confined places and are difficult to water while they are becoming established. Mulch the soil around young plants with chippings to keep it moist and smother any tiny weed seedlings. Mulch plants which like acid soils with peat or leaf-mould. Weed regularly – it is easy for a small choice alpine to be smothered by such fast-growing annual weeds as chickweed and annual meadow grass.

Scree Gardens

To the geologist, a mountain-side scree is an accumulation of small rocks, small stones and grit formed by the weathering of natural rocks. To the alpine gardener, the

Opposite: marginal and bog plants around a small pond

term 'scree' is used to describe an area of the garden, usually near a rock garden, which contains a very high proportion of grit and stone in the soil. A scree differs from a moraine, with which it is often confused, in that the latter is formed from the debris of stones and rocks left in the track of a glacier and generally has water running continuously beneath its surface.

Natural screes (and moraines) are inhabited by plants which are able to live with a minimum amount of nourishment and have adapted to cope with having more than enough moisture in the spring when the snow covering them melts and having little at other times of the year because of the very efficient drainage the open nature of a scree provides. When these plants are grown in the garden, they will not succeed unless they are provided with as near as possible their natural conditions. The best time to build a scree garden is when you are constructing a rock garden. Try to find a position for it in the rock garden where it will look natural. One built following a gulley, where there are no over-hanging trees or shrubs to drip rain on to plants causing damage, is ideal. A level scree never looks as pleasing as one which has been contoured to resemble a natural one. The scree can face north, south, east or west but if possible it should not be exposed to full sunlight all day. Most scree plants benefit from a little shade during some part of the day and in the northern hemisphere a north-west facing scree appears to be the best compromise (south-east in the southern hemisphere).

When you come to choose the materials for constructing a scree, be guided by the type of plants you want to grow. For exam-

ple, lime-loving plants should be grown in a limestone scree, whereas acid-loving plants are better grown in a sandstone scree. But be careful when choosing the type of sandstone: it must not be too soft or it will disintegrate. If you want a neutral scree (neither acid nor alkaline) then you should use granite or some other similar rock. Sandstone and limestone are much more sympathetic to the roots of plants than granite or most other types of rock because they absorb and retain moisture. This reservoir of moisture can be used by the plants and also helps to keep the scree mixture cool.

The construction of a scree is basically the same for all sizes. If the subsoil is well drained and you do not envisage having a drainage problem, excavate the ground to a depth of about 45 to 60cm (1½ to 2ft). If, on the other hand, the soil is heavy and not very well drained, make the hole much deeper, say 1m (just over 3ft), and dig a drainage pit at the base of the scree to allow the excess water to drain away freely. The principles outlined in *Soil* for making a sump can be adapted for use here. The scree should be narrow at the top and fan out towards the base with the sides scalloped for effect. Do not let the scree tumble straight down the side of the rock garden, but instead let it wind its way down in a series of gentle slopes. Start work on the scree by removing the top soil and setting it aside for mixing in later. Then remove the remainder of the soil to the desired depth. This soil can be used for building mounds in other parts of the rock garden.

When the ground has been dug out to the desired depth, start filling the scree. Fill the excavated area to within 30 or 40cm (12 to

Above: When building a rock garden, bear in mind the natural contours of rocky landscapes

Right: a scree garden

Making a garden pool

Dig a hole the required shape and depths. Line the hole with a layer of fine sand

Lay a plastic or rubber sheet designed for pools over the hole and hold it in place with large bricks

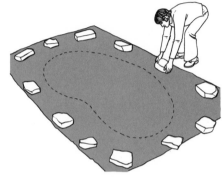

Slowly fill the pool

Finish by hiding the edges of the sheet with coping stones

put in position now. Large rocks can look very attractive by allowing the scree mixture to flow up and around them but make sure that the type of rock used is the same as the chipped material. Position the rocks so that they give the impression of distance by placing the smaller ones at the top, falling away gradually to larger ones at the bottom.

When all the rocks are in position the scree should be filled almost to the top with the growing medium. A good basic medium can be made from a 50:50 mix of 6 to 12mm (¼ to ½in) stone chips with a mixture of equal parts of soil, leaf-mould and peat with 50g (2oz) of a slow-acting general-purpose fertilizer added to every barrow load. Try to avoid standing on the growing medium while you are filling the scree and avoid standing on it later when you are planting or maintaining by setting a number of stepping-stones flush with the surface of the growing medium. Finally, cover the growing medium with a 25mm (1in) layer of stone chips before planting.

Choose small plants with as little soil on them as possible so that they will grow away quickly. Avoid planting rapid-growing plants with slower-growing ones as the latter will become overgrown and lost. A few dwarf shrubs such as *Erinacea anthyllis*, *Ilex crenata*, 'Mariesii' and *Betula nana* will give extra dimensions to the scree. After planting add a further 25mm (1in) layer of stone chips to keep the necks of the plants dry.

Each or every alternate year, top-dress the scree with a 25mm (1in) layer of the growing medium to prevent the plants from becoming starved. Remove the stone chippings before spreading the growing medium out and replace them afterwards. Screes generally need little maintenance and this mainly consists of watering and weeding when necessary.

Plants for Screes
Some suitable plants for a scree are *Androsace*, *Aquilegia*, *Arenaria*, *Asperula*, *Campanula*, *Dianthus*, *Douglasia*, *Draba*, *Edraianthus*, *Lewisia*, *Linaria*, *Morisia*, *Papaver*, *Penstemon*, *Petrocallis*, *Phlox*, *Saxifraga*, *Thlaspi* and *Viola*.

Water Gardens
A water garden is a design in which areas of water, and the plants that associate naturally with water or damp spots, are dominant.

Positioning and Design
Positioning the water garden is most important. It must have maximum exposure to the sun and, if possible, it should be built well away from overhanging trees. If trees can-

15in) of the top with stones, 5 to 10cm (2 to 4in) in diameter. Put a layer of coarse peat, up-turned turves or other bulky organic matter over these larger stones to stop the scree mixture being washed down into the lower level and blocking the drainage. If you want to water this area from below then put perforated pipes of metal or plastic in place at this stage. If you want some large rocks in the scree then they too should be

not be avoided, inspect the pool regularly for fallen leaves and remove them immediately. If they are left, they give off gases during their decomposition which are harmful to fish and plants. Covering the pool with 1cm (½in) mesh netting in the autumn will prevent this. Tree roots may breach the pool lining. Pools need maximum sun to help the water to warm up quickly in the spring to keep the fish and aquatic plants in the pool healthy. Shallow water warms more quickly than deep water and still water warms more quickly than moving water. A pool fed naturally from a stream will always be cold but re-circulated water warms up quite quickly. A fountain will prevent water warming up quickly due to the temperature loss by evaporation.

Formal water gardens can be designed from simple geometric shapes such as well-proportioned rectangles, squares, circles, and ellipses and 'L'-shapes. Informal water gardens consisting of pools and connecting streams are much more popular and are often built in association with a rock garden. To be seen at its best, an informal water garden should follow the terrain, using undulations and bluffs to give a natural design. Water collects naturally at low points and so informal areas of water should be produced in the lowest part of the garden, paying due care to the need to empty the pool and to deal with any overflow of surplus water (usually by a sump).

Construction

It is essential to make sure that a pool is waterproof. For large pools, brick with cement rendering or reinforced concrete should be used. For smaller pools, short-term linings are cheap, easy to use and practical.

A pool should always be made in solid, undisturbed soil. Do not attempt to make a pool in soil which has been built up or moved, since even the most carefully compacted soil will sink in time. Before starting to dig the hole, mark out the proposed shape of the pool on the ground using string, garden hose or even scratching it in the soil or grass. This will help you decide whether it is big enough (or too big) and whether it is in the right position and can be easily seen.

If you want to grow a number of different types of aquatic plants the excavated pool should be of varying depths. Some water lilies will tolerate water up to 1m (3ft) deep but generally 60cm (2ft) will prove quite adequate. If a pool is to be really large – over 10m^2 (100sq ft) then the depth of water at the middle could be increased to around 1m (3ft). Marginal plants – see *Ornamental Plants*: *Aquatic Plants* – pre-

fer much shallower water and the pool should have ledges from 15 to 30cm (6 to 12in) deep to accommodate them. The pool can be designed so that about 15cm (6in) of soil can be spread over both ledges and bottom giving a water depth of zero to 15cm (6in) on the ledges. Or the plants for deeper water can be grown in baskets and the overall depth of the pool at the centre can be reduced by some 15cm (6in). Giving an informal pool sloping sides will make it easier to build – about 20° from the vertical is adequate – but the slope should not be more than 45° from the vertical to minimize soil slip.

After excavation, use a spirit level to check that the pool rim is level. This will prevent unsightly edges showing when the pool is filled; and will also prevent water running out of the pool at a low point.

Plastic and rubber sheeting For speedy lining after excavation, plastic and rubber lining sheets are very suitable. There are three main types: butyl rubber, plastolene and polyvinylchloride (pvc). All three materials are satisfactory and are much superior to polythene, being generally thicker, much more elastic and much less likely to be punctured. Polythene-lined pools generally have to be re-lined after two to three years, but pools lined with the other materials could last from ten years to as long as eighty years for the thicker butyl rubber. A rough idea of the size of sheet needed can be obtained by adding twice the maximum depth of the pool to the overall length and the overall width. The materials should be laid over 3cm (1in) of builder's sand spread over the excavated hole to stop sharp stones from puncturing them. The sheeting should be laid over the hole with a generous overlap at the edges (this can be tucked into a trench at the edge of the pool after it has been filled with water or it can be disguised with stones or plants). Use large stones around the edges of the pool to hold the sheeting in place and slowly fill the pool with water. As it fills, the lining will stretch and mould to the contours of the hole. It will not need any additional fixing when it is full.

Glass fibre Ready-made glass-fibre pools are very useful but are generally too shallow for many aquatic plants, and are expensive. They should be installed as for sheeting pools: careful excavation, lining with sand, then backfilling with sand after a check on levels.

Clay If there is access to good clay, a clay pool is excellent providing it is not allowed to dry and crack. Clay pools should not be built near trees or large shrubs as the clay is easily breached by roots. The hole should be dug some 20cm (8in) deeper than required to allow for the thickness of clay.

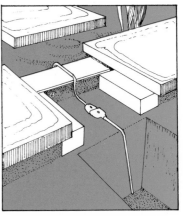

Electric cable to the pool. The cable to the main supply should be buried at least 45cm (18in) deep and laid on fine sand. The coupler of the cable to the pump should be covered by one of the pool coping stones

Right: a pond does not have to be large to incorporate a fountain

Opposite: a water garden with a collection of aquatic plants

Spread the clay lining by treading generous amounts of it mixed with water on to the bottom and sides of the pool. All cracks should be sealed. Clay pools are always muddy when filled, and will not clear. A solution of burnt lime in water should be poured into the pool to flocculate the particles and make them sink.

Concrete and brick pools Excavations for these must be deep enough to allow for the thickness of concrete. In large pools, the concrete should be spread to a minimum depth of 15cm (6in) on top of consolidated hardcore. In smaller pools, 8cm (3in) is adequate. A 3:2:1 mix of concrete – see *Construction* – with a waterproofing additive should be used. If the pool has to be concreted in stages, leaks may develop where the different layers join. To minimize the risk of this, allow one lot of concrete to become firm before the next lot is applied and moisten the older concrete thoroughly at the joins. Make sure that the concrete dries slowly by covering it with moistened sacking. Shuttering will be needed for constructing nearly vertical sides. After construction concrete pools should be painted with a sealer to prevent leakage, and the water used to fill them should be allowed to stand for two to three weeks before plants and fish are put in.

Other materials Half barrels and sinks sunk into the ground make excellent pools though only small plants may be grown in them. Barrels should be charred inside with a blowlamp before use.

Planting Pools

The best time for building and planting a pool is late April and May. The soil used for planting must be free from animal manures to prevent the build-up of gases. Large areas of water should have 15cm (6in) of sand and soil in equal parts laid on the bottom. Smaller pools should have plants growing in baskets or containers for easier maintenance, and they should have smaller-growing plants. Do not cover more than one-third of the water surface with foliage plants or reflections will be lost. Water lilies need a rich soil and free root run and they appreciate regular division in spring for good flowering. For further details see *Ornamental Plants: Aquatic Plants*.

General Maintenance

Good hygiene is essential. All fallen or rotting leaves must be removed as soon as possible. Excessive plant growth should be controlled by regular division. Ice on the pool is rarely detrimental to plants or fish, but when it is necessary to break the ice, do not use a hammer since the sound waves will harm the fish. Hot water poured on the ice is better or, more practical, is a floating ball or piece of polystyrene which will stop ice forming beneath it and can be moved to allow air to the surface. Once a year drain off about two-thirds of the water, remove any algae and re-fill the pool. Take care when removing excessive plant growth, debris or algae not to throw away small water snails which help to keep a pool clean.

Fountains

A fountain is a column of water ejected upwards under pressure. The height of the

Plants growing in rich, moisture-retaining growing mix held in a clay trough

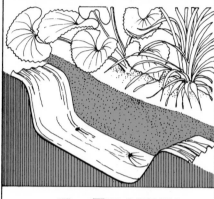

Heavy gauge plastic sheet (with drainage holes) used to hold the growing mix

A small bog garden can be built using a glass fibre water cistern (with drainage holes)

column is largely determined by the pressure, the form of the column and the way it splays outwards are primarily determined by the nozzle it curves out of. A spout ejects water outwards or downwards – over some projection to create a waterfall, say. Water from a spout may be free falling or driven by artificially created pressure. In the USA the word fountain is used to cover both fountain and spout.

A fountain or spout can be purely ornamental, purely functional or a combination of both. In its functional mode water falling into a bowl, dish or pond will increase the supply of oxygen in that water. This will help aerate the water for fish. The action of falling water will also help to prevent the complete freezing of the water during winter. Fountains can also be used to increase the humidity over a small area,

particularly indoors. But, it is not easy to grow aquatic plants in pools which have a fountain. They do not like the rippling effect caused by a water jet nor the sudden temperature drop of the water which fountains can cause, particularly in the evening.

In formal pools the jet can be set at the centre – the pool can then be square, circular or polygonal. Placing a fountain in an informal pool is much more difficult. As a rough guide, at the point at which the fountain is installed, the basin of the pool should be at least twice as wide as the fountain jet is high. If the fountain is in a windy position then this ratio should be increased to one to three to prevent the surrounding area becoming saturated.

Fountains and spouts can work directly from the main water supply or by a pump which re-circulates water from the pool.

Mains water fountains and spouts are simple and cheap to install but they have a number of drawbacks. Because water is constantly being poured into the pool, it is necessary for the pool to have some sort of overflow. Mains water pressure can vary from day to day and from time to time within the same day so at one time a fountain or spout could be reduced to a pathetic trickle, at another it could be watering all the marginal plants surrounding the pool. The more jets or orifices that are installed and the larger they are, the more water will be needed to run them (and to get rid of). The smallest jets or orifices generally use about 5l (1 gal) of water a minute but larger ones can use many times this amount. If you live in an area where water is metered, running a fountain or spout from the mains water supply can prove very costly. In many areas mains water fountains and spouts are not allowed.

In almost every case it is better to run a fountain or spout from a re-circulating pump. These pumps work by electricity and should be installed by a qualified electrician if you are not absolutely sure of your competence to set it up yourself. Most pumps can be submerged in the pool and hidden from view. They have a length of waterproof electricity cable and a water-supply pipe. The waterproof cable should be led out of the pool and connected to the mains electricity supply. The water-supply pipe feeds the fountain or spout.

When a fountain is being used in a large pool a non-submersible type is generally better. These have two water pipes – one supplying water to the fountain head and the other taking water from the pool. They should be primed by filling the pipes with water before turning them on. Non-submersible pumps should be hidden from view in a reasonably weather-proof place.

They can often be used to run a number of different fountains, or a fountain and a spout driving a waterfall at the same time. When they are used like this each water supply pipe should be generally fitted with a stopcock.

A number of different fountain heads are available. Simple nozzles should be set at least 5cm (2in) above the surface of the pool. More complicated, statue fountains are simply connected to the supply pipe from the pump.

In larger gardens, formal, stone-edged pools on a terrace with regular jets are very satisfying. If your garden is on a sloping site then water can be made to gush via channels into a whole series of pools, each with a different architectural effect or different marginal plants, culminating in a bold out-pouring of water from a well-designed fountain head into a grand basin. Since plants are not easy to grow where the water moves, it is often pleasant to ornament the base and sides of the basin with stone pebbles, or with cut and dressed stone slabs or mosaic.

Bog Gardens

A bog garden can provide a suitable environment for growing a wide range of exotic plants which will not grow well in any other part of the garden – lysichitons, many primulas, *Gunnera manicata*, many ferns, grasses and some meconopses, for example. It should simulate the conditions found near marshes and rivers and should be planted with the specialized plants which grow in these places. Most bog plants like a fairly constant supply of water – they will not tolerate long periods of over-wetness nor drought. In the garden bog plants can be planted: 1) where you have a naturally boggy area – near a stream for instance, 2) in the ground around a garden pool which can be kept in a permanently moist state. In this way you can use a bog garden to break up the harsh edges of a pool with growing plants, 3) in a separate part of the garden which you can build as a feature of the garden in its own right.

Many pools are constructed by using a plastic sheet to line a depression in the ground – see *Water Gardens*. If this is the case, it is a fairly simple matter to extend the plastic sheet at a shallower depth along the sides of the pool. This area can be up to 15cm (6in) deep and should be filled with a spongy soil mixture which can be prepared by mixing equal proportions of a rich loamy soil with horticultural peat. This will make an acid bog garden.

To make a separate bog garden take out a pit about 60cm (2ft) deep at the middle with sides which slope gently upwards and out-wards to normal ground level. Line this pit with plastic sheeting, concrete or mortared bricks. (Concrete gardens should be painted with a concrete sealer). For bank construction see *Water Gardens*. For large bog gardens put foundations or sand beneath the lining material. Fill the whole pit with the soil/peat mixture. Small bog gardens can even be constructed by using an earthenware sink filled with the peat/soil mixture.

In these artificial bog gardens you can maintain the water supply by building in perforated pipes of metal or plastic and covering these with crocks to prevent the holes becoming blocked. Or you can supply it by hand. In either case some method of draining away the excess water must be built into the bog garden.

Many bog plants like partial shade so an ideal place for a bog garden would be close to a group of trees. Alternatively, you can plant trees around the bog garden. The swamp cypress, *Taxodium distichum*, or members of the willow family, particularly the weeping willow, *Salix babylonica*, or the silver birch, *Betula pendula*, are particularly suitable if you have a lot of space.

Where there is already a natural bog in your garden some of the plants, particularly the rushes, may be something of a nuisance and these should be kept cut back so that the more interesting and colourful plants can become established. A series of stepping stones should be set across the bog so that the plants can be reached when trimming or replanting is necessary.

Plants for Bog Gardens

The plants for bog gardens can be divided into two groups: moist-soil plants which usually thrive in moist soil and some shade but do not like waterlogged conditions and wet soil plants which will actually tolerate being grown in water.

Moist soil *Astilbe*, will thrive in a moist soil in sun or shade. The plants need cutting back in the autumn and can be divided every two or three years. Attractive hybrids are *A.* × *arendsii* 6, *fls* 60cm (2ft), July, August: *A.* × *crispa* 6, *fls* to 20cm (8in).

Hemerocallis 2 and 3, day lily, very suitable for moist soil but prefers a sunny position or light shade. Cut down the stems after flowering. Vars 'Golden Orchid'; 'Pink Damask'; 'Dark Flame'.

Hosta, there is a wide range of varieties available and in most cases the foliage is attractive with white or pink *fls*. *H. fortunei* 3 and *H. sieboldiana* 3 are particularly good.

Mimulus 5, herbaceous, *M. × burnettii*, *fls* reddish with yellow throats, June to September; 'A. T. Johnson' *fls* yellow flowers with a crimson blotch: *M. cardinalis*, *fls* reddish with yellow throats, June to September.

Primula, a number of species are particularly suitable for waterside planting in association with hostas and astilbes and provide attractive displays of colour provided the soil does not dry out during the summer. *P. bulleyana* 6 is particularly useful, growing to about 70cm (2½ft), *fls* light orange, June, July: *P. burmanica* 6, is similar, *fls* dark red, June.

Wet soil A very wide range of plants is available and many of these come under the heading of marginal plants – see *Ornamental Plants: Aquatic Plants*. Plants suggested below are a selection of those most successfully grown by the beginner.

Lysichitum americanum 6, hardy herbaceous plant, *fls* golden yellow, similar to an arum lily, March to May, *lvs* very large to 60cm (2ft) long, late summer. It is usually necessary to purchase two-year-old plants which take time to become established.

Mentha aquatica 4, water mint, crushed leaves give the aroma of mint, to 20cm (8in), *fls* pink, small clusters, summer.

Primula japonica 5, to 60cm (2ft), *fls* white, pink and red, May to July. Not as long-living as some of the primulas but will usually tolerate wetter conditions than some other varieties.

Typha angustifolia 3, small reed mace, catstail, *lvs* narrow, graceful with poker-like dark brown heads. It will grow either in wet soil or in the water itself.

There are also some ferns which are suitable for growing in wet soil and can be useful for stabilizing the banks of ponds or streams. These include *Matteuccia struthiopteris* 2 with fronds golden-green in colour with an inner circle of darker fronds. They have an elegant arched type of habit while *Onoclea sensibilis* 3 has long, pale green fronds which turn brown at the first sign of frost, hence the common name of sensitive fern.

Heather Gardens

Heaths and heathers are the hardy evergreen shrubs of the three genera, *Erica*, *Calluna* and *Daboecia*. They are mostly lime-hating plants but a few of the species tolerate neutral and even alkaline soils. Heathers offer a colourful display all the year round of foliage or flowers and have attractive form. They are known chiefly for their ground-cover characteristics and little maintenance.

When building a heather garden the aim should be to create a cultivated 'moorland' scene. The heather beds should be informal, using natural contours and rock outcrops and the heathers should be planted in large drifts containing several plants of the same variety. Plant specimen trees or shrubs at strategic positions to break the uniformity of the drifts but be careful to make sure that they complement the heathers and do not dominate them. The dwarfer types of conifers, rhododendrons and evergreen shrubs are particularly suitable.

Choose an open situation for the heather bed in full sun to encourage the heathers to form compact growth and to flower freely – heathers flower poorly in dense shade. A south-facing position is necessary to bring out the brilliant colours of the red-orange foliaged varieties in winter while the more tender ones require some shelter.

Once a heather bed is established perennial weeds can be very difficult to eradicate, so before planting thoroughly prepare the soil and remove all weeds. If you can afford the time it is a good idea to let the ground stand fallow for a season so that all the perennial weeds can be removed. Heathers tolerate a wide range of soil conditions as long as the pH is suitable, and are often better on poorer soils because their growth is not soft and rampant. Whatever the soil, dig in plenty of peat before planting: it increases the moisture retention of sandy soils, opens up clay soils and will help provide the acid conditions which so many heathers like.

Arrange the beds informally and into manageable sizes by using narrow paths, akin to the sheep tracks of the moors. Devote the larger level interspaces to lawn.

Planting

Choose young bushy plants which, if possible, have been grown in containers as this will help you to avoid damaging their roots when you plant them out. Two- to three-year-old cuttings are ideal. Select a few choice varieties to complement and contrast with each other.

Container-grown heathers can be planted at any time but bare-root heathers should be planted from October to March. Avoid planting in predictable dry spells. If you plant heathers in the autumn, this will allow them to establish themselves before they have to withstand any dry and windy spells which might occur during the rest of the year. Plant them deeply with their lower foliage resting on the soil, and firm them in well. Mulch them with peat covering their lower foliage and any bare stems.

The distance you should leave between plants depends on the ultimate height and width of the variety but, in general, if you space them 30 to 45cm (1 to 1½ft) apart this should give ground cover in about three years. Make allowances for the vigorous growers so that they do not smother the dwarf varieties.

Looking after Heathers

Weeding Heathers have delicate roots so when the plants are close together you will have to weed between them by hand. A peat mulch around the heathers will suppress many weeds and make extracting those that do grow an easier task. If the plants are widely spaced you can use a hoe or a contact weedkiller. Selective weedkillers can be used but it is not known yet whether they affect the growth of the heathers.

Feeding and mulching If you add organic matter to a heather bed as a mulch it will encourage the heathers to surface root and self-layer so that young growth and flowering is increased and wind damage becomes minimal. A mulch will also help to conserve soil moisture during dry spells. It is not essential to feed heathers, mulching is sufficient, but a dressing of a slow-release, general-purpose fertilizer may have some benefit. Sequestrols should be used on alkaline soils or on acid soils where mineral deficiencies are suspected. They should be applied just before the new growth begins in spring.

Watering Heathers benefit considerably from watering during long dry spells and it is essential to keep newly-planted ones well watered until they are established.

Pruning Some heathers are easier to maintain than others. *Erica carnea* hugs the soil, is very resilient, and only needs trimming every few years. Others with very brittle wood, for instance *E. vagans*, are easily damaged by wind and snow. For this reason, legginess should be discouraged by clipping off the dead flowers each year. This will also encourage heathers to produce more flowering wood. Winter- and spring-flowering heathers should be clipped after they have flowered and before new growth begins. Summer- and autumn-flowering heathers should not be clipped until the following spring – the flowers offer some winter protection and some provide attractive year-end colours. Ideally pruning shears/secateurs should be used, but as this is not practical with large beds, clippers/shears used upside down will keep a 'natural' effect. If the heathers grow misshapen and produce flowers of reduced quality, prune them back hard to encourage young flowering wood to grow from the base of the plant.

With taller heathers, for example *E.*

arborea, pruning should be aimed at improving their shape and removing unhealthy branches.

Propagation

Heathers last for many years especially if they are mulched and pruned regularly but eventually they become old and misshapen and need replacing, and some heathers can not be rejuvenated by severe pruning. Heathers may be propagated on a small scale by layering and division but both techniques often produce misshapen plants which are prone to die-back. This method is also difficult with upright and brittle species. Propagation by cuttings is better as these produce vigorous and bushy plants. Cuttings should be taken from June to November using half-ripened shoots, varying in length from 2 to 60cm (1 to 24in) depending on the species. Smaller cuttings root better but may take two to three years to reach planting-out size. All types of propagating equipment can be used but a lime-free rooting medium is essential for most species. Hormone rooting powders are not essential. Cuttings taken in October and November can be overwintered in a cold frame and will have rooted by the spring. The rooted cuttings should be potted or planted out in nursery beds providing them with some shelter and shade.

Heather Species

Listed below are the major species with their general characteristics and a few examples of the outstanding varieties. The numbers after the botanical names are the North America hardiness zone ratings – see *Climate*.

Calluna vulgaris 4, ling or heather, dislikes lime, depending on variety, 8 to 75cm (3in to 2½ft), *fls* single or double, white, pinks, reds and purples, July to November, *lvs* green, grey, yellow, orange and red. 'Alba Plena' *fls* double white; 'Beoley Gold' *fls* white, *lvs* golden; 'Californian Midge' *fls* purple, dwarf and compact form; 'Darkness' *fls* bright crimson; 'Fred J. Chapple' *lvs* beautiful in spring with green, pink and coral tips; 'H.E. Beale' *fls* double pink; 'John F. Letts' *lvs* golden, turning orange-red in winter, spreading habit; 'Robert Chapman' *lvs* golden, turning red in winter.

Daboecia cantabrica 5, Irish bell heather, dislikes lime, tolerates partial shade and moist conditions, to 60cm (2ft), *fls* white, pinks, reds and purples, June to October. 'Atropurpurea' *fls* rich purple; 'Alba Globosa,' *fls* large white.

Erica arborea 'Alpina' 7, tree heath, tolerates lime, 1·8 to 2·4m (6 to 8ft), *fls* small, scented, white, March to May, *lvs* bright green: *E. carnea* 5, alpine heath, tolerates lime and heavy shade, very hardy, 15 to 25cm (6 to 9in), *fls* white, pinks and reds, November to May: *E. ciliaris* 7, Dorset heath, moist, sunny position, dislikes lime, easily damaged and does not transplant well, 30 to 45cm (12 to 18in), *fls* white, pinks and red, June to October: *E. cinerea* 5, Scotch heath or bell heather, tolerates dry positions but dislikes lime, 25 to 30cm (9 to 12in), *fls* white, pinks, reds and maroon, June to October; 'Alba minor' *fls* white, compact form; 'Golden Drop' *lvs* orange-copper turning red in winter; 'Pink Ice' *fls* clear pink, compact form; 'Velvet Knight' *fls* very dark maroon, *lvs* very dark: *E.* × *darleyensis* 6, tolerates lime, very hardy, 30 to 60cm (1 to 2ft), *fls* white and pinks, December to May; 'J.W. Porter' *fls* red-purple, young *lvs* red in spring; 'Silberschmelze' *fls* silvery-white: *E. erigena* (*mediterranea*) 7, Mediterranean heath, tolerates lime, 60 to 180cm (2 to 6ft), *fls* white and pinks, February to May; 'Superba' *fls* rose-pink, well-shaped shrub; 'W.T. Rackliff' *fls* white, rounded bush: *E. terminalis* 3, Corsican heath, tolerates lime, 1·2 to 1·8m (4 to 6ft), *fls* pink: *E. tetralix* 3, cross-leaved heath, cool moist position, dislikes lime, 15 to 30cm (6 to 12in), *fls* white, pink and red, June to October; 'Pink Star' *fls* pink, *lvs* soft grey: *E. vagans* 5, Cornish heath, tolerates slightly alkaline soils, 30 to 90cm (1 to 3ft), *fls* beautiful white, pinks and reds, August to October; 'Mrs D.F. Maxwell' *fls* deep rose-cerise.

Peat Gardens

Many interesting plants will not thrive in most garden soils and the only successful way of growing them is to provide them with their own isolated environment which recreates, to some extent, the conditions under which they grow naturally. To this end, peat gardens have been developed. Plants for peat gardens are usually low-growing and flourish in acid soils. They include some high alpine genera as well as woodland species.

Before the first peat gardens were built, most small plants were accommodated in rock gardens or woodland gardens. But rock gardens are really too dry, too well drained, too exposed to wind and too open to the sun to support woodland plants well and woodland gardens are often too shaded or have too many vigorous growing inhabitants for slow-growing dwarf plants to survive.

A peat bed positioned on a north-facing slope, clear of overhanging trees, gives

Right: an attractively planned heather garden with conifers

Bottom: choose heathers to give colour throughout the year

these particular plants the extra moisture, partial shade and safeguard from rampant neighbours which they need.

Building Peat Beds

Peat beds built on a slope are basically a series of flat terraces supported by informal walls. A peat bed can also be constructed in a flat garden as a raised bed. The walls can be made of peat blocks, stone or bricks, and both the peat walls and the crevices between blocks should be colonized by plants.

Peat block walls should be constructed using solid blocks of peat measuring about 20 to 30cm all round (8 or 12in cubes). The best blocks are obtained from the top layer of a sphagnum-heath moor after the surface vegetation has been removed but with the roots of the heathland flora still present. The dense greasy peat available in the lower strata is not as satisfactory.

Place the blocks in layers in a curving, informal design with the object of reconstructing in miniature, or at least giving the illusion of, a gouged-out, fissured heath. Make sure that the tops of the walls are level. If the points of the blocks are set so that they protrude into the air, they will dry out and the peat will be unable to support growing plants. The distance between each wall or step is determined by the slope of the ground: the greater the slope the closer together the walls should be positioned. See that the blocks fit tightly together. Where a gap appears seal it with moist peat to prevent draughts passing through the crevices and further drying out the peat.

Do not use alkaline soil to fill in behind the walls as the natural flora in this type of habitat is comprised of acid lovers. Soil texture too is important as none of the dwarf shrubby species or low-growing herbaceous perennials grow satisfactorily in a purely mineral soil. Mixing granulated peat with about an equal proportion of good loamy (acidic) soil will provide an excellent growing medium, encourage rooting and provide adequate moisture. This medium will make cultivation easy to carry out and the removal of weeds from this rich, open, spongy soil is relatively simple.

Planting

There is such a wide selection of acid-loving plants available that choosing plants for a peat bed is mainly a matter of personal taste. If you intend to raise a wide selection of acid-loving plants then those which are woody and permanently visible should be planted first. Arrange these more densely towards the middle or rear of the peat garden, leaving the front more open. This woody material plays many parts. First, by itself, it is decorative; second it acts as a background against which other plants may be displayed; third by its nature, it helps to protect plants from drying winds; and fourth it helps to confine micro-climates in which a large variety of decorative bulbous and herbaceous plants may be grown.

Once the woody plants are in place, the front of the beds can be planted with smaller plants and some can be set into the walls themselves.

Because many of the plants for a peat garden will be expensive to replace, the garden should be weeded by hand. Provision should be made for access at the start by laying small, flat pieces of sandstone at intervals to act as stepping stones. These should be arranged to let you cross the bed without having to tread on soil.

As the peat garden will contain some of the rarest and most attractive plants in the garden, it will probably receive a great deal of visual inspection from friends and relations. Once the bed has been planted it will need quite a lot of attention to keep the plants in tip-top condition. Certain species will require to be replaced more often than others, for example, some dwarf primulas are short-lived and must be replaced, others need frequent division. As a result of constant weeding, replanting and so on, fairly large amounts of soil will be removed and this must be replaced. Spring is the ideal time for this and it is best applied as a top dressing of granulated peat. You should also take the opportunity to add extra peat while attending to other cultural needs.

Plants for Peat Beds

Rhododendrons immediately come to mind but they constitute only a small fraction of the possible plant population. *Arcterica, Cassiope, Epigaea, Gaultheria, Kalmia, Kalmiopsis, Leucothoe, Menziesia, Pernettya* and *Phyllodoce* are other woody genera.

Herbaceous and bulbous plants should be drifted amongst the shrubby types and some useful ones include *Calceolaria, Cornus, Gentiana, Lilium, Linnaea, Meconopsis, Nomocharis, Notholirion, Omphalogramma, Orchis, Ourisia, Paris, Primula, Rhodohypoxis, Streptopus* and *Trientalis*.

Winter Gardens

When the first winter frost comes to blacken summer annuals, it can strike a chill and depressing note for the summer-only gardener. But for those who enjoy their garden the whole year through, it heralds a change of season that can be as pleasurable and just as exciting as the first stirrings of growth in the spring. However, to enjoy a garden fully in winter, it must be properly planned.

Struggling around, knee-deep in mud, or

slipping on sodden grass, can be uncomfortable and dangerous. Good paths of paving, concrete or gravel, especially where traffic is likely to be heavy, will protect you, the grass and the soil structure but make sure that the materials used are non-slip. A smooth concrete or paving finish can be quite dangerous, particularly in icy weather and, for the same reason, steep slopes should be avoided, steps at intervals being infinitely preferable.

Nearly all the plants that provide winter colour are perennial which means that they will be growing in the same spot for many years, so before planting them prepare the soil well paying particular attention to drainage. A heavy application of organic matter such as peat, compost or straw supplemented by regular mulching will improve the drainage of all but the most extreme soils. Where this is not sufficient use land drains. See *Soil*. Try to position the plants near a door of the house or the drive so that they can easily be seen without having to walk across the garden to find them.

Many plants will benefit from protection against cold winter winds and protection also makes conditions more comfortable for the gardener. Fences and walls will provide some protection but are not as effective as hedges. Winds tend to sweep over the top of solid screens and down again, protecting only a narrow strip. Hedges will reduce the force, while allowing the wind to pass through. The hedges must be very hardy, but the choice is quite wide. × *Cupressocyparis leylandii* is a very fast-growing conifer that provides an excellent, dense windbreak and a good backing for shrubs. *Berberis darwinii* is a hardy, evergreen flowering shrub that will stand quite hard clipping, while its cousins *B. julianae* and *B. stenophylla* make excellent informal hedges. Common beech, *Fagus sylvatica*, though not evergreen, will retain its dead leaves in winter but has the disadvantage of being rather slow growing.

There are many other hardy shrubs useful for hedging – see *Design and Planning: Hedges*.

Plants for the Winter Garden

There are four main qualities of plants that can provide interest and beauty in winter – flower, foliage, bark colour and form.

Shrubs and trees Viburnum is perhaps the most useful of winter flowering shrubs. *V. × bodnantense* will brighten the gloom of many a winter day with its bright, rose pink blossom, heavy with scent, from September to April. *V. × burkwoodii*, though not quite as spectacular, has the advantage of being evergreen, and will produce abundant pink, scented flowers in February. Also ever-green is *V. tinus*, which produces bright pink flower buds opening into white, and is particularly useful as a hedge.

An unusual winter-flowering shrub is the strawberry tree, *Arbutus unedo*. This bears panicles of white flowers in early winter, followed very quickly by the 'strawberry' fruits. Some rhododendrons such as *Rh.* 'Lee's Scarlet' flower through winter.

Of the low-growing shrubs, the most floriferous is *Erica carnea*. Varieties of this superb shrub can produce flowers of many colours throughout the winter, and, unlike many of the other varieties of heather, it will tolerate a little lime in the soil.

The yellow 'spidery' flowers of *Hamamelis mollis*, the graceful silvery catkins of *Garrya elliptica*, the abundant yellow flower of *Cornus mas* and the shrimp pink shoots of *Acer pennsylvanicum* 'Erythrocladum' will all bring a touch of spring to the greyest winter day.

Bark should not be forgotten as an extra source of colour. Perhaps the most striking example is the contrast of the bright yellow stems of *Cornus stolonifera* 'Flaviramea' and the almost luminous red of *C. alba* 'Sibirica'. Many of the willows have brightly coloured bark, the showiest being *Salix alba* 'Chermesina', with stems of orange to vermilion, and one of the loveliest winter sights of all is, *S.a.* 'Vitellina Pendula', the golden weeping willow. The weeping habit and delicate tracery of branches of the weeping silver birch *Betula pendula* 'Youngii' make it almost more attractive in winter than summer, to say nothing of the papery silver bark. When trees such as these are planted for the beauty of their shape, they must be given plenty of room. To crowd them would not only detract from that beauty, but also, in time, spoil the shape of the tree. To add interest, there are a few plants of peculiar habit, perhaps the most striking being the corkscrew hazel, *Corylus avellana* 'Contorta'. The grotesque twisting of the branches is highlighted and complemented by catkins in March.

Conifers Planted in groups, the great range of colours and leaf forms of *Chamaecyparis lawsoniana* varieties will complement each other well. These are all very hardy and range from the emerald green of *C.1.* 'Erecta' through the glaucous blue of *C.1.* 'Allumii', to the brilliant gold of *C.1.* 'Lanei'. Junipers, too, will provide not only a contrast of colour, but a great variety of form, and a 'must' for any large winter garden is the graceful, sweeping form and blue foliage of the blue cedar, *Cedrus atlantica glauca*. Many conifers change leaf colour in winter – for example *Chamaecyparis thyoides* and *C.t.* 'Ericoides' in particular.

Bulbs These are a necessity for a winter

garden and though from January onwards there are many bulbs to choose from, in the early winter months, crocuses are the only ones which will provide flowers. *C. asturicus purpureus* has purple flowers with scarlet stamens, while the lavender-coloured *C. longiflorus* can also be recommended.

Blooming in relays from early winter to spring are the varieties of hardy cyclamen. While, during the first three months of the year snowdrops, crocuses, winter aconites, anemones, irises such as *I. unguicularis*, scillas, narcissi, chionodoxas and hyacinths can all provide colour.

Seaside Gardens

Seaside gardens pose two main problems for plants: 1) they are generally exposed, and 2) the wind may be laden with salt. Trees and shrubs generally have to bear the brunt of these two hazards. Herbaceous perennials and other plants can often be given more sheltered situations. To make sure that trees and shrubs survive, they should be given some sort of shelter, only those types which are known to have some wind and salt-resistance should be planted and their cultivation may have to be modified to cope with their environment.

If evergreen trees and shrubs are planted in exposed coastal gardens in the autumn they may have to face up to six months of intermittent gales before they can attempt to grow and, during this time even the most wind- and salt-tolerant ones may die. Consequently they should not be planted until after the April gales so that they get at least six months of good growing weather to become established and acclimatized before they have to face the next bout of wind and salt. Prepare their planting positions before the drier weather sets in.

Deciduous plants being dormant and leafless in winter remain fairly immune from damage until they start to grow in spring. At this stage, most become extremely vulnerable and may be killed outright by the next salt-laden gale. Notable exceptions include hydrangeas and roses.

See *Cultivation* and *Ornamental Plants* for details of planting and staking.

The plants which are most likely to succeed in a coastal area are those with a maritime inheritance whose forerunners have become adapted to coastal exposures often in other maritime climates. Most of the reliable plants come from the coasts of Spain and from the Mediterranean, Japan, New Zealand and South America.

Providing Shelter

This can be done by using either artificial or natural screens.

Artificial screens Those which let about one half of the wind through are of great benefit since they provide considerable shelter without causing the turbulence which can be attributed to totally non-permeable screens and walls. Fine mesh wire netting (especially when folded double) and fine plastic mesh are excellent. A simple screen can be constructed by nailing laths vertically to a rigid framework of cross-members about 3m (10ft) long. The laths should be about 1·5m (5ft) high, spaced their own width apart and the cross-members should be held up by posts not less than 1·8m (6ft) long by 8cm (3in) square. The posts should be dipped in, or pressure treated with preservative before they are put up.

Natural screens These may consist of shelter hedges or trees or a combination of both with the hedges outermost. Unfortunately the three most salt tolerant evergreen shrubs, *Olearia traversii*, *Pittosporum crassifolium* and *Hebe × franciscana*, are the least cold hardy and are liable to severe frost damage if exposed for long periods to freezing winds.

Shelter hedges The plants listed on the right can be used as a hedge to provide shelter in coastal areas. Restrict trimming to a spring tidy-up in late April or early May followed by a closer trim immediately after flowering and a second main trim between mid-July and mid-August. Do not trim any later than August as this may produce young growth which will not mature before the winter gales set in. Escallonias are an exception as these often make considerable growth in September and October. The numbers after the botanical names are the North American hardiness zone ratings – see *Climate*. E means evergreen; M means suitable for milder coastal areas only.

Tree screens A shelter hedge or, where space permits, irregular groups of shrubs (as recommended for shelter hedges) should be planted along the exposed face of a tree screen to lift the wind and streamline the growth contour.

Shrubs for Primary Plantings

Once adequate shelter has been established, an ever-increasing range of ornamental shrubs can be tried but those likely to withstand the initial exposure are limited in variety.

(E)*Arbutus unedo* 6, Irish strawberry tree, 3 to 6m (10 to 20ft), *fls* clusters, creamy white, October to November, fruits same time, red, strawberry-like. *Propagation* seed, or half-ripe cuttings under intermittent mist. Tender when young, plant from pots in spring. *Pruning* trim only to shape when necessary.

Plants for shelter hedges

(E)	*Arundinaria japonica* 8
	Atriplex halimus 7
(E)	*Berberis darwinii* 7
	Berberis thunbergii 4
(E)	*Cotoneaster lacteus* 6
(E)	× *Cupressocyparis leylandii* 5–6
(E, M)	*Cupressus macrocarpa* 7
(E, M)	*Cupressus macrocarpa* 'Lutea' 7
(E)	*Elaeagnus × ebbingei* 4
(E, M)	*Escallonia* 'Apple Blossom' series 7
(E, M)	*Escallonia* 'Crimson Spire' 7
(E, M)	*Escallonia macrantha* 8
(E, M)	*Escallonia* 'Red Hedger' 7
(E)	*Euonymus japonicus* 7
(M)	*Fuchsia magellanica* 'Riccartonii' 5–6
	Genista hispanica 6
(E, M)	*Griselinia littoralis* 9
(E)	*Hebe × franciscana* 'Blue Gem' 9
(E)	*Lavandula spica* 5
(E)	*Ligustrum ovalifolium* 5
(E)	*Olearia haastii* 8
(E, M)	*Olearia macrodonta* 8
(E, M)	*Olearia solandri* 'Aurea' 8
(E, M)	*Olearia traversii* 9
(E, M)	*Pittosporum crassifolium* 10
(E)	*Pittosporum ralphii* 8
(E)	*Pittosporum tobira* 8
(E)	*Quercus ilex* 9
(E)	*Rhododendron ponticum* 6
	Ribes sanguineum 5
	Rosa rugosa 2
(E)	*Rosmarinus officinalis* 6
(E)	*Ulex europaeus* 'Plenus' 6
(E)	*Viburnum tinus* 7–8

Trees for screens

(E)	*Acer pseudoplatanus* 5
(E)	*Almus glutinosa* 3
(E)	× *Cupressocyparis leylandii* 5–6
(E, M)	*Cupressus macrocarpa* 7
(E, M)	*Cupressus macrocarpa* 'Lutea' 7
(E, M)	*Eucalyptus coccifera* 9
(E)	*Picea sitchensis* 6
(E)	*Pinus contorta* 2
(E)	*Pinus nigra austriaca* 4
(E)	*Pinus pinaster* 7
(E, M)	*Pinus radiata (insignis)* 7
(E)	*Pinus sylvestris* 2
(E)	*Pinus thunbergii* 4
(E)	*Populus alba* 3
(E)	*Populus nigra* 'Italica' 2
(E)	*Populus* 'Robusta' 2
(E)	*Quercus ilex* 9
(E)	*Salix acutufolia* 6

Artemisia abrotanum 5, southernwood, 90cm to 1·2m (3 to 4ft), *lvs* aromatic, finely divided, grey. *Propagation* hardwood cuttings in autumn or winter. *Pruning* cut back in March to promote bushy growth.

(E)*Arundinaria japonica* 8, Japanese bamboo, 3 to 3·5m (10 to 12ft), *lvs* large. *Propagation* by division May to July. *Pruning* older canes may be cut for use as plant supports.

Atriplex halimus 7, sea purslane, 1·2 to 1·8m (4 to 6ft), rapid grower, *fls* inconspicuous, *lvs* soft, silvery grey. *Propagation* hardwood cuttings in July. *Pruning* cut back to shape in spring and repeat as necessary during growing season.

(E)*Ballota pseudodictamnus* 7, low compact bush, may die in a wet winter, 60 to 90cm (2 to 3ft), *fls* small pink in spikes with persistent grey-green bracts, June, July, *lvs* orbicular, grey, heavily felted. *Propagation* soft cuttings in May. *Pruning* cut back older growth to basal shoots in April, remove flowered growth in July.

(E)*Berberis darwinii* 7, Darwin's barberry, dense bush, 1·8 to 2·4m (6 to 8ft), *fls* orange-yellow in pendant racemes, March to May, *lvs* small, holly-like, berries purple. *Propagation* seed, or cuttings in a cold frame in winter. *Pruning* to shape if necessary in spring, older plants may be pruned in May after flowering: *B.* × *ottawensis* 'Superba' 5, hybrid purple barberry, 1·8 to 2·4m (6 to 8ft), *fls* pale yellow, May, June, *lvs* orbicular, plum-purple, young shoots crimson-purple. *Propagation* soft cuttings in intermittent mist or hardwood cuttings in the open in autumn. *Pruning* to shape in winter or spring: *B. thunbergii* 4, Thunberg's barberry, all forms of this variable species are wind and salt tolerant. Compact bush, up to 2·4m (8ft), *fls* pale yellow, May, June, *lvs* orbicular. *Propagation* and *Pruning* as for *B.* × *ottawensis* 'Superba'.

Buddleia davidii 5, most varieties are suitable, 1·8 to 3m (6 to 10ft), *fls* either lavender, purple, black-purple, rosy-purple or white, July, August. *Propagation* seed or cuttings. *Pruning* remove twiggy growth and shorten longer shoots in March: (E) *B. fallowiana* 7, compact grower, 1·8 to 2·4m (6 to 8ft), *lvs* silvery grey usually persistent; 'Lochinch', *fls* broad blue spikes; 'Alba', *fls* long slender white spikes, June, July, *lvs* white-felted. *Propagation* cuttings. *Pruning* shorten flowered shoots if desired: *B. globosa* 7, Chilean orange ball tree, very rapid growing, 1·8 to 3m (6 to 10ft), *fls* in racemes of orange balls, June, July, *lvs* long, pendant; 'Lemon Ball', *fls* stiff erect panicles, habit more vigorous and densely bushy. *Propagation* half-ripe or hardwood cuttings. *Pruning* spent growth may be removed after flowering in July.

(E)*Cassinia fulvida* (*Diplopappus chrysophyllus*) 5, golden heath-like bush, 1·2 to 1·5m (4 to 5ft), *fls* small, white in dense terminal heads, July, August. *Propagation* half-ripe or hardwood cuttings. *Pruning* cut back in spring to promote bushy growth.

(E)*Choisya ternata* 7, Mexican orange blossom, 1·8 to 2·4m (6 to 8ft), *fls* white in dense panicles, May to November, *lvs* dark green and glossy with peppery aroma. *Propagation* half-ripe or hardwood cuttings. *Pruning* seldom necessary, old plants may be pruned severely in April.

(E)*Cistus*, rock rose, most species are wind and salt tolerant. *Propagation* seed or soft cuttings. *Pruning* trim lightly after flowering to reduce seed setting: *C. crispus* 7, 75 to 90cm (2½ to 3ft), *fls* rose pink, May to September, *lvs* grey, crinkled: *C.* × *cyprius* 7, 1·2 to 1·5m (4 to 5ft), *fls* in clusters, white blotched maroon, June, July, *lvs* grey-green, aromatic: *C. ladaniferus* 7,

A peat garden. At the back is *Rhododendron* 'Elizabeth'

resembles *C.* × *cyprius*, 1·5 to 1·8m (5 to 6ft), more erect growth, *fls* not in clusters, May, June, *lvs* narrower, gummy: *C. laurifolius* 7, hardiest species, 1·5 to 1·8m (5 to 6ft), *fls* white, June, July, *lvs* lance-shaped, leathery: *C.* × *pulverulentus* 7, 'Sunset', 'Warley Rose', 60 to 90cm (2 to 3ft), *fls* carmine pink, May, June, *lvs* grey.

(E)*Convolvulus cneorum* 9, small compact bush, needs full sun and good drainage, 60 to 90cm (2 to 3ft), *fls* white, funnel-shaped, buds pink, May to September, *lvs* small, silvery-grey, silky. *Propagation* half-ripe cuttings July, August. *Pruning* seldom necessary, trim to shape in April.

(E)*Cordyline australis* 10, dracaena palm, very wind tolerant tree palm of sub-tropical appearance, 4·5 to 7·5m (15 to 25ft), *fls* tiny white, heavily scented in immense terminal panicles, June, July, *lvs* long and sword-like in dense plumes at end of vertical trunk which branches after flowering. *Propagation* seed. *Pruning* remove spent flower panicles to prevent seeding.

(E)*Corokia virgata* 9, dense erect bush, 1·5 to 1·8m (5 to 6ft), *fls* small golden, starry, berries orange, sparse, May, June, *lvs* small bronze-green on grey stems. *Propagation* seed or half-ripe or hardwood cuttings. *Pruning* seldom necessary, best after flowering in June.

Cortaderia (*Gynerium*) 8, pampas grass, all species will tolerate full coastal exposure, 1·8 to 2·4m (6 to 8ft), *fls* in silvery plumes on long stems, autumn, *lvs* long, grass-like in dense clusters. *Propagation* seed, or by division in April or May. *Pruning* remove old *fls* in spring. Old plants may be set alight whilst dormant to clear dead matter.

Cotoneaster, most species and hybrids will tolerate considerable exposure to wind and salt, *fls* white to pink, June. *Propagation* seed or hardwood cuttings. *Pruning* to shape where necessary in winter. Most tolerant are: (E) *C. lacteus* 6, rounded bush, 1·8 to 2·4m (6 to 8ft), *lvs* large, oval, leathery, grey-backed, berries small in broad clusters: (E) *C. microphyllus* 5, prostrate or pendulous ground-hugging species, berries extra large but sparse, useful for exposed banks and walls: (E) *C. wardii* 6, stiff, erect shrub with slender grey shoots, 1·5 to 1·8m (5 to 6ft), *lvs* small, glossy dark green, white beneath, fruits orange.

(M)*Cytisus*, most brooms (including *Genista* and *Spartium*) are tolerant of coastal exposure, particularly recommended are the dwarfer hybrids of *C.* ×

praecox 5, 90cm to 1·2m (3 to 4ft), April, May; 'Albus', *fls* white early; 'Allgold', *fls* bright yellow; 'Hollandia', *fls* deep rose with pale pink; 'Zeelandia', *fls* deep pink and cream. *Propagation* half-ripe cuttings. *Pruning* cut back immediately after flowering in summer but not into old hard wood. *C.* × 'Porlock', remarkably hardy tall-growing hybrid, 1·8 to 3m (6 to 10ft), *fls* yellow in rounded clusters, February to July. *Propagation* half-ripe cuttings or seed. *Pruning* cut back spent flowered growths in June.

Deutzia, more tolerant of coastal exposure than most other deciduous shrubs, *fls* in paniculate clusters. *Propagation* soft cuttings. *Pruning* remove spent growth after flowering. *D.* 'Mont Rose' 5, 1·2 to 1·5m (4 to 5ft), *fls* rose pink, June, July; *D. scabra* 4–5, see *Ornamental Plants: Shrubs*.

(E)*Elaeagnus*, extremely tough, wind and salt tolerant shrubs thriving in almost any soil or situation, excellent as gap-fillers at foot of established trees. The inconspicuous white bells are very fragrant in autumn. *Propagation* half-ripe cuttings. *Pruning* to shape in spring. *E.* × *ebbingei* 4 (*E. macrophylla* × *pungens*), 1·8 to 2·4m (6 to 8ft),

A winter garden will consist mainly of foliage plants

lvs large, glossy dark green, silvery beneath, fruits orange flecked silver; 'Salcombe Seedling', a more compact and freer-flowering clone: *E. pungens* 7, compact bush, 1·8 to 2·4m (6 to 8ft), *lvs* dark green with silvery brown-speckled underside; 'Maculata' 5, slower grower, 1·2 to 1·8m (4 to 6ft), *lvs* with central splashes of gold; 'Variegata', a more vigorous form, 1·8 to 2·4m (6 to 8ft), *lvs* dark green, glossy with creamy yellow margins: *E.* × *reflexa* 3 (*E. glabra* × *pungens*), 1·8 to 3m (6 to 10ft), *lvs* narrow with margins usually undulated, undersides burnished gold. Branches often long and scandent, capable of climbing adjacent trees.

(E)*Erica*, all species are considerably wind and salt tolerant as are *Calluna*. Coastal sites usually have alkaline soil due to adulteration with sea, sand and salt spray. *Propagation* half-ripe cuttings or from layers. *Pruning* clip off spent flower heads if desired. Lime tolerant kinds include: *E. carnea* 5: *E.* × *darleyensis* 6: *E. mediterranea* 7: *E. terminalis* 3: and *E. vagans* 5. See *Heather Gardens* for further details.

(E, M)*Escallonia* 7–8, includes the most colourful and useful of wind and salt tolerant evergreen shrubs combining rapid growth with massed displays of red, pink or white *fls*. The 'Apple Blossom' series of Irish origin have the largest chalice-shaped blossoms with compact bushy growth. 'Pride of Donard' is the best bright red, 1·2 to 1·8m (4 to 6ft). *Propagation* hardwood cuttings in autumn. *Pruning* remove spent flowering growth in July, prune to shape in March. Taller growing kinds include 'C.F. Ball', 1·8 to 2·4m (6 to 8ft), *fls* large, scarlet; 'Crimson Spire' and 'Red Hedger', similar hedging vars of vigorous, erect growth: *E. macrantha* 8, 1·8 to 2·4m (6 to 8ft), *fls* rose-crimson, June to November, *lvs* large, glossy, sticky, aromatic.

(E, M)*Eucalyptus* 8 and 9, most species are considerably wind and salt tolerant trees. *Propagation* seed. *Pruning* seldom necessary, heading back should be in March or April. *E. coccifera*, slow bushy habit, *lvs* small, grey lanceolate, silvery young shoots: *E. gunnii*, *lvs* silver-blue orbicular when young, on adult trees sickle-shaped, sage-green: *E. parvifolia*, erect, *lvs* narrow, blue-green.

(E)*Euonymus japonicus* 7, Japanese spindleberry, tough hedge plants of slow erect growth, 1·8 to 3m (6 to 10ft). *Propagation* hardwood cuttings in autumn or winter. *Pruning* spring and July, August where desirable.

(E)*Euphorbia characias* 6, giant shrubby spurge, 1·2 to 1·8m (4 to 6ft), *fls* in large cylindrical heads lime green with chocolate centres, March to June, *lvs* long and narrow, sea-green with coffee-like aroma: *E. veneta* 6, *fls* very large, spherical, lime-green. *Propagation* seed or cuttings. *Pruning* remove spent flower stems May, June.

(M)*Fuchsia magellanica* 'Riccartonii' 5–6, hedge fuchsia, vigorous grower, *fls* pendulous, sepals red, corollas purple; 'Mrs P. Wood', 1·5 to 2·4m (5 to 8ft), *fls* deep pink, July to November, *lvs* light green. *Propagation* soft or hardwood cuttings. *Pruning* prior to growth initiation in spring.

Genista, allied to *Cytisus* (broom) and *Ulex* (gorse). *G. hispanica* 6, Spanish gorse, low compact bush, 45 to 60cm (1½ to 2ft), *fls* golden yellow very profuse, May, June. *Propagation* hardwood cuttings in February. *Pruning* seldom necessary, after flowering.

(E, M)*Griselinia littoralis* 9, erect grower, makes good hedges, 1·8 to 2·4m (6 to 8ft), *lvs* bright green orbicular. *Propagation* seed or hardwood cuttings. *Pruning* April or August if necessary.

(E)*Hebe*, shrubby veronica, includes the most wind and salt tolerant of evergreen flowering shrubs. *Propagation* cuttings or seed. *Pruning* seldom necessary, March or August. *H. dieffenbachii* 9, spreading hummock-like bush, 1·2 to 1·8m (4 to 6ft), *fls* long spikes, off-white or pale purple, June, July, *lvs* long, sea-green: *H.* × *franciscana* 9 (*H. elliptica* × *speciosa*), dense, rounded bush, 90cm to 1·8m (3 to 6ft), *fls* fragrant, purple, midsummer to midwinter, *lvs* dark green, glossy, hardy on coasts in all but coldest areas of British Isles; 'Variegata' is a dwarfer grower with *lvs* broadly margined creamy yellow, *fls* lilac-pink to purple in short, fragrant racemes: *H. speciosa* 10, *fls* ranging from white through shades of pink to crimson, and lavender to dark purple – large number of garden varieties.

(E)*Helichrysum*, grey or white-leaved shrubs tolerant of extreme coastal exposures. *Propagation* soft or half-ripe cuttings. *Pruning* remove spent branches after flowering. Delay hard pruning until April. (M) *H. petiolatum* 10, vigorous cascading species, not suitable for colder areas, *fls* pale yellow, *lvs* woolly grey: *H. plicatum* 10, dense low bush, 60 to 90cm (2 to 3ft), *fls* flat golden heads radiating on long slender stems, June, July, *lvs* long, narrow, silvery white: *H. lithospermifolium* 9, similar to *H.*

plicatum with *fls* paler and *lvs* broader and whiter: *H. rosmarinifolium* 'Violaceum' 10, tall, erect, heath-like shrub, 1·8 to 2·4m (6 to 8ft), *fls* small, dense heads, lilac-purple in bud opening pure white, May to July, *lvs* small, narrow on white-felted stems: *H. serotinum* 10 (*angustifolium*), curry bush, 60 to 90cm (2 to 3ft), *fls* small, yellow, July to September, *lvs* sage-green with curry-like aroma.

Hippophae rhamnoides 3, sea buckthorn, tall, erect shrub, *lvs* silvery-blue and willow-like. Females have orange-yellow berries where both sexes are grown. Largely wind-pollinated so site male to windward of females. *Propagation* seed, or suckers in autumn or winter. *Pruning* seldom necessary, winter.

(E)*Hoheria*, New Zealand lacebark, tender, develops rapidly into tall, erect shrub or small tree considerably wind and salt tolerant, *fls* white, nectar-scented in dense clusters resembling mock orange, late summer. *Propagation* seed, soft cuttings or layers. *Pruning* seldom necessary, spring.

Hydrangea macrophylla 5 and 6, remarkably tolerant of coastal exposure, *fls* of two distinct types. The lacecap forms represent the wild or primitive type with central bosses of small fertile florets (usually purple) more or less surrounded by conspicuous florets either white or shaded pink to blue. The mophead or Hortensia forms have large globular heads of white, pink, red or blue or a combination of these shades. White varieties may scorch pink in hot sunlight, blue varieties turn pink in alkaline soils, on acid soils pink varieties flower blue and red varieties flower purple. The redder varieties are usually the more compact and dwarf growers. 'Ayesha' is distinct in having heads of thick-petalled cup-shaped florets, with a faint fragrance that resemble those of a giant lilac coloured silvery blue or pink. *Propagation* soft, half-ripe or hardwood cuttings. *Pruning* cut old *fl* heads back to first pair of growth buds in April, hard pruning leads to vigorous but flowerless growth.

(E)*Ilex* 5 to 7, holly, mainly tolerant of coastal exposure and many have attractively variegated foliage. Most are unisexual so that female plants will not berry without male pollination; 'J.C. van Tol' and 'Pyramidalis' are hermaphrodite (self-fertile); 'Golden King' is the best variegated variety. For ilex oak see *Quercus ilex*. *Propagation* half-ripe cuttings. *Pruning* seldom necessary, spring.

(E)*Juniperus* 2 to 9, juniper, probably the most wind and salt tolerant of the conifers, ranging from small trees to low ground-hugging forms. They provide interesting contrasts in both colour and form. *Propagation* half-ripe cuttings or layers. *Pruning* seldom necessary, spring.

Kniphofia 'Atlanta' 7, Giant Cape torch lily or red hot poker, non-woody not strictly a shrub, 90cm to 1·2m (3 to 4ft), *fls* scarlet torchlike spikes with pale yellow throats, May, June, *lvs* bold whorls, persistent, excels in full coastal exposure. *Propagation* by division. *Pruning* spent flower stems can be cut away in June.

(E)*Laurus nobilis* 7, sweet bay, erect and compact bush, 3 to 4·5m (10 to 15ft), *lvs* large, dark-green, aromatic, *fls* small, creamy-yellow, berries black. *Propagation* half-ripe or hardwood cuttings, or seed. *Pruning* trim to required shape in April and/or July.

(E)*Lavandula*, lavender. *Propagation* hardwood cuttings or seed. *Pruning* trim immediately after flowering. *L. spica* 5, Old English lavender, 60 to 90cm (2 to 3ft), *fls* in dense spikes on long slender stems. There are forms with white or pink flowers, also dwarf and compact growing varieties.

Lavatera olbia 7, shrub mallow, vigorous grower often attaining full stature in first season after planting, 1·8 to 2·4m (6 to 8ft), *fls* large pink, July to November, *lvs* soft and downy. *Propagation* cuttings or seed. *Pruning* shorten all growths in the late autumn, prune plants more severely in April.

(E)*Ligustrum*, privet, flourishes in coastal exposures, *fls* white in dense panicles, berries black. *L. ovalifolium* 5, oval-leaf hedge privet, 1·8 to 3m (6 to 10ft); 'Aureomarginatum', golden privet, slower growing than green form, 1·8 to 2·4m (6 to 8ft), a striking source of bright golden foliage. *Propagation* hardwood cuttings. *Pruning* March and July as necessary.

(E)*Medicago arborea* 7, moon trefoil, dense bush, 1·5 to 1·8m (5 to 6ft), *fls* small, orange, April to December, *lvs* small grey. *Propagation* half-ripe cuttings or seed. *Pruning* seldom necessary, spring.

(E)*Myrtus apiculata* (*luma*) 8 and 9, Chilean tree myrtle, tall shrub or small tree, 3 to 6m (10 to 20ft), *fls* white, August to October, *lvs* small, oval, dull green, aromatic when crushed, fruits black, bark peeling, rust brown. *Propagation* seed or half-ripe cuttings. *Pruning* seldom necessary, spring.

325

(E)*Olearia*, daisy bush, some of the toughest and most salt tolerant evergreen shrubs. *O. albida* 8, 1·8 to 2·4m (6 to 8ft), August to September, *lvs* tough, grey green, privet shaped: also *O. haastii* 8, *O. macrodonta* 8 and *O.* × *scilloniensis* 9 – see *Ornamental Plants: Shrubs* for details: *O. solandri* 'Aurea' 8, dense bush, 1·5 to 2·1m (5 to 7ft), *fls* creamy white, fragrant, October, November, *lvs* golden thyme-like on matching stems. *Propagation* half-ripe or hardwood cuttings. *Pruning* trim after flowering, severe pruning March, April.

(E)*Phlomis fruticosa* 7, Jerusalem sage, rounded bush, 90cm to 1·2m (3 to 4ft), *fls* golden whorls of bright yellow on stiff stems, June, July, *lvs* soft, woolly. *Propagation* seed or hardwood cuttings. *Pruning* remove spent branches after flowering.

(E, M)*Phormium* 9, New Zealand flax, to 4·5m (15ft), *fls* borne on stout arching stems, bronze-red, *lvs* large, sword-shaped, sea-green, bronze, purple or striped creamy yellow on different forms and from 75cm to 2·4m (2½ft to 8ft) long, sub-tropical appearance. *Propagation* seeds or division. *Pruning* remove spent flower stems.

(E)*Pittosporum crassifolium* 10, tall-growing, 3 to 4·5m (10 to 15ft), *fls* deep purple in terminal clusters, May, June, *lvs* leathery, downy-backed, recurved at the edges, not very winter-hardy: *P. ralphii* 8, resembles *P. crassifolium* but has thinner leaves and is more frost-resistant: *P. tobira* 8, Japanese species, 1·8 to 3m (6 to 10ft), *fls* conspicuous clusters of fragrant creamy-white orange-blossom, May to September, *lvs* rhododendron-like. Likes hot dry summers. *Propagation* seeds, cuttings. *Pruning* seldom necessary, April or July.

Potentilla 2 to 5, shrubby cinquefoils, compact bushes, 60cm to 1·2m (2 to 4ft), *fls* like tiny single roses opening over long period, white, blush pink, cream, yellow, tangerine-orange, May to November, *lvs* small, divided. *Propagation* soft cuttings or seed. *Pruning* seldom necessary, January.

(E)*Quercus ilex* 9, evergreen or holm oak, bushy, *lvs* dark green, finely-toothed, can be grown as a clipped hedge or allowed to develop to a large tree. *Propagation* acorns. *Pruning* seldom necessary, April or July.

(E)*Rhododendron ponticum* 6, common purple rhododendron, very wind and salt tolerant shrub for acid and neutral soils, 1·8 to 3m (6 to 10ft), June, July. *Propagation* seed or layers. *Pruning* seldom necessary, July (after flowering).

Ribes sanguineum 5, flowering currant, 1·8 to 2·4m (6 to 8ft), *fls* in pendulous racemes, white, pink or red, February to April. *Propagation* hardwood cuttings. *Pruning* cut back in late spring after flowering, April, May.

Rosa 2 to 10, several shrub-roses are extremely wind and salt tolerant, particularly *R. rugosa*. See *Ornamental Plants: Roses*.

(E)*Rosmarinus officinalis* 6, rosemary, shrubs varying in stature from erect bushes to prostrate and pendulous types, to 1·8m (6ft), *fls* small in numerous axillary clusters, white, grey-blue, rich blue or lilac-pink, January to April, *lvs* small with white undersides. *Propagation* cuttings or seed. *Pruning* trim after flowering.

(E)*Santolina chamaecyparissus* 6 and 7, cotton lavender, dwarf hummock-shaped bush, 60 to 75cm (2 to 2½ft), *fls* orange-yellow in button-like heads on tall slender stalks, July, *lvs* silvery white. *Propagation* hardwood cuttings. *Pruning* remove spent flowering growth, can be severely pruned in March.

(E)*Senecio greyii* 4 and 5 (*S. laxifolius* can also be sold under this name), a rare, low spreading bush, 90cm to 1·2m (3 to 4ft), *fls* golden-yellow, daisy, in large panicles, July, August, *lvs* grey and silver. *Propagation* hardwood cuttings. *Pruning* remove spent flowering growth, can be severely pruned in March: (E) *S. monroi*, 75 to 90cm (2½ to 3ft), *fls* golden, daisy-like, July, August, *lvs* small, bright green, finely toothed, rippled along the margins: (E) *S. reinoldii*, tall, large-leaved shrub of unusual architectural character, 1·8 to 3m (6 to 10ft), *lvs* large, rounded, tough and leathery with felted undersides. Intolerant of dry situations. *Propagation* hardwood cuttings. *Pruning* seldom necessary, spring.

Spartium junceum 7, Spanish broom, one of the fastest-growing shrubs with almost leafless bright green stems, 1·8 to 2·4m (6 to 8ft), *fls* yellow, large, fragrant in pointed terminal spikes, May to November. *Propagation* seed. *Pruning* can be pruned severely in autumn or spring.

Tamarix 2 to 8, tamarisk, thrives in exposed coastal areas, 1·8 to 2·4m (6 to 10ft), *fls* slender racemes, April to September, *lvs* feathery and cypress-like on slender whippy shoots. *Propagation* hardwood cuttings. *Pruning* summer-flowering kinds should be pruned in late spring, later ones immediately after flowering.

(E)*Teucrium fruticans* 6, shrubby germander, attractive white-stemmed shrub, 1·2 to 1·8m (4 to 6ft), *fls* pale blue in terminal racemes, June to September, *lvs* ovate with white undersides. *Propagation* half-ripe cuttings, or seed. *Pruning* severe pruning in spring and/or trim to shape in July.

(E)*Ulex europaeus* 6, gorse, furze or whin, best when growing in poor soil, the non-seeding form 'Plenus' with double flowers is that most usually available from nurseries, 1·2 to 1·8m (4 to 6ft), *fls* massed, chrome yellow, March to May. *Propagation* hardwood cuttings (or seed of the wild form). *Pruning* cut back after flowering.

Veronica see *Hebe*.

(E)*Viburnum tinus* 7 and 8, laurustinus, this winter-flowering evergreen stands coastal exposure well, 1·8 to 3m (6 to 10ft), *fls* white, buds pink in flattened cymes, November to April, *lvs* dark glossy green, oval. *Propagation* half-ripe or hardwood cuttings, or seed. *Pruning* seldom necessary, spring.

(E)*Yucca gloriosa* 7, Adam's needle, 1 to 2m (3 to 7ft), *fls* conical panicles, creamy white, sometimes tinged pink on stout erect stems, July to October, *lvs* broad, stiff, glaucous green. *Propagation* offsets, 'cuttings' comprising broken off crowns, or seed. *Pruning* remove spent flower spikes.

Gardening in the Shade

Shade can be defined as an absence of direct sunlight, but the amount of light available in shaded spots can vary from the light, sun-broken shade of lightly branched trees such as birch, to the deep shade found under low, spreading conifers like cedars. Tall buildings can create shade; in these cases the light may be reasonably good but with no direct sunlight. The amount of sun a garden gets will vary with the position of shade-causing objects and the time of year. In winter the sun is lower in the sky than in summer. The further you go from the equator, the larger the difference between summer and winter. So part of the garden which might get a reasonable amount of sunshine in the summer might be in shade most of the winter. The shadiest parts of a garden are often the driest ones – the cover which keeps sun out can keep rain out too.

Shade is a natural condition and many plants have adapted themselves to growing in shade conditions. Many have large leaves to utilize to best advantage the reduced levels of light reaching them. Some, like ferns, have very finely divided leaves to catch the available light. Most true shade plants are to be found growing along the fringes of deciduous woodland or forests, or in older woodlands where the branch canopy is high and a reasonable level of diffused light reaches the woodland floor.

Deep shade The deepest shade in a garden can be found under evergreen trees and shrubs, particularly those planted in groups and those with low, spreading branches. Under these the light remains poor and the soil remains dry throughout the year. Weeds rarely grow and it is usually impracticable to attempt to grow plants in such situations. It is better to plant a screening shrub or small conifer in the foreground to hide any dark gaping opening. Conditions under deciduous trees may vary considerably in the course of a year. For example, when *Fagus sylvatica*, common beech, is in leaf it casts dense shade, but during the winter and early spring months it is leafless and the soil underneath becomes blessed with sunshine and thoroughly moistened by rain. So, in theory, some plants will establish beneath a beech but, in practice, those which do are usually plants of little visual attraction and of little garden value. They generally make their growth early in the year and die down again as the tree comes into full leaf. Other deciduous trees present much less of a challenge – their shade is not quite as dense during the summer and many of the plants listed below such as camellias and daffodils will grow well. Conditions towards the outside of the branch spread of most trees are much more favourable to plant growth. In summer dappled sunlight may penetrate the foliage cover and the ground is less sheltered from the rain. Low-growing, shade-tolerant plants will thrive.

Light shade (open shade) Parts of the garden which are not sheltered by overhanging branches but are shaded from direct sun by tall trees or buildings are much easier to deal with than those in deep shade. Soil dryness is not usually a problem and there is considerable scope in the choice of plants. Most hardy plants will grow in sunless situations in the open but because they do not usually flower with the freedom of similar plants growing in sunny situations, you should restrict your choice of plants to those you know will tolerate shade.

Shade and Planning

In planning any garden one of the first steps is to determine which parts of the garden receive maximum sunshine and which parts remain shaded or sunless for the whole day or part of the day.

Annual flowers and bedding plants These require full sun and, with very few exceptions, do not grow or flower well in shade. Many will only open their flowers in sunlight. A few, such as *Collinsia*, *Nemophila*, *Nicotiana* and *Tropaeolum peregrinum*, may succeed reasonably well in light shade.

Bulbous plants Most are tolerant of light shade or sunless situations including: *Galanthus* 3 and 4; *Scilla* 2 to 4; *Endymion non-scriptus* 5; *Chionodoxa* 4; *Narcissus* 4 to 6; *Lilium* 2 to 10; *Erythronium* 2 to 5. The following require sunny situations and only open their flowers in direct sunlight: Tulips, *Gladiolus*, *Colchicum* 4 to 6 and *Crocus* 4 to 6, *Cardiocrinum* 6.

Herbaceous plants There are many herbaceous plants which tolerate sunless situations. Amongst those tolerant of deeper shade are: *Anemone nemorosa* 5, *Astrantia* 6, *Bergenia* 2 and 3, *Convallaria majalis* 2 and 3, *Corydalis lutea* 5, *Galeobdolon luteum* 'Variegatum' 4, *Tellima grandiflora* 4, and several species of hardy ferns.

Shrubs Many shrubs need full sun – see *Ornamental Plants: Shrubs* – but the following can be planted in open shade or in the deeper shade under the outer branch spread of larger trees. *Aucuba japonica* 7, *Berberis verruculosa* 5, *Buxus sempervirens* and vars 5, *Camellia japonica* and vars 7, *Elaeagnus macrophylla* 7, *Euonymus japonicus* and vars 7, *Euonymus fortunei* 5, × *Fatshedera lizei* 7, *Hedera helix* and vars 4, particularly 'Hibernica', *Hypericum calycinum* 6, *Ilex aquifolium* and vars 6, *Ligustrum* species and vars 4 to 7, *Lonicera nitida* and vars 7, *Mahonia aquifolium* 5, *Osmanthus heterophyllus* and vars 6, *Pachysandra terminalis* and vars 5, *Prunus laurocerasus* 6 and 7, *Prunus lusitanica* and vars 7, *Ribes alpinum* 2, *Rubus odoratus* 3, *Ruscus* species 7, *Sarcococca* species 5 to 7, *Skimmia* species 7, *Symphoricarpos* species 3, *Viburnum davidii* 7, *Vinca* species and vars 4 to 7.

Roses These prefer a sunny situation but a few climbing ones will flower reasonably well in sunless situations (see below).

Wall plants North-facing walls are invariably sunless in the northern hemisphere, except perhaps for a little low-angled sunlight in the early morning and late evening at the height of summer. Hardy climbers or wall shrubs suitable for training against north-facing walls (south-facing in the southern hemisphere) include: *Chaenomeles speciosa* vars 4, *Clematis* (most early flowering deciduous kinds, particularly *Clematis montana* and vars 6 and *Clematis* × *jackmanii* vars 5), *Cotoneaster henryana* 7, *Cotoneaster lacteus* 6, *Forsythia suspensa* 5, *Garrya elliptica* 8, *Hedera helix* vars 4, *Hydrangea petiolaris* 4, *Jasminum nudiflorum* 5, *Lonicera japonica* 4, *Parthenocissus henryana* 8, *Pyracantha* 5 to 7,

climbing roses such as 'Parkdirektor Riggers', 'Danse du Feu', 'Guinée', 'Hamburger Phoenix', 'Paul's Lemon Pillar'. Where there is relatively little or no winter frost, *Berberidopsis corallina* 10 and *Lapageria rosea* 10 are excellent climbers for sunless situations.

Glasshouses These should nearly always be positioned in full sun. (The exception is when you want to grow ferns or some orchids exclusively.) Direct sunlight is particularly important in the early part of the year when seedlings and young plants are being raised and days are short and the angle of sunlight is low. Maximum sunlight is essential for satisfactory growth – see *Greenhouses*.

Lawns Lawn grasses do not grow well under trees. They tend to die out or become sparse and moss-infested in the reduced light and dry conditions. Mixtures of shade-tolerant grasses can be bought for light shade, but if they are mown closely they will soon die out. Do not cut them closer than 4cm (1½in) from ground level. You could use ground-cover plants like *Ophiopogon japonicus* instead of grass – see *Design and Planning: Banks*.

Fruit Fruit needs sun to ripen properly. Worth trying in sunless situations are culinary (cooking) apples and pears, and gooseberries. All can be grown as espaliers or cordons against sunless walls.

Vegetables All vegetables should be planted in sunny positions. The yields may be considerably reduced in sunless situations.

House Plants

A house plant is broadly any plant that will grow well in the home. The range of plants which can be grown indoors is almost as diverse in size, shape, form and colour as those which can be grown outside. Most are foliage plants but they vary from those which are bushy and rounded in shape, to upright, climbing or even trailing ones. There are plants for sunny window-sills, shaded halls, humid kitchens and bathrooms, cool north-facing rooms with good light and for rooms with gas fires. None is difficult to grow, provided their needs are known and supplied.

Watering In the artificial conditions of pot cultivation watering has to be done very carefully. Water the plants only when the surface of their growing mix becomes dry; give sufficient water each time to fill the space between the surface of the mix and the rim of the pot, let the excess drain away and then leave the plant until the surface becomes dry again. Dribbles of water every day will do more harm than good. If possible use soft water (rain water) and let it reach room temperature by standing it in a warm room for half a day. Much more water is needed by plants while they are actively growing and flowering than in their rest period (usually November to March in the northern hemisphere). When possible, water from a can with a narrow spout.

Feeding Plants absorb food in solution, so they should only be fed when the growing mix is damp. Liquid foods or fertilizers can be used when the nutrients in the growing mix begin to run short – see *Soil*. Some plants need more food than others. Feeding is necessary while plants are in active growth and often when flowering but not when resting. Proprietary liquid fertilizers, foliar feeds and slow-release pellet feeds are available with instructions for rates of dilution with water and frequency of feeding on the container.

Temperature In general the minimum winter temperature should not be less than 4°C (40°F). The more tender plants need at least 10°C (50°F). Winter temperature is rather crucial for house plants but they can stand a slightly lower one than normal if the growing mix is kept on the dry side. Evenness of temperature is important (see Troubles). In most countries the summer temperature should be kept below 24°C (75°F) because there is not sufficient light and humidity in the home to balance higher temperatures. Some countries – Australia, South Africa and parts of the USA like California – have ample light, and much higher temperatures can be tolerated.

Humidity Moisture in the atmosphere is essential at all times. You can achieve this by several methods but the simplest are: standing plants on gravel in saucers of water with the pots clear of the water; placing shallow trays of water close to them; positioning the plants in groups; and placing the plant pot in a larger one and packing wet peat in the space between the two. Spray plants overhead with clear water frequently and sponge large-leaved plants regularly. Give them a steam bath, or stand them outside in summer rain occasionally.

Light House plants vary enormously in their light requirements; most ferns will grow well in those parts of the home which receive little light while succulents need all the light you can give them. Two aspects of light are particulary important – intensity and duration. Duration is important because, among other things, it controls flowering. Intensity is important because it controls the rate of growth and too high an intensity of sunlight can damage plants severely. The amount of light necessary for a plant to survive does not vary greatly from plant to plant but the intensity neces-sary to make it grow well does. Most houses have a limited supply of light available so do not waste light on plants which will not benefit much – give it to those which will. Plants can roughly be divided into those which prefer light shade, those which will grow in a good deal of shade and those which must have full sun. Unfortunately the definition of shade varies from country to country – what could be called shade in San Francisco, USA, would probably be defined as light shade or even sun in the northern-most parts of the UK. Use the ratings for shade in the plant summaries comparatively – if one plant you grow does not do well in the shade in your house it is unlikely that one we have rated similarly will do well in shade either.

If you grow plants in full sun, turn them a little occasionally, otherwise they will grow towards the light and become lopsided.

Holiday care Water plants thoroughly and stand them in even temperature out of the sun and in a frost-free place in winter. Take off flowers and flower buds. Put plants into large shallow boxes, with wet peat packed between pots and on the surface of the growing mix. Make a framework and drape polythene sheeting over the whole box but make sure that it does not touch leaves and stems.

Potting

Most plants should be potted (when necessary) in March and April, or whenever new growth is starting. When the roots have penetrated all through the ball of growing mix to the outside, pot into a size larger pot or, if the plant has reached its full growth, repot it into one of the same size. If the plants are left longer, the roots will grow round and round the outside of the root ball, and the top growth will become pale, stunted and poorly flowered. Very frequent watering will be necessary. Beware of repotting too early: this can be about as harmful as repotting too late.

To repot, put some broken pieces of crock, curved side up, in the bottom of a clay pot – not in a plastic pot – and put a little growing mix on top. Turn the plant and pot upside down and with the fingers of one hand across the surface of the growing mix and supporting the plant, knock the pot rim against a firm surface. The root ball should then fall cleanly out of the pot. Sit it on top of the growing mix in the new pot, put more down the sides of the pot and firm it with the fingers so that the surface is level with that of the root ball. Leave a 1 to 3cm (½ to 1in) space at the top of the pot for watering and tap the pot on the working surface to settle the growing mix. Water and put in a shaded place for a few days.

If space is limited, try growing house plants in tower pots

Growing mixes Soil-based growing mixes (such as the John Innes formulations in the UK) are suitable. They contain loam, peat and sand, chalk and powdered fertilizer in specified proportions and can be bought ready made up. Buy an acid mix for acid-loving plants. Soilless growing mixes are also good, containing much peat, a little sand and some fertilizer but, in general, they should not be used for plants with much top growth. Supplementary feeding is needed soon after potting in these mixes.

Pruning and Propagation

Few house plants need pruning. Any that is needed is usually done in February and should be aimed at either keeping climbing plants in bounds or encouraging the new season's flowering shoots by cutting out the previous year's shoots. Pruning needs are individual and will be given as necessary in each plant summary.

Most home plants can be propagated by 7·5 to 10cm (3 to 4in) tip cuttings, or leaf cuttings, in early summer; by division in spring; or by offsets, plantlets or suckers in spring or summer. Use growing mixes designed for rooting and small 7·5cm (3in) pots. Put a polythene bag over the top and secure it with a rubber band, place the pot in a shaded, warm place and keep the growing mix moist until rooting has occurred – then pot on the cuttings into individual pots.

House Plants

MWT means minimum winter temperature

Aechmea rhodocyanea, 30cm (1ft), *lvs* grey-green with white bands, *fls* blue in pink spike, May to August. *Cultivation* good light to sun, some humidity, MWT 10°C (50°F); keep peaty growing mix moist, feed occasionally. *Propagation* detach rooted offsets when 15cm (6in) long.

Troubles

Symptom	Possible fault
Yellowing leaves and wilting followed by leaf fall	Too much water
Leaf wilting and bud drop	Too little water
Bud and flower drop, brown leaf edges and tips followed by leaf drop	Too dry an atmosphere
Pale, spindly stems and leaves, no flowers, no variegations on variegated leaves	Too little light
No flowers, small pale leaves, stunted slow growth	Lack of food and need for repotting
Sudden leaf or bud drop, withering of young growth	Change of temperature and draughts

Pests	Control
Greenfly, red spider mite, white fly	Spray with aerosol containing derris or malathion
Scale insects	Scrape off and spray as above
Mealybug	Paint white coating with methylated spirits

For fungus diseases, cut out any mildewed or rotting parts, and change cultural conditions.

House plants add life to a home. A pot chrysanthemum is here grouped with *Sansevieria*, *Tradescantia*, *Chlorophytum* and ferns

House plants

Key to common and botanic names

African violet	*Saintpaulia ionantha*
Aluminium plant	*Pilea cadierei*
Busy lizzie	*Impatiens*
Croton	*Codiaeum variegatum*
Friendship plant	*Pilea cadierei*
Grape ivy	*Rhoicissus rhombifolia*
Ivy	*Hedera* spp.
Kangaroo vine	*Cissus antarctica*
Mother-in-law's tongue	*Sansevieria trifasciata laurentii*
Poinsettia	*Euphorbia pulcherrima*
Rubber plant	*Ficus elastica*
Spider plant	*Chlorophytum comosum variegatum*
Sweetheart vine	*Philodendron scandens*
Swiss cheese plant	*Monstera deliciosa*
Urn plant	*Aechmea rhodocyanea*
Wandering jew	*Tradescantia fluviatilis*
Zebra plant	*Aphelandra squarrosa louisae*

Planting a hanging basket

Line the basket with sphagnum moss

Half fill the basket with growing mix and push plants through the sides spreading their roots out well

Push more plants through the sides as you fill the basket. Finally plant more plants in the top

Aphelandra squarrosa louisae, 30cm (1ft), *lvs* white striped, *fls* yellow, December to January. *Cultivation* good light, plenty of humidity, MWT 10°C (50°F), spray overhead, feed while flowering, water freely. *Propagation* from tip cuttings.

Aspidistra elatior, 30 to 45cm (1 to 1½ft), *lvs* large, glossy, dark green, *fls* purple, seldom produced, seeds orange berries. *Cultivation* good light or shade, some humidity, MWT 4°C (40°F), sponge leaves occasionally. *Propagation* by offsets or division.

Azalea, evergreen shrub, 23cm (9in), *fls* pink, red, white, December to February. *Cultivation* good light, plenty of humidity, MWT 13°C (55°F); spray overhead, feed while flowering, use acidic mix and soft water, repot after flowering, put outdoors in summer in light shade, bring in before danger of frost. *Propagation* 7·5cm (3in) tip cuttings in spring.

Chlorophytum comosum variegatum, 30 to 40cm (12 to 16in), *lvs* narrow, grass-like, striped white longitudinally, *fls* small, white, May to July. *Cultivation* good light to sun, some humidity, MWT 7°C (45°F), feed while growing, keep dryish in winter, spray overhead occasionally. *Propagation* detach plantlets when roots appear, divide crown.

Cissus antarctica, climber, *lvs* glossy, handsome, serrated edges. *Cultivation* shade or good light, some humidity, MWT 4°C (40°F), sponge leaves occasionally, water moderately in winter, freely while growing. *Propagation* 10cm (4in) tip cuttings.

Codiaeum variegatum, 45 to 60cm (1½ to 2ft), *lvs* brilliantly and variously coloured, sometimes lobed, in a variety of decorative shapes. *Cultivation* good light, plenty of humidity, MWT 13°C (55°F), keep temperature even, spray overhead frequently with warm water. *Propagation* tip cuttings.

Cyclamen persicum, not the true *C. persicum* but a result of intensive breeding, 25cm (10in), *lvs* green or marbled grey, *fls* pink, red, magenta, white, winter and summer. *Cultivation* good light, plenty of humidity, MWT 10°C (50°F), feed while flowering and keep at 13°C (55°F) while flowering, then dry off, put in shade in garden late spring, repot in autumn and bring in. Needs acidic mix, no coal gas. *Propagation* by seed.

Euphorbia pulcherrima, 30 to 60cm (1 to 2ft), *lvs* large, attractively shaped, *fls* red, pink or white November to January. *Cultivation* good light, plenty of humidity, MWT

13°C (55°F), spray overhead occasionally, water moderately with tepid water, maintain even temperature, no coal gas. If you want to grow from it for a second season cut it down to 5cm (2in) after flowering. Next season's plant will be leggier. *Propagation* by cuttings of new shoots.

Ficus elastica, 30cm to 3m (1 to 10ft), *lvs* glossy, oval, large, and handsome. *F. e. doescheri*, cream-variegated margins. *Cultivation* shade or good light, some humidity, MWT 10°C (50°F), sponge leaves occasionally, keep dryish in winter and water moderately in summer, give *F. e. doescheri* more warmth. *Propagation* by cuttings of top growth 15 to 23cm (6 to 9in) long – roots in two weeks.

Hedera spp, trailing or climbing, attractive small or medium-sized, lobed leaves, plain green or variegated. *Cultivation* shade or good light, some humidity, MWT 4°C (40°F), spray overhead and feed occasionally while growing, water moderately in summer. *Propagation* by tip or by stem cuttings.

Impatiens, 30 to 45cm (1 to 1½ft), *lvs* green, *fls* pink, white, red or purple, most of year. *Cultivation* good light or sun, plenty of humidity, MWT 10°C (50°F), pinch growing tips out to increase flower production, feed while flowering, water freely. *Propagation* tip cuttings in water at any time.

Monstera deliciosa, climber, slow-growing, *lvs* 30cm (1ft) long, deeply serrated and perforated, very handsome. *Cultivation* shade or good light, plenty of humidity, MWT 10°C (50°F), large pots and good growing mix essential, no draughts, train aerial roots on to moss-covered bark or sticks. *Propagation* by cuttings of top at any time.

Peperomia sp, 15 to 23cm (6 to 9in) *lvs* corrugated, plain or variegated, glossy, *fls* white tail-like spikes, at any time. *Cultivation* shade to good light, plenty of humidity, MWT 7 to 10°C (45 to 50°F), water moderately in saucer with tepid water, spray overhead, keep dryish in winter, and supply even temperature. *Propagation* by leaf cuttings or division.

Philodendron scandens, climbing, *lvs* evergreen, heart-shaped. *Cultivation* shade to good light, some humidity, MWT 4°C (40°F), spray overhead occasionally, train aerial roots on to bark. *Pruning* stop if required to make bushy growth. *Propagation* by stem cuttings at any time in 24°C (75°F).

332

Pilea cadierei, 15cm (6in), *lvs* oval, dark green with silver patches. *Cultivation* shade to good light, plenty of humidity, MWT 10°C (50°F), no draughts or coal gas, spray overhead frequently, feed while growing. *Pruning* pinch back tips occasionally to make bushy. *Propagation* by tip cuttings.

Rhoicissus rhombifolia, climbing, *lvs* diamond-shaped, serrated edges, glossy. *Cultivation* shade to good light, some humidity, MWT 7 to 10°C (45 to 50°F), spray overhead and feed occasionally in summer, keep dryish in winter. *Propagation* by cuttings taken in summer.

Saintpaulia ionantha, 7·5cm (3in), *lvs* round hairy, *fls* purple, white, blue-violet, pink, July to January. *Cultivation* good light to sun, plenty of humidity, MWT 10°C (50°F), supply even temperature, water moderately from below with tepid water, feed while flowering, give occasional steam bath, use soilless mix, rest from January to May. *Propagation* by division or leaf cuttings.

Sansevieria trifasciata laurentii, 30 to 60cm (1 to 2ft), *lvs* fleshy, stiff, narrow, erect, mottled green with yellow margin, *fls* white, seldom produced. *Cultivation* sun or shade, some humidity, MWT 10°C (50°F), keep dryish in winter, especially if temperature is low, water moderately in summer. *Propagation* leaf cuttings 3cm (1½in) long in June to July produce plants with mottled green leaves, suckers give plants with yellow-margined leaves.

Tradescantia fluviatilis variegata, trailing, *lvs* small, oval, striped white or cream, pink tinged if kept on the dry side, stems fleshy, *fls* white, summer. *Cultivation* good light, plenty of humidity, MWT 4°C (40°F), remove plain green shoots, spray overhead, feed when flowering and repot. *Pruning* take out tips to prevent straggling. *Propagation* tip cuttings at any time.

Terrariums and Bottle Gardens

A terrarium is a transparent container with a removable cover in which a collection of plants in soil can exist for long periods without additional moisture, nutrition or air. A terrarium protects plants from household dust, fluctuations in water and temperature, draughts and poisonous fumes from gas and coal fires. It is an ideal environment for small tropical plants. A bottle garden is similar but the narrow neck of the bottle limits the range of plants which can be grown.

Containers

Cubes or globes no less than 5cm (2in) in diameter are the smallest practical terrariums. There is no limit to larger containers except space and cost. The largest we have seen is a plastic globe 1·5m (5ft) in diameter. The vessels can be plastic or glass. Plastic vessels are often moulded two-part globes on cubic and polygonal shapes made from welded sheet. Plastics do not resist the action of soil and acids for any length of time and soon lose their transparency. Glass is the superior material. Tropical fish tanks, wide mouth glass storage jars, vases and laboratory glass beakers or tubs, make excellent terrariums if they are covered with a pane of glass or a sheet of plastic.

Choose bottles of clear glass. Tinted glass is less transparent, distorts the colour of the plants and usually does some harm to them. Any size bottle may be used from a perfume bottle to a large chemical carboy. Choose bottles which expand outward from the base all the way to the shoulder. Those with their broadest diameters in the middle are less useful. Bottles should be thoroughly washed inside and out to remove any residue of chemicals or other previous contents.

The Traditional Terrarium

These used a soil consisting of garden loam and leaf-mould, a drainage material and woodland hardy plants, such as small ferns, mosses, lichens, wintergreen and club moss. Plants were set directly in the soil and the main objective was to carry some of the summer greenery through the winter.

The Modern Terrarium

This should contain a soilless growing mix. There is no need for drainage and plants can remain in their pots. Only tropical foliage and flowering plants should be used. The advantages of the modern over the traditional are: 1) soilless compost is the better aerated, more adaptable medium, 2) drainage merely wastes space, 3) with potted plants replacement no longer involves pulling up roots and disrupting a whole arrangement, and 4) tropical plants are much more varied and those which flower add colour.

In bottle gardens, plants are usually grown directly in the growing mix and drainage provided by coarse grit is essential.

Tools

Terrariums need relatively few tools – a brush, small trowel or large spoon and a long-necked, small watering can are adequate. The tools for bottle gardening require a little more imagination and most people make their own.

Plan the garden out on paper before you put the plants in the container

The six listed below offer a good starting point. The length of the handles on these tools depends on the depth of the bottles you want to work on. Dowel is an ideal extender of handles.

A long funnel This is used to get drainage material and the growing mix into the bottle with the minimum of mess. The simplest and most efficient funnel is a stiffish sheet of paper rolled into a cone.

A miniature shovel is needed to dig holes for the plants. Use the narrow indoor gardening type, or a spoon attached to a dowel.

A tamper This is used to firm plants in. Make one from a bottle cork attached to the end of a dowel.

Tweezers These are used for holding and positioning plants. Split a length of bamboo cane and bind with rubber bands or twine at the top of the split. A tool used by mechanics consisting of a flexible metal tube, a plunger and a metal claw is very useful. When the plunger is pressed the claw is extruded and spread. On release the claw contracts and grips the object.

A pruning knife Attach a razor or craft cutting blade to the end of the dowel.

Brush This is needed for cleaning up plants. A long-handled, very soft paint brush is best.

Making a Terrarium

The design should be planned to use the full height of the container and it may be one-sided, angled or concentric. Before starting to plant, trace the container on to a sheet of paper and roughly plan out the positions of the plants. Plan to build up the soil in one or more directions by means of terraces to high points. The more the terracing the greater the planting area. Styles range from natural realism, through Japanese effects to modern, essentially abstract, arrangements. For the soilless mixture, mix equal parts of peat moss, perlite and vermiculite with one tablespoon of horticultural lime or two tablespoons of fine lime chips added to each 3l (2pt). Add just sufficient water to the soil so that it does not remain compacted after being squeezed in the hand. Put the soil into the container by the handful, build up the high points of your design and buttress them against slippage by using strategically placed stones. When the general shape of the 'landscape' is complete you can start to plant. A good point to remember is that the soil should always rise slightly as it approaches the glass.

Use plants in plastic pots and cover the holes in the bottom. Set the pots out in their position on the sheet of paper used for the design. Make a hole in the soil in the container for your most important plant in the design and set the pot in place but do not cover it completely. Do the same with other plants, shifting them around until you have them exactly placed to your liking. Do not overcrowd them. Remember that plants grow so leave plenty of space around the quick-growing ones and less in the vicinity of slow ones. Pots can be angled inward from the slopes. In fact all plants should be placed so that they grow away from the walls of the container towards the centre.

When your arrangement looks right, increase the size of the holes so that the pots disappear into the soil, or build the soil up around and over the rims. Use stones as support. Perspective effects can be achieved by reducing the size of a series of stones as they are placed further toward the rear of the design. To finish off, carefully contour the soil and pave the base with ornamental pebbles. Clean the plants with a soft brush and sweep the base area. Give the plants a misting and then pour water along the inside of the glass all around the terrarium from a watering can with a long, thin spout. Use a minimum of water and then close the terrarium completely.

Making a Bottle Garden

A small bottle may contain only a single tiny plant while larger ones permit elaborate landscaping. The design principles are the same as those given above for terrariums and the outline of the widest part of the bottle should be traced on to a piece of paper. Put the plants on this paper in the same arrangement as you want to have them in the bottle.

Ambitious bottle gardeners succeed in embellishing their landscapes with miniature features. Some indulge in figures, animals, bridges, boats, rustic houses and so on in the Japanese manner. Others build up rocks, walls, mountains, for example, by gluing small components together piece by piece.

Moisten the soil but make sure that it does not remain compacted if you squeeze it in your hand. Do not add too much water – it is much better to err on the dry side. Fold the funnel so that it reaches nearly to the bottom of the bottle, and pour in coarse grit or perlite for drainage. A depth of 4 to 8mm (⅛ to ¼in) is enough for small bottles but 50 to 75mm (2 to 3in) may be necessary in carboys. Shake the bottle to spread the material evenly over the bottom.

The growing mix should consist of two parts of peat moss to one of perlite and one of vermiculite. Before pouring it in decide whether you want a flat soil surface inside the bottle or a sloping one. Sloped surfaces allow for more variation in the height of the plant and more space for their roots. If the soil is to be flat, simply pour it in and shake the bottle to smooth it out. About 15mm (½in) is needed for smaller bottles: about 10cm (4in) for larger ones. If you want to have a slope simply hold the bottle at an angle as you pour.

Dig little holes with your shovel to indicate where you plan to place your plants. When planting start from the outside of the bottle and work inwards. Shake off as much soil from the roots as possible. Grip the plant with the tweezer at the joining of root and stem, poke it through the neck of the bottle and set it in place. A rougher, but actually simpler, method is to squeeze the roots into a tube and fold the leaves upward and together so that they will pass through the opening of the bottle. Then tilt the bottle so that the plant is directly over the spot it is to occupy, force it through the opening and let it go. With a little practice it will always land in the right place.

Shovel and tamp the earth around the roots of the plant. Clean and moisten the plants and clean the glass as described for terrariums.

If you water carefully the inside of the glass will be clean and there will be the barest film of water on the bottom of the vessel, no more. The relatively dry medium will absorb this. If you water excessively and it accumulates in the drainage material, use a glass tube to suck it out. The medium should absorb all free moisture within a day. Cap or cork the bottle.

Maintenance

Bottles and terrariums will need opening from time to time. In any ornamental arrangement plants need occasional trimmings and replacement and the soil in pots in terrariums will eventually dry out. Inspect them every couple of weeks and water them lightly when necessary.

Occasionally the outer air becomes excessively warm and the cover must be opened 3cm (1in) or more to prevent fungus diseases. The base soil must also be kept under observation and water must be added to it when the top becomes dry. Remember that moisture in one part will be distributed throughout the bottle or terrarium within a few days once it is closed. Always add a minimum of liquid.

Fertilizers are neither necessary nor desirable. Maintain the temperature between 16 and 30°C (60 and 85°F) for tropical plants and from 7 to 24°C (45 to 75°F) for hardy, wild plants.

Never set bottles or terrariums in direct sunlight unless the surrounding air is sufficiently cool to prevent the interior temperatures from rising over 30°C (85°F). Bright reflected light is ideal. A terrarium can be maintained without daylight by suspending a two-tube fluorescent light with a power of 40 watts about 10cm (4in) above the cover. Flowering is much more certain under artificial light especially in winter and the lamps should burn for 14 to 16 hours each day.

Children in the Garden

As far as most children are concerned, the most important function of a garden is to provide them with a place to play. From their parents point of view it must be a safe place. The application of some of the following ideas depends on the size of the garden concerned but every garden in which children play should have some provision for their enjoyment of fresh air, and for increasing their experience of life.

Plants

Children often enjoy helping their parents around the garden learning about growing plants and about how to respect and take care of what is being grown by others. You can cater for this need by providing them with a small area of the garden which they know is their own, and where they can grow whatever they like. But this does not mean giving them a patch in a neglected corner of the garden which you can then forget about. A child's garden may need carefully provided attention and frequently shared effort to maintain interest and to develop ideas. Much will depend on the age of the children and their own interests and inclinations. A three year old might plant lettuces today and walk all over them tomorrow; a six year old might give them more care and attention than any adult. A child's pleasure in eating food grown in his own garden, or in cutting flowers from it for use in the house, will certainly not be less than the satisfaction felt by an adult, and this may encourage tremendous effort. The tools needed for children's gardening must be carefully selected and generally smaller and lighter in weight than adult ones, but they must be adequate to do the work and not just easily broken toys.

The choice of plants for children to grow needs careful thought too. It should result in fairly sure success for the first season at least. Plants that can be eaten by the family and which are easy to raise include: radishes, beetroot, carrots and runner and dwarf beans. Some of the weeds that will have to be removed, such as groundsel, dandelions and some of the less spiny thistles can provide food for pets. Flowers for spectacular appearance or use indoors could include any of the easy annuals, such as sunflowers, nightscented stocks and various poppies.

Animal Life

A garden should also cater for a child's interest in animal life. A bird table, or some other point at which birds can be encouraged to feed, will develop powers of observation, and the different kinds of birds can be recorded as they are seen. Any such structure must, of course, be well clear from danger of attack by cats and dogs. If a garden has trees in it then nesting boxes can also be provided so that ultimately families of birds can be seen becoming established.

There are many wild animals which can be found even in fairly small town gardens, and these include hedgehogs, toads, and many invertebrates like slugs, snails, worms, grasshoppers, butterflies and moths (and their larvae), beetles, other insects and spiders. Not all of these are welcome guests as far as the gardener is concerned, but many will be of interest to someone. Wild life can be encouraged by leaving part of the garden somewhat less well tidied than the rest, so that animal and bird habitats can develop without too much disturbance. A small pond adds attraction and allows newts, fish and toad and frog tadpoles to be kept but some sort of protection is necessary for young children.

Apart from wild animals, pets also have an important place in the garden. In town areas in particular, where cats and dogs are not really suitable pets, a small space for a hutch for rabbits or guinea pigs is possible. It is generally best to accommodate pets somewhere away from the house and probably to avoid those which may encourage vermin in the home. Before pets are kept by children, however, there must be some form of agreement on who keeps them clean, how often the work has to be done and how it is to be shared.

An Adventure Garden

Some of the most enjoyable of all children's games involve places to hide from each other and places which they can claim as 'secret' from their parents. The amount of space available is a limiting factor for any such provision, but even room on a lawn for a small tent will make an ordinary garden into all sorts of wild, wide open spaces for the children who can use it. If a large safe tree is available, a tree house can be constructed. It need only be a simple wooden shelf firmly fixed in a horizontal position for the children to add to as they wish, but keep such structures out of fruit trees because of the possible damage to a fruit crop. Trees too are ideal supports for swings and climbing ropes, but use only those limbs which you know are sound and strong.

When you build any form of climbing or swinging apparatus try, wherever possible, to stand it on grass or on reasonably soft ground, in spite of the probable damage to turf. A fall from the top of a climbing frame on to grass is much less dangerous than such a fall on to concrete or a path. Slides are easily constructed out of strong wooden planks covered with a non-splintering material to avoid injury.

Pieces of trees which have had to be removed need not be discarded, but can be used to form the basis of a castle, fort or hill for climbing. Such pieces can be cut into various lengths and set upright in concrete, with no spaces between the pieces of wood (to avoid the danger of feet slipping between them). Pieces of tree trunk left as climbing objects must be firmly fixed and should not be capable of movement when children are climbing on them. This also applies to logs used for a see-saw.

Sand pits and paddling pools may be permanent or temporary structures, although it is usually found that sand is best left in one place for use as required. An old kitchen sink filled with sand can be just as effective as a true pit but it is important to use only clean, washed sand and not ordinary builders' sand. The former will do no harm to the garden when it is spread around, whereas the latter may. Some sort of netting or board will have to be spread over the sand pit when it is not in use to keep cats away. A paddling pool should be emptied when not in use because algae will tend to grow very rapidly in the water and will make the bottom and sides of the pool dangerously slippery. For this reason, and because of the possible damage to plant and animal life, a garden pond is not a suitable place to use as a paddling area.

17. Miscellaneous

Garden Calendar

The ideal time to sow seeds, take cuttings, prune shrubs and so on varies from year to year and there are no hard and fast rules about when to do it. This garden calendar should only be taken as a general guide for horticultural operations throughout the year. The calendar is based on hardiness zones five, six and seven from the zones established by the United States and Canadian Departments of Agriculture – see hardiness zone map on page 340.

The climate in North America has tremendous variations. Every known climatic condition exists within the Continent – from the sub-tropical climates of Florida and Hawaii to the northern polar regions. There are also steppe, Mediterranean, humid, cool and warm temperature climates and local variations of each. Differences in elevation, latitude, prevailing winds, day length, rain and snowfall, soil conditions, quantity and quality of sunshine make it very difficult to devise an accurate garden calendar for all these variables. Zones five, six and seven cover a major part of North America in relation to population. The cities of New York, Philadelphia, Washington, D.C., Chicago, St Louis, Toronto and Montreal all fall within these zones.

The calendar explains what you could and, in some cases, should be doing month by month. Planting dates for geographical areas outside zones five, six and seven will have to be moved forward or backward as dictated by common sense. The subtropical climates have not been included because of their completely contrasting climatic conditions from the rest of the continent.

January

General Repair tools, garden furniture and irrigation equipment. Have power equipment checked and serviced. (Simple maintenance can often be done by yourself).

Under glass Make sure that house plants are receiving enough sunlight and humidity. Reduce watering in most cases and inspect for mealybugs. Start forcing paper-white narcissus and lily of the valley by mid-January. Sow slow-growing annuals such as begonia in seed flats. When temperatures are above 7°C (45°F) ventilate cold frames. On very cold nights add extra protection such as straw matting to cold frames.

Flowers Order flower seeds for the coming year from seed catalogues. Order roses, shrubs and trees. On warmer days, inspect outdoor plants for rodent damage, scale infestations and snow damage. Early in the month complete the winter protection mulch if it was not done the previous year. Near the end of the month cut stems of forsythia, pussywillow and other early spring flowering plants to force indoors.

Vegetables Prepare cropping plans and order seeds as soon as the appropriate catalogues are available.

February

Under glass Sow early vegetables such as head lettuce, early cabbage, onions and leeks. Inspect cold frames for damage and prepare to convert them into hotbeds for growing annuals and vegetables during the coming weeks. Make artificial soil mixes for growing annuals and vegetables.

Fruit During moderate weather prune fruit trees such as apples and pears. Cut back grapevines. On days when the temperature is above 7°C (45°F), spray with dormant oil to control the various scale insects that cause damage in the coming season.

Lawns Apply limestone if necessary.

Flowers February and March are usually the times of the 'heavy' wet snows. Be alert

337

to remove heavy snow quickly from shrubs and small trees or severe damage may result. Prune late-flowering trees and shrubs. Look for early-flowering herbaceous and woody plants such as *Galanthus nivalis*, *Crocus* sp, *Chionodoxa luciliae*, *Scilla* sp, *Erica carnea*, *Hamamelis* sp, *Jasminum nudiflorum*, *Corylopsis pauciflora* and *Cornus mas*.

March

General This is spring clean-up month for most gardeners. On moderate days remove leaves that remain from the previous autumn. Near the end of the month remove winter-protective materials, such as burlap screens or plastic coverings.

Under glass Move small plants started from seed during January and February to hotbeds. Sow many annuals, such as verbena, marigold and salvia. Watch slow-growing seedlings carefully to make sure that they are not overcrowded. Transplant and repot them when they have their first sets of true leaves.

Lawns Begin lawn renovation, thatching and apply fertilizers (start with a highly soluble form of nitrogen such as ammonium nitrate in order to start the grass growing vigorously). Use chemical controls for broadleaf weeds. Apply a top dressing and reseed where necessary.

Flowers Prune deciduous plants. Check plants for winter damage and, if necessary, prune them. Thin old flowering shrubs. Buy bare-root shrubs, cut back and plant.

Vegetables If the ground permits, work the soil in the vegetable garden and prepare it for the coming season. Plant peas, spinach, turnips and onion sets.

Fruit Buy bare-root fruit trees at garden centres, cut back, and plant. Apply dormant sprays if not done in February. In zones five and six prune peach, cherry and plum trees. Thin old blackberries and raspberries.

April

General In zones five, six and seven April is the month generally regarded as the first month of spring. It is a very busy time for the serious gardener. Start landscape construction jobs. Check masonry and repair if necessary.

Flowers Transplant trees and shrubs and buy new ones from garden centres or nurseries. Start spray schedules for insects and diseases. Gardeners should check with local horticultural extension agents for a proper spray programme. End pruning of deciduous plants during this month. Cut back summer-flowering shrubs such as *Abelia grandiflora* and *Buddleia davidii* to the ground if the past winter was a particularly hard one. Hybrid tea and hybrid perpetual

roses should be cut back hard. Dig up perennials, separate, and replant in the garden. Apply fertilizers to shrub and flower beds. A 5–10–5 fertilizer fortified with bonemeal would be a good choice for most shrubs and flowers.

Vegetables Work organic materials such as humus, peat moss, compost, rotted manure, and leaf-mould into the soil wherever they are needed. Check the soil pH and, if need be, correct it with limestone (too acid) or iron sulphate (too alkaline).

May

General May is a very active month.

Lawns Lawn maintenance for controlling weeds, diseases, and insects begins now. See *Pests and Diseases*: *Herbicides* for weedkillers for controlling various lawn weeds. See also *Fungicides* (same section) for lawn fungicides. Fungus infestations usually begin during humid, cool and wet weather. Clinch bugs, grubs and sod-webworm can be controlled by chlordane.

Flowers Complete planting shrubs, evergreens and trees. Mulch them well for summer protection and decoration. Prune early spring-flowering shrubs as soon as they have finished flowering. Be careful to remove the old ones completely. Narrow-leaved evergreens, such as yews, junipers, arbor-vitae and hemlock can be lightly sheared. Cut lilac sprays and bring them into the house. Start hoeing shrub and flower gardens to keep down weeds. Spray for caterpillars, aphids, inch-worms, birch and holly miners. Spray roses for black spot disease.

Fruit Keep fruit trees free of fungus diseases by spraying with captan.

Vegetables From mid to late May sow snap beans, celery, sweet corn, squashes, soya beans and tomatoes.

June

General After the end of May the gardening pace slows down. The weather turns very warm and there are many hot days. Flower boxes and ornamental pots can be planted with annuals and set in place in the garden. Garden chairs, picnic tables, grills and hammocks can be set out.

Lawns Lawn mower blades must be adjusted from 4 to 5cm (1½ to 2in).

Flowers Prune flowering shrubs after flowering. Remove dead floral clusters from rhododendrons, azaleas and lilacs. Tulip leaves should be removed as soon as leaves go limp. Remove the remains of flowering heads from perennials. Water ornamentals and watch for June droughts. Prune pine, spruce and fir. To combat Taxus weevil spray the soil with chlordane during the last two weeks of the month.

North American Hardiness Zones

**AVERAGE MINIMUM
WINTER TEMPERATURE**

Zones 1 and 2,
below —40°C (—40°F)

Zones 3, 4 and 5,
—23° to —40°C (—10° to —40°F)

Zones 6 and 7
—12° to —23°C (10° to —10°F)

Zones 8, 9 and 10,
5° to —12°C (40° to 10°F)

Fruit Protect cherries and strawberries from birds by covering them with cheese-cloth.

Vegetables Set up stakes to support tomatoes and pole beans. A heavy straw or salt hay mulch can be applied to the small vegetables that are starting to grow rapidly. Black plastic sheeting, which has become very popular, is another good weed control mulch. Hoe weeds regularly. Spray and dust to keep down pests and diseases.

July and August

General As the weather turns hot, full time gardening becomes more of a chore than a pleasure. Try to work during the early morning and in the evenings.

Lawns Weed and insect problems in the lawn will require post-emergent chemical treatments. Watch for dollar spot and brown patch diseases in lawns. Warm days and cool nights are major factors in the spread of these diseases.

Flowers Continually growing evergreens such as juniper, cypress and arbor-vitae need periodic light shearing. Yews and hemlocks need one shearing during the summer in order to maintain symmetry. Red spider mites (dry weather), lace bugs, and powdery mildew are common summer ailments for many plants. Check local horticulture bulletins for population build-up of these insects. Prune hedges to keep them in good health and appearance. Autumn flowers such as chrysanthemums and asters should be pinched back to ensure bushiness. Watch for plants that may need water.

Vegetables July and August are the harvest months for the vegetable garden. If an autumn vegetable crop is wanted make sure the proper vegetable seeds have been sown by August 1st. Weeding becomes less of a problem as the summer wears on. Tend and periodically turn the compost heap.

September

General Cooler weather will make gardening easier again.

Lawns This is a lawn month. The latter part of August and all of September are the best times for building either a new lawn or renovating the old one. Start as early as possible because September has a way of slipping by and October is really too late to do any major lawn work (in northern areas). The lawn can be limed and fertilized now.

Flowers This is a good time to transplant evergreens. Be sure these plants are properly planted and that they get mulched later on in the autumn (after the ground freezes). Many flowering shrubs are now showing beautiful fruits. Enjoy them and use them in autumn floral arrangements.

Vegetables Clean out the vegetable garden of old vegetables, turn over the soil and plant rye grass to keep the soil in good tilth.

October

General A marvelous month, weatherwise, to get a lot of work done. Beware of an autumn drought. Watch weather; it could be cool and dry and if so plants will need supplementary water.

Lawns Lawn work that was not done in September should be done as soon as possible in October.

Flowers Dahlia tubers and gladiolus corms should be dug up, dried and stored until next spring. Spring bulbs should be planted in well-prepared beds. Most deciduous shrubs and trees that have lost their leaves can now be safely transplanted. Those deciduous trees and shrubs that have fleshy root systems such as birch, dogwood, and magnolias, should not be moved until spring. This is a good month to do major pruning on trees. Be sure that the cuts are clean or they may become infected later.

November

General There are still plenty of fine days during November to get things done. However, this month is the precursor of winter, so tasks must be completed.

Set snow fencing in place. Accumulation of leaves should be raked into beds, or into piles to be removed.

Lawns Apply a 2, 4–D weed killer to the lawn to prevent dandelions next spring.

Flowers Pruning continues on deciduous trees and shrubs. It is usually more pleasant work now than in late winter or even early spring. These plants can also be fed now that all likelihood of new growth is past. Spring bulbs can be planted until hard frost. Wrap broad-leaved evergreens with burlap, if these trees are in any way subject to winter damage. The branches of plants that are susceptible to snow damage like conical evergreens should be drawn together with plastic twine to prevent splitting.

December

General Holidays are usually the main consideration this month. Most garden operations should be over by now. Finish mulching operations. Bird feeders should be in place and wild bird food stocked.

Under glass House plants have to be watched carefully. Cut down on watering and try to supply extra humidity. The biggest problem for most plants during the winter is a dry atmosphere. Give them as much light as possible.

Flowers Fir, hemlock, and pine can be cut for Christmas sprays and wreaths. Cut sprigs of berried plants for the house.

Windbreaks

Windbreaks are particularly important in a continental climate, where gardens have exposure to high winds in winter and summer. There is a much wider variety of trees and shrubs suitable for windbreaks than is generally realized, even of deep-rooting ones suitable for the Great Plains and Prairies, and of varieties that are hardy up to Zone two. The factors to be considered – see *Design and Planning: Plant Screens* – are:

1) height and spread
2) soil preference
3) what attention will they need
4) is all-year protection required
5) hardiness
6) drought resistance
7) how deep rooted are they

Listed below are plants that are recommended for North America. Those listed as suitable for the Great Plains can of course be planted wherever other conditions are suitable.

Windbreaks suitable for Great Plains (USA) – all deep rooted

over 18m (60ft)	10 to 18m (35 to 60ft)	4·5 to 9m (15 to 30ft)
Acer saccharum 3	*Acer negundo* 2	*Caragana arborescens* 2
Juglans nigra 4	*Celtis occidentalis* 2	*Elaeagnus angustifolia* 2
Juniperus virginiana 2	*Fraxinus pennsylvanica*	*Juniperus scopulorum* 5
Picea pungens 2	*lanceolata* 2	*Prunus americana* 3
Pinus ponderosa 5	*Maclura pomifera* 5	*Prunus virginiana* 2
Populus sp 1 to 4	*Quercus macrocarpa* 2	
Pseudototsuga menziesii	*Salix pentandra* 4	
4 to 6	*Ulmus pumila* 4	
Salix alba 2		
Ulmus americana 2		

Windbreaks not suitable for Great Plains (USA)

over 18m (60ft)	10 to 18m (35 to 60ft)	4·5 to 9m (15 to 30ft)
Acer platanoides 3	*Pinus resinosa* 2	*Cornus mas* 4
Acer pseudoplatanus 5	*Quercus imbricaria* 5	*Ligustrum lucidum* 7
Acer rubrum 3	*Tilia* sp 2 to 5	*Syringa amurensis*
Carpinus betulus 5		*japonica* 4
Eucalyptus sp 9 to 10		*Thuja* sp 2 to 5
Fagus sp 3 and 4		*Viburnum prunifolium* 3
Fraxinus americana 3		
Picea abies 2		3 to 4·5m (10 to 15ft)
Picea omorika 4		*Acer ginnala* 2
Pinus nigra 4		*Juniperus* sp 2 to 7
Pinus strobus 3		
Quercus phellos 5		
Tsuga caroliniana 4		

Index

Entries for main sections and topics – see page 7 – are in **bold** type